WESTERN CIVILIZATION
Recent Interpretations

Volume II
FROM 1715 TO THE PRESENT

P9-AOV-787

Volume II
FROM
1715 TO THE PRESENT

Edited by
C. Stewart Doty
UNIVERSITY OF MAINE

WESTERN CIVILIZATION
Recent Interpretations

THOMAS Y. CROWELL COMPANY
NEW YORK   ESTABLISHED 1834

Library of Congress Cataloging in Publication Data

HAMILTON, CHARLES DANIEL comp.
   Western civilization: recent interpretations.

   Includes bibliographical references.
   CONTENTS: v. 1. From earliest times to 1715.
Edited by Charles D. Hamilton.—v. 2. From 1715 to the
present. Edited by C. Stewart Doty.
   1.   Civilization—History. 2.   Civilization,
Occidental. I.   Doty, Charles Stewart. II.   Title.
CB59.H34 1973   910′.03′1821   72-13456
ISBN 0-690-87470-7 (v. 2)

Copyright © 1973 by
Thomas Y. Crowell Company, Inc.
All Rights Reserved

Except for use in a review,
the reproduction or utilization of this work
in any form or by
any electronic, mechanical, or other means,
now known or hereafter invented,
including photocopying and recording,
and in any information storage and
retrieval system is forbidden without the written permission
of the publisher.
Published simultaneously in Canada
by Fitzhenry & Whiteside, Ltd., Toronto.

Manufactured in the United States of America

1 2 3 4 5 6 7 8 9 10

For
David, Ted and Peter

Preface

The purpose of this volume is to bring together a variety of short supplementary readings in western civilization that are not always accessible in order to introduce students to the nature and importance of historical investigation and to stimulate further thought and discussion about history. Three general groups of materials have been chosen for these readings: those containing new interpretations or research on fundamental themes in western civilization not yet incorporated into the textbooks; those setting forth the basic positions on current controversies in historical interpretation of major events; and those provocatively or evocatively probing those historical events, people, or developments which students find difficult to understand and which, as a result, are often too briefly treated by teachers with too little time and textbooks with too few pages. Rather than being an anthology of snippets, this volume is composed of complete, readable essays which originally appeared as articles, scholarly papers, lectures, or self-contained chapters in larger works. Moreover, the selections are up-to-date, a majority of them having been published in the last decade.

Each selection is introduced by a headnote pointing out the importance of the subject and the significance of the selection to understanding the issue under discussion. Each headnote raises questions for individual study and class discussion. The author's footnotes are eliminated except where they are necessary to the understanding of his message, and the editor has added some explanatory footnotes to aid the student. Each selection contains a full bibliographic citation so that the student can consult the original.

We hope that this book will correct the impression too often conveyed by textbooks that history is a narrative, to be unfolded once and for all. No matter how learned any man is, no matter how skillfully, objectively and comprehensively he can write, a single man's view of any historical period will always remain personal, and will reflect his personal interests, concerns, and abilities, as well as his limitations. The same may be said of a collaborative effort to write on something as diverse as "Western Civilization." "Everyman his own historian," or "each generation must write its own history"—however one states it, the proposition remains valid that history is in some sense a personal thing. What is important or significant to one person or one age may be meaningless to another. Hence this collection is meant to introduce the student to a broad range of historians and historical writing. In this way the student's appreciation of western history may be enriched, and he may be exposed to a variety of viewpoints and interpretations. At the same time, it must not be thought that historical investigation, that is, formulation of questions, the research and weighing of evidence, and the drawing of conclusions, is done without method. As any practicing historian knows, there are certain canons of historical scholarship, and definite methods of approaching and interpreting evidence. Another objective of the present collection, therefore, is to make the student aware of some of the difficulties the historian faces in the pursuit of his craft and to illustrate how some of the best contemporary historians have pursued their investigations. Methodology, evaluation of evidence, historical inference and generalization—these and other aspects of historical writing are touched on in these selections.

In short, the idea of this anthology is to stimulate and stretch the minds of this generation of students with provocative, recent interpretations of basic historical problems in western civilization that will be meaningful to them and to their teachers.

Contents

THE EIGHTEENTH CENTURY

PART I

THE eighteenth century is often difficult to understand. One would think, for example, that because we are still very much the intellectual descendants of Voltaire, Rousseau, and Montesquieu, the Enlightenment would pose few difficulties. Yet, because the Enlightenment's complexities and seeming contradictions have caused historians to interpret it so variously, the selections which follow include two explanations of it, by Peter Gay and Alfred Cobban. Although both were published in recent years, they doubtless will remain standard interpretations for some time.

Perhaps even harder to understand than the cultural life of the eighteenth century has been its social and political life. Frequently it has been a historical no-man's-land between Louis XIV's Versailles and the French Revolution's Bastille. So often our view of the century has been determined by one end of it or the other that we see it either as an extension of royal absolutism or as the bourgeois revolution in embryo. The selection by Leonard Krieger serves to correct that view and to take a fresh look at eighteenth-century politics and society.

1. An Age of Kings

LEONARD KRIEGER

*Nothing is more revelatory than to read the rich tapestries of such standard
works as M. S. Anderson's* Europe in the Eighteenth Century *(London, 1961) or
R. R. Palmer's* Age of Democratic Revolution *(Princeton, two volumes, 1959,
1964) to discover that neither end of the eighteenth century dominated the
politics or society of the whole. The tide of absolute monarchy in most of
Europe, for example, crested with the deaths of Louis XIV (1715), Peter I of
Russia (1725), and Frederick William I of Prussia (1740). The rest of the century
was characterized politically more by a noble resurgence than by absolutism.
Nor was society as modern, bourgeois, or individualistic as one might expect
in an age that produced Voltaire and de Sade. There remained all kinds of
premodern group loyalties described variously as "corporations" or "constituted bodies or authorities," bodies which had either a legal or customary status
and self-perpetuating membership. French hegemony over Europe, a striking hallmark of the eras of Louis XIV and Revolutionary France after 1792,
was in fact absent in much of an eighteenth century which saw an emerging
balance among several European powers.*

*These and other characteristics of the eighteenth century are excellently
summarized in this selection by Professor Leonard Krieger of the University of Chicago. Why, in Krieger's view, was this an age of kings rather
than of emperors, dukes, or counts? What were the "constituted authorities
and corporations," what powers did they have, and why did their members*

Source: Leonard Krieger, *Kings and Philosophers, 1689–1789* (New York: W.
W. Norton Co., 1970), pp. 1–12. By permission of W. W. Norton & Company,
Inc. Copyright © 1970 by W. W. Norton & Company, Inc.

consider them useful? What was causing them to break down in the eighteenth century? How does Krieger account for the resurgence of the nobility, and what forms did it take? What was the effect of this resurgence on kingship?

It was an age of kings. Never before had so much effective power accompanied the prestige of kingship and never again would this power prevail with so little resistance as in the half century that spanned the last years of the seventeenth century and the first part of the eighteenth century. For Louis XIV, that paragon of monarchs, to be a king was a "delightful" profession, and the Continent was to be crowded with colleagues who obviously enjoyed it almost as much as he. The unbridled gusto of their reigns has made Peter the Great and Charles XII the individual heroes of Russian and Swedish history. The Electors Frederick August of Saxony and Frederick III of Brandenburg were sufficiently envious of the royal title to intrigue earnestly for the acquisition of one, the Saxon ruler by converting to Catholicism and getting himself elected to the vacant Polish throne (1697) and the Hohenzollern by arranging for the recognition of his self-announced elevation from duke to king in Prussia (1701). Less spectacular but more far-reaching in their effects were the achievements of the kings Charles XI, Frederick William I, and Charles VI, in establishing bases of unified authority in Sweden, Prussia, and the Habsburg dominions respectively. And if the Glorious Revolution of 1688 had frustrated what seemed like the Stuart attempt to institute a continental type of monarchy in England, still at the start of our period William of Orange, as the English King William III, did take with him, from the covert military dictatorship which he had exercised in the Netherlands as their general *stadholder* since 1672, the jealous care for royal prerogative that helped to moderate the constitutional results of the revolution.

The vogue of kingship meant something very definite in the history of Europe. In its most general meaning, to be sure, it was simply part of that respect for order that had dominated European political life since the early Middle Ages and that persuaded men to accept a network of undisputed authorities by the end of the seventeenth century. If we think of monarchy in its broadest sense as government by a single ruler, whatever his title, then we may well say that, with a few minor exceptions of which the Swiss cantons were the most important, Europe as a whole was organized into monarchies by 1700. But if this fact testifies to the prevalence of political authority in general, the particular emergence of kings out of the welter of monarchs testifies to the precise kind of political authority that was becoming prevalent. The practical conditions of government and the attitudes of men now converged to establish an actual hierarchy among the monarchs, and the rise of the kings to the top of the pyramid illuminated the conditions and the attitudes that were at work.

Grand dukes, dukes, counts, and Electors could exercise the same kind of supreme or even absolute dominion over their subjects as the kings over theirs, but the days were long since a Duke Henry of Rohan (1579–1638) could wage a regular war against and conclude a peace with a king of France, or when a duke of Bavaria (Maximilian I, 1573–1651) could be a preeminent power in Germany, or when an Albrecht von Wallenstein (1583–1634) would get himself invested as duke of Friedland, the better to play an independent role in a war between the great powers. Even more impressive in underlining the distinctive role of kingship was the relatively sad plight of emperors in this age of kings. The once-powerful Ottoman Empire entered now into the long period of decline which later led to its personification as the Sick Man of Europe: the treaties of Karlowitz (1699) and Passarowitz (1718) affirmed the military defeats that marked the definitive end of the centuries-old Turkish threat to Europe, and the sultans responsible for them were ultimately deposed. The Holy Roman Empire, which Voltaire was tellingly to characterize as neither holy nor Roman nor an empire, remained the nominal political organization of the 360-odd principalities that comprised the German nation. It was, indeed, by now more usually referred to simply as the German Empire (as it will henceforward be called here), but it added little beyond the title to the Habsburgs who were usually elected its Emperors. It was precisely during our period, indeed, during the reign of Charles VI, that the Habsburgs began deliberately to choose southeastern expansion on the basis of their real ducal and royal powers in Austria, Bohemia, and Hungary over central European hegemony on the basis of their imperial function in Germany.

Only Russia, where Peter confirmed the imperial implications of the traditional title, Tsar ("Caesar"), when he proclaimed himself Imperator (1721), seemed to escape the derogation of empires. But even here, after Peter's death in 1725, the strain of imperial expansion developed flaws in the structure of state and society that made the position of tsar (or tsarina) unstable in a way that European kingship no longer was.

The advantage which the conditions of the time gave to kings over both dukes and emperors was more than a matter of preferred nomenclature. In the theoretical terms of traditional public law, kings ranked above dukes and below the emperor. It was precisely this intermediate position, paradoxically enough, which established the preeminence of kings in the first half of the eighteenth century, for it was the intermediate region, larger than a city, city-state, county, province, or duchy, smaller than the multinationed span of an empire, and usually identified with the "realm" of a king, that now proved itself to be the most effective unit for the exercise of political power abroad and the organization of social energies at home.

Internationally, the hallmark of the period was the ascendance of a plural system of great powers which would dominate the destiny of Europe until the Second World War of the twentieth century. This system was a practical response to a series of real challenges. It evolved as the fittest means of repelling the claims or aggressions of *de jure* empires like the German and the Ottoman and of aspirants to *de facto* empires like sixteenth-century Spain and seventeenth-century France. Just as a system of independent realms became superior to a hegemonical empire, so the powers which composed this system began now clearly to dominate the several city-states and smaller principalities whose competitive position until recently had rivaled their own. England, France, Austria, Prussia, and Russia—this was the pentarchy whose relations were to determine the issue of war and peace in Europe for two centuries, and it was in the age of kings that it appeared as an authoritative institution on the international scene. The countries whose political decline it signified included, to be sure, kingdoms like Spain, Sweden, and Poland as well as the republican Netherlands and the Electorate of Bavaria, but whatever the titles of the excluded sovereigns the essential fact was that inclusion within the circle of great powers henceforward required the possession of physical and human resources great enough, and the government over them unified enough, to be fit for a king.

Domestically, the hallmark of the period was the development of the king's realm from a set of legal claims to an actual district of administration and of the king's government from a superior magistracy to a supreme authority. At different times in different countries over the previous two centuries, kings, like sovereigns by any other name, had already succeeded in abridging the autonomy of such constituted authorities and corporations as governors, syndics, bailiffs, assemblies, churches, aristocracies, and municipalities, and in asserting, by fair means and foul, a lawful dominion over them. The individual constituted authorities— "subordinate magistrates" in customary legal parlance—were either successors of earlier royal agents who had settled down into local autonomy or the heads of self-administering corporations who exercised public functions. The corporations themselves remained, at the end of the seventeenth century, closer to what they had been in the Middle Ages than to what we now recognize by the term. Each corporation was still a combined social and political association which reflected in its organization the order of rank of a hierarchical society and in its function the interpenetration of private and public services. Each still was sanctioned by a legal charter which authorized it to exercise a monopoly of its assigned function in the community of its assigned region and which guaranteed both its right of governing its own members and its privilege of policing the community in the administration of its function. The most characteristic of the seventeenth-century corporations were the "estates," which referred to both the organized ranks of the society at large and the political organization of representative bodies ("parliaments" or "diets") by social rank; but villages, guilds, churches, and nobility (except in Russia and England, where for different historical reasons nobility as a social corps had no legal standing) equally exemplified the combination of internal hierarchy, self-governing association, and public-service administration which defined the pre-nineteenth-century corporation. At the turn of the eighteenth century most Europeans were still members of such corporations, high and low, but the tendencies were already at work which were limiting both their social monopoly and their administrative rights. As their hierarchical structure hardened into oligarchic exclusiveness the excluded men turned to individual enterprise, and whether as capitalists or day laborers increased the numbers of the unincorporated. As the political and economic demands upon public administration increased, the more mobile and open-minded response of the royal bureaucracies led to the community's acceptance of the king's sovereignty both over the members and over the functions of the corporations.

But the actual administration of this legal power had traditionally been left in the hands of the intermediate authorities and corporations except for those particular matters such as war, diplomacy, high justice, and finance, in which the sovereign had an urgent and continuous interest. As long as the public domain was shared out in this fashion, the difference between kings and other authorities was, in fact if not in law, a difference of degree rather than of kind. Toward the end of the seventeenth century, however, this system of indirect rule was increasingly overlaid by agencies of direct government responsive to the will of the sovereign. The realm of the sovereign became the effective unit for the exercise of political power, claiming jurisdiction over public business of all kinds and administering a growing share of it. The sovereign now became an authority different in kind from all others, and since this development pointed unmistakably to a single center of overall responsibility, it redounded to the advantage of kingship over the plurality of intermediate aristocracies and corporations. The key fields for the transition from particular regalian to general sovereign powers were justice and economics, for these were the activities in which the royal bureaucracies now established direct contact with the mass of the subjects and through which the state became a real force. The traditional authorities in these fields either became themselves instruments of the king's government or witnessed the appearance of new supervisory provincial and local organs that were such instruments.

Although the establishment of governmental agencies and policies that looked to the realm as a whole, and the parallel reorganization of myriad local and provincial communities into larger polities of citizens who looked to the regional state as the primary source of benefits and obligations, were the novel elements in the exaltation of kingship around the turn of the eighteenth century, they were not the only domestic factors in the veneration of kings. Historical changes rarely come in wholesale lots, and in this situation too men clung to accustomed practices and attitudes not simply out of nostalgia or inertia but because there was still a vital need for them. The bureaucratic service state that was coming into its own did not, after all, require a king at its head. That kings, with the regional scope of their legal authority and the practical convenience of their mediating position above competing social groups, should have been more appropriate to this function than more circumscribed nobles and oligarchs is clear, but other, more traditional functions explain why the new needs did not bypass kings as well. These functions were rooted in the psychology of early-eighteenth-century Europeans, in the structure of their society, and in necessary conditions of administration.

However real the activities of its organs, the state as such was an abstraction of which most Europeans were barely aware. Of the three elements that constitute a state—territory, people, and government—territories shifted with the fortunes of wars and dynasties, the people usually had no visible organs of direct participation in the state, and the government was made up of a congeries of authorities undertaking a variety of activities which added up to no visible system. For a minority of intellectuals, trained by philosophy to see abstractions as real things and by legal studies to see a rational order behind the apparent confusion of current practices, the state was the tissue of relationships that actually existed. Another small group, composed of politicians and administrators in the central governments, recognized the reality of the state as a whole because they had increasingly to deal with it in practice. The great majority of men, however, accustomed to recognize reality only in what was visible, tangible, or incarnate, dimly sensed the effects of this new institution which was providing security and services from afar, but could identify it only through its incorporation in the royal person who led and symbolized it. Thus the divine right of kings, which had been replaced among the vanguard of intellectuals by a secularized natural-law theory of sovereignty, remained well into the eighteenth century at the root of the popular attitude toward monarchs. The idea of divine right, in its application to *kingship,* went back to the Middle Ages; in this sense it signified the sacred origination of the royal office, or the king's "body politic." The divine right of *kings,* however, was a more modern product, developing during the sixteenth and seventeenth centuries to extend the sanctity of the king's "body politic" into his "natural body." This extension was a response both to the psychological need for a visible symbol of the ever more palpable activities of the invisible state ("body politic") and to the political need for a distinctive blessing upon kings vis-à-vis the more indiscriminate anointment of any officeholder in the hierarchy of public authorities. Through the dynasty, personal heredity became the natural counterpart of the permanence of the state and the person of the king the embodiment of the state itself.

There were good social as well as psychological reasons for the particular exaltation of kings in the early eighteenth century. The growth of the state, with its exercise of power from one central agency or set of agencies upon all subjects alike, inevitably extended the fields where traditional social distinctions were irrelevant. Economically, this meant the official encouragement of the commerce and industry run by commoners at least as much as of the agriculture dominated by aristocrats. Legally, it implied a community of subjects equal in their common subjection to the laws of the state. Administratively, it entailed the construction of a bureaucratic apparatus which required a technical training and a standard of practical efficiency transcending class origins. In all these ways the seventeenth century had witnessed an improvement in the fortunes of the middling sectors of society in contrast with the nobility. But, not for the first time in history and not for the last, what appeared to be the linear course of an apparently simple progressive development came a cropper during the early eighteenth century. Not that the bourgeoisie either declined or diminished. Powered by the dramatic expansion of overseas trade and by the first stage of the modern population explosion that continues to this day, the European economic growth of the eighteenth century infused wealth, leisure, and culture into an ever-widening circle of enterprising burghers. Nor was the centralizing process of state making reversed. The claims and effective force of bureaucracies continued to increase, and with them the opportunities for trained and talented commoners on the way up.

What was reversed was the precipitous descent of the aristocracy, a descent that had accompanied, and that had seemed a necessary counterpart to, the rise of the bourgeoisie and the emergence of national sovereigns during the sixteenth and seventeenth centuries. In the eighteenth century, surprisingly, aristocracies—or at least important parts of them—were resurgent. Appreciating the principle of what would later become a proverbial prescription for men to join what they could not beat, nobles in the several countries of Europe picked themselves up and began to appropriate commanding positions in the governmental structures of the new states and even in the network of commercial relations. The Whig oligarchy that ruled Britain without serious challenge between the accession of the Hanoverian dynasty in 1714 and George III's assertion of royal influence after 1760 represented a landowning aristocracy that was sponsoring a capitalized and scientific agriculture in response to demands of the market and that had economic ties with merchants and bankers of the City. The French peers, refueled by Louis XIV's calculated infusion of subsidies, made a serious bid to refashion the monarchy in their own image after the death of the Sun King in 1715, and when this attempt failed, a more economically progressive and modern-minded judicial and administrative aristocracy (*noblesse de robe* and *noblesse d'office*) rose to continue the counteroffensive on behalf of the privileged. In Russia various sections of the military and landed nobility dictated the succession to the throne—in general they preferred tsarinas in the expectation that they would behave consistently as members of the "weaker sex"—and dominated the social policy of the government from the death of Peter the Great in 1725 through the accession of Catherine the Great in 1762. The long period from 1718 to 1772 that the Swedes euphemistically called their "era of liberty" was actually an age of aristocratic sovereignty, exercised constitutionally in a nominal monarchy through the nobles' oligarchic control over both the *Riksdag,* or parliament, and the bureaucracy. The Dutch gave the same high-flown label to the period from 1702 to 1747, when the small but influential class of Regents, an oligarchy comprised of urban patricians, resumed its sway after the death of William III and kept the office of *stadholder* vacant. The seven provinces that made up the Dutch "Republic" were, in this respect, expanded versions of the independent city-states in Europe. Concentrated mainly in Switzerland and Germany, they too were stabilized during the first half of the eighteenth century under the rule of exclusive patrician oligarchies.

Only in Spain—an early achiever of state building—and in Austria and Prussia—two relative latecomers to the field—did the aristocracy register no visible resurgence, but the reason was the lack of need or occasion rather than of will or capacity. With Philip V (ruled 1700–1746), the first of the Bourbon line, the attempt was indeed made to rejuvenate the Spanish monarchy through bureaucratic centralization on the French model, but Philip's own political lethargy and the persistence of the Spanish predilection for government by committee throughout the administrative system enabled the nobility to carve their niches of influence in and around the reformed bureaucracy. Austria's Charles VI did obtain the legal recognition of the variegated Habsburg dominions as a single monarchy, but the Pragmatic Sanction of 1720, which secured an indivisible succession, was finally enacted only with the approval of the sundry aristocratically dominated estates of his realms, and their power sufficed to prevent the establishment of any real institutional unity on the basis of it during his reign. When, under the pressure of military defeat, his daughter, Queen Maria Theresa (ruled 1740–1780), did create unified institutions extending throughout Austria, she had to operate through an ambiguous policy of "gentle violence" which spared both the organizations and the feelings of the different kinds of aristocrats in the various Habsburg territories. The Prussian aristocracy, finally, could offer only passive resistance to the implacable mopping-up operation conducted by Frederick William I against the remnants of their political autonomy, but despite the hostility and grim satisfaction he expressed in his statement: "I am destroying the authority of the *Junkers*," Frederick William never even attempted to divest the *Junkers* or any other section of the Prussian aristocracy either of their social privileges in the army and on their estates or of their monopoly in the exercise of the state's administrative and judicial power over the local countryside. Thence they could be returned by Frederick the Great after 1740 to their wonted posts in the upper echelons of the government.

The aristocracies' new lease on life for the eighteenth century was thus predicated upon the modernization of their premises, and they thereby shifted the arena of social conflict from outside to inside the structure of the state. Where they had formerly defended their privileged rights to land-ownership, manorial lordship, judicial immunities, and tax exemptions by denying the jurisdiction of the central governments, they now defended these privileges by occupying and controlling the governmental agencies which exercised the jurisdiction. This aristocratic penetration of the state ran counter to the standards of general law, equal citizenship, and uniform administration which had served and continued to serve bureaucrats as guides in extending the scope of central government. But the hierarchical tendency was no mere atavism. Despite the obvious and reciprocal hostility between it and the leveling tendency with which it shared the state, the coexistence of the two tendencies, however mismatched in logic, was a faithful response to a fundamental social demand of the age. European society required, for the military security of its inhabitants, for the direction and subsidization of its economy, and for the prevention of religious turbulence and popular disorder, the imposition of unified control over a larger area and more people than the contemporary instruments of government could manage. Hence the employment of the traditional social and corporate hierarchies by the government as extensions of the governing arm into the mass of inhabitants. All people were subject, but some were more subject than others.

The necessity both for a social caste and for a bureaucracy which undermined the social caste redounded to the advantage of the kings. For effective political operation an authority was required which was recognized by bureaucrats and aristocrats alike as their representative in the adjudication of rival claims and in the allotment of appropriate powers. This authority could only be the king, for only the king combined in himself a social position as the highest-ranking noble with a political position as the supreme magistrate of the community. For centuries the notion of kingship had joined the idea of a natural man who was preeminent among aristocrats with that of a political man who symbolized the unity of the entire civil society, and the development of the aristocracy as well as the growth of bureaucracy in the late seventeenth century made this two-headed monarch indispensable.

And if the king was necessary to this anomalous mixture of hierarchy and equality in early-eighteenth-century society, he had an interest in perpetuating the anomaly, for it was equally necessary to him. The king's development of organs and policies to perform services needed for the security and welfare of the whole community was an obvious means of combating the dispersion of public power among the traditional corporations, but just as essential albeit not so obvious was the interest of the king in maintaining and even sustaining the privileged corporations— not simply for his administrative convenience but in their own social right. He needed the support of a hierarchy against the dangers of leveling as much as he needed the support of middle-class officials against the ambitions of the notables. The continuous threat and frequent outbreak of popular disorders through the seventeenth and eighteenth centuries were a constant reminder of how unreliable a basis of loyalty the appreciation of governmental services could be. The existence of a hierarchy which made the inequality of rights and functions an ultimate and unquestionable necessity of social organization accustomed men to accept the relationship of inferiors to superiors as a primary fact imbedded in the very nature of things. For kings, their position at the apex of the divinely constructed social ladder called for obedience even when the benefits of their government were not in evidence, and they never dreamed of destroying a support which linked their own preeminence with the general constitution of human society.

Thus peoples were related to their kings in two different ways, one primarily political and uniform, the other primarily social and pyramidal; and each of these relations in its own way supported the king and was in turn supported by him. But such a general characterization should not mislead. The development of kingship into this form may be clear to us, but it was not so clear to the men who developed it and lived under it. For this shape of the institution was being defined as a result of piecemeal practical necessities rather than of a deliberate program. It was no accident, then, that in the period from 1690 to 1748, between Locke's *Second Treatise on Civil Government* and Montesquieu's *Spirit of the Laws,* no important political theory emerged that commanded consensus: the mixture of institutions and principles that were going into the monarchical state was too new, too loose, and too attached to the particular circumstances of its origin for contemporaries to conceive it as a system. There were standard political theories for each of the ingredients, but their basic ideas stemmed from earlier periods.

2. The Enlightenment's "Little Flock of Philosophes"

PETER GAY

The Enlightenment and its philosophes have always had their friends and enemies. Alternately decried as impractical visionaries and destroyers of religious faith and praised as the first to advocate all that is good in modern man, they are currently enjoying a "good press." That they are is in large part due to the efforts of Yale University's Peter Gay. His twenty years of studying the Enlightenment have borne abundant fruit in his two-volume study, The Enlightenment: An Interpretation (*New York, 1967 and 1969*). *The first volume, subtitled "The Rise of Modern Paganism," deals with the education of the philosophes by way of their substitution of a "pagan" world view for a Christian one. The second volume, subtitled "The Science of Freedom," examines their social, political, and aesthetic program and places their thought in its social setting. In doing this, Professor Gay will doubtless shape the historical understanding of the Enlightenment for years to come.*

The size and range of Gay's study make it difficult to choose an excerpt for this anthology. The selection which follows is the introductory chapter of his first volume, and it sets the stage by describing the European Enlightenment as an instrument of "the little flock of philosophes," a little flock which can only be described as a family. In reading it, consider why Gay believes "family" to be an appropriate term for the philosophes. On what matters were they unified, and why did they quarrel? In what ways did both take on the quality of a family affair? What does Gay mean when he describes the philosophes as

Source: Peter Gay, *The Enlightenment: An Interpretation* (New York: Knopf, 1967), vol. I, pp. 3–19. [Footnotes omitted.] Copyright © 1966 by Peter Gay. Reprinted by permission of Alfred A. Knopf, Inc.

modern pagans? Why does he not give them a different characterization? What does the term philosophe *mean, and why should that French terminology be applied to non-Frenchmen? What were the characteristics of the philosophes' ideas and attitudes? As a result of reading this one excerpt from Gay's work, can you get a feeling of the personalities of the philosophes, their value system, and the intellectual climate in which they functioned?*

I

There were many philosophes in the eighteenth century, but there was only one Enlightenment. A loose, informal, wholly unorganized coalition of cultural critics, religious skeptics, and political reformers from Edinburgh to Naples, Paris to Berlin, Boston to Philadelphia, the philosophes made up a clamorous chorus, and there were some discordant voices among them, but what is striking is their general harmony, not their occasional discord. The men of the Enlightenment united on a vastly ambitious program, a program of secularism, humanity, cosmopolitanism, and freedom, above all, freedom in its many forms—freedom of arbitrary power, freedom of speech, freedom of trade, freedom to realize one's talents, freedom of aesthetic response, freedom, in a word, of moral man to make his own way in the world. In 1784, when the Enlightenment had done most of its work, Kant defined it as man's emergence from his self-imposed tutelage, and offered as its motto *Sapere aude*—"Dare to know": take the risk of discovery, exercise the right of unfettered criticism, accept the loneliness of autonomy. Like the other philosophes—for Kant only articulated what the others had long suggested in their polemics—Kant saw the Enlightenment as man's claim to be recognized as an adult, responsible being. It is the concord of the philosophes in staking this claim, as much as the claim itself, that makes the Enlightenment such a momentous event in the history of the Western mind.

Unity did not mean unanimity. The philosophic coalition was marked, and sometimes endangered, by disparities of philosophical and political convictions. A few—a very few—of the philosophes held tenaciously to vestiges of their Christian schooling, while others ventured into atheism and materialism; a handful remained loyal to dynastic authority, while radicals developed democratic ideas. The French took perverse pleasure in the opposition of church and state to their campaigns for free speech and a humane penal code, and to their polemics against "superstition." British men of letters, on the other hand, were relatively content with their political and social institutions. The German *Aufklärer* were isolated, impotent, and almost wholly unpolitical. As Georg Christoph Lichtenberg, essayist, wit, physicist, and skeptic, wrote in the privacy of his notebooks: "A heavy tax rests, at least in Germany, on the windows of the Enlightenment." In those Italian states that were touched by the new ideas, chiefly Lombardy and Tuscany, the reformers had an appreciative public and found a sympathetic hearing from the authorities. The British had had their revolution, the French were creating conditions for a revolution, the Germans did not permit themselves to dream of a revolution, and the Italians were making a quiet revolution with the aid of the state. Thus the variety of political experience produced an Enlightenment with distinct branches; the philosophes were neither a disciplined phalanx nor a rigid school of thought. If they composed anything at all, it was something rather looser than that: a family.

But while the philosophes were a family, they were a stormy one. They were allies and often friends, but second only to their pleasure in promoting the common cause was the pleasure in criticizing a comrade-in-arms. They carried on an unending debate with one another, and some of their exchanges were anything but polite. Many of the charges later leveled against the Enlightenment—naïve optimism, pretentious rationalism, unphilosophical philosophizing—were first made by one philosophe against another. Even some of the misinterpretations that have become commonplace since their time were originated by philosophes: Voltaire launched the canard about Rousseau's primitivism, Diderot and Wieland repeated it; Hume was among the first to misread Voltaire's elegant wit as sprightly irresponsibility.

To the delight of their enemies, the philosophes generated a highly charged atmosphere in which friendships were emotional, quarrels noisy, reconciliations tearful, and private affairs public. Diderot, generous to everyone's faults except Rousseau's, found it hard to forgive d'Alembert's prudent desertion of the *Encyclopédie*. Voltaire, fondest of those who did not threaten him with their talent, gave Diderot uneasy and uncomprehending respect, and collaborated on an *Encyclopédie* in which he never really believed; in return, Diderot paid awkward tributes to the literary dictator of the age. He honored Voltaire, he told Sophie Volland, despite his bizarre behavior: "Someone gives him a shocking page which Rousseau, citizen of Geneva, has just scribbled against him. He gets furious, he loses his temper, he calls him villain, he foams with rage; he wants to have the miserable fellow beaten to death. 'Look,' says someone there, 'I have it on good authority that he's going to ask you for asylum, today, tomorrow, perhaps the day after tomorrow. What would you do?' 'What would I do?' replies Voltaire, gnashing his teeth, 'What would I do? I'd take him by the hand, lead him to my room, and say to him, "Look, here's my bed, the best in the house, sleep there, sleep there for the rest of your life, and be happy."'" There is something a little uneasy beneath this charming fable: Diderot thought well of Voltaire's writings and Voltaire's humane generosity, but he somehow never quite trusted him, and the two men did not meet until 1778, when Voltaire came back to Paris to die. For their part, the Germans, like Lessing, had distant, correct, or faintly unpleasant relations with the French: they admired them judiciously and from afar. Rousseau, at first indulged by all, came to reject and to be rejected by all, even by David Hume. Only Hume, corpulent, free from envy and, in society, cheerfully unskeptical, seems to have been universally popular, a favorite uncle in the philosophic family.

The metaphor of a philosophic family is not my invention. The philosophes used it themselves. They thought of themselves as a *petite troupe,* with common loyalties and a common world view. This sense survived all their high-spirited quarrels: the philosophes did not have a party line, but they were a party. Some of the harshest recriminations remained in the family, and when they did become public, they were usually sweetened by large doses of polite appreciation. Moreover, harassment or the fear of harassment drove the philosophes to remember what they had in common and forget what divided them. The report of a book burned, a radical writer imprisoned, a heterodox passage censured, was enough. Then, quarrelsome officers faced with sudden battle, they closed ranks: the tempest that burst over Helvétius's *De l'esprit* in 1758 and the prohibition issued against Diderot's *Encyclopédie* in the following year did more to weld the philosophes into a party than Voltaire's most hysterical calls for unity. Critics trying to destroy the movement only strengthened it. In 1757 the journalist Fréron denounced Diderot to the chief censor, Malesherbes, as the "ringleader of a large company; he is at the head of a numerous society which pullulates, and multiplies itself every day by means of intrigues," but Malesherbes continued to protect the philosophes to the best of his considerable ability. In 1760, Palissot, a clever journalist with good political sense but doubtful taste, wrote a meager comedy entitled *Les philosophes,* in which he lampooned Rousseau as an apelike savage and brutally satirized Helvétius, Diderot, and Duclos as an unprincipled gang of hypocrites who exploit idle, gullible society ladies with pretentious schemes. Palissot took it for granted that "everybody knows that there is an offensive and defensive league among these *philosophic* potentates." Obviously, the potentates survived this assault: Horace Walpole, who did not like them, had no hesitation in identifying the little flock when he reached Paris in 1765. "The *philosophes,*" he wrote to Thomas Gray, "are insupportable, superficial, overbearing, and fanatic: they preach incessantly. . . ."

Walpole's characterization is too bilious to be just. In fact, the philosophes tolerated a wider range of opinions than fanatical preachers could have: Voltaire was happy to admit that while atheism is misguided and potentially dangerous, a world filled with Holbachs would be palatable, far more palatable than a world filled with Christians, and Holbach, who thought little of deism, returned the compliment. There was one case, to be sure, that seems to shatter the unity of the movement: the philosophes' persecution of Rousseau. But the persecutors did not see it that way. They rationalized their ruthlessness by arguing that Rousseau had read himself out of the family to become that most despicable of beings, an ex-philosophe. "No, my dear," wrote Diderot reassuringly to his Sophie Volland in July 1762, shortly after Rousseau's *Émile* had been condemned and burned, "no, the Rousseau business will have no consequences. He has the devout party on his side. He owes their interest in him to the bad things he says about philosophes. Since they hate us a thousand times more than they love their God, it matters little to them that he has dragged Christ in the mud—as long as he is not one of us. They keep hoping that he will be converted; they're sure that a deserter from our camp must sooner or later pass over into theirs." While, in general, arguments among philosophes were conducted in the tones Voltaire used about Holbach rather than the tones used by Diderot about Rousseau, Diderot's rhetoric in this letter—"we" against "they," the military metaphors, and the virulent hatred of the opposition—reveals at once the anxiety concealed behind the confident façade and the cohesion achieved by the men of the Enlightenment by the 1760's.

The Enlightenment, then, was a single army with a single banner, with a large central corps, a right and left wing, daring scouts, and lame stragglers. And it enlisted soldiers who did not call themselves philosophes but who were their teachers, intimates, or disciples. The philosophic family was drawn together by the demands of political strategy, by the hostility of church and state, and by the struggle to enhance the prestige and increase the income of literary men. But the cohesion among the philosophes went deeper than this: behind their tactical alliances and personal fellowship there stood a common experience from which they constructed a coherent philosophy. This experience—which marked each of the philosophes with greater or lesser intensity, but which marked them all —was the dialectical interplay of their appeal to antiquity, their tension with Christianity, and their pursuit of modernity. This dialectic defines the philosophes and sets them apart from other enlightened men of their age: they, unlike the others, used their classical learning to free themselves from their Christian heritage, and then, having done with the ancients, turned their face toward a modern world view. The Enlightenment was a volatile mixture of classicism, impiety, and science; the philosophes, in a phrase, were modern pagans.

II

To call the Enlightenment pagan is to conjure up the most delightfully irresponsible sexual license: a lazy, sun-drenched summer afternoon, fauns and nymphs cavorting to sensual music, and lascivious paintings, preferably by Boucher. There is some reality in this fantasy: the philosophes argued for a positive appreciation of sensuality and despised asceticism. But these preachers of libertinism were far less self-indulgent, far more restrained in their habits, then their pronouncements would lead us to believe. Rousseau had masochistic tastes which he apparently never gratified, Hume had an affair in France; young Benjamin Franklin "fell into intrigues with low women" and fathered an illegitimate son; Diderot wrote a pornographic novel to keep a mistress in the style to which she hoped to become accustomed; La Mettrie, a glutton, died at the Prussian court shortly after eating a spoiled game pie, thus giving rise to the delicious rumor that he had eaten himself to death; Voltaire had a passionate, prolonged affair with his niece—one of the few well-kept secrets of the eighteenth century. But this rather scanty list almost exhausts salacious gossip about the Enlightenment. Generally, the philosophes worked hard

—made, in fact, a cult of work—ate moderately, and knew the joys of faithful affection, although rarely with their wives. When Diderot found his Sophie Volland in middle age, he found the passion of his life. His disdain of prostitutes or "loose women," which is such a curious theme in his correspondence, was not motivated by mean fear of venereal disease: it was the cheerful acceptance of obligation, the self-imposed bond of the free man. David Hume testified in 1763 that the French "Men of Letters" were all "Men of the World, living in entire or almost entire Harmony among themselves, and quite irreproachable in their Morals." As a group, the philosophes were a solid, respectable clan of revolutionaries, with their mission continually before them.

In speaking of the Enlightenment as pagan, therefore, I am referring not to sensuality but to the affinity of the Enlightenment to classical thought. Words other than pagan—Augustan, Classical, Humanist— have served as epithets to capture this affinity, but they are all circumscribed by specific associations: they illuminate segments of the Enlightenment but not the whole. "Augustan" suggests the link between the first and eighteenth centuries, the parallel between two ages of literary excellence, mannered refinement, and political corruption. "Classical" brings to mind Roman temples, Ciceronian gravity, and Greek myths translated into French couplets. "Humanists" recalls the debt of the Enlightenment to Renaissance scholarship, and a philosophy that places man in the center of things. Yet I do not think that any of these terms makes, as it were, enough demands on the Enlightenment; they have about them subtle suggestions of parochialism and anemia of the emotions. "Augustan" properly applies to Great Britain in the first half of the eighteenth century, "Classical" is the name for the noble, artificial literary style and for a preference for antique subject matter, "Humanism" in all its confusing history has come to include an educated piety. The Enlightenment was richer and more radical than any of these terms can suggest: Diderot's plays, Voltaire's stories, Hume's epistemology, Lessing's polemics, Kant's Critiques—which all belong to the core of the Enlightenment— escape through their meshes.

III

For Walpole or Palissot, as for most historians since their time, a philosophe was a Frenchman. But *philosophe* is a French word for an international type, and that is how I shall use it in these pages. To be sure, it is right that the word should be French, for in France the encounter of the Enlightenment with the Establishment was the most dramatic: in eighteenth-century France, abuses were glaring enough to invite the most scathing criticism, while the machinery of repression was inefficient enough to permit critics adequate room for maneuver. France therefore fostered the type that has ever since been taken as *the* philosophe: the facile, articulate, doctrinaire, sociable, secular man of letters. The French philosophe, being the most belligerent, was the purest specimen.

Besides, Paris was the headquarters and French the lingua franca of European intellectuals, and philosophes of all nations were the declared disciples of French writers. In Naples, Gaetano Filangieri, the radical legal reformer, acknowledged that he had received the impetus for writing his *Scienza della Legislazione* from Montesquieu. Beccaria, Filangieri's Milanese counterpart, told his French translator, Morellet, that he owed his "conversion to philosophy" to Montesquieu's *Lettres persanes,* and that d'Alembert, Diderot, Helvétius, Buffon—and Hume—were his "constant reading matter," every day and "in the silence of night." Hume and Gibbon attributed much of their historical consciousness, Adam Ferguson and Jean-Jacques Rousseau, most of their sociological understanding, to their delighted discovery and avid reading of Montesquieu's works. D'Alembert's *Discours préliminaire* to the *Encyclopédie* was widely read in Scotland and on the Continent. Adam Smith, without being a physiocrat himself, learned much from the physiocrats during his French visit from 1764 to 1766. Bentham derived his utilitarianism partly from Helvétius; Kant discovered his respect for the common man by reading Rousseau; while Voltaire's campaigns against *l'infâme* and on behalf of the victims of the French legal system had echoes all over Europe. Even Lessing, in rebellion against the French neoclassical drama of Corneille, Racine, and Voltaire, assailed it with weapons supplied to him by Diderot. And it is significant that monarchs like Catherine of Russia and Frederick of Prussia, who forced themselves on the movement to whose ideals their policies owed little, incessantly proclaimed their indebtedness to French models.

But while Paris was the modern Athens, the preceptor of Europe, it was the pupil as well. French philosophes were the great popularizers, transmitting in graceful language the discoveries of English natural philosophers and Dutch physicians. As early as 1706, Lord Shaftesbury wrote to Jean Le Clerc: "There is a mighty light which spreads itself over the world, especially in those two free nations of England and Holland, on whom the affairs of all Europe now turn." Shaftesbury himself, with his optimistic, worldly, aesthetic, almost feminine Platonism, exercised immense power over his readers: over the young Diderot; over Moses Mendelssohn, Wieland, and Kant; over Thomas Jefferson; all in search of a philosophy of nature less hostile to the things of this world than traditional Christian doctrine. The propagandists of the Enlightenment were French, but its patron saints and pioneers were British: Bacon, Newton, and Locke had such splendid reputations on the Continent that they quite overshadowed the revolutionary ideas of a Descartes or a Fontenelle and it became not only tactically useful but intellectually respectable in eighteenth-century France to attribute to British savants ideas they may well have learned from Frenchmen. In an *Essai sur les études en Russie,* probably by Grimm, we are told that ever since the revival of letters, enlightenment had been generated in Protestant rather than Catholic countries: "Without the English, reason and philosophy would still be in the most despicable infancy in France," and Montesquieu and Voltaire, the two

French pioneers, "were the pupils and followers of England's philosophers and great men."

Among scientists, poets, and philosophers on the Continent, this admiration for England became so fashionable that its detractors coined a derisive epithet—Anglomania—which its devotees applied, a little self-consciously, to themselves. Skeptics like Diderot and Holbach, who ventured at mid-century to find some fault with British institutions, were in a distinct minority: in the German-speaking world of poets Hagedorn and Klopstock and the physicist Lichtenberg confessed to *Englandsehnsucht,* while Lessing discovered Shakespeare and patterned his first bourgeois tragedy, *Miss Sara Sampson,* on an English model. In the Italian states, reformers idealized the English constitution and the English genius for philosophy: Beccaria's friends could think of no more affectionate and admiring nickname for him than *Newtoncino*—little Newton. But *Anglomanie* was practiced most persistently and most systematically in France: Montesquieu constructed a fanciful but influential model of the British government for other, less favored nations to imitate; Voltaire, well prepared by his early reading, came back in 1728 from his long English visit a serious deist and firm Newtonian and in general a lifelong worshipper of England: "A thousand people," he wrote in 1764, "rise up and declaim against 'Anglomania.' . . . If, by chance, these orators want to make the desire to study, observe, philosophize like the English into a crime, they would be very much in the wrong."

For all of Voltaire's earnest claims, it must be admitted that this cosmopolitan dialogue was not always conducted on the highest level. Hume's influence on the French and the Germans is a study in missed opportunities: Kant, for all his much-advertised debt to Hume, seems never to have read the *Treatise of Human Nature;* except perhaps for d'Alembert and Turgot, the Parisian philosophes, whom Hume greatly liked and who gave him a rousing reception during his stay in the 1760's, neither shared nor fully understood his skepticism; Voltaire, who told an English visitor in his quaint accent that "I am hees great admeerer; he is a very great onor to Ingland, and abofe all to Ecosse," appears to have been as ignorant of Hume's epistemology as he was amused by Hume's quarrel with Rousseau. Still, not all philosophic intercourse was gossip and triviality. British empiricism transformed French rationalism, French scientific and political propaganda transformed Europe.

The philosophe was a cosmopolitan by conviction as well as by training. Like the ancient Stoic, he would exalt the interest of mankind above the interest of country or clan: as Diderot told Hume in an outburst of spontaneous good feeling, "My dear David, you belong to all nations, and you'll never ask an unhappy man for his birth-certificate. I flatter myself that I am, like you, citizen of the great city of the world." Rousseau's intense patriotism was exceptional. Wieland, with all his pessimism, still thought *Weltbürgertum* a noble ideal: "Only the true cosmopolitan can be a good citizen"; only he can "do the great work to which we have been called: to cultivate, enlighten, and ennoble the human race." Gibbon explained in his magisterial tones that "it is the duty of a patriot to prefer and promote the exclusive interest and glory of his native country; but a philosopher may be permitted to enlarge his views, and to consider Europe as a great republic, whose various inhabitants have attained almost the same level of politeness and cultivation." As products of the best schools, with a solid grip on a classical culture, the philosophes, the most privileged citizens in Gibbon's great republic, spoke the same language —literally and figuratively.

The typical philosophe, then, was a cultivated man, a respectable scholar and scientific amateur. The most distinguished among the little flock were academics like Kant, Lichtenberg, and Adam Smith, or men of letters like Diderot and Lessing and Galiani, who possessed an erudition a professor might envy. Some of the philosophes were in fact more than amateurs in natural philosophy. Franklin, D'Alembert, Maupertuis, Lichtenberg, and Buffon first achieved reputations as scientists before they acquired notoriety as philosophes. Others, like Voltaire, advanced the cause of scientific civilization with their skillful popularizations of Newton's discoveries.

At the same time, learned as they were, the philosophes were rarely ponderous and generally superbly articulate. It was the philosophe Buffon who coined the celebrated maxim, *Le style est l'homme même;* the philosophe Lessing who helped to make German into a literary language; the philosophe Hume who wrote the most elegant of essays as well as the most technical of epistemological treatises. Rigorous Christians found it a source of chagrin that practically all of the best writers belonged to the philosophic family. Even men who detested Voltaire's opinions rushed to the bookseller for his latest production. This concern with style was linked to an old-fashioned versatility. The philosophes remained men of letters, at times playwrights, at times journalists, at times scholars, always wits. Adam Smith was not merely an economist, but a moralist and political theorist—a philosopher in the most comprehensive sense. Diderot was, with almost equal competence, translator, editor, playwright, psychologist, art critic and theorist, novelist, classical scholar, and educational and ethical reformer. David Hume has often been accused of betraying his philosophical vocation for turning in his later years from epistemology to history and polite essays. But this accusation mistakes Hume's conception of his place in the world: he was exercising his prerogative as a man of letters qualified to pronounce on most aspects of human experience, and writing for a cultivated public in which he was consumer as well as producer.

Such a type could flourish only in the city, and in fact the typical philosophe was eminently, defiantly, incurably urban. The city was his soil; it nourished his mind and transmitted his message. His well-publicized visits to monarchs were more glittering than the life of the coffeehouse, the editor's office, or a salon, which was often little more than a gathering of congenial intellectuals. But they were also less productive. The philosophe belonged to the city, by birth or adoption: if he was born in the country he drifted to the city as his proper habitat. "The Town," observed David Hume in his autobiography, is "the true Scene for a man of Letters." What would Kant have been without Königsberg, Franklin without Philadelphia, Rousseau without Geneva, Beccaria without Milan, Diderot without Paris, or for that matter, Gibbon without Rome? When the philosophe traveled, he moved from urban society to urban society in a pleasant glow of cosmopolitan communication. When he retired to the country, as he often did with protestations of his love for the simple life, he took the city with him: he invited like-minded men of letters to share his solitude, he escaped rural boredom by producing plays, he lined his walls with books, and he kept up with literary gossip through his correspondents in town—his letters were almost like little newspapers. For many years Holbach gathered an international company around his dinner table: Diderot and Raynal were regular visitors, joined from time to time by Horace Walpole, David Hume, the abbé Galiani, and other distinguished foreigners who would sit and talk endlessly about religion, about politics, about all the great forbidden subjects. In Milan, Beccaria, the Verri brothers, and other like-minded *illuministi* founded a newspaper, *Il Caffé;* it was short-lived, but its very existence documents the alliance of sociability and reformism in the Enlightenment everywhere. The leaders of the Scottish Enlightenment—a most distinguished society—were personal as well as intellectual intimates: Adam Smith, David Hume, Adam Ferguson, William Robertson, Lord Home—political economists, aestheticians, moralists, historians, philosophers and philosophes all— held continuous convivial discussions during the day and often through the night in libraries, clubs, coffeehouses, and when these closed, in taverns. Voltaire presided over a literary government-in-exile in Ferney. He stayed away from Paris for twenty-eight years in succession, but that did not matter: where he was, *there* was Paris. The best of the urban spirit— experimental, mobile, irreverent—was in the philosophes' bones.

But this urbanity was colored and sometimes marred by a sense of mission. The philosophes were threatening the most powerful institutions of their day, and they were troubled by the nagging anxiety that they were battling resourceful enemies—for one, a church (as Voltaire said ruefully) that was truly built on a rock. That is why the philosophes were both witty and humorless: the wit was demanded by their profession, the humorlessness imposed on them by their belligerent status. Obsessed by enemies, not all of whom were imaginary, they were likely to treat criticism as libel and jokes as blasphemy. They were touchy in the extreme; Diderot's correspondence and Rousseau's *Confessions* record bickerings over matters not worth a moment of a grown man's attention. David Hume, who saw through the press a polemical pamphlet directed against himself, was quite uncharacteristic; far more typical were d'Alembert, who petitioned the censors to stifle his critics, or Lessing, who pursued scholars of opposing views and inferior capacities with his relentless, savage learning. This is what Goethe had in mind when he called the Berlin *Aufklärer* Nicolai a "Jesuitenfresser"; and this is why Horace Walpole observed in 1779 that "the *philosophes,* except Buffon, are solemn, arrogant, dictatorial coxcombs—I need not say superlatively disagreeable." No doubt Walpole, the fastidious spectator of life, saw the philosophes clearly, but what he did not see is that this intensity and self-assurance (which often make men disagreeable) are occupational hazards which reformers find hard to avoid.

IV

In drawing this collective portrait, I have indiscriminately taken evidence from the entire eighteenth century, from Montesquieu to Kant. This procedure has its advantages: it underlines the family resemblance among the little flock. But it may obscure the fact that the Enlightenment had a history. Its end was not like its beginning precisely because the last generation of philosophes could draw on the work of its predecessors.

It has been traditional to delimit the Enlightenment within a hundred-year span beginning with the English Revolution and ending with the French Revolution. These are convenient and evocative dates: Montesquieu was born in 1689 and Holbach died in 1789. To be sure, these limits are not absolute, and there have been repeated attempts to move the boundaries, to demote the Enlightenment by calling it the last act of the Renaissance, or to expand it by including Bayle, or even Descartes, among the philosophes. But while these attempts have thrown much light on the prehistory of eighteenth-century polemics, I intend to stay with the traditional dates: I shall argue that while characteristic Enlightenment ideas existed long before, they achieved their revolutionary force only in the eighteenth century. Hobbes, and even Bayle, lived and wrote in a world markedly different from the world of Holbach or Hume.

The Enlightenment, then, was the work of three overlapping, closely associated generations. The first of these, dominated by Montesquieu and the long-lived Voltaire, long set the tone for the other two; it grew up while the writings of Locke and Newton were still fresh and controversial, and did most of its great work before 1750. The second generation reached maturity in mid-century: Franklin was born in 1706, Buffon in 1707, Hume in 1711, Rousseau in 1712, Diderot in 1713, Condillac in 1714, Helvétius in 1715, and d'Alembert in 1717. It was these writers who fused the fashionable anticlericalism and scientific speculations of the first generation into a coherent modern view of the world. The third generation, the generation of Holbach and Beccaria, of Lessing and Jefferson, of Wieland, Kant, and Turgot, was close enough to the second, and to the survivors of the first, to be applauded, encouraged, and irritated by both. It moved into scientific mythology and materialist metaphysics, political economy, legal reform, and practical politics. Criticism progressed by criticizing itself and its own works.

So the Enlightenment displays not merely coherence but a distinct evolution, a continuity in styles of thinking as well as a growing radicalism. The foundations of the philosophes' ideas did not change significantly: between the young Montesquieu's essay on ancient Rome and the aging Diderot's defense of Seneca there is a lapse of half a century, and interest in ancient architecture and sculpture had risen markedly during the interval; yet for the two philosophes, the uses of antiquity remained the same. Similarly, the devotion to modern science and the hostility to Christianity that were characteristic of the late Enlightenment had been characteristic of the early Enlightenment as well. The dialectic which defined the philosophes did not change; what changed was the balance of forces within the philosophic coalition: as writer succeeded writer and polemic succeeded polemic, criticism became deeper and wider, more far-reaching, more uncompromising. In the first half of the century, the leading philosophes had been deists and had used the vocabulary of natural law; in the second half, the leaders were atheists and used the vocabulary of utility. In Enlightenment aesthetics, in close conjunction with the decay of natural law, the neoclassical search for the objective laws of beauty gave way to subjectivity and the exaltation of taste, and especially in France, timid and often trivial political ideas were shouldered aside by an aggressive radicalism. Yet the scandal the later books caused was no greater than that caused by the pioneering efforts: had Montesquieu's *Lettres persanes* been published in 1770, the year of Holbach's *Système de la nature,* rather than in 1721, it would have seemed tame beside that materialist tract, and would have offered nothing new to a world long since hardened to cultural criticism.

One reason the educated world of eighteenth-century Europe and America had come to accept these polemics, or at least to read them without flinching, was that the hard core of the Enlightenment was surrounded by an ever-growing penumbra of associates. The dozen-odd captains of the movement, whose names must bulk large in any history of the European mind, were abetted by a host of lieutenants. Some of these, little read today, had a considerable reputation in their time. They were men like the abbé de Mably, precursor of socialism and propagandist of the American cause in France; Jean-François Marmontel, fashionable, mediocre playwright, careerist protégé of Voltaire and d'Alembert elected to the Académie française and chosen Royal Historiographer despite his participation in the *Encyclopédie* and his pronounced views in favor of toleration; Charles Duclos, brilliant and widely respected observer of the social scene, novelist, and historian; the abbé Raynal, ex-priest turned radical historian, whose *Histoire philosophique et politique des établissements et du commerce des Européens dans les deux Indes,* first published in 1770, and immediately proscribed, went through several editions, each more radical than its predecessor; the abbé Galiani, a Neapolitan wit who became an ornament of the Parisian salons and a serious political economist; Moses Mendelssohn, Lessing's friend and Kant's correspondent, aesthetician, epistemologist, and advocate of Jewish emancipation; Baron Grimm, who made a good living purveying the new ideas to monarchs and aristocrats rich enough to afford his private news service; Louis-Jean-Marie Daubenton, a distinguished naturalist whose contributions to science were eclipsed by Buffon, with whom he collaborated; Freiherr von Sonnenfels, a humane political economist, professor at the University of Vienna and, for all his advanced ideas, advisor to the Hapsburgs; Nicolas-Antoine Boulanger, who died young, but left behind him two unorthodox scientific treatises on the origins of religion for his friend Holbach to publish. These men were philosophes of the second rank. Beyond them were the privates of the movement, the hangers-on, consumers and distributors rather than producers of ideas: men like Étienne-Noël Damilaville, Voltaire's correspondent in Paris, who basked in borrowed prestige or second-hand notoriety by running humanitarian errands, smuggling subversive literature through the mails, hiring theatrical claques, or offering disinterested friendship in a harsh world. As the century progressed, these aides grew in number and influence: to embattled Christians, they appeared to be everywhere, in strategic positions—in publishers' offices, in government posts, in exclusive salons, in influential university chairs, near royal persons, and even in the august Académie française. By the 1770's and 1780's, precisely when the philosophes had grown intensely radical in their program, they had also achieved a respectable place in their society.

25

Gay

ENLIGHTENMENT'S "LITTLE FLOCK OF PHILOSOPHES"

3. The Politics of the Enlightenment

ALFRED COBBAN

"*The* philosophes," *writes the late Alfred Cobban in this selection, ". . . took as their end the happiness of individuals. This they believed to be largely dependent on environment and education, and these in turn on social institutions and government, which therefore held the key to a happier society." For Professor Cobban, then, the "culminating feature" of the Enlightenment was its political stance. And so it has been for most historians. Enlightenment politics undergirded the political thought of the American and French Revolutions and, if we are to believe Cobban, "it legislated for posterity" through its last great figure, Bentham. But in politics, as in so many other aspects, Enlightenment thought was extremely diverse and seemingly contradictory. It extended from the followers of Locke to thinkers as varied as Montesquieu, d'Holbach, Rousseau, and Bentham.*

In the following selection Alfred Cobban describes Enlightenment political thought and its importance. Until his recent death he was professor of modern history at the University of London. He was the author of an important history of France as well as a number of works which fundamentally reinterpreted the French Revolution. This selection is a chapter from his book on the Enlightenment in which he expresses views similar to those of Peter Gay, believing that the philosophes were neither utopians nor fawning celebrators of despotism, as some historians have held. In Cobban's view, why did Voltaire,

Source: Alfred Cobban, *In Search of Humanity* (New York: George Braziller, 1960), pp. 161–79. Reprinted with permission of George Braziller, Inc. and Jonathan Cape, Ltd. Copyright © 1960 by Alfred Cobban. [Footnotes omitted.]

Diderot and d'Holbach object to absolute monarchy even if it were "en-
lightened despotism?" How were their arguments shaped by the ideas of
Locke and Montesquieu? In Rousseau's thought, what is the relationship be-
tween the individual and society? What, for him, is the nature of and necessity
for the General Will, and how does it differ from both the government and the
will of all? In England how did the contract theory of Locke give way to utili-
tarianism under the influence of Price, Hume, and Burke? What were the tenets
of Bentham?

With Diderot and Rousseau, though it would be impossible to separate them from the main stream of the Enlightenment, there are signs
that we are moving into a new intellectual climate; but before concluding
even [a] short survey of the Enlightenment there is one major aspect
which remains to be discussed. This is its political thinking, which may
be regarded as its culminating feature. The *philosophes, . . .* took as
their end the happiness of individuals. This they believed to be largely
dependent on environment and education, and these in turn on social
institutions and government, which therefore held the key to a happier
society. The neglect of the political thinking of the Enlightenment can
be attributed to various causes. The history of thought, because of
the political historian's general lack of interest in ideas, has tended to
be left to students of literature, who are naturally less interested in politics. It is also true that, so long as the explanation is kept on a fairly superficial level, a consistent account can be provided of the political history
of Western Europe in the eighteenth century, up to 1789, without introducing any consideration of political ideas. Thirdly, between Locke and
Burke and Bentham there are no outstanding names in the history of
British political thought; while in France, Montesquieu does not fit easily
into the accepted pattern and Rousseau has often been taken as belonging
to the subsequent period. Finally, it has been assumed, ever since the 'enlightened despots' was invented as a text-book category, that the political
thought of the Enlightenment must be summed up as a justification of
their despotism. This last, since it is the most common prejudice, is perhaps the best point from which to start a discussion of the politics of the
Enlightenment.

The rise of contractual and Natural Law thought, and its culmination
in the work of Locke, have already been described, as well as the decline
of the influence of these ideas in the practical politics of Europe. . . .
The period from the sixteenth to the eighteenth century, which saw the
triumph of the great European monarchies, witnessed the culmination of
ideas of divine right and absolutism. The Natural Law school of thought
itself, with Grotius assimilating the rights of government to property, and
Pufendorf preserving the forms of the natural law—social contract pattern but abandoning the right of resistance, seemed to be moving towards
a justification of absolute sovereignty.

To set against these great names of European political thought there
was only the translation of Locke's *Second Treatise* into French, but it

was enough. The clue to French eighteenth-century ideas on politics is provided, in the absence of genius, which cannot be made to order, by second-hand and second-rate writers such as Barbeyrac and Burlamaqui, who were not the less influential at the time for lacking the originality of their greater predecessors and successors. Barbeyrac's translations into French of Pufendorf and Grotius, which went through many editions, might easily be supposed to have spread the absolutist tendencies of these writers; but in fact, the effect of the text is largely counteracted by the translator's notes, in which are given long extracts from Locke, opposing his views to those of Pufendorf. Barbeyrac claims that there is always a tacit right of resistance, which comes into operation when the prince abuses his power or uses it against the people's interest. Obedience may be refused on moral grounds, even by state officers. For example, the Parlements of France may refuse to register a law; again, there is a right to refuse to bear arms in an unjust war. Unlike Pufendorf, Barbeyrac favours the division of powers. He admires the English constitution. He criticizes Grotius' equation of sovereignty with the right of property.

Burlamaqui was an able Swiss popularizer. His *Principes du droit naturel* (1747) and *Principes du droit politique* (1751), with little or no original thought in them, became standard treatises in the eighteenth century. He followed Montesquieu in praising the balance of powers and mixed government, either in the form of limited monarchy as in England, or of aristocracy tempered by democracy as in Geneva. Like Montesquieu he insisted that there were limitations on the rightful authority even of absolute monarchy. He declared:

> We must not confound an absolute power with an arbitrary, despotic, and unlimited authority. For, from what we have now said concerning the origin and nature of absolute sovereignty, it manifestly follows, that it is limited, from its very nature, by the intention of those who conferred it on the sovereign, and by the very laws of God.

This is an assertion of fundamental law, and that it is not an appeal to an abstract, unenforceable platitude is shown by what follows:

> The fundamental laws, which limit the sovereign authority, are nothing else but the means which the people use to assure themselves that the prince will not recede from the general law of the public good.

The significant point, of course, is not the recognition of the general good as the end of sovereignty, but of the right of the people to enforce it. A similar assertion of the right of resistance to tyranny is to be found in the Genevan Vattel, one of the greatest of the successors of Grotius in the field of international law.

Geneva and England were the chief sources of constitutional ideas in eighteenth-century Europe. Montesquieu in particular was responsible for the general admiration of the English constitution. The view that such admiration came to an end about 1760 has been shown to be mistaken. The change came rather with the American War. It was partly a result of Whig attacks on the corruption of the House of Commons and the despotism of George III, partly of the propaganda of the American colonists, and partly of the prestige resulting from their victorious revolt. They offered an alternative ideal, and one which, it might be argued, was closer to true Lockian ideals and at the same time more in line with the literary cult of republicanism.

This cult should not be misunderstood. By a republic was understood a country ruled by laws and not arbitrary will; it was not necessarily incompatible with limited monarchy. Classical education, and the classical revival in the second half of the century, contributed to the growing favour of the republican ideal, which is reflected in the definitions in the Dictionary of the French Academy. In 1694 republican equals seditious; in 1718 this unfavourable definition is suppressed; and from 1740 favourable examples of the term appear. Voltaire was a good monarchist, but he could write *Brutus,* a republican tragedy, as early as 1730, and even in his later years did not abandon his admiration for the English constitution.

Since Voltaire is often taken as a representative of the supposed bias of the *philosophes* in favour of enlightened despotism, it will be useful to examine in a little more detail his political ideas. They are not the less significant for being unsystematic and incidental, expressed in works which for the most part are not primarily concerned with politics. His praise of Catherine of Russia and Frederick II should not be forgotten, nor his contempt for the masses—the people 'sera toujours sot et barbare'. 'Quand la populace se mêle de raisonner, tout est perdu.' Faced with the question whether a republican government is preferable to that of a king, he concludes, with characteristic political Pyrrhonism, 'la dispute finit toujours par convenir qu'il est fort difficile de gouverner les hommes'. On the other hand, he can write, 'La liberté consiste à ne dépendre que des lois'. When Voltaire says, 'I will admit to you that I would adapt myself well enough to a democratic government . . . I like to see free men themselves making the laws under which they live,' he puts this in the mouth of a citizen of the Dutch Republic. Such pious sentiments do not take us very far, and on the other hand Voltaire criticized Montesquieu's definition of republics; they were founded, he said, not on virtue but on pride and ambition, and were suited only to small States. He opposed intermediate powers in the State, such as the Parlements, and was almost the only *philosophe* who understood the real political needs of France well enough to defend the suppression of these courts by Maupeou and Louis XV. He was more interested in practical reforms than in constitutional safeguards, and he saw the Parlements for the obscurantist defenders of vested interests that they were. From all this no consistent picture or systematic political view emerges. On the whole we must conclude that Voltaire was not very politically minded. He was intensely liberal, but hardly appreciated how much personal liberties depend on political forms. In spite of this, to take him as an advocate of despotism would be to do violence to his thought.

For more developed political ideas we must look elsewhere. The political articles in the *Encyclopédie* were largely compiled by the chevalier de Jaucourt out of the works of Locke and Montesquieu, and express a contractual theory of government. Diderot himself argues that man being made for society, the common good should be his supreme law. By nature men are equal, and for the establishment of government there is needed either a formal or a tacit contract between them and their rulers. Government is necessary for society, but it is only legitimate in so far as it promotes the general happiness. While condemning democracy as chimerical, or at best only possible in tiny States, he is bitter against despotism. It is sometimes claimed, he says, that the best government is that of a just and enlightened despot. This is to forget that, 'on peut abuser de son pouvoir pour faire le bien comme pour faire le mal'. A man is never entitled to treat his fellow beings as a troop of cattle. If a legislator does not consult and respect the general will, he destroys the bonds of society. Although Diderot wrote no political treatise, an anthology of such apothegms could be selected from his works.

The most systematic political theorist among the *philosophes,* apart from Montesquieu and Rousseau, is d'Holbach, in whom can be traced the same development that was occurring in English political thinking. This was the almost complete substitution of the principle of utility for the idea of the contract. It is not difficult to trace in d'Holbach the main stages in the eighteenth-century progress to utilitarianism. It begins from the generally accepted view that the function of politics is to put moral principles into practice. Since 'nature makes men neither good nor bad', it is the task of parents, teachers, rulers to do that. Thus politics is 'the art of regulating the passions of men and directing them to the good of society', which d'Holbach defines in strictly utilitarian terms:

> Laws, to be just, must have as their invariable end the general interest of society, that is to say, to ensure to the greatest number of citizens the advantages for which they are associated together. These advantages are liberty, property and security. *Liberty* is the capacity of doing for one's own happiness whatever does not injure the happiness of others . . . *Property* is the ability of each member of the society to enjoy the advantages which his labour and industry have obtained for him . . . Justice . . . prevents members of a society from using against one another the inequality in strength, which nature or industry may have created.

Like Bentham later, d'Holbach, having decided that it is the function of government to reconcile the self-interest of individuals with the good of society, is faced with the problem of ensuring that it shall want to do so. At this point, where the thought of Bentham passes over into democracy, d'Holbach falls back on the traditional Lockian argument of a negative control over government: 'Since government only derives its authority from society, and is only established for the good of society, it is evident that society can revoke this authority when its interest so demands.'

Like Locke, he has a profound suspicion of political power. He writes, in Actonian language: 'The experience of all ages will convince nations that man is always tempted to abuse power.' From this emerges a full-scale onslaught on despotism. D'Holbach argues in Lockian fashion that the despot is the true revolutionary. The evils of despotism he sees equally in the state of national and international affairs. In their relations with one another, rulers are in that Hobbesian state of nature which is simple anarchy:

> Do not their continual wars; their quarrels, often unjust and puer-
> ile; the unconsidered passions and caprices to which these sover-
> eigns sacrifice so lightly both their own happiness and that of their
> subjects, declare that they are still for the most part Caribs or true
> cannibals?

From his attack on despotism, d'Holbach passes on, in a spirit not dissimilar from that of Diderot and Rousseau, to a general denunciation of the whole existing order of things. His references in this vein are brief and scattered, but they are violent. Are nations made, he asks, 'to work without respite to satisfy the vanity, the luxury, the greed of a pack of useless and corrupt blood-suckers'?

What hope is there then? His answer brings us back to what was the panacea of the *philosophes*—enlightenment or education. D'Holbach's faith is in the power of truth, which nothing, he says, can destroy. 'The love of truth is only the love of the human race.' The power of truth is greater than that of any armed rebellion. Nor is this a mere forlorn hope: there are signs that enlightenment is spreading. Everywhere can be seen the effects of the 'progrès des lumières', he believes.

> If error and ignorance have forged the chains of the peoples, if prej-
> udice perpetuates them, science, reason, truth will one day break
> them. The human mind, benumbed for a long succession of centu-
> ries by superstition and cruelty, has at last reawakened.

D'Holbach's political views may be excessively optimistic; they are not ignoble. Nor is the advocacy of despotism or governmental tyranny of any
kind to be drawn from his writings.

For even a plausible attribution of a theory of benevolent despotism there is only one group of thinkers to be found in eighteenth-century France. This is the Physiocratic school, who were economists rather than political theorists. Their thought was basically Cartesian. They were rationalists who believed in a natural order of things. Evil is the result of breaking this order, which, if it is allowed to operate freely, ensures the maximum degree of welfare. In economic matters laissez-faire was the corollary of this faith in natural laws. On the other hand, politically they took absolute monarchy to be the best form of government, being that in which the interests of the ruler in the maximization of the wealth of his State is identical with those of his subjects. His power has nothing arbitrary about it because his function is simply to proclaim and enforce natural laws. The result is a combination of total economic liberty for the individual with total political power for the ruler. That this added up to simple nonsense became evident even to the second generation of Physiocrats themselves, such as Mercier de la Rivière, and they abandoned the idea of enlightened despotism.

The greatest name, after that of Montesquieu, in the history of French political thought during the eighteenth century is that of Rousseau. Whether he belongs to the pattern of enlightened thought that has been sketched, or anticipates the ideas of the Romantic and Idealist thinkers of the following century, is a matter of dispute. Sir Ernest Barker declares:

> We may almost say that the vogue of Rousseau depends on the fact that a great master of style gave to the world of letters, and the general reader, a system of thought which had hitherto been expressed mainly in Latin, and written by lawyers for lawyers.

There are two defects in this analysis of the importance of Rousseau as a political writer. The first is that the works of the great authors of the Natural Law school were either written in English or French, or else translated into those languages; and that, as the number of editions they went through shows, some of these works were widely read. The second point is that far from popularizing their ideas, the *Contrat social* was, of all the works of Rousseau, that which received the least notice, at least up to 1789. This was suggested long ago by Mornet's analysis of a large number of eighteenth-century libraries. Whereas he found, for example, 165 copies of the *Nouvelle Héloïse,* and even eighty-two of such a bulky and expensive work as the *Encyclopédie,* of the *Contrat social* he found only one. Stories such as that of Marat reading the *Contrat social* to admiring crowds at the street corner are such patent nonsense that it is a wonder that any reputable historian should ever have troubled to repeat them. Whatever political influence Rousseau had is a result of the Revolution, and then it is to be found in the beginning as much, if not more, on the counter-revolutionary as on the revolutionary side. In spite of these qualifications, however, Sir Ernest Barker is right in associating Rousseau with the Natural Law school of thought. He asks the same questions and he uses the same language. It might almost be held that the whole school culminates in the work of Rousseau, which, it has been said, crowns 'the struggle against royal absolutism and enfranchisement from the traditional doctrines of the Catholic Church on the divine origin of civil authority'.

The basis of Rousseau's political theory is the essentially individualist conception of the State of Nature, to which he gives his own particular interpretation in the *Discourse on Inequality*. It follows that for him the State cannot be more than an 'être moral' or 'corps artificiel'—a body, that is, with only an 'abstract and collective existence'. Wherever Rousseau uses what appears to be organic language in dealing with the State, it is clearly only as an analogy.

It would be a mistake, however, to suppose that for Rousseau man in society is still the isolated, atomistic individual of his hypothetical State of Nature: the creation of society has involved a psychological revolution:

> This passage from the state of nature to the civil state produces in man a very remarkable change, substituting in his conduct justice for instinct, giving to his actions the morality which was lacking in them hitherto. It is then only that, the voice of duty succeeding to physical impulse, and justice to desire, man, who up to this point had only considered himself, sees himself compelled to act on other principles and to consult his reason before listening to his desires.

In other words, once he has entered into society man has become a moral and political animal, with possibilities for good and evil which he did not previously possess. This is the basic fact of the situation. Quite early Rousseau had written that the vices of man 'do not belong so much to man as to man badly ruled'. In other words, the key to the good life is in politics. In the *Confessions* he put down as one of the discoveries that had most influenced his thinking that of the basic importance of politics, that 'tout tenait radicalement à la politique'. It was indeed only in the eighteenth century with the rise of the idea of absolute sovereignty and the emancipation of government from the restraints that had formerly bound it, that this began to be true. The sovereign State was at last becoming a fact and Rousseau's political theory was an attempt to come to grips with the problem it presented. His theory of the General Will represents an attempt to reconcile liberty with sovereignty and he demonstrates his affiliation with his century in regarding this as fundamentally a moral issue.

As Rousseau states it, the problem is that the natural goodness, or compassion, of man, his *bonté naturelle,* is not adequate to resist the temptations which arise out of social life. These are the result of the moral crisis which comes with the passage from the isolated individualism of the State of Nature to life in society, which brings with it also the change in motivation from natural self-preservation—*amour de soi*— to *amour propre,* which one might call, in Hobbesian language, pride. To all the innocent if amoral passions, *amour propre* adds an element of perversion, to cope with which man's individual *bonté naturelle* has to be supplemented by *vertu,* which is the triumph of reason over the passions. In the individual this is the moral and rational conscience; in society the General Will, which, like the conscience in the individual, is always present, even when its voice is not heard. For the laws of the State to be legitimate, Rousseau holds, the General Will must find expression in them.

The General Will is reconcilable with liberty, first because it is the exteriorization in politics of the moral will of the individual; and secondly, because of limitations Rousseau introduces, which may also possibly be taken as evidence of his appreciation of the dangers implicit in the idea. It must be emphasized that the idea of a sovereignty which is both absolute and limited is a commonplace of the Natural Law school of thought; there is nothing paradoxical in the title Rousseau gives to one of his chapters—'On the limits of the sovereign power'. Thus his General

Will has only the function of laying down and maintaining the laws of society, by which he means fundamental, constitutional laws, not day-to-day regulations. It cannot take any particular decision affecting individual persons or acts. Secondly, a clear distinction is drawn between the General Will, which operates only by general laws and is sovereign, and the Government, which exercises all the usual executive powers but has no sovereign authority. Thirdly, the General Will is not the will of all: it is the will which is inspired by good motives and directed only to the common interest. It is indeed an ideal of perfection, which Rousseau expects to see realized on earth rarely if ever.

These are all safeguards against the use of the idea of the General Will to justify tyrannical power, but they also carry Rousseau far beyond his starting-point. If he began with all the normal presuppositions of the school of Natural Law, he has now moved away from them. The particular quality of Natural Law thought, as represented, for example, by its most influential exponent in this period, Locke, had been that it rigorously limited the scope of politics and therefore of political power. The criteria by which political action was judged were outside politics. The real problem was to discover what they were. After those laid down by revealed religion had been seen as patently unsatisfactory, theorists fell back on the rational and moral judgment of the individual; and while the State was restricted to more or less utilitarian ends, they could be measured satisfactorily by utilitarian standards. Rousseau reintroduced an ideal of perfection into politics, the effect of which was to bring back dangers similar to those of religious politics, which the Enlightenment believed it had eliminated. Voltaire, however unfair and worse he was to Rousseau, saw truly that there was something alarming in his genius, even if he did not understand what it was.

But in the last resort Rousseau still belongs to the world of the Enlightenment and shares its liberal ideals. Defending himself against Genevan critics, he declared that Locke had treated the same subjects in exactly the same manner as himself; and if this seems a little exaggerated, we may agree that Locke, along with Montesquieu, certainly exercised the greatest influence over his political thinking. Rousseau's later political writings, the *Lettres écrites de la montagne,* dealing with the Genevan constitution, his *Projet pour la Corse* and *Considérations sur le gouvernement de Pologne,* are proof of this. If the *Contrat social* points in a different direction, it stands alone. But it shows that while Rousseau did not follow where his genius led, he was conscious, like Diderot, of coming changes.

The immediate influence of the *Contrat social* was negligible. To attribute to Rousseau the intention of revolutionizing political life, or even of promoting an actual revolution, is moreover to misunderstand him and his thought. Of course, he *was* misunderstood, even at the time. As he complained, men persisted in seeing a revolutionary 'in the man of the world who has the truest respect for national laws and constitutions, and the greatest aversion for revolutions'.

A change was coming over political thinking in the last quarter of the eighteenth century. Anticipations of it may be detected in such writers as Diderot, Rousseau, Mably and even d'Holbach; but they still belong essentially to the Enlightenment. For the continuation and culmination of its political thinking, however, we shall have to recross the Channel and see what had been happening to the tradition of Locke in his own country. For England in the eighteenth century was not immune from the growing influence of the idea of sovereignty, though it was parliamentary and not monarchical sovereignty as on the Continent. The temper of the age can be detected in Blackstone, when he writes: 'There is and must be [in every state] a supreme, irresistible, absolute uncontrolled authority, in which the *jura summa imperii,* or the rights of sovereignty, reside.'

In the second half of the eighteenth century this idea of sovereignty was to come into rough conflict with the still surviving influence of the Lockian tradition, in such episodes as the Middlesex election of 1768, General Warrants, and above all the dispute with the American colonies, where the pure milk of Lockian doctrine was still undefiled. In America, ideas of social contract, natural rights, government as trusteeship, and so on, continued to dominate political thinking. The writers of the American Revolution, it has been said, had a theory of society, a theory of government, and a theory of the relation of the one to the other: but of the State in the modern sense they knew little. If a summary of the ideas of the revolutionary pamphleteers, of greater figures like Jefferson, and of the Declaration of Independence are not recited here as illustrative of the political thought of the Enlightenment, it is only because to do so would be merely to repeat what has already been said in treating of Locke and the political thinking of the seventeenth century.

In England, too, the dispute with the colonies provided the occasion for protests against the assertion of parliamentary sovereignty. Thus the great lawyer Lord Camden declared: "Taxation and representation are inseparable; this position is founded on the laws of nature.' And, quoting Locke: 'The supreme power cannot take from any man any part of his property without his own consent.' Among British writers on politics also the ideas of Natural Law survived. This has only been forgotten because, in the absence of great names, these writers, like Barbeyrac and Burlamaqui in France, have dropped out of text-book currency. But Thomas Rutherford upheld the right of resistance in his *Institutes of Natural Law* (1754–6). The Swiss Delolme, in his widely read eulogy of the British constitution, described resistance as 'the ultimate and lawful recourse against the violences of Power', and attributed the 'freedom of the Constitution' to 'an equilibrium between the ruling Powers of the State'. Similar ideas are to be found in Adam Ferguson's *Essay on the History of Civil Society* (1782), and many other works.

Again, Richard Price, in *Observations on the Nature of Civil Liberty* (1776), which went through eight editions in ten years, declared: 'Government . . . is in the very nature of it, a trust; and all its powers a delegation for gaining particular ends.' Price, however, and the English democrats such as Priestley, Cartwright, Paine, tend to drop the formal social contract out of their theory; and though retaining and emphasizing natural rights, they give them a more patently utilitarian turn. This development may be explained in terms of the general eighteenth-century bias away from the abstract, rationalist, a priori thinking of the previous age, and towards a more historical and empirical attitude. The contract now comes under criticism as unhistorical. Soame Jenyns, denying the State of Nature and the original contract, writes in Burkian language: 'The natural state of man is by no means a state of solitude and independence, but of society and subordination; all the effects of human art are part of his nature.'

The most devastating, though not necessarily the most influential criticism of the contractual argument was that of Hume. He put the case in both philosophical and pragmatic terms. To be valid, he said, a contract implies a preceding agreement that contracts should be kept. In other words, it requires as a necessary preliminary the conditions that it is supposed to create. The result is to plunge us into an infinite regress. Secondly, in practice men do not, Hume points out, obey government because of some hypothetical contractual obligation to do so; their real motive is utility 'because otherwise society could not subsist' and this is enough by itself. This verdict is the only one compatible with Hume's philosophy, with his refusal to accept hypothetical constructions, or fictions masquerading as truth, to account for what can be explained much more directly by the plain facts of observation. As he puts it:

> If the sense of common interest were not our original motive to obedience, I wou'd fain ask, what other principle is there in human nature capable of subduing the natural ambition of men, and forcing them to such a submission?

Adam Smith and Bentham accept Hume's arguments on the contractual theory as decisive, and whether we attribute it to the effect of Hume's criticism or not, this was the end of the contract.

The consequence of its abandonment, however, was not to set up an absolute right of sovereignty. On the contrary, even for the conservative Hume, resistance to government, when it is a case of self-preservation or of defending the public good, is more than a right, it is an inescapable fact. Although political thinking in Great Britain in the second half of the eighteenth century bifurcated into two streams—the democratic, natural right, and the conservative, utilitarian trends—they both retained essential marks of their origin. And just as they had already been largely fused into a single theory by d'Holbach in France, so ultimately they were to come together in the political ideas of Bentham in England.

Meanwhile, we find with Burke, as with Rousseau, the limits of enlightened thought stretched to the point at which new ideas are clearly breaking through. Burke follows Hume in abandoning the State of Nature and the Lockian contract. 'Art', he says, 'is man's nature.' To the idea of the abstract natural rights of man he opposes that of practical utility, in the form of concrete, attainable interests. He retains the idea of government as trusteeship, and allows a right of resistance. This is not merely in theory, for while regretting the causes of revolution, Burke justified it in America and India, and only condemned it in Ireland on the practical ground that it was bound to fail. The French Revolution he regarded as falling into a different category: he saw it not as a defence of the interests of the people but as an attempt on the part of one section of the nation to acquire dominance over the rest. It was a struggle for sovereignty, not liberty. It took the form of the assertion of theoretical principles against practical interests, and consequently was unjustifiable on utilitarian grounds.

Burke follows Hume in the conservative interpretation of utilitarianism. His might be described as an historical utilitarianism. The fact that an institution has survived for many centuries is the best proof of its utility. It may have been set up for a purpose which it no longer serves, but this is no ground for condemning it; if it survives, that is evidence that it still serves some other, perhaps even fortuitously acquired, useful end. For this reason, rational calculation cannot reveal all the purposes of social institutions, to say nothing of the fundamental ends of society. What we call prejudice is a deeper kind of wisdom. 'The individual is foolish . . . but the species is wise.' And so, starting from sound eighteenth-century beginnings, we find ourselves with Burke, and much more drastically than with Rousseau plunged into a new intellectual climate. In Burke, though the interests of individuals remain the basic factor in social ethics, political society has regained the emotional aura which Locke had deliberately excluded. Social values begin to challenge individual ones. The past is reinstated in the name of historical tradition. Natural Law reacquires its medieval religious connections, because religion is for Burke the oldest and greatest of social institutions, the most universal of prejudices. It is the basis of morality and of the whole social order. But at this point we must stop, for Burke, much more than Rousseau, straddles the old age and the new.

It would be a mistake to conclude the history of the political thought of the Enlightenment at this point. Even if it was drawing to an end, or being transformed into something different with Rousseau and Burke, the greatest and most influential, after Locke, of enlightened political thinkers was only to appear towards the end of the century, and not to achieve recognition until the nineteenth century, when his ideas were to exercise by far the greatest single influence that British social and political institutions have ever experienced.

Jeremy Bentham's importance for the history of the nineteenth century is such that one is sometimes tempted to forget how thoroughly by birth and education he belonged to the eighteenth. He was born in 1748 and bred on a diet of French *philosophes,* to whom he subsequently acknowledged his indebtedness for his basic utilitarian ideas. His first work, an onslaught on Blackstone's *Commentaries,* begins with an invocation to the true spirit of the Enlightenment:

The age we live in is a busy age; in which knowledge is rapidly advancing towards perfection. In the natural world, in particular, every thing teems with discovery and with improvement. The most distant and recondite regions of the earth traversed and explored —the all-vivifying and subtle element of the air so recently ana- lysed and made known to us,—are striking evidences, were all others wanting, of this pleasing truth.

Correspondent to *discovery* and *improvement* in the natural world, is *reformation* in the moral.

He proceeds to abandon all the familiar presuppositions of the Natural Law school. The 'chimera' of the Original Contract, he says, has been 'ef- fectually demolished by Mr. Hume': 'I think we hear not so much of it now as formerly. The indestructible prerogatives of mankind have no need to be supported upon the sandy foundation of a fiction.' The Law of Nature is 'nothing but a phrase'. The State of Nature, or natural society, in which there is no government, is an imaginary extreme at one end of the scale, just as a 'perfectly political' state is at the other. Government is based not on such hypotheses as the contract, but on the habit of obedi- ence.

Before proceeding to discuss Bentham's more positive political ideas, it will be helpful to try to place him in the general setting of eighteenth- century moral philosophy. . . . The Enlightenment approached the problem of morals from two angles, which were not always mutually ex- clusive. Locke believed that moral truths, like mathematical truths, could be discovered with certainty by the deductive reason. He failed to dem- onstrate this by deducing any system of moral truths himself, and it might be held that this cannot be done. In particular, it may be said that moral judgments are always practical—that is, they are intended to eventuate in action, or in judgments about action. If moral are to be equated with mathematical truths, on the other hand, while a beau- tiful, self-contained system, such as that of Descartes, may be created, we can have no proof that it has any relation to the actual world. The appre- ciation of this difficulty is one reason why the eighteenth century pre- ferred to speak of reason in the field of moral philosophy as 'practical rea- son', but the failure to deduce a system of moral truths by any kind of reason led in due course to the abandonment of this line of approach.

Secondly, instead of deductive reason, appeal was made to a 'moral sense', by which, it was argued, moral truths were recognized. The diffi- culty here was to attribute any positive and stable content to this sup- posed sense. Historical and geographical discoveries seemed to indicate the relativity of all moral codes. The eighteenth-century Enlightenment therefore found itself driven back, as a third line of defence of morality, on utilitarianism. The moral value of actions was to be judged by their consequences on the happiness of individuals, or of society as a collection of individuals. The problem of the nature of happiness, and its relation to the pleasure-pain motivation was, on the whole, side-stepped; and it was possible to reach agreement on a good many practical issues before it presented itself in an acute form. In the last resort, of course, the appeal to expediency is not quite satisfactory, but generally, in the eighteenth century, the last resort was not reached.

These different trends in moral philosophy produced similarly divergent trends in political thinking. Intuitionists, like Price, supported policies of political and social reform; while utilitarians, like Hume, were more conservative in their political views. This, however, is only a very loose generalization. Utilitarianism had its reforming side from the beginning. The influential Italian advocate of reform of the criminal law, Beccaria, wrote, in 1764:

> It is better to prevent crimes, than to punish them. This is the fundamental principle of good legislation, which is the art of conducting men to the *maximum* of happiness and to the *minimum* of misery, if we may apply this mathematical expression to the good and evil of life.

The object of legislation, said Beccaria, before Bentham, should be 'the greatest happiness of the greatest number'. For d'Holbach in France utilitarianism was associated with social amelioration in a broad sense; while for Bentham it became a specifically reforming system of thought, the effects of which penetrated into every corner of the political and social system.

With Bentham the object of political thinking undergoes a major change. The aim ceases to be to justify the existence of society and government; their necessity is taken for granted. Instead, Bentham, assuming that government is justifiable only in terms of its consequences, wants to find out how to improve these consequences. He begins with a classic statement of the pleasure-pain motivation.

> Nature has placed mankind under the governance of two sovereign masters, *pain* and *pleasure*. It is for them alone to point out what we ought to do, as well as to determine what we shall do. On the one hand the standard of right and wrong, on the other the chain of causes and effects, are fastened to their throne.

This hedonistic analysis is translated, on the first page of his first book, into the formula which has been identified with Bentham's name, though it was not a new one in eighteenth-century thought, of the greatest happiness: 'It is the greatest happiness of the greatest number that is the measure of right and wrong.' This is, in other words, the principle of utility, and Bentham regards it as self-evident. It is 'the principle which furnishes us with that *reason*, which alone depends not upon any higher reason, but which is itself the sole and all-sufficient reason for every point of practice whatsoever.' There follows a simple statement of the problem of government: 'The business of government is to promote the happiness of the society, by punishing and rewarding.' It may be said that this is far too simple, that, like Locke, Bentham narrows the scope of politics and excludes from it much of what makes life worth living. In a general system of moral values this might be a defect, in a political theory it is an advantage . If we criticize Bentham for holding that 'push-pin is as good as poetry', at least it saved him from the danger of trying to make men poetical by Act of Parliament.

The utilitarian doctrine also safeguards Bentham from an easy acceptance of the rising idea of sovereignty. He condemns Blackstone's assertion of the principle of absolute sovereignty. Political authority, if it is not limited by an express agreement, he admits to be indefinite, but it is not infinite. There is an echo of Montesquieu when Bentham says that the difference between a free and a despotic government depends on the manner in which political power is distributed in the State, on the frequent interchange of position between rulers and ruled, on the blending of their interests, on the responsibility of those who exercise the government, and on such liberties as those of the Press, of association, and of peaceful opposition. In the last resort there is a point at which active resistance becomes 'commendable':

> It is *then* . . . when, according to the best calculation he is able to make, *the probable mischiefs of resistance* (speaking with respect to the community in general) *appear less to him than the probable mischiefs of submission.* This then is to him, that is to each man in particular, the *juncture for resistance.*

It is not necessary to pursue further the development of Bentham's thought, to trace the manifold developments to which his simple primary ideas were subject, or the realizations, stretching through the next century and a half to the present day, of the plans his immensely fertile and benevolent mind produced for bettering the lot of his fellow beings. It is sufficient to say that Bentham's is the last great name in the history of the political thinking of the Enlightenment. Through him it legislated for posterity.

THE AGE OF REVOLUTION, 1789-1848

PART II

A T the end of the eighteenth century something new, an age of revolution, came into western civilization. In large measure western history since then has been dominated by the continuing thrust of the energy set in motion by this age's French Revolution and Industrial Revolution, which Eric J. Hobsbawm has lumped together as a "dual revolution." "Industrial Revolution" very rapidly became the norm for economic and social life. Although the French Revolution may not have become the norm for political life, western civilization after it would be to some extent the story of those who made, prevented, or crushed revolutions. The pattern of those choices was established between the French Revolution and the Revolutions of 1848. The selections which follow will deal with some of those themes: Lawrence Stone takes up the nature of modern revolutions, of which the French Revolution was the first, in the light of the insights of the social sciences; George Taylor and George Rudé examine the roles of the two social forces, the bourgeoisie and the crowd, which gave the French Revolution its drive; Harold Parker deals with how even in a revolutionary age of social forces a "great man," Napoleon, could emerge; Henry Kissinger looks at peacemaking in an age of revolution. Eric Hobsbawm and Phyllis Deane investigate the process of industrialization and its effect on the standard of living. Finally, William Langer discusses the dynamics of the Revolution of 1848, which saw the "dual revolutions" merge.

4. The Nature of Modern Revolution

LAWRENCE STONE

*Because of the large role played by revolution in modern times, historians have
been fascinated with such questions as, What causes men to resort to revolution?
By what mechanisms are revolutions successful? Why are some governments
or societies able to resist revolutions while others fall to them? In recent years
historians have sought to answer these questions by attempting to discern some
pattern common to all revolutions or common to different kinds of revolutions.
One way to do this is to see if the social scientists, who have likewise been in-
trigued by the phenomenon of modern revolution, have any useful answers
to offer the historian.*

*The following selection by Princeton University Professor Lawrence Stone,
whose influential* Crisis of the Aristocracy *reevaluated the social change leading
to the English Puritan Revolution of the seventeenth century, describes and
evaluates the more recent efforts of these social scientists. As he points out,
their efforts sometimes offer only "ingenious feats of verbal juggling in an
esoteric language, performed around the totem pole of an abstract model, surrounded as far as the eye can see by the arid wastes of terminological definitions
and mathematical formulae." Yet, he continues, "they can ask new questions
and suggest new ways of looking at old ones. They can supply new categories,
and as a result may suggest new ideas." To understand their arguments you
might consider how the revolutions of your own time—the American civil*

Source: Lawrence Stone, "Theories of Revolution," *World Politics*, XVIII, No.
2 (January 1966), 159–76. Copyright © 1966. Reprinted by permission of Princeton University Press. [Some footnotes omitted.]

rights and student movements of the 1960s, the 1968 uprisings in Prague and Paris, and the fighting in Northern Ireland—fit their models. In particular you might want to address yourself to questions such as these: What models of revolution does the behaviorist approach, represented here by Johnson and Eckstein, set forth? What problems does that approach solve and what does it leave unsolved? How do Marx, Tocqueville, Lewis, Olson, and Davis seek "to relate dysfunction to relative changes in economic prosperity and aspirations"? What problems does their approach solve or leave unsolved and how does Davis's "J-Curve" work? To what extent is it more fruitful to view "Great Revolutions" in stages as Brinton, Amman, and Hopper do?

In attacking the problem of revolution, as most others of major significance in history, we historians should think twice before we spurn the help offered by our colleagues in the social sciences, who have, as it happens, been particularly active in the last few years in theorizing about the typology, causes, and evolutionary patterns of this particular phenomenon. The purpose of this article is not to advance any new hypothesis, but to provide a summary view and critical examination of the work that has been going on.

The first necessity in any inquiry is a careful definition of terms: what is, and what is not, a revolution? According to one view, it is change, effected by the use of violence, in government, and/or regime, and/or society.[1] By *society* is meant the consciousness and the mechanics of communal solidarity, which may be tribal, peasant, kinship, national, and so on; by *regime* is meant the constitutional structure—democracy, oligarchy, monarchy; and by *government* is meant specific political and administrative institutions. Violence, it should be noted, is not the same as force; it is force used with unnecessary intensity, unpredictably, and usually destructively. This definition of revolution is a very broad one, and two historians of the French Revolution, Crane Brinton and Louis Gottschalk, would prefer to restrict the use of the word to the major political and social upheavals with which they are familiar, the "Great Revolutions" as George S. Pettee calls them.[2]

Even the wider definition allows the historian to distinguish between the seizure of power that leads to a major restructuring of government or society and the replacement of the former elite by a new one, and the coup d'état involving no more than a change of ruling personnel by violence or threat of violence. This latter is the norm in Latin America, where it occurred thirty-one times in the ten years 1945–1955. Merle Kling has arrived at a suggestive explanation of this Latin American phenomenon of chronic political instability, limited but frequent use of violence, and almost complete lack of social or institutional change. He

---

[1] Chalmers Johnson, *Revolution and the Social System*, Hoover Institution Studies 3 (Stanford, 1964).

[2] Brinton, *The Anatomy of Revolution* (New York, 1938); Gottschalk, "Causes of Revolution," *American Journal of Sociology*, 1 (July 1944), 1–8; Pettee, *The Process of Revolution* (New York, 1938).

argues that ownership of the principal economic resources, both agricultural and mineral, is concentrated in the hands of a tiny, very stable, elite of enormously wealthy monoculture landlords and mining capitalists. This elite is all-powerful and cannot be attacked by opposition groups within the country; externally, however, it is dependent on foreign interests for its markets and its capital. In this colonial situation of a foreign-supported closed plutocracy, the main avenue of rapid upward social mobility for nonmembers of the elite leads, via the army, to the capture of the government machine, which is the only accessible source of wealth and power. This political instability is permitted by the elite on the condition that its own interests are undisturbed. Instability, limited violence, and the absence of social or institutional change are therefore all the product of the contradiction between the realities of a colonial economy run by a plutocracy and the facade of political sovereignty—between the real, stable power of the economic elite and the nominal, unstable control of politicians and generals.

The looser definition of revolution thus suits both historians of major social change and historians of the palace coup. It does, however, raise certain difficulties. Firstly, there is a wide range of changes of government by violence which are neither a mere substitution of personalities in positions of power nor a prelude to the restructuring of society; secondly, conservative counterrevolutions become almost impossible to fit into the model; and lastly, it remains hard to distinguish between colonial wars, civil wars, and social revolution.

To avoid these difficulties, an alternative formulation has recently been put forward by a group of social scientists working mainly at Princeton. They have dropped the word "revolution" altogether and put "internal war" in its place.[3] This is defined as any attempt to alter state policy, rulers, or institutions by the use of violence, in societies where violent competition is not the norm and where well-defined institutional patterns exist. This concept seems to be a logical consequence of the preoccupation of sociologists in recent years with a model of society in a stable, self-regulating state of perpetual equipoise. In this utopian world of universal harmony, all forms of violent conflict are anomalies, to be treated alike as pathological disorders of a similar species. This is a model which, although it has its uses for analytical purposes, bears little relation to the reality familiar to the historian. It looks to a society without change, with universal consensus on values, with complete social harmony, and isolated from external threats; no approximation to such a society has ever been seen. An alternative model, which postulates that all societies are in a condition of multiple and perpetual tension held in check by social norms, ideological beliefs, and state sanctions, accords better with historical fact, as some sociologists are now beginning to realize.

The first objection to the all-embracing formula of internal war is that,

[3] Harry Eckstein, ed., *Internal War* (New York, 1964), and "On the Etiology of Internal War," *History and Theory,* IV, No. 2 (1965), 133–63. I am grateful to Mr. Eckstein for allowing me to read this article before publication.

by covering all forms of physical conflict from strikes and terrorism to civil war, it isolates the use of violence from the normal processes of societal adjustment. Though some of the users of the term express their awareness that the use of violence for political ends is a fairly common occurrence, the definition they have established in fact excludes all times and places where it *is* common. It thus cuts out most societies the world has ever known, including Western Europe in the Middle Ages and Latin America today. Secondly, it isolates one particular means, physical violence, from the political ends that it is designed to serve. Clausewitz's famous definition of external war is equally applicable to internal war, civil war, or revolution: "War is not only a political act, but a real political instrument; a continuation of political transactions, an accomplishment of them by different means. That which remains peculiar to war relates only to the peculiar nature of its means."

It is perfectly true that any means by which society exercises pressure or control, whether it is administrative organization, constitutional law, economic interest, or physical force, can be a fruitful field of study in its own right, so long as its students remain aware that they are looking at only one part of a larger whole. It is also true that there is something peculiar about violence, if only because of man's highly ambivalent attitude towards the killing of his own species. Somehow, he regards physical force as different in kind from, say, economic exploitation or psychological manipulation as a means of exercising power over others. But this distinction is not one of much concern to the historian of revolution, in which violence is a normal and natural occurrence. The concept of internal war is too broad in its comprehension of all types of violence from civil wars to strikes, too narrow in its restriction to normally nonviolent societies, too limited in its concern with one of many means, too arbitrary in its separation of this means from the ends in view, and too little concerned with the complex roots of social unrest to be of much practical value to him.

The most fruitful typology of revolution is that of Chalmers Johnson, set out in a pamphlet that deserves to be widely read.[4] He sees six types, identified by the targets selected for attack, whether the government personnel, the political regime, or the community as a social unit; by the nature of the carriers of revolution, whether a mass or an elite; and particularly by the goals and the ideologies, whether reformist, eschatological, nostalgic, nation-forming, elitist, or nationalist. The first type, the *Jacquerie,* is a spontaneous mass peasant rising, usually carried out in the name of the traditional authorities, Church and King, and with the limited aims of purging the local or national elites. Examples are the Peasant Revolt of 1381, Ket's Rebellion of 1549, and the Pugachev rebellion in Russia in 1773–1775. The second type, the *Millenarian Rebellion,* is similar to the first but with the added feature of a utopian dream, inspired by a living messiah. This type can be found at all times, in all parts of the

[4] *Revolution and the Social System.*

world, from the Florentine revolution led by Savonarola in 1494, to the Anabaptist Rebellion in Münster led by John Mathijs and John Beukels in 1533–1535, to the Sioux Ghost-Dance Rebellion inspired by the Paiute prophet Wovoka in 1890. It has attracted a good deal of attention from historians in recent years, partly because the career of Hitler offered overwhelming proof of the enormous historical significance of a charismatic leader, and partly because of a growing interest in the ideas of Max Weber. The third type is the *Anarchistic Rebellion,* the nostalgic reaction to progressive change, involving a romantic idealization of the old order; the Pilgrimage of Grace and the Vendée are examples.

The fourth is that very rare phenomenon, the *Jacobin Communist Revolution.* This has been defined as "a sweeping fundamental change in political organization, social structure, economic property control and the predominant myth of a social order, thus indicating a major break in the continuity of development." This type of revolution can occur only in a highly centralized state with good communications and a large capital city, and its target is government, regime, and society—the lot. The result is likely to be the creation of a new national consciousness under centralized, military authority, and the erection of a more rational, and hence more efficient, social and bureaucratic order on the ruins of the old ramshackle structure of privilege, nepotism, and corruption.

The fifth type is the *Conspiratorial Coup d'État,* the planned work of a tiny elite fired by an oligarchic, sectarian ideology. This qualifies as a revolutionary type only if it in fact anticipates mass movement and inaugurates social change—for example the Nasser revolution in Egypt or the Castro revolution in Cuba; it is thus clearly distinguished from the palace revolt, assassination, dynastic succession-conflict, strike, banditry, and other forms of violence, which are all subsumed under the "internal war" rubric.

Finally, there is the *Militarized Mass Insurrection,* a new phenomenon of the twentieth century in that it is a deliberately planned mass revolutionary war, guided by a dedicated elite. The outcome of guerrilla warfare is determined by political attitudes, not military strategy or matériel, for the rebels are wholly dependent on broad popular support. In all cases on record, the ideology that attracts the mass following has been a combination of xenophobic nationalism and Marxism, with by far the greater stress on the former. This type of struggle has occurred in Yugoslavia, China, Algeria, and Vietnam.

Although, like any schematization of the historical process, this sixfold typology is concerned with ideal types, although in practice individual revolutions may sometimes display characteristics of several different types, the fact remains that this is much the most satisfactory classification we have so far; it is one that working historians can recognize and use with profit. The one obvious criticism is semantic, an objection to the use of the phrase "Jacobin Communist Revolution." Some of Johnson's examples are Communist, such as the Russian or Chinese Revolutions; others are Jacobin but not Communist, such as the French Revolution or the

Turkish Revolution of 1908–1922. It would be better to revert to Pettee's category of "Great Revolutions," and treat Communist revolutions as a subcategory, one type, but not the only type, of modernizing revolutionary process.

Given this classification and definition of revolution, what are its root causes? Here everyone is agreed in making a sharp distinction between long-run, underlying causes—the preconditions, which create a potentially explosive situation and can be analyzed on a comparative basis—and immediate, incidental factors—the precipitants, which trigger the outbreak and which may be nonrecurrent, personal, and fortuitous. This effectively disposes of the objections of those historians whose antipathy to conceptual schematization takes the naïve form of asserting the uniqueness of each historical event.

One of the first in the field of model-building was Crane Brinton who, as long ago as 1938, put forward a series of uniformities common to the four great Western revolutions: English, French, American, and Russian. These included an economically advancing society, growing class and status antagonisms, an alienated intelligentsia, a psychologically insecure and politically inept ruling class, and a governmental financial crisis.[5]

The subjectivity, ambiguity, and partial self-contradiction of this and other analyses of the causes of specific revolutions—for example the French Revolution—have been cruelly shown up by Harry Eckstein.[6] He has pointed out that commonly adduced hypotheses run the spectrum of particular conditions, moving from the intellectual (inadequate political socialization, conflicting social myths, a corrosive social philosophy, alienation of the intellectuals) to the economic (increasing poverty, rapid growth, imbalance between production and distribution, long-term growth plus short-term recession) to the social (resentment due to restricted elite circulation, confusion due to excessive elite recruitment, anomie due to excessive social mobility, conflict due to the rise of new social classes) to the political (bad government, divided government, weak government, oppressive government). Finally there are explanations on the level of general process, such as rapid social change, erratic social change, or a lack of harmony between the state structure and society, the rulers and the ruled. None of these explanations are invalid in themselves, but they are often difficult or impossible to reconcile one with the other, and are so diverse in their range and variety as to be virtually impossible to fit into an ordered analytical framework. What, then, is to be done?

Fundamental to all analyses, whether by historians like Brinton and Gottschalk or by political scientists like Johnson and Eckstein, is the recognition of a lack of harmony between the social system on the one hand and the political system on the other. This situation Johnson calls *dysfunction,* a word derived from the structural-functional equilibrium model of

[5] *Anatomy of Revolution.*
[6] "On the Etiology of Internal War."

the sociologists. This dysfunction may have many causes, some of which are merely cyclical, such as may develop because of personal weaknesses in hereditary kingships or single-party regimes. In these cases, the revolution will not take on serious proportions, and will limit itself to attacks on the governing institutions, leaving regime and society intact. In most cases, however, including all those of real importance, the dysfunction is the result of some new and developing process, as a result of which certain social subsystems find themselves in a condition of relative deprivation. Rapid economic growth, imperial conquest, new metaphysical beliefs, and important technological changes are the four commonest factors involved, in that order. If the process of change is sufficiently slow and sufficiently moderate, the dysfunction may not rise to dangerous levels. Alternatively, the elite may adjust to the new situation with sufficient rapidity and skill to ride out the storm and retain popular confidence. But if the change is both rapid and profound, it may cause the sense of deprivation, alienation, anomie to spread into many sectors of society at once, causing what Johnson calls multiple dysfunction, which may be all but incurable within the existing political system.

In either case the second vital element in creating a revolutionary situation is the condition and attitude of the entrenched elite, a factor on which Eckstein rightly lays great stress. The elite may lose its manipulative skill, or its military superiority, or its self-confidence, or its cohesion; it may become estranged from the nonelite, or overwhelmed by a financial crisis; it may be incompetent, or weak, or brutal. Any combination of two or more of these features will be dangerous. What is ultimately fatal, however, is the compounding of its errors by intransigence. If it fails to anticipate the need for reform, if it blocks all peaceful, constitutional means of social adjustment, then it unites the various deprived elements in single-minded opposition to it, and drives them down the narrow road to violence. It is this process of polarization into two coherent groups or alliances of what are naturally and normally a series of fractional and shifting tensions and conflicts within a society that both Peter Amman and Wilbert Moore see as the essential preliminary to the outbreak of a Jacobin Revolution.[7] To conclude, therefore, revolution becomes *possible* when a condition of multiple dysfunction meets an intransigent elite: just such a conjunction occurred in the decades immediately before the English, the French, and the Russian Revolutions.

Revolution only becomes *probable* (Johnson might say "certain"), however, if certain special factors intervene: the "precipitants" or "accelerators." Of these, the three most common are the emergence of an inspired leader or prophet; the formation of a secret, military, revolutionary organization; and the crushing defeat of the armed forces in foreign war. This last is of critical importance since it not only shatters the prestige of the ruling elite, but also undermines the morale and discipline of the soldiers

[7] Amman, "Revolution: A Redefinition," *Political Science Quarterly,* LXXVII (1962).

and thus opens the way to the violent overthrow of the existing government.

The first defect of Johnson's model is that it concentrates too much on objective structural conditions, and attempts to relate conditions directly to action. In fact, however, as Eckstein points out, there is no such direct relationship; historians can point to similar activity arising from different conditions, and different activity arising from similar conditions. Standing between objective reality and action are subjective human attitudes. A behaviorist approach such as Brinton's, which lays equal stress on such things as anomie, alienation of the intellectuals, frustrated popular aspirations, elite estrangement, and loss of elite self-confidence, is more likely to produce a satisfactory historical explanation than is one that sticks to the objective social reality. Secondly, Johnson leaves too little play for the operation of the unique and the personal. He seems to regard his accelerators as automatic triggers, ignoring the area of unpredictable personal choice that is always left to the ruling elite and to the revolutionary leaders, even in a situation of multiple dysfunction exacerbated by an accelerator. Revolution is never inevitable—or rather the only evidence of its inevitability is that it actually happens. Consequently the only way to prove this point is to indulge in just the kind of hypothetical argument that historians prudently try to avoid. But it is still just possible that modernization may take place in Morocco and India without revolution. The modernization and industrialization of Germany and Britain took place without revolution in the nineteenth century (though it can be argued that in the latter case the process was slow by twentieth-century standards, and that, as is now becoming all too apparent, the modernization was far from complete). Some think that a potentially revolutionary situation in the United States in the 1930s was avoided by political action.

Lastly it is difficult to fit into the Johnson model the fact that political actions taken to remedy dysfunction often themselves precipitate change. This produces the paradoxical hypothesis that measures designed to restore equilibrium in fact upset equilibrium. Because he begins with his structural-functional equilibrium model, Johnson is a victim of the fallacy of intended consequences. As often as not in history it is the *unintended* consequences that really matter: to mention but one example, it was Louis XVI's belated and half-hearted attempts at reform that provoked the aristocratic reaction, which in turn opened the way to the bourgeois, the peasant, and the sans-culotte revolutions. Finally the dysfunction concept is not altogether easy to handle in a concrete historical case. If societies are regarded as being in a constant state of multiple tension, then some degree of dysfunction is always present. Some group is always in a state of relative deprivation due to the inevitable process of social change.

Recognition of this fact leads Eckstein to point out the importance of forces working *against* revolution. Historians, particularly those formed in the Western liberal tradition, are reluctant to admit that ruthless, efficient repression—as opposed to bumbling, half-hearted repression—involving the physical destruction of leading revolutionaries and effective control of the media of communication, can crush incipient revolutionary movements. Repression is particularly effective when governments know what to look for, when they have before their eyes the unfortunate example of other governments overthrown by revolutionaries elsewhere. Reaction, in fact, is just as infectious as revolution. Moreover diversion of energy and attention to successful—as opposed to unsuccessful— foreign war can ward off serious internal trouble. Quietist—as opposed to activist—religious movements may serve as the opiate of the people, as Halévy suggested about Methodism in England. Bread and circuses may distract popular attention. Timely—as opposed to untimely —political concessions may win over moderate opinion and isolate the extremists.

Basing himself on this suggestive analysis, Eckstein produces a paradigm for universal application. He sees four positive variables—elite inefficiency, disorienting social process, subversion, and available rebel facilities—and four negative variables—diversionary mechanisms, available incumbent facilities, adjustive mechanisms, and effective repression. Each type of internal war, and each step of each type, can, he suggests, be explained in terms of these eight variables. While this may be true, it is fair to point out that some of the variables are themselves the product of more deep-seated factors, others mere questions of executive action that may be determined by the accidents of personality. Disruptive social process is a profound cause; elite inefficiency a behavior pattern; effective repression a function of will; facilities the by-product of geography. One objection to the Eckstein paradigm is therefore that it embraces different levels of explanation and fails to maintain the fundamental distinction between preconditions and precipitants. Secondly, it concentrates on the factors working for or against the successful manipulation of violence rather than on the underlying factors working to produce a revolutionary potential. This is because the paradigm is intended to apply to all forms of internal war rather than to revolution proper, and because all that the various forms of internal war have in common is the use of violence. It is impossible to tell how serious these criticisms are until the paradigm has been applied to a particular historical revolution. Only then will its value become apparent.

If we take the behaviorist approach, then a primary cause of revolutions is the emergence of an obsessive revolutionary mentality. But how closely does this relate to the objective material circumstances themselves? In every revolutionary situation one finds a group of men—fanatics, extremists, zealots—so convinced of their own righteousness and of the urgent need to create a new Jerusalem on earth (whether formally religious or secular in inspiration is irrelevant) that they are prepared to smash through the normal restraints of habit, custom, and convention. Such men were the seventeenth-century English Puritans, the eighteenth-century French Jacobins, the twentieth-century Russian Bolsheviks. But what makes such men is far from certain. What generates such ruthlessness in curbing evil, such passion for discipline and order? Rapid social mobility, both horizontal and vertical, and particularly urbanization, certainly produces a sense of rootlessness and anxiety. In highly stratified societies, even some of the newly-risen elements may find themselves under stress. While some of the *arrivistes* are happily absorbed in their new strata, others remain uneasy and resentful. If they are snubbed and rebuffed by the older members of the status group to which they aspire by reason of their new wealth and position, they are likely to become acutely conscious of their social inferiority, and may be driven either to adopt a pose *plus royaliste que le Roi* or to dream of destroying the whole social order. In the latter case they may try to allay their sense of insecurity by imposing their norms and values by force upon society at large. This is especially the case if there is available a moralistic ideology like Puritanism or Marxism to which they can attach themselves, and which provides them with unshakable confidence in their own rectitude.

But why does the individual react in this particular way rather than another? Some would argue that the character of the revolutionary is formed by sudden ideological conversion in adolescence or early adult life (to Puritanism, Jacobinism, or Bolshevism) as a refuge from this anxiety state. What is not acceptable is the fashionable conservative cliché that the revolutionary and the reformer are merely the chance product of unfortunate psychological difficulties in childhood. It is possible that this is the mechanism by which such feelings are generated, though there is increasing evidence of the continued plasticity of human character until at any rate post-adolescence. The main objection to this theory is that it fails to explain why these particular attitudes become common only in certain classes and age groups at certain times and in certain places. This failure strongly suggests that the cause of this state of mind lies not in the personal maladjustment of the individuals or their parents, but in the social conditions that created that maladjustment. Talcott Parsons treats disaffection or "alienation" as a generalized phenomenon that may manifest itself in crime, alcoholism, drug addiction, daytime fantasies, religious enthusiasm, or serious political agitation. To use Robert Merton's formulation, Ritualism and Retreatism are two possible psychological escape-routes; Innovation and Rebellion two others.

Even if we accept this behaviorist approach (which I do), the fact remains that many of the underlying causes both of the alienation of the revolutionaries and of the weakness of the incumbent elite are economic in origin; and it is in this area that some interesting work has centered. In particular a fresh look has been taken at the contradictory models of Marx and de Tocqueville, the one claiming that popular revolution is a product of increasing misery, the other that it is a product of increasing prosperity.

Two economists, Sir Arthur Lewis and Mancur Olson, have pointed out that because of their basic social stability, both preindustrial and highly industrialized societies are relatively free from revolutionary distur-

bance.[8] In the former societies, people accept with little question the accepted rights and obligations of family, class, and caste. Misery, oppression, and social injustice are passively endured as inevitable features of
life on earth. It is in societies experiencing rapid economic growth that
the trouble usually occurs. Lewis, who is thinking mostly about the newly
emerging countries, primarily of Africa, regards the sense of frustration
that leads to revolution as a consequence of the dislocation of the old status patterns by the emergence of four new classes—the proletariat, the
capitalist employers, the urban commercial and professional middle class,
and the professional politicians—and of the disturbance of the old income patterns by the sporadic and patchy impact of economic growth,
which creates new wealth and new poverty in close and conspicuous juxtaposition. Both phenomena he regards as merely transitional, since in a
country fully developed economically there are strong tendencies toward
the elimination of inequalities of opportunity, income, and status.

This model matches fairly well the only detailed analysis of a historical
revolution in which a conscious effort has been made to apply modern sociological methods. In his recent study of the Vendée, Charles Tilly argues
that a counterrevolutionary situation was the consequence of special tensions created by the immediate juxtaposition of, on one hand, parish
clergy closely identified with the local communities, great absentee landlords, and old-fashioned subsistence farming, and, on the other, a large-
scale textile industry on the putting-out system and increasing bourgeois
competition. Though the book is flawed by a tendency to take a ponderous sociological hammer to crack a simple little historical nut, it is nonetheless a suggestive example of the application of new hypotheses and
techniques to historical material.

Olson has independently developed a more elaborate version of the
Lewis theory. He argues that revolutionaries are déclassé and freed from
the social bonds of family, profession, village or manor; and that these individuals are the product of rapid economic growth, which creates both
nouveaux riches and *nouveaux pauvres*. The former, usually middle-class
and urban artisans, are better off economically, but are disoriented, root-
less, and restless; the latter may be workers whose wages have failed to
keep pace with inflation, workers in technologically outdated and therefore declining industries, or the unemployed in a society in which the old
cushions of the extended family and the village have gone, and in which
the new cushion of social security has not yet been created. The initial
growth phase may well cause a decline in the standard of living of the
majority because of the need for relatively enormous forced savings for
reinvestment. The result is a revolution caused by the widening gap be-

[8] W. Arthur Lewis, "Commonwealth Address," in *Conference Across a Continent* (Toronto 1963), 46–60; Olson, "Rapid Growth as a Destabilizing Force,"
Journal of Economic History, XXIII (December 1963), 529–52. I am grateful to
Mr. Olson for drawing my attention to Sir Arthur Lewis's article, and for some
helpful suggestions.

tween expectations—social and political for the new rich, economic for the new poor—and the realities of everyday life.

A sociologist, James C. Davis, agrees with Olson that the fundamental impetus toward a revolutionary situation is generated by rapid economic growth but he associates such growth with a generally rising rather than a generally falling standard of living, and argues that the moment of potential revolution is reached only when the long-term phase of growth is followed by a short-term phase of economic stagnation or decline.[9] The result of this "J-curve," as he calls it, is that steadily soaring expectations, newly created by the period of growth, shoot further and further ahead of actual satisfaction of needs. Successful revolution is the work neither of the destitute nor of the well-satisfied, but of those whose actual situation is improving less rapidly than they expect.

These economic models have much in common, and their differences can be explained by the fact that Lewis and Olson are primarily concerned with the long-term economic forces creating instability, and Davis with the short-term economic factors that may precipitate a crisis. Moreover their analyses apply to different kinds of economic growth, of which three have recently been identified by W. W. Rostow and Barry Supple: there is the expansion of production in a preindustrial society, which may not cause any important technological, ideological, social, or political change; there is the phase of rapid growth, involving major changes of every kind; and there is the sustained trend toward technological maturity. Historians have been quick to see that these models, particularly that of Rostow, can be applied only to a limited number of historical cases. The trouble is not so much that in any specific case the phases—particularly the last two—tend to merge into one another, but that changes in the various sectors occur at irregular and unexpected places on the time-scale in different societies. Insofar as there is any validity in the division of the stages of growth into these three basic types, the revolutionary model of Olson and Lewis is confined to the second; that of Davis is applicable to all three.

The Davis model fits the history of Western Europe quite well, for it looks as if in conditions of extreme institutional and ideological rigidity the first type of economic growth may produce frustrations of a very serious kind. Revolutions broke out all over Europe in the 1640s, twenty years after a secular growth phase had come to an end. C. E. Labrousse has demonstrated the existence of a similar economic recession in France from 1778, and from 1914 the Russian economy was dislocated by the war effort after many years of rapid growth. Whatever its limitations in any particular situation, the J-curve of actual satisfaction of needs is an analytical tool that historians can usefully bear in mind as they probe the violent social upheavals of the past.

As de Tocqueville pointed out, this formula of advance followed by re-

[9] "Toward a Theory of Revolution," *American Sociological Review*, XXVII (February 1962), 1–19, esp. the graph on p. 6.

treat is equally applicable to other sectors. Trouble arises if a phase of liberal governmental concessions is followed by a phase of political repression; a phase of fairly open recruitment channels into the elite followed by a phase of aristocratic reaction and a closing of ranks; a phase of weakening status barriers by a phase of reassertion of privilege. The J-curve is applicable to other than purely economic satisfactions, and the apex of the curve is the point at which underlying causes, the preconditions, merge with immediate factors, the precipitants. The recipe for revolution is thus the creation of new expectations by economic improvement and some social and political reforms, followed by economic recession, governmental reaction, and aristocratic resurgence, which widen the gap between expectations and reality.

All these attempts to relate dysfunction to relative changes in economic prosperity and aspirations are hampered by two things, of which the first is the extreme difficulty in ascertaining the facts. It is never easy to discover precisely what is happening to the distribution of wealth in a given society. Even now, even in highly developed Western societies with massive bureaucratic controls and quantities of statistical data, there is no agreement about the facts. Some years ago it was confidently believed that in both Britain and the United States incomes were being levelled, and that extremes of both wealth and poverty were being steadily eliminated. Today, no one quite knows what is happening in either country. And if this is true now, still more is it true of societies in the past about which the information is fragmentary and unreliable.

Secondly, even if they can be clearly demonstrated, economic trends are only one part of the problem. Historians are increasingly realizing that the psychological responses to changes in wealth and power are not only not precisely related to, but are politically more significant than, the material changes themselves. As Marx himself realized at one stage, dissatisfaction with the status quo is not determined by absolute realities but by relative expectations. "Our desires and pleasures spring from society; we measure them, therefore, by society, and not by the objects which serve for their satisfaction. Because they are of a social nature, they are of a relative nature." Frustration may possibly result from a rise and subsequent relapse in real income. But it is perhaps more likely to be caused by a rise in aspirations that outstrips the rise in real income; or by a rise in the *relative* economic position in society of the group in question, followed by a period in which its real income continues to grow, but less fast than that of other groups around it. Alternatively it may represent a rise and then decline of status, largely unrelated to real income; or if status and real income are related, it may be inversely. For example, social scientists seeking to explain the rise of the radical right in the United States in the early 1950s and again in the early 1960s attribute it to a combination of great economic prosperity and an aggravated sense of insecurity of status. Whether or not this is a general formula for right-wing rather than left-wing revolutionary movements is not yet clear.

Moreover the problem is further complicated by an extension of the reference-group theory. Human satisfaction is related not to existing conditions but to the condition of a social group against which the individual measures his situation. In an age of mass communications and the wide distribution of cheap radio receivers even among the impoverished illiterate of the world, knowledge of high consumption standards elsewhere spreads rapidly, and as a result the reference group may be in another, more highly developed, country or even continent. Under these circumstances, revolutionary conditions may be created before industrialization has got properly under way.

The last area in which some new theoretical work has been done is in the formulation of hypotheses about the social stages of a "Great Revolution." One of the best attacks on this problem was made by Crane Brinton, who was thinking primarily about the French Revolution, but who extended his comparisons to the three other major Western revolutionary movements. He saw the first phase as dominated by moderate bourgeois elements; their supersession by the radicals; a reign of terror; a Thermidorian reaction; and the establishment of strong central authority under military rule to consolidate the limited gains of the revolution. In terms of mass psychology he compared revolution with a fever that rises in intensity, affecting nearly all parts of the body politic, and then dies away.

A much cruder and more elementary model has been advanced by an historian of the revolutions of 1848, Peter Amman.[10] He sees the modern state as an institution holding a monopoly of physical force, administration, and justice over a wide area, a monopoly dependent more on habits of obedience than on powers of coercion. Revolution may therefore be defined as a breakdown of the monopoly due to a failure of these habits of obedience. It begins with the emergence of two or more foci of power, and ends with the elimination of all but one. Amman includes the possibility of "suspended revolution," with the existence of two or more foci not yet in violent conflict.

This model admittedly avoids some of the difficulties raised by more elaborate classifications of revolution: how to distinguish a coup d'état from a revolution; how to define the degrees of social change; how to accommodate the conservative counterrevolution, and so on. It certainly offers some explanation of the progress of revolution from stage to stage as the various power blocs that emerge on the overthrow of the incumbent regime are progressively eliminated; and it explains why the greater the public participation in the revolution, the wider the break with the habits of obedience, and therefore the slower the restoration of order and centralized authority. But it throws the baby out with the bathwater. It is impossible to fit any decentralized traditional society, or any modern federal society, into the model. Moreover, even where it might be applicable, it offers no framework for analyzing the roots of revolution, no pointers for identifying the foci of power, no means of distinguishing be-

[10] "Revolution: A Redefinition."

tween the various revolutionary types, and its notion of "suspended revolution" is little more than verbal evasion.

Though it is set out in a somewhat confused, overelaborate, and unnecessarily abstract form, the most convincing description of the social stages of revolution is that outlined by Rex D. Hopper.[11] He sees four stages. The first is characterized by indiscriminate, uncoordinated mass unrest and dissatisfaction, the result of dim recognition that traditional values no longer satisfy current aspirations. The next stage sees this vague unease beginning to coalesce into organized opposition with defined goals, an important characteristic being a shift of allegiance by the intellectuals from the incumbents to the dissidents, the advancement of an "evil men" theory, and its abandonment in favor of an "evil institutions" theory. At this stage there emerge two types of leaders: the prophet, who sketches the shape of the new utopia upon which men's hopes can focus, and the reformer, working methodically toward specific goals. The third, the formal stage, sees the beginning of the revolution proper. Motives and objectives are clarified, organization is built up, a statesman leader emerges. Then conflicts between the left and the right of the revolutionary movement become acute, and the radicals take over from the moderates. The fourth and last stage sees the legalization of the revolution. It is a product of psychological exhaustion as the reforming drive burns itself out, moral enthusiasm wanes, and economic distress increases. The administrators take over, strong central government is established, and society is reconstructed on lines that embody substantial elements of the old system. The result falls far short of the utopian aspirations of the early leaders, but it succeeds in meshing aspirations with values by partly modifying both, and so allows the reconstruction of a firm social order.

Some of the writings of contemporary social scientists are ingenious feats of verbal juggling in an esoteric language, performed around the totem pole of an abstract model, surrounded as far as the eye can see by the arid wastes of terminological definitions and mathematical formulae. Small wonder the historian finds it hard to digest the gritty diet of this neo-scholasticism, as it has been aptly called. The more historically-minded of the social scientists, however, have a great deal to offer. The history of history, as well as of science, shows that advances depend partly on the accumulation of factual information, but rather more on the formulation of hypotheses that reveal the hidden relationships and common properties of apparently distinct phenomena. Social scientists can supply a corrective to the antiquarian fact-grubbing to which historians are so prone; they can direct attention to problems of general relevance, and away from the sterile triviality of so much historical research. They can ask new questions and suggest new ways of looking at old ones. They can supply new categories, and as a result may suggest new ideas.

[11] "The Revolutionary Process," *Social Forces*, XXVIII (March 1950), 270–79.

5. The Bourgeoisie in the French Revolution

GEORGE V. TAYLOR

The French Revolution is one revolution that both Marxists and anti-Marxists have enjoyed interpreting with a Marxist analysis, because in that revolution capitalism was both the cause and the victor. Since the middle ages, so goes the argument, capitalism had been on the rise. As it rose, the capitalist class, or bourgeoisie, grew, became more aware of itself as a class and more revolutionary in its struggle against the aristocracy and the aristocracy's system, feudalism. Finally, in France of 1789 the revolutionary bourgeoisie possessed enough social and economic power to seize political power from the aristocrats and establish capitalism under a bourgeois state. The only remaining question, one that would separate the Marxists from their enemies, was whether the bourgeoisie's revolution was permanent or whether it would give way to a new working class revolution.

In recent years this version of the French Revolution has come increasingly under attack, particularly by Alfred Cobban and his followers. The next selection, by George V. Taylor of the University of North Carolina, has been influential in this attack. Taylor does not question the fact that the bourgeoisie profited from the French Revolution, but he demonstrates that the results of the revolution do not have to have anything to do with its causes. For him "the fundamental question is certainly whether the bourgeoisie of 1789, however defined, had any economic consistency that opposed it to other classes."

Source: George V. Taylor, "Non-Capitalist Wealth and the Origins of the French Revolution," *American Historical Review*, LXXII (January 1967), 469–96. Reprinted by permission of the author. [Some footnotes omitted.]

Like Cobban and others, he concludes that it did not and that, as a result, "the whole classic concept of a bourgeois revolution has become unnecessary and impossible to sustain."

In following his argument one should keep several questions in mind: Why does he use the term "proprietary wealth" instead of "feudal wealth"? What kind of property was proprietary wealth, what attitudes did it foster, and why does the author consider it noncapitalist? What kind of property was capitalist wealth and what attitudes would it foster? What proportion of French wealth was "proprietary" and how much was capitalist? Given the nature of the economy, how were the middle classes and nobles alike and different? After Taylor rejects the notion of a bourgeois revolution, how does he demonstrate that "the struggle against absolutism and aristocracy was the product of a financial and political crisis that it did not create" and that the struggle "was essentially a political revolution with social consequences and not a social revolution with political consequences"? Finally, one might consider which of the social science models of revolution described in Stone's article best fit the evidence amassed by Taylor. In particular, is Davis's "J-Curve" useful here?

Taylor's article is also useful for its summary of the major trends in the writing of the history of the French Revolution from Jaurès and Lefebvre to Cobban. Their work further illustrates the historian's continuing dialogue with the past.

To call the French Revolution of 1789 a "bourgeois revolution" invokes ideas which, by common consent, are inseparable from that phrase. It implies, for example, a social class created and nurtured by capitalism, with its wealth preponderantly capitalist in form and function and its values largely derived from capitalism. It implies that the relation of this class to the processes of production differed substantially from that of other classes and that, allowing for a reasonable number of eccentricities, the bourgeoisie showed an over-all unity of goals and outlook, related significantly to capitalism, that made its political action meaningful, powerful, and revolutionary. Stripped of these associations, the phrase "bourgeois revolution" (or "revolutionary bourgeoisie") loses most of its interpretive value, including particularly its involvement with a concept of economic change and class struggle ranging from the Middle Ages to the cold war and beyond.

The ideas that comprise this interpretation have now come under criticism, chiefly from Alfred Cobban. In his London inaugural lecture of 1954, in an article of 1957 on "The Vocabulary of Social History," and in his *Social Interpretation of the French Revolution*,[1] Cobban argues that the concepts embodied in the words "bourgeois revolution" disagree with what research has brought to light. He believes that the phrase incorpo-

[1] Alfred Cobban, *The Myth of the French Revolution* (London, 1955), "The Vocabulary of Social History," *Political Science Quarterly*, LXXI (Mar. 1956), 1–17, and *The Social Interpretation of the French Revolution* (Cambridge, Eng., 1964); see also his *Historians and the Causes of the French Revolution* (rev. ed., London, 1958).

rates a self-confirming system of deception. Taken in its ordinary sense, it acts as a standard for selecting, interpreting, and arranging evidence, and because of this the research usually ends by confirming assumptions that creep in with the terminology. In the writings of Albert Soboul and the late Georges Lefebvre, Cobban finds assertions and data that can be turned against their conclusions, and he attributes these discrepancies to unperceived conflicts between their premises and their evidence. As a corrective, he calls for a reform of the vocabulary, challenging, among other things, the equivalence of "bourgeois" to "capitalist," and of "noble" to "feudal," and there are others who share his dissatisfaction. I have myself found that there were under the old regime not one kind of capitalism but three, that in comparison with nineteenth-century capitalism they were relatively primitive, and that nobles held a heavy stake in two of them. It also seems clear that the speculation and stockjobbing of the 1780s at Paris, so conspicuously capitalist in appearance, was built not on the modernization of industry and trade but on the financial needs and policies of the monarchy. It was heavily penetrated by the nobles, and its center of gravity included the royal court as well as the Bourse. Herbert Lüthy complains that a "quasi-Marxist" preoccupation with capitalism as peculiarly bourgeois has obscured the capitalism of the court and the great nobles and diverted research from the study of the fortunes of the "grandees." [2] Finally, in a recent article, Elizabeth Eisenstein shows that Lefebvre, in his *Coming of the French Revolution,* attributed the initial stimulus of the "bourgeois revolution" to a group of nobles, the Committee of Thirty, apparently without noticing the contradiction between their status and the class character of the revolution they were supposed to have set afoot.[3]

All this suggests that what has long seemed a settled explanation of the French Revolution has become the source of growing dissatisfaction and is up for a reappraisal like that which J. H. Hexter has applied to the concepts of the gentry and the middle class in Tudor England.[4] This reappraisal is far from complete. The range of topics involved in a full examination of the bourgeois revolution model is very broad; the issues are economic, social, political, and even intellectual. The problem can be taken up at several points. Cobban, in his *Social Interpretation,* reopens the question of how the bourgeois revolution was related (if at all) to that of the peasants, whether the Revolution strengthened capitalism or weakened it, and whether the real winners of the Revolution were not the

[2] Herbert Lüthy, *La banque protestante en France de la Révocation de l'Édit de Nantes á la Revolution* (2 vols., Paris, 1959–61), II, 687.

[3] Elizabeth L. Eisenstein, "Who Intervened in 1788? A Commentary on *The Coming of the French Revolution,*" *American Historical Review,* LXXI (Oct. 1965), 77–103.

[4] J. H. Hexter, "The Myth of the Middle Class in Tudor England" and "Storm over the Gentry," which are conveniently brought together in his *Reappraisals in History: New Views on History and Society in Early Modern Europe* (New York, 1963), 71–162.

landowners rather than the commercial-industrial entrepreneurs. Another issue is posed by recent studies of social structure that show wide ranges of property and income within each of certain vocational groups of the upper Third Estate and suggest that the members of each vocational category may have been distributed among two or more degrees of status. But the fundamental question is certainly whether the bourgeoisie of 1789, however defined, had any economic consistency that opposed it to other classes grounded in different forms of wealth. This paper has to do with distinctions between capitalist and noncapitalist wealth and what these imply about the revolution of the upper Third Estate, the movement that began with the demand for doubling the representation of the Third Estate and voting by head rather than by order. It also offers a way of explaining that revolution without having recourse to the present terminology.

There was in the economy of the old regime a distinct configuration of wealth, noncapitalist in function, that may be called "proprietary." It embodied investments in land, urban property, venal office, and annuities. The returns it yielded were modest, ranging between 1 and 5 percent, but they were fairly constant and varied little from year to year. They were realized not by entrepreneurial effort, which was degrading, but by mere ownership and the passage of calendar intervals. Risk was negligible. Although bad harvests lowered rents in kind, they never destroyed capital, and the rents in money, like annuities and salaries of venal office, were payable regardless of natural hazards. In the proprietary sector investments were almost fully secure.

Historically and functionally, proprietary wealth was aristocratic. Under the old regime, gentility required a stable fortune that left one free to live with ease and dignity on his revenues. In the fortunes of the Toulouse nobles studied by Forster [5] and of the magistrates of the Paris Parlement studied by Bluche [6] it was precisely land, urban property, venal office, and annuities that furnished the income on which these families maintained their way of life. Two considerations discouraged nobles from investing in commerce. First, the social values of aristocracy included a notorious aversion to business as practiced by merchants, merchant manufacturers, and bankers. To invest in "trade" was to risk losing status. The only industries that nobles felt entirely free to develop were those rooted in the land and its resources and growing out of certain exploitations of the medieval fief—mines, metallurgy, paper, glass, and canals—and in developing these they adopted practices and forms of organization substantially different from those employed by the merchants. Second, the risks inherent in business endangered the solidity and continuity con-

[5] Robert Forster, *The Nobility of Toulouse in the Eighteenth Century* (Baltimore, 1960), 17–119.
[6] François Bluche, *Les magistrats du parlement de Paris au* XVIIIe *siècle (1715–1771)* (Paris, 1960), 143–239.

sidered essential to wealth meant to support a family for several generations. Fundamentally, the fortune that best served the interests of an aristocratic family was an endowment. Like an endowment, it was carefully managed, and risk was kept to a minimum. The preference for this kind of wealth, based on ingrained social attitudes that have powerfully retarded French economic growth, survived the Revolution. When the Napoleonic aristocracy was established, a landed endowment or *majorat* was required of anyone raised to the peerage, and he and his heirs were forbidden to alienate it except in exchanges of land. Both before and after the Revolution, the social values of the old elite dominated the status-conscious men and women of the wealthy Third Estate. Avid for standing, they had little choice but to pursue it as the aristocracy defined it, and the result was a massive prejudice that diverted *roturier* as well as noble wealth into comparatively sterile proprietary investments.

In describing this system of wealth, the word "proprietary" does better than "feudal." Cobban has pointed out that, in terms of property, "feudalism" could refer only to the seigneury. The seigneury, consisting of dues, monopolies, and rights surviving from the fief, was an order of property superimposed on property in fee simple, and it could be and was acquired by nonnobles. But seigneurial rights figured marginally in a larger preference for all long-term assets yielding secure revenues and standing, a taste for "property" in every form, not only seigneuries but domains, farms, *métairies,* meadows, fields, stands of timber, forges and mills that could be rented out, houses, buildings, venal offices, and loans of indefinite duration producing annuities called *rentes perpétuelles.* Such properties were enduring. Combined into endowments yielding assured revenues, carefully managed, they could be made to support a family indefinitely in a genteel style of living. They guaranteed a status, by no means exclusively noble, that Professor Palmer has called aristocratic. The term "proprietary" describes these fortunes not only because it is derived from "property" but also because it echoes the old regime term *propriétaire,* a prestige counter claimed by those who owned land, even in trifling amounts.

The fondness for land penetrated all levels of French society. Profoundly rural, most eighteen-century Frenchmen had an atavistic attachment to the soil, and "living nobly" was habitually identified with at least seasonal residence in the country. The aristocracy by tradition and the wealthy urban groups by emulation showed an incurable esteem for rural property. The novelist Stendhal, raised in the 1780s at Grenoble, recalled his father, an *avocat au parlement,* as a man constantly preoccupied with acquiring rural land and expanding his holdings. His father's wigmaker (*perruquier*), on missing an appointment with a client, would explain that he had been visiting his "domain," and his excuses were well received. People bought land yielding 1 or 2 percent with funds that could have been deposited with merchants at 5, and borrowed at 5 to buy land that yielded 1 or 2. This passion for land was by no means limited to Grenoble. Nobles, *avocats, procureurs,* financiers, officials, and merchants in all parts of France bought and held urban and rural properties that qualified them for local acceptance, advancement, and privileges. There were shopkeepers, artisans, and even peasants who invested in land and *rentes* that gave them small incomes for old age. In every town those without a business or profession who lived on such investments were taxed on a separate roll, that of the bourgeois, and in 1789 in most towns they voted as a separate electoral group of the Third Estate. A study by Vovelle and Roche shows that the qualification bourgeois disappeared during the Revolution from official acts, and that persons listed under the old regime as bourgeois reappeared in documents of the Directory and the Consulate as *rentiers* and *propriétaires* demonstrating as well as anything can that before the Revolution the fiscal group called bourgeois was non-capitalist.

Nearly all wealthy landowners exploited their land indirectly, through tenants. They saw their properties not as profit-making enterprises but as sources of rental income. Rent, in fact, was at the center of all calculations. It was what determined the value of a property: as rent increased, the value grew proportionately, so that, curiously enough, the rate of return on capital remained about the same. Generally speaking, rental income seems to have ranged between 2 and 4 percent of capital value, and Necker wrote in 1784 that the net revenue from land was 2½ percent, which is to say that, as an investment, land provided the low but assured return typical of proprietary wealth. When an eighteenth-century proprietor set out to increase the revenue of his properties he thought not in terms of increasing the productivity of the soil but of raising the rent, and in the late eighteenth century a significant rise of the peasant population made this easy to do. As land hunger grew and candidates for leases multiplied, rents rose handsomely. Labrousse has found that, from the base period 1726–1741 to the "intercyclic" period 1785–1789, rural money rents advanced by 98 percent, and in a paper on the royal domains submitted to the Assembly of Notables in 1787 mention was made of "the Revolution which, in twenty years, has nearly doubled the revenues of all land." Where the rent was paid in kind, as in *métayage*, the rise in rents is difficult to measure, but there is no doubt that it took place. Forster has written that in the Toulouse region the old phrase "half-fruits" that signified the owner's share was a euphemism; at the end of the century the owners took as much as three-fourths. It is perhaps possible to say that the French landowner of the old regime was an exploiter of persons rather than of the soil. The circumstances of the prerevolutionary period did nothing to change his traditional attitudes. Indeed, by enabling him to raise his income without raising production they reinforced them.

If in the eighteenth century France had had an agricultural revolution comparable to that in England, it would be possible to speak of agricultural capitalism and to discover an entrepreneurial mentality that saw income as profit and was prepared to increase profits by investing in productivity. Unfortunately for the old regime, no such thing took place. There was, of course, much interest among certain upper-class intellectuals in British agricultural innovations, and, beginning in 1750, there began to appear a large body of publications on the subject. Agricultural societies were formed, and experiments were undertaken. Nevertheless, the results were meager. The peasants distrusted innovations and sabotaged experiments, and proprietors who wished to install improvements failed because, in order to succeed, they would have had to learn to work and think like peasants, which was exactly what their values prevented them from doing. But it was not only the disinterest of landowners or their unfitness to provide leadership that aborted the French agricultural revolution. There were many other obstacles which, taken together, would have defeated the boldest plans of agricultural reform: the fragmentation of domains into small, dispersed parcels of property; the stubbornness with which country people defended common rights and broke down enclosures; the burden of the taille, which penalized initiative; the hostility of peasants to new crops, crop courses, and methods of cultivation; the tyranny of the leases, which fixed the crop courses in the old patterns; and finally the shortage of livestock, which assured a shortage of manure, which assured a shortage of improved meadows, which in turn assured a shortage of livestock. Given all these barriers to improvement, the proprietary mentality, with its noncapitalist orientation, was not terribly unrealistic. In 1788 the scientist-financier Lavoisier, a careful student of agriculture, told the provincial assembly of the Orléanais that the productivity of British agriculture was about 2.7 times that of French agriculture and that the capital invested per unit of land was two or three times greater in Britain than in France. He owned an experimental farm. In four years he had invested 120,000 livres in it. In his judgment, which would seem well established, the improvements needed to raise productivity in the Orléanais would require much more of an outlay than the proprietors could or would invest. All these deterrents—legal, psychic, and social—checked economic growth and increased the danger of breakdowns like that of 1788–1790, which in its origins was largely, though not wholly, agrarian and unleashed the rural and urban disorders of the common people, disorders without which the Revolution of 1789 could not have succeeded.

In the proprietary scale of preference, the passion for property in office was nearly as strong as that for property in land. A venal office was a long-term investment. Usually it brought a low but stable return, and, as long as the owner regularly paid the *droit annuel* (in earlier times the *paulette*), he could, under restrictions applicable to each office, sell it to a buyer, bequeath it to an heir, or even rent it out to someone, such as a judge, who, though admitted to practice, was unable to buy the required *charge*. The number and variety of venal offices that existed at the end of the old regime is incredible. An investigation that Necker launched in 1778 disclosed no less than 51,000 venal offices in the law courts, the municipalities, and the financial system, and their capital value, as revealed by voluntary declarations made under an edict of 1771, totaled 600,-000,000 livres, although this should be increased by as much as 50 percent because the declarations, taxable at 1 percent per annum, were notoriously undervalued. These offices included those held by the personnel of the parlements and their chancelleries, the judges of the other royal courts, and the multitude of clerks, beadles, sergeants, surveyors, assessors, and concessionaires that surrounded these courts. They also included the offices held by the notaries and *procureurs,* who could practice their professions only be acquiring the appropriate *charges.* They did not, however, include the offices of the royal household, venal military appointments, or places in the financial companies and the higher financial concessions like those of the *receveurs généraux des finances,* and for these we should probably add another 200,000,000 or 300,000,000 livres to the total indicated above. Also excluded from these figures were the offices held by guild officials, inspectors, and masters, and particularly by the wigmakers. Given the present state of research we have no precise idea of how many adult males owned offices, but it would not be surprising to find that they came to 2 or 3 percent of the total.

Ordinarily, the declared value of an office was only part of the cost of buying and exercising it. Nearly always, it was sold for a price higher than that recorded in the declarations and contracts, and the investment was increased by heavy taxes, fees for registration and reception, and the honoraria, gratuities, and *pourboires* that a candidate had to distribute to officials, clerks, beadles, and even doormen in obtaining his nomination. Philip Dawson has brought to light the case of a young *avocat* who in 1781 purchased a magistracy in the *sénéchaussée* of La Rochelle. In the contract of sale, filed with a notary, the price was put at 10,167 livres. But the buyer's notes show that he really paid 14,000 livres, plus another 4,150 in taxes, dues, fees, and gratuities, all of which means that the total investment exceeded the stated value of the office by 78 percent. When an office gave admission to a profession, the disproportion between its acknowledged value and the full investment was apt to be still greater. In March 1787 the future revolutionary Danton bought the office of *avocat au Conseil du Roi* for 10,000 livres; at the same time, however, he paid the seller 68,000 livres for his practice, including the clientele and the accounts receivable. In short, the additional costs and professional outlays that accompanied investments in venal office raised the total French private funds committed to this purpose far above the more than 600,-000,000 livres with which the Revolution compensated those whose offices it abolished.

Few venal offices were genuinely lucrative. On the 51,000 judicial, municipal, and financial offices covered by the 1778 investigation, the salaries, after deducting for the *droits annuels, vingtièmes,* and transfer taxes (*droits de mutation*), averaged only 1 percent of the values declared in 1771, although in most cases there were fees, perquisites, and gratuities that made up the interest on the declared capital. Whatever economic value they had depended on how the owners used the opportunities that accompanied them. For a notary or *procureur,* the income from a practice could constitute a very decent return on the total outlay. But for the magistrates it was likely to be a different story. Although it was taken for granted that a Parisian *conseiller au parlement* cleared 5 percent per annum on his investment, the *présidents à mortier* made only 2 percent, and the First President, burdened with costs of maintaining the dignity of his position, probably spent more than he received. Generally speaking, an investment in office was an investment in standing. What made it desirable was the status, the respectability that it conferred. For a solid gain in prestige, the holders of *charges* would usually settle for a low return and even a loss of capital. In 1790, for example, the National Assembly was told that the magistrates of some parlements, by excluding *roturiers* from admission, had so narrowed the market for their offices as to reduce the purchase price from more than 50,000 livres to as little as 15,000. In effect, they sacrificed capital for status, which was not unnatural in a society afflicted with a mania for prestige. Apparently, it meant a great deal to be a *lieutenant-civil*, a *lieutenant-criminel*, a *procureur du roi*, a *grand-maître des eaux et forêts*, or even a *conseiller au grenier à sel*. To the *roturiers* it meant still more to acquire an office that gave noble rank. According to Necker, there were more than four thousand of these, although perhaps half of them, like the magistracies of the parlements, were inaccessible to commoners. For example, a *secrétaire du roi* was ennobled by his office and, if he held it twenty years or died possessed of it, acquired *noblesse transmissible* for his heirs and descendants. A *trésorier de France* enjoyed *noblesse personnelle;* although his family did not share this, there was nothing to prevent him from bequeathing his office to his eldest son, and it appears that some of these offices gave *noblesse transmissible*. According to Necker, there were 900 *secrétaires du roi* attached to the chancelleries of the parlements and 740 places that one takes to be those of the *trésoriers de France* in the financial apparatus. Nothing indicates that the propensity of these offices for creating new nobles had been cut off at the end of the old regime.

In addition to land, urban properties, and office, proprietary wealth was invested in *rentes*. In the broadest sense, a *rente* was an annual revenue that one received for having transferred something of value to someone else. A *rente foncière* was rent for land. A *rente hypothécaire* was an annuity the payment of which was secured by property. A *rente perpétuelle* was an annuity of indefinite duration, terminated only when the debtor chose, on his own initiative, to refund the principal and thereby free himself from paying the *rente*. A *rente viagère* was a life annuity: the principal was entrusted to someone who paid the annuity until the person or persons named in the contract died; at that point the principal became finally and irrevocably his. Because the *rente viagère* was essentially a speculation that destroyed all or part of the capital accumulated for a family endowment, most of those living on proprietary wealth believed it reckless and immoral, and a man who converted his fortune into life annuities was considered to have defrauded his heirs.

To an American student, the rationale of this vocabulary is elusive. Everything is clarified, however, by the fact that the vocabulary took shape during the late Middle Ages, when those who wished to borrow, and those who wished to lend, had to find ways of disguising loans at interest so as to circumvent the laws against usury. The terminology of the *rente* made this possible, at least during the sixteenth and seventeenth centuries. One spoke, for example, of purchasing a *rente:* this modulated the smell of avarice and exploitation by making it seem that the lender, who bought the *rente,* had solicited it from the borrower, who sold it, and obtained it on the borrower's terms. The vocabulary also improved appearances by assimilating all these transactions to land rents, which were undoubtedly on the right side of the law. Schnapper has shown that the *rente perpétuelle* began as an annual rent paid to a seller of land by a buyer who could not furnish the full price and, in effect, paid rent on that part of the property he did not own. In the sixteenth century, however, the *rente perpétuelle* acquired an existence apart from real-estate transactions. It then became a perpetual annuity paid for a grant of capital that an investor (the lender) "abandoned," and this was its legal character through the end of the old regime. In the contract, whatever the parties may have agreed verbally or in separate instruments, to stipulate a time of repayment was forbidden, and no such stipulation could be enforced in the courts, for the Church insisted upon a permanent alienation of the capital. Only the borrower, the "seller" of the *rente,* could decide whether the capital would be restored, and, if so, when. No doubt, if he failed to pay the *rente* he could be forced into ceding property that might equal or even exceed the original capital, and perhaps there were other pressures that creditors could employ. Whatever the truth may have been, it seems probable that in the eighteenth century many borrowers gave assurances that the capital would be repaid at a stipulated time. Those who lived up to these assurances probably did so in large part so as to protect their credit and reputations.

The indefinite duration of the *rente perpétuelle* ruined it for commerce, industry, banking, and the short-term credits that the financiers furnished the royal treasury. In these sectors, advances at interest were indispensable, and, although they were nominally illegal, the parties were shielded from prosecution by a national conspiracy, abetted by the administration, to keep the usury laws from being invoked. Merchants gave and took interest on the balances of their accounts with one another and paid interest on time deposits put up by investors. Bankers took interest for many kinds of accommodations. The King himself, violated the usury laws, and there was even a royal rate of interest which, since the time of Louis XIV, was fixed at 5 percent. Under these circumstances it is difficult to see why the archaic *rente perpétuelle* survived. It survived, of course, because it met most of the demands for long-term credit operations in the traditional or proprietary sector, where there were few pressures for collection and payment and where people took satisfaction in avoiding the questionable practices of *traitants* and *commerçants.* Its proper domain was that of accommodations within and between families and investments in annuities sold by municipalities, provincial estates, and the royal treasury. Although economically obsolete, it not only survived, but left a mark on the management of royal and private wealth. Among other things, it engendered that characteristic insouciance toward debt for which the old regime was famous and induced a dangerous negligence in royal finance. "The abundance of claims and credits of indefinite duration," writes Schnapper, "is a characteristic trait of old economies. The creditor prefers a fixed revenue to a capital for which he cannot easily find use. The debtor, himself, never repays because he does not have sufficient monetary means." It is impossible to read this without thinking of the old French royal debt and the bankruptcy in which it finished. On January 1, 1789, the registers of the Paris Hôtel de Ville showed 52,119,537 livres in *rentes perpétuelles* to be paid out during the year; of this more than 44 percent represented annuities on funds borrowed before 1721. In large part, the chronic and ultimately fatal disinclination to amortize the long-term debt is attributable to the fact that the capital of a *rente perpétuelle* did not have to be repaid. Neither, of course, did that of a *rente viagère*. It was therefore easy to drift into bankruptcy. Only when service on the long-term debt was so large as to make deficits inescapable would a controller general have to consider refunding principal, but then, of course, he would find it impossible to pay. That was precisely the quandary of the controllers general of finance after the American war.

It should now be clear that there was a fairly consistent pattern of non-capitalist wealth, that it was traditionally aristocratic, and that "feudalism" is a bad name for it. It was governed by institutional survivals and social values that opposed the progressive and expansive tendencies of capitalism, preferring rent to profit, security to risk, tradition to innovation, and, in terms of personal goals, gentility to entrepreneurial skill and renown. It displayed nearly all the traits of what Rostow has called a traditional society, one dominated by landowners and their values and governed, as far as production was concerned, by pre-Newtonian modes of thought. All these institutions, values, and fixations promoted, as Rostow has suggested, a "long-run fatalism" and a "ceiling on the level of obtainable output per head." [7] In England, no doubt, such deterrents to growth existed, but in ways that are not yet clearly explained they were being outflanked or overcome. In France, however, they flourished. The question of why there should have been such a disparity deserves much more study than it has received.

Compared with proprietary wealth, eighteenth-century commercial capitalism seems a vastly different thing. In commerce, banking, and domes-

[7] W. W. Rostow, *The Stages of Economic Growth: A Non-Communist Manifesto* (Cambridge, Eng., 1960), 4–7. The idea, which Rostow considers essential to growth, that economic progress is possible and necessary was entrenched in the more imaginative and responsible circles of royal administration and certain clusters of intellectuals who tried to influence public policy. But the reformers were frustrated by inalterable privileges and concessions. That is essentially what blocked the abolition of internal tariffs. (See the excellent study of J. F. Bosher, *The Single Duty Project: A Study of the Movement for a French Customs Union in the Eighteenth Century* [London, 1964].)

tic industry fixed assets were negligible, and investments were put into circulating wealth. Goubert has written of the Motte family of Beauvais:

> One is tempted to write that what was always important to those merchants-born [*marchands-nés*] was wealth in motion, the rather intoxicating impression that must have come to them from the merchandise, credits, and cash that moved, circulated, fluctuated, and constantly transformed themselves: a kind of ballet of linens, paper, and money.

This engaging description of commercial wealth is justified by entrepreneurial records in many archives. At Lyons merchants rented the houses and warehouses in which they did business. With the *armateurs* of Bordeaux and Marseilles, ships were short-term assets; bought by a syndicate organized to finance the voyage, the ship was sold at the end of the venture, sometimes at auction, sometimes simply to the syndicate the *armateur* had formed for the next voyage. Industrial machinery was simple and made mostly of wood. In textiles, which accounted for about two-thirds of industrial production by value, it was owned chiefly by the artisans to whom the work was distributed, and when merchants loaned it to them it was not serious enough to warrant carrying in the accounts. All this explains why the ledgers of the old regime carry no accounts for depreciation costs. The day of heavy fixed commercial and industrial investment was yet to come.

Risk, nearly unknown in the proprietary sector, was a central fact of business life. The merchant speculated in commodities, paper, and credit, and, no matter how prudent he was, his fate depended largely on events he could not control. Shipwrecks, acts of war, sudden changes in style, unforeseeable bankruptcies, or unfavorable shifts in exchange rates could wipe him out, and if it was bad luck that broke him it was largely good luck that made him rich. Established merchants, known for caution and probity, went under, while new men, starting with borrowed money and the savings of a clerk's salary, became well to do. Commerce, therefore, was a zone of fortune building and social mobility. But because it lacked the stability of the proprietary sector, it was dangerous for established wealth. "All that I have seen," wrote the Comte de Villèle, ". . . leaves me with the opinion that every man with an acquired fortune who desires only to keep it, must keep at a distance from people, of whatever class or profession they be, who strive to make a fortune; . . ."

> he must avoid all business, all relations with them, because they will not fail to make him their dupe. Furthermore, to each man his *métier,* as the proverb says: look at the proprietor trying to speculate, and at the merchant trying to enter agriculture. . . . Never have I participated in the least speculation.

Finally, in contrast to proprietary wealth, business capital gave low dividends in prestige. The public image of the merchant that Molière exploited rather brutally in *Le bourgeois gentilhomme* was profoundly ignoble, and it afflicted the merchants themselves with feelings of inferiority that probably troubled them more than the contempt they actually encountered. To some extent their unhappiness was self-induced. In 1700–1701 merchant deputies to the Council of Trade complained that merchants were held in low esteem, that the public ignored the superior status of a wholesale merchant or banker, and that because of this their sons avoided business and their daughters preferred nonmerchants as husbands. "Our young people," wrote one of them, "concentrate on the social graces rather than on the really substantial things in life, [and] our children are ever fearful lest it become known that their fathers were once merchants." About thirty years before the Revolution the Abbé Coyer wrote: "Only the Merchant perceives no luster in his career, & if he wants to succeed in what is called in France *being something,* he has to give it up. This misunderstood expression does a lot of damage. In order to be *something,* a large part of the Nobility remains nothing." The merchants felt that the intense practical training of business, the constant supervision and attention it required, and its remoteness from the leisure and finesse of the proprietary round of life kept them from cultivating the social and intellectual qualities that brought respect. Savary, whose *Le parfait négociant* remained throughout the eighteenth century a desktop oracle of business practice and morality, warned merchants not to educate their sons in the liberal arts and not to let them mingle with young nobles and men of the robe in the *collèges,* because the self-esteem they would acquire in those milieux would ruin them for trade. Because these attitudes existed, anyone who remained in business, no matter how creditably he lived, suffered some discount in prestige. Even in the values of the Third Estate, diverse as they may have been, esteem was associated with proprietary wealth. Capitalism, which offered neither the assurance nor the standing that went with land and office, was simply a way, direct and dangerous, of getting rich.

The merchants, although they complained of the prejudices against trade, had to accept them as part of the status system and ground rules in the competition for standing. That is why they so often diverted profits into the purchase of country properties and offices, and why so many of them, once enriched, converted their commercial fortunes entirely into proprietary possessions. At an appropriate stage, the richest and most ambitious bought offices that conferred nobility. The members of the Danse family, linen merchants of Beauvais, constantly put business profits into country properties, acquired nobility, and, in 1757, liquidated their last partnership. During the Revolution, like other nobles and wealthy commoners, they lost their seigneurial dues, but purchased *biens nationaux* and remained until the Second Empire a family of provincial gentlemen. But this is only a sample of what was going on. The conversion of commercial capital into proprietary wealth was a regular feature of French history, from the sixteenth century to the eighteenth and even beyond. Apparently, the purpose of succeeding in business was to get the means of becoming a proprietor and a gentleman, and both Colbert and Necker, a century apart from one another, complained that this tendency drained off commercial and industrial capital and undermined economic growth. In order to counteract this, the government frequently authorized nobles to enter maritime and wholesale commerce and banking, thereby permitting ennobled merchants to continue in trade without losing status. This remedy, however, was only partly effective. It protected the juridical status of an ennobled merchant, but, since it had little impact on social values and attitudes, his sons were likely to drift into the administration, the armed forces, the judiciary, or country life, where sooner or later their ignoble origins would be forgotten.

There is no conclusive way of comparing the mass value of proprietary and business wealth in prerevolutionary France. Beginning with what passed in those days for statistics, supplementing them with estimates made by well-informed men who say little about their derivation, making inferences on assumptions which, though reasonable, can be endlessly debated, one concludes that the traditional modes of property—land, buildings, office, and *rentes*—accounted for more than 80 percent of French private wealth. This indicates a substantial preponderance for the proprietary sector. It is in no way astonishing. The day of heavy fixed industrial investment in factories and railroads, which would have altered the balance, lay far ahead. Meanwhile, most Frenchmen lived on the land, which yielded most of the taxable income and the gross national product. That is why the *économistes* not unreasonably attacked agricultural problems first, often to the neglect of the others.

For our purposes it is desirable to know the relative weight of the two kinds of capital not only for the society as a whole but in the upper Third Estate. Unfortunately, studies of the notarial records are not sufficiently advanced to show this. For the moment, all one can do is count persons, and from this it appears that even in the most heavily commercialized cities the proprietors and professional men in the Third Estate outnumbered the merchants. At Bordeaux, the second most active port, there were 1,100 officials, professionals, *rentiers,* and property owners against only 700 merchants, brokers, and sugar refiners. At Rouen, a prime center of industry, banking, and maritime and wholesale trade, the administrative and judicial officers, professionals, and proprietors-*rentiers* outnumbered the merchants and brokers by more than three to one. At Toulouse, an agricultural, legal, and ecclesiastical capital, the ratio was about eleven to four, but the four included merchants who for the most part traded on small capital and in little volume and did much retail business, so that one hesitates to call them capitalists. There is, however, a further consideration. Because the merchants and industrialists owned, along with their commercial capital, considerable proprietary wealth, we could, with better data, divide them fractionally between the two sectors, and, by such a procedure, the share of commercial and industrial capital in the upper Third Estate would seem much lower than the impression we get by counting heads.

Soundings like these are merely straws in the wind, but they drift always in one direction. They confirm what seems to have been implicit in the consciousness of eighteenth-century France—that even in the well-to-do Third Estate proprietary wealth substantially outweighed commercial and industrial capital. This would not have surprised a Frenchman of the old regime and should not surprise us. The reason for stressing it here is to lay the ground for an assertion that is fundamental in analyzing the causes of the Revolution: there was, between most of the nobility and the proprietary sector of the middle classes, a continuity of investment forms and socioeconomic values that made them, economically, a single group. In the relations of production they played a common role. The differentiation between them was not in any sense economic; it was juridical. This situation, in the historiography of the Revolution, has received practically no serious attention and remains, in Orwellian language, an "unfact." The reason for this is that it contributes nothing to what Cobban rightly calls "the established theory of the French Revolution," the theory that the Revolution was the triumph of capitalism over feudalism. In that context the configuration of proprietary wealth that pervaded both the second and Third Estates has no place and remains unwanted, unused, and therefore, in effect, unknown.

It deserves, however, to be recognized, and its claims are strengthened by bringing forward a second unfact: that a substantial number of nobles participated as entrepreneurs in commerce, industry, and finance. There was indeed, before the Revolution, a *noblesse commerçante,* though not, perhaps, the one that the Abbé Coyer called for in 1756. Provincial, military, and court nobles, peers, and members of the royal family invested in the General Farm, speculated on the Bourse, and developed and exploited mines, canals, and metallurgical establishments, including the great foundry of Le Creusot. On the other hand, there was, to reverse the phrase, a *commerce anobli,* a sizable group of merchants ennobled through the municipal offices of certain cities and the two thousand or more venal offices that conferred nobility on the buyers. For the most part, these ennobled merchant families were in a transitional stage. As enterprises were liquidated, or generations arose that were no longer trained for business, they dropped out of trade to live, as other nobles did, on their revenues. All the same, merchants or not, they were nobles and sat in the noble assemblies of 1789. To sum up, there were nobles who were capitalists. There were merchants who were nobles. As the proprietary wealth traditionally identified with aristocracy extended far down into the Third Estate, so the capitalism traditionally identified with the wealthy Third Estate penetrated into the second, and into its highest ranks.

This means that the old diagram by which we envision prerevolutionary society must be changed. There was a clear juridical boundary that separated nobles from commoners, and a commoner crossed it by registering a legal document, his letters of nobility. On the other hand, the frontier between capitalist and proprietary wealth ran vertically through both orders. The horizontal line marked a legal dichotomy, the vertical line, an economic one. To think of them as coinciding, even roughly, is to misunderstand the situation completely. The concept of two classes, at once economically and juridically disjunct, can be sustained only by ignoring the weight of proprietary wealth in the Third Estate and that of capitalism in the second, or, in other words, by continuing to ostracize them as unfacts.

From this follow two important conclusions. The first is that when the word bourgeois is used to indicate a nonnoble group playing a capitalist role in the relations of production it includes less than half the well-to-do Third Estate and excludes the proprietary groups that furnished 87 percent of the Third Estate deputation to the Estates-General. In other words, it embraces only a minority of the upper middle classes and explains almost nothing about the origins of the revolutionary leadership. In this sense it should be discarded as inadequate and misleading. But there are other senses, loaded with eighteenth-century implications, in which the word will continue to be employed because it alone translates what the documents have to say. One may, for example, speak of bourgeois who lived nobly on their revenues and comprised a fiscal category; these constituted a small portion of the Third Estate and counted entirely in the proprietary group. One may also speak of bourgeois as persons who, being inscribed in the registers of the bourgeoisie of a town, enjoyed what Anglo-Saxons call "the rights of the city," including political advantages and fiscal exemptions worth having, but in this sense the bourgeoisie included nobles and noncapitalist commoners and was not entirely of the Third Estate. Finally, one may adopt a peasant usage, applying the word bourgeois to townsmen who collected rents in and near the village and were felt to be an alien and adverse interest. All three meanings convey realities of the old regime and are useful on condition that one makes clear which of them he has in mind.

The second conclusion is that we have no economic explanation for the so-called "bourgeois revolution," the assault of the upper Third Estate on absolutism and aristocracy. No one denies that such an assault took place or that it left a powerful imprint upon French society. The struggle for the doubling of the Third Estate and the vote by head, the demand for a constitution and an elected legislature, the intimation of political equality in the Declaration of the Rights of Man, the liquidation of intendancies, provinces, parlements, fiscal inequalities, forms of nobility—all these, put in series with the emigration, the expropriation of Church and *émigré* wealth, and the Terror, have to be made credible on some basis. By one of the unexamined postulates of current historiography we expect them to be explained by a conflict of social classes and the contradictions between a "rising" economic order and the order that it challenges. The position taken here is that we have now learned enough to see that this cannot be done, that to divide the wealthy elements of prerevolutionary society into a feudal aristocracy and a capitalist bourgeoisie forces the concealment of too much evidence, and that the whole classic concept of a bourgeois revolution has become impossible to sustain.

This leaves in our interpretation of the Revolution a somewhat painful void. Our instinct is to fill it with a new class struggle interpretation like Cobban's "revolution of the propertied classes," which explains some results of the Revolution but not, apparently, its origins. There may, however, be more plausibility in a political approach than in a reorganization of social categories. The gist of such an approach can be set down in two propositions that probably amount to the same thing. First, the struggle against absolutism and aristocracy was the product of a financial and political crisis that it did not create. Second, it was essentially a political revolution with social consequences and not a social revolution with political consequences. Because these assumptions suggest a backward step in historiography, it will take a few paragraphs to make them respectable.

The Revolution resulted from a bankruptcy that left the monarchy discredited and helpless. The disclosures of the first Assembly of Notables shocked everyone capable of reacting to public affairs, set off an expanding discussion of reforms, and raised hopes for a national regeneration. The government's reform program, which threatened privileges and seemed tainted with the supposed negligence and dishonesty of the Controller General Calonne, was rejected by the Notables. For more than a year the parlements and other constituted bodies opposed it. This resistance, the so-called *révolte nobiliaire,* taught the upper Third Estate the language, tactics, and gallantry of opposition. It made the convocation of the Estates-General inevitable. When in August 1788 this convocation was announced (along with a partial suspension of payments), there was thrust upon the nation a new political issue: whether royal power would pass to the privileged orders or would be shared with those who, until then, had been disfranchised. By inviting his subjects to advise him on how to organize the Estates-General, the King precipitated a landslide of publications that touched off a growing outcry for the doubling of the Third and the vote by head. This generated a political struggle between democracy, as Palmer has defined it, and aristocracy, substantially as he has taught us to understand it.* The stakes were very high. They included the question of at whose expense the financial problem would be solved, and whether careers in the military, the clergy, and the judiciary, and, above all, in politics would be opened to commoners, rich and poor, whose main resources were talents, education, and ambition. In explaining the democratic assault on despotism and aristocracy it is unnecessary to conjure up a social struggle rooted in economic change. The paralysis of the monarchy, the apprehensions of the taxable groups and creditors of the state, and the hopes and ambitions of the professional classes, combined with the slogans, myths, and images generated by the struggle, seem

* Taylor refers here to the important work of R. R. Palmer, *The Age of Democratic Revolution* (Princeton, two volumes, 1959 and 1964), especially volume I, pp. 4–5. By "democratic" Palmer means the eighteenth century opposition to government by "privileged, closed, or self-recruiting groups of men," recruited by right of status, "history," custom, or inheritance and ordinarily members of what Krieger, in his selection, called "constituted authorities and corporations." In other words, "democrats" were opposed to "aristocrats" and to universal suffrage for the poor and uneducated. [Editor.]

quite enough. The revolutionary mentality was created by the crisis. It was, in fact, the writing of the *cahiers* that forced a crystallization of issues and their formulation in ideological terms. For the mass of the upper Third Estate, the school of revolution were the electoral assemblies of 1789, not the salons and *sociétés de pensée* of the old regime.

What this interpretation restores is the sense of an unplanned, unpremeditated revolution that in many ways exceeded the aims expressed in the *cahiers de doléances* of March and April 1789. Take, for example, the abolition of nobility, which may be understood here as aristocracy constituted juridically as an order. If in the spring of 1789 the upper Third Estate had seen nobility as an intolerable institution it would certainly have called for its destruction. But this was never attempted until the revolutionary leadership had concluded, from more than a year of political experience, that the nobility was an incorrigible enemy of the new regime. Certainly there was friction in the quarrel of 1788 over how the new provincial estates would be constituted and whether nobles and commoners would deliberate there together. It was intensified by the dispute over how the Estates-General should be organized. But in the spring of 1789 middle-class feelings toward nobility were still benign. Far from wanting to abolish nobility, the Third Estate wished to rehabilitate it. One reads in the Third Estate *cahiers* of the major towns and cities that nobility was to be reformed, that nobles should be given opportunities to replenish their fortunes, and, still more remarkable, that nobility must be saved from adulteration by abolishing the venal offices and making ennoblement depend not on money but on service to the nation. Then came the quarrels and confrontations of 1789, the destruction of the constituted bodies, and the reform of the army and the Church, which was dispossessed to protect the creditors of the state. These events made the oppositon to the Revolution, inside and outside the National Assembly, formidable. In all three orders it developed considerable strength. On June 19, 1790, after a year of struggle, nobility, as such, was abolished in order to disarm and probably to punish the most conspicuous element of the opposition. Nothing in the *cahiers* forecasts such a decree. The intention to smash the legal basis of nobility and, along with it, the whole system of language, symbols, images, and formalities that reinforced the subservience of the lower groups, was a product of the revolutionary crisis, not a cause. To argue that it came about through long years of economic change, class formation, and the gradual growth of class consciousness in a bourgeoisie that played a capitalist role in the relations of production is not only out of keeping with the evidence, but superfluous.

The present crisis in the interpretation of the French Revolution results from the maturing of social history as a discipline. This specialty, in its present form, was virtually created in France. Its methods are as distinctive as the sources it employs, and its findings are most convincing when expressed in quantitative form. Applied to the history of the Revolution, it has yielded a mass of data on economic interests and conditions, standards of living, population change, corporate structures, social values, and the complex mentalities found at various levels of society. Much of this material disagrees with the vocabulary in use when the effort began. But the vocabulary is still in force. The problem is how to rescue the data from a language that misrepresents it and imprisons it in categories that can no longer be justified.

Although interest in the social history of the Revolution is very old, its progress as a specialty began during 1901–1904, when Jaurès published the first four volumes of the *Histoire socialiste* and procured the establishment of the Commission of the Economic History of the Revolution. "It was Jaurès," Lefebvre once wrote, "who habituated historians to see [in the Revolution] a fact [that is] social and, consequently, of economic origin." Jaurès had no doubt that the Revolution was the political triumph of a bourgeoisie matured by the growth of capitalism, and, with an erudition that is astonishing, given the literature available to him, he rewrote the history of the Revolution on this theme. Lefebvre, who avowed a deep indebtedness to Jaurès, never renounced this view. In the first two paragraphs of *Quatre-vingt-neuf,* paragraphs that dominate the reading of the whole book, he identified the "primary cause" of the Revolution as a conflict between an aristocratic society, grounded historically in the ascendancy of landowners, and a new class, the bourgeoisie, enriched on liquid forms of wealth. In this passage Lefebvre left no doubt that capitalism was the economic basis of the bourgeoisie and the source of its growing power. Out of this socioeconomic configuration had come, he said, the ideology of the philosophes and the *économistes,* expressing the values and aspirations of a revolutionary class. These developments were fundamental. The royal bankruptcy and the aristocratic resistance that forced the King to convoke the Estates-General were treated as an "immediate cause" which explained many of the characteristics of the Revolution and why it began when it did.[8]

Lefebvre's work, however, led him to modify considerably the original overview of Jaurès. Writing in 1932, he found that overview already too simple. As an explanation, he observed, it was credible only when supplemented with the financial crisis, the *révolte nobiliaire,* and the economic distress that produced the popular disturbances without which the Revo-

[8] Georges Lefebvre, *Quatre-vingt-neuf* (Paris, 1939), 5–6; *id. The Coming of the French Revolution,* tr. R. R. Palmer (Princeton, N. J., 1947), 1–2. Also a passage of 1937: "The origins of the Revolution involve several problems. It was the bourgeoisie that took control of it and gave it juridical form, inspired by its ideology, which agreed with its interests. The problem—which Jaurès stated clearly and for which he outlined the solution—is to know how the bourgeoisie finally came to understand, thanks to the progress of the capitalist economy, that feudal institutions opposed to the triumph of capitalism an obstacle that it was absolutely necessary to eliminate; and how at the same time it acquired the strength, the knowledge, and the talent, which, with the consciousness of its social superiority, gave it the will and the means to seize power and keep it." (Lefebvre, "Le mouvement des prix et les origines de la Révolution française," *Études,* ed. Soboul, 233–34.)

lution could not have succeeded. In *Quatre-vingt-neuf,* passing well beyond the thesis announced in the preface, he described four revolutions: aristocratic, bourgeois, popular, and peasant. In *La Révolution française,* the synthesis that he contributed in 1951 to the series "Peuples et civilisations," he described an aristocratic revolution, a bourgeois revolution, and a popular revolution, the last being composed of a Parisian revolution, a municipal revolution, and a peasant revolution; all these were treated under the heading "L'avènement de la bourgeoisie en France." He was also troubled, far more than less perceptive historians, by the problem of relating the bourgeoisie, with all its diversity, to the derivation assigned it in Jaurès' writings and his own preface to *Quatre-vingt-neuf.* Twice he wrote that it was not "homogeneous." In *La Révolution française* he saw it as composed of bourgeois living on investments in land and, to some extent, liquid capital; holders of venal offices; financiers, maritime merchants, and manufacturers; a "middle class" or *petite bourgeoisie* of tradesmen and petty officials; and a bourgeoisie of intellectual capacities ranging from savants and artists to law clerks and office employees. The determinants of status, he believed, included birth, corps, vocation, and, occasionally, talent. In his last study, an analysis of the urban society of Orléans, he laid out social categories in terms of order, vocation, and wealth or income, but Soboul tells us that he was not satisfied with either the method or the results. It is not difficult to see why. Classification by wealth conflicted with classification by role, and both conflicted with classification by order. Nearly a fifth of the nobles who enjoyed revenues of more than five hundred livres per year, for example, were merchants and sugar refiners; "bourgeois" by vocation, they shared the privileges of the second estate. To put the matter another way, half the refiners and a third of the merchants named in the tax rolls of 1791 were nobles; giving priority to the system of orders, Lefebvre classified them with the nobility. The Third Estate he divided into a *haute bourgeoisie* and a large category called *moyenne et petite bourgeoisies,* but for lack of tax rolls did this entirely on the basis of vocations and corporate groupings. All nonnoble merchants, refiners, brokers, officials, and manufacturers were assigned to the *haute bourgeoisie,* although Lefebvre observed that, if the tax rolls had survived, some of them would have had to be demoted. On that principle, of course, the same documents would have elevated many professional men from the lower group to the higher. Finally, one reads that the *cahier* of the Third Estate of the *bailliage* was drawn up by the elite of the bourgeoisie, but that elite, a political entity, remains unreconciled with the socioeconomic groupings.

Apparently, what the emerging data have made impossible is to equate the identifiable leadership of the upper Third Estate—the "revolutionary bourgeoisie"—with a social class that played a common role in the relations of production, or, more precisely, owned the instruments of production in an emergent capitalist economy. Soboul, in his masterful study of the sans-culottes, faced a comparable situation. He found the sans-cu-

lottes a political bloc composed of diverse economic elements; he therefore pronounced them not a social class.[9] The same step may now be
taken with regard to the "revolutionary bourgeoisie." Jeffry Kaplow has,
in fact, moved toward this solution by defining the bourgeois on juridical
and political lines.[10] They were, he says, well-to-do people excluded from
the privileges of the nobles and from powerful positions in the state, the
army, the Church, and the parlements. Yet they had access, not enjoyed
by the common people, to local political office. "They were beginning to
become conscious of themselves as a class," he observes, "and shared a definite set of values." That is certainly true. Yet, if this is a social class, it is
not one in the sense recognized by the last two generatons of social scientists in this country. Nor is it the bourgeoisie as we commonly think of it.

Hexter has recently pointed out that one of the peculiarities of historical rhetoric is the use of words that he calls "evocative" because they signal
the historian to summon up whole categories and sequences of associations with which professional thought identifies them.[11] Terms like
"aristocracy," "bourgeoisie," "feudalism," "capitalism," and "social class"
have this quality. It is what gives them interpretive value. Each is
freighted with implications that make it operative in the machinery of the
bourgeois revolution model, so that, as Cobban points out, to accept the
language is to accept the theory. In ordinary usage, whoever says "class" is
heard to say "productive role," and whoever says "bourgeois" is heard to
say "capitalist." Unless he adds an emphatic disclaimer, he should expect
to be understood in this sense. But even emphatic disclaimers can be ineffectual if, as in the case of "class" and "bourgeois," special meanings have
been welded on by more than thirty years of writing, teaching, and discussion. Under those circumstances, there is little prospect of revising professional usage. That is particularly true of a vocabulary which, among
many millions of the world's people, has a content that is ideologically
obligatory and is thereby frozen into alliance with an obsolete interpretation. Obviously, the project of solving this problem by giving new meanings to old words is more or less utopian. The phrases "bourgeois revolution" and "revolutionary bourgeoisie," with their inherent deceptions, will
have to go, and others must be found that convey with precision and
veracity the realities of social history.

[9] Albert Soboul, *Les sans-culottes parisiens en l'an II: Mouvement populaire et
gouvernement révolutionnaire, 2 juin 1793–9 thermidor an II* (Paris, 1958), 427.

[10] In his introduction to *New Perspectives on the French Revolution: Readings
in Historical Sociology,* ed. Jeffry Kaplow (New York, 1965), 14.

[11] J. H. Hexter, "The Rhetoric of History," a paper read at the Annual Meeting
of the American Historical Association, San Francisco, Dec. 28, 1965, to be published shortly in *History and Theory.*

6. The "Popular Movement" in the French Revolution

GEORGE RUDÉ

*Just as terms like "bourgeoisie" and "bourgeois revolution" are undergoing
more precise definition and evaluation in recent years, the role of the revolutionary crowd or popular movement in the French Revolution is being looked
at more carefully. If historians have not always been neutral toward the revolution itself, they have been even less neutral toward the crowd.*

Opponents of the French Revolution have termed the crowd the canaille,
mob, *or* rabble. *The revolution's sympathizers, on the other hand, have spoken
imprecisely of the crowd as the* peuple (*people*), menu peuple (*common people*),
or sans-culottes (*those who did not wear knee-breeches*), *or else they have
tried to turn its members into* bras nus, *a "bare armed" budding proletariat.*

*Beginning especially with Georges Lefebvre, historians increasingly have
suggested that these terms will not do, or that they must be given more precise
definition. Lefebvre saw that the French Revolution was a series of successive,
sometimes mutually hostile revolutions of the nobility, bourgeoisie, popular
movement, and peasantry, each of which had its own aims, social composition,
and political action. Lefebvre, perhaps more than anyone, convinced historians that the bourgeoisie, however defined, could not have succeeded had it
not been for the periodic great urban uprisings of the popular movement or
those peasant disturbances in 1789 called the "Great Fear." Because he put*

Source: George Rudé, *The Crowd in History, 1730–1848* (New York: John
Wiley, 1964), pp. 93–107. Copyright © 1964 by John Wiley & Sons, Inc. Reprinted by permission. [Some footnotes omitted.]

such great stock in the role of these latter two "revolutions," his work inspired historians to look at the French Revolution "from below." Studies in English which have done this include Albert Soboul's The Parisian Sans-Culottes and the French Revolution *(Oxford, 1964), R. B. Cobb's* The Police and the People *(London, 1970), and George Rudé's* The Crowd in the French Revolution *(Oxford, 1959). All of them have used seldom studied archival materials, such as police records, to discover who participated in the revolutionary urban crowds, what they did for a living, what issues and organizations mobilized them into action, and what they hoped to achieve by going out into the street.*

This selection is an example of this approach. It is by George Rudé, an English historian presently teaching at Sir George Williams University in Montreal, and it summarized his larger study just mentioned. In reading his account consider why he sometimes refers to the crowd as the menu peuple *and at other times as* sans-culottes. *What was the relationship between bread prices and revolutionary activity? How did the social composition of the revolutionary crowd change during the revolution? Did its politics change and, if so, in what direction? At what points or with which* journées *("days" of revolutionary activity) did these changes occur? What evidence is there that the crowd's violence was rational rather than mindless? What were the political results of the various* journées? *Who benefited most from them? How and by whom was the crowd brought under control? Again, do the revolutionary models described by Lawrence Stone seem helpful in understanding the role of the crowd?*

. . . It was through the *parlements* that the Parisian *menu peuple* learned their first political lessons and . . . under their influence city, unlike rural, riots tended to develop into political demonstrations. This was particularly so in the last two years of the Old Régime, when the *parlement* of Paris, locked in its final dispute with Louis XVI's ministers, provoked enthusiastic and noisy celebrations on the island of the Cité after returning to the capital from exile. Yet this was only a beginning. The crowds that assembled to greet the *parlement* were limited to students, lawyers' clerks, and journeymen of a number of districts. The lessons learned were still rudimentary and skin deep. Above all, they were restricted to the city and had not, as yet, aroused a response among the peasants in the countryside. The onset and course of the Revolution were to change all this. In challenging the "privileged" orders (including the *parlements*) for control of the Estates General of 1789, the *bourgeoisie,* or Third Estate, appealed to the whole nation; its ideas and slogans were seized upon by the rural as well as by the city population; and, under this impact, the food riot of the countryside and the occasional political demonstration of the city became converted into the great popular *jacqueries* and *journées* (or "days") of the summer and autumn of 1789. In turn, these early "spontaneous" demonstrations began to grow into more sophisticated political movements of the urban sans-culottes: these reflected both the intensity of the struggle of parties and the growing political experience and awareness of the sans-culottes themselves. This was a long-drawn-out process, and no detailed examination will be attempted here.

The purpose of this chapter is rather to illustrate the transition from one type of riot to the other and to indicate the main stages by which the political *journées*,* the most characteristic of all the forms of popular participation in the Revolution, originated and took shape.

After its first challenge to the Ministry in the "aristocratic revolt" of 1787, the Paris *parlement* won an early victory and, having spent a week or two in exile, was allowed to return to Paris. The returning magistrates received a tumultuous welcome on the island of the Cité, in the Place Dauphine, in the Rue du Harlay, and at the approaches to the Law Courts. The authorities had been prepared for disorder, and the courts were ringed with 500 Gardes de Paris, supported by a regiment of the Gardes Françaises. Crowds, composed of the clerks of the Palais de Justice and the apprentices and journeymen of the luxury trades of the Cité, filled the Pont Neuf and its approaches, let off squibs and fireworks, and pelted the troops with stones. On September 28, when the disturbances reached their climax, the troops were stung to open fire: there were no casualties, though a passing lawyer had his coat pierced by a stray bullet; and four young men were arrested. The disorders lasted for a week, during which bonfires were lit before the Law Courts, anti-royalist tracts were distributed, and Calonne, former Comptroller General, and the Comtesse de Polignac, governess of the royal children, were burned in effigy. On October 3, the *parlement* itself called a halt to the riots by proscribing all meetings and firework displays in the vicinity of the Law Courts. It had been a limited and localized affair. Its main support had been drawn from the lawyers' clerks and journeymen of the Cité; and the faubourgs and markets had not yet become involved.

In the following months the crisis deepened, both because of the sharpening political tension and the rising price of bread. In May, the *parlement* courted further popularity by condemning the hated *lettres de cachet*, whereby the Ministry's opponents were incarcerated without trial, and the whole system of arbitrary government. The government riposted by surrounding the Law Courts with troops; an edict drafted by Lamoignon, Keeper of the Seals, vested a great part of the *parlement's* jurisdiction in other courts; and the rebellious magistrates were once more packed off to the provinces in exile. But such was the support for the *parlements*—in Paris and in other cities—that the ministers were

---

* The most important of these revolutionary *journées* were:
In *1789:* Réveillon riots (April 28–29), Paris revolution and capture of the Bastille (July 12–14), march to Versailles (October 5–6).
In *1791:* March to Vincennes (February 28), Champ de Mars demonstration and petition (July 17).
In *1792:* Invasion of Tuileries (June 20), overthrow of monarchy (August 10), September massacres (September 2–4).
In *1793:* Expulsion of "Girondin" deputies (May 31–June 2), insurrection of September 4–5.
In *1794:* Overthrow of Robespierre (9th Thermidor—July 27).
In *1795:* Popular riots of Germinal (April 1) and 1st–4th Prairial (May 20–23), royalist rising of 13th Vendémiaire (October 5).

compelled to bow before the storm: Brienne, the Chief Minister, was dismissed and replaced by Necker; the Estates General was promised for the following year; Lamoignon's edict was withdrawn; and the Paris *parlement* was recalled soon after. The victory was hailed by further celebrations in the Cité: fireworks were let off in profusion, bonfires were lit, and the occupants of coaches crossing the Pont Neuf were made to bow low to the statue of Henri IV, most popular of France's Kings, and to shout "A bas Lamoignon!" and "Vive Henri Quatre!"

This time, the disturbances assumed a new and more serious note: the price of the 4-pound loaf had risen in three weeks from 9 to 11 sous; and, at the end of August, the clerks of the Palais de Justice were joined by the *menu peuple* of the faubourgs and markets. The riots became more violent and spread into other districts; guard posts on both sides of the Pont Neuf, which spanned the Cité, were ransacked and burned to the ground. The Guards were ordered to meet force with force; and, in the Place de Grève on the north bank of the river, 600 demonstrators were fired on by troops, who killed seven or eight and put the rest to flight. After a fortnight's intermission, the riots resumed with further celebrations in the Cité and further bloody clashes between troops and journeymen and students at places as far apart as the Rue St. Martin in the north and the university quarter in the south. Over 50 persons were arrested, but the crowds won the day: both the unpopular Lamoignon and the Chevalier Dubois, commander of the Garde de Paris, were dismissed from office before the riots came to an end.

The Paris *parlement* had therefore succeeded, in its duel with government, in harnessing to its cause the energies of a significant part of the capital's sans-culottes; and with their support it had won notable successes. But both the alliance and the achievement proved short lived. Even before the disturbances were over, the *parlement* had antagonized a large part of its supporters by insisting that the Estates General should be composed as it had been when it last met 175 years before—that is, that each "order" should meet separately and have equal representation. Thus the Third Estate would always be outvoted and the "privileged" orders would, as traditionally, call the tune. The Third Estate, seeing its hopes endangered, replied with a pamphlet war that in a remarkably short time turned the tables on the *parlements* and won nationwide support for its own aims, which included double representation for the Third Estate (a demand soon conceded by the government itself) and the merging of all three separate orders into one. The high hopes raised, even in country areas, by the prospect of an Estates General similarly constituted is illustrated in Arthur Young's encounter with a peasant woman of Champagne, who told him that

> It was said at present that *something was to be done by some great folks for such poor ones, but she did not know who, nor how,* but God send us better, *car les tailles et les droits nous écrasent.*

Young's entry in his journal of this conversation dates from July 12; but long before that the militant slogan of "tiers état"—the symbol of the popular challenge to privilege—had begun to circulate among the Parisian *menu peuple:* the earliest example that I have found in police records dates from early April [1789]. Two to three weeks later, it was to be voiced in a popular riot; but one in which the *menu peuple* were largely rioting to promote their own ends and were not yet completely won for the aims of the *bourgeois* politicians of the Third Estate. This was the bloody fray that broke out in the Faubourg St. Antoine—soon to be distinguished as the most revolutionary of all the faubourgs—at the end of April, a week before the long-awaited Estates General met at Versailles. On April 23, two manufacturers, Réveillon and Henriot, both prominent members of the local Third Estate, had, in their respective assemblies of electors, regretted the high wages paid in industry. Whether or not they advocated a reduction in wages is not certain (and both were said to be good employers), but so it was interpreted by the wage earners of the faubourg; and their remarks, made at a time when the price of bread was phenomenally high,* provoked a violent outburst of disorder. Five or six hundred *ouvriers* gathered near the Bastille and, having hanged Réveillon (the most prominent of the culprits) in effigy, paraded dummy figures of both their intended victims round the various districts of the capital. Gathering reinforcements at the docks and in the manufactories and workshops, they arrived at the Hôtel de Ville in the Place de Grève some 2,000 strong. Finding Réveillon's house barred by troops of the Royal Cravate Regiment, they made for Henriot's house and, like the English Gordon rioters, destroyed his furniture and personal effects. Dispersed by the military, they re-formed the following morning, and while more troops were summoned bands of workers went round the districts recruiting fresh supporters by intimidation or persuasion. The climax came between 6 and 8 o'clock in the evening, when Réveillon's house was stormed, the Guards of the Royal Cravate were brushed aside, and the destruction of the previous night was repeated on a greater scale. The Duc du Châtelet, commanding the Gardes Françaises, gave the order to fire, and a massacre followed in the narrow congested streets, where thousands crowded the roofs and windows, while the crowd fought back with shouts of "Liberté . . . nous ne cèderons pas." Others shouted "Vive le tiers état!" and "Vive le Roi et vive M. Necker!" Thus the new "patriot" slogans of the day, strangely at variance with the rioters' behavior, were already being absorbed by the Paris *menu peuple* and turned, if need be, to their own advantage.

As yet, then, the activities of the Parisian sans-culottes had not been fully harmonized with those of the revolutionary *bourgeoisie.* The latter hoped, no doubt, to realize their aims without resorting to the hazardous expedient of calling in the masses. These hopes, however, were frustrated by the obstinate refusal of the aristocracy to make concessions and by the feeble vacillations of the King. Persuaded by the Queen and his younger brother, the Comte d'Artois, Louis decided to call in troops, dismiss the newly formed National Assembly, overawe Paris, and replace Necker,

* The price of the 4-pound loaf had, since February, been 14½ sous.

considered too tender to the "patriot" cause, by Breteuil, a nominee of Marie Antoinette. It was the arrival of the news of Necker's dismissal at noon on July 12 that touched off the popular revolution in the capital. Crowds assembled in the gardens of the Palais Royal, the home of the popular Duc d'Orléans, heard Camille Desmoulins and other orators give the call to arms. Groups of marchers formed and paraded busts of Necker and Orléans, the heroes of the hour, along the boulevards. Theatres were closed as a sign of mourning. Besenval, commander of the Paris garrison, withdrew to the Champ de Mars and left the capital in the hands of the people. The first operation was to destroy the hated *barrières,* or customs posts, that ringed the city and whose tolls on food and wine were bitterly resented by the small consumers: in four days' rioting directed from the Palais Royal , 40 of the 54 posts were systematically destroyed. The monastery of the St. Lazare brotherhood was broken into, looted, searched for arms and grain, and its prisoners were released. Other religious houses and gunsmiths were raided for guns, swords, and pistols. All night long (as we learn from the eyewitness account of a tallow chandler's laborer), milling throngs of civilians and disaffected troops surged through the streets, shouting the newly learned "patriot" slogans, sounding the tocsin, and searching for grain and arms. Meanwhile, the Paris electors of the Third Estate, who had formed themselves into a provisional city government at the Hôtel de Ville, thoroughly alarmed at the turn of events, began to enroll a citizen's milita, or National Guard, as much to guard the capital against the riotous poor as against the military threat from Versailles.

So the search for arms and ammunition continued. It was, in fact, to search for arms, far more than to release prisoners and even more than to settle old scores and a hated symbol of the past, that led Parisians on July 14 to assault the ancient fortress of the Bastille. The insurgents were short of powder, and it was known that stocks had recently been sent there from the arsenal. Besides, the air was thick with rumors of impending attacks from Versailles, while the Bastille's guns were ominously trained on the crowded tenements of the St. Antoine quarter. So, after 30,000 muskets had been removed from the Hôtel des Invalides across the river, the cry went up, "To the Bastille!" The siege—or rather negotiations with the Bastille's governor, the Marquis de Launay—was directed, with fumbling uncertainty, by the Committee of Electors at the City Hall; but the initiative to take the fortress by storm, when peaceful parley led to no result, was taken not by them but by the armed citizens that crowded round its walls. The Bastille's guns had already killed and wounded 150 of the citizens' number when Hulin, a former noncommissioned officer, marched two detachments of the Gardes Françaises, who had recently joined the insurrection, up to the main gate and, joined by a few hundred armed civilians, prepared for a direct assault. Persuaded by his garrison, de Launay ordered the main drawbridge to be lowered; and the fall of the Bastille marked the culmination of the first great popular *journée* of the Revolution.

The Bastille's surrender, though by no means a military feat of great importance, had remarkable political results. The National Assembly was saved and received royal recognition. In the capital, power passed to the Committee of Electors, who set up a City Council (the Commune) with Bailly as mayor. On July 17, the King himself came to Paris attended by fifty deputies and making a virtue of necessity donned the red, white, and blue cockade of the Revolution. For a great deal of this the Paris crowds, in which the sans-culottes played the major part, had been responsible. Yet the Revolution was not yet secure and the gains of July had to be fought for again in October. As long as Court and King remained at Versailles and an active minority of deputies could, in alliance with the Court, frustrate the constitutional program of the Assembly (and this ability became all too evident in August and September), effective power still remained divided between the old Third Estate and its liberal aristocratic allies, and the adherents of the Old Régime. Once more the King, succumbing to the pressure of what remained of the old Court party, tried to break the deadlock by a further display of force, and summoned troops —this time the Flanders Regiment—to Versailles. At a banquet given in their honor, the national cockade (at least, so it was reported in Paris) was trampled underfoot. To avenge the insult, the Paris "patriots" called for a march to Versailles—either to deliver an ultimatum or to fetch the royal family to Paris. Meanwhile, there had been another crisis in the supply of bread; and on October 5 a food riot of angry market women developed into the great women's march which, supported by the battalions of the National Guard, brought the King, soon followed by the National Assembly, back in triumph to the capital. Thus, for the second time in a dozen weeks, the Parisian *menu peuple* had come to the Assembly's rescue and saved the Revolution.

The year 1789 was not only a year of city riots and revolutions. The country also had its share; and here, too, the riot underwent a similar transformation. After the grain riots of 1775, the countryside had been relatively undisturbed. There had, of course, been the usual crop of bread riots: at Toulouse and Grenoble in 1778, at Bayeux in 1784, and at Rennes in 1785; but they had been scattered and sporadic. There was no further generalized movement of rural protest until the winter of 1788–9; and then it occurred in response to a dual crisis. On the one hand, there were the disastrous harvests of 1787 and 1788, which sent prices rocketing in nearly all the main grain-producing regions. On the other hand, the government had, under pressure of the "aristocratic revolt," summoned the provincial Estates to meet and was preparing to convene the electors, of whom the peasants formed the overwhelming majority, to draw up their *cahiers de doléances,* or notebooks of grievances, in every part of France. The peasants' response assumed, in the first place, the traditional form of a revolt against shortage and rising prices. Starting in December 1788, it expressed itself in attacks on grain boats and granaries; assaults on customs officials, merchants, and *laboureurs;* rioting at town halls and at bakers' shops and markets; *taxation populaire* of bread and wheat; and widespread destruction of property. Reports of such activities came in from nearly every province: in December and January, from Brittany and Touraine; in March and April, from Burgundy, the Ile de France, Languedoc, Nivernais, Orléanais, Picardy, Poitou, Provence, and Touraine; in July, from Normandy and Champagne. North of Paris, the fight against famine developed into a movement against the game laws and hunting right of the nobility, the first for many years. On the estates of the Prince de Conti at Pontoise and Beaumont (scenes of the riots of 1775), at Conflans Ste. Honorine and other villages, the peasants set traps for the rabbits infesting their fields, leading to clashes with the rural constabulary. In Artois, a dozen villages combined to exterminate the Comte d'Oisy's game and refused to pay him traditional dues. South and west of Paris, near Fontainebleau and St. Germain, whole parishes were disarmed under suspicion of poaching the game in the royal forests. In Lorraine and Hainault, landless peasants and small proprietors joined forces to oppose plans to clear the woodlands and enclose the fields. Meanwhile, after lying dormant for nearly a century, peasant anger against royal taxes and seigneurial dues had broken out in Provence in March, at Gap in April, and in the Cambrésis and Picardy in May.

Thus, under the impact of economic crisis and political events, the peasant movement developed from early protests against prices, through attacks on enclosure, gaming rights, and royal forests, to a frontal assault on the feudal land system itself. This was by no means a purely spontaneous development: in part, it grew out of the strange phenomenon known as *la Grande Peur,* the Great Fear, of the late summer of 1789. The Great Fear had its origins in rural vagrancy, the product of the economic crisis; the dispersal of royal troops after the popular victory in Paris; and in the peasants' deep-grained belief, which they shared with many townsmen, in the existence of an "aristocratic plot." The conviction grew that "brigands," be they village poor or disbanded soldiers, were being armed ravage the countryside and to destroy the peasants' property. As in the riots of 1775, the rumor spread from market to market and along the course of rivers and during July and August inflamed the rural population in every province outside Brittany in the north and Alsace and Lorraine in the east. So the peasants armed and awaited the invaders. But the "brigands," the product of panic and excited imagination, failed to materialize; and the peasants in many districts, cheated of one quarry, turned against another, and directed their weapons against the manors of the lords instead. For the châteaux housed not only the seigneurs (who were largely left unscathed) but the hated manorial rolls on which were inscribed the feudal rents and obligations, many of them recently invented or revived, that placed a heavy burden on the small proprietor's land. Thus the peasants, bitterly resentful of age-old seigneurial exactions, responded to the appeal of the Third Estate by staging their own particular kind of revolution. They left a trail of burning châteaux in every part of France. The movement yielded quick results. Prodded into action, the National Assembly issued its decrees of August 4 and 5, which abolished, or made redeemable, all seigneurial burdens on the land. Where such burdens were commuted to a money payment, the peasants refused to pay; and three years later the Jacobin government accepted the accomplished fact and annulled the peasants' debt.

The peasant revolution simmered in the countryside throughout the revolutionary years; yet it generally relapsed into food riots or attacks on enclosure and never regained its early scope and vigor. In Paris, as in other cities, the situation was altogether different. The great riots of 1789, though rich in consequence, were only a beginning. The political indoctrination of the sans-culottes with the new ideas of the Revolution had barely yet begun. Clubs and "fraternal" societies were formed, which, after 1790, opened their doors to wage earners and craftsmen. By such means the ideas of the democrats and later of the republicans were transmitted to and absorbed by the people of the faubourgs and the markets. An early outcome of this new stage of political indoctrination was the great rally and petition in the Champ de Mars in July 1791, which called for the abdication of the King after his ill-fated flight to Varennes and for the substitution of a new "executive authority." The many thousands of signatories included a majority of sans-culottes; and we know from other evidence that a great number of them, at least, understood perfectly well what the petition was about. They, too, formed the bulk of the demonstrators who had gathered from every section in the capital, and of whom fifty were shot dead and another twelve wounded by Lafayette's National Guard.

This "massacre," like the war that followed nine months later, deepened the divisions among "patriots"; and the sans-culottes, who were admitted to the meetings of the Sections in July 1792, came more and more under the influence of the Jacobins, republicans, and democrats. It was they who planned and directed the armed attack on the Tuileries in August 1792, which ended the monarchy and ushered in the Republic, and it was carried through by the regular battalions of the National Guard, which were largely composed of the shopkeepers, tradesmen, and journeymen of Paris. The same force was used by the Jacobins in June 1793, this time under Hanriot, a sans-culotte general, to expel their "Girondin" opponents from the National Convention. And so, by stages of political indoctrination and experience, through attendance at meetings of sectional assemblies, societies, and committees and through service in the National Guard and the *armée révolutionnaire,* formed to assure the city's food supply, trained militants and leaders were emerging from among the sans-culottes themselves. They were by no means docile agents of the Jacobins or any other ruling party: they had their own social aspirations, outlook, clubs, and slogans, and their own ideas on how the country should be governed. This being so, it was inevitable that the political riot, when still resorted to, should undergo a further transformation.

This process reached its climax in the great popular insurrection of Prairial of the Year III (May 20–23, 1795). The sans-culottes, by this time divided among themselves and antagonized by the Jacobin govern-

ment's policies, had offered no effective resistance to Robespierre's overthrow in July 1794. But the inflation that followed, accompanied by the
closure of the remaining revolutionary clubs and the persecution of former
"terrorists" and "patriots," gradually roused them to take action. A first
skirmish took place on 12th Germinal (April 1, 1795), when the National Convention was invaded by an angry crowd of men and women,
shouting for bread and wearing in their caps and bonnets the insurgent
slogan, "Bread and the Constitution of 1793." * The intruders, having received some verbal support from the few Jacobin deputies that remained
in the Assembly, were soon ejected by loyal detachments of the National
Guard; and the movement temporarily subsided.

But, as the food situation went from bad to worse, the stirrings in the
streets and markets and among the militants in the sections became more
pronounced; and on 1st Prairial (May 20), there was a new outbreak, this
time of a far more violent and dangerous character. On this occasion, as
in October 1789, it was the women that took the lead and urged their
menfolk to take action. Again, as in October, it started with riots at bakers' shops that developed into a march on the Assembly. But this was a
combined military and political demonstration that reached a higher pitch
of political maturity than that of 1789. In October, the women chanted as
they marched to Versailles (or so tradition has it), "Let us fetch the baker,
the baker's wife and the little baker's boy": thus the political intention,
though evident in the outcome, was never clearly underlined. In May
1795, however, the insurgents bore political slogans in their caps and
blouses and had clearly defined political aims: these were to release the
political prisoners, to reestablish the Paris Commune (suppressed after
Robespierre's fall), to implement the Constitution of 1793, and to reim-
pose the abandoned controls on the price and supply of food. And, unlike
the participants in the *journées* from 1789 to 1793, they received no
marching orders from revolutionary leaders or outside political groups:
they acted on their own account under their own banners and slogans. It
was, in fact, the first, and the last, great political demonstration both initiated and carried through by the sans-culottes themselves.

Yet they failed completely, and were ignominiously defeated and sav-
agely repressed. Once more, as in April, they were ejected from the Assembly; but they regrouped their forces in the Faubourg St. Antoine, the
center of rebellion, and the following afternoon marched on the Convention with a force of 20,000 National Guards. For the first time in the
Revolution, however, a regular army, loyal to the government, was drawn
up to meet them; and to avoid a massacre both sides agreed to negotiate
rather than to fight it out. So lulled by false promises the insurgents retired to their sections. The Faubourg St. Antoine was invested next day,
and on the fourth day of the rebellion the insurgents surrendered without

* This was the democratic Constitution of June 1793, which the Jacobins, who
had drafted it, put into cold storage "for the duration" and their successors re-
pealed in September 1795.

having fired a shot. Defeat was followed by a heavy toll of reprisals and proscriptions: 36 rebels were condemned to death and 37 to prison or deportation by a military court; some 1,200 alleged "terrorists" (not all of them insurgents) were arrested and 1,700 disarmed in a single week; and many followed later.

Thus beheaded, the sans-culotte movement died a sudden death; and, having, like the cactus, burst into full bloom at the very point of its extinction, it never rose again. There was a final insurrection in October; but this time the sans-culottes were passive spectators and the participants were civil servants, lawyers, clerks, shopkeepers, and army officers of the royalist or near-royalist sections. After this the army, called in by the Convention, remained in occupation, and the days of revolutionary crowds and riots, whatever their complexion, were over for thirty-five years.

7. The "Great Man" in an Age of Revolution: Napoleon

HAROLD T. PARKER

One of the highest hurdles faced by the writers of western civilization textbooks is the "great man." History is full of powerful personalities who appear larger than life, who seem to grab civilization by the collar, shake it, and send it off in a new direction. Entangled in the historian's concern with whether the times make the man or the man makes the times, the real *"great man" invariably suffers. Too often in the textbook the man of flesh and blood becomes either a heroic marble statue or a cardboard cutout.*

Napoleon Bonaparte is a case in point. He has probably been the subject of more biographies than has any other man, and perhaps the greatest of them is Georges Lefebvre's brilliant study, Napoleon, *translated into English in 1969. As in the case of any great man the formation of Napoleon's personality is difficult to know, and the following selection, by Harold T. Parker, professor of history at Duke University, is an attempt to pin it down. Professor Parker's essay illustrates the increasing tendency of historians to use the work of psychologists to throw light on a figure in the past. In an omitted footnote, Parker notes that he has based his study on the views of psychologist Joseph Katz, who holds that "personality refers to an organized, interacting system of underlying dispositions (e.g. goals and ways of realizing them, impulses and means of controlling them, ways of experiencing, thinking, and evaluating)." Professor Parker is unable, of course, to put Napoleon on the psychiatrist's couch or run*

Source: Harold T. Parker, "The Formation of Napoleon's Personality: An Exploratory Essay," *French Historical Studies,* VII (1971), 6–26. Reprinted by permission of the author and publisher. [Footnotes omitted.]

him through a battery of psychological tests. He relies, instead, principally on the historical evidence presented by Frédéric Masson and Guido Biagi, Napoléon inconnu: Papiers inédits (1786–1793) *(Paris, 1895) and Arthur Chuquet,* La Jeunesse de Napoléon *(Paris, 1897). "Although this evidence," writes Professor Parker, "is insufficient to enable us to describe Napoleon's personality as a totality at any moment of time prior to 1796, when he came under study public gaze, it is probably sufficient to enable us to notice when the major underlying and enduring dispositions of his adult personality came into existence and under what circumstances."*

In his essay Parker traces Napoleon's career from his Corsican birth and childhood to the military schools at Brienne and Paris, where he led a kind of "double life" between French military service and a struggle for Corsican independence, to his marriage to Josephine, and on to the Italian campaign of 1796–1797. The reader should evaluate the effect of each of these stages on the formation of Napoleon's personality around the questions the author asks: Through these stages was Napoleon's personality formed by a "combination of basic oedipal drive with partial applause"? Was it formed, rather, by a "continuing psychological-social process which closed out the fulfillment of some potentialities while accentuating the development of others"? What was the role of rejection and the importance of rewards in the formation of his personality? Why was Napoleon unable "to achieve satisfying intimate human relationships"?

I do not know much about Napoleon's childhood, but then neither does anyone else. We do know that he was born on August 15, 1769, the second son of Charles and Letizia Bonaparte, in Ajaccio, Corsica. Beyond that the evidence concerning his childhood, the first five years so precious to psychologists, is so slight that much of it can be presented here.

In 1813 Emperor Napoleon smilingly chided his two-year-old infant son: "Lazy bones, when I was your age, I was already beating up Joseph," Napoleon's elder brother. Later, in 1817, Napoleon at St. Helena confided to his intimates a few childhood memories. He frequently spoke of his mother and said to his physician, Antommarchi, "She was all her life an excellent woman, and as a mother was without equal." On another occasion, observing the "tenacity" of little Bertrand, the son of his aide, he remarked: "I was as stubborn as he at his age; nothing stopped or disconcerted me. I was a quarreller, a fighter; I feared nobody, beating one, scratching another, making myself redoubtable to all. It was my brother Joseph who most often had to suffer. He was slapped, bitten, scolded, and I had already complained against him before he had time to recover himself. But my quickness was of no avail with Mamma Letizia, who soon repressed my bellicose humour. . . . She was both tender and severe; she punished wrongdoing and rewarded good conduct; she recognized impartially our good and bad actions."

In the same year, 1817, Joseph was writing his memoirs at Point Breeze, New Jersey. He recounted that on one occasion when the two boys were at school together at Ajaccio, one-half of the class were made to act the part of the Romans, while the other half were Carthaginians. The master placed Joseph, the elder, with the victorious Romans and Napoleon among the defeated Carthaginians. Napoleon begged Joseph to change places with him, to let him be on the winning side, which Joseph willingly did. But then the little Napoleon was remorseful all the way home that he had been unjust to his brother.

Toward the end of her life, in 1834, Napoleon's mother, at the age of eighty-four, dictated a few reminiscences to her companion, Rose Mellini. She early noted in Napoleon, she said, an "esprit de principauté"—a spirit of mastery. She nursed all her children except the infant Napoleon, who was put out to a wet nurse.

Such family reminiscences of 1813, 1817, and 1834 were in each case set down long after the event, but they were apparently independent and they agree. Together with family records the reminiscences enable us to establish that:

the infant Napoleon entered the family as the second son and the second child to live, Joseph (b. January 7, 1768) being one and two-thirds years older, the third child, Maria Anna (b. July 14, 1771), being nearly two years younger; five other children followed;

the parents were young and very much in love; they had been married (June 2, 1764) when Charles (b. March 27, 1746) was eighteen and Letizia (b. August 25, 1750) was not yet fourteen; she was still eighteen when Napoleon was born;

the father, strong, manly, and handsome, conducted the negotiations with the outside world but within the family the mother was dominant and the father was indulgent and easy-going;

the mother was a famous beauty ("brown chestnut hair, brown-black eyes, nose straight and rather long, mouth refined and expressive, good teeth, small ears, hands, and feet, a lovely complexion, white, with a delicate peach tint to the cheeks, an expression that was serious and reflective, with a touch of nobility, of refinement, and an aspect of steadfastness of character") and her beauty endured through the years; she took no nonsense from her children and commanded their respect and affection;

the first two children were lost in infancy; Joseph, the third child and the first one to live, was very much wanted, Letizia nursed him, he slept in the parents' room until he was age three and a half when he was put out for Maria Anna; he was a pretty, likeable baby and boy, and the relations between his mother and him were always warm and close;

Letizia tried to nurse Napoleon, a small, delicate baby, but the milk failed, and he was suckled by a wet-nurse and slept with her in a back room; the relations between the nurse and Napoleon were always warm and affectionate;

in his first months Napoleon had a sweet and gentle disposition, but from at least age two he became irritable, self-assertive, quarrelsome, violent, quick in sizing up human situations and in responding, rivalrous, though also affectionate and remorseful.

Now, in terms of modern psychology what might the data mean? In general the family was warm and affectionate, and its members were usually supportive of each other. From that support might come self-assurance and even clannish pride. Specifically, it might be speculated that the trusting relationship with the wet nurse gave the infant Napoleon a trust in himself and laid the foundation for a fundamental self-assurance that would sustain him in later events. However, Napoleon's position in the family was challenging. When he emerged from these early relations with the nurse he discovered, so to speak, that he was a member of two triangles (Napoleon, Mother, Joseph; Napoleon, Mother, Charles) in which the adored mother had warm and close relations with Joseph and with Charles of a type from which he was excluded. Simply to secure her attention and win her applause he began to assert himself—to jump up and down, to compete with Joseph, and to play tricks. However, in granting approval she early set standards: you do not win my favorable attention by tricks but by performance and achievement. He was thus bound to his mother not by reciprocal warmth and closeness but by a satisfaction of his own needs for approval. He was also given a slant toward obtaining approval through achievement. And achievement in the early years meant overtaking his brother and being the victor, even though Napoleon might be remorseful at being victorious over Joseph, whom he liked.

Thereafter, the early growth of Napoleon depended on his companionship with Joseph and their interrelations with the mother. Let us consider two brothers, aged five and three, playing together. Five performs a gymnastic feat on the sofa, perhaps in the mother's presence. Three imitates it, with success but with difficulty. Both are in a standard learning situation: the acquired drive for both is desire for mother's approval; the cue for five is the sofa and mother's presence, and his response is to perform the feat; the cue for three is mother's presence and his brother's performance, which he imitates; the reward for both is mother's applause. Both children will learn from a succession of such incidents. However, five with a secure superiority will grow up to be assured, self-satisfied, mild, and, since he is pressed by the younger, perhaps a capable man. Three has had to assert himself, to strain after an uncertain prestige, and to force his abilities by exercise, in order, on occasion, to capture the mother's attention. In any case, as an adult Joseph had the self-confidence of one who had enjoyed an assured position in childhood. He was capable, and he enjoyed having public approval, but he did not drive for it. Napoleon, of course, was self-assertive and drove to overtake and to overcome.

It might also be speculated that Napoleon's early self-assertiveness grew out of the rivalry of the child with the father for the mother's attention. There may have been indeed an oedipal situation, but there is little evidence to prove it. The importance of the father in the formation of Napoleon's personality may lie elsewhere. Charles Bonaparte was an intriguer and a self-promoter. He supported the Corsican hero, Pasquale Paoli, in the war of Corsican independence against the French. But when the Corsicans lost, he did not follow Paoli into exile in England but joined the winning side. He assiduously cultivated the favor of the French governor, Marbeuf, while seeking to keep on good terms with Marbeuf's enemy, Narbonne. He established his family's claim to nobility for eleven generations, became a deputy of the Corsican nobility in the Corsican States-General, was elected to the Commission of Twelve that acted for the nobility between sessions, and in 1777 was leader and spokesman of a three-man Corsican delegation that waited on the king at Versailles. Through the influence of Marbeuf he was able to secure in 1778 the appointment of Napoleon as royal scholarship pupil in the French preparatory school of Brienne. He inspired each member of the family to have pride in being a Bonaparte, which was another reason for Napoleon's self-assurance, and he set an example of aggressive, persevering, self-serving intrigue in the invidious French and Corsican cultures. By the time Napoleon left Corsica for France as a child of nine he must have been aware of his father's importance in Franco-Corsican relations and of some of the adroit maneuverings by which this position was maintained.

For the child of nine, small and slight for his age, scion of a person of importance in a little world, Brienne was a shock. The French minister of war, Saint-Germain, had decided that 650 young gentlemen, poor but noble, would be educated at the king's expense in twelve *collèges* or preparatory schools. Those who appeared most gifted would then be admitted to the Royal Military School at Paris. The French conquest of Corsica had just been completed in 1769. To conciliate the Corsicans a few scholarships were granted to sons of relatively impecunious Corsican nobles. Napoleon was the first Corsican recipient of one of these scholarships. There was nothing military about the *collège* of Brienne. It was a typical French boarding school, taught by a Catholic teaching order, the Minims. There were 110 pupils of whom fifty were royal scholars. Instruction in the ancient classics was stressed. No Greek was taught, but Latin was the chief study, year after year, for six years. The other subjects were French composition, elementary mathematics, German, geography, and history. One of the strictest rules at the "military" schools was that except in rare cases of extreme urgency no boy was ever to leave the school during the six years for which he was entered; he could not go home. In September there was relaxation: only one lesson a day and freedom for long walks, but there were no holidays. Parents at long intervals might be permitted to enter the school to see their boy, but he could not leave it to see them. It was an intense, monastic life.

Napoleon was a child of the south: he was transported to a climate that was cold and damp. He spoke Italian: the lessons were conducted in French, which he was just learning. He was a Corsican, a member of a conquered people: he was scorned and derided by his fellow French students. He was by French standards a poor, provincial noble: the sons of French aristocrats snubbed him. His very self-assurance and self-assertiveness may have provoked the older French boys to torment him. More profoundly, he may have been subjected to French ways of managing children that a young Corsican would not immediately understand. In any case, living alone in the midst of the enemies of his country, the conquerors of his nation, he was thrown back upon himself. Resourceful, he developed mechanisms of defense that enabled him psychologically to keep going in a situation of stress and to emerge stronger for the experience. He minimized his contacts with other inmates of this school-prison. He rarely joined their sports; he had only one or two friends, Charles Le Lieur and perhaps Bourrienne; over two or three summers he built a garden and arranged the plants, vegetation, and palisades to form a bower of seclusion to which he could retire. He learned to control his rage. As a boy in Ajaccio he had always been flaring into anger and into street fights. At Brienne such angry outbursts would only amuse his tormentors, and, though he might still flare out on occasion, he usually kept his temper. He accepted the Corsican identity thrust upon him: yes, I am a Corsican, and I am proud of it; today we are vanquished, but tomorrow we shall be free. Paoli was his hero. "Paoli will return," he cried one day, "and if he cannot break our chains, I shall go to his aid as soon as I am strong enough and perhaps the two of us together will deliver Corsica from the odious yoke it bears."

He had won his mother's approval through achievement, and now he worked at those subjects which interested him. He was excellent in mathematics, good or very good in history and geography, and deficient in Latin, a subject he refused to study seriously as having no practical value. During play hours he read, borrowing book after book from the school library, chiefly history books, and particularly Plutarch. Work paid off in knowledge and sense of accomplishment, in prestige, in tangible reward, and presumably, in reduction of anxiety. He had learned to read (in Italian) at the primary school of Ajaccio, and now at Brienne he became practiced in French and also in mathematics. At successive exhibitions he was quizzed first on arithmetic, then on geometry and algebra, and finally on trigonometry and conic sections. He came to be known as the ablest mathematician of the school and its most indefatigable reader. After five-and-a-half years at Brienne he was one of those selected to advance to the Royal Military School at Paris. He worked, and he also dreamed and planned. He dreamed of the liberation of Corsica and of his heroic rôle in it. In his last year he may have planned a history of Corsica, for he requested his father to send him histories of the island.

Notably, under stress Bonaparte turned neither to religion, which might have afforded consolation and support, nor to sexual pleasure, which might have taken the edge off his hostilities. He received his first communion at Brienne, was confirmed during his year at the Royal Military School, and always dutifully attended daily chapel, but at some point his childhood belief dissolved to be succeeded by a vague, inoperative deism. There were homosexual "nymphs" at Brienne, but he was not attracted. Later, after graduation, when heterosexual opportunities became available, he remained chaste, perhaps from memory of the perfect woman, his mother. His personality remained integral, basically self-assured and self-assertive, sturdy and aggressive, but with aggressiveness finding outlets and significance in work and in dreams and plans.

Napoleon left Brienne for the Royal Military College at Paris on October 30, 1784, at the age of fifteen. The patterns of behavior that had been set and hardened under five-and-a-half years of stress at Brienne continued at the Royal Military School. To be sure, his withdrawal from association with Frenchmen moderated. There was a certain camaraderie among the cadets of the school and probably greater acceptance of the Corsican who had established his right to be there. Also, once he had forged a personality that stood up under stress he could be more at ease with himself and, hence, with others. He made friends among the French cadets and had one chum, Alexander des Mazis. However, he still identified with Corsica and dreamed of its heroic liberation by Paoli and himself. He worked, even harder than at Brienne, and was again rewarded in knowledge, prestige, and advancement, thus confirming a habit of industry already formed. He again was known as "one of the ablest mathematicians of the school," and he passed his certifying examination for a commission as second lieutenant in the royal artillery after only a year of study instead of the usual two or three.

He left Paris to join his regiment La Fère at Valence on October 30. One is tempted to say that for the next seven-and-three-quarters years, until June 11, 1793, he led a double life, had a double identity, and wrote two literary styles. One life was that of an officer in the French royal artillery. When not on leave to Corsica, he resided with his regiment at the garrison town of Valence from November 1785 to September 1786; at the artillery school of Auxonne from June 1788 to September 1789 and again from February 12, 1791, to June 14, 1791; then again at Valence from June 16, 1791, to the end of August 1791. He performed his duties punctually, conducted exercises and experiments, wrote analytical, intelligent, and cogent reports, learned the new strategic theories of mobile warfare of Bourcet and Guibert, and received the gratifying praises of the commandant of the artillery school, Baron du Teil, for intelligent work and accomplishment. He continued his companionship with Alexander des Mazis, the chum of the Royal Military College, and he made other friends within the regiment and in town. He had come from an affectionate family, and now that he was more at ease he was, in his personal relations with Frenchmen, chatty, amiable, grateful. In off-duty hours he read and read, chiefly history, political science, and Rousseau, taking notes and gaining knowledge.

Yet all the while he was leading another life, having another identity, and writing another literary style, that of an imaginative dreamer and actor for Corsica. After a day of dutifully and punctually obeying orders in the French Royal Army, Bonaparte would retire to his room to write an analytical declamatory essay à la Rousseau, proving that by the social contract the Corsicans could justly shake off the hateful yoke of the Genoese and now that of the French, "Amen." Or, perhaps after chatting amiably one evening with his landlord and landlady, he would retire to compose a declamatory essay on suicide: how can one go on living when one's country is subdued and one is condemned to live among a people whose vain and corrupt manners are so different from one's own! A little later, he contrasts the republican love of country with the love of glory to the detriment of the latter, thus rejecting the invidious values of the society in which he moved. At Auxonne, after he had completed his second memoir for Du Teil, he wrote out a gory fantasy of a single Corsican knifing a band of French marauders and consuming their bodies in fire.

Notably, he usually composed these fantasy-essays while on garrison in France. In Corsica he was acting out the fantasy. His first Corsican leave began on September 11, 1786. He had left his Corsican home at the age of nine. He now returned to Ajaccio, a young second lieutenant of seventeen, short, dark, and energetic. He now adored once again his mother, a vital, mature southern beauty and widow at thirty-six. He resumed relations with Joseph, who also had had a French education, at the *collège* of Autun. As the oldest son Joseph was now the head of the family, but Napoleon, with the prestige of a French commission, had drawn even with him. Affectionately they together declaimed the tragedies of Corneille, Racine, and Voltaire. Living in his Corsican dream Bonaparte gathered materials for the history of his native land and began to write it. His second Corsican leave started in September 1789. When he reached home, France was free, but Corsica was still in subjection. He organized a revolutionary club in Ajaccio, persuaded it to draft a petition to the National Assembly, and fomented a riot in the port of Bastia to support the petition. The petition precipitated the decision of the Assembly to accord equality to Corsica, as a French department, and to recall Paoli from exile. Bonaparte was a leader in the action, Paoli was returning, and presumably he would accept Bonaparte as his youthful aide and collaborator. The dream, it seemed, was becoming real.

But the ensuing events did not follow the script. From the first fateful interview between the two men Bonaparte antagonized Paoli. The interview occurred on the battlefield of Pont Nuovo, the scene of Paoli's decisive defeat by French troops in 1769. Paoli described to the young man his disposition of the Corsican forces; Bonaparte, the analytical professional soldier, shortly after observed, "Well, with those dispositions, defeat was inevitable," a tactless remark that soon reached Paoli. Paoli, a perspicacious old man in his sixties, could sense in Bonaparte's love of country the challenge and ambition of a self-assertive love of self, and he was in no mood to share his undoubted moral leadership over the Corsicans with a youngster. Besides, while Paoli and a few Corsican "pures" had spent twenty years of exile in London, the Bonapartes had bowed and scraped to the French and eaten at the conqueror's trough. Bonaparte, to win the old man, defended him in a pamphlet from the calumnies of an enemy; Paoli coolly observed that such calumnies had better be left unanswered. Bonaparte asked Paoli for documents to complete his history; Paoli replied that he was too busy and tired to ransack his archives, and besides, writing history was not for young people. Bonaparte, participating in the island quarrels, imagining all sorts of schemes, using ruse, calumny, and violence in the face-to-face contacts of mobile, unstructured, intense island intrigues, secured his election as lieutenant-colonel of a Corsican battalion of volunteers; Paoli remained indifferent and even hostile. Meanwhile, Bonaparte kept open the French route, returning to France often enough to keep his commission in force. Meanwhile, too, Frenchmen were becoming acceptable to him as they recovered the vigor of a free people, granted equality to Corsica, and accorded him promotion to first lieutenant and then to captain. The war of France with other European powers and the emigration of noble officers were opening a route to his ambition for a professional career. Frenchmen were moving into a position once occupied by his mother: a respected but not intimate source of satisfaction of his need for approval and applause. When in June 1793 his quarrel with Paoli flared into an open break, and the Paolists expelled Bonaparte and his family from Corsica and condemned them to Corsican execration, Bonaparte realistically accepted defeat and sought a career in France. After that, with the death of his adolescent dream of fighting for his native land, he could regard most events, people, and institutions impersonally. Freed from the lesser prejudices of factional and national feeling, he could regard ordinary men as figures to be used swiftly and imaginatively for the accomplishment of his ambition.

At first his ambition was for advancement in the army. After performing various military missions in 1793 he distinguished himself by his activity and intelligence at the siege of Toulon and attracted the attention of the deputy Barras. He received the gratifying promotion to general of a brigade and was given command of the artillery of the Army of Italy. But after the overthrow of Robespierre the officers of that army were suspect as Jacobins. Bonaparte was recalled to Paris and ordered to proceed to the Vendée and there take command of an infantry brigade. "Here he would be engaged as an officer in an arm not his own, in a civil war at once desperate and inglorious, against irregular bands of royalist nobles and peasantry. He came to Paris and then boldly refused to go. . . . After a heated argument with the Commissioner of Public Safety he was struck off the army list for refusal to proceed to his post." In the ensuing days of gloom and unemployment in Paris, Bonaparte spent his time paying calls, keeping up his connections, cultivating the society of Barras. Several memoir accounts describe him at this period: the memoirs of the Duchesse d'Abrantès, who was a child of eleven years in 1795 and whose mother the young Bonaparte frequently visited; those of Bourrienne, a former companion of the Brienne days; and those of Thiébault, an army officer who observed him at Paris headquarters. They all describe him as short, dark, energetic, intense, rather poorly dressed, socially awkward, diffident, fundamentally friendly and good-natured but ambitious to command. In moments of frustration in Corsica he had proposed to enlist in the British service in Bengal. Now, fantasy-like, he thought of visiting Turkey to offer his services to the Grand Seignior, or more practically he planned to go there as chief of the French military mission. The lucky accident of a Paris insurrection and his success in subduing it on 13th Vendémiaire

(1795) rescued him. He was restored to the army, and due largely to the influence of Carnot he was given command of the Army of Italy.

Two days before he left Paris to take command he married a woman older than himself, a thirty-two-year-old widow named Josephine. Bonaparte may have married his mother. Josephine was a brown-eyed southern charmer and to an infatuated man a fading Josephine at thirty-two may have resembled a vital Letizia at thirty-six. However, Josephine was not Letizia. She had been born in 1764 on the island of Martinique, the daughter of the supervisor of a sugar plantation. She never received much education—"a little feather instruction at a West Indian convent," and that was all. At the age of fifteen she was brought to France by her aunt, who was the mistress of the Marquis de la Ferté Beauharnais and who married her niece to the Marquis' son, Alexandre, then seventeen. The household was quite irregular—Alexandre had married the niece of his father's mistress, and all four lived in the same residence. Josephine, young, ignorant, and impressionable, began like her aunt to enjoy life and to have friends. A tall, slender girl of considerable sweetness and charm, she was pliable and adopted the immorality of her group, apparently without any shock. As Alexandre grew up he realized the irregularity of his position, denounced Josephine's aunt and then Josephine, and denied the paternity of one of the two children she had. There was a separation but no divorce. During the Revolution first he and then she were arrested and sent to the Carmelite prison. Alexandre was guillotined, but after seven months Josephine was set at liberty. She was now a widow with two children to support. She was generous, and she had a natural and an extravagant taste for clothes; they were her form of self-expression. So, falling in with the current immorality of the new ruling group in France, she became the mistress of General Hoche and then of the deputy Barras. She finally attracted and married Bonaparte, five years her junior.

Bonaparte was infatuated. The honeymoon of two days was just long enough: it left him in transports. From the army he wrote Josephine the most passionate letters. Indeed, his passion for her may have been a factor in the ensuing Italian campaign. His desire to please and impress her may have inspired him to exalted efforts "which the senile generals opposed to him could not by any woman's smiles be galvanized into" emulating. However, Josephine had married him to provide security for her children. She not only did not love Bonaparte, she scarcely even cared for him. Put off by his awkward aggressiveness, she was even a little afraid of him. While he waited feverishly for the mail, as soldiers do, she seldom answered his letters or dropped only a line or two, "cool as friendship," as Bonaparte remarked. She delayed coming to his camp in Italy and, once she arrived, planned on returning. She was having her own pleasant affairs with other men in Paris. Gradually it dawned on the young Bonaparte that he was not receiving the response, the devotion which he desired. Finally, when in Egypt he learned circumstantially from his family of her latest affair, he was bitterly disillusioned. If Josephine was false, who could be true? He continued to live with her, but the old feeling was gone. Instead of a passion she was only a comfortable tranquilizing habit. The intensity of Bonaparte's initial passion, his slowness to recognize Josephine's infidelity, and the bitterness of his disillusionment may indicate an oedipal relation. The failure of his first and only serious venture toward intimacy and sexual union with a woman no doubt accentuated his drive for power and accomplishment.

The new French government, the Directory, had entrusted Bonaparte in the winter of 1796 with the command of one of its main armies, the army that was assembled in the Ligurian Alps for the invasion of Italy. It was no ordinary army that Bonaparte took over. "Its soldiers, its officers, its generals were hardened veterans. They were survivors of a multitude whose ranks had been thinned again and again by fighting, by hardships, by disease," and by desertion. Its divisional generals had been selected by war. The young Bonaparte faced the problem of imposing his personality and will on the generals. The mobile improvisations employed in the face-to-face contacts of Corsican intrigues were inadequate. To solve his problem Bonaparte adopted the rôle of commanding officer and a manner of reserve, brevity, and command.

Three incidents reveal his new approach. An old comrade met Bonaparte at Marseilles, as the latter was proceeding to his post. The old friend moved to embrace him, but a glance from Bonaparte checked him. As Bonaparte approached the Army of Italy, its seasoned generals, Masséna, Berthier, and Augereau, "decided they would ignore the young upstart," to them merely a political appointee. "Augereau especially, a large blustering man, said that he would show this 'General Vendémiaire' his proper place. On April 11, near Genoa, the old generals had their first interview with young Bonaparte. The new general kept them waiting. Then he came quietly into the room, in his general's uniform, hat on head. 'He began to speak at once. In a hard voice, in brief, precise, trenchant phrases, he gave his orders, explained what he proposed to do, and with a gesture dismissed his subordinates.' The generals said not a word but saluted and went out. It was not till he was outside that Augereau recovered his voice. With a loud oath, he said to Masséna: 'This little runt of a general frightened me. It is impossible to understand how he made me feel that he was the master from the moment he looked at me.' "

After the army crossed the Alps, a deputation from Milan, headed by the diarist Melzi, waited upon the young general at Lodi on May 11, 1796. Melzi wrote in his journal:

> General Bonaparte entered; upon seeing us, his countenance assumed a willed expression of severity. Here is the dialogue which followed, half in French, half in Italian, between him and me, who had been named the spokesman of the delegation.
>
> Me.—The town of Milan sends us to present you its wishes for peace and friendship. It wishes openly to express to you the admiration which your luminous qualities as well as your zeal for the

service of the French army have inspired. The sincerity of its sentiments and of its past conduct, exempt from any kind of wrong toward France, give it hope that you will be the protector of its tranquility, its laws, its property, and its religion.

Bonaparte.—Your powers?

Me.—Here they are.

Bonaparte (after having fixed his eyes on the paper longer than it was necessary to read it).—-I receive with interest the expression of the sentiments of the town of Milan but (and he made his tone dry and severe) I cannot dissimulate my surprise at your arming at my approach.

Me.—Milan has not armed and does not dream of doing so.

Bonaparte.—How's that? Do I not have in hand the edict of the archduke ordering you on his departure to call out the militia?

Me.—The edict to which you make allusion indicates, general, that the only object of the militia is to preserve internal order.

Bonaparte assumed a manner of reserve, brevity, and command to impose on others. The manner was really imposed on him first by the army and then by society, that is, if he was to have his way. French officers and other Frenchmen, reared in an authoritarian family and under authoritarian government, would understand and obey only a person who gave orders. Had Bonaparte been reared in contemporary American society, where the father is only a discussion leader and a politician must be one of the boys, he would have assumed another manner to get his way. In any case he assumed this manner to impose on others, and the manner eventually imposed on him. Joseph, his brother, observed that Bonaparte had two characters: a private one, rather sunny, chatty, amiable, friendly, and the artificial one, of authority. That was true. But with the years the public one ceased to be artificial. The manner became the man, the man became the Emperor, and the public character devoured the private one. As political activity more and more filled his life, his political character was exercised more, his amiable one less, until he became the political, calculating man.

Applying the methods of Guibert with amazing resourcefulness, Bonaparte led his army to brilliant victories over the Austrians in the north Italian plain, and eventually he compelled them to sign the peace of Campo Formio (1797). But as he took over the government of the Italian natives, he was ignorant of civil administration, and he knew nothing of Italians. He was entering, like conquerors before and since, a tangle of motives and personal relationships that were largely unknown to him, and some of his early experiences were strange. In the interview at Lodi with the Milanese deputation he tried to tempt them with the offer of liberty, the greatest gift within the power of the great French Republic to bestow. He said, "What do your people desire?" Melzi replied, "Tranquility." Bonaparte: "And nothing else?" Melzi: "And have you sought for anything else in your revolution and your victories?" There was no meeting of minds here. Bonaparte indicated that the Milanese might desire the freedom of a democratic republic. The deputation did not appear interested. Four or five days later Bonaparte, now in Milan, asked another municipal delegation what the dispositions of the Milanese were with regard to liberty. He was told that the people had no notion of liberty. Still trying for his own purposes to set these people in motion Bonaparte instigated the overnight formation of a democratic club of obscure Milanese. They in turn organized a "civic festival" with parades celebrating liberty after the French revolutionary manner. The populace at this time regarded their antics with a "tranquil irony." The word "liberty" and a festival which in France had evoked delirious enthusiasm from millions of people, in Italy moved at first very few.

In his quandary the young Bonaparte, brilliant but green, improvised. He talked, watched the faces of these mystifying Italians, and revised his talk. He acted, provoked response, and revised his action. Or he failed to act, was caught, and recovered. He also read Frederick the Great, a practical prince of his own century. Bonaparte gradually elaborated during his two years in Italy strategies for the manipulation of people as individuals, as groups, and en masse from outside and from above and for the purposes of control. Perhaps unification of his Corsican tactics with his new imposing manner fulfilled once again his need for applause.

The Italian experience was crucial in the development of Bonaparte's career and personality. The campaign rendered him famous and popular in France. The smashing victories over superior enemy forces and the booty he and private soldiers sent to France made him the hero of the hour. The campaign also enlarged his ambition. He had gone forth from Paris simply desirous of being a successful general. His successes led him to dream of greater things, of mastering France. He confided to a civil official, Miot: "I should not want to leave the Army of Italy except to play an [independent] role in France resembling the one I am playing here, and the time is not yet ripe." After the peace, on the way back to France, he told the same individual that he was no longer capable of obedience. "I have tasted supremacy, and I can no longer renounce it." At the same time the day-to-day manipulation of the Italians had given him strategies for mastery and affirmed in him the habit of manipulating people not intimately as persons but externally as facts or figures for the achievement of his career.

The Italian experience thus completed the formation of the main lines of his personality. Madame de Staël described him as she remembered his appearance upon his return to Paris in December 1797:

> I saw him for the first time, [she later wrote], upon his return
> to France after the treaty of Campo-Formio. When I was a little re-

covered from the confusion of admiration, a pronounced sentiment of fear followed. Yet at that time Bonaparte had no power; he was even believed to be menaced by the suspicion of the Directory; so that the fear he inspired was caused only by the singular effect of his personality on almost all who approached him. I had seen men very worthy of esteem; I had likewise seen ferocious men. There was nothing in the effect which Bonaparte produced upon me that could recall to me either the one or the other. I perceived rather quickly, in the different occasions I had of meeting him, that his character could not be defined by the words which we commonly use; he was neither good nor violent, neither gentle nor cruel after the manner of individuals of whom we have any knowledge. Such a being, having no fellow, could neither feel nor excite fellow-feeling; he was more or less than a man. . . .

Far from recovering my confidence by seeing Bonaparte more frequently, I was constantly intimidated by him more and more. I felt that no emotion of the heart could act upon him. He regarded a human being as a fact or a theory, and not as a fellow creature. He did not hate any more than he loved; there was only himself for himself; all other creatures were figures [to be manipulated]. The force of his will consisted in the imperturbable calculation of his egoism; he was an able chess-player for whom the human race was the opposite party. . . . Every time that I heard him speak I was struck by his superiority; yet it had no resemblance to that of men instructed and cultivated by study or society, such as those of whom France and England can furnish examples. But his discourse indicated a tact for circumstance, like the hunter for his prey. . . . He was a man who could be natural only in a position of command.

A human personality, it has been said, is a running function in time. One such function started running on August 15, 1769, in Ajaccio, Corsica, and was named Napoleon Bonaparte, an ego seeking satisfaction, a stubborn ego as it turned out. His life in a warm, affectionate family and his relations with his wet nurse gave him a basic self-assurance. From the time he was weaned his development can be explained by either one of two major hypotheses. One hypothesis derives Napoleon's fundamental dispositions from the combination of a basic oedipal drive with partial applause—winning achievements and successes. The theory runs as follows. The child, Napoleon, wishing to dispossess father and possess mother, drove to have her sole attention but never quite obtained it. Yet he received enough applause for his achievements to encourage him to keep on trying. He sought to outbid Joseph, whom mother liked. He may have succeeded momentarily and repeatedly in attracting the mother's approval, but he could never be sure that she did not prefer Joseph. And besides, even if he won over Joseph, there was always father, whom he could not dispossess. The unconscious wish for mother, the disposition to drive for her approval while knowing one can never fully obtain it, and the encouragement of repeated partial successes was displaced on to other objects in later life and came to form a pattern of behavior. Thus, Corsica became mother, Paoli, the father to be dispossessed, but while momentarily Napoleon won Corsican attention, he did not displace Paoli in Corsican affection. Josephine became mother, the other men in her life the father to be replaced, but Napoleon did not make it with Josephine. Or again France became mother, the potential source of applause, but despite Napoleon's astonishing achievements he could never be sure that he had her, and yet his rewards encouraged him to continue. The combination of an unconscious oedipal drive with repeated, partial successes will explain both his never-satisfied, ever-expanding ambition for ever more unattainable goals and his continuing effort. The way the drive was manifested and expressed was affected by the configurations and resources of the culture and the running events of his life, the schooling at Brienne, the acquisition of knowledge of the new strategies at Auxonne, the opportunities opened by the French Revolution, the accident of 13th Vendémiaire, and the experiences of army command and of governing north Italians.

A second hypothesis would recognize, to be sure, the importance of the drives and dispositions of Napoleon's early years, but it would add that Napoleon's personality was not fully formed by age five. Rather, it was formed en route through many years in a continuing psychological-social process which closed out the fulfillment of some potentialities while accentuating the development of others. This theory, like the first, starts with his life in an affectionate family and his relations with the wet nurse, which gave him a basic self-assurance. But, the second theory continues, his early position in the family as an outsider in the relations of the adored mother with Joseph and perhaps with Charles nurtured the desire to secure applause from people with whom he was not intimately connected and through self-assertive achievements. Later events confirmed this central drive while atrophying the more friendly aspects of his character. His very self-assertiveness later put off some of the people he most wished to win—the aristocratic Brienne classmates, Paoli, Josephine. Resourceful, he invented and borrowed from the culture ways to cope with himself and with other members of the human race. He learned to control his rage, to find satisfaction and praise in work accomplishment, to dream, to fantasy, and to plan, to use available theories of mobile warfare and a seasoned army to win military victories, and to contrive strategies for the management of people from above and by appeal, usually, to egoistic motives. Meanwhile, French society in revolution, by opening careers to talent, loosening the bonds of law and tradition, engaging in war and losing its noble army officers, and passing from one political regime to another, was offering opportunities and occasions to the fulfillment of his ambition and enlarging its scope. By 1797 the values he had accepted for his own life and the rôles and strategies he was employing in managing others coincided with his basic self-assured, self-assertive personality and with the salient values of an invidious, competitive French culture.

In this psychological-social process in which Napoleon's personality was formed, one is impressed by the importance of rejection—the relative inattention of the mother, which the infant might interpret as rejection and which provoked self-assertiveness for applause without associated reciprocal warmth and closeness; the harassment of the Brienne classmates, which fixed the patterns of control of rage, work accomplishment, and proneness to dreams, fantasies, and plans; Paoli's antagonism, which killed the adolescent Corsican dream and focused his energy on a career; and Josephine's infidelity, which closed out his one serious attempt to reach trustful sexual intimacy with a woman. Napoleon was badly hurt four times. No wonder, whether "friendly" and "amiable" or reserved, he kept a distance from human beings. One is also impressed by the importance of rewards—in the mutually trustful relationship with the nurse, which gave him a basic assurance; in the praise and recognition accorded his work, at Brienne, the Royal Military School, and the artillery school at Auxonne, which fixed habits of industry; and in the successive army promotions from second lieutenant of the third and lowest degree to commander of the Army of Italy, which confirmed the focus of his energy on a career in a competitive military structure and endorsed his final acceptance of the values of an egoistic culture. A self-assured, self-assertive, outwardly oriented ego seeking satisfaction, continually coming into contact with people, at times rejected and trying something else, at other times rewarded and continuing what was rewarded, finally reached a solution that coincided with both its central drive for approval and society's values.

One is in addition impressed that this is the story of an ego which failed to achieve satisfying intimate human relationships and which learned to cope with and to master other members of the human race instead. One gains the impression that in these years Napoleon was rarely automatically liked (he had to "win" or "charm") and seldom loved. Of himself he later remarked, "I have never loved anyone except Joseph, and him only a little." Failing in intimate relationships, he learned to find satisfaction in work and mastery of other human beings. Since outside of work relationships and the army he never really understood other people, he contrived strategies to manipulate them as figures for the purpose of control.

What was it like to be Napoleon? What were the inner qualities of his psychic life? We shall never really know, but we can guess. To be Napoleon was to be fundamentally deep down self-assured, quick and wary, quick and meditative, quick to perceive aspects of a social situation, quick to imagine a multiplicity of manipulative responses, some realistic, some wild, and yet meditative in selecting responses and planning; to be desirous of approval, first of mother, then of France, and finally of posterity; to enjoy praise, to enjoy having power over human beings, to enjoy dreams and fantasies that through work could be turned into plans, and to enjoy work and accomplishment. The expedition to Egypt, the Napoleonic Code, the Continental System, and the Grand Empire itself were the achievement of a hard-working, contriving dreamer whose patterns of behavior and underlying dispositions had been set before he came to power.

8. International Stability in an Age of Revolution:The Congress of Vienna

HENRY A. KISSINGER

Of what use is history? This selection is one kind of answer to that persistent question. It is by Henry A. Kissinger, who taught international relations at Harvard University before becoming a foreign policy advisor to President Richard M. Nixon. Kissinger examines the Congress of Vienna of 1814–1815, which made the peace settlement after the downfall of Napoleon Bonaparte's empire.

For a number of reasons the Congress of Vienna has been held up as a "historical lesson" for our own time, for no major war followed it for one hundred years. It was conducted in an age of revolution in which a kind of "cold war" raged between the forces of liberal nationalism and conservative internationalism. It established a fairly lasting international order after a single nation, Bonaparte's France, had come to dominate the entire European continent as did Hitler's Germany later. Finally, it is a classic case of the establishment of a "balance of power." In part for these reasons the Congress of Vienna has enjoyed a "good press" in recent years, but that has not always been so. In the first half of this century historians condemned it for denying self-determination to peoples seeking nationalism and liberalism. One of its chief architects, Metternich, was called the "coachman of Europe" for convincing European powers to crush

Sources: Henry A. Kissinger, "The Congress of Vienna: A Reappraisal," *World Politics,* VIII, No. 2 (January 1956), 268–80. Copyright © 1956 by Princeton University Press. Reprinted by permission of Princeton University Press. [Footnotes omitted.]

*every liberal or national uprising or movement in the 1815–1848 period
and, by so doing, setting back the progress of liberal and national emancipation of European peoples.*

*One of the first efforts to reevaluate the Congress of Vienna in the Cold
War era was the following article by Henry A. Kissinger. In it Kissinger raises
a number of questions useful to understanding both the Congress of Vienna and
the conduct of international affairs in our own time. For example, how do
international politics differ from domestic politics? According to Kissinger, what
are the ingredients of an international settlement which the great powers will
consider "legitimate"? Why is "relative security" preferable to "absolute security"? Why and how are "status quo" powers to be achieved and "revolutionary" powers to be avoided? What problems made it difficult for the leaders
of the great powers—Austria's Metternich, Prussia's Hardenberg, Russia's Tsar
Alexander I, Britain's Castlereagh, and France's Talleyrand—to achieve these
goals at the Congress of Vienna? In particular, why were the Polish and Saxon
problems so sticky for each of the powers and how were those problems able to
be resolved? Finally, what principles for conducting international affairs does
Kissinger set forth in his discussion of the Congress of Vienna which might indicate why President Nixon has relied on him so much? Does the Nixon foreign
policy seem to be based on Kissinger's principles? Who are Kissinger's heroes
at Vienna? On the other hand, how important does he consider diplomats to
be in the achievement of a stable international order?*

I

It is only natural that a period anxiously seeking to wrest peace from the
threat of nuclear extinction should look nostalgically to the last great successful effort to settle international disputes by means of a diplomatic conference, the Congress of Vienna. Nothing is more tempting than to ascribe its achievements to the very process of negotiation, to diplomatic
skill, and to "willingness to come to an agreement"—and nothing is
more dangerous. For the effectiveness of diplomacy depends on elements
transcending it; in part on the domestic structure of the states comprising
the international order, in part on their power relationship.

Any international settlement represents a stage in a process by which a
nation reconciles its vision of itself with the vision of it by other powers.
No state can doubt its own good faith; it is the vehicle of its social cohesion. But, equally, no power can stake its survival entirely on the good
faith of another; this would be an abdication of the responsibility of
statesmanship. The whole domestic effort of a people exhibits an effort to
transform force into obligation by means of a consensus on the nature of
justice. But the international experience of a state is a challenge to the
universality of its notion of justice, for the stability of the international
order depends on the reconciliation of different versions of legitimacy.
Could a nation achieve all its wishes it would strive for absolute security,
a world order free from the consciousness of foreign danger, and one
where all problems have the manageability of domestic issues. But since
absolute security for one power means absolute insecurity for all others, it

is obtainable only through conquest, never as part of a legitimate settlement.

An international settlement which is accepted and not imposed will therefore always appear *somewhat* unjust to any one of its components. Paradoxically, the generality of this dissatisfaction is a condition of stability, because were any one power *totally* satisfied, all others would have to be *totally* dissatisfied and a revolutionary situation would ensue. The foundation of a stable order is the *relative* security—and therefore the *relative* insecurity—of its members. Its stability reflects, not the absence of unsatisfied claims, but the absence of a grievance of such magnitude that redress will be sought in overturning the settlement rather than through an adjustment within its framework. An order whose structure is accepted by all major powers is "legitimate." An order containing a power which considers its structure oppressive is "revolutionary." The security of a domestic order resides in the preponderant power of authority, that of an international order in the balance of forces and in its expression, the equilibrium.

But if an international order expresses the need for security and an equilibrium, it is constructed in the name of a legitimizing principle. Because a settlement transforms force into acceptance, it must attempt to translate individual demands into general advantage. It is the legitimizing principle which establishes the relative "justice" of competing claims and the mode of their adjustment. This is not to say that there need be an exact correspondence between the maxims of legitimacy and the conditions of the settlement. No major power will give up its minimum claim to security—the possibility of conducting an independent foreign policy—merely for the sake of legitimacy. But the legitimizing principle defines the marginal case. In 1919, the Austro-Hungarian Empire disintegrated not so much from the impact of the war as from the nature of the peace, because its continued existence was incompatible with national self-determination, the legitimizing principle of the new international order. It would have occurred to no one in the eighteenth century that the legitimacy of a state depended on linguistic unity. It was inconceivable to the makers of the Versailles settlement that there might be any other basis for legitimate rule. Legitimizing principles triumph by being taken for granted.

Although there never occurs an exact correspondence between the maxims of the legitimizing principle and the conditions of the settlement, stability depends on a certain commensurability. If there exists a substantial discrepancy *and* a major power which feels disadvantaged, the international order will be volatile. For the appeal by a "revolutionary" power to the legitimizing principle of the settlement creates a psychological distortion. The "natural" expression of the policy of a status-quo power is law—the definition of a continuing relationship. But against a permanently dissatisfied power appealing to the legitimizing principle of the international order, force is the only recourse. Those who have most to gain from stability thus become the advocates of a revolutionary policy. Hitler's appeal to national self-determination in the Sudeten crisis in 1938 was an invocation of "justice," and thereby contributed to the indecisiveness of the resistance: it induced the Western powers to attempt to construct a "truly" legitimate order by satisfying Germany's "just" claims. Only after Hitler annexed Bohemia and Moravia was it clear that he was aiming for dominion, not legitimacy; only then did the contest become one of pure power.

The major problem of an international settlement, then, is so to relate the claims of legitimacy to the requirements of security that no power will express its dissatisfaction in a revolutionary policy, and so to arrange the balance of forces as to deter aggression produced by causes other than the conditions of the settlement. This is not a mechanical problem. If the international order could be constructed like a mathematical axiom, powers would consider themselves as factors in a balance and arrange their adjustments to achieve a perfect equilibrium between the forces of aggression and the forces of resistance. But an exact balance is impossible, and not only because of the difficulty of predicting the aggressor. It is chimerical, above all, because while powers may appear to outsiders as factors in a security arrangement, they appear domestically as expressions of a historical existence. No power will submit to a settlement, however well-balanced and however "secure," which seems totally to deny its vision of itself. There exist two kinds of equilibrium then: a general equilibrium which makes it risky for one power or group of powers to attempt to impose its will on the remainder; and a special equilibrium which defines the historical relation of certain powers among each other. The former is the deterrent against a general war; the latter the condition of smooth cooperation. An international order is therefore rarely born out of the consciousness of harmony. For even when there is an agreement about legitimacy, the conceptions of the requirements of security will differ with the geographical position and the history of the contending powers. Out of just such a conflict over the nature of the equilibrium the Congress of Vienna fashioned a settlement which lasted almost exactly a century.

For the problem at Vienna was not simply how to protect Europe against a renewed French onslaught. There was general agreement about the extent of France compatible with the peace of Europe, but this only sharpened the disagreements *within* the victorious coalition about the relative spheres of influence of Austria, Prussia, Russia, and Great Britain. And this contest was made all the more intractable because each of the protagonists meant something different by the term "equilibrium" so frequently invoked: When the British Foreign Minister, Castlereagh, spoke of the equilibrium, he meant a Europe in which hegemony was impossible; but when Metternich appealed to the equilibrium, he included a Germany in which Prussian predominance was impossible. Russia's demand for Poland threatened the equilibrium of Europe and Castlereagh could, therefore, hardly believe that any other problem was worth discussing before the Tsar's pretensions were thwarted. Prussia's insistence on Saxony merely imperiled the balance within Germany, but this was enough to absorb the full energy of Metternich. Castlereagh was interested in creating a Central Europe which would be strong enough to resist attack from both the West and the East; Metternich desired the same thing, but he was also concerned about Austria's relative position *within* Central Europe. To Castlereagh, the Continental nations were aspects of a defensive effort; but to the Continental nations the general equilibrium meant nothing if it destroyed the historical position which to them was the reason for their existence. To Castlereagh, the equilibrium was a mechanical expression of the balance of forces; to the Continental nations, a reconciliation of historical aspirations.

This led to a diplomatic stalemate, made all the more intractable because Britain and Austria had secured most of their special objectives during the war so that few bargaining weapons were left to Russia and Prussia, a stalemate which could be broken only by adding an additional weight to one side of the scales. Since the sole uncommitted major power was France, the former enemy emerged as the key to the European settlement. Thus grew up a myth about Talleyrand's role at the Congress of Vienna, of the diabolical wit who appeared on the scene and broke up a coalition of hostile powers, who then regrouped them into a pattern to his liking by invoking the magic word "legitimacy" and from an outcast emerged as the arbiter of Europe. To be sure, since the Treaty of Paris had settled France's boundaries, Talleyrand could afford perhaps the most disinterested approach. His wit and caustic comments became famous, so that Gentz could say of him that he had both the laughers and the thinkers on his side. But these efforts would have availed little, had not the threat of France been eclipsed by the danger from the East, had not the differences among the Allies become greater than their common fear of France. So long as the Coalition still believed that the memory of the common wartime effort would provide the motive force of a settlement, Talleyrand was powerless. Once this illusion was shattered, the issue became one of the limits of self-restraint, whether a power would fail to add a factor to its side merely for the sake of the appearance of harmony. The logic of the situation provided the answer: France came to participate in European affairs, because they could not be settled without her.

II

As the plenipotentiaries were assembling in Vienna, however, the course of events seemed by no means this clear. It was still thought that the settlement would be rapid, that France would appear as but a spectator, that the rest of Europe would only be called upon to ratify an instrument drafted in relative harmony. This was reflected in the procedural scheme agreed to at preliminary conferences between Austria, Prussia, Russia, and Great Britain which placed the effective control of the Congress in the hands of the "Big Four." Talleyrand protested strenuously against the exclusion of France and the minor powers from the deliberations of the Congress, but despite his brilliance and sarcasm, he achieved only a few minor concessions. It was decided to adjourn the formal opening of the Congress until November 1, 1814, and to have the pending questions examined in the meantime by the eight signatories of the Treaty of Paris, the "Big Four" plus France, Spain, Portugal, and Sweden. The "Big Four" left no doubt, however, that they intended to continue their private discussions and to treat the "Eight" merely as a ratifying instrument or as one for settling peripheral issues.

Talleyrand's first sally failed, because a logical inconsistency is not sufficient to dissolve coalitions. Only after the claim of special righteousness, which is characteristic of coalitions, had disappeared in a conflict which indicated that the relations of the Allies among each other were simply those of contending powers, could Talleyrand emerge as an equal partner. But first one more effort to determine whether the Tsar could be induced to limit his claims without the threat of force had to be made. So well had Castlereagh established himself as the prime contender for the European equilibrium that it was he who entered the arena to try the Tsar's resolution.

There ensued a strange and unreal series of interviews between Castlereagh and Alexander; strange, because their bitterness was accompanied by protestations of unending friendship, and unreal, because Alexander and Castlereagh could never agree on basic premises. In order to obtain a framework for negotiation, the protagonists constantly shifted positions, pretending to agree with the other's principles, but interpreting them in a manner which reduced them to absurdity. Thus Castlereagh at one stage became an avid defender of a completely independent Poland, while Alexander on another occasion defended his Polish plan as a contribution to European security. That Alexander did not propose to let protestations of Allied unity deprive him of his Polish spoils became apparent on the occasion of his first interview with Castlereagh on the day after his arrival. For the first time, he avowed his Polish plans in detail. He proposed to keep all of the Duchy of Warsaw with the exception of a small portion to be ceded to Prussia. These claims, Alexander argued, were not the result of ambition, but the outgrowth of a moral duty and motivated by the sole desire of achieving the happiness of the Polish people. In short, since they were not advanced in the name of security, they could not threaten anyone. Castlereagh, in reply, urged that a Russian appendage extending deep into Central Europe would constitute a constant source of disquiet for the rest of Europe. But the Tsar left no doubt that he was unwilling to withdraw from his Polish possession. The interview between Castlereagh and Alexander had thus made evident that persuasiveness would not suffice and that the next stage of the negotiations would have to be based on force or the threat of force.

III

While Castlereagh was negotiating with the Tsar, he made every effort to assemble such a force. As an abstract problem in diplomacy his task seemed simple. But although the equilibrium might be indivisible, it did not appear so to its components. The Tsar could not be resisted without a united front of the rest of Europe, but the powers of Europe were not at all in accord regarding the real danger. They did not wish to see the general equilibrium overturned, but they were not prepared to resist at the sacrifice of that part of it on which their historical position depended. A strong Russia might dominate Europe, but a too powerful Prussia would outstrip Austria and a united Germany might menace France. Hardenberg, the Prussian minister, was more interested in Saxony than in Poland; Talleyrand was almost as afraid that the problem of Poland would be settled *without* him as that it would be settled *against* him; and Metternich, while not indifferent to the extension of Russia into Central Europe and of Prussia into Central Germany, did not wish to resist openly since this would cause the brunt of the effort to fall on Austria, the most exposed power, while surrendering the policy of close cooperation with Prussia which Metternich considered the key to Austrian security. "I barricade myself behind time," Metternich told the Saxon envoy, "and make patience my weapon."

Thus Castlereagh's effort to create a united front against Russia led to an ambiguous series of constellations, of half-hearted coalitions and tentative betrayals, of promises of unyielding support coupled with hedges against bad faith. Matters were finally brought to a head by Prussia, the power which could least afford delay. For although the treaties of Kalish, Teplitz, and Chaumont had guaranteed Prussia its territorial extent of 1805, they had never specified where Prussia might find the requisite territories, particularly if it lost its Polish possession to Russia. The available compensations, composed of former provinces or former satellites of France, primarily in the Rhineland, were inadequate. And they were undesirable because of their geographic separation from the main part of the Prussian monarchy and the Catholic religion of their inhabitants. Thus Prussia came to look toward Saxony, coveted since the time of Frederic the Great, contiguous with its own territories and with a predominantly Protestant population. But Prussia's negotiating position was the weakest of those of the major powers. Unlike Russia, it was not in possession of its prize. Unlike Austria, it had not made its participation in the war dependent on obtaining its special conditions. If now the Polish question was settled before that of Saxony, Prussia would have paid the penalty for its total commitment; of having fought the war with so much fervor that its participation had never been negotiable, of neglecting the peace because the war, in effect, had become an end in itself. And Prussia required Austrian acquiescence in the annexation of Saxony, because the organization of Germany, the indispensable condition of Prussia's security, would become illusory if Austria emerged on the Saxon issue as the protector of the secondary German powers.

It is not surprising, therefore, that on October 9, 1814, Hardenberg submitted a memorandum agreeing to an "intermediary system based on Austria, Prussia and Britain," and directed against Russia. But he made

Prussia's cooperation on the Polish question dependent on Austrian agreement to the annexation of Saxony and to the provisional occupation of Saxony by Prussia as a token of good faith. In its tentative quest for allies, in its pedantic effort to achieve the advantage of every course of action, the Hardenberg memorandum merely served to illustrate Prussia's dilemma: Russian support might gain it Saxony, but not legitimacy; while Austrian support might yield it Poland, but not Saxony. The Hardenberg memorandum was a plea not to leave Prussia dependent on the good will of the Tsar; to create a European order based on Austro-Prussian friendship, but also on Prussian possession of Saxony.

But this effort to combine incompatible policies provided Metternich with the means to separate the Polish and Saxon questions by one of his intricate maneuvers. On October 22, he transmitted two notes to Hardenberg and Castlereagh whose tone of grudging agreement to Hardenberg's proposal obscured the fact that the moral framework which was being created to resist in Poland would prove equally effective to resist in Saxony, and that Hardenberg, in his effort to hedge his risks, had made his defeat inevitable. For Castlereagh in his overriding concern with the balance of power and Hardenberg in his obsession with Saxony overlooked two subtle and mutually inconsistent reservations in Metternich's despatches: that Prussia's annexation of Saxony should not lead to a "disproportionate aggrandizement," a condition clearly impossible of fulfillment if Prussia regained her Polish provinces, and that Austria's agreement on the Saxon point was conditional on the *success* of the effort to thwart the Tsar's design on Poland—which, in turn, would leave Prussia isolated in the inevitable contest over the interpretation of the first reservation.

But while Metternich was preparing the moral framework for an effort to separate Prussia and Russia, Castlereagh was looking only to Poland, as if the European equilibrium could be created with the necessity of a mathematical equation. On October 23, he finally succeeded in getting Prussia to agree to a common plan of action against Russia on the basis of Metternich's memoranda. The three powers undertook to force the issue by confronting the Tsar with the threat of bringing the Polish question before the full Congress if a reasonable settlement could not be obtained by direct negotiations. They proposed three acceptable solutions: an independent Poland as it existed prior to the first partition, a rump Poland on the scale of 1791, or the return of the three partitioning powers to their former possessions.

The threat of an appeal to Europe in Congress was the last effort to settle the European equilibrium by a combination *within* the anti-French coalition. When Metternich called on the Tsar to present the ultimatum on the Polish question, he was dismissed haughtily and even challenged to a duel. And when, on October 30, the three sovereigns left to visit Hungary, Alexander appealed to his brother monarchs against their ministers. He failed with the Austrian Emperor, but it did not prove too difficult to convince the stodgy and unimaginative Prussian King that the secret negotiations of the three ministers were an act of bad faith. When the monarchs returned to Vienna, Hardenberg was ordered, in the presence of the Tsar, to refrain from any further separate negotiations with his Austrian and British colleagues. In this manner, on November 5, the contest over Poland ended for the time being. The effort to achieve an international order based on agreement and not on force seemed to have returned to its starting point.

IV

But this was a mistaken impression. For if Castlereagh's failure had proved that the equilibrium could not be achieved through a demonstration of its necessity, Metternich's almost imperceptible complementary effort had created the moral framework for reopening the issue by an appeal to legitimacy. The procrastination which had proved so maddening to Castlereagh had in fact been Metternich's most effective means to overcome his dilemmas, for delay strengthened Austria's chief bargaining weapon, that legitimacy can be conferred but not exacted, that it implies agreement and not imposition. So the weeks had passed while Europe complained about the frivolity of the Austrian minister and the old school of Austrian diplomats raged that their "Rhenish" minister, whom they nicknamed Prince Scamperlin, was betraying the Empire to Prussia. But in the admiration for the famous phrase of the Prince de Ligne: "Le Congrès danse, mais il ne marche pas," it was overlooked that the Congress was dancing itself into a trap.

When Hardenberg offered Metternich his cooperation, he believed that he was clinching his gains and that he was obtaining a guarantee of Saxony, however the Polish negotiations ended. But because Metternich's reply had made Austrian agreement to the annexation of Saxony conditional on the *success* of their common measures, the effort to connect the two issues became a means to separate them. For if the Polish negotiations succeeded, Prussia would lose her moral claim to Saxony in the eyes of Europe. If Prussia regained her Polish possessions, the annexation of Saxony would represent the "disproportionate aggrandizement" against which Metternich had warned Castlereagh. But if the Polish negotiations failed, Prussia would lose her moral claim to Saxony in the eyes of Austria. Prussia's isolation was assured none the less surely, because the fact of resistance was almost as certain to alienate the Tsar as its success. Having demonstrated Austria's European concern by yielding in Saxony, intransigence could not be defended by the requirements of the European and not the German equilibrium. And Castlereagh, having obtained Austrian support in the Polish negotiations, would no longer be able to treat the Saxon issue as an internal German affair. There could be no doubt of the attitude of France or of the smaller German states. Prussia, in its effort to obtain reinsurance, had only succeeded in achieving its isolation.

When, on November 7, Hardenberg informed Metternich of the King's orders and of the difficulty of carrying out the agreed plan with respect to Poland, Metternich finally had the moral basis for action. Austria was interested in the closest relationship with Prussia, he replied, but no longer at the price of the destruction of Saxony. After being forced to tolerate Russian aggrandizement in Poland, Austria could not acquiesce in Prussian aggrandizement within Germany without upsetting the equilibrium completely. Metternich suggested an alternative plan which maintained a nucleus of Saxony, while giving a large part of it to Prussia, together with other compensations in the Rhineland. But all protestations of friendship could not hide the fact that Prussia was outmaneuvered, that Metternich had lost out in Poland only to win in Saxony and then partially to restore the situation in Poland by means of Saxony.

It did not matter that, on November 8, the Russian military governor of Saxony turned over the provisional administration to Prussia, or that the Prussian military were threatening war. Russia, at the periphery of Europe, might rest its claim on Poland on the fact of possession, but a power situated in the center of the Continent could survive only as the component of a "legitimate" order both within Germany and in Europe. Thus, although by the middle of December the Congress of Vienna seemed to have reached a complete stalemate, behind the scene a fundamental transformation was preparing itself. A stalemate is not total until all the factors are engaged and France was still uncommitted. The contests during October and November had exploded the myth of Allied unity and the threat of France no longer loomed larger than that of the erstwhile ally. While Castlereagh was despairing about the Polish failure and accusing Metternich of never having really intended to resist, a combination was forming on the Saxon question which was to give a new direction to the contest. For the coalition which could resist in Saxony was, by definition, also the coalition which could resist in Poland. And the claims of power defeated in one quarter would, almost necessarily, limit the assertions of arbitrariness in the other. So it was proved, after all, that the equilibrium was indivisible, although the solution did not come about through a consciousness of this. It was not in the name of Europe that Europe was saved, but in the name of Saxony.

V

But before this new combination could be formed, domestic pressures on Castlereagh nearly wrecked Metternich's finely spun plan. An insular power may fight its wars in the name of the European equilibrium, but it will tend to identify the threats to the equilibrium with threats to its immediate security. Because its policy is defensive and not precautionary, it will make the cause of war depend on an overt act which "demonstrates" the danger. But the danger to the equilibrium is never demonstrated until it is already overturned, because an aggressor can always justify every step, except the crucial last one, as the manifestation of limited claims and exact acquiescence as the price of continued moderation. To be sure, Britain had entered the fray against Napoleon at an early stage and continued the contest with great persistence. But the threat to the equilibrium had become manifest through an attack on the Low Countries and a challenge to Britain's command of the seas. Now the issue was Poland, however, a "distant" country both geographically and psychologically. It was not clear until it was "proven" that the Rhine was best defended along the Vistula or that there existed any threat to peace except France. In this frame of mind the Cabinet considered the Polish dispute an irritating outgrowth of Continental rivalry, threatening a peace dearly won, and dealt with it primarily under the aspect of its impact on British domestic politics.

On October 14, Liverpool, the British Prime Minister, wrote Castlereagh that the "less Britain had to do with [Poland] . . . the better" and he transmitted a memorandum by the Chancellor of the Exchequer, Vansittart, who simply denied the reality of the Russian danger. With the petulance of mediocrity convincing itself that the easy way out is also the course of wisdom, Vansittart argued that the absorption of Poland would add an element of weakness to the Russian state while proving conducive to British commerce. Finally, on November 22, the Cabinet sent its first instructions to Castlereagh since his arrival in Vienna: "It is unnecessary," wrote Bathurst, "for me to point out to you the impossibility of . . . consenting to involve this country into hostilities . . . for any of the objects which have hitherto been under discussion at Vienna."

Thus, at the crucial point in the negotiations, Castlereagh was deprived of his only means of exerting pressure and at a moment when the issue was becoming one of pure power. For Prussia was being drawn by Metternich's temporizing into precipitate action. As it observed its moral and material basis slipping away, its tone became increasingly bellicose. Its military were openly speaking of war and even the more moderate Hardenberg hinted at extreme measures. But if possession without legitimacy was illusory, legitimacy through force proved chimerical. Castlereagh was merely defining Prussia's dilemma when he told Hardenberg that "he [Hardenberg] could not regard an unacknowledged claim as constituting a good title and that he never could in *conscience* or *honor* . . . make the mere refusal of a recognition a cause of war. . . ." In this situation Castlereagh did not propose to follow his Cabinet's instructions. To announce British disinterest would remove the major deterrent to war and, in its effort to guarantee peace, the Cabinet would have brought about what it feared most. Or else, a British withdrawal from the contest would have led to an Austrian surrender and to a complete overturn of the equilibrium.

So it happened that Castlereagh and Metternich found themselves on the same side in a battle whose moral framework had been defined by the wily Austrian Minister. The more intransigent Prussia's attitude, the stronger became Metternich's position. Without the necessity for abstract discussion, Austria emerged as the protector of the secondary powers. When Metternich proposed an alliance to Bavaria and Hanover and the construction of a German League without Prussia, he was simply giving expression to a general consensus. It was at this point, when the last vestiges of the Alliance were disappearing, that Talleyrand reappeared on the scene. He emerged because Metternich put him on the stage and his eloquence was but a reflection of Metternich's desire for anonymity, for Metternich was not interested in appearing as the agent of Prussia's humiliation. It was Metternich's desire that events should come about "naturally," because that would minimize the danger of personal schisms; it was Talleyrand's effort that they should appear "caused," for that would cement his shaky domestic position.

Talleyrand was given his opportunity by Metternich, who communicated to him the Austrian note to Hardenberg and thus made clear that the Big Four had not been able to settle the issue. Talleyrand replied in a trenchant memorandum, which asserted the superiority of the claims of legitimacy over the requirements of the equilibrium and denied the possibility of deposing kings, because sovereigns could not be tried, least of all by those who coveted their territories. It was not for Prussia to state what she would take, Talleyrand argued boldly, but for the "legitimate" King of Saxony to define how much he would yield. It was a masterly summary of all the inconsistencies of two months of acrimony, but this was not its significance. Talleyrand had served France better by remaining "available" than by writing memoranda. The real importance of the exchange lay in the fact that France was once again part of the concert of Europe.

Only a short step separated Talleyrand from full participation in the deliberations. Castlereagh, who had hoped to avoid so drastic a step, finally agreed on December 27. When, on December 31, Castlereagh and Metternich proposed that henceforth Talleyrand participate in the meetings of the Big Four, it was clear that the special claims of the Alliance had ceased before Prussia had gained the fruits of its war effort. Even the Tsar, in Castlereagh's words, "would not advise Prussia to resist now that he has secured his own arrangement in Poland." Thus driven back on its last resources, Prussia threatened war.

But the reaction merely served to indicate Prussia's impotence. Castlereagh replied sharply that "such an insinuation might operate upon a power trembling for its own existence but must have the contrary effect upon all alive to their own dignity; and I added that if such a temper really prevailed, we were not deliberating in a state of independence and it was better to break up the Congress." That same day, Castlereagh proposed a defensive alliance between France, Austria, and Britain. To be sure, Talleyrand was required to guarantee the Low Countries and to reaffirm the provisions of the Treaty of Paris. But Talleyrand's greatest achievement at Vienna was precisely this exhibition of self-restraint, this refusal to attempt to sell French participation in the alliance for a territorial advantage, an effort which would have united all the other powers against him. As a result he gained something more important, the end of the isolation of France and the real recognition of its equality.

If the defensive alliance provided the crisis of the Congress of Vienna, it also paved the way for its resolution. In any negotiation it is understood that force is the ultimate recourse. But it is the art of diplomacy to keep this threat potential, to keep its extent indeterminate, and to commit it only as a last resort. For once power has been made actual, negotiations in the proper sense cease. A threat to use force which proves unavailing does not return the negotiation to the point before the threat was made. It destroys the bargaining position altogether, for it is a confession not of finite power but of impotence. By bringing matters to a head, Prussia found itself confronted by three powers whose determination could not be doubted, although the treaty itself remained secret. And the Tsar proved a lukewarm ally. A series of partial settlements had isolated Prussia because "satisfied" powers will not fight for the claims of another, if an honorable alternative presents itself.

Castlereagh, therefore, took up the proposal of Metternich's memorandum of December 10 by which Prussia was to obtain part of Saxony and extensive territories in the Rhineland. It soon became apparent that Prussia would not carry out her threat of war. By January 3, 1815, after Metternich and Castlereagh had refused to negotiate without Talleyrand, Hardenberg, to save face, himself recommended Talleyrand's participation. On January 5, Castlereagh could report that "the alarm of war is over." The Saxon question was henceforth officially discussed by the now Big Five and was resolved largely through unofficial negotiations in which Castlereagh played the role of the intermediary between Metternich and Talleyrand on the one side and the Tsar and Hardenberg on the other.

In his endeavor to achieve a final settlement, Castlereagh had to resist an attempt by Prussia to move the King of Saxony to the left bank of the Rhine and an effort by Austria to save the Elbe fortress of Torgau for Saxony. But with the aid of the Tsar, he convinced Prussia that in the interest of the European equilibrium she would have to assume the defense of the Rhineland, and he made clear to Austria that the defensive alliance extended only to an actual attempt to overthrow the European equilibrium, not to internal German arrangements. The danger of war had also made the Tsar more pliable. When Castlereagh suggested some concessions in Poland in order to make the Saxon arrangement more palatable to Prussia, Alexander agreed to return the city of Thorn to Prussia. On February 11, a final agreement was reached. In Poland, Austria retained Galicia and the district of Tarnopol, while Cracow was constituted a free city. Prussia retained the district of Posen and the city of Thorn which controlled the upper Vistula. The remainder of the Duchy of Warsaw with a population of 3.2 million became the Kingdom of Poland under the Tsar of Russia. In Germany, Prussia obtained two-fifths of Saxony, Swedish Pomerania, much of the left bank of the Rhine, and the Duchy of Westphalia. Austria had already been assured compensation in Northern Italy and predominance in all of Italy through the establishment of dependent dynasties in Parma and Tuscany.

On June 9, 1815, the final acts of Vienna were ratified by Europe assembled in congress. It was the only meeting of the Congress of Vienna.

There are two ways of constructing an international order: by will or renunciation, by force or legitimacy. For twenty-five years Europe had been convulsed by an effort to achieve order through force and to contemporaries its lesson was not its failure but its near success. Under Napoleon Europe had been unified from the Niemen to the Bay of Biscay but its cohesion was supplied by the power of the Grande Armée. It is not surprising, then, that in their effort to create an alternative the statesmen of Vienna looked back to a period which had known stability and that they identified this stability with its domestic arrangements. Nor was this assessment as ludicrous as a self-righteous historiography made it appear later on. For one of the reasons which had impelled Napoleon ever further was his often repeated conviction that the survival of his dynasty in a world of "legitimate" monarchs depended on the success of his arms. In short, Napoleon confronted Europe with a revolutionary situation because he considered the unimpaired maintenance of the other sovereign states as incompatible with his own existence.

By contrast, one of the reasons for the success of the Vienna settlement was precisely the absence of such an ideological gulf. When a power considers the domestic notion of justice of another sovereign state a mortal threat to its own survival, no basis for negotiation exists. Safety can then only be found in physical extent; diplomacy is reduced to maneuvering for position and such adjustments as do occur have but a tactical significance: to prepare the ground for the inevitable showdown. This is not to say that domestic structures must be identical before meaningful negotiations can take place. It is enough that there exists no power which claims both exclusiveness and universality for its notion of justice. For diplomacy the art of relating powers to each other by agreement can function only when each major power accepts the legitimacy of the *existence* of the others.

In Vienna, of course, the consensus went further than this. There existed a general agreement about the nature of "just" domestic arrangements, which by limiting risks made for flexibility of relationship. The problem of relating a state's vision of itself to the vision of it by the powers, defined in the beginning as one of the key problems of an international settlement, was rarely simpler than at Vienna. This was the reason for the success—for the possibility—of "secret diplomacy," that intangibles were understood in the same manner. To be sure, the result of the Vienna Congress reflected to no small degree the skill of the diplomats in making use of their opportunity. Both Metternich and Castlereagh were extraordinary negotiators capable of shaping a conference to their ends: Castlereagh through his ability to reconcile different points of view and a singlemindedness which enabled him to keep discussions focused on essentials; Metternich through the art of defining a framework which made concessions appear, not as surrenders, but as sacrifices to the common cause. But whatever the skill of the diplomats, the second reason for the success of the Congress is no less fundamental: that in the face of all protestations of friendship and of a real measure of ideological agreement the importance of power-relationships was never lost sight of. The conviviality of the statesmen must not obscure the fact that the European order emerged from the threat of war and the formation, however temporary, of two hostile alliances. The issue was decided not only by the persuasiveness of the statesmen but by the relative strength of the opposing camps.

The settlement proved all the more lasting because the negotiation at Vienna did not confuse the atmosphere of the conference table with the elements of stability of the international system. A statesman cannot make the survival of his charge entirely dependent on the continued good will of another sovereign state; not only because he has no control over the continuation of this good will, but more importantly because the best guarantee for its remaining good is not to tempt it by too great a disproportion of power. The Vienna settlement took into account this relationship of security and legitimacy. It did not rest on unsupported good faith, which would have put too great a strain on self-limitation; nor on the efficacy of a pure evaluation of power, which would have made calculation too indeterminate. Rather, there was created a structure in which the forces were sufficiently balanced, so that self-restraint could appear as something more than self-abnegation, but which took account of the historical claims of its components, so that it met general acceptance. No power felt so dissatisfied that it did not prefer to seek its remedy *within* the framework of the Vienna settlement rather than in overturning it. Since the international order did not contain a "revolutionary" power, either ideologically or in power terms, its relations became increasingly spontaneous, based on the growing certainty that a catastrophic upheaval was unlikely. The result was a century without a major war.

9. The Industrial Revolution

ERIC J. HOBSBAWM

Although the rapid European industrialization begun at the end of the eighteenth century had no datable revolutionary events like the storming of the Bastille, it is usually called the Industrial Revolution all the same. Hand in hand with the French Revolution it transformed western civilization. By "Industrial Revolution" historians have meant the transformation of an agricultural and commercial economy into an industrial one marked by high rates of economic and population growth, machine power, the factory system, urbanization, capital accumulation, and the expansion of the middle and working classes, all of which occurred in the period from the end of the eighteenth century to the middle of the nineteenth. Historical discussion of these changes has usually focused on two issues. One has been the economic process of industrialization. This question is dealt with here. The other issue has been the social effect of this Industrial Revolution, particularly its impact on the life of the workers, and this will be discussed in the selection following this one.

Some historians have objected that the process of industrialization was neither rapid enough nor extensive enough to deserve being called an Industrial "Revolution." J. H. Clapham's Economic History of Modern Britain *(1926) pointed out that not only was general industrialization hardly complete in 1850, the date usually denoting the end of Industrial Revolution, but that the revolution was to a large extent to the iron and cotton industries. An*

Source: Eric J. Hobsbawm, *The Age of Revolution 1789–1848* (London: Weidenfeld and Nicolson, 1962), pp. 27–52. Reprinted by permission of The World Publishing Company and George Weidenfeld and Nicolson. Copyright © 1962 by E. J. Hobsbawm. [Footnotes omitted.]

influential article of 1934 by John U. Nef, which he revised and reprinted in
The Conquest of the Material World *(Chicago, 1964), showed that the sixteenth
and seventeenth centuries saw such significant economic changes that the Industrial Revolution should be seen as a process extending over several centuries. T. S. Ashton's brilliant* Industrial Revolution *(1948) concluded that
industrialization had taken too long to be called "revolutionary," but that the
term "has become so firmly embedded in common speech that it would be
pedantic to offer a substitute."*

*By the 1950s, however, increased concern with theories of economic growth
caused historians to return to the notion of the Industrial Revolution as dis-
continuous with what came before. One of the best short statements of that
current position is this selection by British historian Eric J. Hobsbawm, whose
article in the first volume of this anthology also touched on this problem. His
writings range from studies of premodern protest in* Primitive Rebels *(1959),
to modern working class movements in* Labouring Men *(1964), and an economic and social history of Britain in* Industry and Empire *(1968). The
selection is a chapter from his* Age of Revolution 1789–1848, *and it raises
and deals with the basic questions of how the Industrial Revolution came about:
What are its characteristics? How did it begin? Why did it begin in Britain
and at the time it did? What industries initiated it and how were those, instead of
others, able to do it? What problems or, in Hobsbawm's words, "inherent flaws
in the economic process" did industrialists have to overcome once industrialization was under way? How did the initial industries trigger development in
other industries? In what ways were the total economy and society changed by
the Industrial Revolution?*

I

Let us begin with the Industrial Revolution, that is to say with Britain.
This is at first sight a capricious starting-point, for the repercussions of
this revolution did not make themselves felt in an obvious and unmistakable
way—at any rate outside England—until quite late in our period;
certainly not before 1830, probably not before 1840 or thereabouts. It is
only in the 1830s that literature and the arts began to be overtly haunted
by that rise of the capitalist society, that world in which all social bonds
crumbled except the implacable gold and paper ones of the cash nexus
(the phrase comes from Carlyle). Balzac's *Comédie Humaine,* the most extraordinary literary monument of its rise, belongs to that decade. It is not
until about 1840 that the great stream of official and unofficial literature
on the social effects of the Industrial Revolution begins to flow: the major
Bluebooks and statistical enquiries in England, Villermé's *Tableau de
l'état physique et moral des ouvriers,* Engels's *Condition of the Working
Class in England,* Ducpetiaux's work in Belgium, and scores of troubled
or appalled observers from Germany to Spain and the USA. It was not
until the 1840s that the proletariat, that child of the Industrial Revolution, and Communism, which was now attached to its social movements
—the spectre of the Communist Manifesto—walked across the conti-

nent. The very name of the Industrial Revolution reflects its relatively tardy impact on Europe. The thing existed in Britain before the word. Not until the 1820s did English and French socialists—themselves an unprecedented group—invent it, probably by analogy with the political revolution of France.

Nevertheless it is as well to consider it first, for two reasons. First, because in fact it 'broke out'—to use a question-begging phrase—before the Bastille was stormed; and second because without it we cannot understand the impersonal groundswell of history on which the more obvious men and events of our period were borne; the uneven complexity of its rhythm.

What does the phrase 'the Industrial Revolution broke out' mean? It means that some time in the 1780s, and for the first time in human history, the shackles were taken off the productive power of human societies, which henceforth became capable of the constant, rapid and up to the present limitless multiplication of men, goods and services. This is now technically known to the economists as the 'take-off into self-sustained growth.' No previous society had been able to break through the ceiling which a pre-industrial social structure, defective science and technology, and consequently periodic breakdown, famine and death, imposed on production. The 'take-off' was not, of course, one of those phenomena which, like earthquakes and large meteors, take the nontechnical world by surprise. Its pre-history in Europe can be traced back, depending on the taste of the historian and his particular range of interest, to about AD 1000, if not before, and earlier attempts to leap into the air, clumsy as the experiments of young ducklings, have been flattered with the name of 'industrial revolution'—in the thirteenth century, in the sixteenth, in the last decades of the seventeenth. From the middle of the eighteenth century the process of gathering speed for the take-off is so clearly observable that older historians have tended to date the Industrial Revolution back to 1760. But careful enquiry has tended to lead most experts to pick on the 1780s rather than the 1760s as the decisive decade, for it was then that, so far as we can tell, all the relevant statistical indices took that sudden, sharp, almost vertical turn upwards which marks the 'take-off.' The economy became, as it were, airborne.

To call this process the Industrial Revolution is both logical and in line with a well-established tradition, though there was at one time a fashion among conservative historians—perhaps due to a certain shyness in the presence of incendiary concepts—to deny its existence, and substitute instead platitudinous terms like 'accelerated evolution.' If the sudden, qualitative, and fundamental transformation, which happened in or about the 1780s, was not a revolution then the word has no commonsense meaning. The Industrial Revolution was not indeed an episode with a beginning and an end. To ask when it was 'complete' is senseless, for its essence was that henceforth revolutionary change became the norm. It is still going on; at most we can ask when the economic transformations had gone far enough to establish a substantially industrialized economy, capable of producing, broadly speaking, anything it wanted within the range of the available techniques, a 'mature industrial economy' to use the technical term. In Britain, and therefore in the world, this period of initial industrialization probably coincides almost exactly with the period [1789–1848] for if it began with the 'take-off' in the 1780s, it may plausibly be said to be concluded with the building of the railways and the construction of a massive heavy industry in Britain in the 1840s. But the Revolution itself, the 'take-off period,' can probably be dated with as much precision as is possible in such matters, to some time within the twenty years from 1780 to 1800: contemporary with, but slightly prior to, the French Revolution.

By any reckoning this was probably the most important event in world history, at any rate since the invention of agriculture and cities. And it was initiated by Britain. That this was not fortuitous, is evident. If there was to be a race for pioneering the Industrial Revolution in the eighteenth century, there was really only one starter. There was plenty of industrial and commercial advance, fostered by the intelligent and economically far from naïve ministers and civil servants of every enlightened monarchy in Europe, from Portugal to Russia, all of whom were at least as much concerned with 'economic growth' as present-day administrators. Some small states and regions did indeed industrialize quite impressively, for example, Saxony and the bishopric of Liège, though their industrial complexes were too small and localized to exert the world-revolutionary influence of the British ones. But it seems clear that even before the revolution Britain was already a long way ahead of her chief potential competitor in *per capita* output and trade, even if still comparable to her in total output and trade.

Whatever the British advance was due to, it was not scientific and technological superiority. In the natural sciences the French were almost certainly ahead of the British; an advantage which the French Revolution accentuated very sharply, at any rate in mathematics and physics, for it encouraged science in France while reaction suspected it in England. Even in the social sciences the British were still far from that superiority which made—and largely kept—economics a preeminently Anglo-Saxon subject; but here the Industrial Revolution put them into unquestioned first place. The economist of the 1780s would read Adam Smith, but also —and perhaps more profitably—the French physiocrats and national income accountants, Quesnay, Turgot, Dupont de Nemours, Lavoisier, and perhaps an Italian or two. The French produced more original inventions, such as the Jacquard loom (1804)—a more complex piece of apparatus than any devised in Britain—and better ships. The Germans possessed institutions of technical training like the Prussian *Bergakademie* which had no parallel in Britain, and the French Revolution created that unique and impressive body, the *Ecole Polytechnique*. English education was a joke in poor taste, though its deficiencies were somewhat offset by the dour village schools and the austere, turbulent, democratic universities of Calvinist Scotland which set a stream of brilliant, hard-working, career-seeking and rationalist young men into the south country: James Watt, Thomas Telford, Loudon McAdam, James Mill. Oxford and Cambridge, the only two English universities, were intellectually null, as were the somnolent public or grammar schools, with the exception of the Academies founded by the Dissenters who were excluded from the (Anglican) educational system. Even such aristocratic families as wished their sons to be educated, relied on tutors or Scottish universities. There was no system of primary education whatever before the Quaker Lancaster (and after him his Anglican rivals) established a sort of voluntary mass-production of elementary literacy in the early nineteenth century, incidentally saddling English education forever after with sectarian disputes. Social fears discouraged the education of the poor.

Fortunately few intellectual refinements were necessary to make the Industrial Revolution. Its technical inventions were exceedingly modest, and in no way beyond the scope of intelligent artisans experimenting in their workshops, or of the constructive capacities of carpenters, millwrights and locksmiths: the flying shuttle, the spinning jenny, the mule. Even its scientifically most sophisticated machine, James Watt's rotary steam-engine (1784), required no more physics than had been available for the best part of a century—the proper *theory* of steam engines was only developed *ex post facto* by the Frenchman Carnot in the 1820s—and could build on several generations of practical employment for steam engines, mostly in mines. Given the right conditions, the technical innovations of the Industrial Revolution practically made themselves, except perhaps in the chemical industry. This does not mean that early industrialists were not often interested in science and on the look-out for its practical benefits.

But the right conditions were visibly present in Britain, where more than a century had passed since the first king had been formally tried and executed by his people, and since private profit and economic development had become accepted as the supreme objects of government policy. For practical purposes the uniquely revolutionary British solution of the agrarian problem had already been found. A relative handful of commercially-minded landlords already almost monopolized the land, which was cultivated by tenant-farmers employing landless or smallholders. A good many relics of the ancient collective economy of the village still remained to be swept away by Enclosure Acts (1760–1830) and private transactions, but we can hardly any longer speak of a 'British peasantry' in the same sense that we can speak of a French, German or Russian peasantry. Farming was already predominantly for the market; manufacture had long been diffused throughout an unfeudal countryside. Agriculture was already prepared to carry out its three fundamental functions in an era of industrialization: to increase production and productivity, so as to feed a rapidly rising nonagricultural population; to provide a large and rising surplus of potential recruits for the towns and industries; and to provide a mechanism for the accumulation of capital to be used in the more modern sectors of the economy. (Two other functions were probably less important in Britain: that of creating a sufficiently large market among the agricultural population—normally the great mass of the people—and of providing an export surplus which helps to secure capital imports.) A considerable volume of social overhead capital—the expensive general equipment necessary for the entire economy to move smoothly ahead—was already being created, notably in shipping, port facilities, and the improvement of roads and waterways. Politics were already geared to profit. The businessman's specific demands might encounter resistance from other vested interests; and as we shall see, the agrarians were to erect one last barrier to hold up the advance of the industrialists between 1795 and 1846. On the whole, however, it was accepted that money not only talked, but governed. All the industrialist had to get to be accepted among the governors of society was enough money.

The businessman was undoubtedly in the process of getting more money, for the greater part of the eighteenth century was for most of Europe a period of prosperity and comfortable economic expansion; the real background to the happy optimism of Voltaire's Dr. Pangloss. It may well be argued that sooner or later this expansion, assisted by a gentle inflation, would have pushed some country across the threshold which separates the preindustrial from the industrial economy. But the problem is not so simple. Much of eighteenth-century industrial expansion did not in fact lead immediately, or within the foreseeable future, to industrial *revolution,* i.e. to the creation of a mechanized 'factory system' which in turn produces in such vast quantities and at such rapidly diminishing cost, as to be no longer dependent on existing demand, but to create its own market. For instance the building trade, or the numerous small scale industries producing domestic metal goods—nails, pots, knives, scissors, etc.—in the British Midlands and Yorkshire, expanded very greatly in this period, but always as a function of the existing market. In 1850, while producing far more than in 1750, they produced in substantially the old manner. What was needed was not any kind of expansion, but the special kind of expansion which produced Manchester rather than Birmingham.

Moreover, the pioneer industrial revolutions occurred in a special historical situation, in which economic growth emerges from the criss-crossing decisions of countless private entrepreneurs and investors, each governed by the first commandment of the age, to buy in the cheapest market and to sell in the dearest. How were they to discover that maximum profit was to be got out of organizing industrial revolution rather than out of more familiar (and in the past more profitable) business activities? How were they to learn, what nobody could as yet know, that industrial revolution would produce an unexampled acceleration in the expansion of their markets? Given that the main social foundations of an industrial society had already been laid, as they almost certainly had in the England of the later eighteenth century, they required two things: first, an industry which already offered exceptional rewards for the manufacturer who could expand his output quickly, if need be by reasonably cheap and simple innovations, and second, a *world* market largely monopolized by a single producing nation.

These considerations apply in some ways to all countries in our period. For instance, in all of them the lead in industrial growth was taken by the manufacturers of goods of mass consumption—mainly, but not exclusively, textiles—because the mass market for such goods already existed, and businessmen could clearly see its possibilities of expansion. In other ways, however, they apply to Britain alone. For the pioneer industrialists have the most difficult problems. Once Britain had begun to industrialize, other countries could begin to enjoy the benefits of the rapid economic expansion which the pioneer industrial revolution stimulated. Moreover, British success proved what could be achieved by it, British technique could be imitated, British skill and capital imported. The Saxon textile industry, incapable of making its own inventions, copied the English ones, sometimes under the supervision of English mechanics; Englishmen with a taste for the continent, like the Cockerills, established themselves in Belgium and various parts of Germany. Between 1789 and 1848 Europe and America were flooded with British experts, steam engines, cotton machinery and investments.

Britain enjoyed no such advantages. On the other hand it possessed an economy strong enough and a state aggressive enough to capture the markets of its competitors. In effect the wars of 1793–1815, the last and decisive phase of a century's Anglo-French duel, virtually eliminated all rivals from the non-European world, except to some extent the young USA. Moreover, Britain possessed an industry admirably suited to pioneering industrial revolution under capitalist conditions, and an economic conjuncture which allowed it to: the cotton industry, and colonial expansion.

II

The British, like all other cotton industries, had originally grown up as a by-product of overseas trade, which produced its raw material (or rather one of its raw materials, for the original product was *fustian,* a mixture of cotton and linen), and the Indian cotton goods or *calicoes* which won the markets that the European manufacturers were to attempt to capture with their own imitations. To begin with they were not very successful, though better able to reproduce the cheap and coarse goods competitively than the fine and elaborate ones. Fortunately, however, the old-established and powerful vested interest of the woollen trade periodically secured import prohibitions of Indian calicoes (which the purely mercantile interest of the East India Company sought to export from India in the largest possible quantities), and thus gave the native cotton industry's substitutes a chance. Cheaper than wool, cotton and cotton mixtures won themselves a modest but useful market at home. But their major chances of rapid expansion were to lie overseas.

Colonial trade had created the cotton industry, and continued to nourish it. In the eighteenth century it developed in the hinterland of the major colonial ports, Bristol, Glasgow but especially Liverpool, the great centre of the slave trades. Each phase of this inhuman but rapidly expanding commerce stimulated it. In fact, during the entire period . . . slavery and cotton marched together. The African slaves were bought, in part at least, with Indian cotton goods; but when the supply of these was interrupted by war or revolt in and about India, Lancashire was able to leap in. The plantations of the West Indies, where the slaves were taken, provided the bulk of the raw cotton for the British industry, and in return the planters bought Manchester cotton checks in appreciable quantities. Until shortly before the 'take-off' the overwhelming bulk of Lancashire cotton exports went to the combined African and American markets. Lancashire was later to repay its debt to slavery by preserving it; for after the 1790s the slave plantations of the Southern United States were extended and maintained by the insatiable and rocketing demands of the Lancashire mills, to which they supplied the bulk of their raw cotton.

The cotton industry was thus launched, like a glider, by the pull of the colonial trade to which it was attached; a trade which promised not only great, but rapid and above all unpredictable expansion, which encouraged the entrepreneur to adopt the revolutionary techniques required to meet it. Between 1750 and 1769 the export of British cottons increased more than ten times over. In such situations the rewards for the man who came into the market first with the most cotton checks were astronomical and well worth the risks of leaps into technological adventure. But the over-

seas market, and especially within it the poor and backward 'under-developed areas,' not only expanded dramatically from time to time, but expanded constantly without apparent limit. Doubtless any given section of it, considered in isolation, was small by industrial standards, and the competition of the different 'advanced economies' made it even smaller for each. But, as we have seen, supposing any one of the advanced economies managed, for a sufficiently long time, to monopolize *all* or almost all of it, then its prospects really were limitless. This is precisely what the British cotton industry succeeded in doing, aided by the aggressive support of the British Government. In terms of sales, the Industrial Revolution can be described except for a few initial years in the 1780s as the triumph of the export market over the home: by 1814 Britain exported about four yards of cotton cloth for every three used at home, by 1850 thirteen for every eight. And within this expanding export market, in turn, the semi-colonial and colonial markets, long the main outlets for British goods abroad, triumphed. During the Napoleonic Wars, when the European markets were largely cut off by wars and blockades, this was natural enough. But even after the wars they continued to assert themselves. In 1820 Europe, once again open to free British imports, took 128 million yards of British cottons; America outside the USA, Africa and Asia took 80 millions; but by 1840 Europe took 200 million yards, while the 'under-developed' areas took 529 millions.

For within these areas British industry had established a monopoly by means of war, other people's revolutions and her own imperial rule. Two regions deserve particular notice. *Latin America* came to depend virtually entirely on British imports during the Napoleonic Wars, and after it broke with Spain and Portugal it became an almost total economic dependency of Britain, being cut off from any political interference by Britain's potential European competitors. By 1820 this impoverished continent already took more than a quarter as much of British cotton cloths as Europe; by 1840 it took almost half as much again as Europe. The East Indies had been, as we have seen, the traditional exporter of cotton goods, encouraged by the East India Company. But as the industrialist vested interest prevailed in Britain, the East India mercantile interests (not to mention the Indian ones) were pressed back. India was systematically deindustrialized and became in turn a market for Lancashire cottons: in 1820 the subcontinent took only 11 million yards; but by 1840 it already took 145 million yards. This was not merely a gratifying extension of Lancashire's markets. It was a major landmark in world history. For since the dawn of time Europe had always imported more from the East than she had sold there; because there was little the Orient required from the West in return for the spices, silks, calicoes, jewels, etc., which it sent there. The cotton shirtings of the Industrial Revolution for the first time reversed this relationship, which had been hitherto kept in balance by a mixture of bullion exports and robbery. Only the conservative and self-satisfied Chinese still refused to buy what the West, or western-controlled economies offered, until between 1815 and 1842 western traders, aided by western gun-boats, discovered an ideal commodity which could be exported *en masse* from India to the East: opium.

Cotton therefore provided prospects sufficiently astronomical to tempt private entrepreneurs into the adventure of industrial revolution, and an expansion sufficiently sudden to require it. Fortunately it also provided the other conditions which made it possible. The new inventions which revolutionized it—the spinning-jenny, the water-frame, the mule in spinning, a little later the power-loom in weaving—were sufficiently simple and cheap, and paid for themselves almost immediately in terms of higher output. They could be installed, if need be piecemeal, by small men who started off with a few borrowed pounds, for the men who controlled the great accumulations of eighteenth-century wealth were not greatly inclined to invest large amounts in industry. The expansion of the industry could be financed easily out of current profits, for the combination of its vast market conquests and a steady price-inflation produced fantastic rates of profit. 'It was not five percent or ten percent,' a later English politician was to say, with justice, 'but hundreds percent and thousands percent that made the fortunes of Lancashire.' In 1789 an ex-draper's assistant like Robert Owen could start with a borrowed £100 in Manchester; by 1809 he bought out his partners in the New Lanark Mills for £84,000 *in cash*. And his was a relatively modest story of business success. It should be remembered that around 1800 less than 15 percent of British families had an income of more than £50 per year, and of these only one-quarter earned more than £200 a year.

But the cotton manufacture had other advantages. All its raw material came from abroad, and its supply could therefore be extended by the drastic procedures open to white men in the colonies—slavery and the opening of new areas of cultivation—rather than by the slower procedures of European agriculture; nor was it hampered by the vested interests of European agriculturalists. From the 1790s on British cotton found its supply, to which its fortunes remained linked until the 1860s, in the newly-opened Southern States of the USA. Again, at crucial points of manufacture (notably spinning) cotton suffered from a shortage of cheap and efficient labour, and was therefore pushed into mechanization. An industry like *linen,* which had initially rather better chances of colonial expansion than cotton, suffered in the long run from the very ease with which cheap, non-mechanized production could be expanded in the impoverished peasant regions (mainly in Central Europe, but also in Ireland) in which it mainly flourished. For the *obvious* way of industrial expansion in the eighteenth century, in Saxony and Normandy as in England, was not to construct factories, but to extend the so-called 'domestic' or 'putting-out' system, in which workers—sometimes former independent craftsmen, sometimes former peasants with time on their hands in the dead season—worked up the raw material in their own homes, with their own or rented tools, receiving it from and delivering it back to merchants who were in the process of becoming employers. Indeed, both in Britain and in the rest of the economically progressive world, the bulk of expansion in the initial period of industrialization continued to be of this kind. Even in the cotton industry such processes as weaving were expanded by creating hosts of domestic handloom weavers to serve the nuclei of mechanized spinneries, the primitive handloom being a rather more efficient device than the spinning-wheel. Everywhere weaving was mechanized a generation after spinning, and everywhere, incidentally, the handloom weavers died a lingering death, occasionally revolting against their awful fate, when industry no longer had any need of them.

III

The traditional view which has seen the history of the British Industrial Revolution primarily in terms of cotton is thus correct. Cotton was the first industry to be revolutionized, and it is difficult to see what other could have pushed a host of private entrepreneurs into revolution. As late as the 1830s cotton was the only British industry in which the factory or 'mill' (the name was derived from the most widespread preindustrial establishment employing heavy power-operated machinery) predominated; at first (1780–1815) mainly in spinning, carding and a few ancillary operations, after 1815 increasingly also in weaving. The 'factories' with which the new Factory Acts dealt were, until the 1860s, assumed to be exclusively textile factories and predominantly cotton mills. Factory production in other textile branches was slow to develop before the 1840s, and in other manufactures was negligible. Even the steam engine, though applied to numerous other industries by 1815, was not used in any quantity outside mining, which had pioneered it. In 1830 'industry' and 'factory' in anything like the modern sense still meant almost exclusively the cotton areas of the United Kingdom.

This is not to underestimate the forces which made for industrial innovation in other consumer goods, notably in other textiles, in food and drink, in pottery and other household goods, greatly stimulated by the rapid growth of cities. But in the first place these employed far fewer people: no industry remotely approached the million-and-a-half people directly employed by or dependent on employment in cotton in 1833. In the second place their power to transform was much smaller: *brewing,* which was in most respects a technically and scientifically much more advanced and mechanized business, and one revolutionized well before cotton, hardly affected the economy around it, as may be proved by the great Guinness brewery in Dublin, which left the rest of the Dublin and Irish economy (though not local tastes) much as it was before its construction. The demand derived from cotton—for more building and all activities in the new industrial areas, for machines, for chemical improvements, for industrial lighting, for shipping and a number of other activities—is itself enough to account for a large proportion of the economic growth in Britain up to the 1830s. In the third place, the expansion of the cotton industry was so vast and its weight in the foreign trade of Britain so great, that it dominated the movements of the entire economy. The quantity of raw cotton imported into Britain rose from 11 million lb. in 1785 to 588 million lb. in 1850; the output of cloth from 40 million to 2,025 million yards. Cotton manufacturers formed between 40 and 50 percent of the annual declared value of *all* British exports between 1816 and 1848. If cotton flourished, the economy flourished, if it slumped, so did the economy. Its price movements determined the balance of the nation's trade. Only agriculture had a comparable power, and that was visibly declining.

Nevertheless, though the expansion of the cotton industry and the cotton-dominated industrial economy 'mocks all that the most romantic imagination could have previously conceived possible under any circumstances,' its progress was far from smooth, and by the 1830s and early 1840s produced major problems of growth, not to mention revolutionary unrest unparalleled in any other period of recent British history. This first general stumbling of the industrial capitalist economy is reflected in a marked slowing down in the growth, perhaps even in a decline, in the British national income at this period. Nor was this first general capitalist crisis a purely British phenomenon.

Its most serious consequences were social: the transition to the new economy created misery and discontent, the materials of social revolution. And indeed, social revolution in the form of spontaneous risings of the urban and industrial poor did break out, and made the revolutions of 1848 on the continent, the vast Chartist movement in Britain. Nor was discontent confined to the labouring poor. Small and inadaptable business-men, petty-bourgeois, special sections of the economy, were also the vic-tims of the Industrial Revolution and of its ramifications. Simple-minded labourers reacted to the new system by smashing the machines which they thought responsible for their troubles; but a surprisingly large body of local businessmen and farmers sympathized profoundly with these Luddite activities of their labourers, because they too saw themselves as victims of a diabolical minority of selfish innovators. The exploitation of labour which kept its incomes at subsistence level, thus enabling the rich to ac-cumulate the profits which financed industrialization (and their own ample comforts), antagonized the proletarian. However, another aspect of this diversion of national income from the poor to the rich, from con-sumption to investment, also antagonized the small entrepreneur. The great financiers, the tight community of home and foreign 'fund-holders' who received what all paid in taxes—something like 8 percent of the en-tire national income—were perhaps even more unpopular among small businessmen, farmers and the like than among labourers, for these knew enough about money and credit to feel a personal rage at their disadvan-tage. It was all very well for the rich, who could raise all the credit they needed, to clamp rigid deflation and monetary orthodoxy on the economy after the Napoleonic Wars: it was the little man who suffered, and who, in all countries and at all times in the nineteenth century, demanded easy credit and financial unorthodoxy. Labour and the disgruntled petty-bour-geois on the verge of toppling over into the unpropertied abyss, therefore shared common discontents. These in turn united them in the mass move-ments of 'radicalism,' 'democracy' or 'republicanism' of which the British Radicals, the French Republicans and the American Jacksonian Demo-crats were the most formidable between 1815 and 1848.

From the point of view of the capitalists, however, these social prob-lems were relevant to the progress of the economy only if, by some horri-ble accident, they were to overthrow the social order. On the other hand there appeared to be certain inherent flaws of the economic process which threatened its fundamental motive-force: profit. For if the rate of return on capital fell to nothing, an economy in which men produced for profit only must slow down into that 'stationary state' which the economists en-visaged and dreaded.

The three most obvious of these flaws were the trade cycle of boom and slump, the tendency of the rate of profit to decline, and (what amounted to the same thing) the shortage of profitable investment oppor-tunities. The first of these was not regarded as serious, except by the crit-ics of capitalism as such, who were the first to investigate it and to con-sider it as an integral part of the capitalist economic process and as a symptom of its inherent contradictions. Periodic crises of the economy leading to unemployment, falls in production, bankruptcies, etc. were well known. In the eighteenth century they generally reflected some agrarian catastrophe (harvest failures, etc.) and on the continent of Europe, it has been argued, agrarian disturbances remained the primary cause of the most widespread depressions until the end of our period. Periodic crises in the small manufacturing and financial sectors of the economy were also familiar, in Britain at least from 1793. After the Napoleonic Wars the periodic drama of boom and collapse—in 1825–6, in 1836–7, in 1839–42, in 1846–8—clearly dominated the economic life of a nation at peace. By the 1830s, that crucial decade in our period of history, it was vaguely recognized that they were regular periodic phenomena, at least in trade and finance. However, they were still commonly regarded by businessmen as caused either by particular mistakes—e.g. overspeculation in American stocks—or by outside interference with the smooth operations of the capitalist economy. They were not believed to reflect any fundamental difficulties of the system.

Not so the falling margin of profit, which the cotton industry illustrated very clearly. Initially this industry benefited from immense advantages. Mechanization greatly increased the productivity (i.e. reduced the cost per unit produced) of its labour, which was in any case abominably paid, since it consisted largely of women and children. Of the 12,000 operatives in the cotton mills of Glasgow in 1833, only 2,000 earned an average of over 11s. a week. In 131 Manchester mills average wages were less than 12s., in only twenty-one were they higher. And the building of factories was relatively cheap: in 1846 an entire weaving plant of 410 machines, including the cost of ground and buildings, could be constructed for something like £11,000. But above all the major cost, that of raw material, was drastically cut by the rapid expansion of cotton cultivation in the Southern USA after the invention of Eli Whitney's cotton-gin in 1793. If we add that entrepreneurs enjoyed the bonus of a profit-inflation (i.e. the general tendency for prices to be higher when they sold their product than when they made it), we shall understand why the manufacturing classes felt buoyant.

After 1815 these advantages appeared increasingly offset by the narrowing margin of profit. In the first place industrial revolution and competition brought about a constant and dramatic fall in the price of the finished article but not in several of the costs of production. In the second place after 1815 the general atmosphere of prices was one of deflation and not inflation, that is to say profits, so far from enjoying an extra boost, suffered from a slight lag. Thus, while in 1784 the selling-price of a lb. of spun yarn had been 10s. 11d., the cost of its raw material 2s. (margin, 8s. 11d.), in 1812 its price was 2s. 6d., its raw material cost 1s. 6d. (margin 1s.) and in 1832 its price 11¼d., its raw material cost 7½d., and the margin for other costs and profits therefore only 4d. Of course the situation, which was general throughout British—and indeed all advanced —industry was not too tragic. 'Profits are still sufficient,' wrote the champion and historian of cotton in 1835, in extreme understatement, 'to allow of a great accumulation of capital in the manufacture.' As the total sales soared upwards, so did the total of profits even at their diminishing rate.

All that was needed was continued and astronomic expansion. Nevertheless, it seemed that the shrinking of profit-margins had to be arrested or at least slowed down. This could only be done by cutting costs. And of all the costs *wages*—which McCulloch reckoned at three times the amount per year of the raw material—were the most compressible.

They could be compressed by direct wage-cutting, by the substitution of cheaper machine-tenders for dearer skilled workers, and by the competition of the machine. This last reduced the average weekly wage of the handloom weaver in Bolton from 33s. in 1795 and 14s. in 1815 to 5s. 6d. (or more precisely a net income of 4s. 1½d.) in 1829–34. And indeed money wages fell steadily in the post-Napoleonic period. But there was a physiological limit to such reductions, unless the labourers were actually to starve, as of course the 500,000 handloom weavers did. Only if the cost of living fell could wages also fall beyond that point. The cotton manufacturers shared the view that it was kept artificially high by the monopoly of the landed interest, made even worse by the heavy protective tariffs which a Parliament of landlords had wrapped around British farming after the wars—the *Corn Laws*. These, moreover, had the additional disadvantage of threatening the essential growth of British exports. For if the rest of the not yet industrialized world was prevented from selling its agrarian products, how was it to pay for the manufactured goods which Britain alone could—and had to—supply? Manchester business therefore became the centre of militant and increasingly desperate opposition to landlordism in general and the Corn Laws in particular and the backbone of the Anti-Corn Law League of 1838–46. But the Corn Laws were not abolished until 1846, their abolition did not immediately lead to a fall in the cost of living, and it is doubtful whether before the age of railways and steamers even free food-imports would have greatly lowered it.

The industry was thus under immense pressure to mechanize (i.e. to lower costs by labour-saving), to rationalize and to expand its production and sales, thus making up by the mass of small profits per unit for the fall in the margins. Its success was variable. As we have seen the actual rise in production and exports was gigantic; so, after 1815, was the mechanization of hitherto manual or partly-mechanized occupations, notably weaving. This took the form chiefly of the general adoption of existing or slightly improved machinery rather than of further technological revolution. Though the pressure for technical innovation increased significantly —there were thirty-nine new patents in cotton spinning, etc., in 1800–20, fifty-one in the 1820s, eighty-six in the 1830s and a hundred and fifty-six in the 1840s—the British cotton industry was technologically stabilized by the 1830s. On the other hand, though the production per operative increased in the post-Napoleonic period, it did not do so to any revolutionary extent. The really substantial speed-up of operations was to occur in the second half of the century.

There was comparable pressure on the rate of interest on capital, which contemporary theory tended to assimilate to profit. But consideration of this takes us to the next phase of industrial development—the construction of a basic capital-goods industry.

IV

It is evident that no industrial economy can develop beyond a certain point until it possesses adequate capital-goods capacity. This is why even today the most reliable single index of any country's industrial potential is the quantity of its iron and steel production. But it is also evident that under conditions of private enterprise the extremely costly capital investment necessary for much of this development is not likely to be undertaken for the same reasons as the industrialization of cotton or other consumer goods. For these a mass market already exists, at least potentially: even very primitive men wear shirts or use household equipment and foodstuffs. The problem is merely how to put a sufficiently vast market sufficiently quickly within the purview of businessmen. But no such market exists, e.g., for heavy iron equipment such as girders. It only comes into existence in the course of an industrial revolution (and not always then), and those who lock up their money in the very heavy investments required even by quite modest ironworks (compared to quite large cotton-mills) before it is visibly there, are more likely to be speculators, adventurers and dreamers than sound businessmen. In fact in France a sect of such speculative technological adventurers, the Saint-Simonians, acted as chief propagandists of the kind of industrialization which needed heavy and long-range investment.

These disadvantages applied particularly to metallurgy, especially of iron. Its capacity increased, thanks to a few simple innovations such as that of puddling and rolling in the 1780s, but the nonmilitary demand for it remained relatively modest, and the military, though gratifyingly large thanks to a succession of wars between 1756 and 1815, slackened off sharply after Waterloo. It was certainly not large enough to make Britain into an outstandingly large producer of iron. In 1790 she out-produced France by only forty percent or so, and even in 1800 her output was considerably less than half of the combined continental one, and amounted to the, by later standards, tiny figure of a quarter of a million tons. If anything the British share of world iron output tended to sink in the next decades.

Fortunately they applied less to mining, which was chiefly the mining of *coal*. For coal had the advantage of being not merely the major source of industrial power in the nineteenth century, but also a major form of domestic fuel, thanks largely to the relative shortage of forests in Britain. The growth of cities, and especially of London, had caused coal mining to expand rapidly since the late sixteenth century. By the early eighteenth it was substantially a primitive modern industry, even employing the earliest steam engines (devised for similar purposes in nonferrous metal mining, mainly in Cornwall) for pumping. Hence coal mining hardly needed or underwent major technological revolution in our period. Its innovations were improvements rather than transformations of production. But its capacity was already immense and, by world standards, astronomic. In 1800 Britain may have produced something like ten million tons of coal, or about 90 percent of the world output. Its nearest competitor, France, produced less than a million.

This immense industry, though probably not expanding fast enough for really massive industrialization on the modern scale, was sufficiently large to stimulate the basic invention which was to transform the capital goods industries: the railway. For the mines not only required steam engines in large quantities and of great power, but also required efficient means of transporting the great quantities of coal from coalface to shaft and especially from pithead to the point of shipment. The 'tramway' or 'railway' along which trucks ran was an obvious answer; to pull these trucks by stationary engines was tempting; to pull them by moving engines would not seem too impractical. Finally, the costs of overland transport of bulk goods were so high that it was likely to strike coal-owners in inland fields that the use of these short-term means of transport could be profitably extended for long-term haulage. The line from the inland coalfield of Durham to the coast (Stockton–Darlington 1825) was the first of the modern railways. Technologically the railway is the child of the mine, and especially the northern English coalmine. George Stephenson began life as a Tyneside 'engineman,' and for years virtually all locomotive drivers were recruited from his native coalfield.

No innovation of the Industrial Revolution has fired the imagination as much as the railway, as witness the fact that it is the only product of nineteenth century industrialization which has been fully absorbed into the imagery of popular and literate poetry. Hardly had they been proved technically feasible and profitable in England (c. 1825–30), before plans to build them were made over most of the Western world, though their execution was generally delayed. The first short lines were opened in the USA in 1827, in France in 1828 and 1835, in Germany and Belgium in 1835 and even in Russia by 1837. The reason was doubtless that no other invention revealed the power and speed of the new age to the layman as dramatically; a revelation made all the more striking by the remarkable technical maturity of even the very earliest railways. (Speeds of up to sixty miles per hour, for instance, were perfectly practicable in the 1830s, and were not substantially improved by later steam-railways.) The iron road, pushing its huge smoke-plumed snakes at the speed of wind across countries and continents, whose embankments and cuttings, bridges and stations, formed a body of public building beside which the pyramids and the Roman aqueducts and even the Great Wall of China paled into provincialism, was the very symbol of man's triumph through technology.

In fact, from an economic point of view, its vast expense was its chief advantage. No doubt in the long run its capacity to open up countries hitherto cut off by high transport costs from the world market, the vast increase in the speed and bulk of overland communication it brought for men and goods, were to be of major importance. Before 1848 they were economically less important: outside Britain because railways were few, in Britain because for geographical reasons transport problems were much less intractable then in large landlocked countries. But from the perspective of the student of economic development the immense appetite of the railways for iron and steel, for coal, for heavy machinery, for labour, for capital investment, was at this stage more important. For it provided just that massive demand which was needed if the capital goods industries were to be transformed as profoundly as the cotton industry had been. In the first two decades of the railways (1830–50) the output of iron in Britain rose from 680,000 to 2,250,000, in other words it trebled. The output of coal between 1830 and 1850 also trebled from 15 million tons to 49 million tons. That dramatic rise was due primarily to the railway, for on average each mile of line required 300 tons of iron merely for track. The industrial advances which for the first time made the mass production of steel possible followed naturally in the next decades.

The reason for this sudden, immense, and quite essential expansion lay in the apparently irrational passion with which businessmen and investors threw themselves into the construction of railways. In 1830 there were a few dozen miles of railways in all the world—chiefly consisting of the line from Liverpool to Manchester. By 1840 there were over 4,500 miles, by 1850 over 23,500. Most of them were projected in a few bursts of speculative frenzy known as the 'railway manias' of 1835–7 and especially in 1844–7; most of them were built in large part with British capital, British iron, machines and know-how. These investment booms appear irrational, because in fact few railways were much more profitable to the investor than other forms of enterprise, most yielded quite modest profits and many none at all: in 1855 the average interest on capital sunk in the British railways was a mere 3.7 percent. No doubt promoters, speculators and others did exceedingly well out of them, but the ordinary investor clearly did not. And yet by 1840 £28 millions, by 1850 £240 millions had been hopefully invested in them.

Why? The fundamental fact about Britain in the first two generations of the Industrial Revolution was, that the comfortable and rich classes accumulated income so fast and in such vast quantities as to exceed all available possibilities of spending and investment. (The annual investible surplus in the 1840s was reckoned at about £60 millions.) No doubt feudal and aristocratic societies would have succeeded in throwing a great deal of this away in riotous living, luxury building and other uneconomic activities. Even in Britain the sixth Duke of Devonshire, whose normal income was princely enough succeeded in leaving his heir £1,000,000 of debts in the mid-nineteenth century (which he paid off by borrowing another £1,500,000 and going in for the development of real estate values). But the bulk of the middle classes, who formed the main investing public, were still savers rather than spenders, though by 1840 there are many signs that they felt sufficiently wealthy to spend *as well as* to invest. Their wives began to turn into 'ladies,' instructed by the handbooks of etiquette which multiply about this period, their chapels began to be rebuilt in ample and expensive styles, and they even began to celebrate their collective glory by constructing those shocking town halls and other civic monstrosities in Gothic and Renaissance imitations, whose exact and Napoleonic cost their municipal historians recorded with pride.

Again, a modern socialist or welfare society would no doubt have distributed some of these vast accumulations for social purposes. In our period nothing was less likely. Virtually untaxed, the middle classes therefore continued to accumulate among the hungry populace, whose hunger was the counterpart of their accumulation. And as they were not peasants, content to hoard their savings in woollen stockings or as golden bangles, they had to find profitable investment for them. But where? Existing industries, for instance, had become far too cheap to absorb more than a fraction of the available surplus for investment: even supposing the size of the cotton industry to be doubled, the capital cost would absorb only a part of it. What was needed was a sponge large enough to hold all of it.

Foreign investment was one obvious possibility. The rest of the world —mostly, to begin with, old governments seeking to recover from the Napoleonic Wars and new ones borrowing with their usual dash and abandon for indeterminate purposes—was only too anxious for unlimited loans. The English investor lent readily. But alas, the South American loans which appeared so promising in the 1820s, the North American ones which beckoned in the 1830s, turned only too often into scraps of worthless paper: of twenty-five foreign government loans sold between 1818 and 1831, sixteen (involving about half of the £42 millions at issue prices) were in default in 1831. In theory these loans should have paid the investor 7 or 9 percent; in fact in 1831 he received an average of 3.1 percent. Who would not be discouraged by experiences such as those with the Greek 5 percent loans of 1824 and 1825 which did not begin to pay any interest at all until the 1870s? Hence it is natural that the capital flooding abroad in the speculative booms of 1825 and 1835–7, should seek an apparently less disappointing employment.

John Francis, looking back on the mania from 1851, described the rich man who 'saw the accumulation of wealth, which with an industrial people always outstrips the ordinary modes of investment, legitimately and justly employed . . . He saw the money which in his youth had been thrown into war loans and in his manhood wasted on South American mines, forming roads, employing labour and increasing business. (The railway's) absorption of capital was at least an absorption, if unsuccessful, in the country that produced it. Unlike foreign mines and foreign loans, they could not be exhausted or utterly valueless.'

Whether it could have found other forms of home investment—for instance in building—is an academic question to which the answer is still in doubt. In fact it found the railways, which could not conceivably have been built as rapidly and on as large a scale without this torrent of capital flooding into them, especially in the middle 1840s. It was a lucky conjuncture, for the railways happened to solve virtually all the problems of the economy's growth at once.

V

To trace the impetus for industrialization is only one part of the historian's task. The other is to trace the mobilization and redeployment of economic resources, the adaptation of the economy and the society which
were required to maintain the new and revolutionary course.

The first and perhaps the most crucial factor which had to be mobilized and redeployed was *labour,* for an industrial economy means a sharp
proportionate decline in the agricultural (i.e. rural) and a sharp rise in the
non-agricultural (i.e. increasingly in the urban) population, and almost
certainly (as in our period) a rapid general increase in population. It
therefore implies in the first instance a sharp rise in the supply of food,
mainly from home agriculture—i.e. an 'agricultural revolution.'

The rapid growth of towns and nonagricultural settlements in Britain
had naturally long stimulated agriculture, which is fortunately so inefficient in its preindustrial forms that quite small improvements—a little
rational attention to animal-husbandry, crop-rotation, fertilization and the
lay-out of farms, or the adoption of new crops—can produce dispropor-
tionately large results. Such agricultural change had preceded the industrial revolution and made possible the first stages of rapid population
increases, and the impetus naturally continued, though British farming
suffered heavily in the slump which followed the abnormally high prices
of the Napoleonic Wars. In terms of technology and capital investment
the changes of our period were probably fairly modest until the 1840s, the
period when agricultural science and engineering may be said to have
come of age. The vast increase in output which enabled British farming
in the 1830s to supply 98 percent of the grain for a population between
two and three times the mid-eighteenth century size, was achieved by
general adoption of methods pioneered in the earlier eighteenth century,
by rationalization and by expansion of the cultivated area.

All these in turn were achieved by social rather than technological
transformation: by the liquidation of medieval communal cultivation with
its open field and common pasture (the 'enclosure movement'), of self-sufficient peasant farming, and of old-fashioned uncommercial attitudes towards the land. Thanks to the preparatory evolution of the sixteenth to
eighteenth centuries this uniquely radical solution of the agrarian problem, which made Britain a country of a few large landowners, a moderate
number of commercial tenant farmers and a great number of hired labourers, was achieved with a minimum of trouble, though intermittently resisted not only by the unhappy rural poor but by the traditionalist country
gentry. The 'Speenhamland System' of poor relief, spontaneously adopted
by gentlemen-justices in several counties in and after the hungry year of
1795, has been seen as the last systematic attempt to safeguard the old
rural society against the corrosion of the cash nexus. The Corn Laws with
which the agrarian interest sought to protect farming against the post-
1815 crisis, in the teeth of all economic orthodoxy, were in part a mani-

festo against the tendency to treat agriculture as an industry just like any other, to be judged by the criteria of profitability alone. But these were doomed rearguard actions against the final introduction of capitalism into the countryside; they were finally defeated in the wave of middle class radical advance after 1830, by the new Poor Law of 1834 and the abolition of the Corn Laws in 1846.

In terms of economic productivity this social transformation was an immense success; in terms of human suffering, a tragedy, deepened by the agricultural depression after 1815 which reduced the rural poor to demoralized destitution. After 1800 even so enthusiastic a champion of enclosure and agricultural progress as Arthur Young was shaken by its social effects. But from the point of view of industrialization these also were desirable consequences; for an industrial economy needs labour, and where else but from the former nonindustrial sector was it to come from? The rural population at home or, in the form of (mainly Irish) immigration, abroad, were the most obvious sources supplemented by the miscellaneous petty producers and labouring poor. Men must be attracted into the new occupations, or if—as was most probable—they were initially immune to these attractions and unwilling to abandon their traditional way of life —they must be forced into it. Economic and social hardship was the most effective whip; the higher money wages and greater freedom of the town the supplementary carrot. For various reasons the forces tending to prise men loose from their historic social anchorage were still relatively weak in our period, compared to the second half of the nineteenth century. It took a really sensational catastrophe such as the Irish hunger to produce the sort of massive emigration (one and a half millions out of a total population of eight and a half millions in 1835–50) which became common after 1850. Nevertheless, they were stronger in Britain than elsewhere. Had they not been, British industrial development might have been as hampered as that of France was by the stability and relative comfort of its peasantry and petty-bourgeoisie, which deprived industry of the required intake of labour.

To acquire a sufficient number of labourers was one thing; to acquire sufficient labour of the right qualifications and skills was another. Twentieth-century experience has shown that this problem is as crucial and more difficult to solve. In the first place *all* labour had to learn how to work in a manner suited to industry, i.e. in a rhythm of regular unbroken daily work which is entirely different from the seasonal ups and downs of the farm, or the self-controlled patchiness of the independent craftsman. It had also to learn to be responsive to monetary incentives. British employers then, like South African ones now, constantly complained about the 'laziness' of labour or its tendency to work until it had earned a traditional week's living wage and then to stop. The answer was found in a draconic labour discipline (fines, a 'Master and Servant' code mobilizing the law on the side of the employer, etc.), but above all in the practice where possible of paying labour so little that it would have to work steadily all through the week in order to make a minimum income. In the factories, where the problem of labour discipline was more urgent, it was often found more convenient to employ the tractable (and cheaper) women and children: out of all workers in the English cotton mills in 1834–47 about one-quarter were adult men, over half women and girls and the balance, boys below the age of eighteen. Another common way of ensuring labour discipline, which reflected the small-scale, piece-meal process of industrialization in this early phase, was sub-contract or the practice of making skilled workers the actual employers of their unskilled helpers. In the cotton industry, for instance, about two-thirds of the boys and one-third of the girls were thus 'in the direct employ of operatives' and hence more closely watched, and outside the factories proper such arrangements were even more widespread. The sub-employer, of course, had a direct financial incentive to see that this hired help did not slack.

It was rather more difficult to recruit or train sufficient skilled or technically trained workers, for few preindustrial skills were of much use in modern industry, though of course many occupations, like building, continued practically unchanged. Fortunately the slow semi-industrialization of Britain in the centuries before 1789 had built up a rather large reservoir of suitable skills, both in textile technique and in the handling of metals. Thus on the continent the locksmith, one of the few craftsmen used to precision work with metals, became the ancestor of the machine-builder and sometimes provided him with a name, whereas in Britain the millwright, and the 'engineer' or 'engineman' (already common in and around mines) did so. Nor is it accidental that the English word 'engineer' describes both the skilled metal-worker and the designer and planner; for the bulk of higher technologists could be, and was, recruited from among these mechanically skilled and self-reliant men. In fact, British industrialization relied on this unplanned supply of the higher skills, as continental industrialism could not. This explains the shocking neglect of general and technical education in this country, the price of which was to be paid later.

Beside such problems of labour supply, those of capital supply were unimportant. Unlike most other European countries, there was no shortage of immediately investible capital in Britain. The major difficulty was that those who controlled most of it in the eighteenth century—landlords, merchants, shippers, financiers, etc.—were reluctant to invest it in the new industries, which therefore had often to be started by small savings or loans and developed by the ploughing back of profits. Local capital shortage made the early industrialist—especially the self-made men—harder, thriftier and more grasping, and their workers therefore correspondingly more exploited; but this reflected the imperfect flow of the national investment surplus and not its inadequacy. On the other hand the eighteenth-century rich were prepared to sink their money in certain enterprises which benefited industrialization; most notably in transport (canals, dock facilities, roads and later also railways) and in mines, from which landowners drew royalties even when they did not themselves manage them.

Nor was there any difficulty about the technique of trade and finance, private or public. Banks and banknotes, bills of exchange, stocks and shares, the technicalities of overseas and wholesale trade, and marketing, were familiar enough and men who could handle them or easily learn to do so, were in abundant supply. Moreover, by the end of the eighteenth century government policy was firmly committed to the supremacy of business. Older enactments to the contrary (such as those of the Tudor social code) had long fallen into desuetude, and were finally abolished—except where they touched agriculture—in 1813–35. In theory the laws and financial or commercial institutions of Britain were clumsy and designed to hinder rather than help economic development; for instance, they made expensive 'private acts' of Parliament necessary almost every time men wished to form a joint-stock company. The French Revolution provided the French—and through their influence the rest of the continent—with far more rational and effective machinery for such purposes. In practice the British managed perfectly well, and indeed considerably better than their rivals.

In this rather haphazard, unplanned and empirical way the first major industrial economy was built. By modern standards it was small and archaic, and its archaism still marks Britain today. By the standards of 1848 it was monumental, though also rather shocking, for its new cities were uglier, its proletariat worse off, than elsewhere, and the fog-bound, smoke-laden atmosphere in which pale masses hurried to and fro troubled the foreign visitor. But it harnessed the power of a million horses in its steam-engines, turned out two million yards of cotton cloth per year on over seventeen million mechanical spindles, dug almost fifty million tons of coal, imported and exported £170 millions worth of goods in a single year. Its trade was twice that of its nearest competitor, France: in 1780 it had only just exceeded it. Its cotton consumption was twice that of the USA, four times the French. It produced more than half the total pig-iron of the economically developed world, and used twice as much per inhabitant as the next-most industrialized country (Belgium), three times as much as the USA, more than four times as much as France. Between £200 and £300 million of British capital investment—a quarter in the USA, almost a fifth in Latin America—brought back dividends and orders from all parts of the world. It was, in fact, the 'workshop of the world.'

And both Britain and the world knew that the Industrial Revolution launched in these islands by and through the traders and entrepreneurs, whose only law was to buy in the cheapest market and sell without restriction in the dearest, was transforming the world. Nothing could stand in its way. The gods and kings of the past were powerless before the businessmen and steam-engines of the present.

10. The Industrial Revolution's Effect on Living Standards

PHYLLIS DEANE

The process of industrialization is only one issue in understanding the Industrial Revolution. Of equal importance is the effect of the Industrial Revolution on the standard of living of the workers, for it was this which gave rise to various protest movements in the nineteenth century. It has not been easy, however, for historians to determine the effect of the Industrial Revolution on the standard of living. Although they can agree that the living standard rose in the long run, they disagree about its direction in the early stages of industrialization. Since the Industrial Revolution, some historians, usually called "optimists," have argued that the standard of living rose even in the early stages while others, usually called "pessimists," have insisted that it fell in that period. "Optimists" and "pessimists," have disagreed, in part, because they have tended to use different kinds of evidence. "Optimists" have preferred quantitative data on wages, food consumption, and birth and death rates— data capable of being converted into cost-of-living and wage indices. "Pessimists" have found their case better served by the qualitative accounts written by eyewitnesses investigating early conditions in factories and mines.

This selection, from a book by Phyllis Deane of Cambridge University, deals exclusively with the quantitative data of wages, consumption, mortality, and distribution of national income. Her book and David Landes's The Unbound Prometheus *(1969) are the two most highly acclaimed recent books*

Source: Phyllis Deane, *The First Industrial Revolution* (Cambridge: Cambridge University Press, 1965), pp. 237–53. Reprinted by permission of the author and publisher. [Footnotes omitted.]

on the Industrial Revolution. Deane's approach here, it needs to be remembered, concerns only that material evidence which has always best supported the case of the "optimists." Only in her introduction does she describe the nonmaterial evidence, discussed briefly by Hobsbawm in the preceding selection, which relates to the oppressiveness of child and woman labor, the psychological shock of adapting from handwork to the time clock and factory discipline, sanitary and moral conditions in the growing cities, and the generally recognized—at least short-run—deterioration of family life and leisure. These factors meant that even an improvement in the material living standard could not prevent the rise of social discontent. A fall in that standard, of course, would further heighten social unrest. But, did the material living standard rise, stagnate, or fall? What answers to that question does Deane give us from the data on per capita income of the period? From death rates? From wages? From standards of consumption? From distribution of the work force? From national income estimates? What was the effect of such factors as war, crop failures, unemployment, and urbanization on those data? Finally, why and how does she distinguish three periods— 1780–1820, 1820–1840, and the post-1840 period? What was the character of the material standard of living in each of those periods in relation to the other periods?

Economic growth and economic change involve an expansion of the flow of goods and services produced in the economy and change in its composition. One way of assessing the achievements of an industrial revolution therefore is to measure its consequences in terms of their effects on standards of living. It might be expected that the process of industrial revolution, bringing with it, as it does, a great lowering in costs of production both in agriculture and industry, a perceptible reduction in the amount of human effort required to produce a given unit of output and a consequent increase in the flow of goods and services available for consumption would automatically involve a corresponding rise in the standard of living of the working man. Whether or not it does have these consequences, however, depends on a variety of circumstances, not least of which is the rate of population growth. It is rapidly becoming apparent in today's newly developing countries, for example, that even assuming a fairly brisk rate of technological progress in industry it is only too easy for the number of mouths to be fed to multiply more rapidly than productivity per person in active employment, and hence for the average standard of consumption to fall. If the rising population is due, as it frequently is, to a higher birth rate or a lower infant mortality rate it brings with it a larger *dependent* population and a smaller *proportion* of the total population in active employment. And if technical change begins, as it frequently does, in industries employing a relatively small section of the labour force rather than in, say, agriculture in which a majority of the labour force is engaged, it will have to be very rapid indeed to raise the output of goods and services fast enough to compensate for these factors which are tending to depress average consumption levels. Moreover, if there are important discontinuities in the development process such that the growth of new kinds of industry requires substantial initial expenditures on new capital assets (buildings, harbours, roads, canals, railway-lines, ships and vehicles, plant and machinery) before incomes begin to rise, current consumption may actually have to be reduced so that funds can be diverted to these capital expenditures.

In effect, the evidence suggests that some countries have experienced a period of what has been called a 'swarming' of the population in their early stages of industrialization, a period within which the numbers of the people increased faster than productivity and the flow of consumer goods *per head* actually declined for a time. It is therefore of special interest to ask ourselves whether the English experience included such a period and, if so, when it occurred.

Actually it is quite difficult to produce a conclusive answer to this question and in fact one of the most persistent controversies in the history of the industrial revolution is the argument that has raged around the workers' standard of living. Two schools of thought have grown up in connection with this topic. The pessimistic view, held by a long line of observers from contemporaries of the process to modern historians—by Engels, Marx, Toynbee, the Webbs, the Hammonds and a host of others, more recently Dr. Hobsbawm—is that the early stage of industrialization in England, though it brought affluence to some, caused a net deterioration in the standard of living of the labouring poor. The optimistic view, put forward by an equally long line of observers—by McCulloch, Tooke, Giffen, Clapham, Ashton and more recently Dr. Hartwell—is that although economic change left some workers displaced and distressed, the majority of them were enabled by falling prices, more regular employment and a wider range of earning opportunities to enjoy a rising standard of living.

The controversy has been muddied by political prejudice and the myopic views to which prejudice so often gives rise. It is common to find left-wing writers, their sympathies strongly engaged by the sufferings of the proletariat, holding the pessimistic view; and is equally common to find right-wing writers, more confident of the blessings assured by free capitalistic enterprise, holding the optimistic view. Engels, whose *Condition of the Working Class in England* (originally published in 1844 and recently translated by Henderson and Chaloner) is one of the most vivid and angry denunciations of the factory system, makes no bones about his political motives. In a letter written to Karl Marx he called his book 'a bill of indictment.' 'At the bar of world opinion,' he wrote, 'I charge the English middle classes with mass murder, wholesale robbery, and all the other crimes in the calendar.' The theory of deterioration was buttressed by a somewhat legendary picture of the golden age that was supposed to have preceded the industrial revolution—an England of happy prosperous yeomen and independent domestic craftsmen free from exploitation and care. But in fact the domestic outworker was no less exploited by the master-manufacturer who supplied his family with cotton to spin, or yarn to weave, than the factory worker by the owner: and women and children

145

Deane

THE INDUSTRIAL
REVOLUTION AND
LIVING
STANDARDS

often worked as long hours at the laborious process of domestic industry as they ever did at the factory machines.

The argument has been further complicated by the introduction of 'moral' and 'aesthetic' and other non-economic considerations. The Hammonds, for example, inveighed against the 'curse of Midas.'

> Thus England asked for profits and received profits. Everything turned to profit. The towns had their profitable dirt, their profitable slums, their profitable smoke, their profitable disorder, their profitable ignorance, their profitable despair. . . . For the new town was not a home where man could find beauty, happiness, leisure, learning, religion, the influences that civilize outlook and habit, but a bare and desolate place, without colour, air or laughter, where man, woman and child worked, ate and slept. . . . The new factories and the new furnaces were like the Pyramids, telling of man's enslavement rather than of his power, casting their long shadow over the society that took such pride in them.

There is room for a good deal more sociological research on the social consequences of the industrial revolution, but many of the political and moral assessments are highly subjective. The argument has its parallel today in the modern controversy about whether or not we should seek to bring backward village communities, with their relatively simple scale of wants and pattern of activities, into the rough impersonal competition of a market economy. It is not at all a meaningless problem from the social point of view, though it is not easy to discuss it objectively. But even if we refuse to be drawn into philosophical or moral arguments about whether the workers actually involved in the social and economic upheavals of the industrial revolution grew happier or more civilized, there remains a considerable area of legitimate controversy about whether their material standard of living rose, stagnated or fell.

Here again, as with most of the problems of economic history which are concerned with establishing the facts of growth or decline, or the turning-points which mark their beginning or end, the doubt arises because the historical record is incomplete; in particular the quantitative data are too few or too scattered or too selective to be conclusive. We are again obliged to reconstruct a picture in which various crucial pieces of the jigsaw are missing and to guess at what it means.

Consider, for example, the evidence for a rising standard of living for the working population over the controversial period 1775–1850, within which we can assume that the English industrial revolution largely took place. I have already discussed the evidence on national income. If we juxtapose the contemporary estimates by Arthur Young for 1770 and various authors in the first two decades of the nineteenth century they actually suggest a decline in real incomes per head up to, at any rate, the immediate aftermath of the Napoleonic Wars. But we are justified in regarding these estimates sceptically. They are not strong enough to take the weight of analysis. Attempts to trace the course of total national output on the basis of incomplete production series are more convincing. They suggest a rise which may perhaps date from the 1740's in overall terms and probably accelerated in per-head terms in the last quarter of the eighteenth century under the influence of strongly expanding overseas markets. An index of British industrial production which has been compiled by the German scholar Hoffman, and which is also of necessity heavily dependent on the foreign-trade series, suggest a similar movement. It shows a rate of growth of total *industrial* output averaging under one percent per annum in the first three quarters of the eighteenth century, rising abruptly to over 3 percent per annum in the 1780's and early 1790's, falling back in the period 1793–1817 (probably as a consequence of the war) and recovering to levels of over 3 percent again after 1817.

On the face of it then, we might say that since the evidence points on the whole to an increase in national output per head of the population, beginning probably in the 1780's, muted by the French and Napoleonic Wars and resuming strongly at the end of the second decade of the nineteenth century, it implies a rising standard of living on the average. Actually, whether it does or not depends on whether there were significant changes in the distribution of the national income. It may be that all the value of the increase in national output accrued to the upper income groups—to the mill-owners and the iron-masters, for example, rather than to the workers. Or it may be that the growth in marketed output of corn or meat, say, due to the enclosures, accrued to a small group of owner-farmers, while the cottagers were evicted from their food plots and deprived of the common pasture for cow and pig to become a distressed agricultural proletariat. It is possible for national output to rise faster than population and for the standard of living of the majority of the people to fall because a few people are monopolizing the results of the increase or because the new goods are not consumption goods but capital goods.

147

Deane

THE INDUSTRIAL
REVOLUTION AND
LIVING
STANDARDS

One might also say, of course, as many holders of the 'optimistic' view have said, that the evidence for a sharp decrease in mortality at the end of the eighteenth century points to a rise in the standard of living. If people were becoming more resistant to disease this could have been either because medical skills were improving or because they were living better. The medical historians, however, have discounted the evidence for striking medical advances which could have had this result and they fall back on the view that 'there was a general advance in the standard of living in consequence of the economic developments of the period.' Here again there is a problem of distribution to be taken into account, though in this case it is a question of distribution through time. As Hobsbawm has pointed out:

> It should be remembered that the decrease in mortality which is probably primarily responsible for the sharp rise in population need be due not to an *increase* in per capita consumption per year but to a greater *regularity of supply:* that is, to the abolition of the peri-

odic shortages and famines which plagued pre-industrial economies and decimated their populations. It is quite possible for the industrial citizen to be worse fed in a normal year than his predecessor, so long as he is more regularly fed.

To this improvement in the temporal flow of incomes, investment in communications (better roads, canals, etc.) and regular marketing of foodstuffs may have contributed more than increased productivity in industry or increases in output per acre.

However, the most striking feature of the mortality figures, if we try to use them as an index of standards of living, is that they show the decline in the death rate to have been arrested, probably even reversed, in the period when the industrial revolution was in full swing and began notably to affect the way of life of a majority of the population. Death rates estimated from burial figures reached an average of 35.8 per 1000 in the 1730's and then fell steadily (with an interruption in the 1770's, when there was a slight rise) to reach an average of 21.1 per 1000 in the decade 1811–20. This was an impressive achievement. Then, however, they began to rise again to reach 23.4 in the decade 1831–40 and remained more or less constant at over 22 per 1000 (these are the official figures based on registrations) in the 1840's, 1850's, and 1860's.

The main reason for the rise in the national death rate in the early nineteenth century was the influx of people into the towns which had a high, and in some cases a rising, death rate. The average death rate of the five largest towns outside London (Birmingham, Bristol, Leeds, Liverpool and Manchester) rose from 20.7 in 1831 to 30.8 in 1841. For Liverpool parish the death rate for the decade 1841–50 averaged 39.2 per 1000 and in Manchester it was 33.1. The fact is that the towns had been outgrowing the existing technology of urban living. 'Over half the deaths were caused by infectious diseases alone. . . . Infant diseases, product of dirt, ignorance, bad feeding and overcrowding swept one in two of all the children born in towns out of life before the age of five.' As the towns expanded over the countryside and the population living in their centres multiplied, the existing sanitation systems became so inadequate as to be a growing menace to health. 'Street sewers were immense brick caverns, flat bottomed and flat sided, washed only by a feeble trickle of water,' and cleared by excavation of the streets every 5–10 years. In some cases town sewage was allowed to flow into the rivers from which the water companies were taking their water supply. It took a series of cholera epidemics and some alarming sanitary inquiries to persuade central and local authorities to take positive action to clean filth from the streets and courts, to adopt piped sanitation, and to make the private water-companies chlorinate their water supplies. Meanwhile it is fair to say that in most urban areas the human environment was deteriorating perceptibly through the first half of the nineteenth century and that it probably did not begin to improve generally until the 1870's and 1880's.

To probe more directly the question whether the standard of living of the working classes rose or fell in the course of the Industrial Revolution we need to look at the data on wages. What can we deduce from the way the real incomes of the workers moved over the period of early industrialization? Here the problem of interpreting the incomplete record is twofold—whose wages should we consider and how are we to allow for changes in the value of money?

First of all then, whose wages? For the data do not permit us to compile a national wage bill which might give a measure of overall average earnings from employment. All that is available is a somewhat heterogeneous mass of wage quotations for particular industries, occupations and regions which economists and economic historians may or may not have been able to combine into meaningful aggregates. In general, of course, the wages of workers in industry were higher than those in agriculture, so that as the proportion in industrial employment rose, the average money-wage probably grew. In the expanding industries wages sometimes rose spectacularly; and, conversely, for craftsmen made redundant by mechanization they sometimes fell equally spectacularly. Take cotton, for example. Manchester cotton weavers were earning 7s. to 10s. a week when Arthur Young toured the north of England in 1769—*before* the spinning-jenny provided them with enough yarn to keep their looms going constantly. By 1792, made scarce by the enormous quantities of yarn which the spinning-machines made available, they were earning 15s. to 20s. a week. But these boom wages did not last long. The supply of weavers proved highly elastic and the labour market was soon flooded with them. Their bargaining-power fell steeply. By 1800 'a good workman working 14 hours a day was hardly able to earn 5s. or 6s. between one Sunday and the next.'

Clearly the wage data for specific occupations or industries may shed little or no light on the movement of wages over wide areas of the economy. And as far as the eighteenth-century wage data are concerned there is the additional problem that there was no really integrated national market for labour until the very end of the century. In effect, the outstanding characteristic of eighteenth-century wage history was the existence of wide regional variations in both levels and trends. In Lancashire, for example, the money wages of builders' labourers almost doubled between the 1750's and early 1790's. In London they seem to have risen by less than 5 percent; and in Oxfordshire the increase was of the order of 15 percent. Actually there was a marked narrowing of the regional wage differentials before the end of the eighteenth century, and by the late 1780's Lancashire building labourers whose earning had been two-thirds of the London average in the 1750's were earning about 9s. a week compared with about 8s. 6d. in London and about 9s. 6d. in Oxfordshire.

Of course the typical wage-earner in the late eighteenth century was not the labourer in industry but the labourer in agriculture. Bowley's figures of agricultural earnings suggest that the average agricultural wage increased by something like 25 percent between the late 1760's and 1795. The rise was most marked in the Yorkshire Ridings, Lancashire, Nor-

149

Deane

THE INDUSTRIAL
REVOLUTION AND
LIVING
STANDARDS

thumberland and Staffordshire where the increase exceeded 50 percent; but over a very large part of eastern, middle and southern England in the second half of the eighteenth century agricultural wages seem to have been in a state of relative stagnation similar to that which characterized the London building-trades for this period. When war with France broke out in the early 1790's, however, the economy rapidly moved into a state of relatively full employment and money wages in agriculture soared. Before the end of the Napoleonic Wars a 'national' index of money wages, calculated by combining Wood's index of average money wages in towns with Bowley's index of money wages in agriculture, showed an increase of about 75 percent.

On the other hand if money wages rose steeply over this war period 1792–1815, prices rose even more. For this was a period of galloping wartime inflation. Which brings us to our second major problem of interpretation, the problem of allowing for changes in the value of money. In order to get some measure of the change in the standard of living we must form some view of the movement of *real* wages; that is, to adjust money wages so as to eliminate the effect of the upward movement in prices.

What I have said about the regional variations in the price of eighteenth-century labour applies also to the prices of commodities at this period—sometimes to an even greater extent. For eighteenth-century England in which it took 10–12 days to travel from London to Edinburgh (that was in the 1750's), when the price of coal could vary from 15*s*. a chaldron to over £3 a chaldron according to distance from the pits (this was true even in the 1790's), and when the wages of a building craftsman could vary from 2*s*. to 3*s*. a day according to the region in which he operated, there is no satisfactory way of constructing a general price index which could reflect changes in the value of money for the economy as a whole. Each region had its own price history and its own set of price relationships. Even if we knew enough about the prices of each region to construct a true national average it is doubtful what meaning we could attribute to the result.

On the other hand it is certain that there were important changes in the value of money during the latter part of the eighteenth century and these changes must have had their effect on prices. By the 1790's (probably by the 1760's) the majority of prices had developed an upward trend. Until after the Napoleonic Wars, however—possibly until the beginning of the railway age—the movements of individual prices are so divergent and so variable that the attempt to measure the changes in the form of a general price index is a dubious procedure. Moreover in a period of violent inflation—such as that which developed in the last decade of the eighteenth century when the cumulative effects of a rapidly rising population, a succession of poor harvests and an expensive war drove up the price of many foodstuffs—price indices based on weights relevant to a less disturbed period do not adequately reflect changes in the value of money. This is because they do not take account of the fact that consumers look for substitutes for goods whose prices have soared. They substitute goods which are less vulnerable to harvest and war crises and their standard of living does not fall to the extent that it would have done if they had obstinately persisted in their old patterns of comsumption.

So far I have been considering the conceptual difficulties of constructing price indices that might enable one to allow for changes in the purchasing power of money and so to convert money wages to 'real' wages. But it goes without saying that there are formidable data problems too. We don't have all the price data we need for this purpose. Most of the prices that are regularly available for the period of the industrial revolution relate to commodities which tended to be particularly vulnerable to trade dislocations and harvest crises. In particular they seldom cover the prices of manufactured goods (many of which were reduced by the falling costs associated with industrialization) or of rent, which is generally a fairly steady price even in inflation. And they are rich in the prices of foodstuffs and imported goods, which tended to rise sharply when harvest failure or war made them temporarily scarce. To some extent this bias is inevitable, for it was the vulnerable prices which contemporaries chose to collect and publish regularly and which are accordingly still on record. But it means, of course, that indices based on these selective quotations tend to exaggerate the movements in the general price level and become difficult to use as indications of changes in the value of money during periods of inflation.

The result is that when we try to take out from the wage data the effects of the price rises due to harvest crises and war shortages we completely wipe out any improvement in money wages and it then looks as though average real wages were declining over the period 1782 to 1815. Perhaps indeed they were. When we also bear in mind the burden of war—the British people paid heavy subsidies to their continental allies, one in ten of the labour force was absorbed in the unproductive employment of the armed forces and the growth of industries producing for peacetime markets slackened perceptibly—it is not difficult to believe that consumption standards were actually falling. On the other hand when one takes into account the fact that total war involved full employment of adult males, while the spread of the factory system and the expansion of agricultural acreages widened the employment opportunities for women and children, it seems likely that the decline in the standard of living of the typical working-class family—if decline there was—was less drastic than the wage-price data might lead one to believe.

After the war, however, inflation turned to deflation and the picture changes. Average money-wages declined and so did prices. Within ten years (i.e. between 1816 and 1824, again using the Bowley-Wood indices of agricultural and urban earnings combined into a national average) money wages had fallen by more than 10 percent: by the 1840's the fall was 15 percent. Prices, however, fell faster and at first glance we might deduce that the purchasing power of the worker's wage rose. For the longer period, up to about mid-nineteenth century, this certainly seems to

151
Deane
THE INDUSTRIAL
REVOLUTION AND
LIVING
STANDARDS

be the most plausible interpretation of the data. But for the distressed years of the immediate post-war aftermath when the demobilized soldiers and seamen flooded the labour market and the industries which had thrived in war were facing a slump in demand, it is likely that higher real wages earned by those who were lucky enough to be in regular employment were insufficient to compensate for the loss of earnings experienced by the unemployed or the underemployed. In the tense years between Waterloo in 1815 and the massacre of Peterloo in 1819 it has been said that England was nearer to social revolution than at any other time in her history. It seems probable that the real earnings of the average working-class family were lower in these years than they had been in the 1780's.

Thereafter the evidence for a rise in the average real wage becomes more convincing. It does not become absolutely conclusive because we do not know the incidence of unemployment. In years, in regions or in sectors of the economy where there was trade depression the evidence of acute poverty is overwhelming. But there are three plausible presumptions in favour of a rising standard of living, on the whole, after the end of the war: (1) that as industrialization gathered momentum in the 1820's employment became more rather than less regular than it had been in pre-war years; (2) that the goods that tended to be omitted from the price indices, being largely manufactured goods, were more likely to be falling in price than the goods (largely raw materials) that were included— and hence of course that the price indices understated the post-war price fall; and (3) that the falling weight of taxation would, in a period when most taxes were indirect and hence regressive, give perceptible relief to the working classes.

Actually the conviction of the 'optimists' grows stronger for years towards the end of the controversial period than for periods towards the beginning. Professor Ashton for example is most confident about the period after 1820. 'Let me confess, therefore, at the start,' he says, 'that I am of those who believe that all in all, conditions of labour were becoming better, *at least after 1820,* and that the spread of the factory played a not inconsiderable part in the improvement.' Most observers agree that the 1790's, with war, harvest failures and a rapidly increasing population, was a tragic period for English labour. Clapham, another of the optimists, calls 1795, the year when the Speenhamland system was introduced to augment men's wages out of the rates, 'the blackest year,' and goes on to conclude that,

> whereas on the average the potential standard of comfort of an English . . . rural labouring family in 1824 was probably a trifle better than it had been in 1794, assuming equal regularity of work, there were important areas in which it was definitely worse, others in which it was probably worse, and many in which the change either way was imperceptible. In the bad areas the rates were drawn upon for the deficit.

Not even the most convinced 'optimists' have claimed that working-class standards of living improved perceptibly during the French wars or their immediate aftermath, though full employment financed by income-tax may well have involved some transfer of incomes from rich to poor. On the other hand even the pessimists will allow that perceptible improvements in working-class standards of living set in in the 1840's.

In effect then we can narrow down the area of fiercest controversy to the 1820's and 1830's. Here the data on wage-rates and prices suggest a rising real wage, though not a very great improvement. Between 1820 and 1840, for example, the Bowley-Wood wage data suggest a fall of 10 percent in money wages: and the Gayer-Rostow-Schwartz price index suggests a fall of about 12 percent in prices. Professor Phelps Brown's index of builders' wage rates, expressed in terms of the basket of consumers' goods they might buy, suggests an improvement of about 5 percent over the same period. Now if we assume, as the pessimists do, that 'the period 1811–1842 saw abnormal problems and abnormal unemployment,' then the irregularity of work could easily have outweighed these rather feeble improvements in real incomes suggested by the wage/price data. On the other hand if we assume, as the optimists do, that the price indices understate the price fall (and hence the rise in purchasing power of wages) because they omit the commodities whose prices were influenced most strongly by the cost reductions of the industrial revolution, then we would argue that the wage/price data are only a pale reflection of the true rise in the standard of living. Without a great deal more research in the areas of doubt—the incidence of unemployment for example and the rise in the value of money—it is impossible to resolve this problem, though on the whole the evidence for an improvement in standards seems stronger than the evidence for a fall at this period.

153

Deane

THE INDUSTRIAL
REVOLUTION AND
LIVING
STANDARDS

Nor indeed can we say much about standards of consumption more directly. Figures of imports of tea, sugar and tobacco for example show very little rise (in some cases there are declines) over the controversial period, and the current pessimists' case rests a good deal on this negative evidence. Unfortunately these imported commodities were not consumed in large quantities by the average family and were subject to import duties which made important differences to the rate of consumption. For sugar there is evidence of a stagnant, even a falling consumption: from 29½ lb. per head in 1811 to 15 lb. per head in 1840. For tea there is evidence of a rise from about 1 lb. per head in 1811 (when, however, the duty paid was 4s. per head) to about 1½ lb. in 1841 (when the duty had fallen to under 3s. per head). Consumption of tobacco, on the other hand, went down from 19 oz. per head in 1811 to about 14½ in 1841, but the duty had gone up and no one knows how much tobacco was smuggled in. These consumption figures are inconclusive in their implications therefore, and we have no reliable estimates of the consumption of more important items of working-class expenditure, of bread for example, of milk or meat or butter or eggs. True there are figures of beasts slaughtered at Smithfield market but these are for numbers only, they make no allowance for changes in average weight and they are incomplete even as an index of London consumption, for we have no information on the trade in other London meat-markets.

To sum up, then, what conclusions can we draw from all this? The first is that there is no firm evidence for an overall improvement in working-class standards of living between about 1780 and about 1820. Indeed, if we take into account the harvest failures, growing population, the privations of a major war and the distress of the post-war economic dislocation, we may reasonably conclude that on balance average standards of living tended to fall rather than to rise.

For the period from about 1820 to about 1840 it is difficult to be as definite. Certainly there is no evidence for a substantial rise in real incomes and what rise we can deduce from the statistics is not strong enough to compensate for the wide margins of error in the data. On the other hand the evidence for a fall in standards of living rests *either* on presumptions that we cannot empirically check with the information now accessible to us—like the incidence of unemployment, for example—*or* on data on actual consumption per head of certain not very important commodities whose consumption could as well be attributed to changes in tastes or the weight of duties as to a fall in real incomes. Perhaps on balance the optimists can make out a more convincing case for an improvement in the standard of living than the pessimists can for a fall. But either case is based largely on circumstantial evidence and there is one thing that we can take as reasonably certain—and that is that whichever way it went, the net change was relatively slight.

Finally, beginning in the 1840's we find much stronger evidence of an improvement in the average real incomes of the working class, evidence that has been strong enough to convince even some of the remaining pessimists. It does not rest however on a perceptible increase in real wage rates. Habakkuk, for example, observes that 'The inconclusive nature of the current debate about living standards in this period is perhaps a warrant for supposing that a substantial and general and demonstrable rise in the real wages of industrial workers did not occur until the 1850's and 1860's: it was not until about 1870 that real wages in agriculture began to rise and a steady rise was apparent only in the 1880's.' The argument for an improvement in the average standard of living in the middle of the century rests largely on a change in the composition of the labour force. To quote Hobsbawm, the most recent of the advocates of the pessimistic interpretation of the industrial revolution:

> Little as we know about the period before the middle forties, most students would agree that the real sense of improvement among the labouring classes thereafter was due less to a rise in wage-rates, which often remained surprisingly stable for years, or to an improvement in social conditions, but to the upgrading of labourers from very poorly to less poorly paid jobs, and above all to a decline in unemployment or to a greater regularity of employment.

This shift in the distribution of the labour force from the traditional highly seasonal occupations characteristic of a pre-industrial economy to the modern sector with its mechanical aids to labour, its disciplined working habits and its continuous intensive use of capital equipment in day and night shifts is the true spirit and essence of an industrial revolution. Agricultural labourers, for example, normally earn less per week than factory workers of equivalent skill; hand-loom weavers earn less than power-loom weavers; canal bargemen less than locomotive drivers. Thus a shift in the composition of the labour force—a fall in the *proportion* of workers engaged in the low earning categories and a corresponding rise in the proportion of those in the high earning categories—would raise the average level of earnings per worker even if wage-rates in each occupation remained unchanged. This is the process that seems to have gathered momentum in the 1840's and to have brought with it perceptible improvements in material standards of life for the working classes. It may indeed have begun earlier, but it is not until the 1840's that we can be reasonably certain of its positive effects.

So much for the wage data. What about the national-income estimates? These suggest that between 1801 and 1851 national product per head at constant prices almost doubled. As between the pre-war period (say 1791) and 1851 the improvement was probably somewhat less, for 1801 was already a year of heavy inflation. In the controversial period between 1821 and 1841, however, there was an improvement, it seems, of over a third. Whether this meant a corresponding increase in the average real incomes of the working classes, however, would have depended on the way the increase in the national product was distributed. If the increase in incomes was entirely absorbed by the property-owning classes in the form of profits and rent, and if the increased output of foods and services took the form either of capital goods or of goods and services that were outside the normal budget of the wage-earners, then it is fair to presume that the employed population gained nothing from the process of early industrialization.

155

Deane

THE INDUSTRIAL
REVOLUTION AND
LIVING
STANDARDS

To some extent it is undoubtedly true that there was a shift in the distribution of incomes in favour of profits and rent and a change in the composition of output in favour of capital goods, exports and goods and services for upper-class consumption. But it is manifest that this is not the whole story. The new factories were not producing entirely for the export or the luxury trade or for producers, and the fact that prices of manufactured consumer-goods fell substantially meant that the working classes gained as consumers where they did not gain as wage-earners. So that while on balance the evidence is strongly in favour of the view that working-class standards of living improved by less than the increase in national income per head would suggest over the first half of the nineteenth century; and while there is no doubt that certain sectors of the labouring poor suffered a serious deterioration in their earning-power because they were made redundant by technical progress, nevertheless it would be difficult to credit an overall decline in real incomes per wage-earning family in a period when aggregate real incomes for the nation as a whole were growing appreciably faster than population. In effect the sustained growth of national product to which industrialization gave rise tended to exert an upward pressure on working-class standards of living in three main ways, none of which implied a rise in the price of labour: (1) by creating more regular employment opportunities for all members of the family—this meant high earnings per year and per family even without a rise in wages per man-hour worked; (2) by creating more opportunities for labour specialization and hence for the higher earnings that semi-skilled or skilled labour can command: here again the average earnings can rise without an increase in the wage rate because the composition of the labour force changes in favour of the higher earning group; and (3) the upward pressure on the workers' standard of living also operated through the reductions in the prices of consumer goods and the widening of the range of commodities which come within the budget of the working classes. Finally of course, to the extent that it raised real purchasing power for the masses, industrialization expanded the market for manufactured goods and so justified further increases in investment and output.

11. The Pattern of Urban Revolution in 1848

WILLIAM L. LANGER

The Age of Revolution that began in the late eighteenth century ended with the Revolutions of 1848. Unlike the revolutions at the beginning of the age, the ones in 1848 were neither Atlantic nor merely French. Instead, they occurred throughout most of western and central Europe and constituted almost a European-wide demand for liberal or democratic constitutions, social reform and, especially in central Europe, national states. Unlike the French Revolution of 1789, however, the ones in 1848 met with unrelieved defeat. By 1851 France had a second Bonapartist empire instead of the democratic or social republic it had wanted in 1848. The Austrian empire ended up with the centralized repression of the Bach system instead of the liberalism, federalism, or independence its various peoples had fought for. Italy and Germany eventually achieved national unification, so desired in 1848 by some, but it came at the hands of Cavour and Bismarck instead of through the democratic or liberal process. Of all the major states or regions only Britain had been spared revolution and, if it did not win the democracy championed by the Chartists in 1848, it at least moved peaceably in that direction. The failure of the 1848 Revolutions, if we are to believe the memorable phrase of George Macaulay Trevelyan, marked "a turning point at which modern history failed to turn."

This selection, by the eminent diplomatic historian William L. Langer,

Source: William L. Langer, "The Pattern of Urban Revolution in 1848" in Evelyn M. Acomb and Marvin L. Brown, ed., *French Society and Culture Since the Old Regime* (New York: Holt, Rinehart and Winston, 1966), pp. 90–118. Copyright © 1966 by Holt, Rinehart and Winston, Inc. Reprinted by permission of the publisher. [Footnotes omitted.]

examines that failure. Professor Langer is chief editor of the prestigious multi-volume Rise of Modern Europe *series and he recently contributed to it the monumental volume on the 1832–1848 period. The previous selections on the French Revolution of 1789 in this anthology looked at revolution from the standpoint of its proponents, the revolutionary bourgeoisie and the crowd. Much of the work on the 1848 Revolutions centers on the same groups and forces, even though, by 1848, the bourgeoisie and crowd had been modified by early industrialization. Langer, however, looks at the 1848 Revolutions from the standpoint of the ruling elites or regimes in terms of what we today might call counterinsurgency, pacification, or riot control. He regrets that the revolutions took place at all. It would have been better had the regimes been resilient enough to reform without revolution or to have repressed the revolutions efficiently, that is, with the smallest amount of bloodshed at the earliest possible moment. What, according to Langer, were the conditions which created "chronic social tension" in the crowded cities of nineteenth-century Europe? What options for combating urban disorder did European governments have in the 1840s? What was the composition of the revolutionary crowds? Where did the propertied middle classes stand in the various revolutionary movements? How did they contribute to the revolutionary energies of the crowd? How was revolution prevented in London, one of Langer's four case studies? Why in the other three cases—Paris, Vienna, and Berlin—did the authorities both fail to prevent revolution and respond to it badly, if Britain was so successful? What should Paris, Vienna, and Berlin have done? In sum, why does Langer believe these revolutions to have been both unnecessary and undesired?*

Although the centennial celebrations of 1948 spawned many publications and brought into new relief many aspects of the European upheavals of the mid-nineteenth century, relatively little attention has been devoted to the comparative study of these revolutions. The objective of this essay is to examine the outbreaks of February and March 1848 so as to determine what, if anything, they had in common, and to raise the question whether these famous revolutions were inevitable or even beneficial.

Although there were disturbances in the countryside as well as in many cities, the events in the four great capitals, Paris, Vienna, Berlin, and London, were crucial. It is true that these government centers had been but little touched by the new industrialism and that therefore the proletariat of the factories played but a very subordinate rôle, especially in the early days of the revolutions. Yet the capitals were the seats of traditional industry, with a huge population of craftsmen, tradesmen, and specialized workers of all kinds. London and Paris, in particular, harbored thousands of different industries without having much of a modern industrial proletariat. The workers were mostly what might be termed *menu peuple* (lesser bourgeoisie).

This does not mean that the capital cities were less restless than the new factory towns. In all of them life had become unsettled and precarious, for everywhere the traditional artisan was exposed to the competition of machine industry, located chiefly in the provincial towns. Wages, if they did not actually decline, remained low, while employment became steadily more uncertain. The plight of the urban workers following the economic crisis of 1846–1847 is well known and its bearing on the revolutions of 1848 has been duly stressed by Professor Labrousse and others. Basically it was inevitable that the early stages of industrialization should have brought instability and hardship, but the situation in mid-century was greatly aggravated by the fantastic growth of the European population; this growth entailed an unprecedented movement of rural workers to the cities, which for centuries had held the promise of opportunity.

In the years from 1800 to 1850 the growth of the European capitals was stupendous, with the result that at the end of the period a large proportion of the population was not native born. It consisted largely of immigrants, permanent or temporary, coming either from nearby areas, or from abroad. In the 1840s alone about 250,000 persons came into London, 46,000 of whom were Irishmen, who were particularly disliked and feared by the English workers because of their incredibly low standard of living. In addition, there were substantial numbers of Belgian and German workers.

As for Paris, the researches of Louis Chevalier and others have thrown a flood of light on the nature of the population and the conditions of life. The number of inhabitants just about doubled between 1800 and 1850, due very largely to immigration. Thus, between 1831 and 1836 about 115,000 arrived, and from 1841 to 1846 another 98,000. Most of the newcomers were from the neighboring *départements,* but there were many foreigners as well. Accurate statistics are lacking, but there appear to have been upward of 50,000 Germans (mostly tailors, shoemakers, cabinetmakers) in Paris, to say nothing of large numbers of Belgian and Italian workers and sizable contingents of political refugees from many lands.

The situation in Vienna and Berlin was much the same. The population of the Austrian capital numbered about 400,000, 125,000 of whom had been added between 1827 and 1847. In 1845 there were some 130,000 Czech, Polish, and Italian immigrants. In Berlin the population rose from 180,000 to 400,000 between 1815 and 1847, due largely to the heavy immigration from the eastern provinces.

In all cities the steady influx of people created an acute housing shortage. This was less true of London than of the continental capitals, for there the government offices had long since moved from the Old City to Westminster and the well-to-do had built new homes in the West End and along the main highways to the west and northwest. The 125,000 people who still lived in the Old City were for the most part clerks, runners, cleaners, and other employees of the great banks and business houses. In the continental capitals, however, the exodus of the upper classes from the old central districts had only just begun. The new and fashionable sections of northwestern Paris were still far from complete, while the oldest part of the city was incredibly congested, "an almost impenetrable hive of tenements and shops." The efforts of Rambuteau, the *préfet* of the Seine, to open up the dingiest areas by constructing larger

159

Langer

THE PATTERN
OF URBAN
REVOLUTION
IN 1848

arteries, involved the destruction of much cheap housing, little of which was replaced elsewhere. Under the circumstances, rents rose rapidly. Most immigrant workers were lucky to find even miserable quarters in the center of the town or in the workers' sections of eastern Paris. "The difficulty of finding lodgings," wrote a contemporary, "is for the worker a constant ordeal and a perpetual cause of misery."

In Vienna and Berlin, as in Paris, a great many immigrant workers found refuge in the lodging houses, which enjoyed a golden age at this time. In the low-grade places men and women were housed together, and it was by no means uncommon for eight or nine persons to be crowded into one room. The old Innre Stadt of Vienna, still surrounded by its seventeenth-century walls, was so hopelessly congested that some members of the aristocracy were obliged, most reluctantly, to build new "villas" beyond the Kärntner Tor, while practically all industry, with the exception of the old-established silk trade, was compelled, by government decree, to locate in the suburbs. In Berlin, too, the rapidly developing textile and metallurgical industries were concentrated in the northern areas, while the upper classes lived mostly in the western and southwestern sections. Berlin was notorious for its wretched lodging houses and workers' barracks.

Considering the great instability of the changing social order, it is not surprising that many of the newcomers in the cities failed to find the hoped-for employment. Thousands were chronically out of work, reduced to living in dank cellars or unheated garrets, and often driven by desperation into robbery or other crimes. In Paris, as in most other cities, about a quarter of the population was indigent, dependent on government or private relief. The situation thus engendered was particularly dangerous because as yet in many cities the rich and poor lived cheek-by-jowl. The Paris apartment house, whose lower floors were occupied by the well-to-do while the *petite bourgeoisie* took over the upper stories and the paupers were left the crannies under the eaves, is familiar to us from Balzac's novels, but it must be remembered that in almost every part of Paris prosperous residential areas and pockets of slums were intermingled. There was no strictly aristocratic quarter and no strictly workingmen's quarter. Even in metropolitan London fashionable streets were often backed by abandoned "rookeries." Such existed even in the West End, in the vicinity of Buckingham Palace.

Overall conditions in the crowded cities of the early or mid-nineteenth century were such as to create chronic social tension. Riots by the hungry or unemployed were all too common, as were also clashes between native and foreign workers. It is obvious that these outbreaks could and at times did assume such proportions as to threaten governments, if not the entire social order.

To combat disturbances European governments had traditionally relied upon their military forces. Napoleon's "whiff of grapeshot" was an example of the use even of artillery in breaking up a hostile demonstration. More common, however, was the employment of sabre-charging cavalry. Nicholas I of Russia, though confronted with the most formidable and urgent social problem in Europe, escaped revolution in 1848 by ruthless application of these tactics. His internal defense force, quartered throughout the country, numbered some 200,000 men and beat down any threat of insurrection. The secret police and the Cossack brigades showed the world how to maintain order and vindicated Nicholas's claim to be the gendarme of Europe.

But in western Europe these methods of brutal repression had by the nineteenth century become as difficult to apply as they were objectionable. To ride or shoot down unarmed citizens was hardly the answer to political or social problems, to say nothing of the fact that conscripted soldiers showed ever greater unwillingness to fire upon the people. In Britain, where the problems created by the industrial revolution were most acute, the government had, before 1848, worked out a different procedure or policy. In connection with the very formidable and menacing Chartist demonstrations of 1839 and 1842 freedom of speech and assembly were generally respected, but the authorities made it perfectly clear that any effort to subvert the government or the social order would be ruthlessly suppressed. Furthermore, General Charles Napier, in charge of the forces in the industrial areas of the north, by adroitly placing his troops and by bringing additional soldiery from Ireland to ensure against defection, succeeded in creating a genuine deterrent.

As for London, much greater advances had been made in the direction of public security. In 1829 the first modern civil police force had been established, consisting of selected, uniformed, trained and well-paid constables numbering by 1848 about 5500 men. Despite much popular hostility, the London police soon made itself respected and indeed worked out the tactics of what today are called "riot control formations," that is, the organization and employment of squad or platoon wedges to penetrate mobs, arrest leaders, and break up demonstrations, and of echelons to pry rioters away from buildings and force them to move in specified directions.

161

Langer

THE PATTERN
OF URBAN
REVOLUTION
IN 1848

Chartist Demonstration in London

Some insight into the problems confronting continental governments in February and March 1848 can be gained by reviewing the great Chartist demonstration and petition scheduled for April 10 in London as the culmination of a series of disturbances in Glasgow, Manchester, and even in the capital that echoed the revolutionary events on the continent in the preceding weeks.

In the councils of the Chartist movement there were some who, as in 1839, favored revolutionary action and the use of violence in the event that the great petition were again rejected by parliament. But the majority of the leaders, long since convinced of the government's determination to suppress any attempt at insurrection, still hoped to attain their ends by peaceful demonstration. The plan then was to stage a monster meeting followed by the procession of thousands of workers to the House of Commons. The great day was to be April 10, when contingents of Chartists marched from various assembly points in the metropolis to Kennington Common, in southwestern London. When they gathered, at about 11:00 A.M., the police were already at hand. Feargus O'Connor, the leader, was warned that while the meeting itself was permissible, the law forbade large demonstrations designed to intimidate Parliament and that therefore the crowd would be permitted to recross the river only in small groups. O'Connor, a demagogue braver in words than in deeds, at once urged his followers to accept the police ruling. There was some speechmaking, but presently the whole meeting was washed out by rain. The demonstrators straggled back over Blackfriars Bridge, while the petition, with its millions of signatures, was taken to Parliament by a small delegation riding in three cabs. The day ended without even a window having been broken.

There is every reason to think that the London police could by itself have dealt with the Chartist demonstration. But the government had been unwilling to take the chance and had, with the full support of the propertied classes, made preparations far beyond anything the situation called for. The aged Duke of Wellington had been put in command of the troops, which were brought in from the surrounding areas. At the same time, a call was sent out for special constables, to which all respectable elements, from peers to business and professional men, down to clerks, railroad officials, shopkeepers, and others responded in great numbers. It is said, and was so reported in the *Times,* that no less than 150,000 of these constables were enrolled. They sand-bagged and garrisoned the Bank of England, the Post-Office, India House, and other valuable properties, while the troops, which were kept out of sight as much as possible, occupied the Tower and other strong points. On the river three ships were held in readiness, with steam up, to transport troops or supplies to any threatened spot. The Chartists, as they marched to their rendezvous, could hardly fail to notice the reception that awaited them in case of serious unrest.

So much certainly was to be learned from the London experience: 1) an efficient police force was capable of dealing with even large-scale demonstrations; 2) a government acceptable to the citizenry could count on the support of huge numbers of volunteers; 3) the troops could be kept in reserve, to be used only in an emergency; 4) a clean-cut policy and adequate preparations would serve as an effective deterrent. Harriet Martineau, in her account of the Kennington Common meeting, was not far off the mark when she declared exultantly: "From that day it was a settled matter that England was safe from revolution."

It is true, of course, that the British government had the advantage, in facing the Chartist threat, not only of previous experience but of the experience of the continental governments that had succumbed to revolution. Nonetheless, it will be useful to review the outbreak of insurrection in Paris, Vienna, and Berlin in the light of what could be and was done in another country in what were roughly comparable circumstances. For it is probably a mistake to argue that Britain, because it had no revolution in 1848, was in some mysterious way different and therefore exempt from major social ructions. If there was a great deal of talk of revolution on the continent in the years preceding 1848, there was hardly less of such talk in England. Friedrich Engels, it will be recalled, in 1845 held that social revolution was unavoidable.

The 1848 Revolution in Paris

The events of February 1848 in Paris, which ended with the downfall of the Orleans Monarchy, were conscientiously analyzed by M. Crémieux more than fifty years ago. They were far too complicated to be satisfactorily summarized in a brief essay. Certain features, however, should be highlighted. It is well known, for instance, that Louis Philippe and his chief minister, M. Guizot, were surprised by the insurrection by which they were overtaken. This surprise is at least understandable, for even though opposition to the regime had been mounting, it certainly did not suggest the possibility of a major upheaval. The opposition, insofar as it was organized and directed, was in the main a parliamentary opposition calling for very modest changes: liberalization of the electorate, limitation of political patronage, extension of civil liberties. It is hardly an exaggeration to describe this opposition as a family affair, the struggle of one faction against another within the same social framework. Its leaders did not plan revolution, nor even desire it. For months they had been carrying on a campaign of propaganda and agitation centering about a program of political banquets. But these methods, if they were not directly imitated from the British, were at any rate the counterpart of the great pressure campaigns conducted across the Channel by Daniel O'Connell and Richard Cobden, namely the campaigns that led to the emancipation of the Catholics, to the great Reform Act of 1832, and to the repeal of the Corn Laws in 1846. These victories over a well-entrenched ruling class were watched with the utmost interest by liberals all over the Continent. When Cobden in 1847 made a tour of the continental countries he was everywhere fêted by the enlightened, educated circles, all of which took heart from the British experience. Considering that in the French Chamber most of the prominent members had, by 1848, aligned themselves with the opposition, there is no reason to suppose that in the not too distant future the resistance of even Guizot and Louis Philippe would have crumbled.

Only a few words need be said in this context of the more popular opposition, that of the disfranchised writers, artists, tradesmen, and workers who, ever since their disillusionment with the July Revolution of 1830, had been organized in secret societies and some of whom, certainly, were quite prepared to rise in revolt in the name of democracy or socialism. The unemployment, want, and unrest in Paris were such that a great social uprising seemed to some, like Tocqueville, a real and immediate threat. It will be remembered that the monster opposition banquet that had been planned for the first *arrondissement* was moved to a hall in the aristocratic quarter and that, when it was prohibited by the authorities,

163

Langer

THE PATTERN
OF URBAN
REVOLUTION
IN 1848

the opposition leaders were positively relieved. Far from wanting a popular disturbance, the opposition was intent on remaining within the bounds of legality. But in actuality the popular opposition, while noisy and threatening, was so limited in numbers, so divided and weak, so unprepared as to be quite innocuous. It may be recalled that popular leaders like Louis Blanc positively dreaded an insurrection, knowing that the lower classes were bound to be defeated.

The question now arises: How well equipped and prepared was the government to deal with major disorders? It had faced a series of formidable disturbances in the years 1830–1834 and a concerted attempt at insurrection in 1839. Its security forces were briefly as follows. The regular, uniformed police force (*sergents de ville*) numbered only a few hundred men, but was reinforced by an essentially military *Garde municipale*. This body, recruited largely among army veterans, consisted of sixteen companies of infantry and five squadrons of cavalry (a total of 3200 men), splendidly accoutered, thoroughly drilled, and so notorious for its brutality as to be passionately hated by the population.

The *Garde municipale* was roughly the equivalent of the London metropolitan police, except that it was more pronouncedly military in character. It, in turn, was expected to rely for support on the *Garde nationale* which, again, was intended to play the same rôle as the London special constables. The *Garde nationale* was, however, a permanent force, more or less regularly trained and exercised, for the most part uniformed and armed. It consisted of one legion for each of the twelve *arrondissements*, plus one élite cavalry legion and four suburban legions—all told a force of no less than 84,000 men. All able-bodied men were liable for service in the *Garde nationale*, but actually only those who paid a certain annual tax were enrolled. It was understood that the *Garde* was an essentially bourgeois formation, designed for defense of the regime. Only after it had gone into action against insurgents was the regular garrison expected to take part. This garrison consisted of some 30,000 troops, quartered in barracks scattered throughout the city.

In the July Revolution of 1830 the commander of the forces, Marshal Marmont, had been faced by the refusal of his troops to fire on the populace. The danger of defection in the event of civil strife was a continuing one and for that very reason the government relied chiefly on the *Garde nationale* to quell the disturbances of the 1830s. It proved to be a matter of prime importance, then, that the devotion of the *Garde* to the king had weakened greatly by 1848. Ever since 1835 the upper classes had evaded service, while the legions of the poorer *arrondissements* had become seriously disgruntled. The king was certainly not ignorant of these developments. Indeed, after 1840 he did not even review the *Garde,* though to show his displeasure in this way was probably unwise. The estrangement between the ruler and the formations that were supposedly the mainstay of his regime was to be the crucial factor in the events of February 22–24, 1848.

The crowd that assembled on the Place de la Madeleine on the rainy morning of February 22 was altogether nondescript and evidently moved more by curiosity than by any set purpose. It surged aimlessly to and fro until in the later morning a group of students from the Left Bank led the way to the Chamber of Deputies, where the first minor clashes took place before the crowd was pressed back over the river to the Place de la Concorde. The king and the government clearly did not take the demonstration seriously, for preparatory measures that had been decided on were countermanded, probably from fear that action by the troops would only roil the populace and possibly from uncertainty as to the reliability of the forces. In this connection it is interesting to note that on this very first day of unrest the troops tended to stand aloof. They watched idly while the crowd broke street lanterns and overturned omnibuses, and in some cases stood inactive while barricades were being thrown across the streets.

From the outset the *Garde municipale* acted with its usual energy and ruthlessness and, as might be expected, enraged the populace. It might conceivably have broken up the demonstrations by its own efforts, had it been given appropriate orders. But these were not forthcoming, so the *Garde* found itself reduced to purely defensive operations. Since the disorders continued to spread, the king on the morning of February 23 reluctantly called out the *Garde nationale,* only to find, to his horror, that even the legions from the well-to-do sections had joined the opposition to the Guizot regime and insisted on immediate reforms. The effect of this revelation was to precipitate the rather unceremonious dismissal of Guizot. Had the king then called at once on the opposition leaders, Thiers and Barrot, to form a ministry and had he, at the same time, accepted the modest reforms demanded by the opposition, the situation might well have been saved. But Louis Philippe disliked Thiers and was loath to accept changes. In the sequel he was to agree to a reform ministry but without consenting to reforms and, belatedly, to show a determination to resist that, at an earlier hour, might have stood him in good stead.

For the time being, both the *Garde* and the troops were left without adequate directives. In the growing disorder the officers lost confidence while the men became demoralized. Meanwhile the center of disturbance shifted to the crowded *arrondissements,* where barricades went up by the hundreds. On the evening of February 23 there took place the "massacre" of the Boulevard des Capucines, when a surging crowd of National Guards and people collided with a detachment of troops which, hard pressed, opened fire, leaving some fifty persons dead on the pavement. Only after this tragic episode, which raised the resentment of the populace to fever heat, did Louis Philippe entrust command of both the troops and the *Garde nationale* to Marshal Bugeaud, victor of the Algerian campaigns and a soldier renowned for his toughness, who had been itching for a chance to put the "rabble" in its place. Bugeaud started out bright and early on the morning of February 24 in an attempt to reopen communications between the key points of the city. Yet before noon he proclaimed a cease-fire. The reasons for this *volte-face* on the part of a fire-eating commander have been the subject of much debate, but need not

165
Langer
THE PATTERN
OF URBAN
REVOLUTION
IN 1848

detain us here. The fact is that the weariness and demoralization of the troops, the almost complete defection of the *Garde nationale,* and above all the hundreds of barricades must have shown him the futility of his effort. The king made a last desperate but vain attempt to rally the support of at least part of the *Garde nationale,* after which he was driven to the inevitable decision to abdicate.

In review it must be reiterated that the revolution that developed in Paris was neither planned nor desired. The outbreaks were disjointed, isolated, leaderless, and utterly without plan or coordination. The king, through poor judgment, distrust, and indecision, allowed the disturbances to develop to the point at which suppression became impossible. When he failed to conciliate the *Garde nationale,* he sealed the fate not only of the regime but of the dynasty.

Revolution in Vienna

The situation in Vienna was strikingly similar to that in Paris, despite the vast disparity between France and the Hapsburg Monarchy in terms of political and social development. Opposition to the Metternich system had been growing apace during the 1840s and by 1848 had reached the point at which even the old feudal estates were calling for change and, more importantly, influential officials, army officers, and intellectuals were agitating for reforms along the lines of Western liberalism. The government suffered much from the fact that the Emperor was incompetent to rule, while the imperial family was divided on questions of policy. Certainly Prince Metternich had many enemies, a situation that obliged him to acquiesce in the establishment of the *Gewerbeverein* and the *Leseverein,* organizations that soon became strongholds of the liberal, reforming factions. It is rather hard to believe that, in the natural course of events, Metternich would not soon have been forced out of office and a more liberal, progressive policy adopted.

Naturally the news from Paris, the reports of the ease with which Guizot and Louis Philippe had been driven out by popular demonstration, greatly reinforced the pressure on the Vienna court. A veritable whirlwind of petitions called for an end to repression and the introduction of a liberal system. Most prominent among these was the petition submitted by the 4000 Viennese students, many of whom came from the lower classes, and all of whom suffered under the restrictions of the Metternich system. This, like other petitions, was rejected, largely because of the unwillingness of the Archduke Louis, chief of the council of state, to consider making concessions under pressure.

The Viennese government in no sense faced a threat of revolution. The loyalty of the entire population to the dynasty—even to the half-witted Emperor—was such as to astound contemporaries. The opposition was, as in France, directed against the ministry, hoping that its policy of immobility or stagnation could be gotten rid of by peaceful pressure. The only real danger of upheaval lay in the workingmen of the suburbs, who like workers elsewhere in Europe were suffering, and who, by the spring of 1848, were in such ferment that the government was obliged to set up public works and open soup kitchens to alleviate the unemployment and want. But not even the workers were revolutionary in the sense of having an organization or program. The workers were desperate but knew no course of action besides wrecking the hated machines and occasionally plundering the foodshops.

Besieged by deputations and all but buried under petitions, the government, fearing disturbances, ordered the garrison troops in readiness. These forces numbered about 14,000, mostly quartered in barracks just outside the walls. On these the government would have to rely in case of serious disorder, for the police forces were altogether inadequate. The civil police was almost exclusively a secret police, assigned to the surveillance of dangerous and subversive persons and organizations. Under its supervision was a *Militär-Polizeiwache* consisting of 1100 to 1200 men. On paper, at least, there stood between these police forces and the regular troops something akin to the French *Garde nationale,* namely, a *Bürgerwehr* (Citizens' Guard) that during the French occupation in 1809 had served a useful purpose but that had since 1815 sunk to the status of a ceremonial guard, noted chiefly for the excellence of its band-music. Officially, the *Bürgerwehr* comprised 14,000 men of the upper and middle bourgeoisie, electing its own officers and serving at its own expense. Only about a third of the force was equipped with firearms.

The events of March 13 in Vienna were as confused as the February days in Paris. It was a bright spring morning and many people, including elegantly-dressed ladies, assembled before the palace of the Estates of Lower Austria, because it was known that this influential body was about to proceed to the palace with yet another petition. Presently a large body of students arrived, hoping to enlist the support of the Estates for their own petition. No one knew just what to do. While waiting, some of the students began to make speeches. There was much milling about in the narrow Herrengasse and in the courtyard of the palace. Eventually, toward noon, the president of the Estates appealed to the Archduke Albert, commanding the troops, for relief from popular pressure. The soldiers had a hard time making their way to the center of disturbances. Presently, tiles and other missiles were thrown at them from roofs and windows; guns went off, no one knew how or why; there were five dead. Like the much more horrible "massacre" of the Boulevard des Capucines, this episode was enough to set off a whole series of desultory clashes between the military and the people. At the same time crowds of workers from the suburbs began to invade the Inner City until the gates were closed against them. Some remained outside the walls, howling like hungry wolves. Most of them, however, returned to the suburbs to engage in an orgy of incendiarism and plunder.

Franz Grillparzer, the great Austrian dramatist, was an eye-witness of the events of March 13 and pictured the initial demonstrations at the Ständehaus as a pleasant, good-natured fracas. The whole thing, he wrote

167

Langer

THE PATTERN
OF URBAN
REVOLUTION
IN 1848

in his recollections, could have been snuffed out by two battalions of soldiers, but no troops, in fact not even the police, were to be seen. The military, when at last it appeared, did too much. After the first bloodshed and after the arrival of the workers from the suburbs, the situation became much more ominous. During the afternoon the demand for Metternich's dismissal became deafening. At the same time there were violent clashes between the troops and the populace, led by the students. Efforts to storm the arsenal led to considerable bloodshed, while at the Schottentor the workers actually managed to secure control of the entrance. In the elegant suburb of Wieden the mob sacked Metternich's villa and other aristocratic homes.

In the hope that order might still be restored, a group of prominent citizens in the late afternoon persuaded the Lord Mayor, Count Czapka, to call out the *Bürgerwehr,* of which he was the commanding officer, and if possible induce the military to withdraw from the city while the *Bürgerwehr* took over. The chronology is hopelessly confused and it is hardly worthwhile trying to fix it. Archduke Albert, the commander of the forces, who himself had been badly injured by a block of wood thrown at him from a window, did in fact evacuate the Inner City. For the next several, critical days, the garrison troops stood idle and useless on the parade ground just outside the walls.

The *Bürgerwehr,* meanwhile, was to play the same role as that of the Paris *Garde nationale.* A deputation of *Bürgerwehr* officers at once proceeded to the palace to demand the dismissal of Metternich (allowing the court until 9:00 P.M. to make up its mind) and the arming of the students. These were hard decisions for the court to make, for the emperor was feeble-minded and his relatives were badly divided. Several of the archdukes, led by Archduke John, had long since convinced themselves that Metternich must go and that real reforms must be undertaken. On the other hand, Archduke Louis abominated reforms and was urged by Metternich and Field Marshal Prince Windischgrätz to stand firm. The whole disturbance, argued the aged chancellor, was nothing more than a riot that could be easily mastered by the police and the troops. What led to the downfall of Louis Philippe was his eagerness to dismiss Guizot. Where a policy of concessions would lead no one knew. As for Windischgrätz, he had had years of experience dealing with serious workers' outbreaks in Prague and other Bohemian cities. He was sure that energetic action by the military could quickly suppress the disturbances. To dismiss Metternich, he held, would be nothing short of shameless cowardice.

In the end, "the impotent scarecrows" (Kudlich) were unable to withstand the pressure of *Bürgerwehr,* students, and members of the Estates. In the evening Metternich was obliged to resign and permission was given for the immediate arming of the students, who alone were thought to have any influence with the rampaging workers. In the course of the night thousands of muskets were dealt out to students and citizens. These, in turn, formed patrols and managed to restore some semblance of order.

No good purpose would be served by pursuing the story further. At the end of the first day the court had surrendered to the liberal elements, if only in order to master the radicalism of the workers—that is, to put an end to an unwanted revolution for which the indecision of the court was largely to blame. A few words should, however, be said of the immediate aftermath. Like Louis Philippe in his belated appointment of Marshal Bugeaud, the Viennese court made a hopeless attempt to save the situation by naming Prince Windischgrätz civil and military governor of Vienna (noon, March 14). He was to proclaim martial law, while the government was to revoke all the concessions made under popular pressure on the preceding day. The field marshal apparently thought the situation too far gone, and his efforts to assert his authority did, in fact, prove altogether futile. The court was no longer in a position to refuse the demand for the organization of a national guard, which was to include a separate student corps (*Akademische Legion*). This new national guard was intended to comprise about 10,000 reliable citizens, but popular pressure led to the enrollment of some 30,000, in addition to the 7000 students in the special legion. Windischgrätz was, for the time being, quite helpless. On the following day (March 15) the court had to agree to a constitution, with which the first phase of this rather incredible revolution was brought to a close.

Revolution in Berlin

The story of the Berlin revolution—our last case study—provides a classic example of how *not* to deal with revolutionary situations. Berlin, like other capitals, was in a process of rapid economic transformation and was, in addition, a veritable hotbed of radical philosophical thought. Yet, politically, the population was strikingly inexperienced and apathetic. The rapidly developing liberal movement in Prussia had its stronghold not in Berlin, but in the Rhineland and in provincial cities such as Königsberg and Breslau. The famous United Diet of 1847 had revealed the wide divergence between the aspirations of the rising middle class and the outmoded, traditionalist notions of the ruler. But even then the liberals, for all their discontent, were far from advocating revolution. Like their counterparts elsewhere in Europe, they relied on agitation and pressure to bring about a constitutional regime. A sober evaluation of the evidence suggests that they were probably justified in their expectations. By the beginning of 1848 even so recalcitrant a prince as Frederick William IV was beginning to yield to the constitutionally-directed importunities of his ministers.

Berlin is supposed to have had, in 1848, some 40,000 to 50,000 industrial workers in the textile and metallurgical trades, and certainly far more in the traditional artisan occupations. As elsewhere, the workers suffered acutely from the rapid economic changes; five-eighths of the laboring population is supposed to have been in extreme want. In the years just preceding 1848 some workers' associations had sprung up and some revolutionary groups, such as the *Zeitungshalle,* had emerged. But these were

169

Langer

THE PATTERN
OF URBAN
REVOLUTION
IN 1848

exceptional. The workers were, for the most part, illiterate and apathetic so far as politics were concerned. Class consciousness and subversive activity were practically nonexistent.

It was no doubt inevitable that news of the Paris insurrection should have led to much excitement and that, somewhat later, reports of Metternich's fall should have evoked widespread enthusiasm. From March 6 on, there were many meetings, speeches, resolutions, and petitions, all advancing the familiar liberal demands. The general tone of both meetings and petitions was one of hope and good will. And rightly so, for the Prussian government, like those of the South German states, was on the verge of giving way to popular pressure. There was, to be sure, strong conservative opposition, led by Prince William of Prussia, the king's brother. But there were even stronger forces convinced that fundamental changes were inescapable and that Prussia's future position in Germany depended on leadership of the liberal movement. As early as March 12 the king, albeit reluctantly and with mental reservations, made the basic decision to accept a constitution and a responsible ministry.

Had the Prussian government provided Berlin with an adequate civil police, there is no reason to suppose that the popular meetings and processions would have gotten out of hand. But, incredible though it may seem, in this city of 400,000 there was no police to speak of, nor even anything akin to a civic or national guard. Officially there was a gendarmerie consisting of 40 sergeants and 110 men, but these gendarmes were employed almost exclusively in the law courts, markets, places of amusement, and so forth. For the preservation of public order the government relied on the garrison troops (about 12,000 in number). In short, the government could deal with serious disturbances only by the methods employed in Russia, methods altogether unsuited to the conditions of a large western city. This had become clear during the so-called *Potato Revolution* of April, 1847—large-scale food riots during which some barricades had been erected and severe clashes between troops and people had taken place. At that time the city authorities had petitioned for a modest constabulary, to act in the first instance. But the government had been unwilling to delegate such authority. It therefore remained dependent on the armed forces, which, because of their ruthless and brutal action, were intensely hated by the populace, and which, in turn, despised the "rabble."

As popular excitement grew, the authorities brought more and more troops into the city. Clashes were almost inevitable. They began to take place on March 13 and the ensuing days, with some loss of life and much burning resentment, accompanied by insults and provocations on both sides. Already on March 9 the city authorities renewed the request for formation of a civil constabulary, which was belatedly granted on March 16. Civic guard units (*Bürgerschutzkommissionen*) were hastily enrolled. There was to be a force of 1200 men, patrolling in groups of ten to twenty, armed only with truncheons. It was, however, understood that thenceforth the military should act only if called upon by officers of the civic guard. In a word, they were expected to play the same rôle as the special constables in London.

Actually this improvised constabulary played but a sorry rôle in the Berlin uprising. The men had little more than good will. Neither the military nor the populace paid much attention to them. On the contrary, their efforts met with derision. The crowds grew increasingly restless and the troops more and more eager to beat them into submission. Hence the growing demand on the part of the people for the withdrawal of the military from the city and the formation of a real national guard, which would have been tantamount to the king's putting himself at the mercy of his subjects. This he was naturally unwilling to do, but on March 18, just as a monster demonstration at the royal palace was being organized, the king issued the famous "patent" by which he promised the early convocation of the United Diet, expressed his acceptance of constitutional government, and announced his leadership of the liberal, national movement in Germany. Since this document met most of the popular demands, it called forth general enthusiasm. Huge crowds gathered in the palace square, while the recently established civic guards stood in array before the portals of the palace. Then the sight of troops massed in the courtyard of the palace led to renewed cries for withdrawal of the soldiers. The commotion became so great that the king ordered General von Prittwitz, the commander of the troops, to clear the square. The general's cavalry squadron was so hard pressed by the crowds that infantry was sent out to relieve him. In the din and confusion two rifle shots rang out. No one was hurt, but the crowds suddenly panicked. Like the Paris populace after the massacre of the Boulevard des Capucines, the Berliners were convinced that they had been betrayed: that they had been lured to the palace by promises of reforms, only to be fallen upon by the hated military. Scattering before the advancing troops, they spread all sorts of alarming stories through the city. Everywhere barricades began to go up, and before evening fighting had broken out in many sections of the metropolis.

The king and his military advisers were always convinced that the insurrection of March 18–19 was instigated and planned by foreign agents—French, Swiss, Poles, 10,000 of whom were reputed to have arrived in the city. But this comfortable theory was not supported by solid evidence. No one doubts that there were a great many foreigners, mostly workers, in Berlin, nor that many German workers had spent some years in Switzerland or Paris. Furthermore, there were certainly some confirmed revolutionaries who provided what inspiration and leadership they could. But the insurrection showed little, if any, evidence of planning or organization. All strata of the Berlin population were involved in one way or another. The students played a far less significant rôle here than in Vienna, but they do seem to have been instrumental in bringing workers from the suburbs to help man the barricades. But judging from the losses, the actual fighting was carried on largely by young artisans, the traditional craftsmen of the city.

Prittwitz had at his disposal a total force of about 15,000, consisting of

171

Langer

THE PATTERN
OF URBAN
REVOLUTION
IN 1848

cavalry, artillery, and infantry, with which he proceeded to act with great energy. The insurgents, on the other hand, had but few muskets or munitions and had to make do with improvised weapons. Under these circumstances they could not hope adequately to defend the barricades, many of which were but lightly constructed. Instead, they hurled paving stones and tiles from the roofs or poured boiling water from the windows. The troops invaded the houses, pursued the rebels to the garrets, and there either cut them down or dragged them away captive. The advantage throughout lay with the military, and indeed by midnight of March 18 Prittwitz had established effective control over the center of the city. This is not to say that the completion of the operation would not have been an arduous business. Prittwitz seems to have hoped that he could persuade the king to go to Potsdam, after which he would have concentrated his troops outside the city for establishment of a blockade. Eventually, if necessary, he planned to snuff out the insurrection by bombardment of the disaffected quarters. The king, however, wanted to put an end to the fighting at almost any cost. Hence his pathetic appeal "To my dear Berliners," drafted in the night, offering to discuss the situation with representatives of the people and to withdraw the troops once the barricades had been taken down.

The picture at court on the morning of March 19 was one of utter confusion: The king, in a state of near collapse, was evidently unable to appreciate all the implications of his decisions or in general to provide consistent leadership. Beset on all sides by officials and deputations of citizens and, furthermore, misled by unconfirmed reports that barricades were already being dismantled, he ordered the withdrawal of the troops to their barracks except for the guards at the palace and the arsenal. Through misunderstanding even these critical places were presently abandoned. It seems likely that the king intended to leave Berlin as part of Prittwitz's plan. But all arrangements for his departure were hopelessly upset when, early in the afternoon, a great procession arrived at the palace bearing the bodies of some 200 victims of the street-fighting, their wounds exposed. Eventually the crowd made its way into the courtyard of the palace. On vociferous demand of the throng the king was obliged to appear and even to doff his cap in reverence to the people's dead. Nothing, certainly, could have demonstrated more clearly the complete capitulation of the monarchy. The people, on the verge of defeat in battle, had secured not only the removal of the troops to their barracks but also the establishment of a civic guard. (The king agreed to this immediately after his humiliating appearance on the balcony.)

The *Bürgerwehr,* as the new civic guard was called, was to be organized by districts, each to have roughly 100 men. Only those who had full citizen rights (*Bürgerbrief*) were eligible for enrollment and the old traditional marksmans-guild (*Schützengilde*) was to provide the kernel of the hastily constructed force of 6000 men. Several thousand muskets were immediately supplied from the arsenal. By 6:00 P.M. on March 19 the élite *Schützengilde* and the newly recruited *Bürgerwehr* were able to take over guard duty at the palace. Frederick William had placed himself entirely under the protection of his subjects. He was as defenseless, wrote the American minister in Berlin on March 21, "as the poorest malefactor of the prisons." Early in the morning of March 21 the entire Berlin garrison was withdrawn from the city. For the moment the revolution was triumphant.

Conclusion

By the mid-nineteenth century the economic and social transformation of western and much of central Europe had reached the point at which basic political changes had become imperative.

There was much pressure on the part of the propertied middle classes for such changes, as is shown most vividly by the fact that in both Paris and Vienna the national guard, designed to protect the existing regime, lent their support to the cause of reform.

Yet there was remarkably little organization or planning for revolution. The colorful heroism of a few revolutionary leaders and the occasional spectacular outbreaks of radical elements are apt to be misleading.

The proponents of liberalism and reform expected to attain their ends by peaceful organization and action. They were fascinated by the achievements of O'Connell and greatly heartened by the triumph of Cobden and the free-trade movement.

After 1846 the forces of liberalism were so formidable and insistent as to be almost irresistible.

It was the unpardonable fault of the Continental princes to have failed to gauge the strength of the opposition and to have refused to accept the inevitable. This was particularly true of Louis Philippe, because the reforms called for in France were of a modest nature and the failing loyalty of the national guard must certainly have been known to him.

Ways to avoid serious upheaval were demonstrated not only by the preventive measures taken later in London, but also by the timely concessions made by King Leopold of Belgium, through which his government secured the support of the opposition which enabled it to present a united front to efforts at radical insurrection.

The alternative to concession was systematic repression, as practiced in quite different forms in Britain and Russia. But prevention of insurrection called above all for vigorous action. The situation in the European capitals, with their dislocated artisan economy, widespread unemployment, fluid population, and appalling living conditions, was necessarily explosive. It was imperative, therefore, to prevent ordinary assemblages of people from degenerating into mob action and eventual revolution.

Everywhere on the Continent the civil police was inadequate for the task. As of old, governments still relied on their military forces to prevent major disorders. But the use of troops for police duty, always undesirable because too drastic, had by 1848 become extremely hazardous. For even though the aristocratic officer corps might spoil for a chance to put "the

173

Langer

THE PATTERN
OF URBAN
REVOLUTION
IN 1848

rabble" in its place, the common soldier in conscript armies was understandably reluctant to shoot at unarmed citizens. In the July Revolution Marshal Marmont saw most of his forces melt away. Even in England it was sometimes thought advisable to bring troops from Ireland, lest the English troops assigned to quell disturbances in the industrial areas prove unreliable.

In these circumstances it behooved governments to move promptly and energetically. In all the capitals the initial demonstrations were amorphous, aimless, unaggressive. Yet nowhere did the authorities show the required determination. Troops were left to act as best they could; higher direction was almost completely lacking.

As a result, fairly innocuous aggregations of people quickly turned into bellicose mobs. Open conflict between people and troops ensued, and presently military operations in the narrow, congested quarters of the city became all but impossible. Insurrection fed on itself. Radical elements were able to take advantage of a situation that they by themselves could never have created.

Thus, by ineptitude and indecision the governments provoked revolutions that were as unexpected as they were unwanted, even by the opposition. In discussing this period stress should be laid on the failure of monarchy rather than on the forces of revolution.

To explain this failure presents something of a challenge. We must attribute it chiefly, I think, to the feeling of insecurity common to almost all princes in the period after the French Revolution. Their fear of the actually ineffectual secret societies and their dread of a world conspiracy against the throne and the altar are well-known. Moreover, they were apprehensive of the newly aroused people, the more so in view of the frightful barricade fighting in Paris in July 1830 and, in the 1840s, the growing threat of a desperate proletariat.

The liberal middle classes, too, bear a heavy responsibility for the disastrous revolutions that ensued. In retrospect, it seems almost incredible that the Paris national guard should have carried its dislike of the regime and its desire for reforms to the point of standing aside, allowing the insurrection to develop and opening the door to political and social upheaval that, in turn, provided the opportunity for a repressive dictatorship. In Vienna the *Bürgerwehr* played an equally dubious role, setting the stage for the radicalism of the summer of 1848 and the ensuing counterrevolution.

Finally, one may fairly ask whether the revolutions of 1848 were necessary or even desirable. The work of reform was carried through more rapidly and more smoothly in countries such as Britain, the low countries, Scandinavia and even Russia, in which there were no revolutions. In the last analysis the Continental revolutions, while they achieved some measure of reform, led to grave political and social conflicts, to say nothing of national antagonisms and wars that might otherwise have been avoided. In view of the period of reaction that almost everywhere followed the revolutions it would seem that these upheavals actually delayed many urgently needed changes. Without the revolutions many later tensions might have been forestalled or at least attenuated, and Europe might have escaped a veritable harvest of both internal and external strains and animosities.

175

Langer

THE PATTERN
OF URBAN
REVOLUTION
IN 1848

THE EMERGENCE OF MODERN THOUGHT

PART III

I T has often been pointed out that the nineteenth century invented a number of "isms"—socialism, nationalism, communism, democratic-liberalism, industrialism—which are so much a part of our present-day language that it is difficult for us to comprehend that their ancestry as standard words in the dictionary goes back less than two centuries. More than that, it is hard to imagine how we could describe what we believe in without using the language of these "isms." The next group of selections contains recent examinations of those nineteenth-century "isms" or their creators who were most influential in the emergence of modern thought. These include a study of Individualism by Steven Lukes, an examination of the role of revolution in Marxism by Robert Tucker, an investigation of the *biological* (as compared to *social*) contributions of Darwinism by Michael Ghiselin, H. Stuart Hughes's consideration of Positivism and Anti-positivism, and Erich Fromm's essay on Freud's conception of the nature of man.

12. The Meanings of Individualism

STEVEN LUKES

One of these nineteenth-century "isms," individualism, is both broader and less precise than the others. Its meanings underlay ideas in politics, economics, the literary and cultural attitudes of Romanticism, and social thought. As a result, a study of individualism in the nineteenth century may provide the best avenue for exploring the emergence of modern thought.

The author of this selection, British intellectual historian Steven Lukes, takes on that task. Because few people today argue against individualism, one is struck by the author's evidence that the word was so slow to catch on, that it had such a variety of meanings, and that those meanings tended to develop on national lines. To see why this was so one should keep several questions in mind. Why, for example, did French thinkers of all persuasions, from conservatives like de Maistre, de Bonald, Lamennais, and Brunetière, to liberals like de Tocqueville and socialists like the Saint-Simonians, Cabet, Fourier, Blanc, and Jaurès condemn individualism? How did their critiques agree and disagree? What were the French characteristics of individualism's meaning? How did the idea of individualism held by German Romantics come to constitute the German meaning of individualism? How did it differ from the standard French view of the term? How was it transformed into "an organic and naturalistic theory of community"? How did Burckhardt synthesize the German and French views of individualism? What were the characteristics of American

Source: Steven Lukes, "The Meanings of 'Individualism,' " *Journal of the History of Ideas*, XXXII, No. 1 (January 1971), 45–66. Reprinted by permission of A. D. Peters and Company. [Footnotes omitted.]

individualism and how did that meaning of the word come about? How was the English understanding of individualism similar to and different from the American view?

"The term 'individualism,'" wrote Max Weber, "embraces the utmost heterogeneity of meanings," adding that "a thorough, historically-oriented conceptual analysis would at the present time be of the highest value to scholarship." His words remain true. "Individualism" is still used in a great many ways, in many different contexts and with an exceptional lack of precision. Moreover, it has played a major role in the history of ideas, and of ideologies, in modern Europe and America. The present study seeks to contribute to the analysis Weber desired. But clearly, what is still needed is to carry the analytical task further: to isolate the various distinct unit-ideas (and intellectual traditions) which the word has conflated—unit-ideas whose logical and conceptual relations to one another are by no means clear.

Like "socialism" and "communism," "individualism" is a nineteenth-century expression. In seeking to identify its various distinct traditions of use, I shall concentrate on its nineteenth-century history, for this is what chiefly determined its twentieth-century meanings. My main purpose is to indicate both the variety and the directions of the main paths traced during the term's rich semantic history. The interest of such an account is, however, neither merely semantic nor merely historical. The meanings of words generally incapsulate ideas, even theories. Accordingly, where semantic divergences systematically tend to follow social and cultural (in this case national) lines, to explain those divergences becomes a challenging problem in the sociology of knowledge.

France

The first uses of the term, in its French form *"individualisme,"* grew out of the general European reaction to the French Revolution and to its alleged source, the thought of the Enlightenment. Conservative thought in the early nineteenth century was virtually unanimous in condemning the appeal to the reason, interests, and rights of the individual; as Burke had said: "Individuals pass like shadows; but the commonwealth is fixed and stable." The Revolution was proof that ideas exalting the individual imperilled the stability of the commonwealth, dissolving it into "an unsocial, uncivil, unconnected chaos of elementary principles." Conservative thinkers, above all in France and Germany, shared Burke's scorn for the individual's "private stock of reason" and his fear lest "the commonwealth itself would, in a few generations, crumble away, be disconnected into the dust and powder of individuality, and at length dispersed to all the winds of heaven," as well as his certainty that "Society requires" that "the inclinations of men should frequently be thwarted, their will controlled, and their passions brought into subjection."

These sentiments were found at their most extreme among the theocratic Catholic reactionaries in France. According to Joseph de Maistre, the social order had been "shattered to its foundations because there was too much liberty in Europe and not enough Religion"; everywhere authority was weakening and there was a frightening growth of "individual opinion [*l'esprit particulier*]." The individual's reason was "of its nature the mortal enemy of all association": its exercise spelt spiritual and civil anarchy. Infallibility was an essential condition of the maintenance of society, and indeed government was "a true religion," with "its dogmas, its mysteries, its priests; to submit it to individual discussion is to destroy it." In the earliest known use of the word, de Maistre spoke in 1820 of "this deep and frightening division of minds, this infinite fragmentation of all doctrines, political protestantism carried to the most absolute individualism."

The theocrats agreed in giving to "society" the same exclusive emphasis that they accused the eighteenth-century *philosophes* of giving to "the individual." Society for de Maistre was God-given and natural, and he wished the individual's mind to lose itself in that of the nation "as a river which flows into the ocean still exists in the mass of the water, but without name and distinct reality"; while for de Bonald "man only exists for society and society only educates him for itself." The ideas of the *philosophes* were, they thought, not merely false; they were wicked and dangerous. According to Lamennais, they proclaimed the individual as sovereign over himself in the most absolute sense:

> His reason—that is his law, his truth, his justice. To seek to impose on him an obligation he has not previously imposed on himself by his own thought and will is to violate the most sacred of his rights. . . . Hence, no legislation, no power is possible, and the same doctrine which produces anarchy in men's minds further produces an irremediable political anarchy, and overturns the very bases of human society.

Were such principles to prevail, "what could one foresee but troubles, disorders, calamities without end, and universal dissolution?" Man, Lamennais argued, "lives only in society" and "institutions, laws, governments draw all their strength from a certain concourse of thoughts and wills." "What," he asked, "is power without obedience? What is law without duty?" and he answered:

> *Individualism* which destroys the very idea of obedience and of duty, thereby destroying both power and law; and what then remains but a terrifying confusion of interests, passions, and diverse opinions?

It was the disciples of Claude Henri de Saint-Simon, who were the first to use *"individualisme"* systematically, in the mid-1820's. Saint-Simonism shared the ideas of the counter-revolutionary reactionaries—their critique of the Enlightenment's glorification of the individual, their horror of social atomization and anarchy, as well as their desire for an organic, stable, hierarchically organized, harmonious social order. But it applied these ideas in a historically progressive direction: that social order was not to be the ecclesiastical and feudal order of the past, but the industrial order of the future. Indeed, the proselytizing Saint-Simonians systematized their master's ideas into an activist and extremely influential secular religion, an ideological force serving as a kind of Protestant ethic for the expanding capitalism of the Catholic countries in nineteenth-century Europe.

History for the Saint-Simonians was a cycle of "critical" and "organic" periods. The former were "filled with disorder; they destroy former social relations, and everywhere tend towards egoism"; the latter were unified, organized, and stable (the previous instances in Europe being the ancient polytheistic preclassical society and the Christian Middle Ages). The modern critical period, originating with the Reformation was, the Saint-Simonians believed, the penultimate stage of human progress, heralding a future organic era of "universal association" in which "the organization of the future will be final because only then will society be formed directly for progress." They used *"individualisme"* to refer to the pernicious and "negative" ideas underlying the evils of the modern critical epoch, whose "disorder, atheism, individualism, and egoism" they contrasted with the prospect of "order, religion, association, and devotion." The "philosophers of the eighteenth century"—men such as Helvetius, with his doctrine of "enlightened self-interest," Locke, Reid, Condillac, Kant, and the "atheist d'Holbach, the deist Voltaire, and Rousseau"—all these "defenders of individualism" refused to "go back to a source higher than individual conscience." They "considered the individual as the center" and "preached egoism," providing an ideological justification for the prevailing anarchy, especially in the economic and political spheres. The "doctrine of individualism" with its two "sad deities . . . two creatures of reason—conscience and public opinion" led to "one political result: opposition to any attempt at organization from a center of direction for the moral interests of mankind, to hatred of power."

Partly perhaps because of the extraordinarily pervasive influence of Saint-Simonian ideas, *"individualisme"* came to be very widely used in the nineteenth century. In France, it usually carried, and indeed still carries, a pejorative connotation, a strong suggestion that to concentrate on the individual is to harm the superior interests of society. The latest edition of the Dictionary of the *Académie Française* defines it simply as "subordination of the general interest to the individual's interest," and one recent writer, noting its naturally pejorative sense, has remarked on its "tinge of *'ubris,'* of *'démesuré'* " which "does not exist in English," while another observes that in France "until the present day the term individualism has retained much of its former, unfavorable connotations." It is true that there was a group of French revolutionary republican *Carbonari* in the 1820's who proudly called themselves the "Société d'Individualistes," and that various individual thinkers adopted the label, among them Proudhon—though even Proudhon saw society as "a *sui generis* being" and argued that "outside the group there are only abstractions and phantoms." From the mid-nineteenth century, liberal Protestants and eventually a few *laissez-faire* liberals started to call themselves individualists and one wrote a comprehensive history of "economic and social individualism," incorporating a variety of French thinkers—yet the tone was always one of defensive paradox. Few have welcomed the epithet, and many, from Balzac onwards, stressed the opposition between *"individualisme,"* implying anarchy and social atomization, and *"individualité,"* implying personal independence and self-realization. For the Swiss theologian Alexandre Vinet, these were "two sworn enemies; the first obstacle and negation of any society; the latter a principle to which society owes all its savor, life and reality." The "progress of individualism" meant "the relaxation of social unity because of the increasingly pronounced predominance of egoism," while the "gradual extinction of individuality" meant "the increasingly strong inclination for minds . . . to surrender themselves to what is known as public opinion or the spirit of the age." In general, *"individualisme"* in French thought points to the sources of social dissolution, though there have been wide divergences concerning the nature of those sources and of the social order they are held to threaten, as well as in the historical frameworks within which they are conceptualized.

For some, individualism resides in dangerous ideas, for others it is social or economic anarchy, a lack of the requisite institutions and norms, for yet others it is the prevalence of self-interested attitudes among individuals. For men of the right, from de Maistre to Charles Maurras, it is all that undermines a traditional, hierarchical social order. Thus Louis Veuillot, the militant Catholic propagandist, wrote in 1843 that "France has need of religion" which would bring "harmony, union, patriotism, confidence, morality . . .":

> The evil which plagues France is not unknown; everyone agrees in giving it the same name: *individualism.*
>
> It is not difficult to see that a country where individualism reigns is no longer in the normal conditions of society, since society is the union of minds and interests, and individualism is division carried to the infinite degree.
>
> All for each, each for all, that is society; each for himself, and thus each against all, that is individualism.

Similarly, during the Dreyfus Affair, Ferdinand Brunetière, the strongly *anti-Dreyfusard* literary historian, defended the army and the social order, which he saw as threatened by "individualism" and "anarchy," and poured scorn on those intellectuals who had presumed to doubt the justice of Dreyfus's trial. Individualism, he wrote, was

> the great sickness of the present time. . . . Each of us has confidence only in himself, sets himself up as the sovereign judge of everything . . . when intellectualism and individualism reach this degree of self-infatuation, one must expect them to be or become nothing other than *anarchy.* . . .

Among socialists, individualism has typically been contrasted with an ideal, cooperative social order, variously described as "association," "harmony," "socialism," and "communism"; the term here refers to the economic doctrine of *laissez-faire* and to the anarchy, social atomization, and exploitation produced by industrial capitalism. Pierre Leroux, aiming at a new humanitarian and libertarian socialism, used it to mean the principle, proclaimed by political economy, of "everyone for himself, and . . . all for riches, nothing for the poor," which atomized society and made men into "rapacious wolves"; "society," he maintained, "is entering a new era in which the general tendency of the laws will no longer have individualism as its end, but association." For Constantin Pecqueur, "the remedy lies in association precisely because the abuse springs from individualism" and the utopian Etienne Cabet wrote that

> Two great systems have divided and polarized Humanity ever since the beginning of the world: that of Individualism (or egoism, or personal interest), and that of Communism (or association, or the general interest, or the public interest).

Likewise, the conspiratorial revolutionary Auguste Blanqui asserted that "Communism is the protector of the individual, individualism his extermination."

Other socialists used the term in more complex ways. Louis Blanc saw individualism as a major cultural principle, encompassing Protestantism, the Bourgeoisie, and the Enlightenment, bringing a historically necessary, though false and incomplete, freedom. Its progressive aspect was a new self-assertion, a new independence of traditional structures and rejection of Authority in the religious, economic, and intellectual spheres; but it needed to be transcended and completed, pointing towards a future age of socialist Fraternity. In Blanc's own words:

> Three great principles divide the world and history: Authority, Individualism, and Fraternity.
>
> The principle of individualism is that which, taking man out of society, makes him sole judge of what surrounds him and of himself, gives him a heightened sense of his rights without showing him his duties, abandons him to his own powers, and, for the whole of government, proclaims *laisser-faire*.
>
> Individualism, inaugurated by Luther, has developed with an irresistible force, and, dissociated from the religious factor . . . it governs the present; it is the spiritual principle of things.
>
> . . . individualism is important in having achieved a vast progress. To provide breathing-space and scope to human thought repressed for so long, to intoxicate it with pride and audacity; to submit to the judgment of every mind the totality of traditions, centuries, their achievements, their beliefs; to place man in an isolation full of anxieties, full of perils, but sometimes also full of majesty, and to enable him to resolve personally, in the midst of an immense

struggle, in the uproar of a universal debate, the problem of his happiness and his destiny . . .—this is by no means an achievement without grandeur, and it is the achievement of individualism. One must therefore speak of it with respect and as a necessary transition.

Again, the disciples of Charles Fourier denied any basic opposition between individualism and socialism, while at the end of the century, Jean Jaurès argued that "socialism is the logical completion of individualism," a formula echoed by Emile Durkheim, who saw a kind of centralized guild socialism as a means of "completing, extending, and organizing individualism." For all these socialist thinkers, individualism signified the autonomy, freedom, and sacredness of the individual—values which had hitherto taken a negative, oppressive, and anarchic form but could henceforth only be preserved within a cooperative and rationally-organized social order.

French liberals also spoke of individualism, but they characteristically saw it as a threat to a pluralist social order, with minimum state intervention and maximum political liberty. Benjamin Constant, perhaps the most eloquent exponent of classical liberalism, was clearly groping for the word when he observed that "when all are isolated by egoism, there is nothing but dust, and at the advent of a storm, nothing but mire." It was, however, that aristocratic observer of early nineteenth-century America, Alexis de Tocqueville, who developed its most distinctive and influential liberal meaning in France. For Tocqueville, individualism was the natural product of democracy ("Individualism is of democratic origin and threatens to develop insofar as conditions are equalized"), involving the apathetic withdrawal of individuals from public life into a private sphere and their isolation from one another, with a consequent weakening of social bonds. Such a development, Tocqueville thought, offered dangerous scope for the unchecked growth of the political power of the state.

More specifically, "individualism"—a "recent expression to which a new idea has given birth"—was "a deliberate and peaceful sentiment which disposes each citizen to isolate himself from the mass of his fellows and to draw apart with his family and friends," abandoning "the wider society to itself." At first, it "saps only the virtues of public life; but, in the long run, it attacks and destroys all others and is eventually absorbed into pure egoism." In contrast to aristocratic society, in which men were "linked closely to something beyond them and are often disposed to forget themselves" and which "formed of all the citizens a long chain reaching from the peasant to the king," democracy "breaks the chain and sets each link apart," and "the bond of human affections extends and relaxes." With increasing social mobility, the continuity of the generations is destroyed; as classes become fused, "their members become indifferent and as if strangers to one another"; and as individuals become increasingly self-sufficient, "they become accustomed to considering themselves always in isolation, they freely imagine that their destiny is entirely in their own hands." Democracy, Tocqueville concluded, "not only makes each man forget his forefathers, but it conceals from him his descendants and separates him from his contemporaries; it ceaselessly throws him back on himself alone and threatens finally to confine him entirely in the solitude of his own heart."

Individualism for Tocqueville thus sprang from the lack of intermediary groups to provide a framework for the individual and protection against the State. (As for the Americans, they only avoided its destructive consequences because of their free institutions and active citizenship: they conquered individualism with liberty.) It was, moreover, a peculiarly modern evil: "Our fathers," Tocqueville wrote, "did not have the word 'individualism,' which we have coined for our own use, because in their time there was indeed no individual who did not belong to a group and who could be considered as absolutely alone."

No less diverse than these conceptions of the sources and the dangers of individualism have been the historical frameworks within which French thinkers have placed it. It is variously traced to the Reformation, the Renaissance, the Enlightenment, the Revolution, to the decline of the aristocracy or the Church or traditional religion, to the Industrial Revolution, to the growth of capitalism or democracy, but, as we have seen, there is wide agreement in seeing it as an evil and a threat to social cohesion. Perhaps the role of *"individualisme"* in French thought is partly due to the very success of "individualist" legislation at the time of the Revolution, the elimination of intermediary groups and bodies in the society, and the ensuing political and administrative centralization of the country.

The basis for this had been laid, as Tocqueville observed, in the municipal and fiscal policies of the French kings in the seventeenth and eighteenth centuries, which had systematically prevented the growth of spontaneous, organized activities and informal groupings. One can even reasonably postulate that the lack of such activities and groupings is a basic and distinctive French cultural trait.

However that may be, the mainstream of French thought, above all in the nineteenth century, has expressed by *"individualisme"* what Durkheim identified by the twin concepts of "anomie" and "egoism"—the social, moral, and political isolation of individuals, their dissociation from social purposes and social regulation, the breakdown of social solidarity. General de Gaulle was using it in its paradigm French sense when, in his New Year's broadcast to the nation on 31 December 1968, recalling the *Evènements* of May, he observed:

At the same time, it is necessary that we surmount the moral malaise which—above all among us by reason of our individualism —is inherent in modern mechanical and materialist civilization. Otherwise, the fanatics of destruction, the doctrinaires of negation, the specialists in demagogy, will once more have a good opportunity to exploit bitterness in order to provoke agitation, while their sterility, which they have the derisory insolence to call revolution, can lead to nothing else than the dissolution of everything into nothingness, or else to the loss of everything under the grinding oppression of totalitarianism.

Despite wide divergences in views about the causes of social dissolution and the nature of an acceptable or desirable social order, the underlying perspective conveyed by the term is unmistakable.

Germany

This characteristically French meaning was certainly subject to cultural diffusion beyond the borders of France. It was, for instance, adopted by Friedrich List, precursor of the German Historical School of economics and advocate of economic nationalism, who used it in the sense developed by the Saint-Simonians and the socialists. List's major work, *The National System of Political Economy,* written in Paris, stressed the organic nature of society and the economy, and the historical and national framework of economic activity; and it attacked the classical economists for abstracting economic life from its social context. Thus List accused classical economics, which supported free trade and *laissez-faire,* of "*Kosmopolitismus,*" "*Materialismus,*" "*Partikularismus,*" and, above all, of "*Individualismus*"—sacrificing the welfare of the national community to the individual acquisition of wealth.

There is, however, quite distinct from this French use of the term, another use whose characteristic reference is German. This is the Romantic idea of "individuality" (*Individualität*), the notion of individual uniqueness, originality, self-realization—what the Romantics called "*Eigentümlichkeit*"—in contrast to the rational, universal, and uniform standards of the Enlightenment, which they saw as "quantitative," "abstract," and therefore sterile. The Romantics themselves did not use the term "*Individualismus,*" but it came to be used in this sense from the 1840's when a German liberal, Karl Brüggemann, contrasted with its negative French meaning, as found in List, that of a desirable and characteristically German "infinite" and "whole-souled" individualism, signifying "the infinite self-confidence of the individual aiming to be personally free in morals and in truth."

Thereafter, the term soon became, in this, chiefly German, use, virtually synonymous with the idea of individuality, which had originated in the writings of Wilhelm von Humboldt, Novalis, Friedrich Schlegel, and Friedrich Schleiermacher. Thus Georg Simmel wrote of the "new individualism" which he opposed to "eighteenth-century individualism" with its "notion of atomized and basically undifferentiated individuals"; the new, German, individualism was "the individualism of difference, with the deepening of individuality to the point of the individual's incomparability, to which he is 'called' both in his nature and in his achievement." The individual became "this specific, irreplaceable, given individual" and was "*called* or destined to realize his own incomparable image." The "new individualism," Simmel wrote, "might be called qualitative, in contrast with the quantitative individualism of the eighteenth century. Or it might be labeled the individualism of uniqueness (*Einzigkeit*) as against that of singleness (*Einzelheit*). At any rate, Romanticism was perhaps the broadest channel through which it reached the consciousness of the nineteenth century. Goethe had created its artistic, and Schleiermacher its metaphysical basis: Romanticism supplied its sentimental experiential foundation."

The German idea of individuality has had a remarkable history. Having begun as a cult of individual genius and originality, especially as applied to the artist, stressing the conflict between individual and society and the supreme value of subjectivity, solitude, and introspection, it developed along various lines. In one direction, it led to an uninhibited quest for eccentricity and to the purest egoism and social nihilism. This development found perhaps its most extreme expression in the thought of Max Stirner, whose "individualism" amounted to an amoral and anti-intellectualistic vision of freely cooperating and self-assertive egoists. For Stirner,

> I, the egoist, have not at heart the welfare of this "human society." I sacrifice nothing to it. I only utilize it: but to be able to utilize it completely I must transform it rather into my property and my creature—i.e., I must annihilate it and form in its place the Union of Egoists.

The main development, however, of the idea of individuality was in the direction of a characteristically German *Weltanschauung,* or cosmology, a total view of the (natural and social) world, fundamentally in conflict with the essentially humanist and rationalist thought typical of the rest of Western civilization. In a justly famous essay, Ernst Troeltsch contrasted the two systems of thought, the "west-European" and the German: on the one side, "an eternal, rational, and divinely ordained system of Order, embracing both morality and law"; on the other, "individual, living, and perpetually new incarnations of an historically creative Mind." Thus,

> Those who believe in an eternal and divine Law of Nature, the Equality of man, and a sense of Unity pervading mankind, and who find the essence of Humanity in these things, cannot but regard the German doctrine as a curious mixture of mysticism and brutality. Those who take an opposite view—who see in history an ever-moving stream, which throws up unique individualities as it moves, and is always shaping individual structures on the basis of a law which is always new—are bound to consider the west-European world of ideas as a world of cold rationalism and equalitarian atomism, a world of superficiality and Pharisaism.

Friedrich Meinecke summed up the revolution in thought which he saw Romanticism as bringing to Western civilization in the following way:

Out of this deepening individualism of uniqueness, there henceforth arose everywhere in Germany, in various different forms, a new and more living image of the State, and also a new picture of the world. The whole world now appeared to be filled with individuality, each individuality, whether personal or supra-personal, governed by its own characteristic principle of life, and both Nature and History constituting what Friedrich Schlegel called an "abyss of individuality". . . . Individuality everywhere, the identity of mind and nature, and through this identity an invisible but strong bond unifying the otherwise boundless diversity and abundance of individual phenomena—these were the new and powerful ideas which now burst forth in Germany in so many different ways.

In particular, the personal "individualism" of the early Romantics very soon became transformed into an organic and nationalistic theory of community, each unique and self-sufficient, according to which, as one recent scholar has said, the individual was "fated to merge with and become rooted in nature and the Volk" and would thus be "able to find his self-expression and his individuality." Moreover, individuality was ascribed no longer merely to persons, but to supra-personal forces, especially the nation or the state. Meinecke paints a vivid picture of this transformation:

> This new sense for what was individual resembled a fire which was capable of consuming, not all at once, but gradually, every sphere of life. At first, it seized only the flimsiest and most inflammable materials—the subjective life of the individual, the world of art and poetry; but then it went on to consume heavier substances, above all the state.

The same progression from the individuality of the person to that of the nation or state occurred in countless German thinkers of the early nineteenth century—notably, in Fichte, Schelling, Schleiermacher, and even, in a sense, Hegel. The state and society were no longer regarded as rational constructions, the result of contractual arrangements between individuals in the manner of the Enlightenment; they were "super-personal creative forces, which build from time to time out of the material of particular individuals, a spiritual Whole, and on the basis of that Whole proceed from time to time to create the particular political and social institutions which embody and incarnate its significance." As Simmel wrote, the "total organism" of society "shifts, so to speak into a location high above [individuals]" and, accordingly, "this individualism, which restricts freedom to a purely inward sense of the term, easily acquires an antiliberal tendency"; it is "the complete antithesis of eighteenth-century individualism which . . . could not even conceive the idea of a collective as an organism that unifies heterogeneous elements."

While the characteristically French sense of "individualism" is negative, signifying individual isolation and social dissolution, the characteristically German sense is thus positive, signifying individual self-fulfillment and (except among the earliest Romantics) the organic unity of individual and society. The distinction was drawn with particular force by Thomas Mann, in a passage written at the close of the First World War, which argues that German life reconciles the individual and society, freedom and obligation:

> It remains the uniqueness of German individualism that it is entirely compatible with ethical socialism, which is called "state socialism" but which is quite distinct from the philosophy of the rights of man and Marxism. For it is only the individualism of the Enlightenment, the liberal individualism of the West, which is incompatible with the social principle.

The German variety, Mann thought, "includes the freedom of the individual." To "reject the individualistic Enlightenment does not amount to a demand for the submergence of the individual in society and the state": the German theory of organic community protected freedom, whereas ideas deriving from the Enlightenment (among which Mann included Marxism) led to Jacobinism, state absolutism, political tyranny. "Organism" was a word that is "true to life," for "an organism is more than the sum of its parts, and that more is its spirit, its life." Here one can see that individualism does not, as with the French, endanger social solidarity; it is its supreme realization.

Burckhardt

A striking and influential synthesis of French and German meanings of "individualism" is to be found (appropriately enough) in the work of the Swiss historian Jacob Burckhardt. A central theme of Burckhardt's *The Civilization of the Renaissance in Italy* was the growth of "individualism." Summing up the "principal features in the Italian character of that time," Burckhardt maintained that its "fundamental vice . . . was at the same time a condition of its greatness, namely, excessive individualism." The second part of the work is entitled "The Development of the Individual" and, in general, Burckhardt treated the Italians of the Renaissance as a people "who have emerged from the half-conscious life of the race and become themselves individuals."

Schematically, one can say that Burckhardt's use of "individualism" combines the notion of the aggressive self-assertion of individuals freed from an externally given framework of authority (as found in Louis Blanc) and that of the individual's withdrawal from society into a private existence (as in Tocqueville) with the early Romantic idea, most clearly expressed by Humboldt, of the full and harmonious development of the individual personality, seen as representing humanity and pointing towards its highest cultural development. The Italian of the Renaissance was for Burckhardt "the firstborn among the sons of modern Europe" in virtue of the autonomy of his morality, his cultivation of privacy, and the individuality of his character.

"The individual," Burckhardt wrote,

> first inwardly casts off the authority of a State which, as a fact, is in most cases tyrannical and illegitimate, and what he thinks and does is now, rightly or wrongly, called treason. The sight of victorious egotism in others drives him to defend his own right by his own arm. . . . In face of all objective facts, of laws and restraints of whatever kind, he retains the feeling of his own sovereignty, and in each single instance forms his decision independently, according as honor or interest, passion or calculation, revenge or renunciation, gain the upper hand in his own mind.

As to privacy, Burckhardt wrote of "the different tendencies and manifestations of private life . . . thriving in the fullest vigour and variety" and cited "Agnolo Pandolfini (d. 1446), whose work on domestic economy is the first complete programme of a developed private life." "The private man," he argued, "indifferent to politics, and busied partly with serious pursuits, partly with the interests of a *dilettante,* seems to have been first fully formed in these despotisms of the fourteenth century." Finally, he identified the "impulse to the highest individual development" and saw Italy at the close of the thirteenth century as beginning to "swarm with individuality; the ban upon human personality was dissolved; and a thousand figures meet us each in his own special shape and dress." Dante, "through the wealth of individuality which he set forth," was "the most national herald of his time"; much of Burckhardt's book treats of "this unfolding of the treasures of human nature in literature and art." An acute and practised eye could trace

> the increase in the number of complete men during the fifteenth century. Whether they had before them as a conscious object the harmonious development of their spiritual and material existence, is hard to say, but several of them attained it, so far as is consistent with the imperfection of all that is earthly.

It is worth adding that for Burckhardt this growth of individualism was, as for so many philosophers of history, no accident but a "historical necessity." Transmitted by Italian culture, and infusing the other nations of Europe, it

> has constituted since then the higher atmosphere which they breathe. In itself it is neither good nor bad, but necessary; within it has grown up a modern standard of good and evil—a sense of moral responsibility—which is essentially different from that which was familiar to the Middle Ages.

It was in the United States that "individualism" primarily came to celebrate capitalism and liberal democracy. It became a symbolic catchword of immense ideological significance, expressing all that has at various times been implied in the philosophy of natural rights, the belief in free enterprise, and the American Dream. It expressed, in fact, the operative ideals of nineteenth- and early twentieth-century America (and indeed continues to play a major ideological role), advancing a set of universal claims seen as incompatible with the parallel claims of the socialism and communism of the Old World. It referred, not to the sources of social dissolution or the painful transition to a future harmonious social order, nor to the cultivation of uniqueness or the organic community, but rather to the actual or imminent realization of the final stage of human progress in a spontaneously cohesive society of equal individual rights, limited government, *laissez-faire,* natural justice and equal opportunity, and individual freedom, moral development, and dignity. Naturally it carried widely varying connotations in differing contexts and at different times.

It was imported, in the negative French sense, *via* the writings of various Europeans, among them the socialists, as well as Tocqueville, List, and the Saint-Simonian Michel Chevalier, whose *Lettres sur l'Amérique du Nord* (1836) contrasted the anarchic individualism of the Yankees with the more socially inclined and organizable French. Already in 1839, an article in the *United States Magazine and Democratic Review* identified it positively with national values and ideals seen in the evolutionary and universal terms. The course of civilization

> is the progress of man from a state of savage individualism to that
> of an individualism more elevated, moral and refined. . . . The last
> order of civilization, which is democratic, received its first perma-
> nent existence in this country. . . . The peculiar duty of this coun-
> try has been to exemplify and embody a civilization in which the
> rights, freedom, and mental and moral growth of individual men
> should be made the highest end of all social restrictions and laws.

This abrupt change in the evaluative significance of the term is strikingly illustrated in one of the earliest American discussions of Tocqueville's *Democracy in America* by a Transcendentalist writer in the *Boston Quarterly Review*. The writer, inaccurately but significantly, expounded Tocqueville's concept of individualism as expressing "that strong confidence in self, or reliance upon one's own exertion and resources" and as "the strife of all our citizens for wealth and distinction of *their own,* and their contempt of reflected honors." "Individualism," he continued, "has its immutable laws . . . which . . . when allowed to operate without let or hindrance . . . must in the end assimilate the species, and evolve all the glorious phenomena of original and eternal *order;*—that order which exists in man himself, and alone vivifies and sustains him."

"Individualism" had, by the end of the Civil War, acquired an important place in the vocabulary of American ideology. Indeed, even those who criticized American society, from New England Transcendentalists to the Single Taxers and the Populists, often did so in the name of individualism. The term acquired differing layers of meaning under the successive influences of New England Puritanism, the Jeffersonian tradition, and natural rights philosophy; Unitarianism, Transcendentalism, and evangelicalism; the need of the North to develop an ideological defence against the challenge of the South; the immensely popular evolutionary and *laissez-faire* ideas of Herbert Spencer and the growth of Social Darwinism; and the permanent and continuing impetus of alternative, European-born ideologies. The course of this development has been admirably traced in Yehoshua Arieli's book, *Individualism and Nationalism in American Ideology,* which rightly treats the American version of "individualism" as a symbol of national identification. As Arieli concludes,

> Individualism supplied the nation with a rationalization of its characteristic attitudes, behaviour patterns and aspirations. It endowed the past, the present and the future with the perspective of unity and progress. It explained the peculiar social and political organization of the nation—unity in spite of heterogeneity—and it pointed towards an ideal of social organization in harmony with American experience. Above all, individualism expressed the universalism and idealism most characteristic of the national consciousness. This concept evolved in contradistinction to socialism, the universal and messianic character of which it shared.

It can, indeed, be argued that the lack of a real socialist tradition in America is in part a function of the very pervasiveness of the ideology of individualism.

Certainly, a perusal of the various American uses of the term reveals a quite distinctive range of connotations. For Emerson, contemplating the failure of Brook Farm, individualism, which he endowed with an exalted moral and religious significance, had "never been tried"; it was the route to perfection—a spontaneous social order of self-determined, self-reliant and fully developed individuals. "The union," he wrote, "is only perfect when all the uniters are isolated. . . . Each man, if he attempts to join himself to others, is on all sides cramped and diminished. . . . The Union must be ideal in actual individualism." Society was tending towards a morally superior voluntary social order, a "free and just commonwealth" in which "property rushes from the idle and imbecile to the industrious, brave and persevering." For the historian John William Draper, writing immediately after the Civil War, in celebration of the social system of the North, its

> population was in a state of unceasing activity; there was a corporeal and mental restlessness. Magnificent cities in all directions were arising; the country was intersected with canals, railroads . . . companies for banking, manufacturing, commercial purposes, were often

concentrating many millions of capital. There were all kinds of associations . . . churches, hospitals, schools abounded. The foreign commerce at length rivaled that of the most powerful nations of Europe. This wonderful spectacle of social development was the result of INDIVIDUALISM; operating in an unbounded theatre of action. Everyone was seeking to do all that he could for himself.

And for Walt Whitman, likewise celebrating the democratic system of the North, it incarnated the progressive force of modern history—"the singleness of man, individualism," reconciling liberty and social justice.

In the hands of the Social Darwinists, such as William Graham Sumner, "individualism" acquired a harsher and altogether less idealistic significance. Sumner, who maintained that "liberty, inequality, survival of the fittest . . . carries society forward and favors all its best members," offered a purportedly scientific rationale for a ruthlessly competitive society where the individual "has all his chances left open that he make out of himself all there is in him. This is individualism and atomism." In this context, the influence of Herbert Spencer's doctrines as a justification for unrestrained rivalry in business and unscrupulous dealings in politics was immense; he was widely seen as "the shining light of evolution and individualism." These ideas entered into an evolving ideology of private enterprise and *laissez-faire,* postulating absolute equality of opportunity and the equivalence of public welfare and private accumulation. The word was used in this sense by Andrew Carnegie, and by Henry Clews, author of *The Wall Street Point of View* (1900), who spoke of "that system of Individualism which guards, protects and encourages competition," whose spirit was "the American Spirit—the love of freedom,—of free industry,—free and unfettered opportunity. . . ." It was also used favorably by Theodore Roosevelt, Woodrow Wilson, and William J. Bryan. Despite counter trends to the "Gospel of Wealth" and the "Gospel of Success," the term continued to have wide currency until a temporary eclipse during the Depression and the New Deal. It was in 1928 that Herbert Hoover gave his famous campaign speech on the "American system of rugged individualism"; yet the term regained its resonance, as can be seen by the sales of the writings of the contemporary novelist-philosopher, Ayn Rand, in defence of "reason, individualism, and capitalism."

In short, with regard to the American sense of "individualism," James Bryce was right when he observed that, throughout their history, "individualism, the love of enterprise, and pride in personal freedom, have been deemed by Americans not only their choicest, but their peculiar and exclusive possession."

England

In England, the term has played a smaller role, as an epithet for nonconformity in religion, for the sterling qualities of self-reliant Englishmen, especially among the nineteenth-century middle-classes, and for features common to the various shades of English liberalism. French and German influences can, of course, also be found. Its first use was in Henry Reeve's translation of Tocqueville's *De la Démocratie en Amérique* in 1840. The word was also used pejoratively in the French sense by a great number of thinkers, but especially socialists, to refer to the evils of capitalist competition. Thus, Robert Owen, in specifying his cooperative socialist ideals, argued that to "effect these changes there must be . . . a new organisation of society, on the principle of *attractive union,* instead of *repulsive individualism* . . . ," while John Stuart Mill (who was much influenced by the Saint-Simonians) asserted that "the moral objection to competition, as arming one human being against another, making the good of each depend upon evil to others, making all who have anything to gain or lose, live in the midst of enemies, by no means deserves the disdain with which it is treated by some of the adversaries of socialism. . . . Socialism, as long as it attacks the existing individualism, is easily triumphant; its weakness hitherto is in what it proposes to substitute." Mill, expounding, not unsympathetically, the ideas of "the present Socialists," wrote that, in their eyes,

> the very foundation of human life as at present constituted, the very principle on which the production and repartition of all material products is now carried on, is essentially vicious and anti-social. It is the principle of individualism, competition, each one for himself and against all the rest. It is grounded on opposition of interests, not harmony of interests, and under it every one is required to find his place by a struggle, by pushing others back or being pushed back by them. Socialists consider this system of private war (as it may be termed) between every one and every one, especially fatal in an economical point of view and in a moral.

And the socially-conscious Bishop of Durham, Brooke Foss Wescott argued in 1890 that "individualism regards humanity as made up of disconnected or warring atoms: socialism regards it as an organic whole, a vital unity formed by the combination of contributing members mutually interdependent."

As to the German sense, this can be seen in the writings of the Unitarian minister William McCall, claimed as a precursor in expounding "the doctrine of Individuality" (along with Humboldt, the German Romantics, Goethe, and Josiah Warren) by John Stuart Mill. McCall, who was influenced by German Romanticism, wrote declamatory books and pamphlets, such as *Elements of Individualism* (1847) and *Outlines of Individualism* (1853), in which he preached the gospel of a new way of life dominated by the "Principle of Individualism," which he hoped England would be the first country to adopt.

Among indigenous uses, the term's reference to nonconformity is evident in the condemnation by Gladstone, who for a time advocated a single state religion, of "our individualism in religion" and in Matthew Arnold's contrast between the Catholics' ecclesiastical conception of the

Eucharist and its origin "as Jesus founded it" where "it is the consecration of absolute individualism." The term's reference to the English character can be seen in Samuel Smiles, that ardent moralist on behalf of the Manchester School of political economy. "The spirit of self-help," he wrote, "as exhibited in the energetic action of individuals, has in all times been a marked feature of the English character"; even "the humblest person, who sets before his fellows an example of industry, sobriety, and upright honesty of purpose in life, has a present as well as a future influence upon the well-being of his country." It was this "energetic individualism which produces the most powerful effects upon the life and action of others, and really constitutes the best practical education."

It was as a central term in the vocabulary of English liberalism that "individualism" came to be mainly used in the latter half of the nineteenth century, in contrast with "socialism," "communism," and, especially, "collectivism." Thus the *Pall Mall Gazette* in 1888 spoke of holding "the scales between individualists and Socialists" and the *Times* in 1896 of "the individualists" holding "their own against the encroachments of the State." Though scarcely used by the political economists and the Benthamites, and though, as we have seen, Mill used it in a different and negative sense, "individualism" came to be embraced by the whole spectrum of English liberals, from those advocating the most extreme *laissez-faire* to those supporting quite extensive state intervention.

Among the former was Herbert Spencer, concerned to assist the general course of social evolution by arresting the imminent "drift towards a form of society in which private activities of every kind, guided by individual wills, are to be replaced by public activities guided by governmental will," that "lapse of self-ownership into ownership by the community, which is partially implied by collectivism and completely by communism." Even more extreme than Spencer was Auberon Herbert, author of *The Voluntaryist Creed* (1906) and editor in the 1890's of *The Free Life,* where he described his creed as "thorough-going individualism," advocating among other things voluntary taxation and education, and "the open market and free trade in everything." At the other end of the scale were liberals, such as T. H. Green and L. T. Hobhouse, who favored positive political action for the promotion of a liberal society. For Green, individualism was "the free competitive action of the individual in relation to the production and distribution of wealth," as opposed to "the collective action of society operating through society or the executive"; he believed individualism in this sense to be "a fundamental principle of human nature and an essential factor of the well-being of society." Hobhouse put the matter very clearly: "to maintain individual freedom and equality we have to extend the sphere of social control," and thus "individualism, when it grapples with the facts, is driven no small distance along Socialist lines."

Perhaps the most influential use was that typified by Dicey, who equated individualism with Benthamism and utilitarian Liberalism. For Dicey,

Utilitarian individualism, which for many years under the name of liberalism, determined the trend of English legislation, was nothing but Benthamism modified by the experience, the prudence, or the timidity of practical politicians.

The "individualistic reformers," he wrote, "opposed anything which shook the obligations of contracts, or, what is at bottom the same thing, limited the contractual freedom of individuals" and, in general, they "tacitly assumed that each man if left to himself would in the long run be sure to act for his own true interest, and that the general welfare was sufficiently secured if each man were left free to pursue his happiness in his own way, either alone or in combination with his fellows." "Individualism" has, in this sense, been widely used to mean the absence or minimum of state intervention in the economic and other spheres, and has usually been associated, both by its adherents and its opponents, with classical, or negative liberalism.

13. The Marxian Revolutionary Idea

ROBERT C. TUCKER

Of all the new "isms" of the nineteenth century, socialism is the one most likely to spring to mind first, and the name most closely associated with it is that of Karl Marx (1818–1883). Certainly the work of Marx and his associate, Friedrich Engels (1820–1895), did more to shape the direction of socialism than that of any other thinker.

The non-Communist world's understanding of Marxism has been undergoing considerable change in recent years for two main reasons. For one thing, the political climate has improved to a point where an objective appraisal of Marx is easier to make, thanks to the waning of the ideological Cold War and to the growing "respectability" of west European Socialists. Fewer people automatically equate Marxism with Soviet or Chinese communism, and certainly democratic socialism, the other heir of Marxism, is not so frightening when espoused by such leaders as Germany's Willy Brandt and Britain's Harold Wilson. In short, scholars are no longer restricted to judging Marx either *by the policies of Stalin or Mao, or by the ideological battles within democratic socialism, or by the struggle between socialism and capitalism.*

The second factor bringing about change in Marxist studies has been the rediscovery of forgotten writings of Marx, found in the 1920s and 1930s and translated into English only in the 1960s. These include his Economic and

Source: Robert C. Tucker, "The Marxian Revolutionary Idea," in Carl J. Friedrich, ed., *Nomos VIII: Revolution* (New York: Atherton Press, 1966), pp. 217–39. Copyright © by Atherton Press, 1966. Reprinted by permission of the author and Aldine-Atherton, Inc. [Footnotes omitted.]

Philosophic Manuscripts of 1844 *and his* Grundrisse *of 1857–1858, a complete unpublished draft of the never-completed* Capital. *The comparison of these "new" works with old ones such as the* Communist Manifesto *and* Capital *has caused many commentators, to see, for example, that Marx's early concern was with that fashionable modern term,* alienation. *The* Grundrisse *shows that alienation, moreover, remained a central tenet of Marx's mature thought. Instead of being regarded either as "out of date" or as the harbinger of Leninism and Stalinism, Marx now appears to many to have been a prophet of twentieth-century alienation among affluent labor in an automated economy, or what Marx called "machinofacture." Recent reactions to these themes in Marxism include T. B. Bottomore's and Maximilien Rubel's introduction to their edition of Marx's* Selected Writings in Sociology and Social Philosophy *(1956), Shlomo Avineri's* Social and Political Thought of Karl Marx *(1968), George Lichtheim's* Marxism *(1965), and dissident French communist Roger Garaudy's* Karl Marx: Evolution of His Thought *(1967).*

Some of these new themes are developed in this selection by Princeton University political scientist Robert C. Tucker. He deals here with Marx's social thought and sees a unity in it between the young Marx and the mature Marx. According to Tucker, how does Marxism differ from earlier socialist thought, Soviet Marxism, and the Marxism debated by Kautsky and Bernstein at the turn of the century in the German Social Democratic party? What are the principles of Hegelianism and in what ways and to what extent did Marx depart from them? According to Marx why must society be analyzed in a world context? How and why must this analysis be related to the mode of production and the division of labor? What meanings does Marx give to division of labor anyway? What motivates a class of producers to rise against and revolutionize a mode of production and its social superstructures? How will the communist revolution resemble and differ from all previous revolutions? How do Marx's ideas on individualism and division of labor compare with those expressed in the previous selection on individualism? For example, were his ideas in harmony with the German tradition?

In his parting word about Marx at Highgate Cemetery, Engels characterized his friend as "before all else a revolutionist." This was a true summation of Marx both as a man of action and as a thinker. For as a theorist Marx was before all else a theorist of revolution. The revolutionary idea was the keystone of his theoretical structure. Marxism, as he fashioned it with the assistance of Engels, was in its essence a theory and program of revolution.

Like many a powerful teaching that becomes the ideology of movements carried on in its name and dedicated to its realization, Marxism has not always reflected its original inspiration. It has tended at various times to lose its "revolutionary soul" (to borrow Lenin's phrase). This happened with the revisionist Marxism of Eduard Bernstein, who forsook even the revolutionary theory of Marx in favor of a doctrine of evolutionary socialism. It was reflected too, if less obviously, in the orthodox Marxism of Karl Kautsky, a leading theorist of the German Social Democratic party, whose fidelity to Marxist revolutionism in theory went along with an abandonment of it in practice. A similar if less pronounced discrepancy is becoming apparent in present-day Soviet Marxism. Its exponents rather resemble the German orthodox Marxists of a generation ago in their tendency to talk Marxist revolutionism while pursuing a relatively unrevolutionary policy. But all these instances of the decline of the revolutionary impulse in the Marxist movement belong to the story of what happened to Marxism after its founder's death. Our subject here is Marx's Marxism, and this was the world-view of a revolutionist.

It was so, moreover, from the beginning of his intellectual career. Marx's first independent act of theorizing, contained in notes to his doctoral dissertation of 1841, was an essay on the necessity of a complete revolutionary transformation of the world in the name of the "realization of philosophy," meaning the Hegelian philosophy of humanity's apotheosis in history. Marx was thus in some sense committed to the idea of world revolution prior to his conversion to the notions of socialism or communism, and he only accepted the latter a year or so later when he found a way of assimilating them into the philosophy of world revolution that he had evolved as a member of the school of Young Hegelian philosophers. Marxism was born of this fusion in an intellectual process recorded in Marx's *Economic and Philosophic Manuscripts of 1844*, whose publication in the present century presaged a new era in Marx scholarship in the West.

As a form of socialist doctrine, then, Marxism was inseparable from the idea of revolution. It conceived of socialism or communism (these two terms were always used by Marx and Engels more or less interchangeably) as a radically new state of the world, and of man in the world, which was to be achieved by revolutionary means. This, according to the *Communist Manifesto*, was what distinguished Marxism from the main currents of earlier socialist thought and most earlier socialist movements, which were essentially reformist rather than revolutionary.

The idea of revolution is present in nearly everything that Marx wrote. It is the theoretical axis of his early philosophical writings. It is the leitmotif of his great political pamphlets on the 1848 events, the *coup d'état* of Louis Bonaparte, and the Paris Commune. It informs almost all that he has to say on the strategy and tactics of the communist movement. It is a favorite subject in the voluminous correspondence that he carried on with Engels and others. And his major work, *Capital*, together with his other economic writings, is essentially a political economy of revolution, an inquiry into the conditions of capitalism's revolutionary self-destruction. In a basic sense, therefore, revolution was the master-theme of Marx's thought, and an exposition of the Marxian revolutionary idea in complete form would be nothing other than an exposition of Marxism itself as a theoretical system.

It follows that the Marxian revolutionary idea has as many dimensions of meaning as Marxism itself. Revolution for Marx is a social, an economic, a technological, a political, a legal, and an ideological phenomenon. It is even, in its way, a natural phenomenon, for it involves the appropriation of the man-produced world of material objects that Marx describes in his early writings as "anthropological nature" or the "nature produced by history." Furthermore, revolution means transformation of man himself. In Marx's words, "the whole of history is nothing but a continual transformation of human nature." He especially looks to the future communist revolution as the source of a radical transformation of man or "change of self," and here we touch upon the moral and religious dimensions of the Marxian revolutionary idea. Finally, revolution for Marx is an historical category. The whole of his theory of revolution is set in the frame of the materialist conception of history. His theory of society is a theory of society-in-history, and his theory of revolution is a theory of the transformations of society in history, a theory of history itself as a process of man's revolutionary evolution.

The Genesis of Marxism

Marx always maintained that his theory of history arose as a metamorphosis of Hegel's. The materialist conception of history was the Hegelian idealist conception turned "upside down" or "back upon its feet." The meaning of this enigmatic contention has become clear only in the light of the 1844 manuscripts, which show that Marxism was indeed born as a metamorphosis of Hegelianism.

Hegelianism treats world history as the self-realization of God or Spirit (*Geist*). Historicizing the creation of the world as conceived in the Judaeo-Christian theology, this philosophy pictures creation taking place in historical time as the process by which God becomes fully God *in* the world. Having at first externalized itself in the form of nature, Spirit, acting through humanity, creatively externalizes itself in a succession of historical civilizations or culture worlds, which it appropriates in thought stage by stage through the minds of the great philosophers down to Hegel. History is thus seen as a process of "production." God becomes fully God in the course of it by becoming aware of himself as such, for on Hegel's definition self-knowledge or self-consciousness belongs to the nature (or "concept") of God. For God to become aware of himself as such is, moreover, to become aware of himself as infinite being, or of all reality as Spirit, as subjective. Each historical episode of self-knowledge begins with Spirit confronted by a seemingly objective world of "otherness" outside and beyond it. This experience of being bounded by an object is portrayed by Hegel as an experience of finitude, which in turn is an experience of "alienation" (*Entfremdung*). The knowing mind, in other words, experiences the given objective world as alien and hostile in its otherness before recognizing it as Spirit in externalized form. Hence, knowing for Hegel is de-alienation whereby the given form of external reality produced by Spirit is stripped of its illusory strangeness and made "property of the ego." The terminal point in the historical process of self-knowledge (which Hegel also describes as a progress of the consciousness of freedom through the overcoming of the fetters of finitude) is the stage of "absolute knowledge" when Spirit finally beholds the absolute totality of creation as Spirit and thus achieves complete self-realization in the knowledge of itself as Absolute Being. This self-knowledge, on Hegel's premises, is reached in Hegelianism—the scientific demonstration of the entire process of world history just summarized.

Marx originally formulated his materialist conception of history as a conscious act of *translation* of this Hegelian phenomenology of history into what he considered realistic or truly scientific terms. Following a lead given by Ludwig Feuerbach, he assumed that one had to draw a distinction between the manifest content of Hegelianism, which was mystical, and the latent or "esoteric" content, which was scientifically sound. What Hegel was esoterically talking about in his philosophy of history as the self-realization of God was the self-realization of humanity, the human historical process. Hegelianism was a philosopher's fantasy-picture of real human history. The task was to de-mystify it, which one could do by turning it upside down. That is, one had to switch the subject and predicate in the key propositions of Hegelian theory.

Thus man was not *Geist* in the flesh; rather, *Geist* was the thought-process in the head of real material man. History was not the process by which God becomes fully God in man; rather, Hegel's image of history as such a process was a mental representation of actual history as a process by which man becomes fully human. The world-creating activity going on in history was not thought-production, not something going on in God's mind; rather, the production of the world by Spirit was Hegel's mystified rendition of the real fact that the world is produced in a historical process of *material* production carried on by man in his economic life. Hence the true and scientific conception of history esoterically present in Hegelianism was a "materialist" one that views man as the universal creator and material production—the production of material objects—as the basic kind of human productive activity. By the same token, Spirit's experience of self-alienation in the presence of an alien and hostile world of its own creation was simply Hegel's mystified way of expressing the real fact that working man experiences alienation in the presence of a world of material objects that he himself has created in "alienated labor" in the service of another man—the capitalist—who appropriates the product as his private property. Appropriation (*Aneignung*) was not, therefore, something going on in the philosopher's mind; rather, the Hegelian notion of the cognitive appropriation of the world by Spirit was an inverted representation of the material appropriation of objects in history, the accumulation of capital. Further, the overcoming of alienation was not a process that could take place simply in thought. As the alienated world was a world of real material things and productive powers, the appropriation of it by the exploited and alienated producers, the proletarians, would have to take place in a real revolution—a communist revolution consisting in the worldwide seizure and socialization of private property. And finally, Hegel's picture of the ultimate stage of "absolute knowledge," when Spirit contemplates the whole world as Spirit in the beatific moment of complete self-awareness in freedom, was the philosopher's fantasy of ultimate communism, when man would achieve self-fulfillment in creative activity and aesthetic experience of the no longer alienated world surrounding him.

Such was Marxism, or the materialist conception of history, in its original presentation in Marx's 1844 manuscripts as an inverted Hegelianism. Much was refined and added in the subsequent development of the system by Marx and Engels. Yet this "original Marxism" was the matrix of the mature Marxist *Weltanschauung*. Even where a seeming break occurred, as in the abandonment of the category of "alienation" in the mature restatements of the theory beginning with Marx's in Part I of *The German Ideology,* we find an underlying continuity of thought; for the content of the idea of alienation lives on in the special meaning assigned in mature Marxism to the concept of "division of labor."

The fundamental ideas of original Marxism remained, explicitly or implicitly, the presuppositions of Marx's thought. Having defined history in the 1844 manuscripts as man's "act of becoming," he continued to see it as the process of self-development of the human species or society. For Marx history is the growth-process of humanity from the primitive beginnings to complete maturity and self-realization in future communism. Since man is conceived in this system as a creative being or producer in his essential nature, his developmental process is, as Marx had called it in his early manuscripts, a *Produktionsgeschichte* (history of production), with material production as the primary kind of productive activity. It proceeds through a series of epochs marked by the division of mankind into warring classes towards the postulated communist future. The transitions from epoch to epoch are revolutionary, for "revolutions are the locomotives of history."

Marxism as Social Theory

Understandably, much of the literature of and about Marxism as a revolutionary theory has a political orientation. Marxists, beginning with Marx and Engels, have been deeply concerned with the politics of revolution, and very many students of Marxist thought have interested themselves in this too. It is perhaps a measure and in any event a symptom of this bias that Lenin's principal treatise on Marxist revolutionary theory, *The State and Revolution,* is almost wholly devoted to revolution as a political phenomenon. Now there is no doubt about the great importance of this aspect of the Marxian revolutionary idea. For Marx every revolutionary transition from one social epoch to the next involves a political revolution—the overthrow of the existing state and conquest of political power by the revolutionary class. But to Marx's way of thinking this is not the core of the revolutionary process. Here, indeed, we encounter a certain difference of emphasis between the Marxism of Marx and that of Lenin, for whom the political process of revolution was of supreme importance both theoretically and practically. Without ever slighting the significance of the political dimension, Marx, on the other hand, always saw *social* revolution as the fundamental revolutionary fact. In the analogy between revolution and the birth-process that recurs from time to time in his writings, the social revolution is the whole organic process by which a new society comes into being; the political revolution is merely a momentous incident occurring at the climax of the process. The principal question to be considered here, therefore, is what Marx meant by a social revolution.

In *The Social Revolution,* an influential little volume written in 1902, Kautsky answered this question in behalf of German orthodox Marxism by defining social revolution as "the conquest of political power by a previously subservient class and the transformation of the juridical and political superstructure of society, particularly in the property relations. . . ." As Kautsky himself pointed out, this was a "narrower" view than Marx's own as expressed in the well-known preface to the *Critique of Political Economy.* It also suffered from superficiality. Although the supplanting of one ruling class by another is integral to social revolution as Marx conceives it, this formula fails to convey the substance of what he means by social revolution. To arrive at a more adequate formulation, we must first consider Marx's conception of society.

Marx the sociologist is inseparable from Marx the theorist of history. The view of society presented in his own mature writings and those of Engels is governed at every point by the basic premises of the materialist conception of history. Thus, Marx as a social theorist recognizes the existence of societies on a national scale but does not see in them the fundamental unit of society. For him the real social unit is the species, the human collectivity at a given stage of its historical growth-process. Each such stage constitutes a social epoch dominated by a particular "social formation." Any national society, such as the German, English, or French, is but a concrete expression of human society as a whole in the given epoch, although it may be a case that exhibits the general pattern of the existing or emerging social formation most clearly and in most mature development. Marx, for example, saw contemporary English society as the model and most advanced form of a universally emerging "bourgeois society" of the modern epoch. This bourgeois or capitalist social formation, now becoming dominant on a world scale, had been preceded in history by feudal, antique, and Asiatic social formations, each of which represented the dominant form of human society in its time. An important implication for Marx's theory of revolution is that he always sees a social revolution as universal in scope, as an event of world history. It may express itself here and there on a national scale, as in the French Revolution of 1789, but such a happening is only a partial and local manifestation of a world revolutionary process. For Marx all social revolutions are world revolutions.

The materialist conception of history underlies all other aspects of Marx's sociology. Man being essentially a producer and his history a "history of production," society, to Marx's way of thinking, is in essence a productive system and process. The constitutive fact of society is that human productive activity, especially the material production on which all else depends, is social in nature. In other words, production for Marx is a process going on not simply between man and nature but also between man and man. This "social process of production" is the core of the social process per se. Human society is fundamentally a society of production, a set of "social relations" that men enter in the activity of producing. In the familiar formulation from the *Critique of Political Economy,* the social relations of production constitute the "basis" (*Basis, Grundlage*) of society, over which rises an institutional superstructure and to which there corresponds a social mind expressed in various "ideological forms" (religion, philosophy, art, etc.).

Since primitive times, according to Marx, the society of production has been a divided one. The social relations of production have been property relations between the immediate producers and those who, by virtue of their ownership and control of the means of production, have been able to appropriate the producers' surplus product as private property: slaves and slaveowners in ancient society, serfs and landowning nobles in feudal society, proletarians and capitalists in modern bourgeois society. Each one of these sets of social relations of production has been, in Marx's terminology, a specific form of the division of labor (*Teilung der Arbeit*) in production. This concept has a twofold meaning in Marxist thought. First, it refers to occupational specialization in all its forms beginning with the division between mental and physical labor and between town and country. But it also refers to what may be called the "social division of labor," meaning the division of society as a whole into a nonworking minority class of owners of the means of production and a nonowning majority class of workers. As already indicated, Marx holds that such a social division of labor has been the essential feature of human society so far in history. The prime expression of the division of labor is the class division of society. In Engels' words, "It is . . . the law of the division of labor which lies at the root of the division into classes." Marx makes the same point more concretely when he writes:

> In so far as millions of families live under economic conditions of existence that divide their mode of life, their interests, and their culture from those of other classes, and put them in hostile contrast to the latter, they form a class.

The determination of the class structure of society by the nature of the social division of labor may be expressed in Marxist terms by saying that every society is characterized by its particular "mode of production" (*Produktionsweise*). Contrary to what one might suppose, this key concept of Marx's is primarily social rather than technological in content, although it has a technological element. The mode of production is not equated with the productive techniques or material "productive powers," which are included, rather, under the heading of "means of production" (*Produktionsmittels*). What Marx means by the mode of production is the prevailing mode of labor or productive activity as conditioned by the existing state of technology or means of production. Now productive activity, as already noted, is for Marx exclusively and essentially social activity. Accordingly, the mode of production is equivalent to the social relations of production viewed, as it were, dynamically or in motion, together with the conditioning state of technology. And inasmuch as the social relations of production have so far in history been successive forms of the division of labor in production, the various historical modes of production may be described as forms of productive activity within the division of labor. Production within the division of labor has thus been the *general* mode of production in history. In Engels' formulation, "The basic form of all former production is the division of labor, on the one hand within society as a whole, and on the other, within each separate productive establishment."

The central thesis of Marxist sociology is that every society in history has been characterized and indeed shaped in all its manifold aspects by the nature of its particular mode of production as just defined. In ancient society the mode of production was slave labor, or productive activity performed within the social division of labor between master and slave. In feudal society it was serf labor, or productive activity performed within the social division of labor between nobleman and serf. And in modern bourgeois society it is wage labor, or productive activity carried on within the social division of labor between capitalist and proletarian. In every instance—runs the argument of Marx and Engels—the mode of productive activity has been the definitive fact of the social epoch, the determinant of the character of society in all of its superstructural expressions: political, legal, intellectual, religious, etc. To this way of thinking, every society fundamentally *is* its mode of production. Of wage labor, for example, Marx writes: "Without it there is no capital, no bourgeoisie, no bourgeois society."

It follows that a social revolution in the Marxist definition is a change in the mode of production with consequent change of all subordinate elements of the social complex. The feudal revolution would be defined in these terms as the change from slave labor to serf labor resulting in the general transition to feudal society; the bourgeois revolution as the change from serf labor to wage labor resulting in the general transition to bourgeois society. Historically, argue Marx and Engels, these revolutions in the mode of production and therewith in society as a whole have been changes of the *specific form* of productive activity within the social division of labor. They have been revolutions within the general mode of production based upon the division of labor in society and the production process, i.e., upon the class division of society and occupational specialization.

Turning to the technological aspect of the theory, Marx holds, as pointed out above, that every historical mode of production has been conditioned by the nature of the available means of production or state of technology. As he puts it in a vivid passage, "The windmill gives you society with the feudal lord; the steam-mill, society with the industrial capitalist." According to this view, the rise of a new technology, a new set of material productive powers, will necessarily prove incompatible with the perpetuation of a mode of production associated with an older one. The rise of modern manufacturing techniques led to the bourgeois revolution against serf labor and feudal society and to the enthronement of wage labor as the mode of production. Marx further supposes that the transition from early capitalist manufacture to "machinofacture" in the Industrial Revolution has brought into existence a new set of productive powers—modern machine industry—that must and will prove incompatible with the perpetuation of wage labor as the prevailing mode of production, since the new powers of production cannot be fully developed under the system of wage labor. The destruction of wage labor, and with it of bourgeois society, in a proletarian and communist revolution is the predicted outcome. Reasoning in this way, Marx and Engels frequently define a social revolution as the resolution of a conflict or "contradiction" between the productive powers and the social relations of production, or as a "rebellion" of the former against the latter.

This "rebellion" is not understood in mechanistic terms. A social revolution originates in technological change but actually takes place, according to Marx, in a revolutionary social-political movement of producers as a class. It is not the material powers of production themselves, such as the machines, that rebel against the mode of production; it is the men involved. This presents no problem of inconsistency for Marx, however, because he views working man as the supreme productive power. "Of all the instruments of production," he writes, "the greatest productive power is the revolutionary class itself." It is this productive power whose uprising constitutes the actual revolutionary process. The revolt of the productive powers against the existing social relations of production finds its manifestation in class warfare in the economic arena, culminating in the political act of revolutionary overthrow of the state. If revolutions are the locomotives of history, class struggles are the locomotives of revolution.

The Springs of Revolution

What motivates a class of producers to rise against and revolutionize a mode of production and its social superstructure? Suffering caused by material want and poverty is one of the immediate driving forces of revolutionary action, especially with the modern proletariat. But in Marx's view, material satisfaction as such is never the actual aim of the revolutionary class in its struggle to overthrow and transform an established social formation. What is fundamentally at issue in the class struggle and in social revolution, as in history as a whole, is not the consumption interest but the production interest—this, however, defined in a special Marxist way.

It is man as frustrated producer rather than man as dissatisfied consumer who makes a revolution, and the need of man as producer is to freely develop and express his manifold powers of productive activity, his creative potentialities in material life. Under this heading Marx includes both the productive powers within men, and industry or the material productive forces employed by the human species in its productive interaction with nature. Thus in *Capital* he describes the material forces of production as "the productive organs of men in society" and compares them with "the organs of plants and animals as productive instruments utilized for the life purposes of these creatures." His thesis is that the source of revolutionary energy in a class is the frustration of man in his capacity of producer, his inability to develop new powers of production to the full within the confines of an existing mode of production or socioeconomic order. The bourgeois revolution, for example, results from the inability of the rising capitalist class to develop the new productive powers inherent in manufacture within the cramping confines of feudal relationships. And Marx believes—wrongly as it turns out—that a proletarian revolution will be necessitated by the impossibility of fully developing the productive potentials of modern machine industry within the confines of wage labor as the mode of production. In each instance the effect of the revolution is to eliminate a set of social relations of production that has become, in Marx's Hegelian terminology, a "fetter" upon the evolving productive powers of the species, and thus to "emancipate" these powers. The goal of all social revolutions, according to Marx, is freedom, but freedom in a specifically Marxist sense: the liberation of human creativity.

The obstacle to freedom, the source of human bondage, and thus the evil in history, is the division of labor. This fundamental proposition of Marxist theory has several meanings, all closely interconnected. Not only does each successive historical form of the social division of labor between an owning and a producing class become an impediment to the free development of emergent productive powers; the social division of labor is also a force for enslavement in that it subjects the producer class to the acquisitive urge of the owning class, the insensate greed for possession and power that Marx sees as the dominant motive force of historical development up to now. (We read in Engels: ". . . it is precisely the wicked passions of man—greed and the lust for power—which, since the emergence of class antagonisms, serve as levers of historical development. . . .") Man's life in production is thereby transformed into a life of drudgery, of forced, or "alienated labor," as Marx called it in his manuscripts of 1844, and as he always continued to view it. Above all is this true in modern society, where the worker, although legally free to seek employment wherever he will, is bound down to wage labor, which Marx calls "wage slavery" and describes, in *Capital* and other writings, as productive activity performed in servitude to the capitalist profit mania, the "werewolf hunger" for surplus value.

Finally, every social division of labor is an enemy of human freedom, for Marx, insofar as it enforces occupational specialization as a way of life.

For as soon as labor is distributed, each man has a particular, exclusive sphere of activity, which is forced upon him and from which he cannot escape. He is a hunter, a fisherman, a shepherd, or a critical critic, and must remain so if he does not want to lose his means of livelihood. . . .

It is Marx's view, in other words, that a division of labor under which men are compelled by economic necessity to devote themselves throughout life to one particular form of work activity, be it a specialized economic function, or a noneconomic calling such as a profession or governmental work, or even intellectual activity, is slavery. And this is by no means a view that Marx "outgrew" in the later development of his system. Thus he speaks, in the famous passage of "The Critique of the Gotha Program" on the higher phase of communist society, of the disappearance there of "the *enslaving* subordination of man to the division of labor." Engels is just as explicit and even more concrete when he writes:

> not only the laborers, but also the classes directly or indirectly exploiting the laborers, are made subject, through the division of labor, to the tool of their function: the empty-minded bourgeois to his own capital and his own thirst for profits; the lawyer to his fossilized legal conceptions, which dominate him as a power independent of him; the "educated classes" in general to their manifold local limitations and onesidedness, to their own physical and mental shortsightedness, to their stunted specialized education and the fact that they are chained for life to this specialized activity itself, even when this specialized activity is merely to do nothing.

This is a theme that has not always been much emphasized or even noted in the literature on Marxism. An influential school of Soviet Marxists has even undertaken to expunge it from Marxism, denying that Marx was opposed to occupational specialization as a way of life. But this is to deny the undeniable. The proposition that occupational specialization is slavery and that it can and should be done away with is met constantly in the writings of Marx and Engels, including such major works of mature Marxism as *Capital* and *Anti-Dühring,* and it is of fundamental importance in Marxism as they understood it.

Underlying their condemnation of the division of labor is the philosophical anthropology inherited by Marxism from earlier German philosophy, Hegelianism in particular. Marx's *Mensch* resembles Hegel's *Geist* in that both are imbued with a need for totality of life-experience, for creative self-expression in all possible fields of activity. Thus Hegel speaks of Spirit as "manifesting, developing, and perfecting its powers in every direction which its manifold nature can follow," adding: "What powers it inherently possesses, we learn from the variety of products and formations which it originates." It is the same with the human species in Marx's image of it. And in view of the fact noted earlier that Marx constructed the materialist conception of history on the premise that Hegel's *Geist* was a mystified representation of man in his history of production, it is not at all surprising that the Marxist view of human nature shows this strain of Hegelian philosophical romanticism. Like Hegel's *Geist,* Marx's humanity develops and perfects its productive powers in every possible direction, and man as an individual shows this same tendency. A man's inherent bent—that is, his nature—is to become, as Marx puts it in *Capital,* "an individual with an all-round development (*total entwickelte Individuum*), one for whom various social functions are alternative modes of activity." Consequently, the division of labor is unnatural and inhuman, an impediment to a human being's self-realization. A person who applies himself to one single life-activity is alienated from his real nature, hence a self-estranged man. "In the division of labor," writes Engels, "man is divided. All other physical and mental faculties are sacrificed to the development of one single activity." Even the division between town and country, between urban and rural labor, is on this view "a subjection which makes one man into a restricted town-animal, the other into a restricted country-animal." And to be restricted to a particular kind of life or occupation is to be unfree.

The enslavement and dehumanization of man under the division of labor is a dominant theme of *Capital* and the other writings of Marx and Engels on capitalism and the proletarian revolution. They morally condemn capitalism not for being unjust as a mode of distribution (indeed, they hold that it is the only just one in terms of the sole applicable criterion of judgment), but for being inhuman as a mode of production, an unnatural way for man to carry on his productive activity. What makes it so, they maintain, is above all the hideous extreme to which it develops the division of labor. The capitalist mode of production—wage labor in the service of the drive for surplus value—is a system of division of labor within the division of labor. That is, within the social division of labor between capitalist and proletarian, which Marx calls the "despotism" or "dictatorship" of capital, the worker is subjected to an increasingly oppressive form of occupational specialization. He is reduced to a mere detail worker bound down to a single mindless operation endlessly repeated. As capitalism evolves from the stage of "simple cooperation" into that of manufacture, it brings "the lifelong annexation of the worker to a partial function," which "cuts at the very roots of the individual's life" and "transforms the worker into a cripple, a monster, by forcing him to develop some highly specialized dexterity at the cost of a world of productive impulses and faculties—much as in Argentina they slaughter a whole beast simply in order to get its hide or its tallow."

Moreover, the inner dynamism or dialectic of capitalist production is such—according to Marx's argument—that the functions become increasingly subdivided, the specialization more and more minute, and hence the fragmentation of man more and more monstrous, as the employers, under relentless pressure of the competitive struggle, strive for greater and greater technical efficiency through mechanization of work processes. The total dehumanization of the worker comes about finally under modern "machinofacture," the descriptions of which in *Capital* resemble a "Modern Times" without the Chaplinesque anodyne of humor. Of this stage—which he treats as the stage in which capitalist production becomes wholly unendurable—Marx writes, for example, that here all the means for developing production

> mutilate the worker into a fragment of a human being, degrade him to become a mere appurtenance of the machine, make his work such a torment that its essential meaning is destroyed; estrange from him the intellectual potentialities of the labor process in [the] very proportion to the extent to which science is incorporated into it as an independent power. .

Progress in technological terms thus spells regress in human terms, and man sinks to the nadir of wretchedness and self-estrangement in the production process at the very time in history when his productivity, technically speaking, reaches its peak and—providentially—brings with it the possibility of a thoroughly human way of life in production. The "slavery" and "labor torment" under the division of labor represent a major share of the ever-increasing misery of the proletarian masses that drives them at length, according to Marx's argument, to revolt against their mode of production.

The human history of production is thus also a history of revolution. The growth-process of society is propelled by a series of revolutions that center in major changes in the mode of production as a social process. These changes have been the very substance of the social history of man. It is true that Marx speaks of an "epoch of social revolution" as something occurring when a form of society nears its end. Yet in a way he believes that history has always up to now been a revolutionary process, that man has always been at least incipiently in revolt against his mode of production. This, after all, is the sense of the opening statement of the *Communist Manifesto* that the whole of recorded history is a history of class struggles. Why it should be so on Marx's premises has been made clear. Every mode of production in history has been a form of productive activity within the division of labor, and the division of labor is bondage. In Marx's mind, history is a succession of man's revolutionary breaks out of the prison-house of the division of labor for freedom in the life of production.

No sooner has a new mode of production within the division of labor been established by revolutionary means than it too starts to become a "fetter" upon the ever-developing productive powers of the species. Such is the revolutionary dialectic of the historical process as Marx expounds it. Just as men begin to die biologically as soon as they are born, so societies embark upon their own revolutionary dissolution virtually from the time of their revolutionary "birth pangs." So we shall look in vain in Marx for a sociology in the sense of a theory of how societies work. His is a sociology of revolution, a theory of the internal dysfunctioning of the several historical societies, leading to their disintegration and downfall. Thus *Capital,* which is Marx's principal treatise on society and revolution as well as his chief work of economic theory, treats of the revolutionary rise, development, and fall of bourgeois society. And the whole thrust of the book is toward the "knell" of the proletarian revolution that it tolls in conclusion.

The Revolution of Communism

The proletarian revolution is described in various places by Marx and Engels as the overthrow of the bourgeois state and establishment of a proletarian dictatorship, accompanied by the forcible seizure and socialization of private property in the means of production. But this is only the external manifestation, the "phenomenal form" of the communist revolution. Like all previous social revolutions, the revolution of communism is for Marx and Engels essentially a change in the mode of production. And like all past revolutions, again, it is both destructive in that it does away with an old mode of production and constructive in that it establishes a new one in its place.

This presentation of the socialist or communist revolution, and hence of socialism or communism itself, as turning principally upon production, stands in substantial contrast with the view of most socialists, both of that time and now, that socialism is mainly concerned with the distribution problem. Marx and Engels were well aware of this difference. They often called attention to it in emphatic and even polemical terms. They argued that changes in the mode of distribution, leading to the practice of distribution according to needs in the higher phase of communist society, would only be incidental byproducts of a change in the mode of production that would be the real substance of the revolution of communism. Marx, for example, attacks what he calls "vulgar socialism" for the "consideration and treatment of distribution as independent of the mode of production and hence the presentation of socialism as turning principally on distribution." He states in the same passage that "it was in general a mistake to make a fuss about so-called *distribution* and put the principal stress on it." In the same vein Engels pours scorn on Eugen Dühring for basing his "socialitarian" program on the unacceptable proposition that "the capitalist mode of *production* is quite good, and can remain in existence, but the capitalist mode of *distribution* is evil." He comments in this connection on "how puerile Herr Dühring's notions are—that society can take possession of the means of production without revolutionizing from top to bottom the old method of production and in particular putting an end to the old division of labor."

If the communist revolution resembles all past revolutions in that it primarily revolutionizes the old mode of production, it also, according to Marx and Engels, differs from all other revolutions in history; and this thesis on the uniqueness of the projected world communist revolution is of the greatest importance in Marxist thought. The argument is that what undergoes revolutionizing in the communist revolution is not simply a particular form of productive activity within the division of labor (in this case wage labor), but the division of labor as such. Instead of replacing one form of productive activity within the division of labor by another, as the bourgeois revolution replaced serf labor by wage labor, the communist revolution will pave the way for a radically new mode of production that altogether abolishes and transcends the division of labor and therewith "labor" itself in the sense in which mankind has always known it (i.e., in the sense of "alienated labor" in the terminology of the 1844 manuscripts). As the younger Marx formulated it,

> In all revolutions up to now the mode of activity always remained unscathed and it was only a question of a different distribution of this activity, a new distribution of labor to other persons, whilst the communist revolution is directed against the preceding *mode* of activity, does away with *labor,* and abolishes the rule of classes with the classes themselves. . . .

Over twenty years later the older Marx was saying the same thing when he wrote in *Capital* that the "revolutionary ferments" in modern capitalist society have as their aim "the abolition of the old division of labor."

By the abolition of the old division of labor he and Engels mean, first, the abolition of the class division of society into owners of the means of production and nonowning workers. This will spell the abolition of wage labor after an interim during which old habits of working for a remuneration, and also the lack of full material abundance, will enforce a continuation of wage labor in a noncapitalist form, performed for social needs rather than in the service of the drive for profit. The disappearance of the latter as the motive force of production will make possible the withering away of the division of labor in all its subordinate forms—the division between mental and physical labor, between urban and rural labor, between different trades and professions, and between different functions in each. For as soon as man is no longer compelled by the imperatives of greed and the need to engage in some one form of productive activity all his life, he will give rein to the natural human tendency (as Marx sees it) to become a universal man—"to do one thing today and another tomorrow, to hunt in the morning, fish in the afternoon, rear cattle in the evening, criticize after dinner, just as I have a mind, without ever becoming hunter, fisherman, shepherd or critic." Within the factory the detail worker, annexed for life to a particular specialized function, will give way to the "individual of all-round development" for whom various functions in production are possible. Marx based this expectation, which may have been prophetic, upon the view that in modern industry, where machines themselves do highly specialized work, the technical foundation is established for liberating men from narrow specialization. "Since the integral movement of the factory does not proceed from the worker but from the machine," he reasoned in *Capital*, "there can be a continuous change of personnel without any interruption of the labor process." Machine industry without the division of labor would thus be based upon rotation of jobs among highly trained and versatile machine-operators, whose work would become a form of free productive activity owing to the constant variation and to the "almost artistic nature of their occupation."

Since Marx and Engels believe that every form of society fundamentally *is* its mode of production, most of what they have to say about the future communist society (in its "higher phase") is naturally concerned with the anticipated new mode of productive activity. But the latter, as we see, is not analyzed in economic terms. This omission of an economics of communism from the theory of Marx and Engels is entirely logical considering that part of what they mean by communism is *the end of economics*. They assume that with the emancipation of the immensely potent productive forces inherent in modern machine industry from the "fetters" of capitalist wage labor, there will very soon be created a material abundance so great as to satisfy all proper human needs. At this point, which is the entry-point into the "higher phase," the historic scarcity of goods and resources ceases and therewith the need for economics as a theory and practice of allocation of scarce goods and resources. "And at this point," writes Engels, "man in a certain sense separates finally from the animal world, leaves the conditions of animal existence behind him, and enters conditions which are really human. . . . It is humanity's leap from the realm of necessity into the realm of freedom." For Marx and Engels this "leap" is a take-off not into affluence as such but into the authentically human higher form of existence that man's creative and artistic nature, as they see it, naturally tends toward and for which material well-being is no more than a precondition. The end of economics means the beginning of aesthetics as the keynote of the life of productive activity.

In Marxist theory the communist revolution is the supreme revolution of freedom since it does away not simply with this or that specific form of the division of labor but with all forms, and so with bondage as such. By the same token, this is the last revolution. With production no longer based upon a division of labor in society, there will be no kind of social relations of production that could become a fetter upon the productive powers and thereby precipitate a further revolutionary upheaval. Accordingly, the communist revolution will bring to an end the historical growth-process of humanity—the "prehistory of human society," as Marx called it in a well-known passage. It will mark the maturation of the species, the time when man finally becomes fully human. In his early manuscripts Marx used the terms "humanism" and "transcendence of human self-alienation" to express this idea. Later the German philosophical terminology was abandoned, but the idea was not. The communist revolution continued to be conceived as a revolution of human self-realization.

The self-realization is understood by Marx in both collective and individual terms. On the one hand, it means the completion of the whole historical process of self-development of the species, the becoming of human society. At this point "socialized humanity" (*vergesellschaftete Menschheit*) emerges out of what had been, all through recorded history, a self-divided and inwardly warring human collectivity. The communist revolution, an act of appropriation by the vast majority of the totality of material means of production, is the means by which this final transformation is supposed to take place. The reasoning turns on Marx's view, mentioned earlier, that industry, the total complex of material instruments or powers of production, represents the "productive organs of men in society." Seen in this perspective, the communist revolution is the act by which man in the mass reappropriates his own organs of productive activity, of which he has been dispossessed in history owing to the division of labor in its various forms. By this collective act—runs Marx's argument—the individuals of whom the mass is composed regain their creative potentialities: "The appropriation of a totality of instruments of production is, for this very reason, the development of a totality of capacities in the individuals themselves." This is the basis on which Marx advances the thesis that the change of material circumstances brought about by revolutionary *praxis* coincides with "change of self."

It follows that man must realize himself on the scale of the species before he can do so as an individual, that there is no self-realization without social revolution. Before the communist revolution, no one can be truly human; afterwards, all can and will become so. Then and then only will free creativity become the characteristic human mode of production, will labor become "not only a means of life but life's prime want." Then only will the human society of production become one in which

> productive labor, instead of being a means to the subjection of men, will become a means to their emancipation, by giving each individual the opportunity to develop and exercise all his faculties, physical and mental, in all directions; in which, therefore, productive labor will become a pleasure instead of a burden.

Liberated from the acquisitive urge that has always in the past motivated the production process, and from the slavery of specialization that this has engendered, men will finally become freely creative individuals, accomplished in a multitude of life-activities, who produce without being driven to it by the forces of need and greed and who arrange their world according to the laws of beauty.

That the Marxian revolutionary idea has a moral meaning is clear enough. But this dimension would, it seems, be more accurately described as religious than as ethical in nature. Moral teachers desire man to be virtuous according to one or another understanding of virtue; religious ones —Marx among them—want him to be redeemed. In this connection it must be said that there is a close relation between revolution and religion. Though the founders of revolutionary movements need not be men of religion, the founders of religions tend in their way to be revolutionaries. They envisage for man a goal of supreme worth that involves his total self-tranformation, the revolutionizing of himself as it were, and they give him directions concerning the way to the goal. Marx does the same, and on this account may be characterized as a revolutionist of religious formation. The goal had variously been called the Kingdom of God, Paradise,

Nirvana, Satori, Salvation; he called it Communism. When he wrote in his eleventh thesis that the point was to change the world, the message was that changing the world outside of man, by revolutionary *praxis,* was the way to change man himself, totally. There is little question as to the religious quality of Marx's vision of the goal. The question that one could raise, in an examination of the religious aspect of his thought, is whether he offered valid directions as to the way.

14. The Darwinian Revolution in Biological Science

MICHAEL T. GHISELIN

Anthology selections on Charles Darwin (1809–1882) and Darwinism usually deal either with "Social Darwinism" or with the conflict between evolution and religion. To be sure, the publication of Darwin's Origins of Species *in 1859 reinforced the "Social Darwinist" views of Herbert Spencer and William Graham Sumner—that "survival of the fittest," a slogan invented by Spencer, not Darwin, explained and justified the superiority of laissez-faire capitalists and white men, generally, in their struggle and triumph over the "inferior races" of workers and nonwhites. Although Social Darwinism was all the rage, at least among Anglo-Saxons, its ideas did not add much to Spencerianism, say, and certainly nineteenth-century businessmen would have done as they did without the benefit of Social Darwinism telling them how to meet a payroll. Likewise, although Darwin's discovery dramatized science's conflict with fundamentalist religious views, such a struggle would have occurred from the work of other scientists. That battle, like the one over "Social Darwinism," is largely over now; if science and religion contradict each other it is not over the fact of evolution, but over the conflict between revelation and scientific method.*

Darwin's long-term importance was neither in Social Darwinism nor in the

Source: Michael T. Ghiselin, *The Triumph of the Darwinian Method* (Berkeley and Los Angeles: University of California Press, 1969), pp. 45–57 and 76–77. Originally published by the University of California Press; reprinted by permission of The Regents of the University of California. [Some footnotes omitted.]

struggle of science with religion. Rather, as recent Darwin studies show, his impact on scientific thought has held up far better than either of the other two short-range effects. Once in disrepute thanks to the studies of Gregor Mendel on heredity and the discoveries of mutations by geneticists, Darwin's theory of natural selection was substantiated by R. A. Fisher in 1930 when he found a unity in the thought of Darwin and Mendel. While Fisher's estimate is commonly held by biologists today, historians have seldom taken it into account and customarily still view natural selection as old-fashioned and out-of-date. This reevaluation of Darwin's importance was also spurred by the first publication of his scientific notebooks in 1960.

Typical of this new estimation of Darwin's contribution is this selection by Michael T. Ghiselin, a Stanford University biology professor. Ghiselin feels that Darwin revolutionized biological science and, by doing so, brought "the collapse of the western intellectual tradition." Had Darwin followed that tradition and its "experts" of his day in biology he might never have discovered natural selection. Fortunately, as Sir Gavin de Beer, perhaps the foremost Darwin scholar, points out in his review of Ghiselin's book (New York Review of Books, *December 17, 1970), Darwin's mind had not been prejudiced by the "experts." Ghiselin traces how Darwin arrived at natural selection and the way it revolutionized biological thinking. Because his account is somewhat overly detailed for the student of history, the reader might limit himself to just a few of his questions, such as: What is natural selection, how does it work, and why did Darwin's discovery of it put him in a class by himself among earlier evolutionists? How did his hypothetico-deductive scientific method operate and how did he use it to discover natural selection? How did his use of it overturn the western intellectual tradition of what Karl Popper calls* essentialism? *How did Darwin's classification by population contribute to his discovery?*

The theory of natural selection is certainly Darwin's most important contribution to knowledge. It remains, with such implications as evolution, the dominant organizing principle in biology. Natural selection is a remarkably simple idea—so simple that Huxley, for instance, wondered why he hadn't thought of it himself. Organisms differ from one another. They produce more young than the available resources can sustain. Those best suited to survive pass on the expedient properties to their offspring, while inferior forms are eliminated. Subsequent generations therefore are more like the better adapted ancestors, and the result is a gradual modification, or evolution. Thus the cause of evolutionary adaptation is differential reproductive success. Superficially the principle appears to be so straightforward that it should not be difficult to understand.

Darwin's Priority

In view of the evident simplicity of natural selection, one may wonder why it was not thought of before. In fact, historical research has unearthed a number of anticipations, both real and imaginary. After the publication of *The Origin of Species* some of these were pointed out. Although Darwin had not been aware of them, he appended a "historical sketch" to later editions of *The Origin of Species,* but retained credit for thinking up the idea himself, for seeing its implications, and for establishing it as a recognized theory supported by factual evidence. Yet Darwin's originality has long been, and continues to be, a bone of contention. In the last century, the novelist Samuel Butler attempted to show, in his *Evolution Old and New,* that Darwin had stolen the idea of evolution from his predecessors. Darwin never gave Butler the pleasure of a reply. Even natural selection is held not to be Darwin's original idea. Zirkle has enumerated a number of examples of what seems to be natural selection, or its elements, in the works of many writers, among these: Lucretius, Empedocles, Maupertuis, Buffon, Geoffroy Saint-Hilaire, Naudin, Prichard, Lyell, Lawrence, and Mathew.[1] More recently, Eiseley has attempted to demonstrate that Darwin took the idea of natural selection from the writings of Edward Blyth without giving due credit.[2] Yet de Beer and others have replied that Blyth used natural selection to refute evolution, and it seems clear, therefore, that he cannot really have understood it.[3] The attack by the geneticist C. D. Darlington is largely based upon the notion that natural selection has been suggested by many earlier writers, and his evidence is stated in such a fashion as to make a charge of plagiarism obvious.[4]

A basic approach in all these attacks has been to accuse Darwin of lacking an awareness of history. The literature is culled for passages suggesting evolution or natural selection, and these are easily found. It is then argued that because credit must go to the worker who first conceived of an idea, the discovery should not be attributed to Darwin. Yet in a sense it is the critics, not Darwin, who lack historical perspective. One has no trouble finding other great scientists whose work was anticipated. Copernicus, for example, was not the first to conceive of a heliocentric universe, but there is every reason to consider him the architect of the revolution which bears his name. Darwin likewise accomplished a basic reorientation in our view of the universe, whatever may have been the speculations of his predecessors. With respect to both great revolutionaries, it is clear that their innovations amount to something more than stumbling upon a new idea. They had not only to generate a different hypothesis, but also to invent a new way of dealing with a traditional subject matter, and to demonstrate its advantages by means of a theoretical synthesis. And none of Darwin's supposed forerunners accomplished anything of the sort.

The arguments over Darwin's priority reflect nothing more than the difficulty of understanding his theory. Darwin himself was very much dis-

219

Ghiselin

THE DARWINIAN
REVOLUTION
IN BIOLOGICAL
SCIENCE

[1] C. Zirkle, "Natural Selection Before the 'Origin of Species,'" *Proceedings of the American Philosophical Society,* LXXXIV (1941), 71–123.

[2] L. Eiseley, "Charles Darwin, Edward Blyth, and the Theory of Natural Selection," *Proceedings of the American Philosophical Society,* CIII (1959), 94–158.

[3] G. de Beer, "The Origins of Darwin's Ideas on Evolution and Natural Selection," *Proceedings of the Royal Society of London,* CLV (1961), 321–338.

[4] C. D. Darlington, *Darwin's Place in History* (Oxford: Blackwell, 1960).

couraged in his attempts to explain natural selection to his colleagues, and this may be one of the reasons why he so long delayed publication. He points out, in his autobiography, that the joint paper of Darwin and Wallace was not adequately understood by the audience, and that it took the long discussion of *The Origin of Species* to win many converts. It would seem that there is something about natural selection, in spite of its apparent simplicity, that made it incomprehensible to the vast majority of biologists—at least until they had considered the matter at length. Even after *The Origin of Species* was published, natural selection did not win immediate or universal approval, nor was it understood as well as one might think. Huxley is generally given much of the credit for popularizing Darwin's theories, yet Huxley himself admitted that *The Origin of Species* was most difficult for him. After a lecture by Huxley at the Royal Institution, Darwin wrote to Hooker in 1860 that "He gave no just idea of Natural Selection." Darwin concludes that "After conversation with others and more mature reflection, I must confess that as an exposition of the doctrine the lecture seems to me an entire failure." One may suspect that even though natural selection was accepted by many of Darwin's contemporaries, they nonetheless failed to fully understand it. Indeed, the concept remains an exceedingly difficult one, even for professional biologists. Reflecting upon the genesis of the theory in the minds of its discoverers may help us to see just what has been the problem.

Malthus and the Discovery of Natural Selection

The parallels in the manner in which both Darwin and Wallace discovered natural selection are as striking as the common elements in their evolutionary biogeographies. Wallace records how, during a malarial attack in February, 1858, he meditated about Malthus's *Essay on Population* and considered the powerful effect of mortality on rapidly increasing populations, in both man and animals. He notes that "while pondering vaguely on this fact there suddenly flashed upon me the *idea* of the survival of the fittest—that the individuals removed by these checks must be on the whole inferior to those that survived." In his autobiography Darwin asserts that he approached the problem of evolutionary mechanisms through the study of artificial selection, but was unable to see how to apply selection to organisms under natural conditions. He says:

> In October 1838, that is, fifteen months after I had begun my systematic enquiry, I happened to read for amusement "Malthus on Population," and being well prepared to appreciate the struggle for existence which everywhere goes on from long-continued observation of the habits of animals and plants, it at once struck me that under these circumstances favourable variations would tend to be preserved and unfavourable ones to be destroyed. The result of this would be the formation of new species.

Both Darwin and Wallace thus would seem to have obtained some crucial insight through reading Malthus, yet what this was has not, up to the present time, been adequately explained. De Beer maintains that Darwin overemphasized the significance of Malthus in his discovery.[5] The same general conclusion is reached by Smith, who asserts that Darwin had his theory fully in mind from the outset of his work on species, arguing that the idea of natural selection was implicit in Darwin's notebooks from 1837 onward, as well as in the writings of Lyell.[6] A number of commentators—there seems almost to be a consensus—support the same general point of view.[7] Yet such interpretations seem a bit odd, in the light of the stress laid upon Malthus by Darwin and Wallace alike. Nor does the charge that, in so many words, Darwin lied about Malthus to conceal his own plagiarism seem to be more than an *ad hoc* hypothesis casting doubt on the argument for plagiarism itself.

The key to an understanding of Malthus's importance has already been suggested by Mayr, who points out that Darwin introduced a new way of thinking.[8] The *Essay* of Malthus's provided the stimulus for conceiving of species in a manner totally different from that which had traditionally prevailed. The innovation may be summed up in a single word: *population*.

A Revolution in Metaphysics

In order to see what a difference the new manner of thinking involved, one must compare it with the system it replaced, an intellectual tradition long dominant in Western thought. Indeed, a full analysis must extend to the very foundations of Greek philosophy, especially to the influence of Plato and Aristotle. The group of philosophical ideas that concerns us has been called *essentialism* by Popper, who has traced the impact of Plato's metaphysics on political thinking down to recent times.[9] Even before Plato, Greek philosophy began to experience difficulties in dealing with change. If things grew, or passed away, they seemed somehow unreal, suggesting that they belonged only to a world of appearances. Heraclitus, in adopting the notion that material things are illusory, maintained that all that really exists is "fire"—that is, process. Plato, on the other hand,

221

Ghiselin

THE DARWINIAN
REVOLUTION
IN BIOLOGICAL
SCIENCE

[5] De Beer, "Origins of Darwin's Ideas" (above, n. 3).

[6] S. Smith, "Origin of 'the Origin,' " *The Advancement of Science,* XVI (1960), 391–401.

[7] G. Himmelfarb, *Darwin and the Darwinian Revolution* (New York: Doubleday, 1959); L. Eiseley, *Darwin's Century: Evolution and the Men Who Discovered It* (New York: Anchor, 1961); S. L. Sobol, "Ch. Darwin's Evolutionary Conception at the Early Stages of Its Formation," *Annals of Biology, Moscow Society of Natural History, Section in the History of Natural Sciences,* I (1959), 13–34 (in Russian, English summary); R. C. Stauffer, "Ecology in the Long Manuscript Version of Darwin's *Origin of Species* and Linnaeus' *Oeconomy of Nature,*" *Proceedings of the American Philosophical Society,* CIV (1960), 235–241.

[8] E. Mayr, "Darwin and the Evolutionary Theory in Biology," *Evolution and Anthropology: a Centennial Appraisal,* ed. B. J. Meggers (Washington: The Anthropological Society of Washington, 1959), pp. 1–10.

[9] K. R. Popper, *Conjectures and Refutations* (New York: Basic Books, 1962), p. 19.

elaborated upon a metaphysical world of changeless reality, of which the world as we look upon it is but an imperfect picture. His allegory of the cave, in which all that can be seen are shadows and images, expresses this conception with the utmost vividness and force. To Plato, true reality exists in the essence, Idea or *eidos*. The presumed existence of such a transcendent realm of ideas has profoundly influenced a variety of historically important schools of thought, even down to the present day. It accounts for Plato's adherence to numerology: abstractions of mathematics were envisioned as having more ultimate meaning than mere expedients in dealing with matter and relationships. Even today, many mathematically inclined persons are Platonists, and the philosophies of many physicists are saturated with covert numerology. To Plato, the doctrine of essences had political consequences. His *Republic* seeks to justify dictatorship on the grounds of the reality of an ideal state. The earthly republic exists in order to manifest the perfection of the higher reality. Therefore, the citizen's sole reason for existence is the perpetuation of the state in its divine form. A despotism is necessary because only the best of men can understand the transcendent sphere of existence which the republic must strive to imitate. To anyone who wishes to justify a dictatorship, Platonic essentialism provides an attractive argument. And Platonism has traditionally been the instrument of despots, as may be seen in Hegel's symbiosis with the Prussian monarchy.

In the hands of Aristotle, essentialist metaphysics became somewhat altered. Aristotle retained the notion of essences, but held that they do not exist apart from things. His work embraced concepts of teleology, empiricism, and natural science, making his writings seem far less alien to a modern biologist than do those of Plato. But if the Platonic *eidos* became less transcendent, it retained a fundamental importance in Aristotelian epistemology. For Aristotle, to understand a thing was to know its essence, or to define it. And definition was not of names, but of essences; concepts were "real," their essences were identified with this reality, and the truth could be reached through precise definition. A true system of knowledge thus became essentially a classification scheme, or an ability to relegate things to explicitly delimited categories.

Plato and Aristotle thus both embraced the notion that ideas or classes are more than just abstractions—that is to say, both advocated forms of "realism." Their metaphysics stands in sharp contrast to nominalism, which asserts that classes are mere conveniences, artifacts of man's thought processes. Thus, to a nominalist, the members of a class do not have the same essence; indeed, the only thing they share is a name. Modern philosophy has tended to be strongly nominalistic. Classification, in most circles, is no longer conceived of as the ultimate form of knowledge. Definition is for the most part looked upon as strictly nominal: definition is of names or symbols, and (insofar as nouns are concerned) the names designate not essences, but things. Such a moderate form of nominalism makes a great deal of sense. When one realizes that words are basically expedients of communication, definition is seen to be important only insofar as it helps us to convey our ideas. Yet definition is so intimately bound up with the discovery of the properties of things, or with the analysis of concepts, that one may readily confound it with quite different processes. It is easy to slip into an Aristotelian attitude and think that when we know the definition of a word we have some kind of insight into matter. Many people are inclined to argue fruitlessly over purely verbal issues: in biology, the dispute over the cellular or acellular nature of protozoa is notorious. A certain dose of nominalism is therefore most desirable in preventing the errors which result from thinking that a definition can be true or false. Yet, carried to an extreme, nominalism can be misleading. It tends to assume, although it need not, that since classes "have no real existence in nature," they must be strictly arbitrary, and that one system of classification is as good as another. And it overlooks the significance of relational properties, so that it may treat communities or families as if they were just as much abstractions as the class of red books.

Believing as he did that he could define something more than mere symbols, Aristotle naturally developed a sophisticated philosophy of definition. He advocated hierarchical classification, or systems of classes within classes. The classes were differentiated from each other by properties held in common by all members of each class. A thing was included in the class only if it had the defining properties. The result of such a method of definition was a tendency to conceive of things solely in terms of the defining properties of the class. What was real was the essence and the differentiae, and the peculiarities of individuals were overlooked. An implication, of enormous historical importance, was that it became very difficult to classify things which change, or which grade into one another, and even to conceive of or to discuss them. Indeed, the very attempt to reason in terms of essences almost forces one to ignore everything dynamic or transitory. One could hardly design a philosophy better suited to predispose one toward dogmatic reasoning and static concepts. The Darwinian revolution thus depended upon the collapse of the Western intellectual tradition.

Biological classification was founded in its basically modern form by Linnaeus (1707–1778), who was an Aristotelian. Many of the philosophical difficulties of modern biology are due to the fact that Aristotelian classification and definition have been the unexamined and automatic practice of working biologists. But a variety of philosophical attitudes toward classification are possible, and these have led to much controversy. To the Aristotelian, classes and ultimate reality are one and the same thing. Hence classification consists in discovering the "real" order in nature and in expressing, through a system of classes, the properties that correlate with that order. To the Platonist, the attitude is much like that of the Aristotelian, except that the classes are seen as corresponding to an occult order. The goal of classification is to discover that which is more real than meets the eye—the forms, *eidos,* and so forth—and to erect a system based on it. Just as Plato's politics rested on the notion of an ideal state, Platonic classification is organized in terms of idealized ani-

223

Ghiselin

THE DARWINIAN
REVOLUTION
IN BIOLOGICAL
SCIENCE

mals and plants, and the uniqueness of individual organisms is ignored. For the same reason that Plato advocated a dictatorship ruled by philosophers, Platonic taxonomy relies upon the authority of the systematist's subjective apprehension of the ideal organic form. To the nominalist, who by definition denies the reality of universals, classes have no real existence, and are merely convenient pigeonholes. Classification, to the more radical nominalist, is completely arbitrary, and one order is as good as another. To the modern biologist, the classes may be looked upon as abstractions, but they are not arbitrary, for they represent an order in nature resulting from evolutionary processes. The classes are not real, but the groups of organisms are. In more philosophical terms, this amounts to admitting the "reality" of relational properties. Classification involves the discovery of relationships, and their integration into a system of theoretical knowledge. Perhaps most important of all, biology has ceased to think in terms of abstract classes or idealized forms such as "the horse" and has turned to considering the interactions between "this horse" and "that horse." We owe this shift in emphasis largely to Darwin.

It should thus be clear that metaphysical preconceptions profoundly influence the course of scientific investigation. The effects of divergent philosophical points of view are readily seen in attitudes toward species. Aristotelian definition leaves no room for changes in properties. In a sense the species *is* the set of properties which distinguish between the individuals of different groups. If species change, they do not exist, for things that change cannot be defined and hence cannot exist. A Platonist, by way of contrast, is interested only in the ideal organism, and ignores the individual differences which are so crucial to an understanding of changes in species by natural selection. If one is a radical nominalist, species cannot exist in principle, and any study of change must treat only individuals. It is possible to accept species as real and still embrace a kind of nominalism, if one looks upon species as individuals. Buffon (1707–1788), for example, would seem to have entertained the notion that a species is a group of interbreeding organisms. This point of view has certain analogies with the biological species definition of the modern biologist: "Species are groups of actually or potentially interbreeding natural populations, which are reproductively isolated from other such groups." A species is thus a particular, or an "individual"—not a biological individual, but a social one. It is not a strictly nominal class—that is, it is not an abstraction or mere group of similar things—because the biological individuals stand in relation to the species as parts to a whole. To attain this divergence in attitude required more than simple affirmation. It was necessary to conceive of biological groupings in terms of social interaction and not merely in terms of taxonomic characters.

The new manner of thinking about groups of organisms entailed the concept of a population as an integrated system, existing at a level above that of the biological individual. A population may be defined as a group of things which interact with one another. A group of gaseous molecules in a single vessel or the populace of a country form units of such nature.

Families, the House of Lords, a hive of bees, or a shoal of mussels—in short, social entities—all constitute populations. The class of red books, thanatocoenoses, or all hermaphrodites do not. The best test of whether or not a group forms a population is to ask whether or not it is possible to affect one member of the group by acting on another. Removing a worker from a hive of bees, for example, should influence the number of eggs the queen may lay, and therefore both worker and queen are parts of the same population. The concept in use is often exceedingly abstract. If one is to conceive of a population at all, one must use a logic in which the relationships are not treated in terms of black and white. The emphasis must be placed on dynamic equilibria and on processes. The interaction between the parts may be intermittent, dispositional, or even only potential. Entities are components of the same population to the degree that their interaction is probable. That the definition of "population" allows for no distinct boundary between populations and nonpopulations creates difficulties for traditional logic which can only be surmounted with some effort. And a probabilistic definition of "population," implying as it does a probabilistic conception of the species, has posed even more of a problem to the logician. Thus Hull argues as follows:

> The fact that two groups of organisms *cannot* interbreed (regardless of the isolating mechanisms) is important only in the respect that it follows deductively that they *are not* interbreeding. [He continues:] But taxonomists are not obliged to predict the future course of evolution. Taxonomists are obliged to classify only those species that have evolved given the environment that did pertain, not to classify all possible species that might have evolved in some possible environment. Until potentially interbreeding organisms actually use this potentiality, it is of only "potential" interest in classification. In evolutionary taxonomy unrealised potentialities don't count.

225

Ghiselin

THE DARWINIAN
REVOLUTION
IN BIOLOGICAL
SCIENCE

Hull is here objecting to the kind of vague potentiality talk that proved so misleading and vacuous in the hands of such thinkers as Aristotle. But one needs to draw a line between appropriate and inappropriate contexts, and biologists are fully justified when they employ a terminology loaded with probabilistic implications and expressly designed to convey the idea of potentiality. The probabilistic terminology and manner of thinking that are so characteristic of biology exist for pragmatic reasons and are justified by experience. Their utility is particularly conspicuous in such words as "adaptation" and "environment." The very nature of organic processes demands a probabilistic manner of thinking and a vocabulary adequate to express it. It would be most difficult in embryology, for example, to discuss theory without such terms as "presumptive mesoderm," "regulation," or "potency." And when we are deciding whether or not to eat a wild mushroom, the unrealized potentiality of its poisoning us certainly does count. Just as Aristotelian logic long impeded the progress of biology by necessitating a classification admitting no gradation, modern logic could cope better with systems of thought concerned with probabilistic ideas.

At present, the major source of misunderstanding about the term "population" is a failure to realize the distinction between populations and other kinds of groups. Mayr, for instance, objects to calling a group of asexual organisms a population, although Simpson does not. The divergence of opinion between these two authorities is more than just a disagreement on usage; it reflects differences in attitude of the utmost significance. Simpson uses "population" in an essentialistic or typological sense when he says: "What is classified is always a *population*, defined in the broadest sense as any group of organisms systematically related to each other." At best, this bases "relationship" upon an undefined agreement in taxonomic characters; as stated, the definition is circular. Likewise, Simpson attempts to define "species" in terms of "biological role," which unfortunately does not differentiate between "species" and "subspecies." In Mayr's usage, "population" refers to entities which are more than just nominal classes, and his definition of "species" as particular kinds of populations has the advantage of providing an objective criterion of membership.

Genesis of the Theory

The basic clue in the discovery of natural selection was the realization that biological groups may form populations, or units of interaction in nature. It had further to be understood how the biological and social entities impinge upon each other in their activities, and how changes in the relationships between the components of the population result from such processes. This in turn had to be related to the problem of adaptation—how it is that properties advantageous to the organisms emerge from social interaction. Conceiving of varieties or species as no more than abstract assemblages, founded on their similarities, precluded any such treatment. Nor could an understanding of evolution be obtained from a consideration of individual organisms apart from their relationships to the breeding community. Darwin attained his new conception of biological reality by a series of innovations, each of which brought him gradually nearer to his ultimate synthesis, and each of which was a departure from traditional thought.

The first step was the analogy between the formation of varieties in domestic productions and among organisms in a state of nature. At this stage it was unnecessary to bring in any consideration of adaptive processes. Darwin was by no means original in realizing that artificial selection may produce changes in the properties of organisms. The comparison was discussed at some length by Lyell, to whom many of Darwin's trains of reasoning may be traced. It was clearly possible for a breeder, by selecting individuals with certain attributes, to form a group characterized by whatever combination of properties he might choose. But this procedure would seem to require an intervention by man for its success; the particular forms selected had to be kept separate from others of their species by an act of volition. And there was no obvious way in such a process to account for the origin of adaptive traits, unless one were to invoke an intelligent agent. The comparative reproductive success of individuals within the group or population simply had not occurred to Darwin. All that he had understood at this stage was that a distinctive assemblage may be formed by some action which puts like things together. What the action was, except when man intervened, had yet to be discovered. But even this early in Darwin's investigation, one may see a rudiment of population thinking and a key to the manner in which species are formed. In his first notebook on the transmutation of species, Darwin says: "A species as soon as once formed by separation or change in part of country, repugnance to intermarriage—settles it." In the second notebook he expresses the view that varieties may be formed "without picking"—that is, without selection—and that such a change could produce the sterility necessary to keep species distinct. Thus, Darwin had begun to grasp the notion of speciation, the splitting of populations into permanently separated groups. Yet this was only a beginning.

The next step was an understanding of the relationship between environment and adaptation. Darwin approached this question from the perspective of extinction. Early in his first notebook on transmutation of species, he recognized that the cause of extinction is "non-adaptation of circumstances." In the second he refers to the "wars of organic being," in which one species replaces another. We come to a most crucial distinction. One might think that such a picture of well-adapted species replacing the inferior ones was an adequate conception of natural selection. Many students of Darwin have expressed this view and have constructed sweeping treatments of Darwin's work based on it. But they are grievously in error, and their criticisms of Darwin's work, importance, and even morality collapse with the refutation of their basic premise. It is perfectly true that if a group of organisms had some property, the survival of that group would be favored *once the property had been evolved;* but this does not explain how that property might have originated. Certain workers have proposed what has been called "group selection" to account for altruistic behavior on the part of some animals. The survival of the entire population because of an adaptive trait in any of its members is thought by proponents of this hypothesis to be an effective evolutionary mechanism. Nonetheless, it is not the same as the type of natural selection discovered by Darwin and Wallace, and its importance may be challenged on a variety of grounds.

In its effective form, natural selection depends on the differential reproduction of individuals, especially biological individuals. However, social individuals may also be selected, provided that the component organisms of the social unit have much the same hereditary makeup (kinship selection). Thus, the altruistic behavior of mammals toward their young is explicable in terms of the fact that the family, a social entity, favors the differential survival of the genotype for all its members. Likewise, Darwin treated another kind of family, the hive of bees, as an individual society and a unit of reproduction. He refers to just this kind of relationship when he asserts: "The case being, as I believe, that Natural Selection can-

227

Ghiselin

THE DARWINIAN
REVOLUTION
IN BIOLOGICAL
SCIENCE

not effect what is not good for the individual, including in this term a social community."

To form an accurate theory of natural selection, it was necessary to see how the success or failure of an individual could affect the properties of the species by gradually altering the proportion of individuals with a given characteristic. This required the notions of population dynamics, and extinction was inadequate. For this reason Darwin was fully justified in rejecting the view that his supposed forerunner Naudin understood how selection acts in nature. One may say much the same for a number of alleged precursors of Darwin: they did not appreciate the nature of population phenomena. Nor have some of Darwin's recent critics. For instance, C. D. Darlington criticizes Darwin for expressing uncertainty as to the manner in which the sex ratio has evolved. Darlington invokes group selection: species with a one-to-one ratio of males to females are less likely to become extinct than those with other ratios. But although it is possible to account for the maintenance of an adaptive sex ratio by group selection, it is far less easy to account for its origin by such a mechanism. One might conjecture that it arose quite accidentally, as a consequence of some other process; yet this is not necessary, for recent research shows that the sex ratio is affected by the ordinary kind of natural selection. When there is, say, an excess of males over females, the parents having the largest percentage of female offspring will produce the greatest number of grandchildren, since it will be easier for their children to find mates.

From a consideration of the distinction between "group selection" and the usual kind of natural selection, we may see that Darwin had the necessary components of his theory, but not the theory itself, at a fairly early stage in his investigation. Prior to his reading of Malthus, he was still thinking of species and varieties as mere abstract groupings of things characterized by particular attributes. He had yet to conceive of species as units of interaction composed of biological individuals—as populations, rather than classes. Upon reading Malthus, his attention was drawn to the long-term effects of differences between individuals upon the composition of the population. He ceased to think in terms of idealized forms and became concerned with the activities of individuals. The principle of natural selection was then obvious. Such a shift in emphasis required a fundamental change from the traditional manner of dealing with biological phenomena. It was the beginning of a revolution that transformed not only biology, but man's very conception of the physical universe. It was no longer particularly meaningful to group biological entities merely by enumerating similarities and differences. Knowledge was to be derived from a consideration of how individuals interact with each other, and by the abstraction of the laws governing such activity—laws quite different from those familiar to the science of the times. Darwin never totally escaped from a habit of falling into the old way of thinking, and many times he is inconsistent because of this. Yet he carried out a major portion of the reform himself, and it is this revolution, not the evolutionary one, which most deserves to be called Darwinian.

. . . . .

Innovation and Method

The theory of natural selection, now looked upon as the foundation of evolutionary biology, was the third of Darwin's great syntheses. Darwin deserves full credit for this innovation, as it was he who first conceived of natural selection in terms of a developed, hypothetico-deductive system, capable of explanation, prediction, and experiential testing. All of his so-called forerunners, without exception, either only conceived of elements in the theory, or did not understand its significance. Wallace alone deserves credit for his independent discovery. Darwin and Wallace merit particular respect for having developed the theory of natural selection through a process of "retroduction": that is, they were aware of a phenomenon, and successfully sought out an explanation in superficially unconnected processes. The method through which this insight was obtained would seem to have been orderly and rational. Further evidence for this thesis emerges when we compare the theory of natural selection with Darwin's other major syntheses. All three of Darwin's theories—coral reefs, evolutionary biogeography, and natural selection—invoke a type of order resulting when processes and conditions, random in relation to each other, interact: subsidence and coral growth, barriers and dispersal, variation and fitness. All three are based on abstract models which have numerous implications and can readily be tested. There is a clear-cut series of rational operations leading to each theory, although natural selection differs in having an added difficulty of shifting from groups to populations. The development of thought from invasions to evolution, and from artificial selection and extinctions to natural selection, accompanied by a shift in theoretical perspective, explains the facts of the discovery which have long seemed contradictory. All that we need yield to the notion of intuition is a grasp of the structure of models, an ability to vary them (perhaps at random), and attention to that moment when their implications are significant. Seeing in Malthus how the interaction of individuals in the same species may be affected by the intrinsic properties of each organism, and how there could be cumulative effects, Darwin and Wallace were able to conjoin all the disparate elements into a unitary system which constituted the theory of natural selection. The discovery was, above all else, a triumph of reason. If banishing intuition from our conception of the process of discovery deprives us of a sense of mystery, it nonetheless permits us to analyze that process in a far more satisfying manner than did the mythological accounts.

229

Ghiselin

THE DARWINIAN
REVOLUTION
IN BIOLOGICAL
SCIENCE

15. The Revolt Against Positivism

H. STUART HUGHES

If any one term can describe the central thrust of nineteenth-century western thought after Marx and Darwin, it was positivism. *Its high priest was Auguste Comte (1789–1857), who invented the term. Disdaining metaphysics, Comte advocated the scientific or "positive" method of observing facts and ordering them with hypotheses without seeking any ultimate reality or metaphysic behind them. Watered down into popular culture this meant a widespread belief in science as the bearer of progress and solver of all human problems. It was made to order for a European landscape increasingly dominated by laboratories and smoking factories. Under its impact naturalist novelists like Emile Zola abandoned realism to write "experimental novels" and impressionist painters, notably Seurat, forsook realism to analyze light and shadow scientifically. This is an oversimplification of positivism's influence, but the movement permeated western and especially French culture in the mid to late nineteenth century.*

Toward the end of the century an inevitable reaction set in against positivism, a reaction which fundamentally reoriented western culture and brought forth the fathers of contemporary thought: From symbolism and the psychological novel came the major trends of twentieth-century literature; from the work of Freud came one of the mainstreams of twentieth-century psychology; from the expressionists and cubists came the principal direction of contemprorary

Source: H. Stuart Hughes, *Consciousness and Society: The Reorientation of European Social Thought, 1890–1930* (New York: Knopf, 1958), pp. 33–42 and 63–66. Copyright © 1958, by H. Stuart Hughes. Reprinted by permission of Alfred A. Knopf, Inc. [Footnotes omitted.]

art; from the ideas of Max Weber, Emile Durkheim, Georges Sorel, and Vil-
fredo Pareto was born twentieth-century social thought; from the thought of
Nietzsche and Bergson came existentialism; and from Wilhelm Dilthey and
Benedetto Croce came a new direction in the writing of history.

The climate of opinion that made this reaction possible is the subject of
this selection by Professor H. Stuart Hughes of Harvard University. The
selection includes two excerpts from his Consciousness and Society: The Reconstruction of European Social Thought, 1890–1930, *which remains the*
standard book exploring the impact of this restructuring of western social
thought. In reading it, consider why Professor Hughes objects to the usual
characterizations of the decade of the 1890s as romantic, irrational, or anti-
intellectual. Why does he prefer the term antipositivist? What notions of
positivism did the antipositivists oppose? According to Hughes, what were
"the major ideas that were initially started in the 1890s, preparatory to their
fuller development in the first decade of the twentieth century"? Taken to-
gether, how would you characterize those ideas? Do they still seem adequate
descriptions of present-day culture as you understand it?

There are certain periods in history in which a number of advanced
thinkers, usually working independently one of another, have proposed
views on human conduct so different from those commonly accepted at
the time—and yet so manifestly interrelated—that together they
seem to constitute an intellectual revolution. The decade of the 1890's was
one of such periods. In this decade and the one immediately succeeding it,
the basic assumptions of eighteenth- and nineteenth-century social
thought underwent a critical review from which there emerged the new
assumptions characteristic of our own time. "A revolution of such magnitude in the prevailing empirical interpretations of human society is hardly
to be found occurring within the short space of a generation, unless one
goes back to about the sixteenth century. What is to account for it?"

Nearly all students of the last years of the nineteenth century have
sensed in some form or other a profound psychological change. Yet they
have differed markedly in the way in which they have expressed their understanding of it. In the older, more aesthetically oriented interpretations
(we may think of Henry Adams), the 1890's figured as the *fin de siècle:* it
was a period of overripeness, of perverse and mannered decadence—the
end of an era. We need not stop to ask ourselves how much of this was
simply an artistic and literary pose. For our present purposes, it is irrelevant: the *fin de siècle* is a backdrop, nothing more.

Somewhere between an aesthetic and a more intellectual interpretation, we might be tempted to characterize the new attitude as neo-roman-
ticism or neo-mysticism. This formulation has considerable plausibility.
Unquestionably the turn toward the subjective that we find in so much of
the imaginative and speculative writing of the quarter-century between
1890 and the First World War recalls the aspirations of the original Ro-
manticists. It is not difficult to think of writers who in the 1890's or early
1900's felt that they were reaching back over a half-century gap to restore

to honor those values of the imagination that their immediate predecessors had scorned and neglected. It was writers such as these who established the cult of Dostoyevsky and Nietzsche as the literary heralds of the new era. There is a pathetic paradox in the fact that the year of Nietzsche's madness—1889—coincides with the time at which his work, after two decades of public neglect, first began to find wide acceptance. Again and again in the course of the present study we shall find one or another social thinker elaborating more rigorously and systematically the suggestions with regard to unconscious strivings and heroic minorities which Nietzsche had thrown out in fragmentary form.

Yet to call Nietzsche a neo-romantic is surely misleading. Any such characterization does less than justice to the critical and Socratic elements in his thought. And when it is applied to the social thinkers of the early twentieth century, it fits only a very few—and these are minor figures like Péguy and Jung. The truly great either were hostile to what they took to be neo-romantic tendencies or, like Freud and Weber, sought to curb the romanticism they discovered within themselves. Durkheim was perhaps the most categorical of his contemporaries in protesting against what he called a "renascent mysticism," but he was not an isolated case. It was rather the "mystic" Bergson (whom Durkheim may have been aiming at) who was less typical. Indeed, of the major new doctrines of the period, the Bergsonian metaphysics was unique in having frankly mystical aspects—and even this doctrine was couched so far as possible in acceptable philosophic terminology. It was on the "lower" levels of thought, rather—on the level of semipopular agitation—that the neo-romantic tendencies were to have their greatest effect. And it was here that their application to politics eventually produced that "betrayal of the intellectuals" which Julien Benda assailed with such telling effect three decades later.

If not "romanticism," will "irrationalism" serve as a general description? It is neat, it is frequently used, and it at least begins to suggest the real concerns of early twentieth-century social thought. Unquestionably the major intellectual innovators of the 1890's were profoundly interested in the problem of irrational motivation in human conduct. They were obsessed, almost intoxicated, with a rediscovery of the nonlogical, the uncivilized, the inexplicable. But to call them "irrationalists" is to fall into a dangerous ambiguity. It suggests a tolerance or even a preference for the realms of the unconscious. The reverse was actually the case. The social thinkers of the 1890's were concerned with the irrational only to exorcise it. By probing into it, they sought ways to tame it, to canalize it for constructive human purposes. Even Sorel, who has often been held up as the supreme irrationalist, had as his life's goal the enunciation of a political formula that would fit the new world of industrial logic and the machine.

Sorel, Pareto, Durkheim, Freud—all thought of themselves as engineers or technicians, men of science or medicine. It is obviously absurd to call them irrationalists in any but the most restricted sense. As a substitute, the formula "anti-intellectualist" has sometimes been employed. This characterization is both flexible and comprehensive. It suggests the revulsion from ideology and the *a priori,* from the abstract thought of the century and a half preceding, which served to unite writers otherwise so far apart as Durkheim and Sorel. It recalls the influence and prestige of William James—an influence at the same time comparable, opposed, and complementary to that of Nietzsche. "Anti-intellectualism," then, is virtually equivalent to Jamesian pragmatism. It offers a satisfactory common denominator for grouping a large proportion of the intellectual innovations of the 1890's.

Yet it is at the same time too broad and too narrow. It fails to take account of the unrepentant abstraction and intellectualism in the thought of Benedetto Croce—or, to take quite a different example, the later elaboration by Max Weber of social theory in terms of "ideal types." It suggests, moreover, that the turn from the principles of the Enlightenment was more complete and decisive than was actually the case. The main attack against the intellectual heritage of the past was in fact on a narrower front. It was directed primarily against what the writers of the 1890's chose to call "positivism." By this they did not mean simply the rather quaint doctrines associated with the name of Auguste Comte, who had originally coined the term. Nor did they mean the social philosophy of Herbert Spencer, which was the guise in which positivist thinking was most apparent in their own time. They used the word in a looser sense to characterize the whole tendency to discuss human behavior in terms of analogies drawn from natural science. In reacting against it, the innovators of the 1890's felt that they were rejecting the most pervasive intellectual tenet of their time. They believed that they were casting off a spiritual yoke that the preceding quarter-century had laid upon them.

As a preliminary characterization, to speak of the innovations of the 1890's as a revolt against positivism comes closest to what the writers in question actually thought that they were about. Yet even this last formula has its pitfalls. We must be on guard against the tendency of someone like Croce to use positivism as a philosophic catch-all, to embrace under this epithet every doctrine for which he had a dislike. We must not forget the number of influential thinkers of the period—men like Durkheim and Mosca—who remained essentially in the positivist tradition. And, finally, we must take proper account of the others, like Freud, who continued to use mechanistic language drawn from the natural sciences long after their discoveries had burst the framework of their inherited vocabulary.

How, then, did positivism appear to the young rebels of the 1890's? To understand a new tendency in thought, we must necessarily look first at what the revolt is directed against.

I have already suggested that the late nineteenth-century critics of positivism did not write of it in any very precise terms. Apparently they regarded it as so familiar to their readers as not to require identification: they thought of it more as a diffused intellectual tendency than as a specific set of principles. Hence they used the word "positivism" almost interchangeably with a number of other philosophical doctrines that they regarded with equal disfavor—"materialism," "mechanism," and "naturalism." To describe the dominant tendency in late nineteenth-century thought as materialism was obviously a crude simplification. Few serious thinkers of any period have been true materialists. Indeed, the individual usually pointed to as the nineteenth-century prototype of this attitude—Ludwig Feuerbach—was far from being an unqualified materialist. "Mechanism," on the other hand, was a rather more accurate characterization: it suggested the prestige of explanations drawn from the Newtonian physical universe and in particular from the recently developed field of electricity. Similarly the term "naturalism" evoked the biological explanations that had come increasingly into vogue as the nineteenth century advanced. This had been notably the case since the triumph of Darwinism in the 1860's.

With Darwinism in its applied or "social" form, we come to the central point of intellectual conflict. Some of Darwin's earliest supporters had been followers of Auguste Comte, and the second of the high priests of positivism, Herbert Spencer, had early rallied to Darwinism, sensing its possibilities as support for his own position. With its Darwinian alliance, the positivist way of thinking underwent some curious changes. In its original eighteenth-century or Utilitarian form it had been an intellectualist philosophy, basing itself on the conviction that the problems of man in society were readily capable of a rational solution. Under the influence of Social Darwinism, however, the positivist creed began to shed its rationalist features: "heredity" and "environment" replaced conscious, logical choice as the main determinants of human action. A Hobbesian state of nature (now called "struggle for existence") was substituted for decorous social order as the characteristic view of the relations between man and man. The result was a kind of scientific fatalism—the antithesis of the buoyantly optimistic attitude that had characterized the philosophers of the eighteenth century or the English Utilitarians of the first part of the century following. The ultimate irony of positivism was that what had started as an ultra-intellectualist doctrine became in effect a philosophy of radical anti-intellectualism.

Hence in the perspective of a cultural scene dominated by Social Darwinism, the young thinkers of the 1890's can be regarded as aiming at precisely the opposite of what they have usually been accused of doing. Far from being "irrationalists," they were striving to vindicate the rights of rational inquiry. Alarmed by the threat of an iron determinism, they were seeking to restore the freely speculating mind to the dignity it had enjoyed a century earlier.

From our present-day vantage point, it is difficult to reconstruct in our minds the dominant intellectual temper of the 1890's. It is hard for us to conceive how men who are almost forgotten today could have wielded so much influence in their own time. In Italy, where the anti-clericalism of the governing classes reinforced the teachings of positivism to cast them in their crudest mold, the guardian of the cult was the defrocked priest Ardigo. In Germany, where positivism never took so firm a hold, the physiologist DuBois-Reymond pontificated at the University of Berlin. It was France, perhaps, that had produced the most distinguished positivist minds: the names of Taine and Renan may still command our respect as the exponents of a dedicated search for precise chains of causation and an ethic of dignified, urbane resignation. To the generation that had grown up under their direct influence, however, these teachings appeared rather more sinister. Taine's celebrated precepts—"virtue and vice are products like sugar and vitriol" or "genius . . . is a resultant of race, milieu, and the [proper] moment" or yet again "nature and history are only the unrolling of universal necessity"—these dicta, which today strike us as merely excessive, then seemed crushing burdens under which the youthful imagination felt stifled. Similarly Renan's ultra-civilized relativism acted as an icy bath in which ideal values simply dissolved. The novelist Romain Rolland has recalled how as a young lecturer on art and music at the Ecole Normale Supérieure—the summit of the French educational system—he and his friends had striven for liberation from the prevailing attitude of pessimistic skepticism:

> There we were, huddled together in anguish, scarcely breathing.
> . . . Ah! we spent difficult years together. Our masters do not suspect the anxieties with which our youth struggled under their shadow!

It was not only in respect to the life of the mind that young men began to feel stifled as the 1880's drew to a close. In sober truth it had been a stuffy decade. It was almost literally in order to breathe more freely that Nietzsche had withdrawn to his Alpine heights—away from the smugness, the "philistinism," of upper middle-class society. In the very character of its decorative arts the epoch exuded a sense of heaviness, of material excess, of confinement:

> Men of the seventies and eighties . . . were filled with a devouring hunger for reality, but they had the misfortune to confuse this with matter—which is but the hollow and deceptive wrapping of it. Thus they lived perpetually in a wretched, padded, puffed-out world of cotton-wool, cardboard, and tissue-paper. In all their creations it is with the arts of adornment that imagination is concerned: with the art of the upholsterer, the confectioner, the stucco decorator. . . .

The quotation is from one of the most imaginative and least systematic of cultural historians. But it has deftly caught the material background of bourgeois life in the 1880's.

With the new decade, particularly with its closing years, the circumstances, social and political, that had earlier inspired a sense of sober confidence began to change. Both on the "lower" and on the "higher" levels of intellectual activity, doubts arose as to the reigning philosophy of the upper middle class—the self-satisfied cult of material progress which, in a vulgarized sense, could also be termed "positivism." After two decades of precarious equilibrium, the institutional arrangements of the major Western European states were again brought into question. The artificial, contrived character of the regimes with which unification had endowed Germany and Italy were revealed by their malfunctioning—in the one case by the erratic changes in policy that followed the resignation of Bismarck in 1890, in the other by the social disorders and authoritarian government with which the century came to a close. In France the shock of the Dreyfus case acted as a stimulus to the re-examination of the traditional ideologies on which both the defenders and the enemies of the accused captain had rested their case.

Social disorder, economic crisis, and institutional malfunctioning had contributed to the growth of Socialist parties and to the spread of Marxist doctrines. The decade of the 1890's was to be the great period of expansion in the history of European Socialism. At first sight it might seem that Marxism—a critical as opposed to a positive philosophy of society—could have offered to the intellectual innovators of the 1890's a suitable weapon with which to combat the dominant ideology of the European middle class. Such was, indeed, briefly the case in Italy, under the revivifying influence of the lectures of Antonio Labriola at the University of Rome. But even here Labriola's student Croce was eventually impelled to arrive at his own critique of Marxist doctrine. Basically Marxism was to figure in the intellectual renovation of the 1890's as an aberrant, and pecularly insidious, form of the reigning cult of positivism. It loomed on the cultural horizon as the last and most ambitious of the abstract and pseudoscientific ideologies that had bewitched European intellectuals since the early eighteenth century.

To come to terms with Marxism, then, was the first and most obvious task confronting the intellectual innovators of the 1890's. Some, like Freud, dealt with Marx only by implication—by extending social thought to new areas undreamed of in the socialist ideologies. Others, like Pareto, offered highly skeptical refutations of the central arguments of dialectical materialism. Still others, like Croce and Sorel, while maintaining the Marxist terminology, were to transmute it into something so different from the original intention as to leave little standing but a hollow framework—within which the earlier categories of thought had ceased to be actualities and had become mere symbols and methodological conveniences. Finally, a decade later than the rest, Max Weber was to propose a view of society that brought Marx's economic motivations into a tense and polar relationship to the deepest spiritual values of mankind.

. . . . .

. . . Against this background we may outline in preliminary and schematic form the major ideas that were initially stated in the 1890's, preparatory to their fuller elaboration in the first decade of the twentieth century.

1. Most basic, perhaps, and the key to all the others was the new interest in the problem of consciousness and the role of the unconscious. It

was the problem implicit in the title of Bergson's first book, the *Essay on the Immediate Data of Consciousness*. In it he had tried to distinguish between a "superficial psychic life" to which the scientific logic of space and number could properly be applied, and a life in the "depths of consciousness" in which "the deep-seated self" followed a logic of its own: he had come to the conclusion that the world of dreams might offer a clue to this secret and unexplored realm. "In order to recover this fundamental self," he had added, "a vigorous effort of analysis is necessary." A decade later, and proceeding from a philosophic and professional preparation almost totally in contrast to that of Bergson, Freud began to carry out the program that the former had outlined. Freud's first major work, *The Interpretation of Dreams,* built on his own "vigorous effort" of self-analysis a theory of unconscious motivation to which the life of dreams offered the key.

2. Closely related to the problem of consciousness was the question of the meaning of time and duration in psychology, philosophy, literature, and history. It was the problem to which Bergson was to return again and again in an effort to define the nature of subjective existence as opposed to the schematic order that the natural sciences had imposed on the external world. It represented one aspect of the task that Croce had set himself in trying to establish the qualitative and methodological differences between the realm of history and the realm of science. In somewhat different form it was the problem with which the natural scientists were themselves contending in postulating a universe that no longer strictly conformed to the laws of Newtonian physics. Finally it was the dilemma that obsessed the novelists of the first two decades of the new century— Alain-Fournier, Proust, Thomas Mann—the tormenting question of how to recapture the immediacy of past experience in the language that in ordinary usage could reproduce no more than the fragmentized reality of an existence that the logical memory had already stored away in neat compartments.

3. Beyond and embracing the questions of consciousness and time, there loomed the further problem of the nature of knowledge in what Wilhelm Dilthey had called the "sciences of the mind." In the early 1880's Dilthey had attempted to establish rules that would separate the areas in which the human mind strove for some kind of internal comprehension from the realm of external and purely conventional symbols devised by natural science. A decade later Croce had resumed the task, with his first important essay, *"La storia ridotta sotto il concetto generale dell'arte."* Croce soon abandoned the simple solution of including history among the arts. But his conviction of the radical subjectivity of historical knowledge remained. By 1900 it was apparent to the more imaginative of Croce's contemporaries that the nineteenth-century program of building an edifice of historical and sociological knowledge by patient accumulation and painstaking verification no longer sufficed. By such means it would prove forever impossible to penetrate beneath the surface of human experience. One had, rather, a choice between the exercise of the sympa-

thetic intuition postulated in Croce's neo-idealistic theory of history, and the creation of useful fictions, as Max Weber was later to elaborate them, as models for critical understanding.

4. If the knowledge of human affairs, then, rested on such tentative foundations, the whole basis of political discussion had been radically altered. No longer could one remain content with the easy assurances of the rationalistic ideologies inherited from the century and a half preceding —liberal, democratic, or socialist as the case might be. The task was rather to penetrate behind the fictions of political action, behind what Sorel called the "myths," Pareto the "derivations," and Mosca the "political formulas" of the time. Behind these convenient façades, one could postulate the existence of the actual wielders of power, the creative minorities, the political élites. The discussion of politics, then, had been pushed back from the front of the stage to the wings—from the rhetoric of public discussion to the manipulation of half-conscious sentiments.

Such, indeed, is the most general characterization we may give to the new intellectual concerns of the 1890's. They had displaced the axis of social thought from the apparent and objectively verifiable to the only partially conscious area of unexplained motivation. In this sense the new doctrines were manifestly subjective. Psychological process had replaced external reality as the most pressing topic for investigation. It was no longer what actually existed that seemed most important: it was what men thought existed. And what they felt on the unconscious level had become rather more interesting than what they had consciously rationalized. Or—to formulate the change in still more radical terms—since it had apparently been proved impossible to arrive at any sure knowledge of human behavior—if one must rely on flashes of subjective intuition or on the creation of convenient fictions—then the mind had indeed been freed from the bonds of positivist method: it was at liberty to speculate, to imagine, to create. At one stroke, the realm of human understanding had been drastically reduced and immensely broadened. The possibilities of social thought stretched out to infinity. It was perhaps this that Freud had in mind when in 1896 he spoke of "metapsychology"—the definition of the origin and nature of humanity—as his "ideal and problem child," his most challenging task for the future.

16. Freud's Model of Man and Its Social Determinants

ERICH FROMM

*Of all the intellectual figures of the antipositivist revolt the most command-
ing was Sigmund Freud (1856–1939), the father of psychoanalysis. Not only
have his psychological terms such as subconscious, drive, Oedipus complex,
and sublimation become household words, but Freudianism has come to per-
meate the arts and thought in general. In that way Freud joined such others as
Marx and Darwin to become one of the giants of modern thought.*

*The previous selection sought to show that the antipositivist revolt
grew out of the intellectual climate of the times. This selection, by
Erich Fromm, a psychiatrist and one of the most esteemed and prolific
interpreters of Freud, does the same for Freud as an individual. "One can
best understand the greatness of Freud," writes Fromm in this paper he delivered in 1969, "that of the man and that of his work, only if one sees him
in his fundamental contradictions, and as bound—or chained—to his social
situation." The latter, in particular, is extremely important in understanding
how a thinker came to his ideas. What does Fromm mean when he says that
"Freud saw man as a closed system driven by two forces: the self-preservative and the sexual drives"? To what extent were these ideas determined by
Freud's own environment? How and in what direction did Freud's views
change after 1920? In what ways were these new ideas rooted in his society
of that time? How did he synthesize human rationality and irrationality and*

Source: Erich Fromm, *The Crisis of Psychoanalysis* (New York: Holt, Rinehart
and Winston, 1970), pp. 30–45. Copyright © 1970 by Erich Fromm. Reprinted
by permission of Holt, Rinehart and Winston, Inc. [Footnotes omitted.]

why did that notion have such an impact on the twentieth century? What does Fromm mean by the "conflict between determinism and indeterminism of the will"? Would the women's liberation movement consider Freud a "sexist" or "male chauvinist"? What are the consequences of his view of women, and why did he hold such views? If the current child advocacy movement becomes a children's liberation movement, would it feel the same way toward Freud's view of the child? What was Freud's view of history and why was it "tragic"?

To appreciate the social basis of Freud's views, it is useful to recognize from the outset that he was a liberal critic of bourgeois society, in the sense in which liberal reformers in general were critical. He saw that society imposes unnecessary hardships on man, which are conducive to worse results rather than the expected better ones. He saw that this unnecessary harshness, as it operated in the field of sexual morality, led to the formation of neuroses that, in many cases, could have been avoided by a more tolerant attitude. (Political and educational reform are parallel phenomena.) But Freud was never a radical critic of capitalistic society. He never questioned its socio-economic bases, nor did he criticize its ideologies—with the exception of those concerning sexuality.

As for his concept of man, it is important to point out first that Freud, rooted in the philosophy of humanism and enlightenment, starts out with the assumption of the existence of *man* as such—a universal man, not only man as he manifests himself in various cultures, but someone about whose structure generally valid and empirical statements can be made. Freud, like Spinoza before him, constructed a "model of human nature" on the basis of which not only neuroses, but all fundamental aspects, possibilities, and necessities of man, can be explained and understood.

What is this Freudian model?

Freud saw man as a closed system driven by two forces: the self-preservative and the sexual drives. The latter are rooted in chemophysiological processes moving in a phased pattern. The first phase increases tension and unpleasure; the second reduces the built-up tension and in so doing creates that which subjectively is felt as "pleasure." Man is primarily an isolated being, whose primary interest is the optimal satisfaction of both his ego and his libidinous interest. Freud's man is the physiologically driven and motivated *homme machine*. But, secondarily, man is also a social being, because he needs other people for the satisfaction of his libidinous drives as well as those of self-preservation. The child is in need of mother (and here, according to Freud, libidinous desires follow the path of the physiological needs); the adult needs a sexual partner. Feelings like tenderness or love are looked upon as phenomena that accompany, and result from, libidinous interests. Individuals need each other as means for the satisfaction of their physiologically rooted drives. Man is primarily unrelated to others, and is only secondarily forced—or seduced—into relationships with others.

Freud's *homo sexualis* is a variant of the classic *homo economicus*. It is the isolated, self-sufficient man who has to enter into relations with others in order that they may mutually fulfill their needs. *Homo economicus* has simply economic needs that find their mutual satisfaction in the exchange of goods on the commodity market. The needs of *homo sexualis* are physiological and libidinous, and normally are mutually satisfied by the relations between the sexes. In both variants the persons essentially remain strangers to each other, being related only by the common aim of drive satisfaction. This social determination of Freud's theory by the spirit of the market economy does not mean that the theory is wrong, except in its claim of describing the situation of *man as such;* as a description of interpersonal relations in bourgeois society, it is valid for the majority of people.

To this general statement a specific point must be added with regard to the social determinants of Freud's concept of drives. Freud was a student of von Brücke, a physiologist who was one of the most distinguished representatives of mechanistic materialism, especially in its German form. This type of materialism was based on the principle that all psychic phenomena have their roots in certain physiological processes and that they *can be sufficiently explained and understood* if one knows these roots. Freud, in search of the roots of psychic disturbances, had to look for a physiological substrate for the drives; to find this in sexuality was an ideal solution, since it corresponded both to the requirements of mechanistic-materialistic thought and to certain clinical findings in patients of his time and social class. It remains, of course, uncertain whether those findings would have impressed Freud so deeply if he had not thought within the framework of his philosophy; but it can hardly be doubted that his philosophy was an important determinant of his theory of drives. This means that someone with a different philosophy will approach his findings with a certain skepticism. Such a skepticism refers not so much to a restricted form of Freud's theories, according to which in *some* neurotic disturbances sexual factors play a decisive role, but rather to the claim that *all* neuroses and all human behavior are determined by the conflict between the sexual and the self-preservative drives.

Freud's libido theory also mirrors his social situation in another sense. It is based on the concept of scarcity, assuming that all human strivings for lust result from the need to rid oneself from unpleasureful tensions, rather than that lust is a phenomenon of abundance aiming at a greater intensity and depth of human experiences. This principle of scarcity is characteristic of middle-class thought, recalling Malthus, Benjamin Franklin, or an average businessman of the nineteenth century. There are many ramifications of this principle of scarcity and the virtue of saving, but essentially it means that the quantity of all commodities is necessarily limited, and hence that equal satisfaction for all is impossible because true abundance is impossible; in such a framework scarcity becomes the most important stimulus for human activity.

In spite of its social determinants, Freud's theory of drives remains a fundamental contribution to the model of man. Even if the libido theory as such is not correct, it is, let us say, a symbolic expression of a more general phenomenon: that human behavior is the product of forces which, although usually not conscious as such, motivate man, drive him, and lead him into conflicts. The relatively static nature of human behavior is deceptive. It exists only because the system of forces producing it remains the same, and it remains the same as long as the conditions which mold these forces do not change. But when these conditions, social or individual, change, the system of forces loses its stability and with it the apparently static behavior pattern.

With his dynamic concept of *character,* Freud raised the psychology of behavior from the level of description to that of science. Freud did for psychology what the great dramatists and novelists achieved in artistic form. He showed man as the hero of a drama who, even if he is only of average talent, is a hero because he fights passionately in the attempt to make some sense of the fact of having been born. Freud's drama par excellence, the Oedipus complex, may be a more harmless, bourgeois version of forces which are much more elementary than the father-mother-son triangle described by it; but Freud has given this triangle the dramatic quality of the myth.

This theory of desires dominated Freud's systematic thinking until 1920, when a new phase of his thinking began, which constituted an essential change in his concept of man. Instead of the opposition between ego and libidinous drives, the basic conflict now was between "life instincts" (Eros) and "death instinct." The life instincts, comprising both ego and sexual drives, were placed in opposition to the death instinct, which was considered the root of human destructiveness, directed either toward the person himself or the world outside These new basic drives are constructed entirely differently from the old ones. First of all, they are not located in any special zone of the organism, as the libido is in the erogenous zones. Furthermore, they do not follow the pattern of the "hydraulic" mechanism: increasing tension→unpleasure→detension→pleasure→new tension, etc., but they are inherent in all living substance and operate without any special stimulation. They also do not follow the conservative principle of return to an original state that Freud, at one point, had postulated for all instincts. Eros has the tendency to unite and to integrate; the death instinct has the opposite tendency, to disintegration and destruction. Both drives operate constantly within man, fight each other, and blend with each other, until finally the death instinct proves to be the stronger and has its ultimate triumph in the death of the individual.

This new concept of drives indicates essential changes in Freud's mode of thinking and we may assume that these changes are related to fundamental social changes.

The new concept of drives does not follow the model of materialistic-mechanistic thinking; it can, rather, be considered as a biological, vitalistic oriented concept, a change corresponding to a general trend in biological thought at that time. More important, however, is Freud's new appreciation of the role of human destructiveness. Not that he had omitted aggression in his first theoretical model. He had considered aggression to be an important factor, but it was subordinated to the libidinous drives and those for self-preservation. In the new theory destructiveness becomes the rival of, and eventually the victor over the libido and the ego drives. Man cannot help wanting to destroy, for the destructive tendency is rooted in his biological constitution. Although he can mitigate this tendency to a certain point, he can never deprive it of its strength. His alternatives are to direct his destructiveness either against himself or against the world outside, but he has no chance of liberating himself from this tragic dilemma.

There are good reasons for the hypothesis that Freud's new appreciation of destructiveness has its roots in the experience of the first World War. This war shook the foundations of the liberal optimism that had filled the first period of Freud's life. Until 1914 the members of the middle class had believed that the world was rapidly approaching a state of greater security, harmony and peace. The "darkness" of the middle ages seemed to lift from generation to generation; in a few more steps, so it seemed, the world—or at least Europe—would resemble the streets of a well-lighted, protected capital. In the bourgeois euphoria of the *belle époque* it was easily forgotten that this picture was not true for the majority of the workers and peasants of Europe, and even less so for the populations of Asia and Africa. The war of 1914 destroyed this illusion; not so much the beginning of the war, as its duration and the inhumanity of its practices. Freud, who during the war still believed in the justice and victory of the German cause, was hit at a deeper psychic level than the average, less sensitive person. He probably sensed that the optimistic hopes of enlightenment thought were illusions, and concluded that man, by nature, was destined to be destructive. Precisely because he was a reformer, the war must have hit him all the more forcefully. Since he was no radical critic of society and no revolutionary, it was impossible for him to hope for essential social changes, and he was forced to look for the causes of the tragedy in the nature of man.

Freud was, historically speaking, a figure of the frontier, of a period of a radical change of the social character. Inasmuch as he belonged to the nineteenth century, he was optimistic, a thinker of the enlightenment; inasmuch as he belonged to the twentieth century, he was a pessimistic, almost despairing representative of a society caught in rapid and unpredictable change. Perhaps this pessimism was reinforced by his grave, painful, and life-threatening illness, an illness which lasted until his death, and which he bore with the heroism of a genius; perhaps also by the disappointment over the defection of some of his most gifted disciples— Adler, Jung, and Rank; however this may be, he could never recover his lost optimism. But, on the other hand, he neither could nor probably wished to cut himself entirely loose from his previous thinking. This is perhaps the reason why he never resolved the contradiction between the old and the new concept of man; the old libido was subsumed under

Eros; the old aggression under the death instinct; but it is painfully clear that this was only theoretical patchwork.

Freud's model of man also places great emphasis on the dialectic of rationality and irrationality in man. The originality and greatness of Freud's thought becomes particularly clear at this point. As a successor of the enlightenment thinkers Freud was a rationalist who believed in the power of reason and the strength of the human will; he was convinced that social conditions, and especially those prevailing in early childhood, were responsible for the evil in man. But Freud had already lost his rationalistic innocence, as it were, at the beginning of his work, and had recognized the strength of human irrationality and the weakness of human reason and will. He fully confronted himself with the opposition inherent in the *two* principles, and found, dialectically, a new synthesis. This synthesis of rationalistic enlightenment thinking and twentieth century skepticism was expressed in his concept of the unconscious. If all that is real were conscious, then indeed man would be a rational being; for his rational thought follows the laws of logic. But the overwhelming part of his inner experience is unconscious, and for this reason is not subject to the control of logic, of reason, and will. Human irrationality dominates in the unconscious; logic governs in the conscious. But, and this is decisive, the unconscious steers consciousness, and thus the behavior of man. With this concept of the determination of man by the unconscious, Freud, without being aware of it, repeated a thesis which Spinoza had already expressed. But while it was marginal in Spinoza's system, it was central to Freud.

Freud did not resolve the conflict in a static way, simply allowing one of the two sides to prevail. If he had declared reason the victor, he would have remained an enlightenment philosopher; if he had given the decisive role to irrationality, he would have become a conservative romantic, as were so many significant thinkers of the nineteenth century. Although it is true that man is driven by irrational forces—the libido, and especially in its pregenital stages of evolution, his ego—his reason and his will are also not without strength. The power of reason expresses itself in the first place in the fact that man can understand his irrationality by the use of reason. In this way Freud founded the *science of human irrationality*—psychoanalytic theory. But he did not stop at theory. Because a person in the analytic process can make his own unconscious conscious, he can also liberate himself from the dominance of unconscious strivings; instead of repressing them, he can negate them, that is, he can lessen their strength, and control them with his will. This is possible, Freud thought, because the grown-up person has as an ally a stronger ego than the child once had. Freud's psychoanalytic therapy was based on the hope of overcoming, or at least restraining, the unconscious impulses which, working in the dark, had previously been outside of man's control. Historically speaking, one can look at Freud's theory as the fruitful synthesis of rationalism and romanticism; the creative power of this synthesis may be one of the reasons why Freud's thinking became a dominating influence in the twentieth century. This influence was not due to the fact that Freud found a new therapy for neuroses, and probably also not primarily because of his role as a defender of repressed sexuality. There is a great deal to say in favor of the assumption that the most important reason for his general influence on culture is in this synthesis, whose fruitfulness can be clearly seen in the two most important defections from Freud, that of Adler and of Jung. Both exploded the Freudian synthesis and reverted to the two original oppositions. Adler, rooted in the short-lived optimism of the rising lower middle classes, constructed a one-sided rationalistic-optimistic theory. He believed that the innate disabilities are the very conditions of strength and that with intellectual understanding of a situation, man can liberate himself and make the tragedy of life disappear.

Jung, on the other hand, was a romantic who saw the sources of all human strength in the unconscious. He recognized the wealth and depth of symbols and myths much more profoundly than Freud, whose views were restricted by his sexual theory. Their aims, however, were contradictory. Freud wanted to understand the unconscious in order to weaken and control it; Jung, in order to gain an increased vitality from it. Their interest in the unconscious united the two men for some time, without their being aware that they were moving in opposite directions. As they halted on their way in order to talk about the unconscious, they fell under the illusion that they were proceeding in the same direction.

Closely related with Freud's synthesis of rationality and irrationality is his treatment of the conflict between determinism and indeterminism of the will. Freud was a determinist; he believed that man is not free, but he is determined by the unconscious, the *id,* and the super ego. *But,* and this "but" is of decisive importance for Freud, man is also not wholly determined. With the help of the analytic method he can gain control over the unconscious. With this position of alternativism, which resembles in its essence that of Spinoza and Marx, Freud accomplished another fruitful synthesis of two opposite poles.

Did Freud recognize the moral factor as a fundamental part in his model of man? The answer to this question is in the negative. Man develops exclusively under the influence of his self-interest, which demands optimal satisfaction of his libidinal impulses, always on the condition that they do not endanger his interest in self-preservation ("reality principle"). The moral problem, which traditionally has been that of the conflict between altruism and egoism, virtually disappeared. Egoism is the only driving force, and the conflict is simply between the two forms of egoism, the libidinous and the material. It hardly needs to be demonstrated that in this view of man as basically egotistical, Freud is following the leading concepts of bourgeois thinking. Nevertheless, to say that Freud simply denied the existence of conscience as an effective element in his model of human nature would not be correct. Freud recognizes the power of conscience, but he "explains" conscience, and in doing so deprives it of all objective validity. His explanation is that conscience is the super ego, which is a replica of all the commandments and prohibitions of the father (or the father's super ego) with whom the little boy identifies himself when, motivated by castration anxiety, he overcomes his Oedipal strivings. This explanation refers to both elements of conscience: the formal one—the *how* of conscience formation, and the substantial one, that is concerned with the contents of conscience. Since the essential part of fatherly norms and the fatherly superego is socially conditioned, or to put it more correctly, since the superego is nothing but the personal mode of social norms, Freud's explanation leads to a relativization of all moral norms. Each norm has its significance, not because of the validity of its contents, but on the basis of the psychological mechanism by which it is accepted. Good is what the internalized authority commands, and bad what it prohibits. Freud is undoubtedly right inasmuch as the norms believed in by most people as moral are, to a large extent, nothing but norms established by society for the sake of its own optimal functioning. From this standpoint his theory is an important critique of existing conventional morality, and his theory of the superego unveils its true character. But he probably did not intend this critical aspect of the theory; it may not even have been conscious to him. He did not give his theory a critical turn, and he could hardly have done so, since he was not much concerned with the question of whether there are any norms whose contents transcend a given social structure and correspond better to the demands of human nature and the laws of human growth.

One cannot talk about Freud's anthropology without discussing two special cases: that of man and woman, and that of the child.

For Freud only the male is really a full human being. Woman is a crippled, castrated man. She suffers from this fate, and can be happy only if she finally overcomes her "castration complex" by the acceptance of a child and husband. But she remains inferior also in other respects—for instance, she is more narcissistic and less directed by conscience than man. This strange theory, according to which one half of the human race is only a crippled edition of the other, followed Victorian ideas that woman's desires were almost entirely directed to the bearing and upbringing of children—and to serve the man. Freud gave clear expression to this when he wrote *"the libido is masculine."* Belief in this Victorian idea of woman as being without her own sexuality was an expression of the extreme patriarchal assumption of man's natural superiority over the woman. The male, in patriarchal ideology, is more rational, realistic, and responsible than the female, and hence destined by nature to be her leader and guide. How completely Freud shared this point of view follows from his reaction to the demand for political and social equality of women expressed by J. S. Mill, a thinker whom Freud profoundly admired in all other respects. Here Mill is simply "crazy"; it is unthinkable for Freud to imagine that his beloved bride should compete with him on the market place, instead of allowing herself to be protected by him.

Freud's patriarchal bias had two further serious consequences for his theory. One was that he could not recognize the nature of erotic love, since it is based on the male-female polarity which is only possible if male and female are equals, though different. Thus his whole system is centered around sexual but not erotic love. Even in his later theory he applies Eros (the life instincts) only to the behavior of living organisms in general, but does not extend it to the male-female dimension. The other equally serious consequence was that Freud completely overlooked for the largest part of his life the primary tie of the child (boy or girl) to the mother, the nature of motherly love, and the fear of mother. The tie to mother could be conceived only in terms of the Oedipus situation when the little boy is already a little man, for whom, as for father, mother is a sexual object and who is afraid only of the father, not the mother. Only in the last years of his life did Freud begin to see this primary tie, although by no means in all its importance. It seems that aside from the repression of his own strong fixation to his mother, Freud's patriarchal bias did not permit him consciously to consider the woman-mother as the powerful figure to which the child is bound. Almost all other analysts accepted Freud's theories of sexuality and the secondary role of mother, in spite of the overwhelming evidence to the contrary.

Here, as everywhere else, pointing to the connection between the theory and its social determinants, of course, does not prove that the theory is wrong; but if one examines the clinical evidence carefully, it does not confirm Freud's theory. I cannot discuss it in this context; a number of psychoanalysts, especially Karen Horney's pioneering work with regard to the point, have presented clinical findings which contradict Freud's hypothesis. In general, it may simply be said that Freud's theory in this field, while always imaginative and fascinating because of its logic, seems to contain only a minimum of truth, probably because Freud was so deeply imbued by his patriarchal bias.

Freud's picture of the child is quite a different matter. Like the woman, the child also has been the object of oppression and exploitation by the father throughout history. It was, like slave and wife, the property of the man-father, who had "given" it life, and who could do with it whatever he liked, arbitrarily and unrestrictedly, as with all property. (The institution of the sacrifice of children, which was once so widespread in the world, is one of the many manifestations of this constellation.)

Children could defend themselves even less than women and slaves. Women have fought a guerrilla war against the patriarchate in their own way; slaves have rebelled many times in one form or the other. But temper tantrums, refusal to eat, constipation, and bed-wetting are not the weapons by which one can overthrow a powerful system. The only result was that the child developed into a crippled, inhibited, and often evil adult, who took revenge on his own children for what had been done to him.

The domination of children was expressed, if not in brutal, physical terms, then in psychic exploitation. The adult demanded from the child the satisfaction of his vanity, of his wish for obedience, the adaptation to his moods, etc. Of especial importance is the fact that the adult did not take the child seriously. The child, one assumed, has no psychic life of its own; it was supposed to be a blank sheet of paper on which the adult had the right and the obligation to write the text (another version of "the white man's burden"). It followed from this that one believed it to be right to lie to children. If a man lies to adults he has to excuse it in some way. Lying to the child apparently did not require any excuses, because, after all, the child is not a full human being. The same principle is employed toward adults when they are strangers, enemies, sick, criminals, or members of an inferior and exploited class or race. By and large, only those who are not powerless have the right to demand the truth—this is the principle that has been applied in most societies in history, even though this was not their conscious ideology.

The *revolution of the child,* like that of the woman, began in the nineteenth century. People began to see that the child was not a blank sheet of paper, but a very developed, curious, imaginative, sensitive being, in need of stimulation. One symptom of this new appreciation of the child, in the field of education, was the Montessori method; another, the much more influential theory of Freud. He expressed the view, and could prove it clinically, that unfavorable influences in childhood have the most aggravating consequences for later development. He could describe the peculiar and complicated mental and emotional processes in the child. He emphasized particularly the fact, which was generally denied, that the child is a passionate being, with sensuous drives and fantasies that give his life a dramatic quality.

Freud went furthest in this radically new appreciation of the child when he assumed in the beginning of his clinical work that many neuroses have their origin in acts of sexual seduction of children by adults —and particularly, by their parents. At this moment he became, so to speak, the accuser against parental exploitation in the name of the integrity and freedom of the child. However, if one considers the intensity of Freud's rootedness in the patriarchal authoritarian system, it is not surprising that he later abandoned this radical position. He found that his patients had projected their own infantile desires and fantasies on to the parents in a number of cases and that in reality no such seduction had taken place. He generalized these cases and came to the conclusion, in agreement with his libido theory, that the child was a little criminal and pervert who only in the course of the evolution of the libido matures into a "normal" human being. Thus Freud arrived at a picture of the "sinful child" which, as some observers have commented, resembles the Augustinian picture of the child in essential points.

After this change, the slogan was, so to speak, "the child is guilty"; his drives lead him into conflicts and these conflicts, if poorly solved, result in neurotic illness. I cannot help suspecting that Freud was motivated in this change of opinion not so much by his clinical findings, but by his faith in the existing social order and its authorities. This suspicion is supported by several circumstances, first of all by the categorical fashion in which Freud declared that all memories of parental seduction are fantasies. Is such a categorical statement not in contrast to the fact that adult incestuous interest in their children is by no means rare?

Another reason for the assumption of Freud's partisanship in favor of parents lies in the treatment of parental figures, which is to be found in his published case histories. It is surprising to see how Freud falsifies the picture of parents and attributes qualities to them that are clearly in contrast to the facts he himself presents. . . . In the example of his case history of Little Hans, Freud mentions the lack of threats on the part of Hans' parents who are fully concerned with the welfare of the child, when in fact threats and seduction are so clearly present that one has to shut one's eyes in order not to see them. The same observation can be made in other case histories.

The interpretation of Freud's shift from being an advocate of the child to a defender of the parents is indirectly supported by the testimony of S. Ferenczi, one of Freud's most experienced and imaginative disciples. In his last years, Ferenczi, who never wavered in his loyalty to Freud, was caught in a severe conflict with the master. Ferenczi had developed ideas which deviated from those of Freud in two important points, and Freud reacted with such sharpness that he did not shake hands with Ferenczi at the latter's last visit. One "deviation," which interests us less in this context, was the insistence that the patient needs, for his cure, not only interpretation, but also the love of the analyst (love understood here in a non-sexual, non-exclusive sense). A more important deviation for our present purpose was Ferenczi's thesis that Freud had been right after all in his original view: that in reality, adults were in many instances the seducers of children and that it was not always a matter of fantasies, rooted in the child.

Aside from the importance of Ferenczi's clinical observation, one has to raise the question why Freud reacted so violently and passionately. Was it a matter of something more important than a clinical problem? It is not too far-fetched to suppose that the main point was not the correctness of the clinical theory, but the attitude toward authority. If it is true that Freud had withdrawn his original radical critique of the parents—that is, of social authority—and had adopted a position in favor of authority, then, indeed, one may suspect that his reaction was due to his ambivalence to social authority, and that he reacted violently when he was reminded of the position he had given up, of, as it were, his "betrayal" of the child.

The conclusion of this sketch of Freud's picture of man requires a word on his concept of history. Freud developed the nucleus of a philosophy of history, although he did not intend to offer any systematic presentations. At the beginning of history, we find man without culture, completely dedicated to the satisfaction of his instinctual drives, and happy to that extent. This picture, however, is in contrast to another, which assumes a conflict even in this first phase of complete instinctual satisfaction.

Man must leave this paradise precisely because the unlimited satisfaction of his drives leads to the conflict of the sons with the father, to the murder of the father, and eventually to the formation of the incest taboo. The rebellious sons gain a battle, but they lose the war against the fathers, whose prerogatives are now secured forever by "morality" and the social order (here again we are reminded of Freud's ambivalence toward authority).

While in this aspect of Freud's thinking a state of unrestricted instinctual satisfaction was *impossible* in the long run, he develops another thesis which is quite different. The possibility of this paradisiacal state is not denied, but it is assumed that man cannot develop any culture as long as he remains in this paradise. For Freud, culture is conditioned by the partial non-satisfaction of instinctual desires, which leads in turn to sublimation or reaction formation. Man, then, is confronted with an alternative: total instinctual satisfaction—and barbarism—or partial instinctual frustration, along with cultural and mental development of man. Frequently, however, the process of sublimation fails, and man has to pay the price of neurosis for his cultural development. It must be emphasized that for Freud the conflict that exists between drives and civilization and culture of whatever kind is in no way identical with the conflict between drives and capitalistic or any other form of "repressive" social structure.

Freud's sympathies are on the side of culture, not the paradise of primitivity. Nevertheless, his concept of history has a tragic element. Human progress necessarily leads to repression and neurosis. Man cannot have both happiness and progress. In spite of this tragic element, however, Freud remains an enlightenment thinker, though a skeptical one, for whom progress is no longer an unmixed blessing. In the second phase of his work, after the first World War, Freud's picture of history became truly tragic. Progress, beyond a certain point, is no longer simply bought at great expense, but is in principle impossible. Man is only a battlefield on which the life and death instincts fight against each other. He can never liberate himself decisively from the tragic alternative of destroying others or himself.

Freud tried to mitigate the harshness of this thesis in an interesting letter to Einstein, "Why War?" But in his essential position, Freud, who called himself a pacifist at that time, did not allow himself to be seduced either by his own wishes, or by the embarrassment of expressing deep pessimism in the decade of new hope (1920–1930); he did not change or prettify the harshness of what he believed to be the truth. The skeptical enlightenment philosopher, overwhelmed by the collapse of his world, became the total skeptic who looked at the fate of man in history as unmitigated tragedy. Freud could hardly have reacted differently, since his society appeared to him as the best possible one, and not capable of improvement in any decisive way.

In concluding this sketch of Freud's anthropology I should stress that one can best understand the greatness of Freud, that of the man and that of his work, only if one sees him in his fundamental contradictions, and as bound—or chained—to his social situation. To say that all his teachings, over a period of almost fifty years, are in no need of any fundamental revision, or to call him a revolutionary thinker rather than a tragic reformer, will be appealing to many people, for many different reasons. What is required, however, is to contribute to the understanding of Freud.

POLITICIANS AND THE PEOPLE IN THE NINETEENTH CENTURY

PART IV

O NE cannot but be struck by the abundance of powerful and colorful political leaders in the generation or so following the Revolutions of 1848. Earlier periods often were so dominated by single personalities that eras could be called the Age of Napoleon or the Age of Metternich. But how are we to describe the late nineteenth century which sees side by side such major figures as Napoleon III, Cavour, Alexander II, Bismarck, Gladstone, and Disraeli? No one of them gave his stamp to the entire period. Although all of them were aware of the rapidly changing political, economic, and social forces at work everywhere in the western world, each built his power by being able to assess and respond to those changes as they occurred in his own nation-state.

The following group of selections contains recent evaluations of each of these leaders, by Alan Spitzer, Agatha Ramm, Alfred J. Rieber, Fritz Stern, and Robert Blake, respectively. This, however, is but half of the story. Other selections, those by Charles Tilly and Peter Stearns, rather than looking at these makers of policy, will examine how the consumers of their policy, namely their subjects, perceived the same rapid changes.

17. The Good Napoleon III

ALAN B. SPITZER

*The first of these nineteenth-century politicians to achieve prominence
was Napoleon III—nephew of the great Napoleon, unsuccessful leader of coups
d'état under Louis Philippe, president of the Second French Republic after
the 1848 Revolution, destroyer of that republic, and emperor of the
Second French Empire, captured by the Germans at the battle of Sedan
in 1870 and overthrown as a result. He is the subject of this selection by
Alan B. Spitzer, a University of Iowa historian. It is an excellent example of
the historiographic essay, a medium in which the author describes and evaluates
the work of other historians and the general trends of interpretation on a
problem and then comes to some conclusions of his own. Because of the nature
of the historiographic essay the footnotes have been retained in this reprinting of
it. Spitzer introduces the problem so well, the notion that recent historians
have created a "good Napoleon III," that there seems no need for further introduction here. You might, however, keep in mind some of the questions he
raises: According to Spitzer, what are the arguments of those historians who
evaluate Napoleon III's Second French Empire favorably? What evidence
points in the direction that Napoleon III was a "Saint-Simon on horseback" who
brought unusual prosperity to France? What evidence is there that his policies
did not create this prosperity? To what extent did he have "sympathy for the*

Source: Alan B. Spitzer, "The Good Napoleon III," *French Historical Studies*,
II, No. 3 (Spring, 1962), 308–29. Reprinted by permission of the author and
publisher.

masses" and, if he had, what were his motives? How much did the workers profit from his regime? How would you describe the politics and the political personnel of the Empire at its various levels? To what extent did the "authoritarian Empire" become a "liberal Empire," and what accounts for the shift? What was the Empire's foreign policy and how was it arrived at? Was the defeat at the hands of the Prussians in 1870 a result of Napoleon III's good intentions being undermined by others? What does Spitzer conclude was the chief weakness of the Empire?

H.M. THE EMPEROR NAPOLEON III.—In respectful memory of a beneficent and far-sighted man, died January 9th, 1873. He has found peace; one day he will find true justice.—The Hon. Secretary of the Souvenir Napoleonien in England, Ernest Weal.—In Memoriam notice, The Times *(London), January 9, 1962.*

In the past two decades the standard interpretation of the Second Empire, in England and America at least, has become generally favorable.[1] This approach, often presented as a revision of earlier partisan judgments is based both on fresh research and on changing conceptions of what is politically right and desirable. The classic Bonapartist, republican, and socialist interpretations have been qualified or discarded, but political norms, not always articulated, continue to shape evaluations of the regime.[2]

Much of the recent literature on Napoleon III reflects the conviction that he needs to be rescued from a tendentious historiography. The very persistence of this idea is of some interest when one considers for how long and by how many historians it has been expressed. To mention a distinguished example: Pierre de La Gorce began his classic history of the Second Empire with the observation, "The reign of Napoleon III has been judged until now either by goodwill or hatred. Twice it has undergone the trial of falsehood: the falsehood of adulation in its days of power, falsehood of calumny in its days of misfortune [editor's translation]." [3]

[1] The most notable recent examples of this tendency are: Albert Guérard, *Napoleon III* (Cambridge, 1943) and *Napoleon III, A Great Life in Brief* (New York, 1955); Lynn M. Case, *French Opinion on War and Diplomacy during the Second Empire* (Phila., 1954); Roger L. Williams, *Gaslight and Shadow* (New York, 1957); Theodore Zeldin, *The Political System of Napoleon III* (London, 1958); and, to some extent, J. M. Thompson, *Louis Napoleon and the Second Empire* (New York, 1955). This essay was completed before the author could obtain a copy of T. A. B. Corley, *Democratic Despot. A Life of Napoleon III* (London, 1961). This work also presents a qualified favorable reinterpretation of the Second Empire, concluding, "For Napoleon the 'end' was not, as in Solon's phrase, death, but that posthumous reputation he so desired. Who shall say that this end is not well in sight?"

[2] My own approach to the Second Empire starts from the Left.

[3] Pierre de La Gorce, *Histoire du Second Empire* (7 vols.; 12th ed., Paris, 1912), I, i; *cf.,* Blanchard Jerrold, *The Life of Napoleon III* (4 vols., London, 1874–1882), III, 8; H. Thirria, *Napoléon III avant l'Empire* (2 vols.; Paris, 1895), I, i–iii; Henry Berton, *L'Évolution constitutionelle du Second Empire* (Paris, 1900), I, 739; Paul Guériot, *Napoleon III* (2 vols., Paris, 1933–34), II, 319–321; Hendrik N. Boon, *Rêve et réalité dans l'œuvre économique et sociale de*

De La Gorce's attempt at an objective and critical analysis won general acclaim but it too has been challenged by his successors. F. A. Simpson in his *Napoleon and the Recovery of France* deplored a Catholic bias in de La Gorce and then developed an interpretation which has been influential in establishing the favorable image of Louis Napoleon.[4] Indeed, Albert Guérard could assert in 1943 that "within the last fifty years Napoleon III has won the respect and sympathy of practically every critical historian."[5] Nevertheless, Guérard's successors continue to break lances for the man who, in the words of Roger Williams, has been "the victim of an indifference which has been translated by most writers about him into terms of contempt."[6] In a subsequent issue of *History Today,* the journal in which Williams' remarks appeared, Theodore Zeldin wrote, "It is time, therefore, that the abuse of his enemies should be appreciated in its true light and not accepted as impartial history merely because they happened to be distinguished men."[7]

A hostile tradition does certainly survive. In a sense the unfortunate Emperor is forever represented as Victor Hugo's Napoleon the Little and his partisans as Daumier's "Ratapoil," the rakish, seedy, and sinister adventurer. These images persist in the republican historiography introduced by Taxil Delord's implacable *Histoire du Second Empire*[8] and in the socialist interpretations of Albert Thomas and his successors.[9]

Napoléon III (La Haye, 1936), pp. 164–165; Octave Aubry, *The Second Empire,* trans. A. Livingston (Phila., 1940), 604; J.-B. Barbier, *Outrances sur le Second Empire* (Paris, 1946), pp. 7–9. For a somewhat dated survey of the literature on the Second Empire see Robert Schnerb, "Napoleon III and the Second French Empire," *Journal of Modern History,* VIII (September, 1936), pp. 338–355.

[4] F. A. Simpson, *Louis Napoleon and the Recovery of France, 1848–1856* (London, 1923), viii. De La Gorce has recently been damned as an apologist of the Second Empire: E. Jeloubovskaia, *La Chute du Second Empire et la Naissance de la Troisième République en France,* trans. J. Champenois (Moscow, 1959), pp. 5, 9.

[5] Guérard, *Napoleon III,* p. 282.

[6] Roger L. Williams, "Louis Napoleon. A Tragedy of Good Intentions," *History Today,* IV (April, 1954), 219.

[7] Theodore Zeldin, "The Myth of Napoleon III," *History Today,* VIII (February, 1958), 105.

[8] Taxil Delord, *Histoire du Second Empire* (6 vols.; 5th ed., Paris, 1869–1875). *Cf.* Gabriel Hanotaux, *Histoire politique,* Vol. V of *Histoire de la nation française,* ed. G. Hanotaux (Paris, 1929). For another example of a broadly unfavorable treatment see René Arnaud, *The Second Republic and Napoleon III,* trans. E. F. Buckley (London, 1939). The author claims to stand between Seignobos and de La Gorce. The attitude toward the Second Empire of the academic left (under the Third Republic) is succinctly expressed in the following comment on Bergson's eulogy of Émile Ollivier at the Académie in 1918, ". . . un philosophe pour muscadines, a osé prononcer non pas l'éloge, mais le panégyrique effronté, de M. Émile Ollivier. . . . La même Académie . . . a écouté sans broncher l'insolent défi que M. Bergson a porté à la conscience publique." *Annales Révolutionnaires,* X (1918), 287–288. See also Henry Jaudon, "Émile Olliver," *Revue bleue,* LVI (Feb., 1918), 80–84. For Bergson's speech see Henri Bergson, *Discours de Reception de M. Henri Bergson, Séance de l'Académie française du 24 Janvier 1918* (Paris, 1918).

[9] E.g., Albert Thomas, *Le Second Empire (1852–1870),* Vol. X of *Histoire Socialiste,* ed. J. Jaurès (Paris, 1906); and Vol. XI of the same series, Jean Jaurès, *La*

Possibly the most influential republican evaluation of the reign of Louis Napoleon was engraved by Charles Seignobos on that monument to Sorbonnard historiography, the Lavisse series. He concluded his history of the Empire:

> The Empire, imposed on France by a military coup d'état, had no other defense at its service than the army; the nation did not become imperialist and sustained the Empire only through the force of inertia; voters voted for the Empire because it was there. The government was only a group of bureaucrats superimposed on the nation without becoming a part of it; it remained an official machine without moral authority; the mass of the indifferent obeyed it, but everyone with political life struggled against it. When the army disappeared, the Empire collapsed, without fighting or opposition, from a shove by the mob. Its leaders fled the country and no one tried to defend it [editor's translation].[10]

Perhaps the gap between orthodox republican historiography and the modern revisionists can be measured by two evaluations of Seignobos. While Robert Schnerb refers to his "sufficiently objective analysis" of the Second Empire,[11] Albert Guérard describes his work as "the frankly biased account by the petit-bourgeois Radical Charles Seignobos, a period-piece of the Gambetta age." [12]

The attitudes distressing to Guérard persist, but the extent of partisan animus among contemporary French historians of the Empire can be exaggerated. The monographs of Maurain, Schnerb, Duveau, Guiral, and others probably do add up to a negative presentation of the regime, but they are scrupulously documented, fair, and balanced efforts.[13]

Unfavorable judgments never did go unchallenged in France. Aside

Guerre Franco-Allemande; Paul Louis, Histoire du mouvement syndical en France (2 vols., Paris, 1947), I, 41–42, 98–99; Alexandre Zévaès, "Les Candidatures ouvrières et révolutionnaires sous le Second Empire," La Révolution de 1848, XXIX (mars 1932–février 1933), 132–154. Jeloubovskaia, La Chute du Second Empire. This work is written partly as a corrective to what the author considers to be a tradition of unscientific apologetics. She presents both imperial domestic and foreign policy simply as the political manifestations of capitalist class interests.

[10] Charles Seignobos, Le Déclin de l'Empire et l'établissement de la 3° Republique, Vol. VII of Histoire de France Contemporaine, ed. E. Lavisse (Paris, 1921), p. 248.

[11] Schnerb, "Napoleon III and the Second French Empire," pp. 338–339.

[12] Guérard, Napoleon III, p. 282.

[13] Jean Maurain, La Politique ecclésiastique du Second Empire de 1852 à 1869 (Paris, 1930), and Un Bourgeois Français au XIX° siècle. Baroche, Ministre de Napoléon III (Paris, 1936); Georges Duveau, La Vie ouvrière en France sous le Second Empire (Paris, 1949); Pierre Guiral, Prévost-Paradol (Paris, 1955); Jacques Droz, Lucien Genet, and Jean Vidalenc, L'Époque Contemporaine. I. Restaurations et Révolutions (1815–1871) ("Clio," Paris, 1953). In the Peuples et Civilisations series the volume by Charles Pouthas, Démocraties et Capitalisme (1848–1860) (Paris, 1948) shows no discernible bias; the succeeding volume, by Henry Hauser, Jean Maurain, and Pierre Benaerts, Du libéralisme à l'Impérialisme (Paris, 1939) presents an unfavorable picture of the later Empire.

from Bonapartist apologia, of which the most distinguished was Émile Ollivier's massive and influential justification of the Liberal Empire,[14] scholarly works favorable to the Empire have appeared frequently in the twentieth century—from Lebey's treatment of the early period to Paul Gueriot's well-received volumes, which characteristically concluded on the note of Louis Pasteur's eulogy of the Emperor.[15]

Louis Napoleon has enjoyed an even better press abroad. Notwithstanding occasions of great unpopularity in England and America, he has never, from the time of Bagehot's defense of his coup d'état,[16] lacked defenders—in fact, the major monographs in English have been predominantly sympathetic. A line of hostile interpretation does exist—running from Kinglake's conspiracy theory of the origins of the Crimean War [17] through H. A. L. Fisher's and G. P. Gooch's whiggish distaste for Bonapartist authoritarianism,[18] to various critiques of Louis Napoleon's diplomacy [19] and to J. Salwyn Schapiro's description of the imperial system as a harbinger of Fascism.[20]

The critical literature has been outweighed by works justifying the Empire to the foreign reader. Blanchard Jerrold's semi-official biography based upon materials in the possession of the imperial family was an early example of books exhibiting sympathy for Louis Napoleon and for his tragic Empress, who for many years continued to make documents accessible to sympathetic investigators.[21] The most influential academic rein-

---

[14] Émile Ollivier, *L'Empire libéral, études, récits, souvenirs* (17 vols., and 1 table; Paris, 1895–1915).

[15] André Lebey, *Louis-Napoléon Bonaparte et la Révolution de 1848* (2 vols.; Paris, 1907–08); Guériot, *Napoléon III,* II, 322.

[16] Walter Bagehot, "Letters on the French Coup d'État of 1851," *Literary Studies* (2 vols.; London, 1911), Vol. I.

[17] Arthur William Kinglake, *The Invasion of the Crimea: Its Origin and an Account of Its Progress down to the Death of Lord Raglan* (6 vols., London, 1863–1880). For the most recent of the scholarly refutations of Kinglake, see Brison D. Gooch, "A Century of Historiography on the Origins of the Crimean War," *American Historical Review* LXII (October, 1956), 33–58.

[18] H. A. L. Fisher, *Bonapartism* (Oxford, 1914), pp. 142–163, 198–200; Philip Guedalla's popular success was, if not critical, patronizing. Philip Guedalla, *The Second Empire,* (London, 1922). G. P. Gooch, *The Second Empire* (London, 1960). This recent work is close in tone to a nineteenth-century liberal response to the Empire.

[19] E.g., Franklin Charles Palm, *England and the Rise of Napoleon III* (Durham, 1948); A. J. P. Taylor, *The Struggle for the Mastery of Europe, 1848–1918* (Oxford, 1954), pp. 25, 133, 204 ff.; René Albrecht-Carrié, *A Diplomatic History of Europe Since the Congress of Vienna* (New York, 1958), pp. 82–83, 132–138.

[20] J. Salwyn Schapiro, *Liberalism and the Challenge of Fascism* (New York, 1949), pp. 316 ff. See also J. P. Mayer, *Political Thought in France* (London, 1943), pp. 45–69; Karl-Heinz Bremer, "Der Sozialistische Kaiser," *Die Tat,* XXIX, (Juni, 1938), 160–171; and for a brief assessment of the similarities and differences with Fascism, see Frederick B. Artz, "Bonapartism and Dictatorship," *South Atlantic Quarterly,* XXXIX (Jan. 1940), 48–49.

[21] The flow of works on the tragic Empress, the Gilded Beauties of the Court, and the Prince Imperial still provides a certain moisture.

terpretation was expressed in F. A. Simpson's two distinguished volumes, *The Rise of Louis Napoleon* and *Louis Napoleon and the Recovery of France,* first published in 1909 and 1923, respectively.[22] After Simpson, the current outside of France has continued to flow strongly in Louis Napoleon's favor, swelling into the lush prose of Robert Sencourt:

> . . . even in his weakness and his mistakes, he, as a Bonaparte, proved that there was in him, as in his more famous predecessor, an elasticity, a resilience, which make him a power when he seemed to have left the world branded as a failure. He completed the career of Napoleon I. Who has completed his own?[23]

The recent works of Guérard, Williams, Zeldin, Case, and (to a lesser extent) J. M. Thompson have continued the revision of an excessively critical image of the Second Empire. These works are not uncritical, but they tend to emphasize the desirable consequences of the regime and to present partial justifications for its alleged failures. The arguments most often advanced in the line of this positive revisionism might be represented in the following rather unfair pastiche:

The Second Empire has been too narrowly viewed in the light of republican or socialist predilections. A more just evaluation would recognize that the faction-ridden systems which the Second Empire replaced were only destroyed after they had failed to satisfy the national aspirations for order and unity. The new 18th of Brumaire entailed a certain amount of temporary unpleasantness, but it provided that political stability which was the indispensable context for economic and social advances scarcely possible under any alternative regime. Despite inherited disabilities the Liberal Empire was evolving towards a viable parliamentary system with the support of the vast majority of the nation. Doctrinaire critics overlook the real progress that was made in the face of complex difficulties and with that refractory human material whose last chance to be welded into a truly unified people disappeared with the Empire. Even the condemnation of Louis Napoleon's apparently disastrous foreign policy must be qualified with reference to the pressures of irresponsible political factions and of public opinion which demanded victories abroad without sacrifice at home. And one must take into account Louis Napoleon's vision of a European policy—a noble conception frustrated by the short-sighted Machiavellianism of other princes.

A full discussion of this interpretation would touch on political, economic, social, literary, religious, educational, and diplomatic history. This article will consider only certain questions of economic, political, and foreign policy evoked by the recent literature.

In judging the economic development of the Empire, although it poses the most complex problems of research and interpretation, historians are

[22] F. A. Simpson, *The Rise of Louis Napoleon* (London, 1909); Simpson, *Louis Napoleon and the Recovery of France* (London, 1923).

[23] Robert Sencourt, *Napoleon III: The Modern Emperor* (London, 1933), p. 369.

in agreement unusual in the historiography of the period. Not all would accept Sainte-Beuve's identification of Napoleon III as a "Saint-Simon on horseback," [24] but most admit to some real connection between imperial policies and the striking advance of the French economy. Georges Pradalié's monograph in the *Que sais-je?* series is representative of French historiography in its conclusion that, while France suffered in the long run from Louis Napoleon's foreign and domestic political policies, it owes to him a considerable legacy of national wealth and of effective economic institutions.[25]

The difficulty for a just assessment of the economic contributions of the Empire lies in the obligation to distinguish the economic consequences of government policy from the effects of other factors and to work out the relationship of short-run economic change to long. When, for example, Guérard and Pradalié commended the Second Empire for the accumulation of wealth which made possible the rapid payment of the indemnity after the Franco-Prussian war, they gave to Louis Napoleon's reign all of the credit for that viability which enabled France to make comparable efforts after 1815 and again after the World Wars of the twentieth century. Notwithstanding Guérard's disclaimers he seemed to attribute to Napoleon III the fruits of a century of French secular economic growth.[26]

One might argue that the years of the Empire happen fortuitously to coincide with a period of French, or indeed, world-wide, industrial expansion that would have occurred under any political circumstances. Similar considerations might be applied in favor of the Empire. To evaluate the break with protectionism merely by its consequences in the period 1860–1870 is to ignore the possibly beneficial long-run effects of competition on a traditionally overprotected economy.[27] Other complications arise from varying views of the economic curve of the years 1852–1870. Partisans of the Empire emphasize the burgeoning years between 1852–1857. Opponents look to the depression of 1867–1870.

Most historians have agreed, despite their different points of view, that the signs of economic growth are impressive in relation both to other periods and to other states. The years 1852–1857 particularly were an ex-

[24] Guérard, *Napoleon III,* pp. 193 ff.

[25] Georges Pradalié, *Le Second Empire (Que sais-je?)* (Paris, 1957), p. 124; and for the same assessment see Marcel Blanchard, *Le Second Empire* (Paris, 1950), pp. 7–8.

[26] Guérard, *Napoleon III,* p. 196.

[27] For assessments of the economic consequences of the Second Empire, see Émile Levasseur, *Histoire du commerce de la France* (2 vols.; Paris, 1911–1912); Germain Martin, *Histoire économique et financière,* Vol. X of *Histoire de la nation française,* ed. Gabriel Hanotaux (Paris, 1927), Marcel Marion, *Histoire financière de la France depuis 1715* (5 vols., Paris, 1914–1928), V. Arthur L. Dunham, *Anglo-French Treaty of Commerce of 1860 and the Progress of the Industrial Revolution in France* (Ann Arbor, 1930); Shepard B. Clough, *France: A History of National Economics, 1789–1939* (New York, 1939); Henri Sée, *Histoire économique de la France* (2d ed., 2 vols.; Paris, 1951), II.

ception to a long history of relative stagnation, and the French rate of growth was unmatched by that of any other state.[28] The combined value of French exports and imports almost tripled between the beginning and the end of the Empire, surpassing the rate of expansion for any other European state in those years.[29] Perhaps even more impressive is the evidence of the structural changes which helped to propel France into the industrial era. The Second Empire saw the establishment of what Perroux calls the "triggering industries . . . industries whose creation was decisive for the formation of a French market [editor's translation]," and the striking growth of the railroads and the "great credit institutions."[30]

To establish the existence of these changes is not to demonstrate Louis Napoleon's responsibility for them, but significant relationships between imperial policies and constructive change are persuasively presented in such works as David Pinkney's *Napoleon III and The Rebuilding of Paris*, Louis Girard's *La Politique des Travaux Publics du Second Empire*, and Marcel Blanchard's articles on the railroad policies of the Empire.[31] At any rate, a majority of historians grant Louis Napoleon some of the credit for the unprecedented stimulus to capital formation, credit expansion, and a spirit of enterprise foreign to the crabbed, unimaginative Orleanist economic tradition, and essentially believe with Girard that France still enjoys a legacy of "The work erected by the French of the Second Empire [editor's translation]."[32]

The relevance of these conclusions to a justification of the Empire depends not so much on economic fact as on political value. Did the economic benefits outweigh the accompanying graft, favoritism, and speculation? Did the Morny who floated impressive enterprises compensate for the Morny who enjoyed a slice of Jecker's Mexican investments? Did the improved salubrious and magnificent product of Haussmann's municipal renovation cancel out the inequities, the inconveniences, and the aberrations in taste that attended the rebuilding of Paris? The answers can be founded only on individual postulates of Right and Progress.

[28] Rondo Cameron, "Economic Growth and Stagnation in France, 1815–1914," *The Journal of Modern History*, XXX (March, 1958), 1.

[29] Sée, *Histoire économique*, II, 288. According to Levasseur Belgium was the only state to surpass France. Levasseur, *Histoire du commerce*, II, 331.

[30] François Perroux, "Prise de Vues sur la croissance de l'économie française, 1870–1950," *Income and Wealth*, Series V, ed. Simon Kuznets (London, 1955), p. 55.

[31] David H. Pinkney, *Napoleon III and the Rebuilding of Paris* (Princeton, 1958); cf. J. M. and Brian Chapman, *The Life and Times of Baron Haussmann* (London 1957); Louis Girard, *La Politique des travaux publics du Second Empire* (Paris, 1952). Marcel Blanchard, "La politique ferrovaire du Second Empire," *Annales d'histoire économique et sociale VI* (November, 1934), 529–545.

[32] Girard, *La Politique des travaux publics*. See also Sée, *Histoire économique*, II, 251, "Si Napoléon ne fut qu'une apparition passagère au point de vue politique, par contre son règne fit epoque au point de vue économique; c'est lui qui en France par là sur tout le continent a ouvert la voie au capitalisme." There are similar views in Pierre DuPont-Ferrier, *La Marché financier de Paris sous le Second Empire* (Paris, 1925).

Whatever uniformity obtains for such judgments does not extend to evaluations of Louis Napoleon's social welfare policies, perhaps because the evidence is even more difficult to assess, perhaps because the implicated values are so strongly held and so sharply conflicting.

Louis Napoleon's sympathy for the masses has been one of his strongest claims to the affections of historians. J. M. Thompson dwelt on his sincere intention to provide the workers with "their just share of the national wealth," [33] and concluded that Louis Napoleon ". . . never ceased to clutch the inviolable shade of social equality and justice which still eludes a less corrupt and prejudiced age." [34] This interpretation, of Louis' intentions at least, is widely shared—even Karl Marx, who was scarcely charitable to "the hero Crapulinsky," granted that, "Bonaparte looks on himself as the representative of the peasants and of the people in general, against the bourgeoisie, who wants to make the lower classes of the people happy within the framework of bourgeois society." [35]

More recently, Guérard and H. N. Boon, among others, have identified Louis Napoleon as a Socialist, and in 1938 the German historian, Karl-Heinz Bremer, praised the pioneering authoritarian socialism of the Second Empire, which is not precisely what its recent admirers have in mind.[36] Admiration for Louis Napoleon's brand of socialism has, however, generally been confined to non-socialists. The hostile socialist histories of the Second Empire are analogous to the "ungrateful" electoral behavior of the contemporary French worker, which produced the paradox of "a leader . . . rejected by those whom he was most anxious to benefit." [37]

The apparent working-class preference for republican institutions in spite of the imperial benevolence is often praised, or damned, as a triumph of abstract ideological considerations over strictly material demands. Some historians have argued, however, that the intentions of the government were essentially manipulative, that occasional social reforms were only the means to authoritarian political ends, that the state remained the agency of the possessing classes, that real wages fell, and that the workers showed an increasingly mature awareness of their own material interests when they repudiated the system at the polls.[38]

How the workers actually conceived their interests and how these conceptions influenced their political behavior remain complex and difficult questions. Georges Duveau's remarkable study of working class life under the Empire delineated the "caractère équivoque" of proletarian political

[33] Thompson, *Louis Napoleon and the Second Empire*, p. 103.

[34] *Ibid*, p. 239.

[35] Karl Marx, *The Eighteenth Brumaire of Louis Bonaparte*, Vol. 35, *Marxist Library*, ed. C. P. Dutt (New York, 1936), p. 117.

[36] Guérard. *Napoleon III*, p. 198; Boon, *Rêve et réalité*, p. 154; Bremer, "Der Sozialistische Kaiser," pp. 161–164.

[37] Guérard, *Napoloen III*, p. 218.

[38] This is essentially the position of Édouard Dolléans, *Histoire du mouvement ouvrier* (4th ed., 2 vols., Paris, 1948), I, pp. 251–360; *cf.* I. Tchernoff, *Le Parti Républicain au coup d'état et sous le Second Empire* (Paris, 1906), pp. viii–ix, 404, 410, 493–494; Jeloubovskaia, *La Chute du Second Empire, passim*.

response in which sympathy for the Emperor might accompany hostility to the *patronat,* or resistance to the Empire be expressed not so much from the viewpoint of a worker as from that of a democrat in the tradition of the old radical artisanate.[39] Duveau concluded that, in the obscurity of the contemporary industrial climate, the worker searched for his solutions "in his moral heritage and in utilizing, rather than fighting, the propaganda of the traditional parties which sought to coopt him [editor's translation]." [40]

Other historians have seen an increasing consciousness of class interests developing independently of traditional political alignments. Workers supported Louis Napoleon in 1848 precisely because he was not identified in their eyes with bourgeois interests but they eventually repudiated his paternalism, not so much for some republican ideal but because of their inchoate urge to defend their interests according to their own lights.[41]

On the basis of his findings that real wages remained stagnant during the Empire, Duveau concluded that the general progress of the French economy widened the social gap between the workers and an enriched bourgeoisie.[42] But this in itself cannot explain working-class political behavior because workers reacted not alone to this secular development but also to short-term business fluctuations, to political change, and to the government's successes and failures in international relations. Even in the years of economic depression and social conflict from 1867 to 1870 working-class behavior was variously motivated. The textile workers, for example, combined with their patrons in a campaign against imperial tariff policy,[43] yet in 1870 the alliance was shattered by strikes of unprecedented size and violence.[44]

The government's ambiguous response to the textile strikes indicates some of the complexities of an analysis of the relation between imperial policies and working-class politics. There is evidence of a certain amount of imperial sympathy for the strikers, but the strikes were ultimately met with the intervention of troops.[45] On many other occasions contradictions between Louis Napoleon's benevolence and the actual response of the government to working-class aspirations had been apparent. J. M. Thompson observes that the Emperor's sincere pursuit of social justice assumed an economic expansion essentially dependent upon bourgeois enterprise, and was "mortgaged to capitalism." The idealistic ends were sacrificed to the indispensable means. "Workers' associations and meetings might be prohibited in the name of public order, strikes broken to protect

[39] Duveau, *La Vie ouvrière,* pp. 100–103.

[40] Duveau, *La Vie ouvrière,* p. 550.

[41] Fernand L'Huillier, *La Lutte ouvrière à la fin du Second Empire* (Paris, 1957), pp. 74 ff.; Sreten Maritch, *Histoire du mouvement social sous le Second Empire à Lyon* (Paris, 1930), pp. 266–267.

[42] Duveau, *La Vie ouvrière,* pp. 385–416.

[43] Claude Fohlen, *L'Industrie textile au temps du Second Empire* (Paris, 1956), pp. 410–429.

[44] *Ibid.,* pp. 439–440; L'Huillier, *La Lutte ouvrière,* pp. 64–72.

[45] *Ibid.,* p. 70.

the labour market, wages kept down to stimulate production and public works. The Empire might become the victim of its own *élan vital,* the Emperor the prisoner of his prosperity and progress." [46] It is probable that working-class attitudes were affected more by the actual operation of the imperial system than by Louis Napoleon's conceptions of how it ought to operate.

To understand how Louis Napoleon's government qualified and perverted his most generous conceptions one must be aware of the differences between the Emperor's ideals and the interests of the groups that shared power with him. The Emperor is often praised for standing above the factions and governing for the good of all, but his policies were shaped and executed by men whose values were those of the conservative, propertied minority.[47] Guérard regretted that the conservatives were able to "muscle in and to endorse a winner whose principles were the very reverse of theirs." [48] But Zeldin has shown that the imperial system continuously cooperated with local notabilities and that it recruited its parliamentary candidates "from the highest ranks of society, from the great landowners, wealthy mayors and so on." [49] This élite was scarcely enthusiastic for socialism, even of the Bonapartist brand. If the Empire, as Guérard, Williams, and Zeldin claimed, was not the instrument of the political Right, it certainly did business with and through the traditional supporters of the "party of order."

At the very peak of the imperial structure there was the court, a group which must figure in any examination of the obstacles between Louis Napoleon's good will and positive reform. The imperial entourage is often blamed for major blunders including the fatal decision for war with Prussia. J. M. Thompson is one of the few reasonably sympathetic historians of the Second Empire to point out that the political power of the imperial court was a necessary product of the imperial system. "In a government which left so little initiative to its constitutional bodies, it becomes of special importance to inquire into the relations between the Emperor and those who were his immediate associates: the Empress, his Bonaparte relations, the friends of his youth, his ministers and ambassadors." [50] The ex-

[46] Thompson, *Louis Napoleon and the Second Empire,* p. 239. Duveau, *La Vie ouvrière,* p. 549, "L'Empereur voudrait gouverner pour les masses et avec l'aide des masses . . . mais, non sans raison, il se préoccupe du loyalisme de la classe ouvrière et, finalement, il bride les ouvriers plutôt qu'il ne collabore avec eux."

[47] Duveau concedes the caesarist socialism of Louis himself, but emphasizes the fact that he surrounded himself with "fonctionnaires [qui] gardent le vieil esprit orléaniste et, devinant les contradictions qui assaillent le souverain, ils n'hésitent pas à lui faire souvent la leçon. De là, dans les rouages de la machine impériale, des ratès des saccades qui ont leur répercussions dans la vie ouvrière." Duveau, *La Vie ouvrière,* p. 16.

[48] Guérard, *Napoleon III,* p. 138.

[49] Persigny, quoted by Zeldin, *ibid.,* p. 11. For the view that one of the grave weaknesses of the regime was its failure to rally the established élite, see Simpson, *Louis Napoleon and the Recovery of France,* pp. 372–373, and Hanotaux, *Histoire politique,* pp. 477, 551.

[50] Thompson, *Louis Napoleon and the Second Empire,* p. 246.

tra-constitutional influences exerted by these close associations were contradictory and inconsistent, reflecting personal and ideological cross-purposes, and from them stemmed some of the vagaries of imperial policy.

Perhaps of even greater significance was the cumulative influence of the minor officials who actually executed policy. Indeed, the Empire can well be described, not as a dynastic direct democracy, but as the quintessential administrative state. According to Brian Chapman's useful survey, *The Prefects in Provincial France,* the apogee of prefectoral authority was attained under the Second Empire.[51] In a sense the prefects made the regime, for, according to Chapman, they contrived the Red Scare of 1851, which was a crucial element in Louis Napoleon's coup d'état. This interpretation is reinforced by Howard Payne's detailed analysis of the role of the bureaucracy in preparing for the coup d'état and in inviting Louis Napoleon to seize supreme power and crown the edifice of the administrative state.[52]

In another article Payne described the consolidation and reinforcement of the centralized police system and concluded that "despite the contemporary elaboration of theories of unlimited police powers they were in practice limited to an extent far removed from the totalitarian models of the twentieth century."[53] This observation does not really vitiate the cumulative force of Payne's descriptions of the increase in authority and scope of the imperial police. Louis Napoleon can be defended against rather forced comparisons with the Nazis, but the fact that nineteenth-century dictators fell short of twentieth-century totalitarians can scarcely be a conclusive answer to their liberal critics.

Napoleon III is perhaps most effectively defended against charges of authoritarianism by reference to the evolution of the Liberal Empire after 1860. The Emperor himself is the great protagonist of this transformation, not only creating new institutions but summoning up new men to operate them. Among these men Émile Ollivier was pre-eminent—the hero of those who would trade the doctrinaire insistence on republican forms for the substance of imperial liberties.[54]

[51] Brian Chapman, *The Prefects and Provincial France* (London, 1955), p. 38; see also, Pierre-Henry, *Histoire des préfets* (Paris, 1950), pp. 171–194. Zeldin emphasizes the crucial electoral role of the prefects. "It was not Napoleon, nor Persigny but the prefects, who had the greatest single influence in choosing the official candidates," Zeldin, *The Political System of Napoleon III,* p. 19.

[52] Chapman, *The Prefects and Provincial France,* p. 37; Howard C. Payne, "Preparation of a Coup d'état: Administrative Centralization and Police Powers in France, 1849–1851," *Studies in Modern European History in Honor of Franklin Charles Palm,* ed., F. J. Cox, R. M. Brace, B. C. Weber and J. F. Ramsey (New York, 1956), p. 197.

[53] Howard C. Payne, "Theory and Practice of Political Police during the Second Empire in France," *Journal of Modern History,* XXX (March, 1958), 14–23.

[54] At the conclusion of a chapter devoted to Ollivier, Williams writes, ". . . recalling the despair of the Republicans after the plebiscite in 1870, is it not possible that the reforms were sufficiently promising for the reconciliation of liberty and order that the Republicans after 1870 never dared admit it?" Williams, *Gaslight and Shadow,* p. 298; cf., Berton, *L'Évolution constitutionelle du Second Empire,*

The ambiguities of a constitution which stipulated ministerial responsibility but did not specify its locus, which envisioned a cabinet based on a parliamentary majority but acceptable to, and presided over by, the Emperor, have been defended as necessary aspects of a difficult transition. Both Williams and Zeldin compare the constitutional progress of the Liberal Empire to the complex adjustment of executive to legislature worked out over a much longer period in seventeenth-century England.[55] It would be consistent with this analogy to argue that Louis himself had led France back into the seventeenth century. Perhaps his enemies exaggerated the "crime" of the Second of December, but it is fair to recall that the builders of the Liberal Empire had razed the parliamentary edifice of the Second Republic. The prospects of the parliamentary Empire might have been matched by those of the Republic, had it been allowed the twenty years which the Empire used to return to its point of departure. It is certainly plausible to suppose that a Republic dominated by Thiers and the "Burgraves" would have lacked the democratic ambiance of Bonapartist caesarism.[56] Still, arguments from English analogy might lead one to assume as good a chance for a fruitful evolution under a conservative parliamentary Republic before 1870 as for resolution of the contradictions of a parliamentary empire after 1870.

There is little point in pursuing this rather arid conjecture, but there is some point in examining the actual recruitment for the Liberal Empire, which did not, after all, staff itself with something very different from a reconstituted party of order. Ollivier's ministry of the Right and Left center did not include the great Orleanist paladins but did take in a range of qualified Orleanists and diluted Bonapartists who would have been perfectly at home in earlier oligarchies.[57] Some of the enemies of liberal institutions were dropped, but in the person of Rouher went a powerful partisan of free trade and with Haussmann the personification of public works, to be replaced by protectionists and scrupulous economizers. The last section of Girard's book on public works under the Empire, entitled "L'Abdication de la finance Saint-Simonienne," presents as a concomitant

pp. 381; Pierre de La Gorce, *Napoléon III et sa politique* (Paris, 1933), pp. 156 ff.; Pierre Saint Marc, *Émile Ollivier* (Paris, 1950), pp. 227 ff.; Bergson, *Discours . . . de l'Académie française.*

[55] Williams, *Gaslight and Shadow*, p. 279. Zeldin, *The Political System of Napoleon III*, p. 152. ". . . since so many people believed that France was not ripe for the institutions of nineteenth-century England, it was perhaps not as silly as it might appear to start with those of seventeenth-century England."

[56] See the characterization of Orleanist liberalism in E. Beau de Loménie, *Les Responsabilités des dynasties bourgeoises* (3 vols.; Paris, 1943), I, 171, 185, 200; and in Maurain, *Baroche*, p. 357. "Les chefs de l'ancien parti de l'ordre . . . libéraux en politique parce qu'hostiles au Gouvernement personnel de l'Empereur . . . étaient très conservateurs en matière sociale et réfractaires à l'humanitarisme de Napoléon III."

[57] Zeldin, *The Political System of Napoleon III*, pp. 144–151. De La Gorce quotes one of the deputies of the Right as remarking "Dans le cabinet actuel . . . il ne manque que le duc d'Aumale à la Guerre et le prince de Joinville à la Marine." De La Gorce, *Histoire du Second Empire*, VI, 5.

of liberalization the repudiation of the buccaneering and creative finance of the great period of imperial public works.[58]

According to Maurain the evolution of the Liberal Empire represented not only the triumph of the reconstituted party of order but also of the clergy: "Under the authoritarian Empire the clerical party had exercised only an indirect action, often powerful but always limited, but now it took possession directly [editor's translation]." [59]

Maurain's analysis of the ecclesiastical policies of the Second Empire challenged the representation of the regime as the last hope for a true political community, for he concluded that its shifts and expedients only sharpened the classic conflict between clericals and anti-clericals until, "after 1869 power was disputed between the party of clerical order and the anti-clerical republicans as it had been in 1849 [editor's translation]." [60]

An examination of these conflicts and of the social tensions attendant upon the growth and concentration of French industry reinforces the supposition that the bitter class and political struggle of 1871 must have owed something to the Empire.

Evaluations of domestic developments during the last years of the Second Empire are often affected by the knowledge that imperial foreign policy was to end in disaster. For many critics of the regime, the catastrophe of 1870 damns all of its works. The friends of the Empire, on the other hand, reject this judgment as the narrow standard of the cult of success, and some even defend those policies which led directly to the destruction of the Empire.

Historians generally agree that, notwithstanding autonomous foreign and domestic pressures which shaped imperial foreign policy, the major plans and the ultimate decisions were the Emperor's.[61] This grave responsibility has weighed heavily in the scales of his critics, but it has also served as a kind of palliation for some of his apparent blunders. His partisans emphasize his personal good will—expressed, for example, in his sincere attempt to mitigate the effects of a suicidal international *Realpolitik* by the formation of a new Congress of Europe. Binkley's volume in the Langer series coined the term *Federative Polity* to represent those tendencies which rampant nationalism was to destroy and which Louis Napoleon's foreign policy strove unsuccessfully to preserve and to extend.[62]

[58] Girard, *La Politique des travaux publics,* pp. 359 ff.

[59] Maurain, *La Politique ecclésiastique du Second Empire,* p. 939.

[60] *Ibid.,* p. 959.

[61] Albert Pignaud, "La Politique extérieure du Second Empire," *Revue Historique,* CLV (Sept.–Oct., 1927), 42–43; G. Pagés, "La Politique extérieure de Napoléon III," *Bulletin of the International Committee of Historical Sciences,* V (Feb., 1933), 16; Pierre Renouvin, *Le XIX ° Siècle, I. De 1815 à 1871,* Vol. V of *Histoire des relations internationales,* ed. P. Renouvin (Paris, 1954), pp. 269–270; Charles W. Hallberg, *Franz Joseph and Napoleon III, 1852–1864* (New York, 1955), pp. 23–24.

[62] Robert C. Binkley, *Realism and Nationalism, 1852–1871,* Vol. 16 of *The Rise of Modern Europe,* ed. W. L. Langer (New York, 1935), p. 260.

Binkley's conviction that the Emperor was "the last good European in a position of authority" is widely shared.[63]

The image of Louis Napoleon's visionary internationalism owes a great deal to hindsight. Demolished by a rival which had scarcely begun to realize its satanic strengths, imperial France may not seem terribly threatening in retrospect, but the policies she pursued were not reassuring to contemporaries, whose best evidence for the Emperor's intentions was drawn from his actions. These actions included proposals for international readjustment, often entailing some territorial bagatelle for France; two major wars before 1870, which by no stretch of even the French imagination could be considered defensive; the apparently boundless ambitions of the Mexican policy; [64] and continuous unsettling maneuvers, pronouncements, and projects which seemed to stem not from evident national requirements but from the Emperor's restless will.

Using information not readily available to Louis' contemporaries one can find a kind of consistency in his sincere belief that a revision of the unjust settlement of 1815 entailed, and without contradiction, the liberation of oppressed nationalities, the rightful extension of French territory and influence, and the reconstitution of a European polity. Most critics would now agree that the Emperor was sincere in his nationalities program, and that such policies as the weak, vulgar, and humiliating pursuit of compensations after 1866 were, in opposition to his deepest instincts, the reluctant responses to domestic pressures.[65]

To what extent Louis Napoleon's good intentions justify maladroit actions conducted under his authority is another question that can only be answered in the Emperor's favor if some force outside of the imperial establishment can be shown to have compelled the government to undertake erroneous policies. The defenders of the Empire have identified such a maleficent force in public opinion corrupted by an irresponsible opposition whose very existence depended upon Napoleon's good will.

The most thorough, effective and systematic work embodying such conclusions is Lynn Case's *French Opinion on War and Diplomacy during the Second Empire*. Case's careful analysis, based primarily on reports of the prefects and the procureurs généraux, shows that imperial policy during the springtime of the Empire's success was often carried out in spite of public opposition, but that during the last disastrous phase it was increasingly shaped by popular pressures. This was particularly striking in

[63] E.g., Williams, "Louis Napoleon, A Tragedy of Good Intentions," p. 226; Case, *French Opinion . . . during the Second Empire,* p. vii; Simpson, *Louis Napoleon and the Recovery of France,* p. x: "Essentially he [Napoleon III] was an international figure; too good a citizen perhaps of Europe to be the ultimately successful ruler, of any one country in it." See also Luigi Salvatorelli, "L'Europe de Napoléon III et l'Europe de Mazzini," *Revue historique,* CCXXIII (avril-juin, 1960), 275–286.

[64] The Mexican policy, which will not be examined here, has its defenders, *e.g.,* Sencourt, *Napoleon III: The Modern Emperor,* pp. 271–278; Guérard, *Napoleon III,* pp. 222–242; Barbier, *Outrances sur le Second Empire,* pp. 13–227.

[65] E.g., Taylor, *Struggle for Mastery in Europe,* pp. 173–177.

the case of the Emperor's program of army reform, blocked by a public which with equal zeal demanded bellicose foreign policy and cheap defense.[66] In the light of such behavior Case has no difficulty in casting up the balance of guilt:

> Thus the responsibility for the dilution of the army bill . . . falls directly upon French public opinion and its legislative representatives. This responsibility is all the heavier because at the same time that opinion was opposing the bill, it showed evidence of a universal belief in the inevitability of war with Prussia. . . . The road to Sedan, unlike that to Hell, was not even paved with good intentions. And when the tragedy of defeat finally broke upon the land, the unrepentant people loaded all the blame upon the one man who, accepting captivity to save the lives of his handicapped soldiers, had long before exerted himself more than all the others to spare them that evil day.[67]

The force of this indictment falls not only upon mass opinion but upon a political opposition that was willing to accrue factional advantage by attacking the government both for unpopular policies and for the consequences of suspending them. Still, any judgment of responsibility must take into account the nature and personnel of a watered-down caesarism. One must distinguish between the Emperor, who was eager to pursue a rational policy of acceptance of German aspirations and a prudent policy of rearmament in the face of Prussian power, and both his enemies and his supporters who were willing to accept neither. As Albert Sorel observed,

> But if the projects of Marshal Neil [for army reform] were wrecked, the orators of the opposition should not be blamed for it exclusively. These orators formed only a very restrained minority in the *Corps législatif;* they had no influence on the government, and their speeches, which most of the time were destined only for the public, very rarely modified the opinions of the majority. This majority was composed of official candidates, and it was it, in short, which defeated the marshal's reforms or amended them in such a way that their effect was paralysed [editor's translation].[68]

This observation has been reaffirmed by recent research.[69]

Even if the establishment had spoken with one voice on the reforms, which it did not, it could not present the public with clear alternatives

---

[66] Gordon Wright, "Public Opinion and Conscription in France 1866–1870," *Journal of Modern History.* XIV (March, 1942), 26–45.

[67] Case, *French Opinion . . . during the Second Empire,* pp. 239–240.

[68] Albert Sorel, *Histoire diplomatique de la guerre Franco-Allemande* (2 vols.; Paris, 1877), I, v–vi.

[69] Cf. Zeldin, *The Political System of Napoleon III,* p. 133; Guiral, *Prévost-Paradol,* pp. 483–484; Schnerb, *Rouher,* p. 200.

because it tried to preserve an image of superior strength while soliciting remedies for relative weakness. The presentation of the official case between 1866 and 1870 scarcely contributed to a responsible and informed public evaluation of imperial programs.

These considerations do not lift the responsibility from an opposition that was willing to seek political advantage at the expense of national security, but they indicate the flaws of a system in which supreme responsibility for foreign and military policy was concentrated in the hands of the Emperor and in which the dilution of this responsibility in part reflected the conflicts within an irresponsible entourage. There is still force in Jaurès' observation that a regime praised for ability to override the caprices of the crowd and the tumult of the forum is not also to be justified because it succumbed to public caprice and emotion.[70]

This approach was rejected in principle and in closely reasoned detail by Case, who defended even the last stumbling parade into the trap of the Hohenzollern candidacy. His research into the public response at each stage of the crisis impelled him to revise earlier estimates that public opinion was for peace in 1870.[71] These investigations suggested to Case that perhaps public opinion is inadequate to the formulation of foreign policy and that, indeed, given world realities it is problematical whether democracy can long survive in the present state system of international anarchy.[72]

This brings us back to the foundations of political value. If one does not choose to identify the concept of democracy with the momentary expression of the demos—if one conceives of democracy as a system of rules, processes and guarantees, including the right to form a meaningful opposition, then the aberrations of mass opinion in the short run do not constitute the ultimate test of democratic viability. Case praises the Empire for brushing aside political factions in order to combine authority with direct democracy, but it is precisely this caesarism which enforces an opportunism in relation to public opinion, not all of the time, for often the government flouted the public will, but only when the really difficult and embarrassing decisions had to be made. Then without the background of responsible opposition or continuous informed debate the system desperately husbands its popularity and in effect places the security of the dynasty above the health of the state.[73] In the last years, anxiety regarding public opinion was expressed in terms of the overthrow of the regime, and quite rightly, because when such a regime is repudiated it does not

[70] Jaurès, *La Guerre franco-allemande*, p. 178.

[71] E.g., E. M. Carroll, "French Opinion on War with Prussia in 1870," *American Historical Review*, XXXI (July, 1926), 679–700.

[72] Case, *French Opinion . . . during the Second Empire*, pp. 275–277.

[73] A similar phrase is applied by Guérard to the weaknesses of imperial leadership in his monograph on Napoleon III for the Great Lives in Brief series. This book presents the same general interpretation as his earlier work but is somewhat more critical of the last phase of the regime, particularly in relation to foreign policy. Guérard, *Napoleon III, a Great Life in Brief*, pp. 148, 187–191.

go out of office, it goes out of existence. There was not the margin for error afforded to the notoriously unstable Third Republic which somehow maintained a coherent foreign policy for forty years and, unlike its predecessor, found it to be politically possible to retreat upon Paris and regroup to withstand a German invasion.

It is not the cult of success which makes foreign affairs so relevant to an evaluation of the Empire, although a regime whose actions were so often justified as expedient can only justify its expediencies by success. No French statesman could have contrived a policy to stay the inexorable German advance toward economic and military hegemony but, as de La Gorce justly observes, it is particularly in the realm of foreign affairs that the characteristic weaknesses of the imperial system persist, not in the manifestations of an authoritarian will, but in the old tendencies toward *"infatuation, incohérence and imprévoyance."* [74]

Admirers of the Second Empire sometimes regret the onerous legacy it had to accept from the First. The legend of dynamic imperialism, essentially so foreign to the gentle and visionary Louis Napoleon, forced him into ventures abroad that were eventually disastrous.[75] But there is an element of the testament fabricated at St. Helena which is fully consistent with the spirit of Louis Napoleon's regime. This is the tradition of mendacity, manifested in the first Napoleon's *Memoirs* as contempt for the truth and also apparent in the absence of intellectual courage at the core of the Second Empire. In the long run the regime was not characteristically brutal, nor consistently authoritarian, but meretricious. If the imperial system anticipated any aspect of the twentieth century, it is the tendency to conduct foreign affairs as a branch of domestic public relations and to beg many difficult alternatives of policy formulation by doublethink, self-deception, and cant.

[74] De La Gorce, *Napoléon III et sa politique,* pp. 167–173.
[75] Williams, "Louis Napoleon. A Tragedy of Good Intentions," p. 220.

18. Cavour and the Risorgimento

AGATHA RAMM

*Schoolchildren used to learn—perhaps they still do—that Italian unifica-
tion and the Risorgimento resulted from the "heart" of Mazzini, which instilled in Italians a national spirit through the Young Italy movement,
the "hands" of Garibaldi which swept up the pennisula from Sicily in the
form of the Red Shirts, and the "head" of Cavour, who played his Sardinian
pieces on the Italian and European chessboard of power politics. These
forces combined to make inevitable the grand achievement of Risorgimento.
The flaw in this interpretation, however, appeared fifty years later when
Mussolini turned united Italy into a Fascist dictatorship. That fact by itself
was almost enough to cause historians to reevaluate their answers to the
questions persistently raised by the Risorgimento: Was unification achieved
by the welling up of a national spirit or was it accomplished almost by the
accident of Cavour's Sardinian aggrandizement? Did Cavour's moderates,
by taking the initiative away from the Mazzinians and Garibaldians and by
failing to meet the yearnings of large numbers of Italians for social reforms,
republicanism or federalism, create a* rivoluzione mancata, *or aborted
revolution? Or did Cavour's moderates create the only Italian state that
could be made in the nineteenth century?*

This selection reviews the current state of those controversies. It is

Source: Agatha Ramm, *The Risorgimento* (London: The Historical Association, 1962 and 1967), pp. 16–27. Copyright © 1967 The Historical Association. Reprinted by permission of the author and The Historical Association.

from British historian Agatha Ramm's pamphlet in the Historical Association's admirable series of brief, up-to-date essays on historical problems. In her view, what were Cavour's aims, attitudes, and policies, and to what extent can he be called the architect of Sardinian prosperity and Italian unification? What were the goals and style of his foreign policy? How, when, and why did he become interested in Italian unification? What evidence is there that "Cavour's policy towards southern Italy illustrates more clearly what we now know to have been his characteristic relationship to the Risorgimento"? What people for what reasons were estranged and alienated from his regime as a result of the way unification was achieved?

Cavour followed, in relation to the *Risorgimento,* a course all his own. He was governed by ideas which were rooted in the Lombard and Piedmontese *Risorgimento* of the thirties and forties. He shared all the ideas of the practical reformers of Lombardy and admired William Pitt and Sir Robert Peel. But he rejected the federalist, fusionist, and republican possibilities sketched out by the Piedmontese political writers and the Mazzinians, although these awakened the strongest sympathies outside Sardinia. He was for Sardinian leadership, annexationist and monarchical. But the facts of 1856–61 were not all predetermined in their continuity by his ideas. He was neither the servant of circumstance, who failed to dominate the *Risorgimento,* nor, as was once thought, the master-builder, who understood it and carried it to completion. Cavour's aims widened as the results of his earlier achievements created new possibilities. His policy became Italian as he associated his Sardinian aims with the national movement. He worked with the national movement, but he did not draw out of it latent political and social possibilities. Cavour's policy towards central and southern Italy estranged classes which had been politically active and should have formed part of the political nation after 1861. His individual brand of liberalism blinded him to such aspirations for the redress of social wrongs as were latent in the *Risorgimento.* The idea of creating out of the *Risorgimento* a new political nation and a social revolution was, indeed, beyond the range of his thinking. In short, it was due to Cavour that any of the aims of the *Risorgimento* were achieved, but because it was due to him, some of the richness of the *Risorgimento* was inevitably lost.

Cavour's actions as a member of the Sardinian parliament and a minister were not the result of his intention to unite Italy, but, on the contrary, of his desire for power and his wish to discharge the obligations of power in accordance with the new progressive ideas which filled his mind. A young nobleman, he was like the young Lombard landowners of the previous generation in his belief in the potency of practical scientific knowledge and the value of economic progress. The *connubio* of 1852, whereby Cavour won the premiership through an alliance between the left and right centres of the Sardinian parliament, illustrates his ambition and skill in gaining power. His financial policy illustrates his cautious implementation of current economic ideas. He was responsible for the famous financial statement to the nation of May 1851; he taxed and borrowed heavily; he raised a government loan with Hambro on better terms than those offered by Rothschild or Baring; he encouraged French investment in government securities and private business * until it became an important element in Sardinian prosperity, shown in the building of railways and the development of trade; he encouraged the Chambers to exercise an almost peasant-like scrutiny of expenditure. He was not directly responsible for the reform of the army or for the anti-clerical legislation, which were also part of modernization. In short, Cavour showed no particular originality nor any conscious Italianism. His was a policy of good stewardship, and he showed great ability in profiting from the confidence in Sardinia which it inspired, but he had little to do with the real revolution in Sardinia, which was a social revolution. The opening of the officer corps of the army and posts in the magistracy and the government to all alike caused the old governing aristocracy to withdraw from public affairs. Many of the exiles from other Italian states became industrial *entrepreneurs* and capitalists in Sardinia. They captured the leadership of industry and later of politics, and the old aristocracy was displaced by a rising bourgeoisie, from which it remained isolated. It was as much this social revolution as Cavour's work which prepared Sardinia for the leadership of Italy. The traditional view that Cavour created Sardinian prosperity, in order to prepare Sardinia to govern Italy, is no longer tenable. He did further prosperity, but his especial gift was political perception. He saw that Sardinia's strength, which was derived from many sources, made it possible for her to use the opportunity of the Crimean War, and later to accept the alliance of France, in order to fight Austria for northern Italy.

The Sardinian intervention in the Crimean War was not Cavour's first master-stroke, and still less the predetermined next step in the systematic realization of plans made long before, to unite Italy. Mr. Mack Smith has argued that the intervention was due to the King, and not to Cavour; that if any other influences affected the King's attitude, they were primarily French and secondarily English; that Cavour was only important in the last stage, and that he was then moved by self-interest and not by policy. The evidence, as summarized by F. Valsecchi, shows that de Guiche, the French minister in Turin, was told by the King in June 1854 and again in January 1855 that he wished for intervention and that Cavour did not. But it also shows that Cavour too wished to send troops to the Crimea, and tried to win his colleagues over to this plan. Further, it shows that Cavour from the first took a distinct line of his own. When, in December 1854, serious negotiations were opened by both the French and the English, Dabormida, the Sardinian foreign secretary, first opposed outright and then sought to impose conditions. Cavour's principal concern, was not, however, whether Sardinia should intervene, but that, if she intervened, she

---

* K. R. Greenfield, "The Man who made Italy," in *Studi in onore di Gino Luzzatto,* vol. 3 (1950), p. 191; R. E. Cameron, "French Finance and Italian Unity in the Cavourian Decade," *American Historical Review,* April 1957, p. 552.

should do so on equal terms and not as a hired mercenary. Finally Valsecchi relates how Count Salmour, an intimate friend of Cavour, told him that he had just been informed by de Guiche, a cousin of his wife, that the King intended to dismiss Cavour and replace him by Count Ottavio di Revel, if he did not agree to intervention. Cavour that same evening won the Council of Ministers over to intervention and almost immediately afterwards came to terms with the French and English ministers. It is to this French intrigue and to this display of self-interest that Mr. Mack Smith ascribes the final decision. It ought in fairness to be said that the evidence has been convincingly interpreted another way. Valsecchi argued that Cavour seized the best, though it also happened to be the last, opportunity to do what he had all along intended to do. In either event the intervention was neither an instance of commanding foresight with Italian unity in mind, nor a mere demonstration of self-interest. It was the skilful and courageous use of an opportunity to enlarge Sardinia's European standing. Even although Cavour saw the advantage of representation at the Congress of Paris, he went reluctantly and without knowing the precise gains he would secure.

The Plombières meeting with Napoleon on 21 July 1858 was also, from Cavour's side, unplanned. The initiative was Napoleon's. He had a compelling personal motive in his wish for the hand of Victor Emmanuel's daughter for his cousin Jerome, and Cavour was taken by surprise by the extent and unreserved character of Napoleon's offers and promises. On 3 August Cavour sent to Napoleon a memorandum of what had been decided. During the rest of the summer he made sure of the Princess Clotilde's agreement. On 18 January 1859 a Franco-Italian treaty was signed, and on 30 January the marriage took place. Yet if these successes were unplanned, they were not entirely a matter of luck as Mr. Mack Smith appears to contend. Cavour had been given opportunities, which he used skilfully and flexibly, accepting what Napoleon offered without precisely knowing in advance what he was going to gain, and enlarging his aims as he saw that more was possible. He had given Sardinia a respectable European position; he had now a chance to conquer northern Italy for her.

The second war with Austria undoubtedly made a deeper impact on Italian feeling than that of 1848–49; despite dependence on French help, it was more nearly a national effort and provided some evidence of the resurrection of national vitality. The sequence of events leading from Napoleon's New Year reception of the Austrian ambassador with his famous expression of regret that their relations were not as cordial as they had been, to the Austrian ultimatum of 23 April 1859, is well established. Modern writing has not altered the story of Sardinia's provocation of Austria into war. But the attempt to relate Cavour's work as a whole to the national *Risorgimento* causes considerations other than the diplomatic to emerge more sharply. Cavour, despite his attitude of defensive innocence, as is well known, intended war. From the autumn of 1858 onwards he spoke openly of the inevitability of war with Austria in the following spring. He said this to Odo Russell, unofficial British representative at the

Vatican, and when Russell doubted his assertion, exclaimed: "But I shall *force* her to declare war upon us." Russell, still incredulous, inquired when "he expected to accomplish so great a wonder of diplomacy". Cavour answered, "About the first week of May." This was precisely when war came. The story should not be taken, as it once was, just to prove Cavour's unerring foresight, his infallibility. Cavour's talk was policy and not prophecy. It marks the beginning of his conscious association with a movement, below the level of courts and cabinets, national though never fully popular. Cavour had by 1858–59 come to think and talk in terms of Italy. He had done so diplomatically among the European statesmen at Paris in 1856; in 1858 he seemed to do it before his Italian countrymen. From January to May 1859 he had embarked upon a kind of national propaganda, encouraging the enrolment of volunteers all over Italy, seeking apparently to attach the support of Garibaldi, and constantly talking of the inevitability of war as if it were to be a great life and death struggle. He had embarked on a risky enterprise. In order to appreciate how great the risk was, one need only remember that the Sardinian army, even in 1866, when it had become the Italian army, never defeated the Austrians. His objects were still primarily Sardinian. But in order to ensure victory—a kind of re-insurance, should the French let him down—he pursued a calculated policy of enlarging and exploiting the Italian movement. The war became, what there was little reason at Plombières to think it would become, plausibly, if not actually, a national struggle.

Another reason why this should be so was that, for Austria too, the war was a more serious struggle than that of 1848–49. It was not entirely true that she was provoked into war. She, too, intended war. The intention may have been due in part to ignorance and to expectation of easy victory caused by overestimating her strength. But there was desperation in her intention too. Austria was fighting in 1859, as she was to fight again in 1866, for the idea upon which the Empire was founded. The Empire was a group of nationalities, loosely articulated, claiming to fulfil, in its existing form, a European need. Peaceful withdrawal from Lombardy would have had harmful, perhaps disastrous, effects upon Austria's relationship with Hungary and perhaps also upon her relations with the Germanic Confederation. Franz Joseph believed he was bound to defend the Empire as it existed to the last, and then to yield only at the point of the sword. Austria's stiffness, then, also helped to make it possible for Cavour to propagate the idea of the war as a struggle for a national ideal against a reactionary survival.

The French help did not really blur this picture. Napoleon was almost equally as much a liability as an asset. His wish for territorial aggrandizement encouraged Cavour to hope that he would give sufficient support, and he had been promised Nice and Savoy if Sardinia acquired northern Italy up to the Adriatic. His wish, on the other hand, to draw diplomatic profit from the war made his reliability doubtful. Mr. A. J. P. Taylor has suggested that Napoleon, having gained an *entente* with Russia out of war *against* her in the Crimea, hoped for a similar understanding with

Austria out of a war against *her*. Cavour, of course, could not fathom any such intention, if it existed, but he certainly sensed enough of Napoleon's propensity to pursue contradictory policies simultaneously, to realize that Napoleon would never be consistent or ruthless enough to convince anyone that Sardinia's gains out of the war were the mere gift of France.

The annexation of central Italy, which, after the war, followed the annexation of Lombardy, illustrates a further stage in Cavour's relationship with the national movement. It shows that, in so far as he moved with and furthered the growing sense of national cohesion, he did so less to fulfil a long-cherished intention, than because its independent development suggested the possibility. It shows also how he defeated and estranged from United Italy the more radical elements in the movement and, to some extent, the lower social classes.

After 1848–49 there had been reaction in Tuscany, Parma, Modena, and the Papal Legations. Despite nationalist agitation and liberal pressure, Duke Leopold of Tuscany proclaimed his neutrality in the war against Austria. But he could not continue to stand out, and on 27 April 1859 he retired leaving a provisional government in control. Victor Emmanuel refused the dictatorship, which the provisional government offered him, but took command of the Tuscan army and appointed a royal commissioner for Tuscan affairs. The Duchess withdrew from Parma on 10 June and the Duke from Modena on 12 June. In the Legations, the cities appealed to Victor Emmanuel to assume the dictatorship. Once again he refused, but Sardinian commissioners were ruling in Parma, Modena and the Legations, when the Preliminaries of Peace were signed at Villafranca on 11 July. These provided for the return of the former rulers, but without laying down the method of enforcement. On the other hand, the final peace treaty signed at Zürich, on 10 November 1859, merely reserved the rights of these rulers and did not provide for their restoration.* What had happened between July and November was that Sardinia—Cavour had resigned in July—had accepted the undertaking made at Villafranca to restore the rulers, and set about rendering it impossible of execution with the object of asking to be released from it on the ground that no one could be compelled to perform the impossible. Tuscany was the pivot of this policy and the principal agent, the Baron Ricasoli, who set to work to induce the peasantry throughout the length and breadth of Tuscany to support annexation to Sardinia and eventually to vote for it in a plebiscite. Meanwhile the provisional government resolved to convene an assembly to decide the future of Tuscany, in defiance of the agreement signed at Villafranca. Elections were held on 4–7 August, and the deputies met and voted for annexation to Sardinia, provided that Tuscany retained a measure of self-government.

In January 1860 Cavour returned to office and negotiated a bargain with Napoleon, whereby the French Emperor agreed to accept the Sar-

* This distinction is lost in the *New Cambridge Modern History*, vol. 10, p. 572, by the use of the word "confirm."

dinian annexation of central Italy in return for the cession, after all, of Nice and Savoy, the prize he had forfeited by the over-hasty conclusion of peace in July. Annexation was, however, to be conditional on a fresh consultation of the people. Ricasoli resisted Cavour's pressure for a plebiscite for two months. But he was beaten step by step, and was unable in the end to insist on the condition of Tuscan self-government.

Cavour, then, achieved the annexation of central Italy not by foreseeing how the national movement would develop, but by taking advantage of Ricasoli's power to change the profound mistrust of Sardinia, which Tuscany had shown in 1848–49, into eager and unreserved support. Even if Ricasoli's success owed something to the failure of Montanelli's policy in 1848–49, to the victories of 1859 and to the previous annexation of Lombardy, it was too personal a triumph for Cavour to have foreseen it. But Cavour also achieved the annexation at the cost of losing the support of some elements in the movement. Nor were these elements ever fully reconciled and united Italy was so much the poorer. Among these, of course, were the supporters of the *ancien régime* and of Tuscan autonomy. Many of the latter were men of weight and influence whom it was a pity to lose. Finally, the fusionists, who wanted to create united Italy by a movement from below and a real fusion of the people, circumventing the governments and especially avoiding annexation to the existing Sardinian Kingdom, also now began to hold aloof.* Many of these, especially those who were also Mazzinian republicans, were idealists, who were anyhow alienated by the questionable honesty, as they thought, of Cavour's diplomacy and especially by the new bargain with Napoleon III. There is no doubt that Ricasoli and Farini, his counterpart in the Legations, used much the same methods against these groups, that the governments of 1815–48 had used against suspected conspirators, and with greater stringency, since they acted with such strong conviction of the purity of their motives. In the end the support of the peasantry too was lost; for despite encouragement to hope for advantages from annexation, nothing was afterwards done for them. In this sense socialist regrets that "the revolution" stopped short are well justified.

Cavour's policy towards southern Italy illustrates even more clearly what we now know to have been his characteristic relationship to the *Risorgimento*. The story begins with the rising in Sicily on 4 April 1860. This was not the work of the liberals or nationalists, but of the *bassa gente,* of bands of insurgents out to plunder and loot and to escape taxes, of men on the point of starvation and despair with nothing to lose and ready to continue the revolution against all logic. Garibaldi landed on 11 May and the peasant risings helped his conquest of the island, but unintentionally, and in the end the peasants were excluded, as in the centre, from the benefits of victory, which went to the new landowning gentry

---

* All this is equally true of Parma, Modena, and the Legations, where plebiscites were also held after diligent propaganda by Sardinian commissioners and annexation also followed.

and the merchants. The unification, in the long run, increased the mistrust of the peasantry for all and any government, and did not help, as it possibly might have done, to draw them into a single Italian community. It was characteristic that Cavour by his quarrel with Garibaldi, whom they idolized, should have sacrificed this possibility and also be unaware that he had done so.

Mr. Mack Smith carried conviction in reversing the old view that Cavour, while ostensibly opposing the departure from Genoa of Garibaldi and the Thousand, secretly did all he could to assist it. He proved that Cavour pretended to help and secretly did everything to hinder. But the fact that much the same evidence can be used to support both versions suggests that Cavour's policy, to say the least, was equivocal. Perhaps it was, in the long run, this equivocation which mattered rather than which intention was a feint and which a reality. Such equivocation aroused more mistrust and tended ultimately to estrange the more idealist elements of the national movement. Cavour's failure to fulfil his promise of autonomy to Sicily bore the same alienating stamp of equivocation, and estranged further groups, who should have helped to make the new political nation of the united Kingdom. There was a kind of tripartite struggle for power in Sicily. Garibaldi, in command of armed force whether in Sicily, or, after 19 August, in Naples, and Crispi, until September at the head of the provisional government, constituted one party. Cavour's agents (in succession La Farina, Depretis and Mordini) constituted the second party, and Cavour himself in distant Turin, often out of touch, the third. Cavour twice made promises of autonomy in order to outbid Crispi, and even his own agents, for the support of the Sicilians, and to defeat attempts either to delay annexation or to express the consent of the Sicilians to it through an assembly, which might impose conditions, such as the Sicilians voting individually in a plebiscite, "yes" or "no" to a "loaded" question, could not. The policy of centralization in 1861 amounted to the breach of a promise. When in March 1861 Minghetti's bills imposing a uniform centralized system throughout the peninsula were passed by the Chamber in spite of the presence of the Sicilian deputies, Cavour considered his obligation discharged. His equivocation continued to the end. Negotiations were going on in Turin for a Sardinian-Neapolitan alliance, even while Garibaldi was fighting to conquer Naples. Just before the Sardinian troops invaded the Papal States from the north in order to forestall Garibaldi, and defeated the papal troops at Castelfidardo, Cavour's agents were attempting to provoke an anti-Garibaldian rising such as would afford a pretext for the Sardinian invasion.

Finally, the alienated parties in the south were even more numerous and dangerously estranged than those of central Italy. In Naples the supporters of the *ancient régime,* who were never reconciled to Sardinian rule, included a host of courtiers and office-holders and hangers-on of the old court, aggrieved by the loss of their livelihood. These were a nuisance, but not a serious stumbling-block to national cohesion. The Sicilian federalists and supporters of Sicilian autonomy were, however, many and often important men. The fusionists and the republicans had been much strengthened by the propaganda of the contending parties during the struggle for power from May to September. These groups were not disloyal to the Kingdom of Italy, but after unification were inclined to hold aloof. Cavour's policy towards the South, like the break with the Church, meant that the political life of united Italy included neither the old political classes nor many of those who had supported the national movement, or, if it included them, did so with their ardour cooled. Something of the promise of the *Risorgimento* was lost.

In conclusion, then, Cavour's thinking was rooted in the political movement that was, from the beginning, Sardinia's especial contribution to the *Risorgimento,* and in the practical intellectual movement of Lombardy. Yet he achieved unification by none of the ways foreseen by the great Piedmontese political writers, and in the end he had no economic policy for the serious social problems of central and southern Italy. This, of course (quite apart from the fact that his time was too short), is not surprising. The national movement had developed beyond the range of the earlier thinkers and the social problems that were encountered after unification were more difficult than those for which the early *laisser-faire* economists had solutions. It is more significant that Cavour was at odds, at the end, with Mazzini and Garibaldi and their supporters, who were representative of aspects of the *Risorgimento* in its last phase, when it came nearest to being, what it never was, a truly national movement, touching all classes. Cavour distrusted Mazzini's single-minded devotion to unification as an obsession, while Mazzini scorned Cavour for his want of idealism. Cavour was driven to break with Garibaldi by the pressure of circumstances; for he needed his enmity in order to retain the French alliance and the support of the conservatives of Naples and the Papal States at the time of the Sardinian invasion in the last chapter of the story. Garibaldi's alienation sprang from his conviction of Cavour's double-dealing and above all from the cession of Nice and Savoy to France. Cavour, in short, was a great liberal for whom the writers of the forties were too conservative and the Mazzinians and Garibaldians too radical. Yet even as a liberal his position was distinct. He was never afraid to accommodate his liberal principles to the Sardinian preference and, perhaps, need for a strong executive. The *connubio* of 1852 set the precedent for the later parliamentary practice (called transformism) of Italian governments of buying off the opposition and absorbing so much of it in the government as seemed necessary or possible. He kept much from the knowledge of parliament, and did things even in opposition to it. He was himself at times dictatorial and illiberal. He compelled Carlo Cattaneo, whose economic views he disliked, to find a home in Switzerland; he virtually badgered Mazzini's newspaper, *L'Italia del Popolo,* out of existence; and he quashed parliamentary elections. But Cavour believed in the liberal principle of government by discussion and he bequeathed it to his successors. The bequest was more important than his autocratic actions, which were necessary, if Cavour was to do what he intended, in the circumstances as he understood them. It was unfortunate that Cavour's successors chose, or were obliged, so often to follow the bad rather than the good precedents which he set. But the conservatism, or perhaps realism, which cooled his liberalism, set him still further away from the more radical and the deeper national movement, and meant, as his liberalism itself meant, that some of the generous idealism of the *Risorgimento* went in the end to waste.

282

POLITICIANS AND
THE PEOPLE IN
THE NINETEENTH
CENTURY

IV

19. Alexander II: A Revisionist View

ALFRED J. RIEBER

*By beginning his reign as an autocrat and ending it as a liberal Napoleon III
became for his admirers the "good Napoleon." Tsar Alexander II, the textbooks usually tell us, did just the opposite. He began his rule of Russia in 1855
as a liberal. As the "Tsar Liberator," he emancipated the serfs in 1861, established the local representative assemblies or zemstva in 1864, liberalized the
press, universities, and judiciary by 1864, and extended a measure of autonomy
to some of his non-Russian subjects, such as the Poles and Finns. But, in 1866,
in the face of a revolutionary movement whose members eventually succeeded
in assassinating him in 1881, Alexander II turned to repression and retrograde
autocracy. His reign did unleash the modern forces of economic growth as well
as the modernization of the state's military forces, finances, and administration.
Yet, not even his friends seem to believe that he went far enough as a nineteenth-century version of Peter the Great in bringing Russia into the mainstream
of western civilization's liberalism.*

*This selection, recently published by University of Pennsylvania professor
Alfred J. Rieber, suggests that this view of Alexander II needs to be revised.
Rather than "dividing his reign into reformist and conservative periods" and
contrasting the era of the "great reforms" with that of "the dark forces of reac-*

Source: Alfred J. Rieber, "Alexander II: A Revisionist View," *Journal of Modern
History,* XLIII (1971), 42–58. Copyright © 1971 by the University of Chicago
Press. Reprinted by permission of the author and publisher. [Most footnotes
omitted.]

tion," Professor Rieber insists that we should abandon such western European categories. Instead, we should see that Alexander's policy was consistent in its aim to preserve Russia's unity and strength through military, fiscal, and administrative soundness. How, according to Rieber, did each of Alexander's reforms work to that effect: the military and fiscal reorganization, the emancipation of the serfs, the tariff and railroad policies, the zemstvo *establishment, the dispensing and limiting of civil liberties, the treatment of subject nationalities, and religious and foreign policy? Taken as a whole, were Alexander's policies wise or unwise for Russia's future? If unwise, what alternatives should he have chosen? Why did he choose the alternative he did?*

Few rulers have come to power under less promising circumstances than Alexander II. From the lips of his dying father he received not only the reins of his "command" but also an apology for the lamentable state of affairs in the empire. Nicholas I was not easily moved to ask forgiveness from any earthly being. He left behind a dispirited country, humiliated by military reverses, threatened with bankruptcy, and riddled with corruption. Peasant disorders were increasing ominously, and an even more threatening coalition of foreign enemies was gathering. As Alexander and his closest advisers soon realized, continued fighting offered little hope of success and could easily release the powerful centrifugal forces which had been held in check for so long by the unchallenged authority of the state. By negotiating the Treaty of Paris in 1856, Alexander relieved the pressure of military defeat and avoided possible dismemberment of the empire, but more fundamental changes were needed to save Russia from a similar fate at a later time.

The character and tempo of such changes depended largely upon Alexander's perception both of his own role as autocrat and of the social forces with which he had to contend. His early training and the forceful personality of his father, which deeply influenced his outlook, were themselves rooted in the well-established traditions of the Russian empire. Thus to try, as most historians have, to judge his motives and goals by artificial criteria lifted from the experience of western Europe is to miss the basic continuity in Alexander's reign. Not surprisingly, the charge of inconsistency and weak will often leveled at Alexander by the liberal school has helped preserve the myth that he vacillated constantly between liberal and conservative forces. That the charge has some substance has been amply documented by his tutors' memoirs. "It often happens with the Grand Duke," wrote K. K. Merder to Nicholas in 1829, "that he becomes listless, displays an unusual apathy and a complete absence of firmness and consistency." What has been ignored or forgotten is his considerable success in masking his boyish weakness through a combination of stubbornness, suspicion, and devotion to duty. Instilled since childhood with the belief that the tsar was "the genuine father of his people," "a sacred person," and responsible only to God, Alexander soon developed from experience, as he wrote to his mother in 1857, "a very low opinion of the human race in general and in particular, with very few exceptions." Throughout his life he rejected any form of constitutionalism, "not because he was jealous of his authority," wrote his disappointed minister of interior, P. N. Valuev, "but because he was genuinely convinced that it would harm Russia and would lead to its dissolution." He alone could hold in check the warring interests.

In Alexander's eyes no single class held a monopoly on loyalty by virtue of its past behavior or present status. Loyalty had to be proven by individual acts of unquestioning obedience or personal sacrifice. Although he spoke of himself as "the first noble," he could not forget the nobility's opposition to the emancipation, its constitutional projects, its hostility to the army reforms. He regarded the peasants as naïve but often rebellious children, and he feared that they would anticipate his plans to free them by rising against their hated landlords. To him the youth of Russia was corrupted by the press, and, as he wrote his sister, "in general [they] wish to eliminate all authority." As for the nationalities, he expressed his skepticism of their trustworthiness even before they had proven him right. With the Polish revolt still seven years away, he brooded: "I would very much like and would be happy to believe in the sincere sympathy of the Poles, but I recognize that in spite of my [enthusiastic] reception in Warsaw, I have not the least faith in them." As for the merchantry, he shared the suspicion of the court and the intelligentsia that they lacked initiative and slipped easily into corrupt and dishonest dealings. He despised the intelligentsia.

Many of his advisers tried to play upon his apprehensions by exaggerating one or another form of discontent and opposition. It was not surprising, therefore, that he distrusted the intrigues of his own bureaucrats and, most of all, the court. The confusion of government, lamented D. A. Miliutin, was due to the tsar's unwillingness to "give exclusive influence to any one of us." On occasion Alexander violated his own precepts, as when the clever Peter Shuvalov gained ascendance over the tsar, but his disappointment, disillusion, and revenge were all the greater when Shuvalov failed the ultimate test of loyalty by criticizing Alexander's liaison with Countess Dolgorukaia.

In order to protect himself Alexander devised a method of balancing off the contending groups and personalities who sought his favor. Without surrendering any of his autocratic prerogatives, he placed responsibility in the hands of those who expressed in word and deed their unswerving personal loyalty to him. On matters about which he had made up his mind, he usually found a loyal subordinate, "an instrument of his will," to carry it out. Where he felt himself uncertain, he tossed the issue like a juicy bone into the pack of his squabbling ministers and waited to be convinced by the strongest or most clever of them. Thus, Alexander pursued his own policies by unconsciously exploiting rather than reconciling the conflicting interests within the government and throughout the country. As a result, political alignments constantly shifted on different issues, but all of them revolved around the person of the autocrat.

Despite the inauspicious debut of his reign, Alexander faced his new responsibilities with some concrete advantages. In contrast with three out of his four predecessors, his accession to the throne was legitimate and unopposed. A surge of hope greeted him from all quarters. He responded quickly by relaxing his father's most repressive measures and thus gained much good will, which is valuable even to an autocrat. Alexander had served a long and instructive apprenticeship, having chaired, for example, important secret committees on peasant reform and railroad construction. Consequently, he had a better grasp of administrative and financial matters than most previous grand dukes and, just as important, a more realistic view than his father of Europe's industrial power.

The army, though defeated, was intact and loyal. In fact, only a small proportion had seen service in the Crimea. Fresh line divisions had remained inactive in Poland and the Caucasus. Alexander could still call upon the services of some enlightened if now venerable reformers from his uncle's reign as well as a new generation of technically trained civil servants who, despite Nicholas's repressive educational measures, were well educated and eager to undertake a massive program of reforms from above. Finally, the defeat itself discredited the old rigid social and political system and opened up a broader range of options for the new tsar. The continued existence of serfdom and autocracy well into the nineteenth century rested in no small measure upon the ability of the system to satisfy the pressing demands of the state. What had these demands been and how could they now be met most effectively? By reforms which copied the institutions of western Europe as in the time of Peter the Great? By transforming the autocracy into a parliamentary government and the serf economy into a capitalist one?

Historically, the driving force behind Russia's state policy had been the vital necessity of becoming and remaining a great European power. Only by borrowing from Western forms of culture and technology could Russia resist domination by the West and secure stable frontiers in Asia through conquest and colonization. As the great Russian historian P. N. Miliukov has so persuasively argued, significant social and administrative reforms in Russia since the fifteenth century have sprung from the urgent necessity to mobilize human and material resources—men and money—in order to repel foreign invasion and advance toward the center of civilization. The education and training of Alexander I, Nicholas I, and Alexander II reflected a keen awareness of this compelling tradition. Shaken by the Napoleonic Wars, Alexander I warned his younger brother that he must be a soldier or perish, advice which Nicholas passed on in turn to his son: "He must be a soldier at heart or else in this century he will be lost." The complementary lesson was also driven home by the financial tutor of the young heir, E. F. Kankrin, Nicholas's minister of finance, who repeated Peter the Great's doctrine that "money was the main artery of war." At a staggering cost to society, this policy paid for Russia's membership in the world's most exclusive club, the European Concert.

On many occasions, to be sure, Alexander's predecessors had acknowledged the desirability of reform. As early as 1818 Alexander I authorized the drafting of a peasant reform but insisted that the plan "not include any measure harmful to the landowners and especially that those measures display no sign of force on the part of the government"—a qualification which effectively blocked action except for the landless liberation of peasants in the Baltic provinces. Nicholas regarded serfdom as "an evil, palpable and obvious to all," but despite the warning of his secret police chief, Count A. Benckendorff, that "serfdom is a powder keg under the government," and his recommendation in 1839 that it be gradually abolished, the tsar believed the immediate consequences would "be an even more disastrous evil." Both Alexander I and Nicholas I feared alienating the mass of the nobility upon whom they relied to defeat Napoleon, put down the Decembrists in 1825, and crush the Poles in 1830. The gap between benevolent attitudes and hard politics could not be bridged until defeat or revolution threatened the very existence of the state. Defeat took place first, overcame open resistance by the nobility who had most to lose from the reform, and thrust upon Alexander II, a reputedly weak-willed man, the historic role of "tsar-liberator."

Historians who have subjected Alexander to a liberal critique generally agree on dividing his reign into reformist and conservative periods, neatly separated by the attempt upon his life in 1866 by the student Dmitri Karakozov. Before that fatal date, the argument runs, the "great reforms" were launched: emancipation of the serfs, far-reaching changes in local government, the judiciary, press, and universities. Following the shock of near-assassination, the dark forces of reaction rose again to the surface. Liberal reformers lost their positions, non-Russian nationalities were persecuted, and the revolutionary movement occupied the ground abandoned by the defeated gradualists. Alexander, the liberals concluded, had betrayed the ideals of his age.*

This scheme seeks to explain Alexander's motivation and the direction of his policies with scant regard for the rare consistency of his views on the two vital questions of his reign. Military and fiscal reforms provided the impetus for emancipation and continued to overshadow all other aspects of Russian politics. In the mid-nineteenth century Russia maintained the largest and most expensive peacetime army in Europe. Based on long-term serf recruits, the armed forces lacked a trained strategic reserve and thus could not be expanded in time of emergency. Largely immobile, because of long, exposed frontiers, an unsettled internal situation, and the absence of modern transportation, army units could not be rushed to reinforce the regular forces under attack at an exposed position, like the Crimea, where only a fraction of the men under arms actually fought

* Alexander Kornilov, *Modern Russian History*, trans. Alexander Kaun (New York, 1952), 2:106, 111–12, 179, whence much of the influence on Western secondary accounts. See, for example, P. N. Miliukov, Ch. Seignobos, and L. Eisenmann, *Histoire de Russie* (Paris, 1933), 3:864, 905 (this section was written by Miliukov himself); M. T. Florinsky, *Russia, a History and an Interpretation* (New York, 1953), 2:1033, 1065–66; W. E. Mosse, *Alexander II and the Modernization of Russia* (London, 1958), pp. 132, 178.

the enemy. The huge cost of keeping an army in full readiness meant that sums much needed for modernizing equipment and building strategic railroads and fortresses could not be spared. An unsuccessful war like that in the Crimea added almost a billion rubles to the national debt and shook the monetary stability of the country to its foundations. Alexander and a few of his military advisers recognized that among all the other evils spawned by serfdom, an outmoded army and a crippled treasury were the most intolerable. By liberating the serfs, Alexander could not only free Russia from a moral blight but furnish it with both a smaller, more efficient standing army with a large ready reserve and also a modern fiscal system with a European-style budget.

The architects of these policies were M. Kh. Reutern and D. M. Miliutin, whose activities cannot easily be accommodated by the liberal interpretation. Although both men are traditionally considered liberals, their service careers span the better part of Alexander's reign, Reutern as minister of finance, 1862–78, and Miliutin as minister of war, 1861–81. During this time they worked consistently and often successfully to introduce profound changes in their respective ministries. Both men took an active part in preparing the first two important reforms which followed the emancipation—namely, the creation of a unified treasury, a cost accounting budget, and a territorial system for the army, all of which were introduced in the first year of their tenures as ministers. When Reutern left office, it was not because he had been dismissed, like so many others. He resigned because Alexander had decided to sacrifice fiscal stability to military requirements, to choose Miliutin's advice to go to war with the Ottoman Empire over Reutern's strong opposition. Not only did 1866 fail to interrupt their reforming activity, but it marked a new phase. Reutern's memorandum of September 1866 set forth a plan for Russia's fiscal and economic growth which in part foreshadowed Count Sergius Witte's views a generation later. The same year Miliutin responded to the victory of the Prussian mass army over Austria in the Seven Weeks' War by initiating the changes which culminated in 1874 with the introduction of universal conscription. This he accomplished only with Alexander's unflinching support in the face of a long and stubborn opposition by the leaders of the die-hard nobility. Yet, can there be any doubt that Alexander was less interested in democratizing the army and encouraging capitalism than in utilizing Western techniques to bolster the twin pillars of the Russian autocracy?

A similar unifying thread can be seen running through the broad range of legislation which necessarily followed the decision to free the serfs. It cannot be emphasized too much that the emancipation undermined the whole legal and institutional structure which had existed in Russia since the seventeenth century. Having outlived the purpose for which it was created, the harsh separation of social classes into closed hereditary estates, each with its own set of corporate obligations, could not be swept away entirely by introducing a brand new set of institutions borrowed wholesale from western Europe. The lesson of Peter the Great's indiscriminate haste had not gone unnoticed. Moreover, Alexander lacked his ancestor's demonic energy as well as confidence in the abilities of his people, fettered or corrupted by 200 years of serfdom, to fulfill the role of responsible citizens. The error and frustration of the liberals consisted in their unwillingness to acknowledge the resilience of the traditional cultural pattern. The economic settlement of 1861 is a case in point.

Attempts to measure Alexander's policies against the standards of European capitalism cause far more difficulties than they resolve. On this issue, however, the liberal historians do not stand alone, nor do they occupy the first rank. Soviet historians, in particular, have sought to establish 1861 as the dividing line between feudal and capitalist periods in Russian history, although they have clearly demonstrated that, on the one hand, capitalist relations developed in Russia as early as the late eighteenth century, and, on the other hand, the Russian bourgeoisie remained for some time after 1861 a small and cautious class bound closely to the state bureaucracy. They attribute the peculiar and incomplete character of Russian capitalism to Alexander's subjective defense of the landlords' interests even as his reforms were creating the objective conditions for the growth of capitalism. Ironically, non-Marxist historians have drawn inspiration from Engels's more determinist analysis that the main motive for the emancipation was the economic necessity to free the labor and capital with which to industrialize Russia.*

A close look at the complicated economic terms of the emancipation seriously challenges both interpretations. Although Alexander admitted that "everything possible was done to safeguard the interests of the gentry," he warned the State Council that he would accept revisions in the draft law he laid before them "only if they do not require a manifest sacrifice on the part of the peasantry, . . . for the basis of the entire affair should be the improvement of the peasants' condition, not just in words but in fact." That improvement, however, remained limited by the fiscal interests of the state. The real liberals, like K. D. Kavelin, B. N. Chicherin, and A. I. Koshelev, envisaged a landed peasantry as the basis of a commercial capitalist economy. Another group of landlords who also claimed to represent the capitalist spirit favored freeing the serfs without land and hiring them back as wage laborers. Two staggering difficulties

* Theodore Von Laue, "The State and the Economy," in *The Transformation of Russian Society,* ed. C. E. Black (Cambridge, Mass., 1960), p. 211; Alfred Skerpan, "The Russian National Economy and Emancipation," in *Essays in Russian History,* ed. A. D. Ferguson (New Haven, Conn., 1962). A brilliant modern interpretation of the relationship between the emancipation and industrialization is Alexander Gerschenkron, "Agrarian Policies and Industrialization: Russia 1861–1917," in *The Cambridge Economic History of Europe* (Cambridge, 1965), vol. 6, pt. 2, where the emphasis is placed on the liberation "as an essentially political act" taken primarily "to obviate outbreaks of peasant violence and the threat of catastrophic consequences to the regime." Most important, the author shows that industrialization was initiated "almost as an incidental and not quite desirable by-product of a political action oriented to other goals and inspired by other considerations" (ibid., p. 711).

impelled the government to reject both solutions. Once the landlords' patrimonial authority was removed, who was going to make certain that the landed peasants would pay and that the landless peasants could pay their taxes? The state was still unable to shoulder the cost of collecting its own taxes; and even had it tried, the reaction of both the nobility and the peasantry, who already resented the "bureaucratic invasion" of the countryside, might well have caused serious difficulties. As the *Journal of the Secret and Main Committee* reveals, the decision by the state to maintain the communal forms of landholding by the peasants in the bulk of the European provinces was based upon the dual need to maintain the individual peasant taxpayer on the land and at the same time to preserve the joint guarantee of taxes by the collective. By this ingenious device the government made certain that the peasant, now saddled with redemption dues for his land over a period of forty-nine years as well as the poll tax, could not leave the land without the approval of the other heads of households, who would have to take upon themselves his share of the communal tax burden.

In a different way but to the same effect, the nobility was denied the reality of its compensation for the loss of its serfs and almost half its land. The government did not make outright cash payments to the nobility; indeed it could not have done so without having gone completely bankrupt. Rather, it issued interest-bearing bonds and redemption certificates which could be used only to pay off state obligations in the amount of up to 80 percent of a sum capitalized at 6 percent of the value of previous dues minus the landlord's debt to the credit institutions. In brief, this meant that the landlords obtained very little capital from the transaction that might enable them to reorganize their estates on a capitalist basis. Because of their enormous indebtedness to the state treasury, they received, in fact, only about one-half of the 600 million rubles awarded to them on the basis of the subsequent settlement, and that sum could not be converted into cash but had to be either placed in banks as securities paying 5 percent or turned in to the Treasury as payment for future loans. In the meantime, the district treasury agents received the additional 20 percent of the land value in cash from the peasantry and continued to collect 6 percent of the total capitalized sum while paying back to the landlord only 5 percent of one-half that sum in the form of bonds. Defenders of the nobility and the peasantry lamented the fate of both, and not without good reason. Their interests and the interests of Russian capitalism were sacrificed to the fiscal stability of the state.

More or less consistently throughout Alexander's reign, the same considerations dominated policies in other economic areas such as tariffs and railroad building. From 1856 to 1878 the main strategic lines were built linking the administrative capitals—Moscow and St. Petersburg—with the western frontier—Warsaw—and the Black Sea—Odessa. More to increase trade with western Europe than to develop internal markets, other lines connected the great ports with the grain-producing provinces, for example, St. Petersburg-Moscow-Nizhnii, St. Petersburg-Moscow-Voronezh, Riga-Tsaritsyn, and Kursk-Kharkov-Odessa. By the end of the 1870s the dramatic results justified the high expectations. On the eve of the Russo-Turkish War in 1876 only fifteen days were required for general mobilization, while in 1859 during the French-Piedmontese War against Austria it had taken the army five months to partially mobilize four corps along the Galician frontier. Similarly, in 1861 grain amounted to just under 40 percent of Russia's exports. By 1878 that figure had topped 60 percent. Beginning with the tariff of 1857 duties on pig iron and steel were substantially reduced and free importation of rails and rolling stock was permitted to hasten the construction of the first planned railroad network under French management. In fact, the general purpose of slightly lower Russian tariffs up to 1881 was to raise revenue rather than to protect domestic industries. The main casualty of these policies was the bulwark of industrial development in the modern age—the metallurgical industry, which stagnated for the entire decade of the 1860s as a result of loss of labor due to emancipation, foreign competition due to the tariffs, and absence of direct railroad connections between coal and iron sources. Recovery was slow until the late 1870s and early 1880s, when the first railroad linked the Urals with the Donets Basin, the poll tax on peasants was abolished, increasing their mobility, and a high protective tariff to be paid in gold encouraged domestic industry. The realization was late in coming that only by means of state encouragement and support of industry could both military power and fiscal stability be assured.

The zemstvo reforms under Alexander were no more designed to serve the cause of liberalism—or conservatism, for that matter—than the emancipation was planned to further Russia's capitalist development. Once the patrimonial rights which the landlords had exercised over the peasants had been abolished by the emancipation, the autocracy faced again the recurring dilemma in Russian history of devising some means by which the provinces could be tied to the center. How much local autonomy could be permitted without undermining the authority of the autocrat? On the other hand, how could the state bureaucracy shoulder the enormous burden of maintaining public services through vast and remote areas without modern transportation and communications? The long-delayed opportunity to raise the cultural and economic level of the rural population was now at hand, making the problem more acute than ever before. Yet the autocracy resorted to nothing more imaginative than the traditional forms of local government dressed up in a new guise.

In the most general terms, the zemstvo reform of 1864 can be characterized as a compromise between political centralization and socioeconomic decentralization. Or, as Alexander once stated when rejecting a petition of the Baltic nobility concerning an alleged violation of their local rights, "all legislation takes its authority from the unified autocracy." Russian Liberals praised the elective principle upon which the reform rested. How, then, is one to explain why the reputedly "liberal" (or was he simply enlightened?) N. A. Miliutin submitted a draft of the reform which, in contrast with other plans, substantially increased the power of the bureaucrats at the expense of the locally elected representatives? Was it because he believed that under conditions prevailing at that time the bureaucrats would be more disinterested than the nobility, who, by virtue of their own great personal influence in the countryside and the indirect, three-class voting system, were certain to dominate the zemstvo assemblies and boards? And had not this suspicion been more than justified during the preparation of the emancipation by the landowners' selfish and impassioned defense of their own economic interests? In theory, to be sure, the government could have accepted the principle of "one man, one vote," but in practice this would have meant submerging Russia's only provincial elite in the gray mass of the peasantry. In its final form the zemstvo legislation posted bureaucratic watchdogs over the local elective bodies in the person of the district police chief and the governor, whose duty it was to check the political ambitions of the nobility and protect the peasant against such exploitation by former landlords as might cripple their tax-paying abilities or turn them into desperate rebels. In this way the state continued the policies of the sixteenth and seventeenth centuries, when, as Kliuchevskii explained, it was perfectly willing to turn over the peasant to the tender mercies of the landlord as long as the peasant continued to be able to fulfill his primary obligations to the state.

As it turned out, certain sections of the nobility supported by the zemstvo specialists (teachers, engineers, doctors, agronomists, etc.) proved to be more concerned with improving education, health, transportation, and other public services than were the bureaucrats. They also furnished the cadres for a genuine liberal movement in the western European tradition. Yet, even granting this, it is still a moot point whether these zemstvo liberals reflected the basic interests of the peasantry as the peasantry saw them. It is less doubtful that bureaucratic interference in local government was aimed not so much at the socioeconomic functions of the zemstvos as at the political aspirations of the provincial nobility. In characteristic fashion Alexander never doubted throughout his long reign that representative bodies should function exclusively as administrative arms of the center. When, near the end of his life in the face of terrorist attacks, he placed complete confidence in Count Loris-Melikov to save the regime, he also gave his wholehearted approval to the political philosophy which underlay "the dictatorship of the heart": "for Russia any organization of people's representatives in forms borrowed from the West is unthinkable, [but also] a simple recreation of representative forms of olden times [the zemskii sobor] would be difficult to achieve, and in any case, a dangerous experience in returning to the past."

It may be accepted as an axiom of Alexander's reign that the farther removed an issue from the central concerns of fiscal and military security, the greater the latitude his advisers enjoyed in reforming outmoded and decayed institutions. In the three traditional bulwarks of civil liberties—the press, the universities, and the judiciary—Alexander permitted a degree of freedom never before equaled in Russian history. But as soon as it became evident that journalists, students, teachers, and lawyers were exercising those rights in order to express and defend their own values rather than to prove their devotion to the tsar, as Alexander thought they should, then he turned upon them with wrath and indignation. In his eyes the press ought to serve the government's need to explain its policies to the people. Criticism from either the Right or the Left he considered a betrayal of that obligation. At times, even the most loyal subject, like M. N. Katkov, was warned that unless he refrained from attacking government officials, no matter how justifiable this might seem to him in terms of the true interests of the autocracy, his paper would be closed down. Ivan Aksakov, who supported the autocracy in principle but demanded such conservative measures as russification, had two newspapers he edited shut down on government orders and lost his job on a third. As with the censorship statute of 1865, so with the university statute of 1863; the new regulatory machinery shifted responsibility for upholding order from those who administered the law, the bureaucrats, to those who were supposed to enjoy its protection, the university professors. The basically repressive nature of this device soon became apparent.

Alexander measured out doses of freedom to his subjects in relation to their ability to understand exactly how he wanted them to use it. Like his other reforms, the extension of civil liberties was meant to increase the opportunities of the people to serve and obey him. They would become more devoted and unified by assuming their new role as active citizens in contrast with their previous role as passive subjects. Alexander favored, as did his father, a narrow functionalism in school curricula in order to prepare individuals for a specific bureaucratic job and prevent them from developing a generalized view of society. One concrete and positive aspect of his policies was the dramatic growth of technical cadres in law, education, and other neglected professions. Still, a great distance separated the idea of voluntary acceptance of the will of the tsar from the liberal ideal of the inalienable rights of the individual.

Alexander's attitude toward nationalism also reflected his deep concern over the fragile unity of the empire. The two most prominent aspects of nineteenth-century nationalism were the myth of popular sovereignty and the exclusiveness of a single language and culture. As the absolute ruler of a multinational empire in which the Great Russians were slowly losing their majoritarian position, Alexander refused to endorse either of these principles. This by no means suggests that russification under Alexander can be discounted, much less ignored, but rather that it must be considered in the light of the political and strategic requirements of the autocracy. Only in this way is it possible to explain the variety of response to the nationalities question in Finland, Poland, the Baltic provinces, and the Caucasus. Alexander laconically acknowledged Finland's loyalty: "My father relied on you. All of you have fulfilled your duty." Consequently he rewarded the Grand Duchy by granting a large degree of political and cultural autonomy, far more liberal, for example, than that which the English extended to the Irish. Consistent with this policy, the autocracy offered the Finnish majority important cultural advantages at the expense of the minority Swedish elite, whose sympathies with Stockholm diluted their loyalty to St. Petersburg. By contrast Alexander's initial willingness to extend similar rights to the Poles aimed at winning over the aristoracy. When the revolt of 1863 discredited that policy, Alexander angrily demanded a more thoroughgoing russification of Polish administration and culture than a majority of bureaucratic specialists in the Committee for the Western Region, and he consistently supported N. A. Miliutin's drive to liberate the Russian peasants from their Polish landlords on more generous terms than those enjoyed by the peasantry in the Central and Black Earth Provinces.

Because the Baltic Germans had served the autocracy loyally for so long, Alexander not only upheld their economic and social privileges against the nascent Estonian and Latvian nationalists but also rebuked overzealous right-wing patriots for attacking them with, in his words, "a sharpness which instead of uniting Russia into a single whole involved its division."

In the recently conquered Caucasus, Alexander approved sizable deportations and resettlement of Circassian tribes who forcibly resisted assimilation into the administrative structure of the empire. The problem here as with other Muslim peoples was the powerful attraction of Constantinople and Mecca upon the faithful. At the suggestion of the viceroy of the Caucasus, Prince A. I. Bariatinskii, Alexander established the Society for the Reestablishment of Christianity in the Caucasus, and Orthodox missionaries rather than language teachers took up the main burden of transforming former enemies into obedient subjects. Their quasi-political activities soon spread into the Tatar areas of the Volga. Together with the revival of missionary work in the Western Provinces, the campaign converted over 600,000 by the end of the reign.

Largely at the instigation of his younger brother, Grand Duke Constantine Nikolaevich, the tsar sought to revitalize and modernize the administrative and educational functions of the church in order to prepare it for a more active role beyond the frontiers. In 1876 a twenty-year project to translate for the first time the entire Bible into modern Russian was finally completed. In 1867–69 a large-scale reform of clerical education was undertaken. Overseas missions were dispatched to the Near East and the Americas. In his attempts to use the church as a political weapon, Alexander was gradually drawn into much the same ambivalent position toward the Balkan Slavs as his father. Consistently, if at times reluctantly, he encouraged the belief that Russia would champion Orthodox Christianity against Islam, although he left unclear the extent of that support. "I will do what I can," he answered the request of a visiting delegation of Serbs to help them clear Belgrade of the Turks. Officially Alexander opposed the grandiose designs of the Pan-Slavs, but his moral commitment to Orthodoxy as a kind of substitute for national unity left him helpless to resist their pressure at the decisive moment. By 1877 he reached the point where he had unwittingly staked his own honor and that of the empire upon saving the rebellious Christian population of the Ottoman Empire from their legitimate sovereign.

Rejecting Great Russian nationalism as divisive and Pan-Slavism as adventurist, Alexander relied on the traditional loyalty to tsar, church, and state to carry the empire through the war. But whatever enthusiasm the war generated came from an emotional identification with Russia's mission with which the tsar did not fully sympathize and therefore could not exploit. Victory in the Balkans cost Russia more men and treasure than defeat in the Crimea. In psychological terms the paradox was even greater. European intervention robbed Russia of the choicest fruits of victory, leaving the disgruntled Pan-Slavs without Constantinople and the disillusioned liberals without a constitution. The reformed army had not been ready, and the fragile fiscal structure buckled under the strain. Faced with rising pressure from the postwar revolutionary terror, Alexander appealed in vain for public support. The great reformer had been unable to tap the emotional wellsprings of the people, nor was he willing to provide them with the constitutional rights that even liberated Bulgaria enjoyed. Deeply embittered and frightened, Alexander could not understand why he was being "hunted like a wild beast" in his own country. Ever since he had been a child, he had wanted people to love and respect him. He wept when his tutors gave him poor marks, and he grieved later when his people misunderstood his policies. Above all, it appeared to him he had sought to unite the empire, to reconcile the conflicting interests through compromise; yet in the end he stood alone.

Given Alexander's personal character and the socioeconomic situation in mid-nineteenth century Russia, was it not possible that a policy based upon liberalism, capitalism, and nationalism might have produced exactly the opposite effect in Russia that it did in western Europe? Rather than unifying the country, it might have destroyed it. On the one hand, Alexander clearly lacked the strength of will, imagination, and boldness of Peter or Lenin. He was only too well aware of his own weaknesses. On the other hand, the obstacles to Petrine revolution were far greater than in 1700, and the prospects of a mass revolution, far less than in 1917. The Muscovite state had become a multinational European power with a more stable social and political elite and a more complex economy than at the end of the seventeenth century. Conversely, although Crimea had been a defeat, it had not rent the fabric of society as was to happen during World War I. The risks of upheaval from above outweighed the dangers of disintegration from below.

Alexander worked hard to preserve both the power of the state and the loyalty of his subjects. The two aims proved to be incompatible, and in the end his policy of reconciliation collapsed. We can hardly expect him to have tried revolution instead. Neither he nor the times were suited to it. The heavy responsibility for state security and social order had rested too long upon the shoulders of the autocracy for Alexander to be willing or for society to be able to share it.

Yet Alexander's personal fate would yield more significant insights if his struggle to solve the problems which defeated him were placed in a different historical perspective, one free of the inadequate categories originally defined and best suited for western European history. Surely, it is no longer possible to discuss the politics of Russian autocracy in terms of an artificial dualism, whether liberal-conservative, Westernizer-Slavophil, or rational-national. These no more than capitalism and nationalism suggest the real preoccupations of those who held power as distinct from those who wanted it.

20. Money, Morals, and the Pillars of Bismarck's Society

FRITZ STERN

Otto von Bismarck has troubled historians for the hundred years since his creation of a united north Germany. More recent historians, whether they admit it or not, are always conscious that such a large German state made two world wars possible if not probable, that the German republic after World War I was unable to root itself in German society, that there eventually was Hitler's dictatorship, and that Hitler's demise resulted in a cold war division of Bismarck's Germany into two states. Implicitly or explicitly, then, historians tend to ask whether Bismarck can in some way be held responsible for these German failures.

In recent years German historians have considered the "Bismarck problem" mainly in terms of the internal conditions of his Germany—the undemocratic nature of the constitution, the nondevelopment of parliamentary government and legal party opposition, and the lack of able leadership among his successors. This selection, by Fritz Stern, professor of history at Columbia University, carries this one step further. United Germany's problems, he argues, stemmed from the coinciding of "two related facets of internal weakness." First, "the rise of industrial capitalism brought about a fundamental crisis of moral conscience." Secondly, "Bismarck's style . . . came to have a disastrous effect on the political culture and public morale of the new nation." Germany might have survived one or the other as successfully as France

Source: Fritz Stern, *The Failure of Illiberalism* (New York: Alfred A. Knopf, 1971). Copyright © 1971 by Fritz Stern. Reprinted by permission of Alfred A. Knopf, Inc.

weathered the reign of Napoleon III. Instead, the conjuncture of the two, after an initial political and economic exuberance which German historians call the Gründerzeit *or* Gründerjahre, *"saw a political and psychological faltering that affected the growth of the new nation for decades to come." In other words, Bismarck's Germany, unlike the rest of western Europe, did not develop a flexible and public-spirited ruling class able to carry on after Bismarck was dropped as chancellor in 1890. According to Professor Stern, what difficulties did the sudden rise of industrial capitalism create for the German Junkers or aristocrats? What factors made it difficult for them to adjust to materialism? In what ways did their adjustment color politics? How would you describe Bismarck's political style and his policies? Stern holds that Bismarck "poisoned the atmosphere of political life" in Germany by ignoring the fact that "success and viability of 1871 depended on the transformation of subjects into citizens." In what ways did Bismarck do this? Why did he do it? Given the German people's "fundamental crisis of moral conscience" brought about by unification as well as by the economic and social problems of the 1870s, what kind of corrective policies and political style should Bismarck have pursued?*

Perhaps one of Europe's more remarkable achievements has been the creation of a flourishing bourgeois civilization that has never been free from the most penetrating bourgeois criticism. *"Épater le bourgeois"* was a great pastime of the last century and the sport still seems to be alive. Ibsen's *Pillars of Society,* published in 1877, was a radical analysis of the moral pretensions and the moral burden of bourgeois society. The pillars of that society were rotten; the life of the protagonist was a lie violating his own nature and that of his fellowmen. It is as if Ibsen had written a dramatic commentary on the *Communist Manifesto* without indulging in the comforting hope that a social revolution would create a new man in a newly virtuous society. In the play, salvation came through an improbable act of contrition and self-purgation; at his most revolutionary, Ibsen thought that the feminine slamming of doors sufficed for human improvement.

He had, however, written a powerful indictment of contemporary mores and had exposed the psychic cost of bourgeois striving. Subsequent years provided frequent substantiation of his charge that beneath the façade of prosperous respectability was teeming corruption, produced by the lure of wealth and power. Old virtues—probably always more honored in the breach than the observance—disappeared in all but name; empty labels remained, reminding the world that a new code had yet to be formulated. Unbridled capitalism offered immense advance and taunted people with ever new temptations. Out of greed, men cheated and cajoled, robbed those below them of their just rewards, injured and despised them.

Ibsen situated his conflict between pretense and reality in a Norwegian seaport, as it was gradually being subverted by modern forces. The same discrepancy and the same growing sense of unease and corruption prevailed in Bismarck's new Reich. For a people that had long been exceedingly sentimental about its moral virtues, the dim realization of a transformation of values was painful indeed.

Initially, the mood of imperial Germany was jubilant. The dream of decades had come true on the battlefields of France. Treitschke celebrated that war as a "blessed fate. For truly only such a prodigious event, such an act of violence, so brutal and so insolent that it had to wake even the dullest conscience, would have been able to lead the south back to the great fatherland." [1] God had punished the decadent French and rewarded virile, honest Germans by an imperial crown, won in the very seat of ancient *gloire,* in Versailles, whence Germany had been kept divided. Or so legend adorned victory—for outward façade was sustained by internal legend and by an exaltation of German victory that seemed designed to compensate Germany for its almost uninterrupted experience of defeat. The exaltation of 1871 marked the climax of an ancient tradition—a particularly crass and ugly climax. It was a kind of national intoxication; it was unrestrained hubris. In our century, victory has been too costly to permit exaltation; no great power is likely ever again to have that experience.

Glittering façade, noisy exaltation, and solid achievement persuaded historians—particularly German historians—that the early decades of the Second Empire were one of the great periods of German history. Certainly Germany rose to the pinnacle of her European power—and thanks to Bismarck's skills, did so without provoking another war. The internal scene, however, was more somber: the new nation came to suffer from new conflicts and uncertainties, disappointments and psychic discontents.

The exaltation of victory was followed within two years by a financial crash of unprecedented scope, triggered to some extent by reckless overconfidence and fraudulence. The crash of 1873 revealed the emergent transformation of values: a new capitalistic ethos was in the ascendancy. But the crash, quickly translated into moral terms, produced a shock in German public consciousness that in turn inspired the repudiation of economic liberalism and the rise of new antagonisms. In the political realm, too, crisis and scandals emerged. The triumph of unification was followed by gradual disenchantment with the political life of the new nation. The German people suffered not only from a quick reversal of mood but from an attendant crisis of self-assessment and self-understanding. The old, peculiarly German, question "What is German?" assumed new urgency.

I would like to deal with two related facets of the internal weakness of the new nation. First, I want to suggest that the rise of industrial capitalism brought about a fundamental crisis of moral conscience. The members of the Junker class in particular found it hard to reconcile their old values with the sudden necessity to adapt to a new kind of economy. At the very time when Bismarck seemed to have preserved their political preemi-

[1] Heinrich von Treitschke, *Historische und Politische Aufsätze,* III (4th ed., Leipzig, 1871), p. 612.

nence, a new economic system put in jeopardy their material power and challenged the moral priorities by which they had justified that preeminence. Their role in the crash of 1873 and in its aftermath served as a focus of that moral crisis.

Second, I should like to show that in the long run Bismarck's style—quite aside from his policies—came to have a disastrous impact on the political culture and public morale of the new nation. Far from fostering participation, he gradually became an autocrat who offered little leadership. Having played a central role in creating the new nation, he unwittingly played a central role in keeping it divided.

It was Germany's pecular fate that the crisis precipitated by capitalism coincided with twenty years of Bismarckian rule. That the coming of capitalism brought moral and social dislocation was a common experience in the world; for better or for worse, Bismarck was *not* a common experience. The two experiences together shaped and obscured the political culture of the 1870's. The coinciding of the two illustrated Germany's middle position between the bourgeois-capitalistic world of Western Europe and the backward autocracies of Eastern Europe.

More than the achievement of national unification, the triumph of industrial capitalism changed the reality of German life, although awareness of this fact was partially disguised by the survival of an earlier code of private and public virtues. The material consequences of industrialization were clear-cut: the immense growth of German power, the demographic shifts, the impact on class antagonisms and on politics. We are less familiar with the psychological impact of capitalism on the Junker class with its long-cherished contemptuous disdain for business and bourgeois life. A succinct statement of their predicament can be found in Friedrich Spielhagen's novel *Sturmflut,* which deals with the moral crisis and material temptations of the 1870's. Reminded that the aristocratic motto must always remain *noblesse oblige,* the Junker protagonist demurs, "because our condition has never been so precarious as it is today. In this, our leveling century, we have long been on the same plane, in the same dusty arena with the classes that rush on behind or against us—the very arena in which is fought out the struggle for survival; but sun and wind are unevenly divided. A multitude of means which the bourgeois class uses with the most incredible success is denied us because of *noblesse oblige.* Very nice: privilege we no longer have: God forbid. But unique duties [*Vorpflichten*]: we are supposed to defend our position in state and society and still preserve our moral qualities. This is all too often a difficult thing and sometimes it is impossible: it is nothing but the squaring of the circle." [2]

The rise of industrial capitalism was bound to create difficulties; the very speed with which it swept over Germany multiplied these difficulties. Offering a new way of life and a new means of gaining wealth and

[2] Friedrich Spielhagen, *Sturmflut,* in *Sämmtliche Werke,* XIII, Part I (6th ed., Leipzig, 1886), 47.

power, capitalism prescribed values radically different from previously held attitudes regarding the morality of money, the accumulation of wealth, and the propriety of unearned profits. This conflict of values was to some extent disguised because nineteenth-century Germans were perhaps particularly inhibited in honestly facing or discussing questions of money. In Western Europe, the upper classes also had begun with strong prejudices against the capitalist spirit, but they had had a much longer time and a more congenial political and religious milieu in which to make their compromises. Capitalism burst upon a Germany whose middle class had lost a revolution and whose Junkers still dominated politics and the public ethos. Capitalism took hold in Germany more rapidly than elsewhere, violating deeper prejudices and offering greater opportunities. Three strands in Germany's cultural tradition militated against an easy acceptance of material values. First, there was the legacy of Luther's abhorrence of money as filthy lucre—a different attitude from that of Calvinists or Catholics. The most complicated attitude toward money occurred in regions where Lutheran pastors sought to keep alive this anti-capitalistic spirit. Second, and in the same regions, an unbroken feudal tradition proclaimed that manly virtues of honor and heroism were superior to and in conflict with material ambition. Birth was more important than wealth, though Providence in its wisdom had decreed that the two should be joined by placing Junkers on their manorial estates. The Junkers frowned on business and on most mercantile activities; to live off other people's misfortunes—their definition of money-lenders—was considered parasitical, as was the amassing of profit without work. They shared the common rural prejudice against clever city-folk, against outsiders and Jews who carried on the kind of business that no Junker would touch—or could do without. The third strand was the German ideal of *Kultur* which came to be exalted and institutionalized in the nineteenth century. By its extravagant praise of *Bildung* and spirit, it clearly implied that any man dedicated to the higher things in life would have to be properly scornful of the baser things—of which money or business was a prime example. This third strand was distinctive to Germany and expressed something of the intellectual aspirations and political and material weakness of her middle classes.

German views concerning money described a difference in degree, not kind, as compared to those of other nations. A man's attitude toward money is never simple and never easy to establish. It is embedded in so many other values, it is so often encrusted by hypocrisy and disguised by subterfuges that in the end the person himself is half-deluded. The problem is posed at the outset: does one talk about money, is one embarrassed by one's material interests? Changing attitudes toward money—and obviously I am using money as a shorthand for a more complicated set of questions—tell us a great deal about a society, a class, or an individual. Attitudes toward money often furnish an invaluable index of hypocrisy. Historians—perhaps because of their well-known indifference to money—have slighted some of these questions.

Evidence, of course, is hard to come by, but some historians may have neglected these questions because they assumed that modern men automatically follow the fiction of economic man and that anti-materialist rhetoric can be dismissed as mere rationalization. On the other hand, we know that modern mass movements of the right and left have exploited not only material grievances but also anti-materialist sentiments in society, and that certain cultural movements, such as the German Youth Movement, would be inexplicable without recognition of the anti-capitalist impulse behind them.

Men's attitude toward money is so enormously complicated because it expresses so much of their deeper selves. It fashions and reflects the direction of their lives; it encompasses their attitude toward work and pleasure, toward family and education, toward what is or ought to be the principal goal in a man's life. The pursuit of wealth can stand for drudgery and vanity, it can enslave a man to his workaday life, it can be a crushing experience. It can also beckon as an adventure, a romance, a leap to greatness. It can be a means or an end—but does it ever appear as a satisfying end? The ambivalence of financial success is illustrated by the conflict between Thomas and Christian Buddenbrook, between the tortured and repressed businessman and the idle, self-indulgent brother whose very existence taunts and threatens the successful Thomas. One's attitude toward money bespeaks an inclination to abide by prevailing norms or to rebel against them, to accept one's ticket or to seek another.

The prejudice against money-making is often as great as the love of it—and the contradiction fosters doubt and hypocrisy. Has the notion that money is the root of all evil—that preposterous exaggeration of the importance of the acquisitive instinct and of its relation to sin—ever *not* coexisted with rampant lust for wealth? Has the longing for the simple and austere life, the nostalgia for an Arcadian past, not been a cultural fact of extraordinary power? Money-grubbing and money-hating, the pursuit of wealth and the fear of wealth as a burden and a distraction—these attitudes express deep human and social ambivalences that can help us to understand the tangle of the past.

Some of these ambivalences are illustrated by the Junkers' response to the capitalist challenge. In the relatively calm days of the early nineteenth century, they lived comfortably on and from their estates, and their habitual lack of cash was not particularly noticeable in a country that was generally poor and had made a virtue of sobriety. The Junkers, however, had learned to become punctilious in the running of their estates; necessity had driven them to watch over their income. In fact, they had become remarkably adept at introducing new techniques that promised higher returns. For the rest, they felt or affected disdain for money, even for talk about money. Their reluctance to intermarry with the commercial bourgeoisie suggests something of the tenacity of this prejudice. It left them without the material replenishment that their English counterparts had long since learned to accept graciously. The young Bismarck exemplified this indifference to money; although all his life assiduous in matters of finance, as a young man he affected scorn, and when trying to collect some outstanding debts from a friend, he apologized for his "Jewish kind of calculating character [*Berechnungswesen*]." [3]

Gradually the Junkers came into close contact with the new type of economy. In 1842, the industrialist Friedrich Harkort remarked that "the nobility feels that the railroad locomotive is the hearse in which feudalism will be carted off to the cemetery." [4] But the Junkers were far too practical to indulge in any incipient Luddite sentiment. While most had to be dragged into the mysterious world of modern business, a few charged in, full of hope and greed. Neither the laggards nor the enthusiasts found the experience particularly inspiriting. Some began to participate in the highly speculative enterprise of railway construction—a real departure from their earlier code. The magnates of Silesia, never as reticent as their poorer, purer cousins in the older Prussian provinces, pointed the way. With the advent of a liberal economy, nobles and non-nobles became involved in joint-stock ventures.

By the late 1860's many succumbed to a scheme, at once symptomatic and disastrous, fathered by one of the great Jewish promoters of the time, Dr. Bethel Henry Strousberg. Having successfully built German railroads, Strousberg collected some fifty million talers for the construction of railways in Rumania. Foreshadowing later practice, he enticed great notables to decorate his board of directors, men like the Prince Putbus, the Duke of Ujest, and the Duke of Ratibor.[5] By 1870, the enterprise was on the brink of disaster, and Prussia's *Prominenz* and many ordinary people stood to lose all their investments. It took two bankers and the imperial government some ten years to retrieve these improvidently placed funds.[6]

[3] Bismarck, *Die gesammelten Werke,* XIV, Part I (2nd printing, Berlin, 1933), 179.

[4] Quoted in Dietrich Eichholtz, *Junker und Bourgeoisie vor 1848 in der preussischen Eisenbahngeschichte* ([East] Berlin, 1962), p. 37.

[5] Joseph Maria von Radowitz to Bismarck, Mar. 10, 1871, in Acta betreffend Verhandlungen mit Rumänien, A.A. II, Rep. 6, No. 4205, Deutsches Zentralarchiv, Merseburg. See also Strousberg's self-justification, *Dr. Strousberg und sein Wirken von ihm selbst geschildert* (Berlin, 1876), pp. 337–88.

[6] In 1879, Bismarck gave the French ambassador, the Comte de St. Vallier, a marvelously colorful account of the Strousberg affair. The European powers at the time were trying to force the Rumanian government to grant civic equality to its Jews, as it had promised at the Congress of Berlin. The Rumanians stalled, and Bismarck expressed his anger "at the crooks and savages . . . with the liveliness and brutal energy one often encounters in his assessments." The ambassador reported the conversation *verbatim:* "My other motive [for being anti-Rumanian] has to do with a more private matter which for us however has an urgent and distressing character; you are familiar with the Strousberg affair; you know what bloodletting it has inflicted on German capital; close to 200 million francs have been swallowed up in these Rumanian railways which yield nothing and the value of which is hardly one-tenth of the cost; our greatest lords and our bootblacks believed that Strousberg would present them with a gold mine and a great many risked the best part of what they possessed, believing the promises of this adventurer. All that is buried now in the Rumanian mud, and, one fine day, two dukes, one general who is an aide-de-camp, a half-dozen ladies-in-waiting, twice that many chamberlains, a hundred coffeehouse owners and all the cabmen of Berlin found themselves totally

In the euphoria of the day, the lessons of the Strousberg disaster went unheeded.[7] Instead, his pattern of promotion was widely emulated and the victory of 1871 provided a heady atmosphere for still more promotion. The influx of the French indemnity—an unprecedented five billion francs—added material stimulus. A speculative fever suddenly gripped many Germans—and respected neither rank nor position. Hundreds of new enterprises were spawned, sometimes on flimsy foundations. An aroused public pounced on these creations and drove up the price of the shares—to the great profit of the original promoters, who were usually a group of financiers, including many Jewish financiers, and men of title. For a while, then, there were great profits, and more men were caught up in the frenzy. Prudence gave way to recklessness and occasional fraudulence, as more and more people thought that they could get rich fast.

The extent to which aristocrats were swept along by the same desire

ruined. The Emperor took pity on the dukes, the aide-de-camp, the ladies-in-waiting, and the chamberlains, and charged me with pulling them out of the trouble. I appeared to Bleichröder who, on condition of getting a title of nobility which as a Jew he valued, agreed to rescue the Duke of Ratibor, the Duke of Ujest, and General Count Lehndorf [sic]; two dukes and an aide-de-camp saved—frankly, that is worth the 'von' bestowed on the good Bleichröder. But the ladies-in-waiting, the cabmen and the others were left drowning, and even Bleichröder's three Moses [whom he had dredged out of the water] were not so entirely saved but that they have to face each year some nice trial in which they are sued for two or three million marks which they cannot pay since their domains of Ratibor, Ujest, etc. are totally mortgaged in exchange for the Bleichröder guarantee. There is but one way for everybody to get out of this trouble and that is to try to sell the Rumanian railways. . . . [At present] the Rumanian government exploits the owners' misery with usurious barbarism; by annoyances, injustices, extortions, it wants to force them to abandon the railways to the government for a crust of bread . . . every day our German engineers and workers are being beaten, maltreated, imprisoned, cheated, robbed of everything, and we can do nothing to help them attain justice. That is why I just told you that I wished I could use naval ships as in Nicaragua to obtain satisfactions; but that is impossible, and neither do I have balloons [aerostats] to send in German troops." He urged the dukes to sell the railways, perhaps to Austria or Russia—for cash because to lend money to these great defaulters would be a mistake. The dukes thought that Bismarck might object to the Rumanian railways being sold to Russia, but he had reassured them "that it was a matter of indifference to me if the Rumanian railways and indeed all of Rumania should fall into Russian hands." The French ambassador added to the Quai d'Orsay that this was perhaps not quite so pleasant a prospect for France. Archives du Ministère des affairs étrangères, Correspondance Politique, Allemagne, XXVII, Feb. 26, 1879.

[7] Ludwig Bamberger summed up the Strousberg fiasco with his usual anti-aristocratic bias: "Because charlatanry in all realms has no more credulous adherent than the aristocracy, financial wizards [like Strousberg] always manage to entrap many aristocrats who for their part are ready to contribute the radiance of their name to the sham gilding of an enterprise. In turn, they are rewarded from the first easily acquired profit of that enterprise. Strousberg understood perfectly how to fashion for himself such an aura out of the Prussian aristocracy; the aristocracy's still prevalent view that all financial business really encompasses fraud derives perhaps in part from its recollections [of Strousberg]." Ludwig Bamberger, Erinnerungen, ed. Paul Nathan (Berlin, 1899), p. 527.

has not been properly recognized. For some, it was sheer greed; for others, it was tinged with what might be called professional necessity. The cost, not so much of living, as of living in style, of maintaining status, had suddenly increased enormously. The burden fell most heavily on those impecunious Junkers in public service, whose still frugal salaries ill equipped them to survive in the fiercely competitive society of plutocratic Berlin. At the time of some unwelcome resignations from the government in 1879, Bismarck complained to the king: "Applications for ministerial posts are not very numerous in any case; the salary is too low compared to the external demands and only a *rich* man can be a minister without getting into financial difficulties."[8] Ideally, candidates should be rich, competent, and aristocratic: no wonder the supply was limited and the financial strain pervasive.

Hence the headlong rush into an unknown but infinitely alluring world; people sensed boundless opportunity and fought to take advantage of it. Financiers were besieged with requests and demands, and someone like Gerson Bleichröder had an exceptionally good vantage point from which to see how noble society, despite its anti-materialist ideology, sought instant wealth. His most celebrated client, Bismarck, was something of an exception; he was rather modest, almost old-fashioned, in his expectations. To be sure, he was deeply concerned about his finances. He always wanted more land and a higher return from it; he owned some stocks, but he shunned speculation and had some sense of what we call conflict of interest. He was closer to the old patriarchal Junker traditions than many of his Junker critics.[9]

Most others were less modest. Men wrote to Bleichröder in great secrecy, beseeching him not to reveal their correspondence. Among themselves they still sneered at money-making, especially Jewish money-making. But requests of the most extraordinary diversity poured in. Count Pückler, William's *Hofmarschall*, asked Bleichröder to make up some minor losses he had suffered on an investment. Bleichröder, he wrote, had assured him that a given stock would appreciate and had promised to

[8] Bismarck, *Die gesammelten Werke*, VI c, 156. German diplomats of the time were also underpaid and consistently received lower salaries than the representatives of other great powers. When Count Solms-Sonnenwalde, then Prussian minister in Dresden, wrote Bleichröder concerning the desirability of changing his investment portfolio, he added: "Forgive me, dear Baron, if I trouble you with so small a matter; but since the state cares so little about the improvement of the salaries of *Prussian* diplomats, while the Russian post here has been raised to 20,000 talers, I have to look out for other ways of augmenting my income." Count Solms to Bleichröder, Mar. 9, 1875, Bleichröder Archive in possession of F. H. Brunner, a partner of Arnhold and S. Bleichroeder, New York. I would like to express my gratitude to Mr. Brunner for placing that archive at the disposal of Professor David S. Landes and myself. See also Rudolf Morsey, *Die oberste Reichsverwaltung unter Bismarck 1867–1890* (Münster, 1957), p. 113.

[9] See my "Gold and Iron: The Collaboration and Friendship of Gerson Bleichröder and Otto von Bismarck," *American Historical Review*, LXXV, No. 1 (Oct. 1969), 37–46.

compensate him for any loss if the stock were to fall. He now presented his claim. Count Pückler liked his profits without running any risks.[10] In 1878, one of the richest men in Germany, Count Henckel-Donnersmarck, begged Bleichröder, reputedly the richest man in Germany, to intercede with the government on his behalf. Donnersmarck thought the government the best potential buyer for some land he had bought six years earlier in Berlin's governmental quarter. Buyers were hard to find, even though he was prepared to sell at 30 percent below his purchase price. "I am at your disposition for reciprocal services [*Gegendienste*]." Bleichröder duly intervened with Bismarck and with the commerce minister. There were many uses to Bleichröder's intimacy with Bismarck.[11]

Consider finally as one example among many, the case of Count Paul von Hatzfeldt, whose great talents led Bismarck to call him the best horse in his stable. Scion of an ancient family and son of the Countess Hatzfeldt, who as Lassalle's friend had imbibed some socialist ideas but not bequeathed them, Paul turned to speculation with a vengeance. From the battlefield in France he wrote to his wife that Germans are not as corrupt as Frenchmen, but "at the same time I must say that I should like to earn some money in some honest manner, and I am racking my brains to think of some way to do so. All one has to do is to get a good idea or to discover some good investment." [12] Hatzfeldt finally stumbled on yet another method: all one needed was a friendly banker. Between 1871 and 1873 Bleichröder placed Hatzfeldt on the board of two newly created companies; by these and other means he helped Hatzfeldt to a profit of about 100,000 talers in three years. But Hatzfeldt wanted more, and his letters to Bleichröder constitute a record of imaginative, mounting greed—a perfect symptom of the age. "Would it not be possible for me to try to get a railroad concession? You probably have many such projects before you and you could recommend one or the other of these. I would also count on your advice concerning the ways and means to go ahead with the railroad. I fail to see why I could not succeed as well as Mr. von Kardorf [*sic*] in this kind of enterprise, in which one can always anticipate a considerable advantage." [13] Wilhelm von Kardorff was a highly respected conservative politician who, as an associate of Bleichröder's, had participated in some important promotions. His mounting indebtedness was known to few people; Bleichröder, however, had to perform various salvaging operations.

Hatzfeldt did not get his railroad. Perhaps this saved his diplomatic career: excessive involvement in the promotional frenzy of the *Gründerjahre* would probably have hobbled it. As it is, that career had to over-

[10] Count Pückler to Bleichröder, Sept. 2, 1876, Bleichröder Archive.

[11] Henckel-Donnersmarck to Bleichröder, Oct. 9 and 28, 1878, Bleichröder Archive.

[12] *The Hatzfeldt Letters. Letters of Count Paul Hatzfeldt to his Wife, Written from the Head-Quarters of the King of Prussia 1870–1871*, transl. from the French by J. L. Bashford (London, 1905), p. 282.

[13] Hatzfeldt to Bleichröder, Feb. 9, 1872, Bleichröder Archive.

come widespread gossip about his extravagant debts and his marital irregularities—and one might note in passing that the popular mind tended to link the two as twin failings of frivolous men. Hatzfeldt's debts, however, were but a particularly flagrant and highly publicized example of a common affliction among his fellow nobles.[14] Many of them suffered from the same combination of greed and indebtedness. The simple truth is that money had emerged as a central, though still unacknowledged, concern of Bismarck's contemporaries.

The novels of Theodor Fontane bear witness to this change in attitude. In his *Stechlin,* the old Junker muses that money is indeed the worst of all evils and that "men are in all things mendacious and dishonest, in money matters, too, and almost more than in matters of morals." The son, contemplating various injunctions about whom he, as a nobleman of the Mark Brandenburg, should marry and about how "money debases," thinks to himself, "But I know all this. As long as it is a great deal of money— then it can even be a Chinese woman. In the Mark, everything is a question of money because there is none around—money sanctifies person or cause."[15] In time, money sanctified even Jewish heiresses, as witness Bismarck's delicate remark about the desirability of Christian stallions breeding with Jewish mares, because, as he put it, "The money has to get back into circulation and [the crossbreeding] does not produce a bad race."[16]

Fontane also drew a memorable picture of middle-class hypocrisy. It was one of the paradoxes of German social history that as the Junkers became more realistic in their assessment of money, some of the bourgeoisie forsook their earlier realism, their pride in middle-class appreciation of

[14] And fellow diplomats. Count Harry von Arnim was deeply involved in stock market speculations at the very time when he was fighting for his political survival in the early 1870's. Bismarck suspected Arnim of delaying important negotiations with the French government in order to complete some market operations. Arnim's secretary at the Embassy, Friedrich von Holstein, also showed a lively interest in financial operations. Details will appear in a forthcoming work on Gerson Bleichröder.

[15] Theodor Fontane, *Der Stechlin* (Berlin, 1905), pp. 232 and 208. In Spielhagen's *Sturmflut,* some crafty promoters try to lure a count, heavily in debt, into the shadowy world of promotion. At different stages of submission, the count exclaims: "No, if I am to join the promoters, then it cannot be for a bagatelle. Then I want the coup to be a capital coup which will compensate me for the pangs of conscience that I will feel for having squarely violated the traditions of my family—a coup that will secure my future for all time." When he utters a last gasp of moral hesitation about people, especially ordinary people, getting rich fast, his tempter replies: "On the contrary, this should prove encouraging. If people without names, without connections, without inherited wealth can bring it so far in such a short time . . . what remains unattainable for you gentlemen who, unlike them, have the immeasurable advantages of birth, connections, patronage, an inherited estate —provided that you liberate yourselves from certain prejudices, of course, very honorable prejudices, and seize your chance with energy and relish, as they do." *Sturmflut, op. cit.,* pp. 202 and 219.

[16] Quoted in Otto Jöhlinger, *Bismarck und die Juden* (Berlin, 1921), p. 27.

money as exemplified by thrift, sobriety, and hard work, and began to affect disdain for money.[17] Fontane's Frau Jenny Treibel protests *ad nauseam:* "everything is worthless [*nichtig*]; but the most worthless thing is what all the world so greedily presses for: tangible possessions, property, gold . . . I for one stick to the ideal and will never renounce it." Her old suitor, whom she had abandoned for a man of means, saw through the pretense: "She is a dangerous person and the more dangerous because she does not know it herself and sincerely imagines she has a tender heart, and above all a heart 'for the higher things.' But she has a heart only for the tangible, for everything that is substantial and bears interest. . . . They all constantly liberalize and sentimentalize, but that is all farce: when the time comes for showing one's true colors, then the motto is: Gold is trump and nothing else." [18]

Money became scarce after the great crash of 1873. The stock market dropped precipitously, as many of the new businesses ran into trouble or failed altogether. Most of the original promoters had reaped their benefits; the public, its greed aroused, discovered that what had started out as the lure of participatory profiteering quickly turned into the disaster of participatory bankruptcy. Gone was the dream of acquiring instant wealth; gone, too, was the speculative fever. The great boom turned into an unprecedented depression and Germany's laissez-faire phase—of a few years' standing—was virtually at an end.[19] The actual crisis was serious; the effort at explanation and expiation was worse. The nation had suffered a shock which far from inspiring efforts at reform or reappraisal led to bouts of indiscriminate breast-beating, to mendacious and divisive accusations, to still greater obfuscation and suspicion.

The Junkers reacted with predictable peevishness. The crash had vindicated their prejudices, though not their actions. They blamed others, Bismarck included, for their misfortunes. Capitalism was evil and un-German. To protect themselves in the face of mounting economic difficulties, the Junkers now turned from private initiative to the ruthless exploitation of their collective political power. With Bismarck's encouragement, the upper classes united to demand material help and satisfaction from the state. By the end of the 1870's, an unacknowledged materialism pervaded the political realm, and the gap between professed ideals and actual practice widened—covered by still greater hypocrisy. By the end of

[17] On the earlier realism, see one of the few studies on attitudes toward money that has appeared: Hans-Richard Altenhein, "Geld und Geldeswert. Über die Selbstdarstellung des Bürgertums in der Literatur des 18. Jahrhunderts," in *das werck der bucher. Von der Wirksamkeit des Buches in Vergangenheit and Gegenwart*, Festschrift for Horst Kliemann, ed. Fritz Hodgeige (Freiburg, 1956), pp. 201–13.

[18] Theodor Fontane, *Frau Jenny Treibel* (Berlin, 1905), pp. 32, 96.

[19] We now have three important studies that deal with the place of the depression in German development: Helmut Böhme, *Deutschlands Weg zur Grossmacht. Studien zum Verhältnis von Wirtschaft und Staat während der Reichsgründszeit 1848–1881* (Cologne, 1966); Hans Rosenberg, *Grosse Depression und Bismarckzeit. Wirtschaftsablauf, Gesellschaft und Politik in Mitteleuropa* (Berlin, 1967); Hans-Ulrich Wehler, *Bismarck und der Imperialismus* (Cologne, 1969).

the decade also, conservatism acquired a cramped, repressive character, as embodied in the Puttkamer regime of the next decade.

Men quickly translated the crash into a political and moral indictment of the whole society. Corruption became the common charge of the day —and one to which Germans were perhaps peculiarly sensitive. Eduard Lasker, Germany's foremost liberal parliamentarian and a Jew, was the first to allege collusion between high public servants—including a protégé of Bismarck's—and the so-called promoters. It was assumed that Lasker had meant to strike a blow against the conservatives, and the latter quickly retaliated with a torrent of abuse. They unmasked what they dubbed the promoters' swindle and laid it at liberal doors: liberalism invited corruption, and liberals indulged in it. For years, the charge of corruption remained a conservative monopoly. Nor did the conservatives hesitate to malign Bismarck—in fact, they rejoiced at having found a popular stick with which to beat the renegade Junker. In some celebrated articles of 1875, the *Kreuzzeitung* blamed Bismarck for the depression, because—according to this allegation—he had surrendered the direction of the German economy to his liberal colleagues and to his Jewish banker, from whom he derived vast gains. Bismarck denounced "those most shameless and most mendacious calumnies" but discovered that his erstwhile Pomeranian neighbors—"The most esteemed and most influential men of the Protestant population"—rushed not to his, but to his traducers' defense.[20]

What the elite began, subterranean literati kept alive. The rottenness of the system, the conspiracy behind the system, the horrendous illicit profits made possible by the system: these were the stock-in-trade of pamphleteers and agitators. The closing words of one of these indictments conveys the flavor of all of them: "As long as Prince Bismarck remains the single, powerful idol, the German nation will be sacrificed to the Reich, the Reich will be sacrificed to the Chancellor, and the Chancellor —belongs to the Jews and the *Gründer*. Hence there is but *one* political order of the day for us: remove the present system and its defender."[21] Just as the promoters had played on people's naive confidence, so these writers played on their latent paranoia. People had been lured to believe in the feasibility of quick, certain profits and now grasped at conspiratorial theories that explained why they had fallen for promises that never materialized.

But the early 1870's, the *Gründerzeit,* proved to be more than a financial and moral shock. It was a cultural disaster as well. The rise of a plutocracy set standards of dazzling tastelessness that combined maximum expenditure with minimal artistic integrity. In this realm, too, uncertainty

[20] Siegfried von Kardorff, *Wilhelm von Kardorff. Ein nationaler Parlamentarier im Zeitalter Bismarcks und Wilhelms II., 1828–1907* (Berlin, 1936), p. 100; Dr. H. Ritter von Poschinger, *Fürst Bismarck und die Parlamentarier,* II, 1847–1879 (Breslau, 1895), 202.

[21] Dr. Rudolph Meyer, *Politische Gründer und die Corruption in Deutschland* (Leipzig, 1877), p. 204.

prevailed, disguised by garish ostentation. No wonder Nietzsche condemned the absence of all style: elegance consisted in collecting ill-fitting, expensive creations of the past or of aping them in the present. Even the great artists were touched by the confusion of the age. Richard Wagner was a genius—and a superb promoter. His Bayreuth shrine of 1876 was a monument to the promotional spirit. Magnificently mercenary, he could create the religious spirituality of a *Parsifal* and utter fashionable laments about the materialism of modernity. He was the German anti-materialist materialist *par excellence.* A popular painter of the day, Hans von Marées, once wrote to a friend, "Do you know what I need? The fist of a Rubens and the speculative spirit of a Strousberg," and the linkage of Rubens and Strousberg epitomized something of the cultural climate of the age.[22]

The *Gründerjahre* held up a distorted mirror to a society that had but a blurred vision of its physiognomy. Self-discovery is rarely an undivided pleasure; self-discovery the day after is bound to be painful and misleading. Endless and exaggerated laments about Germany's moral collapse appeared and paved the way for the creation of a new culprit.

The sudden rise and widespread acceptance of a new, virulent anti-Semitism must be seen as a psychological consequence of the great boom-and-bust experience. Aristocratic consciences had been aroused by the discovery that the lure of wealth had drawn their own class into the world of speculation. They too had contributed to the nation's corruption —and some of them experienced stirrings of unease and guilt. To deviate from one's moral code successfully, without being caught, is a very different experience from violating one's code and ending up in failure and public reprobation. Protestant conservatives, moreover, were uneasy about the *Kulturkampf,* about what they regarded as Bismarck's attack on a Christian religion in what once had been a Christian state—though Bismarck's intentions had been quite different. That transgression also ended in failure, and failure often quickens conscience. Is it an accident that these misgivings and stirrings of guilt coincided with the rise of anti-Semitism? The disaster of 1873 would appear less wounding if it could be charged to the machinations of a foreign agent. The cry went up that the Jew tempted and corrupted, that the Jew lured Germans away from their ancient code of virtue. Anti-Semitism had been waning in mid-century; after 1873, it burgeoned in unprecedented fashion. In 1875, the *Kreuzzeitung* indicted imperial politics as *"Judenpolitik,"* insisting that all policies were being conducted by and for Jews. Two years later, people complained about "Jewish domination [*Judenherrschaft*]." [23] Anti-Semitism now became a doctrine that court chaplains could dispense to the elite as well as to the masses. It constituted an avowal of German idealism; it became a means to regain a good conscience.

[22] Richard Hamann and Jost Hermand, *Gründerzeit* ("Deutsche Kunst und Kulturvon der Gründerzeit bis zum Expressionismus," I, Berlin, 1965), p. 46.
[23] *Kreuzzeitung,* June 29, 1875; Dr. Rudolph Meyer, *Politische Gründer,* p. 111.

The scapegoat theory of anti-Semitism is never more than a partial and unsatisfactory interpretation, but in this instance it does seem as if the Jew was made to carry dimly perceived Christian guilt, that the upper classes were vulnerable to the rantings of rabble-rousers because anti-Semitism helped to restore their self-esteem. Was this experience an anticipation of later charges that an undefeated, uncorrupted Germany had been stabbed in the back? All of this is hard to document and easy to exaggerate, but the paranoid underworld of politics in an age of affluence and cultural unease cannot be overlooked.

The pillars of German society were not as strong or as solid as had once been assumed. What Bismarck had sought to save at the visible top of the political system, the spread of capitalism undermined at the largely invisible substratum. The adjustment of the upper classes to sudden and profound change was painful—the more so, perhaps, for being largely disguised. Junkers and *Bürgertum* lacked a certain kind of self-assurance: the Junkers because their position required them simultaneously to despise and acquire the fruits of capitalism, the middle classes because, challenged from below, they protected these same fruits by accepting the anachronistic and politically emasculating domination of an older caste. Capitalism booming created problems; capitalism in a state of protracted crisis created still worse problems. After 1873, the depression shook the economic self-confidence of many Germans and the spectres of corruption and Jew-conspiracy came to trouble anxious people.

The political realm, as we shall see, did not provide the stability, leadership or confidence that the society needed. Quite the contrary. Bismarck sought to handle the political crises of the new nation by making himself the principal arbiter of the country. Here, too, self-reliance and self-governance were gradually corrupted and demeaned—though it is important to remember that this process of political enfeeblement had begun much earlier and had been deeply affected by the outcome of the constitutional struggle of the 1860's. In part, Bismarck became more authoritarian because his opponents were so weak; they grew weaker, as he grew stronger. In the 1860's, he had said that it would be enough to put Germany in the saddle; she would know how to ride. In the 1870's, he thought that it would be best if he stayed in command; Germans turned out to be poor riders, after all. His long and increasingly autocratic rule strengthened existing tendencies to political passivity and submission.

The achievements of 1871 had been extraordinary, and an age that glorified heroes rather than analyzed anonymous social and economic forces attributed them to Bismarck's genius. He had forged institutions that would promote Germany's power by providing for common commercial and foreign policies and that would guarantee Germany's survival by a common military establishment under thinly disguised Prussian hegemony. By creating a national parliament, Bismarck had inserted democratic and popular elements into the structure of the Reich without materially weakening the preceding monarchical-conservative order. By making concessions to modernity, the old order prolonged its life. The new Reich facilitated the immense expansion of material power—though the attendant social transformation undermined Bismarck's political structure. Bismarck was slow to appreciate the danger from that quarter. He was more attuned to foreign dangers. For the great Bismarck was at home abroad, and estranged at home.

He devoted his best efforts to shielding Germany from foreign wars. His greatest accomplishment after 1871 was his assimilation of Germany into the European state system; he persuaded a suspicious Europe that Germany had become a satiated power—and by the time Europe fully believed him, he was dismissed from office, and Germany ceased being satiated.

In the early 1870's, the German Empire was in the historic position of a new nation—even if most Germans, bound by older dynastic loyalties, were unaware of it. It was a time when traditions needed to be founded, patterns set, loyalties formed. A partnership of citizenry and government in the affairs of state needed to be created. In certain tangible concerns —the establishment of a national bank or of a national railroad system —the Reich did make significant progress, and for a few years Bismarck seemed to have overwhelming popular support behind him. But the dominant note was conflict, not consolidation. In his memoirs, Bismarck acknowledged that fact. He entitled the three chapters dealing with the domestic history of the Second Empire: *"Kulturkampf,"* "Break with the Conservatives," "Intrigues." In retirement, he remembered the antagonisms, not the achievements. In retirement, as in power, he thought himself the victim of malevolent rivals, of indolent and stupid subordinates, of scheming politicans, and of ungrateful monarchs. Bismarck was great in everything—self-pity included.

All societies built on rank and inequalities are riddled with intrigue and conspiracy—the greater the consciousness of hierarchy, the stronger the sense of intrigue. Imperial Germany probably exceeded the contemporary norm. Did the newness and brittleness of the Empire, its peculiar political structure, its strident tone and hidden fears, its imbalance between political and economic power, breed a special combination of insecurity, sycophancy, and intrigue? The diaries and letters of the period suggest this, and an amateur psychologist might wonder whether the sexually repressive and largely hypocritical character of the society might not have contributed to its harsh undertone, which all too often was disguised by an official veneer of painful sentimentality. Certainly Bismarck contributed to it: his own contemptuous distrust of others and his often intolerant authoritarianism injected a special kind of poison into Germany's public life.

It was undoubtedly deleterious for the new nation to have its politics dominated by one man. Bismarck had defined his constitutional role in this fashion, and his temperament would scarcely have tolerated any other role. But he found it difficult and unrewarding. It was one thing to improvise the startling victories of the sixties; it was quite another to settle down to institutionalize these gains in the seventies. "I am bored," he complained. "The great deeds are done." [24]

His boredom and his health became matters of national importance, and for most of the 1870's his health was terrible. His ills made him more prone to anger, and anger aggravated his ills. As an admirer, Lord Odo Russell, wrote in 1872: "Bismarck, whose nervous system is shattered by overwork and nocturnal beer and pipe orgies, and who can no longer stand contradiction without getting into a passion, frets and fumes at what he calls the ingratitude of a Sovereign who owes him everything —political power,—military glory and an invincible Empire, and whose confidence ought therefore to be boundless." [25] In his psychosomatic maladies—and perhaps only in them—Bismarck was thoroughly modern. His vicious cycle of complaints was broken intermittently by his ebullient high spirits, his charm, and the resourcefulness of his mind.

Bismarck's capacity for hatred and suspicion is justly renowned and was probably harder on his subordinates than on his foes. He could be incredibly brutal to colleagues as well as unpredictably generous. He said the most devastating things about his fellow ministers, and he vilified some of them with a coarseness that reeked of barnyards. He exaggerated the evil machinations of his putative rivals, and in his celebrated nights of sleeplessness, he endowed these hapless creatures with his own intelligence and toughness. No wonder that the next morning he feared them. But there *were* intrigues against him, even if he vastly exaggerated, for example, the dangers of feminine court conspiracies. Of his favorite target, Queen Augusta, he once said that "her intrigues border on high treason." [26] In the early 1870's, amid various storms and scandals, there was the possibility that Bismarck's rule might not last long, that he might soon be overthrown or resign.[27] In the 1880's, on the other hand, it appeared as if the Bismarck rule would be perpetuated in a Bismarck Dynasty, that there would be no end of Bismarcks. Neither prospect lent a sense of security to his subordinates.

Bismarck's entourage was not the happy little band of devoted assistants that has sometimes been depicted. There were jealousies and animosities, fear and anger, rankling the more for having to be concealed. In his selection and advancement of underlings, Bismarck appeared capricious. He disdained stupidity and rebuffed independence. He wanted intelligent

[24] Poschinger, *Fürst Bismarck und die Parlamentarier,* 1 (2nd ed., Breslau, 1894), 87.

[25] *Letters from the Berlin Embassy 1871–1874, 1880–1885,* ed. Paul Knaplund ("Annual Report of the American Historical Association for the Year 1942," 11, Washington, 1944), p. 58.

[26] *Bismarck-Erinnerungen des Staatsministers Freiherrn Lucius von Ballhausen* (Stuttgart, 1921), p. 110.

[27] *Staatssekretär Graf Herbert von Bismarck. Aus seiner politischen Privatkorrespondenz,* ed. Walter Bussmann ("Deutsche Geschichtsquellen des 19. und 20. Jahrhunderts," XLIV, Göttingen, 1964), p. 15.

servants without private judgment or ambition, well-wrought tools for his master-hands. The loyal Hatzfeldt once complained that Bismarck's appointments bore no relation to merit and that he preferred nullities.[28] Morale was low around Bismarck.

The personal character of his rule outraged many of his thoughtful contemporaries. The letters and diaries of the 1870's express again and again the fear that it was Bismarck's whim, his caprice, that governed Germany and not the counsels of statesmen of the principles of *raison d'état*. At times, observers may have mistaken inscrutable policy for caprice, but what remains is the impression of considerable unease. There were endless variations on Mommsen's celebrated judgment that Bismarck had broken Germany's moral backbone. Franz von Roggenbach, admittedly a foe, often lamented "the moral degradation" that autocratic rule produced in spineless servants.[29] In 1881, he wrote: "Nobody can deceive himself about the fact that if the elections put him at the head of a slavishly subservient majority and if the dynasty is thereby still further put in check, then the Chancellor will become more extravagant than ever in indulging his passions, his caprices, his hatreds, and his wild ambition." [30]

Bismarck came to sense the precariousness of the new nation. The particularist jealousy of the Reich extended deep into Prussian hearts—and if dominant Prussia resented the new imperial authority, why should Catholic Bavaria feel any special loyalty? The major parties constituted latent threats: the National Liberals had not yet consciously surrendered their hopes for a parliamentary regime, hopes that were anathema to Bismarck. The conservatives balked at his seeming closeness to the liberals. Nothing so embittered Bismarck in the 1870's as the sudden enmity of his own class. The Junkers' desertion, which Bismarck largely attributed to their envy of him, left him isolated, without personal friends or dependable political allies. The Junkers, scarred by the financial crash and affronted by Bismarck's liberal and Jewish associates, came to distrust him as a renegade and could not grasp that Bismarck's genius had torn him away from his provincial moorings but that that same genius had devised means to save their political fortunes. The break between the Chancellor and his natural allies illuminates the connections between the social disarray of the early 1870's and the political crisis of the new Reich.[31]

[28] Hatzfeldt to Bleichröder, Apr. 15, 1878, Bleichröder Archive.

[29] *Im Ring der Gegner Bismarcks. Denkschriften und Politischer Briefwechsel Franz von Roggenbachs mit Kaiserin Augusta und Albrecht von Stosch 1865–1896,* ed. Julius Heyderhoff ("Deutsche Geschichtsquellen des 19. Jahrhunderts," XXXV, 2nd printing, Leipzig, 1943), p. 184.

[30] *Ibid.,* p. 213.

[31] In November 1873, Lord Russell reported from Berlin: "While shooting in Silesia I met many great and small landed proprietors. They spoke freely of their hatred of Bismarck whose radical German policy and persecution of the Clergy was alienating the Prussian Aristocracy from the Throne. The Prussian Aristocracy had ever shed their best blood in the hour of danger for the House of Hohenzollern, but in the day of prosperity Bismarck used his ambitious influence to mislead their old King into treating them as enemies etc. etc. Most of them said they would not

It was one thing for Bismarck to fight Catholic priests, all of whom he suspected—to put it with Ems-like brevity—of maintaining simultaneously illicit relations with both the Pope and Queen Augusta. It was easy for him to persecute socialist leaders whom he suspected of being cousins of the Commune, hirelings of the Internationale. It took no emotional toll to break with the National Liberals in 1879 and to remove, one by one, his liberal associates of earlier years. Only the rupture with the conservatives hurt. As Bismarck put it in his memoirs, "To break existing relations with all or almost all friends and acquaintances is a hard test for the nerves of a man in his mature years." [32] His earlier, intermittent misanthropy now became his steady companion and protection. Gradually Bismarck hardened into an autocrat, convinced not so much of his own greatness or of his ability to impose his will on events, as of the pettiness and utter incompetence of his fellowmen.

After the conservatives had broken with him, where were the unshakable pillars of the state—the more needed as new enemies appeared? Or did the putative remark of Count Eulenburg, the Prussian Minister of the Interior, attest a general apprehension? "The old pillars of the government are destroyed. From now on, we have to lean on the Jews." [33]

Bismarck had seen revolution in its liberal and post-liberal guise; he feared it, not so much as the replacement of the monarchical-conservative order, but as the senseless subversion of all order. Hence his genuine fear of democratic socialism, with its revolutionary pretensions. He also manipulated that fear in order to intimidate the electorate. He was no less afraid of the Catholic politicians who would perpetuate a confessional party, under foreign influence, that could mobilize a religious minority and keep it permanently estranged from the state. As Lord Russell once put it: "Thinking himself far more infallible than the Pope he cannot tolerate two infallibles in Europe and fancies he can select and appoint the next Pontiff as he could a Prussian General, who will carry out his orders to the Catholic Clergy in Germany and elsewhere." [34]

Bismarck's response to these threats—which he exaggerated, as he exaggerated all threats—was disastrous. He launched repressive campaigns, dubbed opponents enemies of the Reich, and almost succeeded in converting them into the creatures he imagined them to be. He knew that he could no longer escape domestic difficulties by foreign adventures; instead he applied the tactics hitherto reserved for dealing with foreign nations to his relations with the different factions of the Reich. Worse, he sought to crush domestic enemies in a way that he would not even try to do with foreign foes. His various stratagems proved harder on liberals and

go to Berlin this Winter so as not to mark their disatisfaction [*sic*] with the Court and Government,—but I suspect also, to save money, for Berlin has become simply ruinous." *Letters from the Berlin Embassy*, p. 117.

[32] Otto Fürst von Bismarck, *Gedanken und Erinnerungen*, 11 (Stuttgart, 1898), 156.

[33] Dr. Rudolph Meyer, *Politische Gründer*, p. 27.

[34] *Letters from the Berlin Embassy*, p. 71.

conservatives who always struggled to find reasons to support him than on Catholics and socialists who knew unambiguously that he was their foe. His repressive policies further weakened the principles of the elements that supported the state, even as they strengthened the popular support of the so-called enemies of the state.

The reality of Bismarck's rule, then, was radically different from its appearance. Twenty years of misanthropic autocracy left German politics with a hard, brutal tone and a viciousness that exacerbated the many inherent antagonisms of the new regime. Bismarck's style was as injurious as his policies: need one recall his brutal polemics against political opponents, his systematic denigration of the organs of public life, of parliament and press? The fact that he was superbly skillful in these attacks only sharpened their impact.

Unification was followed by deep divisiveness, much of it caused by social changes beyond the control of any man or government. It is my contention, however, that Bismarck gratuitously added to this divisiveness and made more difficult the resolution of these conflicts. Far from marshalling a consensus behind the new government, far from inspiring trust and tolerance, he poisoned the atmosphere of political life. His critics charged him with promoting the moral degradation and political nonage of the German people. His own diagnosis of the German people was no more complimentary; he would have insisted, however, that he was the victim, not the cause, of these disabilities.

Perhaps we can better assess Bismarck's historic role by looking at it from another perspective. Other new nations had the inestimable fortune that their first leaders also proved to be fathers of their country: one thinks of George Washington and T. G. Masaryk. Bismarck hardly fits that category of leaders, yet his long rule at that particular juncture in his nation's history cast him in the role of a father. He did not play that role, or, at most, he played it occasionally and according to the notoriously different standards of German fatherhood. His talents would inevitably have awed his charges; his autocratic ways confirmed and strengthened their dependence and their fearful adulation of authority. Bismarck, however, should have been aware that precedents were being set, that the success and viability of 1871 depended on the transformation of subjects into citizens, and that subjects, like children, need to learn independence and self-government. Precisely when it was necessary to expand the basis of government, to recruit new talent, to legitimize new institutions, Bismarck, perhaps without realizing it, demeaned the entire political process.

It is ironic to note that Bismarck dead came to symbolize what Bismarck alive could not achieve. The monuments scattered throughout Germany in his honor were intended as mystical representations of national unity: he had become the "Ur-symbol of the nation" he had united. By their massive solidity, these monuments embodied artistic and political protests against the vapid ostentation of Wilhelmine Germany but also sought to express "an insecurity, a secret fear of the dissolution of the national community and of the loss of power because of a hapless *Welt-politik.*" [35]

William II justified all the fears that wise observers voiced about his reign. But his heritage had not been enviable. Bismarck's legacy had set strict limits to the possibilities of subsequent statesmanship—limits that William II never came even close to testing. William's pathetically unbalanced personality dramatized his political ineptness; Bismarck's greatness helped to obscure his failings. The young Bismarck, in particular, had combined an abundance of intelligence, courage, and a certain kind of romantic *Übermut* in so felicitous a fashion that even his critics were understandably awed and captivated by him. The Bismarck of subsequent decades was a curiously changed man, and it had been the Chancellor himself who had set patterns that proved impossible to cast off. It was in the early years of the Empire that a vicious tone crept into German public life, that political institutions were discredited before they had been allowed to develop, that hypocrisy and false self-assessment encouraged suspicion and xenophobic arrogance. Ralf Dahrendorf's suggestive formulation for a later period in Germany history, that Germany was governed by a "cartel of anxiety," has bearing on this period as well: the roots of that fatal anxiety reach back to the weaknesses of German political culture here discussed.[36]

The people of the new nation suffered from a variety of growing pains, all likely to induce anxiety. Adjustment to capitalism proved hard; the discrepancy between idealized self-image and actual, material behavior was difficult to ignore or explain. Frank acceptance of the values of capitalism would have both undermined the ideological pillars of Junker predominance and lent some legitimacy to the claims of the lower classes for better living conditions and some measure of equality. There was a psychological and moral crampedness in the way most Germans in that first generation of the Empire perceived the realities of the new society. Perhaps there was also something symbolic about Bismarck's hardheaded decision to try to cure Germany's ills by erecting protective walls against foreign competitors; Germans needed to be sheltered from the winds of change and from the outside world. At home, too, Bismarck sought to insulate them from the free, competitive play of political forces and arrogated to himself powers that should have been diffused. Yet, he found it harder and harder to offer leadership or to operate successfully the very regime he had himself devised. The first decades of the Empire, then, saw a political and psychological faltering that affected the growth of the new nation for decades to come.

In 1871, Bismarck had unified the German states, not the Germans. He had helped to give Europe peace, but had left his successors a distrust-

[35] Thomas Nipperdey, "Nationalidee und Nationaldenkmal in Deutschland im 19. Jahrhundert," *Historische Zeitschrift,* CCVI, No. 3 (June 1968), 582.

[36] Ralf Dahrendorf, *Society and Democracy in Germany* (New York, 1967), p. 275.

ful, agitated, anxious people who were held together by dynastic traditions, by aggressive nationalist sentiments, and by material prosperity about which they felt intermittently unsure and uneasy. He had done nothing to educate his people in the uses of power; by forging a political culture that bore traces of his own misanthropy and contempt for mankind, he had dulled them to the dangers of unbridled power. All this he bequeathed, but his exquisite skill as diplomat was not hereditary. He had forgotten, as so many statesmen before and after him, that peace, like charity, begins at home, and that power, to be enduring, must have a moral basis.

21. Disraeli and Gladstone

ROBERT BLAKE

*A selection in the first volume of this anthology sought to "bring alive"
Napoleon I. The next does the same for two considerably different "great men"
of the nineteenth century, the rival British politicians Benjamin Disraeli
(1804–1881) and William Ewart Gladstone (1809–1898). Its author, Robert
Blake, has written the most widely acclaimed biography of Disraeli. He delivered the selection which follows as the 1969 Leslie Stephen lecture at
Cambridge University. He knows Disraeli and Gladstone as well as does anyone. He resists the temptation to view Gladstone through the eyes of
Disraeli, although they detested each other. Rather than exploring their hatred,
as such, he deals with "the origins and nature of their conflicts and its consequences on the political scene." He points out that even though they led
their parties against each other for only about eight years, posterity has not
been wrong to see that their conflict of personality, political style, and policy
both personified the Victorian era and shaped much of the direction of British
politics which followed.*

*In examining their conflict and its consequences one might keep certain of
Blake's questions in mind. How, for example, did Disraeli and Gladstone differ
in their youth and its attitudes, their life styles, their marriages, their ability
to be good dinner companions, and their relations with Queen Victoria?
What brought the two men into conflict and why did it run so deep? What*

Source: Robert Blake, *Disraeli and Gladstone* (Cambridge, Eng.: Cambridge
University Press, 1969). Copyright © 1969 by Cambridge University Press. Reprinted by permission of the author and publisher.

*evidence does Blake use to show that the two rivals were leaders of the
"two nations" described by George Kitson Clark—Disraeli of "an old nation
based on the old nobility, upon the squires and upon the Established Church"
while Gladstone represented "a new nation based on commerce and industry,
and in religion mainly dissenting" (i.e. mainly Methodist rather than the
Anglican established church)? What reason does the author give for "why
there has never been another Disraeli or Gladstone at the head of the Right
and Left respectively" in British politics? Finally, to ask another one of his
questions, "how different were the actual policies of the two men, as opposed
to their political styles and public images?"*

The general election of April 1880 resulted in a crushing defeat for Disraeli and his party. On 24 April, just after Gladstone had returned in
triumph to office, Lord Granville wrote to Queen Victoria, who was
deeply distressed. He wished to calm her down with regard to the strong
language which Gladstone had used against the late Prime Minister during the election campaign.

> Lord Beaconsfield and Mr Gladstone are men of extraordinary abil-
> ity; they dislike each other more than is usual among public men.
> Of no other politician Lord Beaconsfield would have said in public,
> that his conduct was worse than those who had committed the Bul-
> garian atrocities. He has the power of saying in two words that
> which drives a person of Mr Gladstone's peculiar temperament into
> a state of great excitement.

Granville had always been on good terms with Disraeli; he was a guest
at Disraeli's first and, as it turned out, last dinner party at his new house
in Curzon Street on 10 March 1881. He was also, perhaps more than any
other Liberal minister, on really intimate terms with Gladstone himself.
He actually persuaded him on one occasion to attend the Derby. So his
verdict is not to be lightly set aside.

There is no point in pretending that the two old statesmen did not de-
test each other. They did. Gladstone, it is true, denied that he actually
hated Disraeli, and said that he did not believe Disraeli hated him. It is
to the credit of Gladstone's heart, rather than his head, that he should
have been under this delusion. Lord Acton who knew Gladstone very well
implored him after Disraeli's death not to propose a public monument to a
man whom, he said, Gladstone regarded as 'the worst and most immoral
Minister since Castlereagh'. If Gladstone did not in his own interpretation
actually hate Disraeli, he certainly regarded him as essentially a force for
evil in public life. 'In past times', he wrote at the end of his life, long
after Disraeli's death, 'the Tory party had principles by which it would and
did stand for bad and for good. All this Dizzy destroyed.' And when Disraeli died, having given instructions in his will to be buried quietly at
Hughenden beside his wife, Gladstone, who had offered Westminster
Abbey to the executors, wrote in his diary: 'As he lived, so he died—all
display without reality or genuineness.' He could not believe that this was

anything but a last theatrical gesture of fraudulent false modesty. It was for Gladstone, the most magnanimous of men, a quite exceptionally unmagnanimous remark.

But Gladstone's language about Disraeli was more moderate than Disraeli's about Gladstone. Just before his death Disraeli had been engaged on an unfinished novel designed to hold up his great rival to odium and ridicule. There is something wonderfully disreputable, undignified and yet engaging about this curious fragment. It is as if Sir Winston Churchill instead of writing his memoirs in 1945 had started a latter day version of *Savrola* in which he lampooned Lord Attlee. The hero, if that is the right word, is Joseph Toplady Falconet. The Christian names are not chosen accidentally: Joseph alludes to Joseph Surface, the immortal hypocrite in the *School for Scandal,* and Toplady was an intolerantly vituperative divine who detested Wesley and—more to the point—wrote 'Rock of Ages' which Gladstone in 1839 had translated into Latin.

Joseph Toplady Falconet, son of Mr. Wilberforce Falconet, a wealthy Evangelical merchant, is 'arrogant and peremptory'; as a boy 'scarcely ever known to smile . . . with a complete deficiency in the sense of humour'; a prodigy of Eton and Oxford where he was 'the unrivalled orator of its mimic parliament'; 'his chief peculiarity was his disputatious temper and the flow of language which even as a child was ever at his command to express his arguments'. He was 'essentially a prig and among prigs there is a free-masonry which never fails. All the prigs spoke of him as the coming man.' Disraeli's opinion of Gladstone earlier had been even worse. Perhaps the nadir of their personal relations was reached during the eastern crisis of 1876–8. In October 1876 he wrote to Lord Derby:

> Posterity will do justice to that unprincipled maniac Gladstone— extraordinary mixture of envy, vindictiveness, hypocrisy and superstition; and with one commanding characteristic—whether Prime Minister, or Leader of the Opposition, whether preaching, praying, speechifying or scribbling—never a gentleman.

Disraeli oscillated between Queen Victoria's view that Gladstone was insane and the more common Tory theory that he was a monstrous hypocrite. On the whole he plumped for the latter—'a ceaseless Tartuffe from the beginning', as he wrote to Lady Bradford, and in his letters Mrs Gladstone not infrequently figures as 'Mrs T.' for short.

Too often biographers of these two extraordinary men have felt it their duty to see their hero's enemy through their hero's eyes, and to denigrate or at least sneer at the opponent almost as if the battle was still raging when they wrote. This is absurd over seventy years after Gladstone's death, and he after all outlived Disraeli by seventeen years. Sir Philip Magnus in his excellent life of Gladstone was one of the first to break this custom. He is indeed generous to Disraeli. We can, surely, today give up archaic partisanship and consider instead the origins and nature of their conflict, and its consequences on the political scene.

Their youthful years could scarcely have been in sharper contrast. Disraeli, unlike Gladstone, did not keep a diary, except for a short period in the early 1830s. But *Vivian Grey* is avowedly and sufficiently autobiographical for our purpose. To Vivian at eighteen surveying the possibilities of his career 'The idea of Oxford was an insult.'

> . . . THE BAR—pooh! law and bad jokes till we are forty; and then with the most brilliant success the prospect of gout and a coronet . . . THE SERVICES in war time are fit only for desperadoes (and that truly am I); but in peace are fit only for fools. THE CHURCH is more rational . . . I should certainly like to act Wolsey; but the thousand and one chances against me! . . .

What Vivian Grey decided to do is irrelevant. What Disraeli did, as we all know, was to entangle himself in a self-woven web of financial, journalistic, and speculative intrigue which left him with a heavy load of debt and ill repute while he was still twenty-one, but in no way diminished that restless ambition, that determination to get to the top of the greasy pole, which dominated all his dreams.

Gladstone for the whole of his life thought about the Church, though scarcely in the spirit of Disraeli's fictitious hero. At Oxford he was convinced that to take Holy Orders was his real career. He was dissuaded partly by his father, partly by the opportune offer of a pocket borough by the Duke of Newcastle, whose son was one of his closest Christ Church friends. To the end of his days he regarded politics as subordinate to religion. No purely political biography of him, however valuable it may be as history, can ever adequately portray him as a man.

His diary is in the course of publication. It is a most remarkable document, and when the whole of it is in print there will be the materials for a reassessment of his entire career. The volumes already out covering 1825–39, and admirably edited by Professor Michael Foot, are in themselves enough to convince anyone of his extraordinary character: the deep obsession with his own sinfulness; the agonizing self-examination; the determination to render account to God for every moment of his life; the guilty consciousness of worldly—or as he put it 'carnal'—backsliding. One of the most revealing passages about his time at Oxford is the entry written on 24 March 1830. The day before, he noted ' . . . had to go to Veysie [one of the Censors, i.e. disciplinary Officers of Christ Church] about a most disgraceful disturbance in Chapel last night'. Evidently the disturbers took umbrage and what followed made Gladstone abandon the normal telegraphese in which he wrote.

> Last night between twelve and one I was beaten by a party of men in my rooms. Here I have great reason to be thankful to that God whose mercies fail not. And this for two reasons.
>
> 1. Because this incident must tend to the mortification of my pride by God's grace; if at least any occurrence which does not border on the miraculous can . . . I hardly know what to think of my own conduct myself. It is no disgrace to be

beaten, for Christ was buffeted and smitten—but though calm reasoning assures me of this my habit of mind, my vicious corrupt nature asserts the contrary—may it be defeated.

2. Because here I have to some extent an opportunity of exercising the duty of forgiveness. So long a time has elapsed since anyone has in any way injured me that I have feared, in repeating the words 'forgive us our trespasses as we forgive them that trespass against us' that I really had no practical knowledge of the nature and spirit of the words I was uttering.

What was it which convinced Gladstone that he was, in his own words on his twentieth birthday, 'the chief of sinners'? We shall probably never know. It may have been connected as Professor Foot suggests, with the impossibly high ideals which he absorbed from his much older sister Anne who died when he was nineteen. It may have been what he called, in an entry written on his twenty-second birthday, 'the blackness of my natural (and vigorous) tendencies'. There are many possibilities. What is certain is that self-mortification, the consciousness of sin, the desire to make amends by bringing the highest moral principles into the political career which he always regarded as second best to the Church were among his principal springs of action. It is an easy step from the particular to the general. If Gladstone more than most statesmen was ready to see the sin of pride in his fellow countrymen, to regard a certain degree of self-mortification as being good for them too, we need not be surprised that he was the very opposite to a jingo, that he found himself ill at ease in a cabinet headed by Palmerston, and that Disraeli's 'alien patriotism' aroused his deepest disapproval.

Disraeli from his youth onwards was a much less complicated character than Gladstone. His life, his affairs, his manoeuvres were of course highly complicated, but his objective was simple, his reactions predictable. His aim was above all to *be* someone, to get to the top. What he did when he was there would be settled by circumstances, pressures, events. If one is to seek the causes of his driving ambition, it is possible to suggest two, though it is impossible to be completely certain of either. One was his sense of being an outsider, an alien, a person who did not belong. He never said this, but no one can read the autobiographical passages of his novels, particulary *Contarini Fleming,* without a strong conviction that he felt it and that he was determined to conquer the great world partly because he knew that he could never belong to it. The other is his unhappy relationship with his mother who regarded him as 'a clever boy but no genius' and who never gave him the devotion which his intensely egotistical nature craved. Again and again through Disraeli's sophistication, his poses, his play-acting one sees the little boy crying out 'look at me' to an unreceptive sceptical mama 'troubled about many things', not unkind or hostile, but not prepared to adore.

Let us trace the way the careers of the two men entwined with one another. Disraeli, as everyone knows, began his many unsuccessful efforts to storm his way into parliament, as a Radical. Gladstone did not have to storm at all. Macaulay later dubbed him 'the rising hope of those stern and unbending Tories'. Gladstone was five years younger than Disraeli and got into Parliament five years earlier—in 1832 when he was just under twenty-three. Their ways did not cross much in those days for they dwelt in totally different worlds: Disraeli moved in the raffish salons of aristocratic bohemia and his time was spent in avoiding his creditors and conducting a prolonged liaison with a married woman, varied at intervals by attempts to get into the House and by the production of literary works which at best never quite came off and at worst were disastrous (his good ones nearly all belong to a later date); Gladstone was deeply involved in theological reading, improving his debating power and searching though not with immediate success for a suitable wife. Sir Philip Magnus quotes two symbolic extracts from their diaries. On 1 September 1833 Disraeli wrote: 'I have spent the whole of this year in uninterrupted lounging and pleasure.' On 29 December 1832 Gladstone wrote: 'I have now familiarized myself with maxims encouraging a degree of intercourse with society, perhaps attended with much risk, nay perhaps only rendered acceptable to my understanding by cowardice and a carnal heart.'

The first recorded occasion on which they actually met was at a dinner party given by Lord Lyndhurst, the Tory Lord Chancellor on 17 January 1835. Gladstone was a junior Lord of the Treasury in Peel's government. Disraeli had given up Radicalism and was a sort of private secretary to Lyndhurst—one of the oddest and least reputable figures to have been keeper of the King's conscience. Disraeli was still without a seat. Gladstone made no note of Disraeli's presence in his diary though years later he declared that he recalled with amazement the foppery of his clothes. Disraeli noted in a letter to his sister that 'young Gladstone' was present. The dinner, he continued, was 'rather dull but we had a swan very white and tender and stuffed with truffles, the best company there'. Two years later he got into the House. Whether Gladstone was present at the fiasco of his maiden speech we do not know. When the Conservatives returned to power in 1841 Gladstone was naturally given office, and soon afterwards entered the Cabinet. Disraeli, not surprisingly, and despite his own importunacy, was left out. He never forgave Peel but there is nothing to show that he and Gladstone had any particular relationship hostile or otherwise at this time. Disraeli did express in a letter to his sister after Gladstone's resignation speech over the Maynooth grant early in 1845 his belief that Gladstone had no future in politics. But many others also found Gladstone's behaviour incomprehensible on this occasion. So far there had been no conflict between the two men.

Yet by summer 1852, seven years later, it is clear that Gladstone had come to entertain profound personal mistrust for Disraeli. Much had happened in politics by then. Gladstone would still have called himself a Conservative but he belonged to the minority of the party who had followed Peel over the repeal of the Corn Laws, and his group was more hostile to the majority of the Conservatives under Derby and Disraeli than to the Whigs. Moreover, Disraeli was Chancellor of the Exchequer, and Gladstone, ever since his pupillage at the Board of Trade when Peel was Prime Minister, had regarded himself as in a peculiar degree the guardian of Peelite fiscal orthodoxy. On 30 July we learn that he regards every speech of Disraeli that summer on finance as being 'more quackish in its flavour than its predecessor.' And for the first time we find that he is entertaining personal feelings of hostility not explicable simply by differences in political outlook. He complains on 5 August to Lord Aberdeen of the government's 'shifting and shuffling' on the Catholic question due, he says, 'partly to the (surely not unexpected) unscrupulousness and second motives of Disraeli, at once the necessity of Lord Derby and his curse'.

Clearly by then Gladstone had a strong personal mistrust of Disraeli's character. There is nothing to show that it was as yet reciprocated. Rather the contrary. As late as September Disraeli was commending his protégé, Lord Henry Lennox, for using his vote in favour of Gladstone at the Oxford University election earlier that year. But he can have had no doubt where he stood with Gladstone two months later. For in December there was a confrontation—and a dramatic one. Disraeli had made the winding-up speech, or so he supposed, in defence of his highly vulnerable budget. He had engaged in personal remarks against his opponents, and, although he had much provocation, he had gone beyond the normal limits tolerated by the House. Gladstone had not been personally attacked but he was indignant for those who had been. When Disraeli sat down most members expected a division. But Gladstone amidst catcalls, hoots and screams—the House of Commons has not changed!—leapt to his feet, and, first delivering a grave personal rebuke to Disraeli, proceeded to cut the budget to pieces. When the division was taken the government was defeated, and Disraeli was to be in opposition for the next five years.

Of course many people mistrusted Disraeli. There was something highly provocative about him, a brazenness, a sarcastic turn of phrase, an insolence, a readiness to discard inconvenient pledges, and a refusal to cover up that process with the normal politician's linguistic cotton wool; all of these enraged his opponents beyond measure—and no wonder. Then there was a particular resentment felt by the followers of Peel. Although Peel really was open to the charge of betrayal—perhaps just because he was—his friends particularly resented the onslaughts upon him; and no one delivered these more tellingly than Disraeli and no one was more loyal to Peel than Gladstone.

But in Gladstone's case there may have been another cause for hostility to Disraeli. Like many great statesmen and almost all successful politicians Gladstone was a master of oratory, only really at home when clothing his thoughts in the spoken word. As Lytton Strachey puts it, 'Speech was the fibre of his being.' Yet at a crucial moment in his own career and in the affairs of the nation this was just what was denied to him. For, although he returned to the Cabinet in 1845 and was Colonial Secretary for six months during the great Corn Law crisis he failed to get himself re-elected to Parliament. So he could not intervene in debate, and come to the aid of his beloved chief. He had to sit in the Strangers' Gallery and listen in silence to Disraeli's brilliant, cruel, and very funny attacks upon Peel. The situation was the more galling because Peel was no good at answering back himself. For whatever reason he simply could not cope with this sort of thing. Years later, after Disraeli's death, Morley asked Gladstone whether Disraeli's famous philippics were really as effective as people said. 'Mr. G.,' he recorded, 'said Disraeli's performances against Peel were quite as wonderful as report makes them. Peel altogether helpless in reply. Dealt with them with a kind of "righteous dullness".' Is it possible that Gladstone's real hostility to Disraeli first stemmed from a sense of frustration at his own forced inability to answer on behalf of a chief to whom he was devoted?

However that may be, there is no doubt about the animosity felt on both sides after the budget of 1852. It was not made any less by the fact that Gladstone succeeded Disraeli as Chancellor of the Exchequer. Almost at once they had a row about two things: first about the Chancellor's robe which Disraeli, believing it to have been Pitt's, was determined to keep: secondly, about the payment for the furniture at 11 Downing Street. It is enough to say that on the robe Disraeli was in the wrong though he got away with it—literally; and it is on exhibit at Hughenden to this day —while on the furniture he seems to have been in the right. The correspondence, which is entertaining, has been published in full. Its tone can be gauged by Disraeli's last letter which was written in the third person and ended: 'As Mr Gladstone seems to be in some perplexity on the subject Mr Disraeli recommends him to consult Sir Charles Wood who is a man of the world.'

This last expression, 'man of the world', brings me to a point about their relations which has sometimes been overlooked. Disraeli consciously prided himself on being a man of the world, sophisticated, unshockable, moving easily in society. In some respects he was a romantic in politics, but in ideas rather than behaviour. For example, he adopted Lord Chesterfield's advice to his wretched son and scarcely ever laughed in public. It was part of the Byronic pose to be both romantic and cynical at the same time. A man's heart could seethe with poetry, drama, rhetoric, but his manners could be cool and urbane, his tone at a dinner party witty and sardonic, his general air that of a somewhat bored man of fashion. This was very much Disraeli's style, and a great deal of his effectiveness in the House of Commons was that of a sensible cool-headed man of affairs, not fussing too much about high moral issues which were a matter for the middle classes, but putting a reasonable case to other reasonable men of affairs. Disraeli and Gladstone both came in one sense from the middle class, though Gladstone was far richer and had a typical upper-class education at Eton and Christ Church, whereas Disraeli went to obscure schools and no university at all. On the face of things, with his marriage into the

Whig aristocracy Gladstone ought to have been socially above Disraeli. True, he always spoke, even as Peel had, with a provincial accent, whereas Disraeli talked in the Queen's English (although in a rather curious way: for example he always said 'parl-i-a-ment', 'bus-i-ness', etc.). But the social nuances of a bygone era are not easy to distinguish. The fourteenth Earl of Derby, the Prime Minister, spoke impeccable English. His son, the fifteenth Earl and Foreign Secretary, spoke, if Disraeli is to be believed, 'in a sort of Lancashire patois'.

In fact Disraeli thought of himself as an aristocrat. He persuaded himself that the Jews were the most 'aristocratic of races'—whatever that expression means; and that he belonged to its most aristocratic branch. His facts were very dubious but this does not affect the genuineness of his belief. Hence some of those curious Disraeliana—or curious as from the son of a middle-class Jewish *litérateur*. 'What can one expect', he wrote once when in opposition, 'with a government that does not move in Society.' Or his comment on his Home Secretary, Sir Richard Cross, who had explained to the House that the Prime Minister was absent 'on account of the *state of his health!!!* What language. This comes of giving high office to a middle class man.' Thus then we have Disraeli a self-promoted member of the upper class, friend of the Queen, repository of her family secrets, consulted on royal marriages, mediator in the great row between Lord Randolph Churchill and the Prince of Wales, and from 1874 to 1880 at the apex of society as well as politics. The social world may have thought him odd but it accepted him.

Now Gladstone for all his background was never 'a man of the world' in Disraeli's sense. And his marriage actually enhanced this unworldliness, for Mrs Gladstone was in some ways socially naïve, though not of course to anything like the degree of Mrs Disraeli. Gladstone's attitude should not be misunderstood. He was not in the least a prig, despite Falconet. He had for himself a standard of the highest moral rectitude, but he did not expect others to conform to it, and he was tolerant of human failings. I often think that some people at the height of the Profumo scandal might with advantage have remembered Gladstone's words to Morley at the height of the Parnell scandal. He refused all pleas to issue a public moral condemnation. ' "What!" he cried, "because a man is what is called leader to a party, does that constitute him a censor and a judge of faith and morals? I will not accept it. It would make life intolerable!" '

The notion that he was an austere, bleak figure—a sort of Sir Stafford Cripps of the Victorian era—is quite untrue. I once asked, in a miniature and highly superficial Gallup Poll of my pupils, whether they thought Gladstone was an abstainer. The great majority did. Quite incorrectly. There is an interesting note in the minutes of Grillions—a very old and still flourishing Parliamentary-cum-literary dining club to which both Gladstone and Disraeli belonged, one of the few places where they sometimes met socially. On one occasion Gladstone was the only member present: the minutes record that a bottle of champagne was consumed. As a young man Gladstone was fond of shooting, cards and wine parties. He took wine with his meals all his life and almost to the end of his days abhorred a teetotal dinner.

Nor was he a severe *pater familias*. His family life was gay and happy. His children adored him. He in return was kind and tolerant to them. He used to try to catch them out. Guests at the family table were astonished when after some deliberately false dictum of their host a childish treble —'a lie, a lie!'—would be heard from the other end, treated with urbane amusement by the GOM himself.

But there was nevertheless something about him which to Disraeli and a great many other Tories was repugnant, and even to many Liberals disconcerting. Gladstone had an intensity, a fervour, a conviction of absolute right and wrong, which astonished and disturbed the aristocratic world that to the end of his life continued to dominate politics. It was the secret of his appeal to the non-conformist conscience, and it was, more often than not, directed against things which most of us now agree to have been either outrageous, like the Bulgarian atrocities and the Armenian massacres, or in the end indefensible—the Irish Church and the preservation of the Union. But there was something about Gladstone's (metaphorical) tone of voice, which enraged the sophisticated, the 'man of the world' in both parties. It enraged no one more than it enraged Disraeli who, just as he overplayed most of his parts, overplayed that of the slightly cynical man of sense. At times one feels that Disraeli's antipathy to Gladstone—and Gladstone's to Disraeli—was not simply caused by the differences of their political outlook on concrete issues, important though these were, rather by their whole approach to politics, their way of thinking, their political style. What Disraeli disliked was the bringing of morality and religion into politics—to him an essentially practical business. By the same token Gladstone deplored the cynical amorality of his old enemy.

The two nations that fought each other during much of the nineteenth century were not Disraeli's 'THE RICH AND THE POOR' but divergent groups among the rich—or moderately rich. As Dr Kitson Clark puts it, 'there were . . . in Britain two nations struggling in the bosom of one land—an old nation based upon the old nobility, upon the squires and upon the Established Church, and a new nation based upon commerce and industry, and in religion mainly dissenting'.

It was not straightforward conflict. There were many cross currents. Yet at the risk of over-simplification it is fair to see in Peel and his disciple Gladstone, symbols and standard bearers of the new nation. Of course they were not dissenters or commercial men; they had an upper-class education, they belonged to upper-class clubs, they possessed, or controlled, or believed in, landed property. But none the less they stood not only for compromise with, but also for sympathy with the new nation. They were at least in part converts to its values and ideals. Gladstone in particular had all its earnestness, its belief in hard work, its attachment to the ideal of godliness and good learning.

Disraeli was a complete contrast. However much later circumstances obliged him to take a Peelite line, despite having led the attack on Peel in 1846, he had no sympathy whatever with the new nation. He might, like every statesman of the age, have to compromise with it, but he was never a convert. His personal values were those of the early-nineteenth-century aristocracy. One paid one's debts of honour but tradesmen had to take their chance—and in Disraeli's case it was a pretty thin chance too. As for religion one conformed outwardly, perhaps even inwardly, but did not make a public display of it. If one was insulted the response was a challenge to a duel. One was not necessarily promiscuous in matters of sex, but one certainly did not worry unduly about the seventh commandment. Politics was a matter of practical management of particular problems with the underlying purpose of keeping things much as they were at home—upholding 'the aristocratic settlement of this country', as Disraeli wrote to Derby—and preserving the honour and grandeur of England abroad.

Gladstone was not, at least in one sense of the phrase, hostile to the aristocratic settlement. He may have disapproved of the 'Upper Ten Thousand' but he never envisaged a social order in which the landed aristocracy would not be in the governing class, and he regarded with horror anything that would tend towards the confiscation of landed property. But he believed profoundly in the need for that class to be imbued with the earnestness, the moral purity, the readiness for hard work which, in his eyes, characterized the best elements of the non-conformist middle class and, as the years went by, the best elements of the non-conformist working class too. Above all, the aristocracy should govern morally and impartially in the public interest, not in any narrow class interest. It was Gladstone's tone of voice more than his actual policies which appealed to the world outside the magic circle. This explains the seeming paradox of the Old Etonian, Puseyite, landowner becoming the hero of the dissenting shopkeeper and the chapel-going artisan.

Not that Gladstone had no influence on the upper class. On all counts Lord Rosebery, who seemed almost a caricature of a Young England aristocrat, ought to have been a Disraelian. Yet, fascinated though he was by Disraeli, he joined Gladstone. And on a more frivolous level there is the sad story of Monckton-Milnes, Lord Houghton, the possessor of a pornographic library which would have satisfied even the exacting demands of a working party of the Arts Council back from a jaunt to Copenhagen. He once dreamed that he was being pursued by Gladstone in a hansom cab. In his effort to escape he fell out of bed and broke his collar bone.

The position which the two men held in relation to particular social classes partly answers the question often asked: why has there never again been another Disraeli and Gladstone at the head of the Right and Left respectively? The reason is partly of course the accident of personality: they were unique figures. But, apart from that, one cannot easily envisage quite such an adventurer again climbing to the top of the Tory party or quite such an Old Testament prophet being swept to the summit of the Liberal or Labour parties. The old aristocracy was never a caste. It was raffish, gay, tolerant of new men as long as they were amusing and justified their keep. But even in Disraeli's lifetime a change was occurring. The aristocracy and the wealthy middle class began to merge. Each accepted something of the other's values. Respectability now became essential. 'I was never respectable', Disraeli truly told one of the Fourth Party. And so the pirates and the buccaneers could no longer get away with it. Lord Salisbury defeats Lord Randolph Churchill. Only the convulsions of war can bring F. E. Smith to the Lord Chancellorship, Lord Beaverbrook to the Cabinet, Winston Churchill to the premiership itself. Otherwise it is the Baldwins and the Chamberlains who win the day. Would the young Disraeli get the nomination today for even a shaky Conservative seat? I doubt it.

A change also took place on the other side of the political divide. Bread and butter issues replaced the great moral questions on which Gladstone thrived. The Bulgarian atrocities had rallied the Liberal Party and created a convulsion in the nation. Twenty years later the Armenian massacres, in comparison, created scarcely a stir; and by then the Irish question—another great moral question—far from rallying the Liberal Party had divided it as damagingly as ever Peel's policy had divided the Tories. There was no longer a place for the religious crusade appealing to the higher moral sentiments. Campbell-Bannerman, Asquith, Lloyd George were the men of the Liberal future.

It is very rare that two political opponents polarize the political sentiments of their day to quite the extent that these two did. Balfour and Campbell-Bannermen, Bonar Law and Asquith, Baldwin and MacDonald, Churchill and Attlee were at times divided politically almost as deeply and were certainly dissimilar characters. But somehow the battle never became quite the same sort of personal combat. So strong an impression has this made to posterity that we tend to see the direct confrontation between them as lasting for a large part of the Victorian era. In fact, it was not for so very long. They faced each other as respective leaders of their parties in the House of Commons for little over eight years. Nevertheless posterity is basically right. Their conflict did affect political attitudes for longer than that, and well beyond Disraeli's death: for example the bitter suspicion with which the Conservatives treated Gladstone's espousal of Home Rule in 1886 is at least partly explained by their resentment at his attacks on Disraeli during the Eastern crisis and the Midlothian campaigns nearly ten years before.

When they actually did confront each other in the House of Commons it was like one of those curious conflicts between incongruously armed opponents, beloved in the circus of ancient Rome—Retiarius against Secutor, Thracians against Mirmillones. Disraeli never tried to meet Gladstone on his own ground. On the contrary, he would listen with half-closed eyes, his hat forward over his head, to the torrential eloquence of his great enemy. But he never missed a trick. Once when Gladstone paused a moment, seeming to lose the thread of his oration, Disraeli leant forward as if to help and said in a voice audible all over the House 'Your last word was re-vo-lut-i-on.' But Gladstone sometimes got his own back. On another occasion Disraeli's manner of speech suggested that he had consumed rather more wine than was prudent. Gladstone in reply said: 'The Rt Hon. Gentleman speaking under the influence . . .'—and he paused— '. . . of great excitement', and the House roared with laughter.

One could probably say of them as parliamentarians that honours were even. As ministers, no. The most ardent admirer of Disraeli must concede that Gladstone was more thorough, more knowledgeable, more energetic, better briefed. One has only to contrast the slapdash nature of Disraeli's first budget (1852), in which he muddled up all the income tax schedules, with the immensely competent carefully planned first budget of Gladstone the following year. And Gladstone who was of course in office far more than Disraeli showed his superiority in the field of legislation again and again. The contrast in the length of their official experience is worth mentioning. Down to Disraeli's death in April 1881, Gladstone had been in office for 19½ years, Disraeli only 11. More strikingly perhaps, Gladstone had had 13 years of official experience before he became Prime Minister, Disraeli less than 4—figures which of course reflect the fact that for half a century or more after 1832 the Liberals were the normal majority party. In common they had their apprenticeship at the Exchequer. Disraeli held no other post before he reached the top. Gladstone held it for 9 years all told. It is partly because of them that the Chancellorship became so important. Hitherto the second man in the government had usually been at the Foreign or Home Office. The Foreign Office remained an important stepping-stone, but the Home Office was replaced by the Exchequer.

But statistics and institutions are dry-as-dust affairs, let us return to personalities. What were they like? Two points are to my mind commonly misconstrued. Most people, basing themselves on his novels and other dicta, would regard Disraeli as the more cosmopolitan and cultivated of the two. In fact it was Gladstone. He travelled much more than Disraeli. In addition to a first-class knowledge of the classics, he was at home in French, Italian and German. He was very widely read, probably more so than any Prime Minister before or since, and he conducted a vast correspondence with theologians and scholars all over Europe.

Disraeli, apart from his famous grand tour of the Mediterranean and Near East in 1830–1, which left an indelible impression on his mind, went abroad very little and when he did it was for the most part to rather conventional places, Paris or the Rhine valley. His classical knowledge had very shaky foundations though he could put up a good show, and managed to pull the wool over the eyes of Sir Stafford Northcote. His command of modern languages was negligible, his French being notoriously atrocious. For example he pronounced the last three letters of the French for grocer—*épicier,* if I may venture to remind my audience of the word—as if it rhymed with 'beer'. When he made his famous breach with diplomatic protocol and addressed the Congress of Berlin in English instead of French, the customary international language, it was not, as was believed at the time, because he wished to make a John Bullish assertion of English prestige but because he was incapable of speaking in any other.

Disraeli, at any rate after he had sowed his wild oats, led a rather parochial life compared with Gladstone. Apart from visits to grand houses —no more nor grander than corresponding visits by Gladstone—he divided most of his time between London and the country. Here the two men did have something in common. Disraeli was as devoted to Hughenden as Gladstone was to Hawarden, and both received the same sort of mental and physical refreshment from their country houses and estates.

My second point is that most people who are asked whether Disraeli or Gladstone was the better company at luncheon or dinner or an evening party would unhesitatingly opt for Disraeli. I doubt whether they would be right. Gladstone was more conversational and easier to talk to— perhaps something of a monologuist but not a person to relapse into embarrassing silence. There was nothing of a stick about him. Rather, he was like quicksilver.

Disraeli's conversational gifts were, at their best, brilliant. But his best was rare. Much depended on the company. He was never good with men only. This was the defect of his education. Leaving an obscure school at sixteen, conscious even then of being in a sense an 'alien', missing Oxford contrary to his father's hopes, Disraeli never made those friendships with boys and men of his own age, which were made by Gladstone and by most of Disraeli's political contemporaries. He had patrons like Lord Lyndhurst in his youth, disciples like Smythe and John Manners when he grew older. Equals were rare: Bulwer Lytton perhaps; and James Clay a forgotten figure and his partner in the dissipations of the Orient. It is hard to think of others. Whatever the reason, Disraeli was on the defensive with men, disliked masculine dinners, and at mixed parties hated the moment when the ladies left and the port circulated amidst bawdy anecdotage and gossip about pheasants. He was far less gregarious than Gladstone. He was apt to shoot some barbed witticism into the air, and leave his listeners vaguely uneasy and unsure how to reply. Even Queen Victoria must have been disconcerted when he said to her apropos of nothing in particular, 'I am the blank page between the Old Testament and the New.'

But in the company of women of all ages he blossomed marvellously. There he was at his most agreeable, amusing and entertaining. However strange some of them must have thought him, they rarely failed to be entranced. Disraeli maintained that his whole career depended upon women. It was an absurd exaggeration, but he certainly had a career in which the opposite sex played a bigger part than in that of his great rival.

Yet they had one great thing in common: both made happy, indeed ideally happy, marriages curiously enough in the same year, summer 1839: Disraeli after more than one dubious amour; Gladstone after two unsuccessful proposals to others. Their marriages were very different.

Gladstone, who was 30, married Miss Glynne, 27, a member of the Whig aristocracy—and married for love. Disraeli, who was 34, married a childless middle-class widow, Mary Anne Wyndham Lewis—twelve years older—and he married for money. The Gladstones were blessed with a large family. The Disraelis had no children, but although Disraeli married for money it is true, as Mary Anne herself said, that 'Dizzy would have married me again for love'. Even Gladstone could find nothing to censure in Disraeli's conduct towards his wife, with whom indeed Gladstone personally got on quite well. His letter to Disraeli on her death is eloquently sympathetic, and Disraeli made a touching reply. There is something engaging too in the fact that the wives of the two great Victorian statesmen could at times make them in the privacy of their homes abandon their habitual grave deportment. Mr and Mrs Gladstone, we are told, in moments of exhilaration could stand on the hearthrug with arms round each other's waists singing the chorus

'A ragamuffin husband and a rantipoling wife,
We'll fiddle it and scrape it through the ups and downs of life.'

On at least one occasion Mr and Mrs Disraeli relaxed in a similar fashion. This was after one of Disraeli's rare visits to Scotland, a country which owing to its inveterate Liberalism he normally regarded with disfavour. 'The Scotch shall have no favours from me', he once wrote, 'until they return more Tory members to the H. of C.' But in November 1867 he successfully addressed a great Conservative banquet at Edinburgh, and the University conferred an honorary degree upon him.

I fancied, indeed, till last night that north of the border I was not loved [he told Sir John Skelton], but last night made amends for much. We were so delighted with our reception, Mrs Disraeli and I, that after we got home we actually danced a jig (or was it a hornpipe?) in our bedroom.

However happy they made their husbands in domestic life, it has to be recorded that neither Mrs Gladstone nor Mrs Disraeli were assets in the social and political world. Mrs Disraeli's gaffes were and are famous, and Disraeli's iron restraint while he listened to them aroused general respect. Less well known is Mrs Gladstone's indifference to the social *convenances*. She was courteous and kind, like Gladstone, but she was casual and bad at returning calls, and did little to counteract her husband's worst political defects, his inability to remember names and faces, his reluctance to conciliate those neutral or wavering figures whose support was sometimes vital to him. Neither of the two ladies kept lavish tables, but Mrs Gladstone's was better than that of Mrs Disraeli, whose reputation among the gourmets could not have been lower.

The subject of the women in the two men's lives leads one inevitably to the Queen. The traditional notion that Gladstone treated her like—I will not say a public meeting—but like the embodiment of an institution, whereas Disraeli treated her like a woman is broadly true. Gladstone certainly lacked tact. His wife saw what was needed. She wrote to him in 1863 before he visited Windsor: 'Now contrary to your ways, do *pet* the Queen, and for once believe you can, you dear old thing.' But, alas, Gladstone could no more have brought himself to pet the Queen than to pet a crocodile. In contrast Disraeli's skill at managing her, whether you call it tact or oriental flattery, is one of the commonplaces of history. Did he seek to consolidate his position, as some members of Gladstone's family came to believe, by making malicious innuendos about Gladstone's rescue work among the London prostitutes? There is no evidence for this in his papers or in the Royal Archives, but negative evidence cannot be conclusive. Much of their most private correspondence was destroyed by Edward VII, and in any case there are things one does not commit to paper.

Nevertheless, I like to think that he did not stoop to this, and on the whole it seems unlikely that he did. For it was unnecessary. The Queen disliked, indeed dreaded, Gladstone, not because he was tactless or because she suspected his morals, but above all, because she deeply disapproved of his policies. Her language about him in private was indeed violent, for example, 'This half mad firebrand who would ruin everything and be a dictator.' But when Rosebery whom she personally liked replaced him, her language was scarcely less extreme. 'Lord Rosebery has made a speech so radical as to be almost communistic', she implausibly wrote on one occasion. The truth was that in the last thirty years of her enormous reign the Queen, however much she called herself 'a true Liberal', was in fact a Conservative Imperialist, and deeply opposed to almost every feature of Gladstonian Liberalism. No amount of 'tact' on Gladstone's part could have overcome this difficulty.

This brings me to a final question. How different were the actual policies of the two men, as opposed to their political styles and public images? The perspective of history tends to diminish political differences. We can see now that their basic views on the monarchy, the rights of property, the importance of landed estates, the enlargement of the electorate did not differ so very greatly. Both would have repudiated the levelling trends of the twentieth century. Gladstone declared that he was 'an out and out inequalitarian'. So was Disraeli. Both were opposed to the extension of the sphere of government, and both would have been horrified by its features today.

Yet, when that is said, important divergencies remain. Gladstone believed intensely in nationalism, in the virtues of 'nations struggling rightly to be free'. He sensed the 'wind of change' in Ireland long before anyone else of his calibre and status. He combined this with a deep conviction that political action should be a moral crusade, and that the great issues were essentially moral issues transcending particular British interests. He believed in the comity of nations, the concert of Europe, obedience to international law, the acceptance of arbitration. His attitude, with its idealism, its contradictions, its dilemmas, has coloured the parties of the Left to some extent ever since.

Disraeli repudiated all this. The only nationalism with which he sympathized was English nationalism. This was in no way incompatible with being singularly un-English himself. All other nationalisms he suspected or ignored. Politics to him was not a question of high morality or crusading zeal. It was a matter of practical problems to be solved by common-sense and a proper assertion of English interests. He believed in *realpolitik* and the use of power. This was why he got on so well with Bismarck. His language may have been high flown, extravagant, fantastic; but it clothed a Palmerstonian attitude of straight English patriotism, no-nonsense with foreigners, and preservation of the Empire. His attitude, with its dilemmas and difficulties, has to some extent coloured that of the Right ever since.

It is largely this contrast which makes study of the two men so fascinating. And we need not today be partisan. Gladstone was not necessarily a superior statesman to Disraeli, though he was morally and intellectually superior, and in courage not inferior. But he was much more a creature of his own period. His language lacks the wit, freshness, the originality of his great rival who is a much more timeless figure. Disraeli could have lived either today or in the era of Gibbon and Lord North. This is not true of Gladstone. Although he was in no sense a typical Victorian, one feels nevertheless that he could only have flourished in the Victorian era.

That is perhaps why Disraeli has fascinated posterity more than Gladstone. But the interest of posterity is not necessarily an index of a person's worth, and precisely because the Victorian era is becoming a matter of such interest today to historians and to the educated public, interest in Gladstone's character and achievement is beginning to revive. Perhaps we should not try to make comparisons between them at all. Perhaps we should end as we began, with Lord Granville—'Lord Beaconsfield and Mr Gladstone are men of extraordinary ability'—and leave it at that.

22. Collective Violence in European Perspective

CHARLES TILLY

Political events in the nineteenth century were made not only by those at the top like Disraeli, Alexander II, Gladstone, Napoleon III, Bismarck, and their ruling elites. They were also made by those at the bottom. When the masses participated in politics they often resorted to a technique likewise used by those at the top: collective violence. That should not surprise anyone. We have already looked at revolutionary violence in the French and 1848 Revolutions, and events of our own time indicate that collective violence is a normal part of the human condition. What is surprising is that historians have virtually ignored the development of collective violence. Somehow violence was not to be discussed for almost the same reason that Victorians avoided talking about sex.

That is not the case, however, with this selection, one of a group of scholarly essays commissioned by the National Commission on Violence (the Eisenhower Commission). Its author, Charles Tilly of the University of Michigan, is claimed by both historians and sociologists for his excellent study of the Vendée uprising against the French Revolution. He is presently engaged in extensive research on the phenomenon described in the essay. He

Source: Charles Tilly, "Collective Violence in European Perspective," in Hugh Davis Graham and Ted Robert Gurr (ed.), *Violence in America: Historical and Comparative Perspectives; A Report to the National Commission on the Causes and Prevention of Violence* (Washington, D.C: Government Printing Office, 1969), I, 5–34. [Footnotes omitted.]

acknowledges, in an omitted footnote, that his formulations were influenced
by George Rudé's The Crowd in History, *which provided a selection in the*
first volume of this anthology, and by E. J. Hobsbawm's Primitive Rebels,
"the two best books on the subject of this essay." Tilly believes that collective
violence both is normal to historical development and passes through "three
broad categories: primitive, reactionary, and modern." The nineteenth
century witnessed the shift from the reactionary to the modern variety.
That is why examination of collective violence is appropriate at this point,
because it changed in response to modernization just as the politicians did.
Why does Tilly say, "Collective violence is normal"? If it is, why has "the
collective memory machine" forgotten some examples of violence and
remembered others? Why does he believe that collective protest is political
rather than "mere side effects of urbanization, industrialization and other large
structural changes"? How do his first two varieties of collective violence—
primitive and reactionary—differ in objectives, organization, and form?
What different types of reactionary collective violence does he see? How
did the authorities cope with this kind of violence in the nineteenth century? In
turn, how do the objectives, organization, and form of modern collective vio-
lence differ from the earlier varieties? What accounts for the shift to modern
collective violence and when did the shift take place? Did the shift vary from
nation to nation? What insights does Tilly's essay throw on where, when, and
why collective violence can occur in our own time and how we can cope with it?

As comforting as it is for civilized people to think of barbarians as violent and of violence as barbarian, Western civilization and various forms
of collective violence have always been close partners. We do not need a
stifled universal instinct of aggression to account for outbreaks of violent
conflicts in our past, or in our present. Nor need we go to the opposite
extreme and search for pathological moments and sick men in order to
explain collective acts of protest and destruction. Historically, collective
violence has flowed regularly out of the central political processes of
Western countries. Men seeking to seize, hold, or realign the levers of
power have continually engaged in collective violence as part of their
struggles. The oppressed have struck in the name of justice, the privileged
in the name of order, those in between in the name of fear. Great shifts
in the arrangements of power have ordinarily produced—and have
often depended on—exceptional movements of collective violence.

Yet the basic forms of collective violence vary according to who is involved and what is at issue. They have changed profoundly in Western
countries over the last few centuries, and those countries have built big
cities and modern industries. For these reasons, the character of collective
violence at a given time is one of the best signs we have of what is going
on in a country's political life. The nature of violence and the nature of
the society are intimately related.

Collective violence is normal. That does not mean it is intrinsically desirable, or inevitable. For century after century, the inhabitants of southern Italy endured malaria as a normal fact of life; today, American city

337
Tilly
COLLECTIVE
VIOLENCE IN
EUROPEAN
PERSPECTIVE

dwellers endure smog and nerve-rending traffic as normal facts of life; few people hail malaria, smog, or traffic jams. Europeans of other centuries often destroyed children they could not provide for. Now infanticide has become rare. Few of us mourn its passing. But the fact that infanticide persisted so long in the face of persuasive teachings and fearsome penalties tells us something about the poverty and population pressure under which people once lived in Western countries. It also may help us understand some apparently barbaric practices of people outside the West today. In a similar way, both the persistence of the phenomenon of collective violence and the changes in its form within European countries over the last few centuries have something to teach us about their political life, and even about contemporary forms of protest.

Ours Is Violent History

Long before our own time, Europeans were airing and settling their grievances in violent ways. "To the historian's eyes," said Marc Bloch, the great historian of feudal Europe, "the agrarian rebellion is as inseparable from the seigniorial regime as the strike from the great capitalist enterprise." The chief moments at which ordinary people appeared unmistakably on the European historical scene before the industrial age were moments of revolt: the Jacquerie of 1358, which lent its name to many later peasant rebellions; Wat Tyler's popular rebellion of 1381; the German peasant wars of 1525; the astonishing provincial insurrection against Henry VIII in 1536 and 1537, which came to be known as the Pilgrimage of Grace; the bloody revolt of the Don Cossacks in the 1660's. Much of the time the peasant suffered in silence. Now and then he found his tongue, and his voice was violent.

Collective violence as a voice is the metaphor that occurs to almost all historians of popular movements before our own time. In their discussion of the English agricultural laborer, J. L. and Barbara Hammond summed it up for all their colleagues:

> The feelings of this sinking class, the anger, dismay, and despair with which it watched the going out of all of warm comfort and light of life, scarcely stir the surface of history. The upper classes have told us what the poor ought to have thought of these vicissitudes; religion, philosophy, and political economy were ready with alleviations and explanations which seemed singularly helpful and convincing to the rich. The voice of the poor themselves does not come to our ears. This great population seems to resemble nature, and to bear all the storms that beat upon it with a strange silence and resignation. But just as nature has her own power of protest in some sudden upheaval, so this world of men and women—an underground world as we trace the distances that its voices have to travel to reach us—has a volcanic character of its own, and it is only by some volcanic surprise that it can speak the language of re-

monstrance or menace or prayer, or place on record its consciousness of wrong.

And then the Hammonds proceed to read the rebellion of 1830 for signs
of what was happening to the agrarian population of England.

Even with the growth of representative political institutions, ordinary
people continued to state their demands through violence. The French
historian of England, Elie Halévy, stated the matter clearly:

> Throughout the eighteenth century England, the sole European
> country where the reigning dynasty had been set up as the result of
> a successful rebellion, had been the home of insurrection. There had
> been an outbreak of anti-Jewish rioting in 1753, when the Govern-
> ment had decided to grant the right of naturalization to the Jews
> domiciled in England. The Cabinet had yielded and repealed the
> statute. . . . . In 1768 there were riots against the Government.
> The popular hero Wilkes triumphed in the end over the opposition
> of court and Cabinet. In 1780 an anti-Catholic riot broke out; dur-
> ing four entire days the centre of London was given up to pillage.
> A government without a police force was powerless either to pre-
> vent these outrages or repress them promptly. The right to riot or,
> as it was termed by the lawyers, "the right of resistance," was an in-
> tegral part of the national traditions.

That "right of resistance" was, in fact, a part of the English legal tradition
upon which the American colonists insisted in the very act of separating
themselves from the mother country, and emphasized in their writings
about the new state they were bringing into being.

Nor did collective violence fade out with the American Revolution, or
the French Revolution, or the multiple revolutions of 1848, or the American Civil War. Western history since 1800 is violent history, full enough
of revolutions, coups, and civil wars, but absolutely stuffed with conflict
on a smaller scale.

The odd thing is how quickly we forget. When Lincoln Steffens visited London in 1910, he found distinguished Members of Parliament convinced that England was on the brink of revolution as a result of the
angry strikes of the time. The strikes and the talk of revolution spread
through Great Britain during the next few years. In prickly Ireland — still
part of the United Kingdom, but barely—a real revolution was shaping
up. Now we look back to England as a country that solved its internal
problems peacefully.

During the American rail strike of 1911,

> In New Orleans railroad workers stole company records, switched
> or destroyed identification cards on freight cars, and cut the air
> hoses of as many as fifteen to twenty cars a day. Mobs of varying
> size constantly bombarded nonstrikers with stones and gunfire. . . .
> In Illinois periodic incursions damaged or destroyed company prop-
> erty. On one occasion, strike sympathizers in Carbondale turned

339
Tilly

COLLECTIVE
VIOLENCE IN
EUROPEAN
PERSPECTIVE

loose a switch engine, which rammed into a freight train on the main line. . . . Turbulence and bloodshed led to a complete breakdown of civil government in sections of Mississippi. . . . For two successive nights hordes swarmed through the streets of Central City, Kentucky. They set upon men in railroad cars and fired at employees lodged in temporary sleeping quarters. . . . In the neighboring state of Tennessee the strike bred a rash of mobbings, stonings, gun battles, and killings.

Following the sacred ritual of such conflicts, the governor of Mississippi declared martial law and blamed his State's troubles on "foreign agitators." Then it was the Americans' turn to speak of revolution. Only comfortable hindsight permits us to congratulate ourselves on our peaceful resolution of conflict.

Few Frenchmen recall that as recently as the end of 1947 revolutionary committees blew up trains and seized control of railroad stations, post offices, city halls, and other public buildings in a dozen major French cities, including Marseille, Grenoble, Nice, and St. Etienne. Then the newspapers proclaimed "revolution" in fear or jubilation. Now November and December of 1947 look like little more than an exceptional period of strike activity—so much so that French and American newspapers alike commonly treated the momentous but essentially nonviolent student protests of May 1968 as "the largest French movement of protest since the war." The collective memory machine has a tremendous capacity for destruction of the facts.

There are many reasons for historical forgetfulness, besides the simple desire to ignore unpleasant events. The record itself tends to cover the rebel's tracks. The most detailed and bulkiest historical records concerning collective violence come from the proceedings of courts, police departments, military units, or other agencies of government working to apprehend and punish their adversaries. The records therefore support the views of those who hold power. Protestors who escape arrest also escape history.

Yet the most important reason is probably that so long as historians concentrate on political history as seen from the top, the only protests which matter are those which produce some rearrangement of power. The Hammonds again make the essential point when discussing the rebellion of 1830:

> This chapter of social history has been overshadowed by the riots that followed the rejection of the Reform Bill. Everyone knows about the destruction of the Mansion House at Bristol, and the burning of Nottingham Castle; few know of the destruction of the hated workhouses at Selborne and Headley. The riots at Nottingham and Bristol were a prelude to victory; they were the wild shout of power. If the rising of 1830 had succeeded, and won back for the labourer his lost livelihood, the day when the Headley workhouse was thrown down would be remembered by the poor as the

day of the taking of the Bastille. But this rebellion failed, and the men who led that last struggle for the labourer passed into the forgetfulness of death and exile.

This selective memory even operates at an international scale. Modern Spain and modern France have acquired reputations as violent nations, while Sweden and England pass for countries of domestic tranquillity. Such differences are hard to measure objectively. But if numbers of participants or casualties or damage done are the standards, then the actual differences are far smaller than the differences in reputation. One international estimate of "deaths from domestic group violence per million population" from 1950 through 1962 rates Sweden and England at 0, Spain at 0.2, and France at 0.3, as compared with 2 for Greece, 10 for Ethiopia, 49 for South Korea, or 1,335 for Hungary. Of course Spain and France acquired their disorderly reputations well before the 1950's. Yet during the very period of these statistics France experienced the great riots brought on by the Algerian war and the series of insurrections that brought down the Fourth Republic. Obviously the amount of bloodshed is not what matters most.

The day-by-day record of these countries over a longer period likewise reveals much more collective violence in Sweden or England than their peaceable reputations suggest. The large difference in notoriety most likely comes from the fact that in Spain and France the protestors sometimes succeeded in toppling the regime. There is a real difference, an important puzzle: How did the British political system survive protest and yet change in fundamental ways, while Spanish regimes snapped and crumbled? But the secret is by no means simply the contrast between anarchic peoples and law-abiding ones.

The record so far available suggests that the histories of collective violence as such in Western European countries over the modern period have had a good deal in common. There have been large differences in the ways the rulers of different states have responded to collective violence, or initiated it, and consequently in its impact on the structure of power. There have been fewer differences in the evolution of the basic forms and conditions of collective violence.

In these circumstances, it is tempting to turn away from reflections on national politics or national character toward ideas about the impact of industrialization. A number of theories proposed to account for various forms of protest in contemporary nations as well as in the Western historical experience suggest a standard cycle: a relatively integrated traditional society breaks up under the stress and movement of industrialization, the stress and movement stimulate a wide variety of violent reactions—at first chaotic, but gradually acquiring a measure of coherence. New means of control and ways of reintegrating the displaced segments of the population into orderly social life eventually develop, and finally a mature industrial society held together by widespread, generally pacific political participation emerges. In such a theory, the stimulus to collective violence

341

Tilly

COLLECTIVE
VIOLENCE IN
EUROPEAN
PERSPECTIVE

comes largely from the anxieties men experience when established institutions fall apart.

Not only scholars hold such a theory. It is our principal folk theory of social change. It reappears almost every time ordinary Americans (and, for that matter, government commissions and well-informed journalists) discuss riots, or crime, or family disorganization. It encourages, for example, the general illusion that highly mobile people and recent migrants to the city have greater inclinations to rioting, crime, or family instability than the general population. It encourages the dubious notion that if poor nations only become rich fast enough they will also become politically stable. But the theory runs into trouble when it turns out that recent migrants are not more disorganized than the rest of the population, that murder is about as common (proportionately speaking) in the country as it is in the city, or that the world's wealthiest nations are quite capable of domestic turmoil.

Politics and Violence

My own explorations of Western Europe, especially France, over the last few centuries suggest a more political interpretation of collective violence. Far from being mere side effects of urbanization, industrialization, and other large structural changes, violent protests seem to grow most directly from the struggle for established places in the structure of power. Even presumably nonpolitical forms of collective violence like the antitax revolt are normally directed against the authorities, accompanied by a critique of the authorities' failure to meet their responsibilities, and informed by a sense of justice denied to the participants in the protest. Furthermore, instead of constituting a sharp break from "normal" political life, violent protests tend to accompany, complement, and extend organized, peaceful attempts by the same people to accomplish their objectives.

Over the long run, the processes most regularly producing collective violence are those by which groups acquire or lose membership in the political community. The form and locus of collective violence therefore vary greatly depending on whether the major ongoing political change is a group's acquisition of the prerequisites of membership, its loss of those prerequisites, or a shift in the organization of the entire political system.

The impact of large structural changes such as urbanization, industrialization, and population growth, it seems to me, comes through their creation or destruction of groups contending for power and through their shaping of the available means of coercion. In the short run, the growth of large cities and rapid migration from rural to urban areas in Western Europe probably acted as a damper on violent protest, rather than a spur to it. That is so for two reasons:

1. The process withdrew discontented men from communities in which they already had the means for collective action and placed

them in communities where they had neither the collective identity nor the means necessary to strike together.

2. It took considerable time and effort both for the individual migrant to assimilate to the large city, and thus to join the political strivings of his fellows, and for new forms of organization for collective action to grow up in the cities.

If so, the European experience resembles the American experience. In the United States, despite enduring myths to the contrary, poor, uprooted newcomers to big cities generally take a long time to get involved in anything—crime, delinquency, politics, associations, protest, rioting—requiring contacts and experiences outside a small world of friends and relatives. These things are at least as true of European cities.

In the long run, however, urbanization deeply shaped the conditions under which new groups fought for political membership, and urbanization's secondary effects in the countryside stirred a variety of protests. The move to the city helped transform the character of collective violence in at least three ways:

1. It grouped men in larger homogeneous blocs (especially via the factory and the working-class neighborhood) than ever before.

2. It facilitated the formation of special-interest associations (notably the union and the party) incorporating many people and capable of informing, mobilizing, and deploying them relatively fast and efficiently.

3. It massed the people posing the greatest threat to the authorities near the urban seats of power, and thus encouraged the authorities to adopt new strategies and tactics for controlling dissidence.

For the people who remained in the country, the rise of the cities meant increasingly insistent demands for crops and taxes to support the urban establishment, increasingly visible impact on individual farmers of tariff and pricing policies set in the cities, and increasingly efficient means of exacting obedience from the countryman. All of these, in their time, incited violent protests throughout Europe.

Of course, definitive evidence on such large and tangled questions is terribly hard to come by. Until very recent times few historians have taken the study of collective violence as such very seriously. As Antonio Gramsci, the Italian socialist philosopher-historian, put it:

This is the custom of our time: instead of studying the origins of a collective event, and the reasons for its spread . . . they isolate the protagonist and limit themselves to doing a biography of pathology, too often concerning themselves with unascertained motives, or interpreting them in the wrong way; for a social elite the features of subordinate groups always display something barbaric and pathological.

Since World War II, however, a considerable number of French and English historians, and a much smaller number of Americans, have begun to study and write history "from below"—actually trying to trace the experiences and actions of large numbers of ordinary men from their own point of view. This approach has had a special impact on the study of protests and rebellions. As a result, we are beginning to get a richer, rearranged picture of the political life of plain people in France and England (and, to a lesser extent, other European countries) over the last few centuries.

The new variety of evidence makes it possible to identify some major shifts in the predominant forms of collective violence in those countries over the modern period. Without too much difficulty we can place the forms of collective violence which have prevailed during that long period in three broad categories: primitive, reactionary, and modern. The primitive varieties once predominated, until centralized states began dragging Europeans into political life on a larger than local scale. As Thorstein Veblen put it in his sardonic *Imperial Germany and the Industrial Revolution,*

> . . . so soon as the king's dominions increased to such a size as to take him personally out of range of an effectual surveillance by neighborly sentiment . . . the crown would be able to use the loyalty of one neighborhood in enforcing exactions from another, and the royal power would then presently find no other obstacle to its continued growth than the limit placed upon it by the state of the industrial arts.

In the process, the king's retinue produced the apparatus of the state, which then acquired momentum of its own. That transformation accelerated through much of Western Europe after 1600. Since then, the primitive forms of collective violence have dwindled very slowly, but very steadily. Now they occur only rarely, only at the margins of organized politics.

The reactionary forms, by contrast, burgeoned as the national state began to grow. That was far from coincidence; they most often developed as part of the resistance of various communal groups to incorporation into the national state and the national economy. But the state won the contest; in most countries of Western Europe the reactionary forms of collective violence peaked and then faded away in their turn during the 19th century. They gave way to modern forms of collective violence, characterized by larger scale, more complex organization, and bids for changes in the operation or control of the state apparatus, rather than resistance to its demands. Although during very recent years we have seen what might be signs of another large shift in the form and locus of collective violence, for in the last century the modern forms have pushed all others aside.

Primitive Collective Violence

Primitive varieties of collective violence include the feud, the brawl among members of rival guilds or communes, and the mutual attacks of hostile religious groups. (Banditry, as E. J. Hobsbawm has said, stands at the edge of this category by virtue of its frequent direction against the existing distribution of power and wealth, and its frequent origin in the state's creation of outlaws as part of the attempt to extend legal authority to formerly ungoverned areas.) Primitive forms of collective violence share several features: small-scale, local scope, participation by members of communal groups as such, inexplicit and unpolitical objectives. Almost regardless of the question at issue, for example, Frenchmen could count on a national political crisis to produce battles between Protestants and Catholics in Nimes and Albi. Attacks on the persons and properties of Jews accompanied 18th-century rebellions in England and 19th-century rebellions in France. The vendetta and the bandit raid, too, took on a degree of political significance in times of national crisis.

The *rixe de compagnonnages*—the battle royal between members of rival craft corporations—often left blood in the streets. In 1830, a characteristic *rixe* in Bordeaux involved 300 artisans; two were reported dead, many were wounded, and the local inns were left a shambles. In 1835, the newspaper *Le Constitutionnel* carried the following story from Châlons-sur-Saône:

> The *compagnons du Devoir,* called *Dévorans,* following an altercation on the previous day and a challenge by letter to fight the *compagnons de Liberté,* called *Gavots,* in the open country, attacked the mother house of the latter in the rue St. Antoine. Huge stones, big enough to kill an ox, were thrown through the windows.

The very prevalence of such fracases gave the inhabitants of 19th-century French cities a wide acquaintance with collective violence. In London, likewise:

> It was usual for the boys of St. Anne's parish to fight those of St. Giles armed with sticks for "a week or two before the holidays." This fact survives, because in 1722 the captain of the boys of St. Giles, a chimney sweep aged twenty-one, was killed by another boy, aged sixteen. Earlier still, "prentice riots were serious and frequent disturbances to the peace of London."

The prevalence of the *rixe* in Europe before modern times simply expressed the intense solidarity of each group of urban craftsmen, for (as has been said of German artisans) "Their group spirit turned against other groups and took an insult to an individual as an affront to the whole association." Something like that solidarity lies close to the core of most of the primitive forms of collective violence.

This does not mean the fighting was always in rage and deadly earnest. Just as today's lumbermen or sailors on a weekend will now and then tear up a bar out of sheer boredom, frustration, or high spirits, the workmen of Berlin or Turin sometimes brawled for the fun of it. On such occasions, the traditional enmities provided no more than the pretext. In the European city of the preindustrial age, funerals, feasts, and fairs provided pub-

345

Tilly

COLLECTIVE
VIOLENCE IN
EUROPEAN
PERSPECTIVE

lic occasions out of which flowed collective violence offering diversion to the young as well as expressing deeply rooted communal rivalries.

Students, and even schoolboys, displayed some of the same violent propensities. At the Jesuit college of La Flèche, during the carnival days of 1646, the boys declared they had been dishonored by the public flogging of some of their number, and staged an armed mutiny. "The rebels . . . stood in the avenues, armed with swords, sticks, blackjacks, and stones, driving back the pupils who came out when the bell rang to get to the classrooms." In England—

> There was indiscipline and rebellion everywhere. At Winchester, in the late eighteenth century, the boys occupied the school for two days and hoisted the red flag. In 1818 two companies of troops with fixed bayonets had to be called in to suppress a rising of the pupils. At Rugby, the pupils set fire to their books and desks and withdrew to an island which had to be taken by assault by the army. There were similar incidents at Eton.

Again, the intense solidarity of the students—a kind of brotherhood in league against their masters—facilitated their indignation and their common action.

A number of the other common primitive forms of collective violence had this curious combination of esprit de corps, recreation, and grim determination, a combination that the English somehow managed to transmute into the sporting spirit. The free-for-all among men from different towns (from which it is said, in fact, that various forms of football developed) has some of this character. So does the rag, charade, or charivari. Yet it would be quite wrong to consider the primitive varieties of collective violence as nothing but early versions of soccer. The deadly vendetta, the endemic banditry of the European highlands, the pervasive Sicilian scourge called Mafia, and the occasional millenarian movements that have racked southern Europe share many traits with the apparently trivial kinds of collective violence. What sets the primitive forms of violence off from the others is not a lack of seriousness, but their activation of local communal groups as such, and usually in opposition to other communal groups.

Reactionary Collective Violence

Reactionary disturbances are also usually small in scale, but they pit either communal groups or loosely organized members of the general population against representatives of those who hold power, and tend to include a critique of the way power is being wielded. The forcible occupation of fields and forests by the landless, the revolt against the tax collector, the anticonscription rebellion, the food riot, and the attack on machines were Western Europe's most frequent forms of reactionary collective violence. The somewhat risky term "reactionary" applies to these forms of collective violence because their participants were commonly reacting to some change that they regarded as depriving them of rights they had once enjoyed; they were backward looking. They were not, however, simple flights from reality. On the contrary, they had a close connection with routine, peaceful political life.

For ordinary Europeans of a few centuries ago, the most persistent political issues were the demands of the nation-state and of the national economy. And the food riot, as unlikely as it seems, illustrates the pressing nature of these demands very well. Seemingly born of hunger and doomed to futility, the food riot actually expressed the indignation of men and women who felt they were being deprived of their rights and who, by rioting, were often able to restore a semblance of those rights—if only temporarily.

The Western European food riot had a classic form: seizure of grain being stored or transported in a town, demonstrations (and sometimes bodily harm) directed against those presumed to be profiteering through the shipment or hoarding of grain, and sale of the grain at a publicly proclaimed just price, the proceeds going to the owner of the grain. Such food riots occurred throughout the 18th century in England, and during the first third of the 19th century. They were, indeed, one of the chief components of England's large agrarian rebellion of 1816. A. J. Peacock describes the beginning of one of the principal incidents of that rebellion:

> A crowd had started assembling in the market place at about nine o'clock that morning. About an hour later some women came along who announced that their men were following them but had stopped along the Thetford road to collect sticks. Eventually fifty or more, all armed, and led by William Peverett, a labourer, marched into the square carrying white and red flags. Whillett, the butcher, who was amongst the crowd, told Peverett that the parish would let them have flour at 2s. 6d. if they would disperse, and asked for a deputation to go along with him to meet the magistrates. Helen Dyer, a married woman, had earlier told Willett that, although she could not read, she had a paper containing the crowd's demands, which she wanted shown to the magistrates. On it was written, "Bread or Blood in Brandon this day."

347

Tilly

COLLECTIVE
VIOLENCE IN
EUROPEAN
PERSPECTIVE

Finally, after several days of milling, grumbling, stoning of windows, and pulling down of buildings, the magistrates—

> guaranteed the price of flour at 2s. 6d. per stone, with an advance of wages to 2s. per head for a fortnight, and unless the millers reduce their prices by that time, the officers of the parish will purchase their grain at the cheapest rate, and furnish the poor with provisions at prime cost.

To modern eyes, the curious feature of this event is that the rioters did not loot, did not steal, but demanded to buy food at a price they could afford. Furthermore, it is clear that the crowd directed their anger at the authorities, expected them to act, and, indeed, bargained with them.

In fact, the food riot was an attempt to make the merchants and the municipal authorities meet their traditional responsibilities: holding grain within the town to meet local needs before permitting it to enter the national market, and assuring the town poor of a supply of grain at a price adjusted to the local level of wages. As great cities grew up in Western Europe during the 17th and 18th centuries, and national markets in grain developed to feed them, it became harder and less profitable for merchants and officials to give priority to local needs. And so men rioted to hold them to the bargain. The geography of the food riot (at least in France, where it has been best mapped) suggests as much: such riots occurred not in the areas of greatest famine and poverty, but in the hinterlands of big cities and grain-shipping ports.

The case of Italy points up the importance of the control (as opposed to the sheer quantity) of the food supply. In England, the classic food riot virtually disappeared after 1830; in France, after 1848; in Italy, toward the end of the 19th century. The timing of that disappearance corresponds approximately to the pace of technical improvements in the production and distribution of grain. It also follows the destruction of traditional controls over the grain trade, but at a significant distance.

The bad harvests of 1853, for example, brought food riots through much of Western Europe. In the Italian peninsula, the riots of that year were concentrated in the prosperous north—Piedmont, Parma, Tuscany—although shortage was at least equally acute in the silent south. The northern authorities had generally adopted policies favoring free trade in grains; in the southern Kingdom of the Two Sicilies, paternalism reigned.

In 1859, however, the new, progressive King Francesco of the Two Sicilies began to liberalize the grain trade. In 1860 he faced widespread food riots of the south. At the time of the October 1860 plebiscite on the unification of Italy there were rebellions in the south, to the theme "The old king fed us." The old king was Francesco's father, who had maintained the traditional controls.

All this may appear unduly complicated for anything so simple as a food riot. That is the point: these recurrent, apparently spontaneous events rested on and grew from the local structure of politics, and the crises of local politics were responses to pressures from the center. Far from being a momentary, rural, local reaction to misery, the food riot recorded the urbanization and centralization of European nation-states.

The food riot had companions. The anticonscription rebellion, the resistance to the tax collector, the violent occupation of fields and forests, the breaking of reapers or power looms all had many of the same characteristics. Although they often appear in clusters, each of the events was more or less local and self-contained. Instead of pitting one communal group against another, they stood a significant segment of the population against the local elite or the representatives of the central power. ("When the French peasant paints the devil," said Karl Marx in 1850, "he paints him in the guise of the tax collector.") The organization of the formations taking part was rudimentary. It was essentially the organization of everyday life: users of a common market, artisans of the same shop, a single commune's draft-age boys, and so on. Because of this tie with everyday groupings, those who took part often included women, children, and old people. The participants were either resisting some new demand (taxes, conscription) laid on them by outsiders, protesting against what they viewed as a deprivation of their traditional rights (the prohibition of gleaning in fields and forests, the introduction of machinery), or both. All of them, in one way or another, amounted to action against the forcible integration of local groupings into the national economy and the national state. I believe—but this is a hunch for which little evidence is yet available—that all the reactionary forms of collective violence will turn out to have had an extraordinary appeal for just those segments of the European population whose political and economic identities these changes were dissolving. The large numbers of rural artisans whose livelihoods disappeared with the expansion of urban industry during the 19th century are the most important case, but agricultural day laborers and petty nobles faced some of the same problems.

The rural unrest of England during the early-19th century falls into this general pattern. In addition to recurrent food riots, the English countryside produced movements of protest in 1816, 1822, 1830, 1834–35, and 1843–44, with the 1830 rebellion covering much of southeastern England. During the events of 1830, the village rebels concentrated on three sorts of action: (1) levying a once-traditional contribution of beer or money on the local rich; (2) imposing a wage agreement on the employers of day laborers; (3) destroying new farm machinery, especially threshers. For those who resisted, the crowds reserved personal attacks, the tearing down of buildings, and the burning of hayricks. During one of the larger outbreaks, in Wiltshire—

349
Tilly
COLLECTIVE
VIOLENCE IN
EUROPEAN
PERSPECTIVE

> The mob destroyed various threshing machines of Mr. Bennet's farms, and refused to disperse; at last, after a good deal of sharp language from Mr. Bennett, they threw stones at him. At the same time a troop of yeomanry from Hindon came up and received orders to fire blank cartridges above the heads of the mob. This only produced laughter; the yeomanry then began to charge; the mob took shelter in the plantations round Pyt House and stoned the yeomanry, who replied by a fierce onslaught, shooting one man dead on the spot, wounding six by cutting off fingers and opening skulls, and taking a great number of prisoners.

As hopeless as this sort of popular agitation may seem, it actually had a measure of success. As E. J. Hobsbawm states it, "the day-laborers succeeded to a large degree in destroying the machines and achieving wage raises and other improvements, and they held onto their gains for some years, mostly because the unexpected sight of their massive force . . . instilled a salutary fear in the rural gentry and farm owners." Of course, this was only a delaying action; the reactionary forms of rural protest did not last much longer, mechanized farming did win out, and millions of agricultural workers eventually left the land. Nevertheless, in the context the actions of 1830 had a logic poorly conveyed by words like "riot" and "protest."

The same may be said of the handloom weavers, whose 19th-century rebellions stirred the countryside in most sections of Europe. What we loosely call Luddism took the form of a well-concerted avenging action. Ned Ludd, the mythical enemy of shearing frames and power looms, who in 1811 and 1812 issued threats and manifestoes from his retreat in Sherwood Forest, had much in common with Captain Swing, the equally mythical leader in whose name the agrarian rebels of 1830 wrote their warnings. Here is a Luddite letter:

> We will never lay down Arms (till) The House of Commons passes an Act to put down all Machinery hurtful to Commonality, and repeal that to hang Frame Breakers. But we. We petition no more —that won't do—fighting must.
> Signed by the General of the Army of Redressers
> Ned Ludd   Clerk
> Redressers for ever Amen.

The Army of Redressers, they called themselves. Their pseudonym epitomizes the defensive, indignant, focused, rule-bound character of their rebellion. "Luddism," says E. P. Thompson, "must be seen as arising at the crisis-point in the abrogation of paternalist legislation, and in the imposition of the political economy of laissez faire upon, and against the will and conscience of, the working people." Far from reacting in aimless confusion, the Luddites, and most of the European machine breakers, knew what they were doing. While the food riot and machine breaking were quite distinct in form and content, they shared the same sort of crude rationality.

Much of the popular protest that took place during the Italian Risorgimento has the reactionary character. During the 1850's there were scattered strikes in the industrial centers and a few revolts of fairly modern variety in cities like Milan, Livorno, and Genoa. But most of the disturbances took the familiar form of the food riot, or consisted of *occupazioni delle terre*—mass squatting on lands formerly held in common as a means of demanding their distribution in compensation for lost rights in the commons. Even as Garibaldi marched up the peninsula on his way to unifying Italy, Sicilians were attacking tax collectors and occupying the commons. At times, villagers in the south shouted "Down with the Constitution," "Down with the Nation," "long live the King"—a set of cries which recalls the much older motif of French tax rebellions, "Vive le roy et sans gabelle."

By this time a rather different (and, to us, more familiar) kind of collective violence had been taking shape in the cities of Italy, as it had been in most cities of Europe. There, political clubs, secret societies, and workers' organizations were organizing collective action through strikes, demonstrations, banquets, meetings, and military coups. The most economically advanced people of the countryside were also being drawn into these newer forms of action. Although the new political and economic forms were not intrinsically violent in themselves, they became increasingly important contexts for collective violence.

When and how fast this happened varied from country to country. But it happened almost everywhere. The numerous disturbances that occurred in France at the middle of the 19th century were mixed in character. The great bulk of them fit the standard reactionary models: tax rebellions, food riots, machine breaking, and so on. The 1848 Revolution notwithstanding, strikes, demonstrations, and revolutionary movements produced only a small share of the collective violence. The violent disturbances of the 1930's, by contrast, grew almost entirely out of organized strikes and demonstrations; with the important exception of the Resistance during the Second World War, the 1940's and 1950's brought little change in this respect. Between the 1840's and the 1940's, transformation of the character of collective violence took place. Even in the mid-19th century, a growing minority of disturbances involved more complex and durable organization, more explicit and far-reaching objectives, a forward-looking perspective. After 1848, these very rapidly became the prevailing characteristics of collective violence.

In the process, solid citizens and national leaders developed an acute fear of the masses and organized a whole set of new means for maintaining public order. The elite feared the ordinary people of country and city alike, although they concentrated their efforts at crowd control in the cities where they themselves lived. This was true in England. Looking back from 1862, Benjamin Disraeli wrote:

351
Tilly
COLLECTIVE
VIOLENCE IN
EUROPEAN
PERSPECTIVE

> Then arose Luddite mobs, meal mobs, farm riots, riots everywhere; Captain Swing and his rickburners, Peterloo "massacres," Bristol conflagrations, and all the ugly sights and rumours which made young lads, thirty or forty years ago, believe (and not so wrongly) that "the masses were their natural enemies, and they might have to fight, any year, or any day, for the safety of their property and the honour of their sisters."

Englishmen and other Europeans of the time developed a set of beliefs that is still widespread today, essentially equating the "working classes" with the "dangerous classes" and arguing that misery, crime, personal disorganization, and rebellion sprang from approximately the same causes and occurred in approximately the same segments of the population. The causes were the breakdown of traditional social arrangements and the demoralizing overpopulation of the great cities.

A unique essay contest run by King Maximilian of Bavaria in 1848 produced hundreds of fearful statements from middle-class Germans concerning the rise of overpopulation, mechanization, and immorality. It matters little that many of the analyses (for example, those attributing the growth of the urban population to the increase in illegitimacy) were wildly mistaken. The fear was there. And in France:

> On bourgeois opinion of the time, we can take the work of Balzac as the most remarkable piece of evidence, above all because it bears the marks of these two facts: on the one hand, the blending of the working classes and the dangerous classes, the proletariat and the underworld misery and crime; on the other hand, the division between two categories of the population, that daily settlement of differences of which criminality is an expression, and that sporadic settlement of differences of which riots and revolution are the expression.

In response, some Frenchmen, Germans, and Englishmen organized inquiries into poverty; others organized police forces.

For several centuries before this time, the central task of the European police had been control of the grain trade, markets, and, by extension, public assemblies. The notion of a professional organization devoted mainly to the detection and apprehension of criminals took hold in the 19th century. But before that professionalism developed, the European States were expanding and reorganizing their police forces very largely as a means of dealing with the new threats from "the masses." The new police began to replace both the army and those older repressive forces which had been fairly well matched to the primitive and reactionary forms of collective violence: the local militias, part-time constabularies, the personal employees of justices of the peace. Sir Robert Peel's organization of the London metropolitan police in 1829 (which immortalized him by transferring his nickname "Bobby" to the police officers themselves) had the well-recognized dual purpose of putting aside thugs and putting down rebellions. It is even clearer that the establishment of a nationwide provincial police by the Rural Police Act of 1839 "was precipitated by the Chartist disturbances of that year and, in particular, by the desire to relieve the military of a pressure which was in the highest degree inconvenient and injurious."

European police forces of the period acquired great political importance, not only as agents of crowd control but also as the organizers of political espionage via networks of spies and informers. Their reorganization throughout Europe in the early-19th century marked a victory of the national over the local, a nationalization of repressive forces. As Allan Silver says, "The police penetration of civil society . . . lay not only in its narrow application to crime and violence. In a broader sense, it represented the penetration and continual presence of central political authority throughout daily life." Although the new police forces by no means succeeded in eliminating collective or individual violence from everyday life, they did speed the decline of the older forms of protest. By matching more complex and specialized organization of repression to the more complex and specialized organization of the newer forms of protest, they probably even earned some of their reputation for staving off revolution.

Modern Collective Violence

The modern varieties of political disturbance (to use another tendentious term) involve specialized associations with relatively well-defined objectives, organized for political or economic action. Such disturbances can easily reach a large scale. Even more clearly than in the case of reactionary collective violence, they have a tendency to develop from collective actions that offer a show of force but are not intrinsically violent. The demonstration and the violent strike are the two clearest examples, but the coup and most forms of guerrilla [activity] also qualify. These forms deserve to be called "modern" not only because of their organizational complexity but also because the participants commonly regard themselves as striking for rights due them, but not yet enjoyed. They are, that is, forward looking.

In England, the modern varieties of collective violence came into their own fairly early. Joseph Hamburger, whose general purpose is to refute the notion that England came close to revolution before the 1832 Reform Bill, nevertheless describes some good-sized disturbances in 1831:

> There were also disturbances in London during the days immediately after the Lords' rejection of the Bill. They mainly occurred in connection with a procession that was organized, with Place's help, by two London Radicals, Bowyer and Powell. Organized by parishes people were to march to the palace and present an address in support of the Bill to the King. When it took place on October 12, 300,000 persons were said to have taken part. The Home Secretary informed the deputations that the King could not receive their petitions, but they could present them through County Members. Hume received some of them in St. James Square and later left them at the palace. The procession then marched past the palace as the demonstration of its size and resolution. It consisted of "shopkeepers and superior artisans"; nevertheless, during the day there were attacks on some Tory peers as well as the usual broken windows.

353
Tilly
COLLECTIVE
VIOLENCE IN
EUROPEAN
PERSPECTIVE

The violence in this case obviously was minor, but the order and size of the demonstration impressive. Much more so than in the case of reactionary disturbances, the extent of violence in this sort of event depends heavily on the reactions of the demonstrators' opponents.

During the widespread Chartist agitation of the following two decades the standard routine involved a fire-eating speech by a Chartist leader, followed by a procession through the streets, whose members spewed threats and displayed weapons. The threats, however, rarely came to anything except when the marchers confronted the Queen's soldiers. While once in a great while a member of the crowd fired at the troops, their usual tactic was to stone them:

> At Preston, during the Plug-Plot disturbances, a mob which had belaboured the soldiers with stones stood its ground for a while when the order to fire was given and several of its members were struck, but the shooting of a ringleader, who had stepped out in front of the mob to encourage his followers to continue the assault, put a damper on the proceedings, and caused the crowd to disperse.

The British army and police soon developed effective, and largely nonviolent, methods of crowd control.

Despite the development of effective policing, England still witnessed much collective violence later in the century. There was a wave of "riots" in London in 1866, another in 1886 and 1887; most of these events consisted of demonstrations that got out of hand. But the real resurgence of this form of violence came early in the 20th century, as the movements for temperance and (more importantly) for women's suffrage began to mount demonstrations in the course of which the women showed unwonted determination:

> . . . they smashed windows, fired pillar-boxes, slashed pictures, threw things at M.P.'s, and even burned down churches and houses; in reply they were treated with great roughness by policemen and worse by crowds. They were kicked and beaten; their hair was pulled and their clothes half-torn off; hatpins were pushed into them; they were knocked down and trampled upon.

It was about this time that Lincoln Steffens heard English leaders talking about the possibility of revolution. For three different movements were swelling and coalescing in the years just before World War I: the demand for women's suffrage, huge (and sometimes insurrectionary) strikes, and opposition to war. A famous leaflet of the time communicates some of what was happening:

> You are Workingmen's Sons.
> When we go on Strike to better Our lot which is the lot also of Your Fathers, Mothers, Brothers and Sisters, *You* are called upon by your Officers to *Murder Us.*
> Don't do it. . . .
> Don't you know that when you are out of the colours, and become a "Civy" again, that You, like Us, may be on strike, and You, like Us, be liable to be Murdered by other soldiers.
> Boys, Don't Do It.
> "Thou shalt not kill," says the Book.
> Don't forget that!
> It does not say, 'unless you have a uniform on.'
> No! *Murder is Murder.*

Think things out and refuse any longer to Murder Your Kindred. Help Us to win back Britain for the British and the World for the Workers.

Some of these movements (like the drive for women's suffrage) succeeded; some (like the various demands of organized labor) met a mixture of success and failure; and some (like pacifism) failed utterly. England survived. But the essential point is that the characteristic forms of collective violence accompanying those movements differed fundamentally from those which had prevailed a century before.

The rise of the strike as a context for collective violence followed a similar rhythm. Although European states often reimposed one restriction or another, most of them legalized the strike sometime during the 19th century: England in 1824, Saxony in 1861, France in 1864, Belgium in 1866, Prussia in 1869, Austria in 1870, the Netherlands in 1872. That did not, however, make all subsequent strikes peaceful. Occasionally the violence began when the workers themselves attacked a factory, mine, or manager's home. Sometimes the workers demonstrated, and the demonstration turned violent. More often the violence grew from a confrontation between strikers assembled at a workplace and troops, police, or strikebreakers sent in to thwart or control them.

In France, occasional strikes broke out in the biggest cities as early as the 16th century. In the first half of the 19th century, several rounds of strikes—notably those of Lyon in 1831 and 1834—bubbled up into bloodily repressed insurrections. But the first sets of strikes approaching a national scale came at the end of the Second Empire, in 1869 and 1870. A major strike movement swept the textile and metalworking plants of Alsace in July 1870, with some 20,000 workers out in the vicinity of Mulhouse. Then:

355
Tilly
COLLECTIVE
VIOLENCE IN
EUROPEAN
PERSPECTIVE

Peaceful parades took possession of the streets. First the carpenters: the evening of 4 July, 400 to 500 men "walked through the city singing, in an orderly fashion." And for three days the processions continued across the city, in groups, men, women, children marching "in a fairly disciplined way."

Then the demonstrations grew. In a number of towns the strikers kept the nonstrikers out by force. Eventually the troops came in, and the minor violence ended. Total: a few injuries, a little property damage, perhaps 70 arrests.

Not all strikes were so peaceful, however. During the same period, a number of mining strikes involved pitched battles between troops and demonstrators. In the course of a strike of 15,000 miners around St. Etienne in June 1869, the troops killed 13 and wounded another nine members of a crowd which attacked them; this encounter went down in history as "the massacre of La Ricamarie." At Aubin (Aveyron), later in the year, the troops shot 30 to 40 strikers trying to break into a metalworking plant, and managed to kill 14 of them on the spot. The point is not so much that people sometimes died in the course of these conflicts as that both the strikes involving trivial damage and those involving loss of life took essentially the same form.

The tremendous Paris Commune of 1871 broke the continuity of modern collective violence to some extent, for its organization greatly resembled that of earlier Parisian rebellions, and its leitmotifs—local control, communal autonomy, equalization of advantages—were contrary to the prevailing nationalization of political conflict and the formation of special-interest associations. But the break occurred as the Prussians marched through northern France, as the government fled, as the rest of the nation, in effect, seceded from Paris. The break was short. With Paris tamed and the National Government reinstalled, Frenchmen returned quickly to the modern forms of violent conflict.

Later on strikes grew in amplitude and frequency. As they spread, they became increasingly common contexts for collective violence, even though a decreasing proportion of all strikes were violent. After 1890, a number of strikes took on an insurrectionary character, with both the doctrine and the practice of the general strike growing in importance. (It was at just this time that Georges Sorel, in his famous *Reflections on Violence,* placed the "myth of the general strike" at the center of revolutionary action.) And the character of strike activity continued to change as the structure of labor unions, the structure of industry, and the relations of labor, management and government all evolved. France's peak years for strike activity—1906, 1919–20, 1936, 1947—have all been years of great social conflict in other regards as well. Each of those crises marked a new stage in the scale and sophistication of conflict.

The Transition to Modern Collective Violence

Unlike the food riot or the *occupazioni,* all this is terribly familiar stuff to the 20th-century reader. In it he can see the collective violence of his own era. The only reason for reviewing it is to notice the deep differences in character among the primitive, reactionary, and modern forms. They lend importance to the fact that so many Western countries shifted from one type to another rapidly and decisively.

The nature, timing, and causes of these shifts from one major type of collective violence to another are complicated, controversial, and variable from one country to another. They are just as complicated, controversial, and variable, in fact, as the political histories of European nations. The transformations of collective violence depended on transformations of nonviolent political life. Rather different political systems emerged in different corners of Europe: communist, socialist, liberal-democratic, corporatist. Each had a somewhat different experience with collective violence. Yet everywhere two things happened and profoundly affected the character of violent protest.

The first was the victory of the national state over rival powers in towns, provinces, and estates; politics was nationalized. The second was the proliferation and rise to political prominence of complex special-purpose associations like parties, firms, unions, clubs, and criminal syndicates. The two trends generally reinforced each other. In some countries, however, the state gained power faster and earlier than the organizational changes occurred; Russia and France are cases in point. In others, the organizational revolution came much closer to the nationalization of politics; Germany and Italy fit that pattern. In either case, the times of overlap of the two trends produced the most dramatic changes in the character of collective violence.

Some of the contrast appears in crude tabulations of disturbances occurring in France during the three decades from 1830 to 1860 and three later decades between 1930 and 1960. This fairly representative set of disturbances includes 1,393 events, involving 3,250 formations (distinct groups taking part in the collective violence). The distribution over time is shown in Table I. The figures show that France by no means became a

Table I

Period	Number of disturbances	Number of formations	Formations per disturbance	Estimated total of participants (in thousands)
1830–39	259	565	2.2	293
1840–49	292	736	2.5	511
1850–60	114	258	2.3	106
1930–39	333	808	2.4	737
1940–49	93	246	2.6	223
1950–60	302	637	2.1	664

357

Tilly

COLLECTIVE
VIOLENCE IN
EUROPEAN
PERSPECTIVE

peaceable nation as urbanization and industrialization transformed her between 1830 and 1960. The two decades from 1850 to 1860 and from 1940 to 1950 produced the fewest disturbances; what actually happened is that during two extremely repressive regimes (following Louis Napoleon's 1851 coup and during the German occupation and Vichy government of the 1940's) there was almost no open large-scale violence. The large numbers for the 1930's include the huge sitdown strikes of 1936 and 1937. Even without them the depressed thirties would look like troubled times. So would the prosperous fifties. In boom and bust, Frenchmen continue to fight.

We can look at the distribution of formations taking part in the disturbances in Table II. The figures show a decided decline in the participation of the ordinary, mixed crowd without any well-defined political or economic identity, and a compensating rise in the participation of crowds labeled as supporters of particular creeds and programs. We find no marked change in the involvement of repressive forces in collective violence, but see an important shift of the task of repression from military forces to police. "Natural" groups like users of the same market (who were typical participants in food riots, invasions of fields, and other small

Table II

Type of formation	1830–39	1840–49	1850–60	1930–39	1940–49	1950–60
Simple crowd	16.5	17.2	8.9	1.5	3.3	1.5
Ideological crowd, activists	17.5	10.4	32.3	48.3	21.5	35.2
Military	20.5	16.2	15.2	3.0	8.5	1.9
Police	10.9	16.9	24.5	24.6	26.4	31.8
Public officials	3.5	6.0	4.3	1.0	3.7	1.5
Occupational group	17.0	17.3	4.7	14.6	24.4	17.7
Users of same market, fields, woods or water	2.5	4.4	1.9	.7	.0	.0
Others	11.7	11.7	8.2	6.3	12.2	10.5
Total	100.1	100.1	100.0	100.0	100.0	100.1

reactionary disturbances) disappeared completely over the 130-year span.

Altogether, the figures show the rise of specialization and organization in collective violence. Just as industry shifted its weight from the small shop to the large factory and population rushed from little town to big city, collective violence moved from the normal congregations of communal groups within which people used to live most of their lives toward the deliberate confrontations of special-purpose associations. Collective violence, like so many other features of social life, changed from a communal basis to an associational one.

As one consequence the average size of incidents went up. Some measures of magnitude for the 1,393 disturbances in the sample are shown in Table III. The figures describe the average disturbance, of course, not the

Table III

	1830–39	1840–49	1850–60	1930–39	1940–49	1950–60
Mean number participating	1,130	1,750	925	2,215	2,405	2,200
Mean man-days expended	1,785	3,295	1,525	2,240	2,415	2,200
Man-days per participant	1.6	1.9	1.6	1.0	1.0	1.0
Percent lasting more than 1 day	18	18	25	4	4	5
Mean killed and wounded	25	22	30	19	34	23
Mean arrests	20	53	327	24	22	43

total amount of violence in a decade. They show a distinct rise in the average number of people taking part in a disturbance, despite a strong tendency for disturbances to narrow down to a single day. As the burden of repression shifted from the army to the police, interestingly enough, the use of widespread arrests declined while the number of people hurt stayed about the same. Relative to the number of participants, that meant some decline in the average demonstrator's chance of being killed or wounded. The main message, once again, is that, although the predominant forms of collective violence changed in fundamental ways, collective violence persisted as France became an advanced industrial nation.

The 20th-century figures from France include almost no primitive violence. By the beginning of the century the primitive forms had been fading slowly through most of Western Europe for three centuries or more. In some countries, however, the transition from predominantly reactionary to predominantly modern forms of collective violence occurred with striking rapidity. In England, the reactionary forms were already well on their way to oblivion by the time of the last agrarian rising, in 1830, although they had prevailed 30 years before. In Germany, demonstrations and strikes seem to have established themselves as the usual settings for collective violence during the two decades after the Revolution of 1848.

The situation was a bit more complicated in Italy, because of the deep division between north and south. The transition to modern forms of collective violence appears to have been close to completion in the north at unification. By the time of Milan's infamous *fatti di Maggio* of 1898, in which at least two policemen and 80 demonstrators died, the newer organizational forms unquestionably dominated the scene. In the south, mixed forms of the food riot and tax rebellion still occurred at the end of the century. Within 10 years, however, even in rural areas the agricultural strike and the organized partisan meeting or demonstration had become the most regular sources of violence on the larger scale.

Spain, as usual, is the significant exception: while the country as a whole displays the long-run drift from primitive to reactionary to modern forms of collective violence, it also displays a marvelous array of regressions, mixtures, and hesitations. Surely, the country's erratic industrialization, uncertain, fluctuating unification, and exceptional military involvement in politics lie behind its differentiation from the rest of Western Europe in this respect. Spain, as Gerald Brenan says,

> . . . is the land of the *patria chica*. Every village, every town is the centre of an intense social and political life. As in classical times, a man's allegiance is first of all to his native place, or to his family or social group in it, and only secondly to his country and government. In what one may call its normal condition Spain is a collection of small, mutually hostile, or indifferent republics held together in a loose federation. . . . Instead of a slow building-up of forces such as one sees in other European nations, there has been an alternation between the petty quarrels of tribal life and great upsurges of energy that come, economically speaking, from nowhere.

Thus Spain becomes the exception that tests the rule. For the rule says the shift from predominantly reactionary to predominantly modern forms of collective violence accompanies the more-or-less durable victory of the national state and the national economy over the particularisms of the past. In Spain, that victory was not durable, and the forms of violence wavered.

The precise timing and extent of the shift from reactionary to modern forms of collective violence in these countries remains to be established. For France, it is fairly clear that the shift was barely started by 1840, but close to complete by 1860. Furthermore, France experienced great, and

359
Tilly

COLLECTIVE
VIOLENCE IN
EUROPEAN
PERSPECTIVE

nearly simultaneous, outbreaks of both forms of collective violence in the years from 1846 through 1851. The well-known events we customarily lump together as the Revolution of 1848 and the less-known but enormous insurrection of 1851 stand out both for their magnitude and for their mixture of reactionary and modern disturbances, but they came in the company of such notable outbreaks as the widespread food riots of 1846–47, the Forty-Five Centime Revolt of 1848–49, and the unsuccessful coup of 1849.

If this account of the transition from reactionary to modern collective violence in Western Europe is correct, it has some intriguing features. First, the timing of the transition corresponds roughly to the timing of industrialization and urbanization—England early, Italy late, and so on. Furthermore, the most rapid phase of the transition seems to occur together with a great acceleration of industrial and urban growth, early in the process: England at the beginning of the century, France of the 1850's, Germany of the 1850's and 1870's, Italy of the 1890's.

Second, there is some connection between the timing of the transition and the overall level of collective violence in a country. Over the last 150 years, if we think in terms of the frequency and scale of disturbances rather than the turnover of regimes, we can probably place Spain ahead of France, France ahead of Italy, Italy ahead of Germany, and Germany ahead of England. France is in the wrong position, and the contrast much less than the differences in the countries' reputations for stability or instability, but there is some tendency for the latecomers (or noncomers) to experience greater violence. If we took into account challenges to national integration posed by such peoples as the Catalans, and differences in the apparatus of repression, the connection would very likely appear even closer.

The information we have on hand, then, suggests that the processes of urbanization and industrialization themselves transform the character of collective violence. But how? We have a conventional notion concerning the life cycle of protest during the course of industrialization and urbanization: an early stage consisting of chaotic responses to the displacements and disruptions caused by the initial development of urban industry, a middle stage consisting of the growth of a militant and often violent working class, a late stage consisting of the peaceful integration of that working class into economic and political life. This scheme has many faults, as we have seen. Certainly we must correct and expand it to take account both of other groups than industrial workers and of the connections between industrialization and urbanization concerning the character of collective violence we have already reviewed raises grave doubts whether the underlying process producing and transforming protest was one of disintegration followed by reintegration, and whether the earlier forms of protest were so chaotic as the scheme implies.

The experience of France challenges the plausible presumption that rapid urbanization produces disruptions of social life that in turn generate protest. There is, if anything, a negative correlation over time and space between the pace of urban growth and the intensity of collective violence. The extreme example is the contrast between the 1840's, with slow urban growth plus enormous violence, and the decade after 1851, with very fast growth and extensive peace. Cities like St. Etienne of Roubaix that received and formed large numbers of new industrial workers tended to remain quiet while centers of the old traditional crafts, like Lyon and Rouen, raged with rebellion. When we can identify the participants in political disturbances, they tend to grossly underrepresent newcomers to the city and draw especially from the "little people" most firmly integrated into the local political life of the city's working-class neighborhoods. The geography of the disturbances itself suggests as much. It was not the urban neighborhoods of extreme deprivation, crime, or vice, George Rudé reports, "not the newly settled towns or quarters that proved the most fertile breeding-ground for social and political protest, but the old areas of settlement with established customs, such as Westminster, the City of London, Old Paris, Rouen, or Lyon." The information available points to a slow, collective process of organization and political education—what we may loosely call a development of class consciousness—within the city rather than a process of disruption leading directly to personal malaise and protest.

As a consequence of this process, the great new cities eventually became the principal settings of collective violence in France. Furthermore, collective violence moved to the city faster than the population did. Even at the beginning of the 19th century, the towns and cities of France produced a disproportionate share of the nation's collective violence. Yet tax rebellions, food riots, and movements against conscription did occur with fair regularity in France's small towns and villages. After these forms of disturbance disappeared, the countryside remained virtually silent for decades. When rural collective violence renewed, it was in the highly organized form of farmers' strikes and marches on Government buildings. This sequence of events was, to some extent, a result of urbanization.

Early in the 19th century, the expansion of cities incited frequent rural protests—obviously in the case of the food riot, more subtly in the case of other forms of collective violence. We have some reason to believe that groups of people who were still solidly established within rural communities, but were losing their livelihoods through the concentration of property and the urbanization of industry, regularly spearheaded such protests. The most important group was probably the workers in cottage industry. Their numbers declined catastrophically as various industries—especially textiles—moved to the city during the first half of the century. Large numbers of them hung on in the countryside, doing what weaving, spinning, or forging they could, seeking out livings as handymen, day laborers, and farmhands, and railing against their fate. Within their communities they were able to act collectively against power looms, farm machines, tax collectors, and presumed profiteers.

Slowly before midcentury, rapidly thereafter, the increasing desperation of the French countryside and the expanding opportunities for work in

361
Tilly

COLLECTIVE
VIOLENCE IN
EUROPEAN
PERSPECTIVE

the new industrial cities drew such men away from their rural communities into town. That move cut them off from the personal, day-to-day contacts that had given them the incentive and the means for collective action against their enemies. It rearranged their immediate interests, placed them in vast, unfamiliar communities, and gave them relatively weak and unreliable relations with those who shared common interests with them.

The initial fragmentation of the work force into small groups of diverse origins, the slow development of mutual awareness and confidence, the lack of organizational experience among the new workers, and the obstacles thrown up by employers and governments all combined to make the development of the means and the will for collective action a faltering time-consuming process. Collective violence did not begin in earnest until the new industrial workers began forming or joining associations—trade unions, mutual-aid societies, political clubs, conspiratorial groups —devoted to the collective pursuit of their interests. In this sense, the short-run effect of the urbanization of the French labor force was actually to damp collective violence. Its long-run effect, however, was to promote new forms of collective action that frequently led to violent conflicts, and thus to change the form of collective violence itself.

This happened in part through the grouping together of large numbers of men sharing a common fate in factories, urban working-class neighborhoods, and construction gangs. Something like the class-conscious proletariat of which Marx wrote began to form in the industrial cities. This new scale of congregation combined with new, pressing grievances, improving communication, the diffusion of new organizational models from Government and industry, and grudging concessions by the authorities to the right of association. The combination facilitated the formation of special-interest associations. At first workers experimented with cramped, antique, exclusive associations resembling (or even continuing) the old guilds; gradually they formed mutual-aid societies, labor exchanges, unions, and national and international federations.

The new associations further extended the scale and flexibility of communication among workers; they made it possible to inform, mobilize, and deploy large numbers of men fast and efficiently in strikes, demonstrations, and other common action. These potentially rebellious populations and their demanding associations proliferated in the big cities, in the shadows of regional and national capitals. They therefore posed a greater (or at least more visible) threat to the authorities than had their smalltown predecessors. The authorities responded to the threat by organizing police forces, crowd-control tactics, and commissions of inquiry. The associations, in their turn, achieved greater sophistication and control in their show of strength. The process took time—perhaps a generation for any particular group of workers. In that longer run the urbanization of the labor force produced a whole new style of collective violence.

The experience of the industrial workers has one more important lesson for us. In both reactionary and modern forms of collective violence, men commonly express their feeling that they have been unjustly denied their rights. Reactionary disturbances, however, center on rights once enjoyed but now threatened, while modern disturbances center on rights not yet enjoyed but now within reach. The reactionary forms are especially the work of groups of men who are losing their collective positions within the system of power, while the modern forms attract groups of men who are striving to acquire or enhance such positions. The reactionary forms, finally, challenge the basic claims of a national state and a national economy, while the modern forms rest on the assumption that the state and the economy have a durable existence—if not necessarily under present management. In modern disturbances, men contend over the control and organization of the State and the economy.

What links these features together historically? The coordinate construction of the nation-state and the national economy simultaneously weakened local systems of power, with the rights and positions which depended on them, and established new, much larger arenas in which to contend for power. In Western European countries, as locally based groups of men definitively lost their struggle against the claims of the central power, reactionary disturbances dwindled and modern disturbances swelled. The rapid transition from one to the other occurred where and when the central power was able to improve rapidly or expand its enforcement of its claims. Accelerating urbanization and industrialization facilitated such an expansion by providing superior means of communication and control to the agents of the central power, by drawing men more fully into national markets, and by spreading awareness of, and involvement in, national politics. In the process, special-purpose associations like parties and labor unions grew more and more important as the vehicles in the struggle for power, whether violent or nonviolent. Thus urbanization and industrialization affected the character and the incidence of collective violence profoundly, but indirectly.

363
Tilly
COLLECTIVE
VIOLENCE IN
EUROPEAN
PERSPECTIVE

The Logic of Collective Violence

Before rushing to apply this analysis of European collective violence to current American experience, we should pause to notice how much of it is a historical analysis—helpful in sorting out the past and identifying the context of the present, but not in predicting the future. Categories like primitive, reactionary, and modern have more kinship with time-bound terms like Renaissance, Liberalism, or Neolithic than with more timeless concepts like urban, clan, or wealth. I would not argue for a moment that forward-looking protests are necessarily larger in scale than backward-looking ones, although that has been the usual experience of Western countries for several centuries. For those were centuries of growth and centralization, in which to look backward meant to look toward the smaller scale. As a general statement, the analysis is too one dimensional.

To take the problem out of time, we must deal with at least two dimensions. One is the organizational basis of routine political life. To simplify the problem, we might distinguish between politics based on small-scale, local, traditional groupings (communal politics) and politics based on large-scale organizations formed to serve one well-defined interest (associational politics). Then we could say that both the primitive and the reactionary forms of collective violence spring from communal bases, although under differing circumstances, while the modern forms of collective violence develop from an associational base. In the primitive and reactionary cases, the links among those who join together in collective action—whether violent or not—come from traditional, localized, inherited, slow-changing memberships. The rhythm of collective violence therefore follows the rhythm of congregation and dispersion of existing communal groups; market days, holidays, harvest days produce more than their share of violence. In the purely modern case, on the other hand, deliberately created formal organizations provide the crucial links. The organizations help shape the aspirations and grievances of their members, define their enemies, determine the occasions on which they will assemble and the occasions on which they will confront their antagonists, and thus the occasions on which violence can occur. The communal/associational distinction is one of the hoariest in the study of social life, and it turns out to apply to such apparently antisocial behavior as violence.

We have to consider another dimension: the relationship of the groups involved to the existing structure of power. Again simplifying radically, we might imagine a division among groups unrepresented in the existing structure of power, groups in the process of acquiring positions in that structure, groups holding defined positions in that structure, and groups in the process of losing defined positions. Then it would be accurate to say that, on the whole, primitive disturbances involve groups holding defined positions in a (certain kind of) structure of power, whereas reactionary disturbances involve groups losing such positions, and modern disturbances involve groups acquiring them.

Strictly speaking, these are not types of violence. The distinctions do not apply to acts of violence, or even to the collective actions characteristically producing violence. They sort out groups of people into differing political situations. Their relevance to violence as such rests on a simple argument: a population's organization and political situation strongly affect its form of collective action, and the form of collective action stringently limits the possibilities of violence. Thus each type of group takes part in a significantly different variety of collective violence.

That clarification gives us the means of putting the two dimensions together. We discover that there are some other possible types not discussed so far, as shown in Table IV. It is not so hard to fill in two of the blanks. There are really two varieties of modern collective violence; a frenzied variety on the part of people like the suffragettes who are trying to storm the system, and a more controlled but massive show of strength by groups like parties already established in the system. Violent movements of protest like Poujadism [a French taxpayer revolt in the 1950's] on the other hand, resemble those I have called reactionary except that they

Table IV

Relation to structure of power

	Acquiring position	Maintaining position	Losing position
Organizational base:			
Communal	(?)	Primitive	Reactionary
Associational	Modern	(?)	(?)

have an associational base. This suggests placing them in the lower right-hand corner: the characteristic collective violence of groups losing position in a system built on an associational basis.

As for acquiring position in a communal system, common sense says it cannot be done. But we might throw common sense aside and speculate that the millenarian, transcendental, and fanatical movements that rack backward areas from time to time provide men with the means of acquiring totally new identities through religious conversion. This would lead us to expect these other-worldly protests to turn into modern protests as the organizational basis shifts from communal to associational. Some features of millenarian movements in such European areas as Andalusia and southern Italy lend this speculation a snippet of plausibility, but it is still only a speculation.

We have filled in the boxes. The table now looks like Table V. The

Table V

Relation to structure of power

	Acquiring position	Maintaining position	Losing position
Organizational basis:			
Communal	Other worldly?	Primitive	Reactionary
Associational	Offensive	Interest-group	Defensive

boxes are not airtight. We can easily locate groups standing halfway between the communal and associational forms of organization, or just barely maintaining their political positions. Organized criminals come to mind as an example of the first; languishing protest parties as an example of the second. The point of the scheme is to suggest that groups' usual collective actions, and therefore their usual forms of collective violence, will also fall halfway between those of their neighbors in the table.

All this box filling would be no more than a scholastic exercise if it were not possible to draw some interesting hypotheses from the discussion. The first is that, regardless of their organizational basis, groups acquiring position are likely to define their problem as the achieving of rights due them on general ground but so far denied, groups losing position to define their problem as the retention of specific rights of which they are being deprived, and groups maintaining position to pay less attention to rights and justice. Second, the actions of those acquiring or losing position are likely to be more violent than those maintaining position. Third, a larger proportion of collective actions on a communal basis results in violence, because the associational form gives the group a surer control over its own actions, and thus permits shows of force without damage or bloodshed. While historically the shift from communal to associational bases for collective violence did not, by any means, stop the fighting, it did bring into being a number of alternative nonviolent mechanisms for the regulation of conflicts: the strike, the parliament, the political campaign.

So when does this line of reasoning lead us to expect that collective violence will be widespread? It suggests that over the very long run the transformation of a population, a movement, or a society from a communal to an associational basis of organization diminishes its overall level of violence, but only over the very long run. If we were to consider external war as well as internal civil disorders, even that timid inference would look dubious. The scheme implies much more definitely that collective violence clusters in those historical movements when the structure of power itself is changing decisively—because there are many new contenders for power, because several old groups of power holders are losing their grips, or because the locus of power is shifting from community to nation, from nation to international bloc, or in some other drastic way. Violence flows from politics, and more precisely from political change.

The extent of violence depends on politics in the short run as well. Violence is not a solo performance, but an interaction. It is an interaction that political authorities everywhere seek to monopolize, control, or at least contain. Nowadays almost all collective violence on a significant scale involves the political authorities and their professional representatives: policemen, soldiers, and others. This happens, first, because the authorities make it their business to intervene and thus maintain their monopoly on the use of force; second, because so much collective violence begins with a direct (but not necessarily violent) challenge to the authorities themselves.

As odd as it may seem, the authorities have far greater control over the short-run extent and timing of collective violence, especially damage to persons rather than property, than their challengers do. This is true for several reasons. The authorities usually have the technological and organizational advantage in the effective use of force, which gives them a fairly great choice among tactics of prevention, containment, and retaliation. The limits of that discretion are more likely to be political and moral —Can we afford to show weakness? Could we fire on women and children?—than technical. If the criterion of success is simply the minimization of violence, repression often works. In recent European experience few countries have been freer of civil disorder than Spain, a normally turbulent nation, when it was under the right dictatorships of Primo de Rivera and Franco. In the heydays of the German and Italian Fascists, virtually the only violence to occur was at the hands of Government employees.

The authorities also have some choice of whether, and with how much muscle, to answer political challenges and illegal actions that are not intrinsically violent: banned assemblies, threats of vengeance, wildcat strikes. A large proportion of the European disturbances we have been surveying turned violent at exactly the moment when the authorities intervened to stop an illegal but nonviolent action. This is typical of violent strikes and demonstrations. Furthermore, the great bulk of the killing and wounding in those same disturbances was done by troops or police rather than by insurgents or demonstrators. The demonstrators, on the other hand, did the bulk of the damage to property. If we sweep away the confusion brought on by words like "riot," "mob," or "violence," a little reflection will make it clear that this division of labor between maimers and smashers follows logically from the very nature of encounters between police and their antagonists.

All this means that over the short run the extent, location, and timing of collective violence depend heavily on the way the authorities and their agents handle the challenges offered to them. Over a longer run, however, the kinds of challenges they face and the strength of those challenges depend rather little on their tactics of crowd control and a great deal on the way the entire political system apportions power and responds to grievances.

Discussions of these matters easily drift into praise and blame, justification and condemnation, fixing of responsibility for violence. If, when, where, and by whom violence should be permitted are inescapably difficult questions of moral and political philosophy. My review of European historical experience has not resolved them. Its purpose was the more modest one of sketching social processes lying behind the actual occurrence of collective violence in Western countries as they have existed over the last century or so. Yet the fact that the analytic and historical questions bring us so close to political philosophy underlines my main conclusions: collective violence is part and parcel of the Western political process, and major changes in its character result from major changes in the political system.

If that is the case, very recent changes in the character and locus of violent protest bear careful watching. Through much of Europe, students have reached a level of activism and anger never before equaled; the French events of May 1968 were only the most spectacular episode of a long series. Separatist movements long thought dead, ludicrous, or at least under control—Welsh, Scottish, Breton, Basque, Slovak, Flemish— have sprung up with energy. Demands for autonomy, cohesion, insulation from state control, which virtually disappeared from European political debate a half-century ago, now appear to be growing rapidly. Of course it is possible that the widespread emergence of autonomist themes in collective violence is a coincidence, a passing fancy, or simply my misreading of the character of the new movements. If none of these is the case, we might consider the possibility that they record a transfer of power away from the national State, perhaps in part because its own weight keeps it from dealing with the most burning aspirations of its own citizens, and in

367

Tilly

COLLECTIVE
VIOLENCE IN
EUROPEAN
PERSPECTIVE

part because power is devolving to international blocs of states. Then we might be witnessing a transformation comparable in scope to the 19th-century shift from reactionary to modern forms of collective violence. These are speculations, but they, too, emphasize the political significance of violence.

I must leave it to the well-informed reader to apply this analysis of European experience to the civil disorders of contemporary America. Naturally, analogies immediately come to mind. Recent studies of ghetto riots have been producing a picture of the average rioter that much resembles what we know of many 19th-century urban disturbances: the predominance of young males, overrepresentation of longtime residents rather than recent migrants, the relative absence of criminals, and so on. But why search for easy analogies? The chief lesson of the European experience is not that riots are all the same. Far from it!

What we have seen, instead, is a close connection between the basic political process and the predominant forms of conflict, both violent and nonviolent. That makes it hard to accept a recent characterization of American ghetto riots as "mainly for fun and profit." It raises doubts about attempts to reduce current student rebellions to one more expression of adolescent anxiety. It makes one wonder whether the recent revival of violent and nonviolent separatist movements in such different Western countries as Belgium, Canada, Spain, France, and Great Britain indicates some larger change in international politics. For the basic conclusion is simple and powerful. Collective violence belongs to political life, and changes in its form tell us that something important is happening to the political system itself.

23. National Character and European Labor History

PETER N. STEARNS

*Long ago Georges Lefebvre urged us to view history "from below," to look
at the consumers of the politics made by the élite. All too frequently his advice has not been followed. Historians simply have found it easier (thanks
to better documentation), more significant, and perhaps more congenial to
work with history "from above." For the most part, cf course, the consumers
of the politics made by Napoleon III, Disraeli, Gladstone, Bismarck, and their
successors were working people. We have already seen that they resorted frequently to collective violence both before and after the heydey of those statesmen. That, however, is but one aspect of their lives and aspirations at the end of
the nineteenth century.*

   *To understand what the life of working people was really like in this period
one needs to keep in mind that it was played out, in the developed countries
at any rate, within the framework of a "second industrial revolution," the
revolution of steel, chemicals, and electricity in which business was organizing itself for the first time into corporations and cartels. At the same time
factory work and urban life were becoming the norm. In turn, because of
vastly enlarged electorates and the rising tide of parliamentary party politics, the period saw the creation of the first viable, genuine, and permanent
socialist parties and trade union movements. These developments took place*

Source: Peter N. Stearns, "National Character and European Labor History,"
Journal of Social History, IV, No. 4 (1970–1971), 333–56. Copyright © 1971 by
Peter N. Stearns. Reprinted by permission of the author and editor. [Footnotes
omitted.]

*within distinct national states, each with its own political and cultural pecu-
liarities. Historians have, then, tended to treat working people's lives in national
terms: workers (like everyone else) take on the "national character" of their
country. Indeed, there has been a veritable epidemic of popular interest in
"national character" in recent years, as witnessed by such best-selling books as
David Frost's* The English, *Luigi Barzini's* The Italians, *and Sanche de Gra-
mont's* The French.

*This selection, by social historian Peter Stearns of Rutgers University
examines the relationship, if any, between "national character" and the life of
working people. Stearns attacks the question as a problem in comparative
history, an approach already illustrated by the Langer and Tilly selections.
At the same time, he tells us much about the lives, hopes, and aspirations of
European workers and their families at the end of the nineteenth century,
when they were becoming a social force to be reckoned with. What evidence
does Stearns use to show that British, French, and German workers did reflect
normally conceived "national characteristics," and what are those characteristics? What data makes him doubt these stereotypes? Were there any national
peculiarities which he suggests might have affected worker outlooks? For
what reasons and on what evidence does he believe it to be more fruitful to
group workers by industry or kind of work rather than by nation?*

The need for comparative study is often invoked, but historians have
more than once demonstrated their ability to withstand invocations. In
the history of European labor, most studies remain purely national. Those
few whose titles suggest a wider scope turn out to be divided into separate national chapters with only a hint of explicit comparison. The national focus has produced widespread assumptions about national characteristics which have not been subjected to any rigorous examination. We
can easily recite the features of French workers, but have we seriously
stopped to investigate whether these features are really uniquely French?
The national focus of most labor history is implicitly comparative, in its
assumption that one nation can be distinguished from the next in this
subject; the comparative approach must now become explicit.

So much for yet another invocation. The next step is to ask, what are
we to compare? What little precedent there is suggests that our purpose
should be to discover what the "national genius" of each country is. We
know that Frenchmen are individualistic; a comparative study might hope
to measure this characteristic with some precision, show its effects in
workers' behavior, and possibly discuss its causes. Yet this sort of approach should be in terms of questions, not a priori assumptions. The
issue is not, at this stage, what was the national character of French workers, but whether there was a national character at all. The problem is of
course immensely difficult. For the period under consideration, 1890 to
1914, there are surprisingly few studies of the working classes, for historians have been bent on hailing the rise of the labor movement. Without
going into detail about the problems of sources, it is obvious that information available about one national working class may not be available

for another. Studies by contemporary German sociologists about the goals and mobility patterns of German workers have no counterparts in other countries, for example. Even precise statistical comparisons, of strike movements or wage patterns, are complicated by different units of measurement from one country to the next. Yet the effort must be undertaken. We must know among other things whether knowledge about the mobility expectations of German workers can be applied to workers elsewhere or whether it must be treated as distinctively German.

One thing is certain: however difficult to handle, the doubts about national character are not all frivolous. Many of the most common stereotypes are open to question. I admit to a fear of belaboring the obvious, both in outlining familiar characteristics that cannot be ignored and in dealing with others that crumble at the first breath of skepticism. Some flimsy straw men have to be attacked with a vigor that in other contexts might seem excessive. Some strangely simple points must be made to jar a framework both simple and pervasive.

Studies of national character have been poorly developed in the social sciences generally. It seems immensely difficult to remove the blinders in this field. It seems immensely difficult to ask questions rather than endlessly to repeat the same conventions. A fine methodological essay on the subject instructs us to look for unusual incidence of personality traits, rather than uniform behavior and to expect great diversity by class and region. But the actual efforts by social scientists who equate the nation with society fall well short of this subtlety. The French are thrifty, individualistic, irritable, rational (does rationality produce irritability?), unusually interested in culture. And what is the evidence? The classical literary tradition, bits and pieces on the artisanal tradition, and above all what everybody says about the French. The Englishman is pragmatic, peaceful, fair. Why? As far as workers are concerned, because somehow in the nineteenth century workers imprinted on the image of the unarmed bobby, who provided a new model for ideal character. It is easy to be amused by the notion of a whole class of would-be policemen, but at least such an explanation leads us in a fruitful direction. The historian cannot measure national character as precisely as a sociologist might hope to do in the present. But even aside from the lack of real measurements to date, a historical dimension will continue to be vital. For national character, if it exists, has to be caused. The historian can hope to get some idea of what national character was in the past, and whether it was; he should also be alert to possible changes, for we tend quite unhistorically to think of national character as a constant. He can and should also ask about causes, even if his inquiries take him into the history of toilet training and child care. In sum, national character, so commonly taken as given, invites elaborate inquiry from many disciplines and historians have a role to play.

The purpose of this essay is more modest, of course. I am discussing a time period, 1890 to 1914, that is very limited, in part so that reasonably precise comparisons are possible. I deal with only four countries—France, Britain, Belgium, and Germany—which were in a reasonably

371

Stearns

NATIONAL
CHARACTER
AND EUROPEAN
LABOR HISTORY

comparable range of industrialization; and it must be insisted, contrary to some national stereotypes, that France was definitely in this range. And I deal only with workers. It is quite possible that the doubts I must suggest about workers' national character do not apply to other groups. Generalizations about national character usually have a distinct upper-class bias, relying on cultural and political criteria. It is conceivable to admit, for example, that German Junkers and industrialists may have had national characteristics and that therefore knowledge of national character is essential to understand Germany at the end of the nineteenth century, but still to question how much all this advances our understanding of German workers. How rapidly and extensively do characteristics filter down? Again, when we begin to question rather than to assume, the existence of national characteristics at one level does not prove their existence at all levels.

We can agree, I believe, on many of the characteristics normally attributed to the national working classes—leaving Belgium aside for a moment since it has failed to produce a national character. The vast majority of these characteristics are institutional, relating to the labor movement. This should in itself be a warning signal, for real national character is a concentration of psychological or personality traits, not the attributes of organizations. But obviously in labor history organizational characteristics—like the pragmatism of British trade unions—are commonly related to the traits of workers themselves. Many of these characteristics cannot easily be dismissed, which is why their summary is more than the establishment of straw men. A few other apparent characteristics can be added, some rather unexpected, that are even farther removed from the formal labor movement.

The British worker was of course pragmatic and tolerant, content with piecemeal gains and nonviolent. His trade union and political representatives mingled amicably with the upper classes; only in Britain can one imagine a unionist's biography entitled "From Workman's Cottage to Windsor Castle"—not that the author managed to establish residence in the latter. So far as we know, the British worker rarely threatened severe violence; even in barroom brawls he refrained from pulling weapons. Not for him the calls to arms of the French syndicalists or even the quiet advice of a worker in Halle: "The best thing is to buy a gun." The vast network of collective bargaining and conciliation agreements reflected the moderate tone of the labor force. Roughly 800,000 workers annually accepted conciliation procedures for their wage rates by 1908, which means that they vowed in advance to compromise; over two million were covered by formal conciliation boards. All of this both explains and reflects the nature of British trade unions and the pragmatic politics of British workers before and after the rise of the Labour party.

The British worker enjoyed and expected a high standard of living. Here is surely one of the causes of the unexcited approach to politics and industrial agitation. In Germany one finds cries of despair from relatively well-paid workers, like the Ruhr miners in 1904 who shouted "we are tired of starving," which have few echoes in Britain. Moreover, consumption patterns in Britain were in some ways more bourgeois than those on the continent. Most obviously, the British worker wanted a three- or four-room dwelling unit, if possible in a separate house. This sort of housing interest may imply and cause comparative stability and acceptance of the established order, an *embourgeoisement* which had not yet penetrated the poorer but also freer-floating workers on the continent. And how much of the tone of the British working class was set by the fact that working class wives, living often in separate dwellings, did not wrangle, and burden their husbands with tales of their battles, as the Germans did who were crowded into tenements? This is not the least important of the ways in which British workers were free from some of the personal acrimony that surrounded their counterparts elsewhere.

The third general characteristic, at least as valid as the first two, is a bit discordant. British workers had a distinctive style of life in many respects, defiant of middle-class norms, and their most distinctive grievances were not those to be expected of a labor force with high but pliant expectations. The British worker was far more interested in sports and in gambling than his continental counterparts. Rugby and boxing were integral parts of the life of Welsh miners. And they and others regularly placed bets on games and races. On the continent only Belgian workers had developed this passion for gambling, and their efforts were limited largely to pigeon racing, whereas the British interest encompassed horses and dogs as well as birds. Working class wives described how placing a bet brought hope and excitement into their lives. Many British workers enjoyed a distinctive appearance on work days. They liked to look like ruffians and refused to use factory wash facilities. The contrast with German workers was striking, as many observers noted; German workers carefully washed and changed clothing before leaving the plant and often agitated for improved wash facilities, though the ones they already had were the best in Europe. British working class wives were considerably more independent than their continental counterparts. Observers (including traveling workers) uniformly noted that the British wife was a sloppier housekeeper than the French or German, more wasteful of food and less capable of sticking to a budget; some claimed that she did not care for her children as well. These elements add up, I think, to a statement that British workers had a more genuine proletarian culture than their continental counterparts in basic matters like washing habits and recreational patterns. They were freer from peasant traditions, more thoroughly urban.

The British worker worried more about unemployment and possibly more about the pace of work than did the French and Germans. Rates of unemployment among union members were not a great deal higher than those in France, but in Britain the unskilled had long crowded into the cities, rather than remaining in the countryside as was the predominant pattern on the continent. Only in Britain were there marches and demonstrations of the unemployed, even in years of prosperity like 1911. In strikes, the pervasive concern over unemployment was reflected in the

373

Stearns

NATIONAL
CHARACTER
AND EUROPEAN
LABOR HISTORY

high—and distinctively British—level of demarcation disputes and the relatively high incidence of demands to curtail hours of work. A more concrete example: cab drivers in both London and Paris struck during this period, but in Paris they stressed wage raises whereas in London they asked for a limit on licenses issued. Here again, distinctive and in this case durable British characteristics emerge, for the fear of unemployment and the desire to protect established skills have been a continuing part of the history of British labor in the twentieth century. Well before 1914 these concerns were affecting British industry, as workers slowed up on the job and resisted technical change.

The characteristics of French workers can be outlined quite easily. Their fabled individualism was revealed in countless ways: the small size of most unions, the resistance to relatively moderate union dues, the small size of the average strike, the almost complete lack—compared particularly to Britain—of solidarity strikes, indeed the whole flowering of revolutionary syndicalism which sets France off vividly from the other industrial countries, for syndicalism was above all a rebellion against organization and bureaucracy. At the same time class consciousness ran high, even if it could not always be effectively organized. One comparative study of French and American labor has stressed that French unions believed that society was hostile and treated the strike as an episode in class war rather than a pragmatic effort at immediate gain; correspondingly, so this line of argument runs, collective bargaining was unimportant. Class tension could lead to violence in France. Four or five strikes in company towns were virtual revolutions in this period, in which workers rushed to seize their employer's home and destroy his property. These incidents it must be stressed, are atypical in France, but it remains interesting that no analogous rebellions occurred in Britain even in the strike wave that swept similarly isolated towns in the Black Country in 1913.

At the same time there was an underlying conservatism that French workers shared with their employers and others. The low birth rate has to be seen as the result of a peculiarly intense desire for stability. Workers' expectations were limited in many ways. They seemed preoccupied with improvements in diet; France is the only country where the percentage spent on food rose markedly with improvements in income. This interest in food is, of course, conveniently in keeping with French character. It meant that French workers consumed almost as much meat as British workers did, despite lower incomes; and it set the French off from the Germans and Belgians, who were relatively content with far poorer diets. But this focus, along with the expectedly high rate of alcohol consumption, also reflected a relative lack of concern about more substantial consumptive items, like housing. French workers also tended to be less interested in issues like hours and conditions of work, judging by the incidence of strike demands compared to patterns in the other industrial countries.

The two strike demands that do stand out from a comparative standpoint sum up, in fact, much of the character of French labor. Twenty-four percent of all French strikes between 1899 and 1914 were over personal issues, such as firing a hated foreman or rehiring a pal. These issues were prominent in other countries too, of course, but the incidence in France was about 25 percent higher than the norm for the industrial zone. The French were preoccupied with personal, individual dignity, like the arsenal workers who claimed the right "to remain absolute masters of ourselves outside the arsenals." One might read into these personal disputes a special French sourness and touchiness as well, plus an obvious distaste for factory discipline. And there is at least a potential class consciousness in the battles with foremen and managers. The French struck unusually frequently over wage questions, a trait that persisted into the interwar period. One reason for this was their quick perception of a rise in food prices. The British were slow to react to inflation after 1900. They were relatively less interested in food and their wives, bad budget keepers, were not quick to report that prices were rising; in one Welsh mining village women began complaining about prices only in 1907, five years after inflation had begun. French women were more alert to the issue. Complaints about food prices appear extensively as early as 1903; and it is only in France that market riots occur. The preoccupation with wages in France may have even deeper significance. The wage is an individual gain, to be used as the individual wishes. In stressing wages over more collective improvements or conditions on the job, the French worker may have been demonstrating his individualism in a very basic sense.

The German worker evokes images of docility, organization-mindedness, a zeal for hard work. In the poems and letters of German workers we can even find hints of the distinctive German imagination and addiction to Romanticism; one metal worker wrote that, when he was on the job, "Forms and pictures pour from my mind's eye. O that I could paint them all. O were I freer," while another simply noted that "wild longings torment me." Certainly the German longing for nature touched the life of workers deeply. Large numbers of workers preferred to commute many miles than to move to the city, while urban workers listed gardening and walks in the countryside as their favorite recreation. A Berlin worker summed up the sentiment: "I believe that every city resident, as soon as time permits, should go to the countryside, go to nature, and fill his lungs with pure, unspoiled air."

Attachment to traditional family structure remained strong. Many workers fought to avoid having their wives work, at least outside the home, although the percentage of working wives was rising. Foreign visitors marveled at the domestic skills of the working class wives, their devotion to cleanliness and their sensible cooking. Many workers remained unaware of birth control practices, while others considered *coitus interruptus* the only sound method; only gradually did knowledge of artificial devices, known as "Parisian articles," spread.

The zeal for hard work was consistent with traditionalist attitudes about the family and nature. Silesian miners thought it was evil to miss a shift, and German miners generally accepted far longer working hours

375

Stearns

NATIONAL
CHARACTER
AND EUROPEAN
LABOR HISTORY

than their counterparts elsewhere. Along with the *Arbeitsfreude,* noted by all foreign observers, was a lack of imagination on the job. German workers had to be told what to do, in contrast to the more inventive but less assiduous French or British. In the textile industry certainly there was a higher ratio of foremen to workers than in France or Britain.

Signs of docility toward authority were everywhere. In the factory German workers had to be obsequious toward their foremen and managers. Some workers who visited Britain contrasted the chumminess of English factories, where employers might attend the same church as their workers and might talk to them in friendly tones, with the rigidity of Germany. Yet the rate of strikes over matters of personal dignity was relatively low, implying that German workers accepted the factory hierarchy. A more specific comparison points to the same condition. Whereas many French metallurgical workers made at least one attempt to protest company paternalism before the war, albeit in vain, German metallurgists were by all indications content. The labor movement obviously built upon the German worker's taste for authority. German unions quickly developed the largest bureaucracies and highest dues. Whereas most French unions left their members free to strike with at most a voice vote at a meeting, German unions carefully required a three-quarters majority in a ballot vote plus authorization of the central executive.

Low expectations complete the picture of the German worker. Oppressed by miserable housing conditions, which were vigorously deplored not only by socialists but by liberal commentators, and by a meager diet, German workers protested only infrequently. Only about 150,000 struck each year, on the average, between 1900 and 1913 in this giant industrial country. This was a rate 25 percent below the French level absolutely and over 100 percent lower per capita of the manufacturing labor force. This relative reluctance to strike persisted in most of the interwar period and after World War II. German workers before 1914 were not addicted to expensive recreations, aside from drinking. They were only beginning to develop an interest in stylish clothing. Unskilled workers normally went without overcoats, and some told investigators that they found it appropriate that skilled workers wore clothing of this sort that they could not afford. Relatedly, many observers found a pervasive lack of ambition among German workers. Paul Göhre, who spent three months in a factory and many years writing about workers as result, stated that the goal of German workers was simply to get through life. More recently Ralf Dahrendorff has cited a lack of mobility, a reluctance to change companies, change jobs, or even move to a different area, as an enduring characteristic of the German labor force.

This, then, is the picture, at least in outline. It reveals that workers as well as formal labor organizations seem to have shared national characteristics of fundamental importance. Contemporary travelers certainly found this to be so. Well before 1914 they had documented the diligence of German workers, the fair play of the English and so on, and almost never was there dissent from the conventions about each nation's character.

Why, in the face of this varied evidence, object? It must be admitted at once that a complete dissent is not possible. The national stereotypes have too great a currency to be entirely wrong and I cannot pretend to dispute all the characteristics just sketched. Yet questions have to be raised. Too many studies, whether explicitly comparative or not, have illustrated national characteristics that were assumed in the first place. Contemporary travelers, thinking in terms of long-established images, naturally found what they knew they would find; their very unanimity should be a warning. Historians have repeated the pattern, and Americans are perhaps particularly vulnerable to this, since in studying abroad they find so much in their own surroundings that fits or seems to fit the familiar stereotypes.

The notion that workers before World War I can be described in terms of national characteristics must be challenged because too many of the characteristics contradict each other, because some important ones are demonstrably false, and because non-national categories of analysis are considerably more accurate than national ones.

Some possible contradictions need only be suggested. Quite a case can be made for French individualism, but note the obvious anomaly: the high rate of personal disputes suggests an unusual sense of small-group solidarity, of sticking up for one's pals. This was not full class-consciousness —indeed I would argue that it often inhibited class-consciousness— but it certainly revealed a sense of common cause. Many French workers may have been unusually unindividualistic in relation to their workmates. The preoccupation with wages may reveal certain national characteristics but also reflects a definite acceptance of the industrial system, a willingness to accept changes in techniques and work organization in return for better pay that in terms of the usual national stereotype seems un-French. The ambivalent picture of the British worker is troubling. Possibly the interest in "respectable" housing can be reconciled with the equally well documented disdain for "respectable" dress, but it is far more probable that different types of workers are being discussed within the same country. British workers had unusually high expectations and British workers were obsessed by fears of unemployment. Again, reconciliation is conceivable but it is more likely that different groups are involved, that the national picture is a false composite.

It is time to add some more facts, without trying to make the list too burdensome. There are many areas where evidence indicates at least that the national stereotypes require qualification. Despite foreign travelers' contentions that British workers were devoted to the city, autobiographical evidence suggests that British workers, too, talked of returning to the countryside; some did go back for village festivals, while the bicycle craze took many workers to the country for recreation. It is impossible to claim that bucolic sentiment was as high as in Germany and certainly recreational interests were more diverse, but the contrast is at least incomplete; yet distinctive rural longings are normally cited as part of German character. The stability and traditionalism of German family life form an-

377

Stearns

NATIONAL
CHARACTER
AND EUROPEAN
LABOR HISTORY

other doubtful generalization. It is true that unskilled workers, freshly in from the country, wanted their wives to quit work as soon as their own wages covered subsistence. But more skilled groups kept their wives at work at least until better housing was obtained (the principal goal was a separate room for the children) and the number of working wives rose very fast. This is quite consistent with close family ties, but not of a purely traditional sort. And there is considerable autobiographical evidence of widespread disruption and anxiety in some German worker families, where traditional male behavior was not changing as rapidly as women's expectations. Many wives made life miserable for their husbands when earnings did not rise or when too many babies came. And in textile regions many wives went into the factories because they hated housework, just as in Lancashire. German workers did not uniformly accept a factory hierarchy; one worker noted "I once gave a foreman the pleasure of giving me notice: I'll never do it again." Here again, we cannot claim to measure docility exactly, but at least considerable diversity can be noted. Nor were German foremen uniformly stiff and overbearing. Many were friendly and many addressed at least their skilled workers with the familiar "du"; even in the larger factories the legacy of artisanal comradeship was visible between master and workers. Is there a clear national picture in these industrial relationships at all?

Questions and qualifications of this sort can be raised almost endlessly. On at least five major points, assumptions about national characteristics have obscured the reality of working class life and activities.

British workers most decidedly did not eschew violence. They were rarely armed and may well have been restrained in barroom brawls—one would like direct police evidence on this—but violence against people and property was a recurrent feature of their protest. Precise comparisons are difficult and evidence remains thus far impressionistic. Still, if there was not more violence in Britain than in France in relation to the degree of strike activity, there was about as much, even before 1910. The British did not carry guns but they did have an unusual penchant for burning that may hark back to older traditions of protest. British miners, on a strike, fought with their fellows less often than was true in France or Germany, for they were better organized, but they were more likely to attack mine property. Cabdrivers and coachmen, builders and dockers clubbed nonstrikers in Britain as elsewhere. Everywhere there were occasional deaths in strikes, five or six in Britain in the late 1890s for example, but again no national pattern emerges.

After 1910 the picture changes. Nothing in France or Germany compares with the uprising of Welsh miners and transport workers in 1910–11, in which Chinese laundries, Jewish shopkeepers, and local magistrates were viciously attacked. Lest this be attributed to Welshness, it must be quickly added that the English too could do their share. The railroad strikes of 1910 and 1911 in France and Britain provide a useful comparison. Prior to the French strike there were widespread syndicalist promptings of sabotage and violence. During and soon after the strike,

1,411 cases of sabotage were reported, most of them (1,187) involving cutting telephone and telegraph wires. There were 10 shots fired, 11 dynamite attempts, 30 stonings of trains, 64 blocked signals, and 82 derailment attempts. Most of these were carried out by individuals and small groups. The British strike a year later had none of the preliminary rhetoric of violence, but bands of 200 or more workers attacked stations in many cities, looted hundreds of wagons, burned several warehouses and damaged at least 150 engines and other vehicles. There is no need to suggest that the character of British workers be altered to read unusually violent. Their grievances were unusually great at this point and their outburst astonished the nation. But the outburst did occur and it was violent, and it had some precedent in the far more limited violence of earlier years. Clearly the existing concept of national character is called into some question.

The French distaste for organization needs similar qualification in labor history. There is no doubt of the revolutionary syndicalist position, though this had to be modified as even these leaders realized that union dues and benefits were essential. But only a few large unions were syndicalist. Groups like the typographers and even many provincial building trades unions had dues and insurance programs comparable to their counterparts elsewhere. The fact that syndicalist programs are regarded as typical is a tribute to the power of their rhetoric and the degree to which they fit the French stereotype, but not to the analytical balance of their students. Some of the habits of workers so often cited as an index of individualism make no sense in a comparative context. Union membership fluctuated, to be sure, but much less than in organization-minded Germany. Annual turnover in the metal workers' union ran at two-thirds the rate of the German metal workers' federation (where it was over 100 percent). French strikes were very small on the average, but the average German strike, with 119 workers, was less than half the size. German workers too fought high dues and discipline. If a generalization is possible here, it has nothing to do with national character: amenability to voluntary organization depends on the length of experience of a labor force with industrialization, and here France led Germany.

The widespread notion that Britain had an immense lead in collective bargaining and that France somehow never developed significant collective bargaining before 1936 is simply in error. The British did have a chronological lead of a decade or two, since collective bargaining began seriously in France only in 1891 and in Germany in the late 1890s; but this follows more from stage of industrialization than from national character. By 1914 almost all French miners, printers, shoe factory workers and the like were covered by collective bargaining agreements as were large numbers of textile workers, dockers, and construction workers. There was virtually no instance in which French workers refused to bargain collectively and only a few where they refused outside arbitration. Of course some workers, whether syndicalist or not, grumbled that they had been "sold-out" by compromises; so they did in every country. There was

379

Stearns

NATIONAL
CHARACTER
AND EUROPEAN
LABOR HISTORY

in fact more grumbling in Germany, including strikes against union leadership on the subject; and where French workers typically accepted three-year contracts, the Germans long held out for one-year agreements that would limit their freedom of action less. Finally there was no suggestion in France of the near-rebellion against conciliation that developed among British miners, engineers, and railroad workers after 1910. In these same years in fact the strike rate in France leveled off in part because workers were so satisfied with the new collective bargaining system. Here without any question the stereotypes resulting from assumptions about French national character, plus unduly restrictive reading of C.G.T. resolutions, have led for this pre-World War I period to neglect of a major development in industrial history.

The Germans were not wild for work. Laments about overwork and fatigue crop up more frequently in Germany than in the other industrial countries. "My eyes burn so—if I can only sleep." Textile workers complained particularly of chronic fatigue. This was a major issue in the great Crimmitshau strike, while in a later survey of Adolf Levenstein 75 percent of all textile workers said they found no joy in their work. And German workers pressed more vigorously and successfully for a reduction of hours than did the French, with the mining industry the one partial exception. It does seem to be true that workers of rural origin seldom complained about long hours, in their gratitude for more regular and remunerative employment, though their pace of work was often slow. The Silesian miners, referred to earlier, who thought that missing a shift was evil are a case in point; but these workers found themselves surrounded by evil when they went to the Ruhr.

German workers, finally, both practiced and expected unusual job mobility. This is an understandable feature of a rapidly expanding industrial system, and it is amazing that assumptions about Germanness blinded even contemporary foreign observers to the phenomenon. Mining companies in the Ruhr faced sixty to seventy percent annual turnover, and many miners avoided company housing so that there would be no barriers to changing jobs; turnover rates in Upper Silesia were a bit higher. Workers left because they were uncomfortable in factory life ("I didn't really feel at home in the big hall") or to escape a harsh director or to gain higher pay. Here also is one reason for the rather low German strike rate—workers tried to solve problems on an individual basis, and the labor market was sufficiently tight for them to have some hope of success. All the inquiries into working class life reveal surprisingly high mobility expectations. Locksmiths, artisanally trained but now at work in machine factories, dreamed of their own bicycle repair shops, and some of them managed to get one. Thirty-three percent of the children of printers, in one large sample, went through secondary school and into the professions. In sum, the vast majority of German workers changed jobs several times and often changed trades; a significant minority, particularly those of artisanal origin, had hopes for substantial vertical mobility.

These revisions of some widely held stereotypes are sufficiently important to impel us to a further question: why should workers have had national characteristics? Much of the rather vague causation usually suggested for national character may have had little bearing on the workers. Did the rationalist traditions of Descartes and Racine reach French workers, whose experience with education was limited? All the evidence would indicate not, at least in any direct way. An interesting minority of workers read seriously and it may have made some difference that intellectual miners in the Ruhr read Goethe while those in Wales read Shakespeare, but this has little applicability to most workers. If there are national characteristics in the genuinely popular culture of the period, these remain to be discovered. At a glance the cheap novels which German workers borrowed from socialist libraries to the exclusion of almost every other kind of reading matter seem much the same in tone as popular literature in Britain. In any event, we can safely omit direct causation by formal national cultures, remembering that most national character studies put much weight on such cultures both as cause and as symptom.

On the other hand, a vastly more plausible cause of worker characteristics, the patterns of family upbringing, did not operate on a national basis. We need to know much more, of course. And it is possible to make references to stereotypes such as the authoritarian German family. But what is striking here is the lack of uniform patterns among workers within a single country. We will return to this point, for it is one of the most telling arguments against the notion of "national causation."

The simplest explanation of worker national character is to say that national characteristics antedated industrialization, whatever their cause, and were brought by peasants and artisans into industrial life. German workers recalled the docility, the respect for social hierarchy, they had learned on the big estates. Rural traditions also accustomed them to low standards of living, in housing and in the types of meat consumed, and this helps explain low levels of protest. Arguments of this sort are hard to refute. They do assume the possibility of proving pre-industrial national characteristics—were French peasants so pervasively individualistic? —and they assume that rural characteristics long persisted. We have seen already signs in Germany that second-generation workers quickly shook off whatever docility toward employers and joy in work they had brought from the countryside. And if journeymen artisans had been distinctively German in the mid-nineteenth century, their goals were no longer so by this time. The fact that most pre-industrial traits— including such basic matters as the type and amount of meat consumed —were regional rather than national add further doubts about the approach. Still, the possibility of persistent pre-industrial national traits sets an obvious task for further serious research.

We turn most readily to late nineteenth-century political and economic forms to explain workers' national characteristics. Surely the paternalism of the German government helps explain docility. Surely its repressiveness, as in the anti-Socialist laws, helps explain the German workers' sense of isolation, their desire to build a separate society through social-

381

Stearns

NATIONAL
CHARACTER
AND EUROPEAN
LABOR HISTORY

ism. But we are back to a familiar dilemma: Can two such diverse effects be posited? Are we talking about the same German workers in each case? Service in the German military helps explain docility and even other habits such as cleanliness. Many German workers, even socialists, looked back on their service fondly; but large numbers of workers hated their stint in the military, the majority of many categories of workers were not called up at all, and many British workers admired the military as fervently as many Germans did. What of the differences in national schooling? Did distinctive curricula, like the conservative-religious program in Germany, have much impact on workers whose experience with education was often recent and still brief? Some evidence indicates that school discipline had more effect—generally to repel young workers—and that it did not vary greatly from one nation to the next. Lack of social insurance in France can be used to explain hostility to the state, but French factory legislation was more advanced than German and gave many workers favorable contacts with the state; it has plausibly been suggested that the moderation of French miners, in comparison with British, stemmed from friendly relations with government inspectors in France. In sum, there are many aspects of state policy to be investigated, including police functions of course. At this point it is permissible to doubt that the national state was yet shaping worker character uniformly or distinctively.

There were of course huge differences from one country to the next in the rights of political participation. These cannot be ignored and they had undeniable influence on labor politics. From the vantage point of worker characteristics, however, they made a great difference only to the minority fervently interested in politics. The agitation of 1910–14, for example, casts doubt on any notion that the flexibility of the British political system had affected worker attitudes outside of politics. Belgian miners struck for political rights, which miners in France and Britain did not have to do, but their purposes in doing so reflect typical miners' economic goals. Different political systems produced notable differences in the impact of worker activity and interests on politics but, if only because politicization was so recent and incomplete, from a standpoint of general worker character they were not clearly decisive.

National economic characteristics are most frequently invoked by students of national character who mention workers at all. There are obvious economic factors that cut across national lines. In this period, the inflation after 1900, the spread of machines to the crafts and the general effort to speed up the pace of work are among the most notable. At the same time, many apparent national peculiarities may be due primarily to differences in the stage of industrialization. Many of the characteristics of German workers stem more from recent exposure to industry than from any Germanness and as we have seen the most stereotypically German workers in terms of zeal for work and so on were those of rural origin.

But there may be some substance to claims of national economic characteristics. If it is possible to argue, in this period, that the relatively low strike rate in Germany was due to less experience with industry and the possibility of higher individual expectations, why has this characteristic persisted? The timidity of the labor movement has played a great role, of course. But perhaps, even before World War I, German workers were forming modest collective expectations because their real wages continued to rise despite inflation and because their unemployment rate was so low compared to that in other industrial countries. In other words distinctive economic conditions in a formative period for the labor movement helped create more durable patterns on the part of workers and their leaders. Possibilities of this sort, which could be extended to cover the persistent French interest in wage gains and the British concern over unemployment, deserve consideration.

The two most common approaches to national economic character, however, are dangerously misleading. It is possible, and by no means entirely inaccurate, to postulate national types of employers, whose traits affected workers in many ways. The British, tolerant of their workers as human beings, willing to bargain; the Germans, tough, well-organized, paternalistic, as evidenced by their undoubted lead in employer associations and lockouts; the French somewhere in the middle, more paternalistic and less willing to bargain than the British but unable to organize well and far less effective than the Germans. But far too much is missed by these simple generalizations. British shipowners were far tougher, less willing to bargain than their counterparts in France or Germany. French metallurgists were almost as effectively tough and paternalistic as German. The rate of compromise in strikes was higher in Germany than in France, the rate of outright loss by workers lower. If German mine owners and machine builders were tougher than those in France and England, manufacturers in textiles, food processing, and in the crafts were at least as softhearted, whether by intent or by necessity.

And this leads to the final point about economic causation. The size and modernity of companies, so dear to the partisans of national character, are national statistical fallacies as far as understanding the working class is concerned. It may be useful, for political and economic history, to know how much bigger the average German company was then the average French company, but it is meaningless for working class history. How many working-class characteristics have been attributed to big business in Germany? Docility, organization-mindedness, sense of class isolation—the list is long. But there were at least two industrial economies in Germany and the more populous sector was unusually backward. Firms in textiles and leather goods were more dispersed and backward than those in France. In printing 50 percent of the French labor force was in units with over fifty workers in 1906, whereas Germany had only 44 percent in this category a year later; and automatic compositing machines were introduced far more rapidly in France. We have fearfully distorted our vision of the German economy and labor force by false national statistics. Correspondingly we have exaggerated the backwardness of the French artisanal sector and, in generalizing about the French small shop economy, have ignored the average size of companies in metallurgy (711 workers in 1906),

383

Stearns

NATIONAL
CHARACTER
AND EUROPEAN
LABOR HISTORY

mining (984 workers) and even textiles (over 300 workers in factory concerns).

Possible causes of workers' national characters are thus as questionable or at least as open to genuine investigation as were the national characters themselves. The burden of proof is on the defenders of national character. For in addition to the doubts about apparent symptoms and possible causes, an alternate framework for understanding worker characteristics can be developed that fits much better than the national approach and which most decidedly crosses national lines.

In all the industrial countries there were parallel divisions within the labor force. There was the gap between skilled and unskilled, in terms not only of earnings and dress but of basic outlook. There were workers who enjoyed hard work—who preferred piece to time rates, for example, in Britain just as in Germany. Most of all, there were traits normally, though of course not invariably, associated with given industries. A docker can be more accurately understood as a docker than as a Frenchman or German.

It has long been known that propensity to strike follows industrial lines; we can now add that, in the portion of Europe considered here, it followed these lines far more than national ones. German building trades workers struck just as often, per capita, as their brethren in France; they cannot be subsumed under the rubric "low German expectations"; the same is true of other groups such as printers, food processing workers, and metal workers. Strike methods, most notably the likelihood of violence, also followed industrial more than national lines. And so did strike goals. Building trades workers everywhere worried about pay. It was very difficult to interest them in other issues; even when they struck for a reduction of hours, they often intended mainly to gain increased overtime. Textile workers stressed pay questions as well, but they strove for less clearly positive gains. Machine builders were haunted by a fear of unemployment (their rate of unemployment was about the same in all the industrial countries, for here again national averages are of limited utility for understanding workers) and by the rising pace of work.

Behind these strike patterns were congruent expectations, again across national lines. Differences in expenditure patterns were far greater from group to group than from country to country. For example, a study of national averages reveals an unusual British interest in health expenditures, consistent with the pattern of high expectations. But unskilled workers spent almost nothing on health, for they feared and ignored doctors and relied on herbalists if they turned to any outsider—quite like the Prussian worker who said "God is the best doctor. If he wishes, I'm healthy; otherwise not." More generally, German artisans were fully as interested in housing as were British artisans. The latter had higher incomes and could indulge in the purchase of pianos and the like, but German artisans spent an even higher percentage of their budget on housing, cutting back on the purchase of food, drink, and sometimes clothes. Workers in the physically strenuous jobs, such as metallurgical workers, everywhere stressed food and drink.

Mobility expectations followed industrial lines as well. The unskilled trained their children to endure rather than to improve; textile workers had little ability to articulate any precise expectations; while of course craft workers had high expectations. Similar patterns united workers in reaction to technological change. French metallurgical workers accepted change without demur, like their counterparts elsewhere; German machine builders, like the French and British, were greatly concerned about it.

Most important, as an index of character traits and their cause, family patterns differed more across industrial than across national lines. A statistical offering: French birth rates were low, of course, but the average printer's family in France, with 1.5 children, was only 25 percent smaller than the average German printer's family with 2.0 children, whereas it was 40 percent smaller than the average French miner's family, which had 2.54 children. Again, a national influence cannot be doubted, but worker characteristics can be far more precisely described by other means. Everywhere miners and the unskilled had the largest families, metallurgical workers were next, and so on to the skilled artisans. Child raising patterns followed similar industrial lines. The unskilled lived amid noise and disorder, and their children slept in the same room as their parents, in London as in Berlin; they were often beaten. Textile families had greater resources, including a separate room for the children, but they were unstable in many ways. Wives worked initially by necessity, eventually by habit; those that did not work were frequently bored and despondent. Children, in either case, were ill-cared for, physically weak and poorly educated. Miners' families were far more structured, albeit highly traditional, while skilled artisans were moving toward essentially bourgeois family patterns, including quite a late marriage age.

These coherences across national lines indicate that the causes that really shaped worker characteristics were industrial rather than national. Levels of unemployment, differences in the methods of pay, and differences in methods of work supervision, as well as relative earnings, were key economic factors that shaped expectations and strike demands. The numbing effect of strenuous outdoor labor helps explain the high birth rates of groups like miners and dockers. Miners were also influenced by their tightly-knit but isolated villages. And as we have seen family patterns tended to perpetuate characteristics within an industry, as in textiles where physically weak workers entered the industry and produced generally frail children.

Industries tended not only to produce workers of a certain type but also to draw workers who shared personality traits in advance. Each mature industrial nation had a pool of diverse personality types who would react quite differently to technological change or to material gain; national stereotypes applied to workers falsely emphasize only one strain of many. The great competition for apprenticeship in printing and other crafts naturally attracted workers whose expectations were already high. The railroads attracted security-minded workers, rather placid people who

385

Stearns

NATIONAL
CHARACTER
AND EUROPEAN
LABOR HISTORY

loved their work and who were very hard to rouse. Metallurgical workers were also placid, in Britain where their employers were not repressive as on the Continent where they were. High pay and profound divisions by skill within the industry help account for this; it was obviously crucial that piece rates were not lowered rapidly amid technological change. Still, there were more than purely economic factors behind the characteristics of these workers. Many passed their trade from father to son; and these were physically big men, self-satisfied with their strength and endurance.

There were, then, in all the industrial countries a comparable variety of personality types within the labor force, each of which tended to be produced by the same sort of industry and also drawn to that industry. Some of the characteristics that seem "national" can be partly explained by this industrial typology. France's emphasis on wage strikes stems in large part from the unusual importance of textile workers in the labor force. And there are cases in which the typology breaks down and this too can explain apparent national anomalies. German miners are not like miners in other countries in this period. This can be explained by the role of the state, the toughness of employers, but above all by the newness of the mining labor force. It took a great deal to rouse German miners and their strike rate was comparatively very low. Almost all the apparent lack of vigor in German labor agitation can be explained by this, for the other major industrial categories fell within the normal range of activity, as determined by comparative standards. Furthermore, more enduring features of German labor may be explained by the miners. It can be argued that the miners would have developed greater zeal with growing experience, as had occurred elsewhere, but the coal slump following World War I prevented their full flowering. Hence the labor movement never received the impulse of miners' disciplined ardor, so vital to unions and socialism in Western Europe. This, I would suggest, is a more probable monocausal explanation than any deriving from national character. It indicates again that most German workers at least before World War I cannot be judged by apparent national characteristics.

The question of workers' national character has not been solved. This must be admitted even at the cost of ending on an irresolute note. If indeed scholars can agree that a question exists, much has been gained. The focus has been limited, it must be recalled. The upper classes may have had a national character when the workers did not. National characteristics may have developed later among workers, as the influence of the national state, national media, and national experiences in war grew stronger, though of course such a development must be studied critically and not simply asserted.

Even for decades before World War I certain national characteristics cannot be blithely dismissed: the Germans' lack of imagination on the job, for example, or the French preoccupation with wages. On the whole the most pervasive characteristics relate primarily to the formal labor movement and particularly to its politics. This was a period when the working class was just beginning to merge with the labor movement, if indeed it ever has. Obviously, to use one example, revolutionary syndicalism has something to do with French characteristics, particularly in politics. But the causes that shaped revolutionary syndicalism, including disgruntlement with the government and with socialism, did not bear on most workers. Had most French workers, even those active in the syndicalist unions, been convinced syndicalists or behaved as such, the whole attack on the national approach would have to be rethought. But they were not, which is why the movement failed so quickly. In other words it is quite conceivable to admit that labor movements had national characteristics, because they were in contact with national political structures and were led by men, whether workers or not, who participated in the formal national culture. Before World War I, at least, the history of workers and their characteristics is not the same as that of the labor movements, though of course in terms of this study it is useful to make the familiar point that labor movements did become increasingly similar, across national boundaries, toward 1914.

Naturally the idea of national character is so deeply embedded and so convenient that it will be dislodged only with difficulty, even as it applies simply to workers during a quarter-century. Yet I would urge that it at least be suspended. Too many presumed national features collapse when subjected to any comparison. Too many contradict each other, which almost certainly means that they derive from different groups within the labor force. Some are better explained by stage of industrialization than by national character. Others turn out to be accurate but to apply to almost all national groups of workers. Workers almost everywhere, for example, showed signs of longing for the countryside. There are few obvious national differences in the zeal for gardening or for rural recreation, though there are important variations among occupational groups. If German workers longed a bit more fervently, it seems more economical to explain this by the recency of urbanization than by Germanness. Most of the measurable characteristics usually applied to each national working class either did not exist or provide at most a very general framework within which the real causes that shaped groups of workers operated.

This may simply mean that we should turn away from measurement, to national essences that more accurately describe human life. We have not discussed national loyalty itself. Many workers in France, Germany, and Britain were nationalistic—this does not have to be minimized by an attack on national characteristics, for it was in many ways a common feature—but was there a distinctive quality to this sentiment in each country? We have not touched on the effects of language, possible national religious traits, or other factors perhaps all the more important because they are hard to grasp. Here, perhaps, is where serious advocates of national character for the lower classes should turn their attention. The question is whether their subject, even at this level, has any reality.

The doubts raised about workers' national character as it is conventionally used add to the complexity of a comparative approach. It has

387

Stearns

NATIONAL
CHARACTER
AND EUROPEAN
LABOR HISTORY

been pleasant to assume a special genius for each nation and to minimize problems of causation by vague reference to the remote past or even to race. Perhaps a coherent national framework can be established for working class history, but it must be very explicitly and carefully done. For the time being, in terms of the factors most historians of the working class normally deal with, the national framework causes more trouble than it is worth. It has led to some monumental empirical errors and to many false assumptions about the factors that shaped working class life. If it seems brash to challenge such long-established conventions, I can only plead that such is the American way.

THE CONTEMPORARY AGE

PART V

OUR contemporary age was not only shaped by the ideas of Marx, Darwin, and Freud. It was also created by a rapidly occurring series of almost cataclysmic events which began at the end of the nineteenth century and most of which could hardly have been foreseen by leaders like Bismarck, Disraeli, or Alexander II. These events have been so traumatic and have occurred in such rapid succession that they have caused at least one observer, Alvin Toffler, to diagnose the ill of our age as "future shock," a difficulty of adapting to fundamental rapid change similar to the "culture shock" of suddenly having to adjust to a foreign country. Whether we suffer from "future shock" or not, our contemporary age is in large measure the product of traumatic events such as those analyzed in the next set of selections: imperialism, two world wars and a cold war, the Russian Revolution, and the counterrevolution of Fascism. Raymond Betts takes up the question of the relationship between imperialism and European power politics. World War I and the peace at Versailles are discussed by Imanual Geiss, George F. Kennan, William Langer, and Arno J. Mayer. The Russian Revolution is the subject of essays by Theodore Von Laue and E. H. Carr, and the Fascist counterrevolution is treated by George L. Mosse, Wolfgang Sauer, and Alan Bullock. Gordon Wright assesses the impact of modern war. Finally, Arthur M. Schlesinger, Jr., and Christopher Lasch take up the orthodox and revisionist views of the Cold War.

24. Late Nineteenth-Century "New Imperialism"

RAYMOND F. BETTS

As early as the beginning of this century some commentators noted something new in the relations between the developed and undeveloped parts of the world. They held that in the 1870s or 1880s a "new imperialism" had begun to replace the "old imperialism," which had run out its course in the eighteenth-century wars for empire between France and England. That imperialism had arisen in the age of discovery and had been preindustrial, mercantilist, and confined principally to the western hemisphere, the west African sources of slave labor, the Indian subcontinent, and the East Indies. The "new imperialism," on the other hand, was carried on by competitive industrial states, highly developed politically, culturally, and economically. It was played out as a veritable "scramble for Africa" and a subdivision of East Asia into colonies or spheres of influence. In only one generation a largely independent Africa became a patchwork of European colonies except for Liberia and Ethiopia. In the same length of time only Japan retained its independence in Asia. The "taproot" of this imperialism, to use the phrase of British liberal J. A. Hobson, remained economic, but to the old lust for markets and raw materials was added a new desire for sources for capital investment.

Source: Raymond F. Betts, *Europe Overseas: Phases of Imperialism* (New York: Basic Books, 1968), Chapter 3, "The New Rush Overseas," pp. 46–76. Copyright © 1968 by Basic Books, Inc., Publishers, New York. Reprinted by permission of the publisher. [Some footnotes omitted].

While this view is by no means dead (see, for example, D. C. M. Platt, "Economic Factors in British Policy during the 'New Imperialism,'" Past and Present, No. 39 [April 1968], pp. 120–38), it has come under attack in recent years from a number of historians who doubt both the "newness" and the economic motivation of nineteenth-century imperialism. Rather, they hold, it was a continuation of earlier imperialism, and whatever changes occurred at the end of the nineteenth century stemmed mainly from political and strategic motives. An able recent synthesis of the question is this selection by Professor Raymond F. Betts, of the University of Kentucky. Its great merit is that it not only reviews the literature of the controversy, but puts it in the broader framework of the cultural conflict between Europe and the colonial areas. According to Betts, what was there in the "power relationship between Europe and the rest of the world" that made imperialism both "possible" and "tempting"? What are the theories of Hobson, Lenin, Schumpeter, Brunschwig, and Gallagher and Robinson, and how does Betts evaluate their theories, especially the economic ones? The fact that imperialism was "possible" and "tempting" for Europe does not mean that it was inevitable. For what reasons did Europe yield to the possibility and the temptation? By what pattern or dynamic, for example, were the initiatives of "a small number of [imperial] enthusiasts" converted into a program of European imperialism? Was this pattern, dynamic, or program "new"? What was the impact of imperial conquest and rule on both colonizers and colonized? In sum, how did the "second phase" of imperialism of the late nineteenth century differ from the "first phase" of the sixteenth century?

Toward the end of the nineteenth century the recrudescence of imperialism occurred, leading to the so-called Scramble for Africa and the nearly final consumption of the remaining noncolonial territories of Asia. Until quite recently, this series of events was analyzed as sudden and new, an outburst after a hiatus of one hundred years of noncolonial, nonimperialist activity. Now historical analysis has shown otherwise.[1] Imperialism was scarcely quiescent during the lengthy interval separating the American Revolution from Stanley's exploration of the Congo. The most familiar form it then assumed, however, was indirect, essentially economic predominance with none of the heavy responsibilities of direct administration. Nevertheless, in this very same period sporadic outbursts of direct imperialism were easily discernible, as witness the French in Algeria and the Senegal or the British in Burma and above all in India. What occurred at the end of the nineteenth century, then, was new only in its intensity, but this alone is sufficient to cause it to be singled out. At no time before or since has "earth hunger" seemed more voracious—or more completely satisfied.

What drove Europe out with such gusto has been a question asked

[1] The principal presentation of this argument is Ronald Robinson and John Gallagher, "The Imperialism of Free Trade," *The Economic History Review*, VI, No. 1 (1953), 1–15.

many times over and provided with an impressive array of answers. There is no need to try to sort these all out, however, for the pattern of this phase of imperialism seems very clear in retrospect.

No matter from what angle observed, the effort appears as a national one. Whether begun by merchant, adventurer, or soldier; whether extolled in religious, sociological, or racial terms, empire was established and maintained by nationalistic European states and directly through their responsible agencies. An appreciation of this new imperialism, therefore, can best be gained by first observing the political setting in which these nation-states acted.

With the unification of Germany and Italy in 1870–1871 the European state system appeared complete. A grouping of independent states, still operating on the principle of balance of power, the system was dynamic, characterized by manipulation and maneuvering, by the exercise of aggressive diplomacy and the assertion of national rights and prerogatives. Unlike its seventeenth- and eighteenth-century predecessor, the late nineteenth-century system was aggravated by a chauvinistic, exclusivist nationalism which suggested that state rivalry was a necessary condition of political life, and which found pseudo-scientific support in the social Darwinian notions of struggle for survival and survival of the fittest. Fear, not complacency; anxiety, not confidence characterized international politics at the end of the nineteenth century, as each country viewed its neighbors' strength with growing concern. The condition of European peace therefore resulted not from relaxation, but from tension. It was the effect of "an equivalent development of power" according to the German historian Friedrich Meinecke.

Admiral Mahan described the situation as "an equilibrium on the Continent, and, in connection with the calm thus resulting, an immense colonizing movement in which all the great powers were concerned." The exciting and daring political activity was now undertaken outside of Western Europe. New zones of friction developed and old ones were intensified: the Middle East, North Africa and Africa south of the Sahara, Southeast Asia. The growing realization of the possible political and economic worth of Africa and Asia to the European states directed national attention thither. Fervid nationalists took new hope in the possibilities of national grandeur and expressed themselves in terms of a "Greater Britain," a *Plus Grande France*, and a *Gross Deutschland*. Active colonial policy seemed a means to renewed national success, a source of new power and world significance. France, recovering from the humiliating defeat by Prussia in 1870, wished to regild her renown abroad. Germany, until recently dismembered, wished to break out of the political encirclement which she imagined to exist and to be a check to her *Weltpolitik*. Italy, also unified and thinking in terms of a Third Rome, dreamed occasionally of Roman Africa. And Great Britain, sensing her relative decline in a world of new great powers, notably the United States and Germany, derived some solace from the notion of an empire upon which the sun never set.

393

Betts

LATE
NINETEENTH-
CENTURY
"NEW
IMPERIALISM"

A flood of political epigrams describing the urgency and glory of imperialistic actions came from the pens of the proponents of empire. "Colonization is for France a matter of life or death," wrote the French colonial theorist Leroy-Beaulieu. The German foreign minister, Prince von Bülow, remarked in a phrase now notorious: "We do not want to put anyone in the shade, but we demand a place for ourselves in the sun." And in a fit of patriotic and poetic verve, Cecil Rhodes intoned: "I would annex the planets if I could."

Soon the European nations again fanned out into the world, hoping that size and breadth of acquisition would assure them leadership or favorable location in this comity of competitive nations. With choice irony, Joseph Conrad's hero Marlowe in *Heart of Darkness* observed the pictorial effects of this effort as he looked at the map of Africa:

> There was a vast amount of red—good to see at any time, because one knows that some real work is done there, a deuce of a lot of blue, a little green, smears of orange, and, on the East Coast, a purple patch to show where the jolly pioneers of progress drink the jolly lager beer.

This colorful activity was politically directed, but its success depended on that awesome *ultima ratio,* power. Just as the major underlying cause of Europe's political unrest was the immense military and economic power that the states were amassing, so the dreams of empire were easily realized by the utilization of this power. In short, the urge to political empire and the realization of such empire can be paired only where the physical means of domination are available. Thus, while one can aver that the new phase of imperialism was the undertaking of the European nation-state, he is obliged to explain the particular nature of national power and the uses to which it was put so as to distinguish it from that which was earlier existent. The qualitative and quantitative differences between the power at the disposal of the sixteenth-century Portuguese and that available to the nineteenth-century Germans, for instance, are of great significance in explaining the rapidity and extent of modern imperialism.

Europe was the first of the world's regions to modernize: to amass, organize, and dispose of its human and natural resources in such a way that human needs were rather easily satisfied and human power was increased manifold. Primarily a nineteenth-century phenomenon, this culturally revolutionary process was both caused by and resulted in the urban, industrial society which we all by common agreement now call "modern." The European political framework within which the process occurred was, of course, the national one, and the value system upon which it was structured emphasized secularism and rationalism: man's independence of fate and nature, his ability to understand and control the world in which he lives. For the first time in history ideas, techniques, and institutions were mobilized in such a way that one small region of the world enjoyed a material cultural superiority that necessitated not comparison but contrast with the many civilizations that were oceans and seas removed from it.

It is in the nature of this contrast that the causes and success of modern imperialism are to be found. The asymmetrical power relationship between Europe and the rest of the world not only made imperialism possible, it also made imperialism tempting. Empire could be acquired "on the cheap," and most often was. Superior military equipment made the subduing of foreign peoples no inordinately grave task. As Hilaire Belloc quipped:

> Whatever happens we have got
> The Maxim gun and they have not.

Superior means of transportation enabled empire to be consolidated and bound. The steam engine propelled the railroad trains that crossed new continents and the freighters which transported goods from empire to mother country and back again. Superior communications ensured greater imperial control: the telegraph became the new line of empire, allowing Whitehall, the Quai d'Orsay, and Wilhelmstrasse to listen in to the world abroad. Technology made the world one, and won most of the world for Europe.

Against this technological and organizational triumph, the economically underdeveloped regions of the world were quite helpless or indifferent. Overseas imperialism occurred only where power had ebbed, as in the decaying empires of Turkey, Moslem India, or China; or where power had never been effectively organized on a large-scale and rather permanent basis, as in parts of Africa. In brief, the new imperialism always involved striking contrasts of potential power. The adjective "potential" is significant, for the stronger power was not always wantonly used; it was often displayed symbolically, as in the form of a beplumed viceroy seated on a carpeted dais, or a mighty ship of war riding gracefully at anchor, or a railroad cutting purposively through jungle or desert. The ways of the West were impressive and were soon to be imitated.

395

Betts

LATE
NINETEENTH-
CENTURY
"NEW
IMPERIALISM"

Yet the very societal organization which brought Europe to its ascendancy over the rest of the world was also responsible for the urge toward empire and the intensity with which it was felt. As the European nations strengthened their national structures and became more aggressively nationalistic, and as their separate industrial economies seemed more and more bent on aggravated competition, particularly with the advent of the United States and Germany as great economic powers, the tendency toward national policies of trade protection was increased. In such an atmosphere fear of dwindling or closed foreign markets and sources of raw materials suggested the need for the acquisiton of national economic preserves. "Without colonies, no more exportation," exclaimed the Frenchman Henri Mager, who almost seemed to be frantically replying to the statement made by United States Senator Albert J. Beveridge: "The trade of the world must be ours."

Such mercantile policy—"neo-mercantilism" it has been labeled by many commentators—reveals an obvious similarity to its seventeenth-century predecessor and implies again a close relationship between economics and politics. How to separate the two is a perplexing question to historians of the subject. However, thanks to the usual dialectics of historical debate, the major distinctions are easily found. At one extreme are those individuals, principally in the Hobson-Lenin tradition, who see modern imperialism as the result of capitalistic economics. To Hobson, in *Imperialism: A Study,* published first in 1902, imperialism principally occurred as a result of maldistribution in capitalist society. A surfeit of capital and goods, not absorbed in the home economy because of the lack of a more equitable distribution of wealth among the social classes, needed an international exit, and hence colonies and areas of domination were sought as places of investment. Trade and the flag went together, or as Hobson wrote:

> It is this economic condition of affairs that forms the taproot of imperialism. If the consuming public in this country [England] raised its standard of consumption to keep pace with every rise of productive powers, there could be no excess of goods or capital clamorous to use imperialism in order to find markets. . . .

For Hobson the problem was not inherent in capitalistic society, for it was susceptible to correction. He was not unduly sanguine, however, about the ease with which the necessary change, to wit the real democratization of society, would be made. In his day imperialism was still displaying great vitality—it is "only beginning to realize its full force," he wrote—and society was far from completely reformed.

In *Imperialism: The Highest Stage of Capitalism,* Lenin viewed the matter differently, asserting that the developing structure of capitalism made imperialism an ineluctable economic necessity. Within his modified Marxist framework, imperialism was another, but the highest, stage of capitalism. The process which he described can be recapitulated in short measure. Capitalist competition had given way to monopolies; large investment banks had appeared and soon were enmeshed with industry in a financial net; great quantities of surplus capital were now accumulated, quantities which could be profitably invested abroad only in those regions where capital was in scarce supply. Along with goods, the capitalist countries now exported capital. In Lenin's own words:

> Imperialism is capitalism in that stage of development in which the dominance of monopolies and finance capital has established itself; in which the division of the world among the international trusts has begun; in which the division of all territories of the globe among the great capitalist powers has been completed.

Throughout the period between the two world wars, when the traditional European political and economic order was assailed, variations of this economic interpretation of imperialism remained the most attractive ones, complete with their moral conclusions.

> The results of the policy of economic imperialism pursued by this country [England] and the other imperialist powers can hardly be

viewed with satisfaction or equanimity. Political subjection, exploitation, and economic slavery are never pleasant to their victims.

These words, written by the British Labourite Leonard Woolf in 1922,
were not unusually severe.

In opposition to this position is found a series of more recent statements of the problem which de-emphasize or discard economic motivations. First and foremost among them is the opinion held by the Austrian
economist Joseph Schumpeter, who described imperialism as essentially a
militaristic problem. "History, in truth, shows us nations and classes—
most nations furnish an example at some time or other—that seek expansion for the sake of expanding, war for the sake of fighting, victory for
the sake of winning, dominion for the sake of ruling." From this Schumpeter concluded that "imperialism is the objectless disposition on the part
of a state to unlimited forcible expansion." [2] Several more recent critics
have placed imperialism in a political mold, thus eliminating Schumpeter's insistence on its "objectlessness." The French historian Henri Brunschwig has found French imperialism of the late nineteenth century to be
the direct result of a recrudescence of nationalism, the concerted effort on
the part of nationalist politicians to regain France's position of peerage
within the circle of the European great powers.[3] Lastly, there is the opinion of two British scholars, Robinson and Gallagher, who have interpreted the partition of Africa as being essentially political. Speaking of
the responsible English ministers of the period, these authors write:
"Their territorial claims were not made for the sake of African empire or
commerce as such. They were little more than by-products of an enforced
search for better security in the Mediterranean and the East." It was England's Egyptian policy which precipitated the partition, they insist. Their
conclusion: "So far from commercial expansion requiring the extension of
territorial claims, it was the extension of territorial claims which in time
required commercial expansion." [4]

Some analysts in this debate had already arrived at conclusions not dissimilar to those of Robinson and Gallagher. They thought the economic
cause to be an *ex post facto* consideration, a means of convincing the vot-
ers and parliamentarians who controlled the nation's purse strings of the
value of investing in the imperialist game. There is much truth in this appraisal, particularly as it applies to French colonial policy. But to suggest
that the economic argument was simply a device is to ignore the expansionist disposition of modern industrial economics. Of course, we now
know that political empire is not a necessity for modern industrialism,
capitalist or otherwise. The successful economic development of both Hol-

397
Betts
LATE
NINETEENTH-
CENTURY
"NEW
IMPERIALISM"

[2] Joseph Schumpeter, "Imperialism," in *Imperialism and Social Classes* (New
York, 1958), p. 6.

[3] See Henri Brunschwig, *Mythes et réalités de l'impérialisme colonial français*
(Paris, 1961).

[4] Ronald Robinson and John Gallagher, *Africa and the Victorians* (New York,
1961), pp. 463, 472.

land and France (not to mention Japan) in their postcolonial phase stands out as irrefutable contemporary proof. But to many late-nineteenth-century thinkers the economic value of imperialism was real and necessary: national markets did seem somewhat limited, industrial competition did seem pressing, and the Colbertian dictum about favorable balance of trade did have a contemporary ring. Yet if trade followed the flag on more than one occasion, the flag was not simply displayed to cover up the financial machinations of a capitalistic middle class. The outstanding proponents of imperialism were principally political visionaries who sought the way to national—political and economic—greatness. In general businessmen only responded to their urging at first; the taste for economic imperialism had to be acquired.

Lenin's thesis rested on the assumption that capital was attracted to the backward regions because of the high returns it would reap, thanks to the paucity of existing capital there—as opposed to the glut found in monopoly-ridden Europe—and thanks also to the availability of cheap labor. That money did flow outward and in enormous quantities, there is no denying, but this money did not head principally to the newly acquired regions of empire. The French in the years before World War I centered their financial activity first and foremost in Europe. Overseas, more money was invested in the United States and Latin America than in the colonies. The English in this same period held great investments in the United States but rapidly developed those in Latin America, Canada, Australia, and even India. As with France, England found her new empire no exceptionally attractive field for capital investment. The real imperialist *champ de manoeuvre* was Africa, and no enormous investment found its way there until after World War II, with the notable exception of South Africa, where mining absorbed considerable sums of capital. In short, there was no nice coincidence between new empire and new foreign investment which would suggest a close causal connection between the two. No pattern emerges which would support the idea that empire provided a financial safety valve for the capitalist machine.

The economic aspects of empire are not thus dispelled, however. The real value of the newly imperialized regions, at least as seen by the strong proponents of imperialism, was as trading areas first and as sources of raw material second. But the latter actually became the chief *raison d'être* as phosphates from North Africa, rubber and ivory from the Congo, hemp from Indochina, and oil from Indonesia all were fed into the gluttonous European industrial machine. Outside of the mining and petroleum industries, very few of these economic activities required great capital investment in order to be realized. Most of the products coming from the colonies were shipped out in a natural or semifinished state and hence needed very little expensive machinery or highly organized productive processes on the spot. It was in Europe where these products were refined and manufactured in already existing industrial complexes. As later critics were to complain, the world of empire was one of a neat division of labor: the colonies providing the raw materials, the colonial powers providing the industry; the former therefore remaining underdeveloped, the latter continuing to modernize.

In review, what conclusions might now be offered? Considered less in the form of history-as-event and more of history-as-process, modern imperialism is perhaps best described in terms of cultural relations, or more accurately, cultural conflict. Unlike earlier European imperialism, when the economic and political structures of colonizer and colonized were not markedly disparate, the difference between nineteenth-century Europe and those areas upon which it arbitrarily imposed its will was exceedingly great. It was the difference between a modern, urban, industrial culture resting on a rather popular base, and traditional, rural, agrarian cultures resting on an aristocratic base. The well-known dichotomy between traditional and modern states has particular relevance for this late-nineteenth-century era, one in which the transitional phase to modernity had not yet been thought of, let alone reached, for the vast non-European world.

European social processes had been so highly developed as a result of the political and industrial revolutions of the eighteenth and nineteenth centuries that European power, in almost whatever form, was vastly superior to that of any other region, with the notable exception of the United States, which for all practical purposes could be considered a part of this civilization. Very few were those areas which were able to resist the outward flow of European power. Japan is the striking example of a non-Western state that did this successfully and by means of a process of modernization which, ironically, enabled her to engage in a robust imperialism of her own.

399
Betts
LATE
NINETEENTH-
CENTURY
"NEW
IMPERIALISM"

Late-nineteenth-century imperialism was the most forceful and obvious manifestation of a modern society technologically advanced and nationalistically organized, a society capable of economic and political domination over much, indeed most, of the underdeveloped world. It was not the outcome of any historical necessity—Marxist or Social Darwinian. It was, however, the outcome of a combination of all-too-human concerns: fear of the power of surrounding states, personal and national ambitions for secular glory, the temptation to dominate the weak.

Despite the fact that imperialism was a conscious policy pursued by the state, it was the handiwork of a small number of enthusiasts, the prophets and politicians at home, the actors and movers abroad. Their vision may of course have been partially of personal gain—"philanthropy is good, but philanthropy at 5 per cent is better," said Rhodes—but it was more of national grandeur and prestige. They accomplished their work chiefly by the unpleasant means of intrigue and force, seizing territories, establishing protectorates, and signing treaties, all with next to no concern about the thoughts and desires of the resident populations. But they also accomplished their work cheaply. Until the Boer War and the Russo-Japanese War, imperial undertakings were not very costly in either men or equipment. Such undertakings may have outraged the consciences of the Socialists or disturbed parliaments from time to time; however, they occasioned no great popular outcries of national indignation and only infrequently gave cause for national alarm. On the contrary, they could and did arouse popular enthusiasm, "jingoism," to employ the favorite nineteenth-century term for the attitude. Only with the Boer War did an ardent debate over imperialism arise, but by then the general lines of colonial empire had been well defined.

As has been said before, in this age of rising nationalist passions which was the last quarter of the nineteenth century, empire was more of a comfort than an irritant, if it was seriously considered at all. And that it was all too seldom seriously—that is thoroughly—considered at the time is a point not without meaning.

Between European intentions and ambitions in pegging out claims to empire and the actual realization of that empire, there was considerable distance. In part this gap was due to the combination of arrogance and ignorance which frequently prevailed in the imperialist camp. Imperialists at home enthusiastically embraced the idea of empire *in abstracto* but too seldom revealed a well-founded knowledge of the territories in which this power was to dominate. Expressions like the Dark Continent and the Mysterious East were descriptive less of the lack of geographical familiarity on the part of the European than of the meager awareness of the social and historical developments of these lands. As a former cabinet minister of Malawi once said: "Stanley didn't discover us; we were here all the time." The cavalier attitude that sometimes accompanied such European ignorance can be gathered from Jules Ferry's comment that modern empire was "an immense steeplechase on the road of the unknown." Far from the scene of the action, European politicians, gathered in comfortably appointed chancelleries, carved out their empires with a pen.

Nevertheless, this does not mean that the geographical configurations of modern empire were the result either of historical accident or of diplomatic whim. The new imperialism was far from patternless. True, the real legwork—the surveying of the real estate—was done by men who sought fame and fortune abroad, who often wished to escape the seemingly humdrum existence of bourgeois Europe. But unlike their predecessors in the Age of Discovery, they enjoyed no immense freedom of action. In general the European powers knew where they were expanding, even if they did not know what their territories contained.

Most of the empires tended to extend from preexisting bases. What happened in the Far East was, most simply put, an enlargement of previously held properties. Britain rounded out her Indian Empire, and France did the same with her incipient Indochinese Empire. Even the new imperialist states intruding into this part of the world followed much the same process. The United States, or at least some of her more rabid citizens, had their eyes fixed on Hawaii well before the end of the century. Korea had already been invaded by Japan in the sixteenth century and continued to attract the attention of those seeking a place upon which the Japanese sun might shine. In Subsaharan Africa, where a supposed scramble had taken place, there really had not been any mad and undirected rush forward. France spread horizontally from Algeria, first eastward to Tunisia, then westward to Morocco. Britain spread vertically from the Cape Colony northward into East Central Africa and, later, from Egypt southward to the Sudan. In the heartland of Africa, a France moving from its littoral possessions gathered around the hump of West Africa clashed in its eastward drive with an England descending from the north. The point of intersection was Fashoda, and the moment of tension between the two imperialist nations has been called the Fashoda Incident of 1898.

.There is no denying that the European newcomers picked up what they could where they could: Italy assumed a few favorable positions along the Red Sea coast; Leopold II of Belgium did quite handsomely with his enormous chunk of Central Africa; and Bismarckian Germany got a few pieces of the west and the east coasts of Africa and a few Pacific islands. This part of the grab was the least anticipated or foregone; yet even here the direction and limits of the expansion were largely conditioned by the positions and intentions of the two superimperialist powers, Great Britain and France.

The pegging out of empire was thus no completely haphazard effort. But the occupation and control of that empire was nonetheless very complicated and very perplexing. The new imperialism was new in the sense that it brought forth a wide range of ecological conditions and social problems to which all previous colonial experience was to contribute all too little by way of happy solutions. Although England had a continued and viable colonial tradition, her real expertise—and it was slow in being developed—was in the white, English-speaking dominions. Africa was initially an enigma. The other major colonial powers of the epoch were without meaningful tradition—the disastrous French policy in Algeria scarcely warranted imitation—and they were really starting *de nouveau.*

401
Betts
LATE
NINETEENTH-
CENTURY
"NEW
IMPERIALISM"

If imperialism is the disposition to expansion and its realization, empire is rule and administration. By the end of the nineteenth century the problems of empire loomed large. These problems derived, first, from particular colonial situations, and, second, from European attitudes toward these situations. Yet empire was always a two-way proposition: European attitudes toward the natives, native attitudes toward the Europeans.

Of the myriad of concerns and interests which soon confronted the European as colonial administrator, the first understood was that the new imperialism had transpired primarily in tropical climes in which large settlement colonies would be out of the question. Either the climate seemed initially to be unhealthy to the white man, or the teeming populations, as in Southeast Asia, allowed of little free space for new intruders. Moreover, the few serious attempts at colonization were not successful in numbers. Somewhat ironic to observe, the greatest era of European emigration had begun shortly before the age of imperialism, but that emigration was directed primarily toward America. The new overseas possessions were to necessitate a new relationship between European administrator and local population. "Tropical dependencies" was the term used by the British to describe many of these newly acquired regions; "dominations" was the French phraseology of the time.

Whatever their affixed generic name, these new areas were to be ruled—or better, administered—not populated, assimilated, or in any way incorporated into the body politic of the metropolitan European state. On this point almost all of the colonial experts agreed. The suggested relationship between colonial ruler and indigenous population might be described euphemistically as an "association of two parties," but it was looked on more rudely as a combination of European brains and native muscle. Above all, the European function was to be directional. The analogy has been made between modern overseas imperialism and medieval feudalism: the European colonial was to play the role of the lord of the manor, while the natives played that of the serfs.

Theoretically, this asymmetrical relationship was justified primarily by the argument that the lands of the world, regardless of present ownership, had to be worked for the benefit of mankind. As one Frenchman rationalized: "A race of men do not have the right to be apart, to refuse all communication with others and to leave their immense territories unused because they do not know how to develop them." And a Belgian later added weight to these words: "On a vast continent, nearly empty, some dozens of savages lived, lost in the immensity of the forests and the savannas, tolerated by a physical environment which they did not dominate, leading—

as it were, on the edge of nature—a precarious existence. . . . The riches of the soil and the sub-soil were ignored, left to abandon, without master." The conclusion drawn from this statement is this: "The great colonial movement of the nineteenth century, the partition of Black Africa, is based not on the right of conquest, but on the right of occupation." In brief, if a people does not know how to work its lands or does not care to, then another people with this knowledge and desire has the right of occupation.

The source of this particular attitude is pretty much derived from prevalent European economic attitudes. The same rationalization of economic activities—regulated labor, specialized functions, managerial direction —which so greatly accounts for European material superiority was found wanting in other parts of the world, a condition deemed disadvantageous. No less a person than Albert Schweitzer fully revealed the European bent of mind with respect to native labor in his *Edge of the Primeval Forest:*

> The negro, then, under certain circumstances works well, but only so long as circumstances require it. The child of nature—here is the answer to the puzzle—is always a casual worker. In return for very little work nature supplies the native with nearly everything that he requires for his support in his village. . . . The negro, then, is not idle, but he is a free man. The wealth of the country cannot be exploited because the native has no interest in the process.

While Schweitzer's interpretation is not noticeably tainted with the racial concepts that are found in the writings of many imperialists of the time, his lines illustrate the ease with which the assumption of European superiority and native inferiority could be made. As Schweitzer also stated: "The negro is a child, and with children nothing can be done without the use of authority." At one with Schweitzer on this point, the imperialists were predisposed to consider their charges immediately incapable of or indifferent to responsible self-development. While Schweitzer restricted his comments to the Africa he thought he knew, such comments frequently appear regardless of the particular continent or people. In their new overseas possessions, the Europeans came to see themselves as indispensable guides, without whom the future would be repetitious of the past: economic stagnation, political anarchy, administrative corruption.

Airing such thoughts, the Europeans soon developed an imperial or colonial mentality, a sense of their own superiority, deriving not only from a superior material civilization but also from the belief in the superiority of their government, educational system, social customs, and the like. They created their own equivalent of manifest destiny, saw themselves as ruling races charged with civilizing missions, assumed they were tutors in the ways of the good life.

The obverse side of this easily assumed sense of European superiority was a similar but enforced sense of native inferiority. The local populations, where they came into contact with the European, were made to see that their customs and institutions were not comparable to those of their conquerors. Nehru bitterly commented on this in *Toward Freedom:*

403

Betts

LATE
NINETEENTH-
CENTURY
"NEW
IMPERIALISM"

> We developed the mentality of good country-house servants. Sometimes we were treated to a rare honor—we were given a cup of tea in the drawing room. The height of our ambition was to become respectable and to be promoted individually to the upper regions. Greater than any victory of arms or diplomacy was this psychological triumph of the British in India.

Several social and psychological theories about the "colonial situation," the confrontation of European and native, have been erected. But no author to date has presented the problem more provocatively than Albert Memmi, a North African novelist, whose assessment of colonialism is often very revealing. It is his thesis that both "colonialist" and "colonized" have to be created, that prior to the advent of colonial rule there is no predisposition of one or the other to assume his particular role.

> There is only a particle of truth in the fashionable notion of "dependency complex" and "colonizability," etc. There undoubtedly exists—at some point in its evolution—a certain adherence of the colonized to colonization. However, this adherence is the result of colonization not its cause. It arises after and not before colonial occupation. In order for the colonizer to be complete master, it is not enough for him to be so in actual fact, but he must also believe

in its legitimacy. In order for the legitimacy to be complete, it is not enough for the colonized to be a slave, he must also accept his role. The bond between the colonizer and the colonized is thus destructive and creative. It destroys and re-creates the two partners of colonization into colonizer and colonized.[5]

Whether it is, as Memmi asserts, that the colonizer must legitimize his initial usurpation in order to be able to live with himself, it is patently clear that a paternalistic attitude at best and a contemptuous attitude at worst developed within the European colonial mind and led to little social or intellectual intercourse between colonizer and colonized. No more striking description of the effects of this attitude is to be found than that of the "bridge party" which takes place in E. M. Forster's *Passage to India*. To accommodate the desires of some newly arrived Englishwomen an official's wife arranges a lawn party to bridge the gap between Hindu and Anglo-Indian. But the party is not a success, as the Anglo-Indians remain haughtily on the higher portion of the lawn while the Hindus hesitatingly stand together on the lower portion. There is no "bridge party" at all. Rather, as Kipling put it earlier, "Never the twain shall meet."

Two communities came to exist in almost every colonial region: the small but dominant European nucleus and the indigenous mass. Juxtaposed they were, but certainly seldom socially interrelated. Even the traditionally nonracial French could, on occasion, find reason for social separation of the races. Speaking of urbanism in Dakar, Senegal, Charles Morazé wrote in 1936:

Formerly Europeans and natives lived mixed together. Innumerable families were heaped together in small rooms, true caravansaries blended together in the European town. This promiscuity was deplorable. Europeans and natives were not subject to the same epidemics; yellow fever, for example, mortal for the white, is benign in the negro. The danger of a mixed population was that epidemics were able to spread without being quickly checked. Finally, the system lacked elegance. Thus, in 1916 it was decided to create the native village of the medina.

The polar extremes which the Europeans thus fixed for themselves and their charges further led to the assumption that colonial rule would of necessity be of long duration. From their comfortable heights many nineteenth-century theorists asserted that the colonial territories would of course eventually become independent, but "eventually" was usually conceived of as meaning many decades, perhaps centuries. Paul Leroy-Beaulieu, the French colonial expert, was sure some three hundred years would be necessary before most of France's new possessions would be ready to handle their own affairs. Even between the two world wars the clearest

[5] Albert Memmi, *The Colonizer and the Colonized* (New York, 1965), pp. 88–89.

feature of British colonial policy was "the tranquil assumption of the long-term character of colonial rule."

What the new imperialists had done was to create their own political dilemma: the continued necessity of their political domination, yet the suggestion of eventual colonial independence. No one better presented this dilemma than did the Earl of Cromer, who stated that the Englishman, in considering imperial objectives ". . . is in truth always striving to attain two ideals, which are mutually destructive—the ideal of good government, which connotes the continuance of his own superiority, and the ideal of self-government, which connotes the whole or partial abdication of his own supreme position." Condescending toward the native populations, the European imperialists and colonial administrators complacently and imperiously assumed the "white man's burden," the "tutelage of the lesser breeds." But, as is well known, nothing is less easily parted with than self-righteousness. As late as the 1950's the Belgians were still speaking of a sacred civilizing mission.

Finally, this prevalent attitude led to something of a self-fulfilling prophecy. Believing that native retardedness was a reality and that colonial rule would endure, the Europeans did all too little toward the preparation of their possessions for eventual self-rule. While the British come out better than most other colonials on this score, their over-all record is not an exceptionally inspiring one. Lord Bryce, viewing India at the end of the nineteenth century, offered this pertinent comment: "The government of India by the English resembles that of her provinces by Rome in being virtually despotic. In both cases, whatever may have been done for the people, nothing is done by the people."

In brief, the colonized peoples were nowhere seriously asked to participate in the decision-making or policy formulation taking place in their own lands. They were directed and guided, often by gentle and well-meaning hands, but they were not allowed to tamper with the administrative machinery. We now know that the European imperialists and colonial administrators who arrived at these conclusions were generally self-deluding. And yet perhaps they had reason to be.

In those rather halcyon days before World War I imperialist policy was not without its appeal to certain elements within the native populations. Once the task of pacifying the area over which the European flags flew had been achieved, the acceptance or acquiescence in colonial rule was rather widespread. The resentment and national fervor which were later to rend apart colonial empires were nowhere in prominent evidence in the new possessions. This is not to say that nationalism did not exist anywhere outside of the West. Interestingly enough, its first far-off reverberations were in old empires: Manchu China with the Revolution of 1911, the Spanish Empire with the uprising of the Philippines, Japan with the Meiji Era, and even the British Empire with Canada's demands for autonomy. If, however, nationalism seemed to appear in incipient form in places such as India and Indochina before World War I, neither European nor native seriously entertained any thoughts about early inde-

405

Betts

LATE
NINETEENTH-
CENTURY
"NEW
IMPERIALISM"

pendence. As Nehru said, to become respectable was still the height of general native ambition. Those few initiated into the ways of the West, either by European education or its colonial facsimile, aspired to be part of this new order. In the French colonies of West Africa they became the *évolués,* those persons brought up sufficiently to Western standards to act as negotiators between ruling minority and dominated mass. And others, less well placed but supposedly blessed with a smattering of the ruler's language and customs, like Joyce Carey's hero in *Mister Johnson,* did all they could to please, even if they could not fully understand.

In this respect Albert Memmi is quite correct: the colonized were created, usually forced to accept a new and inferior status, although on occasion they fell into that status when the European, like Albert Schweitzer, exercised a benign philanthropy. But this statement is something of an anticipation, for the striking feature of the new imperialism in its initial stage was that it really affected no great numbers of natives or Europeans. Just as the European taxpayer could afford imperialism because it was not too expensive a luxury, so the average native could ignore the phenomenon, so remote was it from his daily existence. Would it be presumptuous to suggest as a generalization the following: the seeming initial success of modern imperialism was the result of the ignorance of colonizer and colonized of what imperialism really meant or was to mean?

From the above analysis it might appear that the first and second phases of European overseas expansion were more characterized by their similarities than by their differences. Proclaimed economic needs combined with power politics brought certain portions of the world under European control in the first period, and nearly all of the remaining regions under European control in the second. As was stated at the beginning of this study, causal factors offer little variety even when viewed across the centuries. The trilogy of God, gold, and glory remains a handy way of summing up the entire enterprise.

This much said, there are some other points which should be considered. If causes remain consistent, methods and abilities had changed. First, the older agency of the chartered company as spearhead of the imperialist endeavor had declined. There were, of course, many concessionary companies existing in the first days of the new wave of imperialism, as the Royal Niger Company or Rhodes' South Africa Company indicate. French exploitation of Equatorial Africa and Belgian exploitation of the Congo were ruthlessly initiated by such companies. Nonetheless, their role was far more short-lived and insignificant than that of their predecessors. Their greatest success was in Subsaharan Africa, but elsewhere more direct state control was initiated, and even in Subsaharan Africa the concessionary company was replaced nearly everywhere within the first three decades of the new imperialism. Second, the degree of European success—the ability to lord it over alien populations, the ability to amass huge empires grossly disproportionate to the size of the colonial nation—was very much greater in the nineteenth century than in the sixteenth. The power that made this possible was essentially industrial, and the industries of the new Europe required raw materials from all over the world to feed them. In contrast to the Europe of Queen Elizabeth I and Louis XIV, that of Gladstone and Bismarck was economically very advanced. Domination of the world's trade and resources now became a European objective. But, in truth, empire was less the source of financial investment or the outlet for goods than it was the source of raw materials. Rubber, oil, tin, cocoa, peanuts, and phosphates are all part of the long bill of lading which Europe compiled.

Along with this newfound industrial and political power—indeed, a part of it—was the nationalist fervor with which imperialism was engaged. Although never winning over the majority of the articulate European population, imperialism was nonetheless popular, as is exemplified by the *Kolonial Gesellschaft* of Germany with its 100,000 membership at the turn of the century. Similar organizations existed in other countries, with even the Fabians in England providing a deferential nod in the direction of empire. The prestige of empire was never higher, nor was its power.

Finally, the new imperialism was soon accompanied by a new attitude of responsibility and obligation. We contemporaries probably find this attitude maudlin, and we imagine it to have been often as much pose as sincere intention. But regardless of our appraisal of it, many late-nineteenth-century Europeans convinced themselves that they were discharging a significant burden by helping the "lesser breeds." The condescension, the phlegmatic aloofness with which they carried forth this burden is certainly reproachable, but the point remains that, unlike their earlier imperialist predecessors, they set about working out a "native policy," a suitable rapport between colonizer and colonized. What is most significant in this attitude was its clear-cut implication of responsibility, and this, in turn, meant the injection of moral issues. Perhaps the very acknowledgment of the matter of morality in imperialism made the late-nineteenth-century European effort all the more incongruous, if not grotesque, but with the twentieth century genuine attempts at reform were made, and imperialism began to undergo a transition which was ultimately to lead to its own elimination.

407
Betts
LATE
NINETEENTH-
CENTURY
"NEW
IMPERIALISM"

25. The Outbreak of the First World War and German War Aims

IMANUAL GEISS

26. The Price We Paid for War

GEORGE F. KENNAN

Historians often are hung up on the notion that "big events" must have "big causes." Certainly World War I, like the French Revolution, was a big event as far as its results were concerned. The enormous number of lives lost, bodies maimed, and souls damaged scarred at least one European generation. It was the major cause of the outbreak of the Russian Revolution of 1917, the breakup of the Hapsburg empire, the disruption of the world economy and currencies, the rise of Fascism, and of World War II.

Because the "big event" of World War I turned out to be a "big crime" as well, some person or some nation must have been guilty of it. Or so the peacemakers in 1919 thought. Article 231 of the Treaty of Versailles blamed Germany for causing the war and many historians agreed. This raised what the German people would call the Kriegsschuldfrage or "war-guilt question." By the late 1920s non-German historians began to question Article 231's truth. Work by Harry Elmer Barnes and, particularly, Sidney B. Fay, convinced a large number of historians and students, even to our own time, that every major European power was guilty. As a result, Germany was no more guilty than Austria, Russia, France, and Britain. If every power was guilty, then, the fault was in the breakdown of the alliance systems and the creation of international anarchy. This view even colored the work of those historians,

Source: Imanual Geiss, "The Outbreak of the First World War and German War Aims," *Journal of Contemporary History*, I, No. 3 (July 1966), 75–91. Reprinted by permission of George Weidenfeld and Nicolson. [Footnotes omitted.]

*such as Pierre Renouvin, Bernadotte E. Schmitt, and Luigi Albertini, who
still placed primary responsibility on Austria and Germany.*

*The war-guilt question, once believed dead, was resurrected in the 1960s,
especially for Germans, with the furor raised by the publication of Fritz Fischer's book* Germany's Aims in the First World War *(1961 with English
translation in 1967). Fischer holds that prewar German policy could be described as, to use a literal translation of his book's title, a "grasping at world
power." The aggressiveness of this policy brought about a British, French, and
Russian alliance to check it. Germany wrongly considered this Triple
Entente as "encirclement" and launched a preventive war in 1914 to break it up.
Fischer's thesis alone raised a storm of protest, but the worst of it was that he
and his students substantiated their charges of German culpability with abundant new archival documentation.*

*All of these questions—the tradition of German innocence, the Fischer con-
troversy, and a summary of the Fischer school's position—are treated in the
first of the following two selections on World War I by one of Fischer's stu-
dents, Imanual Geiss. He holds that right after the war the War Guilt Section*
(Kriegsschuldreferat) *of the German Foreign Office* (Auswärtiges Amt *on the
Wilhelmstrasse in Berlin) established a Working Committee of German Organizations* (Arbeitsausschuss Deutscher Verbände) *and Central Office for the
Investigation of the War Guilt Question* (Zentralstelle zur Erforschung der
Kriegsschuldfrage) *to amass and disseminate documentation* (Gutachten) *of
German innocence. According to Geiss, how were they able to do it and how
successful were they in the 1920s and 1930s? How did Fischer's book explain
away "the myth of* Einkreisung" *or "encirclement" and how did belief in it
by Germans in 1914 contribute to the willingness to make "preventive war"?
For Geiss the Sarajevo crisis of 1914 was "hardly more than the cue" for
Germany to make this preventive war against encirclement. What was the*
carte blanche *or "blank check" Germany gave Austria in early July 1914
and why was it given? What was its impact on Austrian leadership? What
pro-war pressures did Germany place on Austria after the "blank check"?
What effect did Austrian shelling of Belgrade have on Russian policy and,
in turn, how did that policy affect German policy? How did Bethmann-
Hollweg and the* Auswärtiges Amt *undercut Wilhelm II's second thoughts
on July 27 and 28? What were the effects of the negotiations with Britain on
Bethmann-Hollweg? What made war "inevitable"? Finally, what two distinctions does Geiss believe need to be made in assessing the responsibility for the
war? How does he evaluate the responsibility of each of the major powers?*

*The selection by George F. Kennan picks up where Geiss's leaves off. In it
Kennan, the distinguished diplomat, historian, and former American ambassador to the Soviet Union and Yugoslavia, examines the underlying causes of
the war and goes on to discuss its long-term consequences. "In the damage it
did to the structure of international life," he writes, with great wisdom, "and
in the even deeper damage it inflicted on the biological and spiritual condition of the European peoples, World War I still looms on the historical horizon as the great determining tragedy of our century." According to Kennan
what were the two "broad historical circumstances out of which the war arose"*

409
Geiss

THE FIRST
WORLD WAR
AND GERMAN
WAR AIMS

and how exactly did they contribute to the war's causation? What nations does he believe to have been most responsible for causing the war and why does he come to his conclusions? In what ways did these political causes of the war stem not from "war guilt" but from the misunderstanding of "the real implications and possibility of major warfare as an instrument of policy in the modern age"? What results came from the war, "results which nobody could have predicted" and which were at variance with every power's reasons for going to war in the first place? What does Kennan believe to be the lessons of the war for our generation? Finally, what parts of Geiss's and Kennan's articles can be reconciled? What ones contradict each other?

IMANUAL GEISS

German innocence—or at least relative innocence—for the outbreak of the 1914 war had for decades been something that could not be questioned in Germany. The function of this taboo varied according to the circumstances: in early August 1914 it was designed to impress both the SPD [Social Democratic Party] and Britain, in order to get the former into the war, and if possible to keep the latter out of it. During the war it was to convince neutrals and Germans alike of the righteousness of the Reich's cause. Immediately after the war, even the left-wing governments of 1918–19 clung in dealing with the Allies to the concept of German relative innocence, in the hope of getting a more lenient peace settlement. When they failed, later governments and public opinion in the Weimar Republic retreated from the relatively critical line of these earlier governments which, after all, had published the German documents and set up a Commission of Enquiry into the causes of Germany's defeat.

The Weimar Republic opened a sustained campaign against article 231 of the Versailles treaty; it hoped, by disputing Germany's responsibility for the war, to dismantle the treaty as a whole. The campaign had started at Versailles itself, where Bülow (later Secretary of State in the Auswärtiges Amt) mapped out and initiated the strategy. In the Auswärtiges Amt a small sub-section, the Kriegsschuldreferat, inspired, directed, and financed the German innocence propaganda. Its chief instruments were two organizations, the Arbeitsausschuss Deutscher Verbände (ADV), and the Zentralstelle zur Erforschung der Kriegsschuldfrage. ADV, a federation of practically all reputable semi-political organizations, including the trade unions, looked after the general propaganda, while the Zentralstelle had to cover the scholarly aspects of the campaign.

The two organizations worked together, notwithstanding occasional rivalries and bickerings behind the scenes, and the Kriegsschuldreferat saw to the necessary finances and co-ordination. Each had a periodical, the more important one for the general historian being the Zentralstelle's *Kriegsschuldfrage;* for its launching it was possible to find money even in summer 1923, at the height of the inflation. The editor of

Kriegsschuldfrage—later renamed *Berliner Monatshefte*—was Alfred von Wegerer, an ex-army officer. For tactical reasons he posed as an independent, but he was in fact employed by the Auswärtiges Amt, in a position ranking in salary and annual leave as a *Ministerialrat*. Both the budget and the literary activities of the Zentralstelle were controlled by the Kriegsschuldreferat, which in its turn gave Wegerer valuable information for pursuing the scholarly struggle against the 'Kriegsschuldlüge'.

A third, more subtle instrument consisted of a host of writers, none of them historians, engaged as part-time propagandists. For a moderate but regular monthly payment of a few hundred marks they wrote three or four articles a month in German dailies and/or periodicals on the war guilt question. The most prominent among them were Bernhard Schwertfeger, an ex-Colonel, and Hermann Lutz, a free-lance writer. The appearance of Lutz on the pay-roll of the Auswärtiges Amt is the more startling since, judging from his *Gutachten* for the work of the Commission of Enquiry, he must have passed as an independent critic of the official line. A fourth means used was to subsidise publications which took the German line, although occasionally books with critical passages were allowed to pass in order not to arouse suspicions abroad. These publications ranged from *Die Grosse Politik* to insignificant pamphlets. The usual method was to buy a number of copies, often several hundred, in advance; these were afterwards sent to German missions abroad which distributed them free to key personalities in the respective countries. Many of the subsidised books were translations into German. (The Auswärtiges Amt subsidy was much sought after by German publishers, and it is quite possible that without the financial assistance of the Kriegsschuldreferat many a book might not have appeared.) Probably only a few foreign authors received more than this kind of subsidy: one, Boghitchevitch, living in Switzerland, was paid by the Auswärtiges Amt in gold francs, a difficult thing to manage in 1919. Most of the foreign authors supporting the German cause were probably unaware of the subsidy, though it is difficult to say how many would have minded if they had known.

The Kriegsschuldreferat decided which publications criticizing the German line were to be attacked, how, by whom, and when and where, or whether they should be simply ignored. This is what happened to a booklet by Walter Fabian, now editor of *Gewerkschaftliche Monatshefte*. Similarly, it acted as internal censor for official or semi-official publications, in particular of the Untersuchungsausschuss, an effort in which it was partly supported by the latter's secretary-general, Eugen Fischer-Baling. Together, they prevented the publication of Hermann Kantorowicz's *Gutachten* for the Untersuchungsausschuss, although it was completed and set up in type as early as 1927. When, in 1932, the Untersuchungsausschuss wanted to publish five volumes of documents on German war aims, the Kriegsschuldreferat vetoed the proposal on the ground that the documents would prove to the whole world that German plans of conquest made nonsense of the German innocence campaign. Finally, the Kriegsschuldreferat prepared the many official statements of German

411

Geiss

THE FIRST
WORLD WAR
AND GERMAN
WAR AIMS

chancellors and of President Hindenburg on the war guilt question during the Weimar period, statements which, perhaps more than anything else, helped to strengthen the taboo.

The campaign was the more effective since German historians lent it their great prestige. Most of them did not need official prompting but had only to follow their natural inclinations. Surprisingly enough, the contribution of professional German historians to a rational analysis of the causes of the war had been fairly slight. Most of the German campaigners were amateurs, and none of the few professionals who were prominently engaged (Hans Delbrück, Friedrich Thimme, Paul Herre, Erich Brandenburg, Richard Fester, Hans Rothfels, Hans Herzfeld) ever wrote anything comparable to the great works of Pierre Renouvin, Bernadotte E. Schmitt, or Luigi Albertini. The defence of the German cause was mostly left either to foreigners, such as Barnes or Fay, or to amateurs such as Wegerer or Lutz.

How effective the German innocence campaign had been became clear after the second world war. To the rest of the world this had only proved German responsibility for the first. Not so in Germany. After a few years of confusion and hesitation, which produced some criticism by Friedrich Meinecke, most German historians swung back to the old line. They contended that Germany (or rather Hitler) was responsible for the second but not for the first. There was no fresh research or re-interpretation of the causes of 1914. Although a few modifications were introduced by Gerhard Ritter, Wegerer's authority was never questioned; Albertini's massive work was almost completely ignored. The German public remained dependent on the meagre fare offered by professional historians in articles, textbooks, and short chapters or sub-chapters in a number of more general works.

It is only against this background that one can understand the terrific outburst of excitement over Fritz Fischer's book, which quickly became known as the 'Fischer controversy'. For Fischer not only questioned the taboo built up over five decades by successive political regimes in Germany; he also broke the monopoly of knowledge held by conservative or mildly conservative-liberal historians, in a historical problem which may well rank as one of the most complicated and bewildering in modern history. He did it just by picking up Albertini and reading the documents published since 1919.

The leading German historians rushed angrily into print to denounce Fischer and closed ranks against the heretic. Vis-à-vis Fischer they all seemed to have forgotten their former squabbles and political disagreements. Erwin Hölzle from the right joined forces with Golo Mann, Ludwig Dehio, and Hans Herzfeld of the 'left', while Gerhard Ritter from his centre position turned out to be Fischer's most persistent critic. Taking real or imaginary defects as an excuse for condemning the effort as such, many concentrated their attacks on the chapter on July 1914. In the very year when their attacks reached an emotional climax in the shrill polemics of Michael Freund and Giselher Wirsing, the discussion took a turn for the better. After the initial formation of a united front against Fischer, three major groups emerged. One, led by Hans Rothfels, stuck to their traditional guns and said there was nothing to revise. A second, headed by Gerhard Ritter and Michael Freund, though criticizing the older German literature on July 1914 as 'too apologetic' (Ritter) or even denouncing the traditional line as the 'Unschuldslüge' (Freund), still maintained most of their old arguments.

A third group, represented by Egmont Zechlin and Karl-Dietrich Erdmann, have at least in part abandoned the old positions, although very discreetly and without giving any credit to Fischer. They now admit that Germany in July 1914 deliberately risked war, even with Britain, but they hedge this vital admission with a number of 'explanations' which only tend to obscure the central issue. Zechlin argues that Bethmann Hollweg, when taking the plunge in July 1914, only wanted a limited, 'rational' war in eighteenth-century style, not a ferocious world war. In two recent articles he has moved even closer to the position of those who criticize the traditional line, so that the differences between him and the Fischer group, on that point at least, have now been reduced to a few subtle shades of interpretation. On the other hand, these slight divergences give even less warrant for Zechlin's (and others') view that Fischer is all wrong, since Zechlin now maintains that Bethmann Hollweg consciously took the risk of British intervention. Erdmann gives a psychological portrait of the Chancellor, based mainly on the diary of Kurt Riezler, Bethmann Hollweg's close adviser, and stresses the Chancellor's subjective honesty, his rejection of world domination for Germany (which, unfortunately, Erdmann confuses with the alleged rejection of achieving the status of a world power). Both harp on the rediscovered story of the proposed Anglo-Russian naval convention. Still, Zechlin and Erdmann have introduced new tones into the debate and have made rational discussion possible. They set the final seal on the demolition of the traditional taboo.

Another myth has also to go for good—the myth of *Einkreisung*. There was no 'encirclement' of Germany by enemies waiting to attack and crush her. The partition of Europe and the world into two power blocks, with the Triple Entente on the one hand, the Triple Alliance on the other, was largely a result of German policy, of the German desire to raise the Reich from the status of a continental power to that of a world power. The Triple Alliance itself came into being as a purely continental arrangement in the years 1879–82, in order to keep France isolated, and the Franco-Russian Alliance of 1894, the nucleus of the Triple Entente, was the French means of escaping that isolation. It was only after Germany started on her ambitious and ill-fated career of becoming a full-fledged world power in her own right that the world situation changed radically. Britain, challenged by Germany's naval programme more than by her territorial claims, notably in Africa, abandoned her 'splendid isolation' and sought alliances, first with Japan in 1902, then with France in 1904, and finally, in 1907, with Russia. What was—and to a certain ex-

413

Geiss

THE FIRST
WORLD WAR
AND GERMAN
WAR AIMS

tent still is—denounced in Germany as *Einkreisung,* amounted to the containment of German ambitions which ran counter to the interests of all other imperialist powers.

The concept of encirclement, however, played an important part immediately before the outbreak of war in 1914. In Germany the idea had become widespread that the only choice for the Reich was between rising to a full-fledged world power and stagnation. The German *Weltanschauung* saw only the unending struggle of all against all; this social-Darwinist concept was not limited to the lunatic fringe, but influenced even the most liberal spokesman of the Wilhelmian establishment, Riezler, Bethmann Hollweg's young protégé. For him all nations had the desire for permanent expansion with world domination as the supreme goal. Since he looked upon any containment of German aspirations as a hostile act, Riezler's ideas, translated into official policy, were bound to make war unavoidable. Even Bethmann Hollweg thought in 1911 that war was necessary for the German people.

The final logical conclusion was the idea of preventive war against those enemies who tried to block Germany's further rise. The traditional school in Germany always indignantly denied the existence of the preventive war concept even among the Prussian General Staff. The prevailing spirit of militarism and social-Darwinism in Wilhelmian Germany made it, however, more than plausible. A new source, the private papers of Jagow, provides the missing link between Germany's pre-war *Weltpolitik* and the outbreak of war. At the end of May or early in June 1914 Moltke, Chief of the General Staff, asked Jagow, the German Secretary of State for Foreign Affairs, to start a preventive war as soon as possible, because militarily the situation for Germany was constantly deteriorating. Jagow refused, pointing to the improvement in the German economic situation. But after the war he admitted that he was never *a limine* against the idea of preventive war—after all, Bismarck's wars had been preventive wars, according to Jagow—and that Moltke's words inspired him with confidence in military success when the crisis did come in July 1914. Another recent find tallies with Jagow's point of view. In February 1918 ex-Chancellor Bethmann Hollweg, questioned privately by the liberal politician Conrad Haussmann, said: 'Yes, My God, in a certain sense it was a preventive war. But when war was hanging above us, when it had to come in two years even more dangerously and more inescapably, and when the generals said, now it is still possible, without defeat, but not in two years time. Yes, the generals!'

Against that background the events after Sarajevo are easy to understand, for Sarajevo turned out to be hardly more than the cue for the Reich to rush into action, although Austria had to deal the first blow against Serbia. The Austrians, however, were originally divided in their counsels. Only the Chief of the General Staff, Conrad von Hötzendorf, pressed for immediate war against Serbia, supported by high officials in the Foreign Ministry and by most of the German press in Austria. Foreign Minister

Berchtold, the Austrian and the Hungarian Prime Ministers, Stürgkh and Tisza, hesitated and were for less radical measures. But even Conrad realized that he could not wage war against Serbia without first making sure that Germany would cover Austria's rear against Russia. Thus the real decision lay with Germany.

After Sarajevo Germany could not at once make up her mind which course to follow. The Auswärtiges Amt clearly saw the danger involved in Russia's trying to protect Serbia if Austria made war, namely, that a world war might result. This is why the Auswärtiges Amt from the first counselled moderation both to Austria and to Serbia. The German General Staff, on the other hand, was ready to welcome Sarajevo as the golden opportunity for risking a preventive war. In this situation it was the Kaiser's word that proved decisive. Wilhelm II was incensed at the murder, perhaps most because it attacked his cherished monarchist principle. When he received the report of Tschirschky, the German ambassador to Vienna, of 30 June, telling of his moderating counsels to the Austrians, the Kaiser commented in his usual wild manner and provided the specious slogan 'Now or never'! which turned out to be the guiding star of German diplomacy in the crisis of July 1914.

On 5 July, Count Hoyos came to Berlin, bringing with him two documents on Austrian policy towards the Balkans. The Austrian ambassador, Szogyeny, handed them to the Kaiser at a special audience at the Potsdam Palace, in which he apparently used fairly warlike language, although the documents of his own government spoke of war, if at all, only by implication. After initial hesitation, Wilhelm II promised German support to the Dual Monarchy, whatever Austria did. His promise soon came to be called the German *carte blanche* to Austria. But the Kaiser was not satisfied with giving his ally a free hand against Serbia. He urged Vienna, which apparently had not made up its mind, to make war on Serbia, and that as soon as possible. Bethmann Hollweg and the Emperor's other civilian and military advisers duly endorsed these imperial decisions.

When Bethmann returned to Hohenfinow, he told Riezler what had happened at Potsdam. From what Riezler recorded in his by now famous diary, it appears that the Chancellor was not only fully aware of the possible consequences when taking his 'leap into the dark'—war with Britain, i.e. world war—but that already at that stage his first objective seems to have been war with Russia and France; a diplomatic victory— France dropping Russia, Russia dropping Serbia—would have been accepted only as a second best.

Impressed by the German stand, Berchtold swung round in favour of Conrad's line. His colleagues in the Cabinet followed suit, last of all Tisza, and so did Emperor Francis Joseph. Preparations were made in Vienna and Berlin for the *coup* against Serbia: it was decided to confront Serbia with an ultimatum which would be designed to be unacceptable as soon as the French president Poincaré and his prime minister Viviani had finished their state visit to Russia. That was to be on 23 July.

Meanwhile, the Austrian and German governments did everything to

415

Geiss

THE FIRST
WORLD WAR
AND GERMAN
WAR AIMS

create a peaceful impression. The two emperors enjoyed their usual sum-mer holidays, as did the leading generals of the Central Powers. But they returned to their respective capitals before or just after the ultimatum was handed over at Belgrade. Austria kept the German government informed of her intentions through the normal diplomatic channels, while the Ger-man government pressed Austria to start the action against Serbia as soon as possible. Privately the Germans aired serious misgivings at the lack of energy Austria displayed, and the Auswärtiges Amt suspected her of being unhappy about Germany's urgency. These suspicions were not un-founded: the Austrians had waited to make a decision until the German declaration of 5 July, but even then they moved slowly. According to Austrian plans, mobilization would begin after the rupture of diplomatic relations with Serbia, but it was originally intended to delay the actual declaration of war and the opening of hostilities until mobilization was completed, i.e., until approximately 12 August. The Wilhelmstrasse, how-ever, deemed such delay absolutely intolerable. It was quick to see that the powers might intervene diplomatically during the interval to save Serbia from humiliation. As the German government was bent on preventing any mediation, it spurred Vienna on, as soon as it learned of the Austrian time-table, to declare war on Serbia immediately after the rupture with Belgrade and to open hostilities at once. On 25 July, Jagow told Szogyeny that the German government

takes it for granted that upon eventual negative reply from Serbia, our declaration of war will follow immediately, joined to military operations. Any delay in beginning warlike preparations is regarded here as a great danger in respect of intervention of other powers. We are urgently advised to go ahead at once and confront the world with a *fait accompli.*

On the other hand, Jagow justified his refusal to pass on British proposals of mediation to Vienna by the alleged fear that Vienna might react by rushing things and confronting the world with a *fait accompli.* Yet when Austria, giving way to German pressure, did declare war immediately, the German Secretary of State told the British Ambassador, Sir Edward Goschen, that now the very thing had happened he had always warned against: namely, Austria rushing things as an answer to proposals of me-diation.

German pressure on Vienna to declare war on Serbia without delay had an immediate and telling effect: on 26 July, Berchtold, who had been wavering and who tended to be timid rather than aggressive, adopted the German idea, and in this he was vigorously supported by Tschirschky. Conrad, however, was far from happy. Although usually thought of as the most warlike on the side of the Central Powers, he would have preferred to stick to the original timetable, but he gave in, and the Austrian government decided on an early declaration of war. On 27 July the final decision was taken to declare war the following day.

Now the German government had accomplished one of its short-term aims: Austria had confronted the world with a *fait accompli* in the form of an early declaration of war against Serbia, which was bound to undermine all attempts at mediation between Austria and Serbia. The following day, 29 July, the Austrians rushed things even more, again following German advice, when they started the bombardment of Belgrade. The immediate effect was catastrophic: the Russians took the bombardment of Belgrade as the beginning of military operations against Serbia, as it was meant to be. They had, on 28 July, already ordered partial mobilization against Austria in order to deter her from actual warfare against Serbia. Now the Russian generals, thinking war with Austria and Germany imminent, successfully pressed for immediate general mobilization, since Russian mobilization was known to be far slower than Austrian or German. The Tsar ordered a halt to general mobilization and a return to partial mobilization after the receipt of a telegram from Wilhelm II late in the evening of 29 July, but the next afternoon the generals and the foreign minister Sazonov renewed their pressure on him. Nicholas gave way and Russian general mobilization was ordered for a second time on 30 July, at 6 p.m.

The German government rushed things also in two more respects. On 27 July Jagow had assured Jules Cambon and Sir Horace Rumbold, the British chargé d'affaires in Berlin, that Germany would not mobilize so long as Russia mobilized only in the south, against Austria. Two days later, however, the Auswärtiges Amt received a lengthy memorandum from General Moltke, whose arguments boiled down to an insistence on German general mobilization. Again the Auswärtiges Amt followed the lead of the generals. After 30 July, Berlin demanded the cancellation of Russian mobilization not only against Germany, but also against Austria, and that demand was expressly included both in the German ultimatum to Russia on 31 July and in the declaration of war of 1 August. When the French ambassador reminded Jagow of his words only a few days earlier, Jagow apparently shrugged his shoulders and replied that the generals wanted to have it that way, and that his words had, after all, not been a binding statement.

The second point was at least as serious: while the Entente powers tried desperately to prevent a local war, in order to avert a continental and world war, by making a whole series of proposals of mediation, the German government not only flatly rejected them or passed them on to Vienna without giving them support, but also stifled the only initiative from the German side which might have saved the general peace. This time, the initiative had come from the Kaiser. Wilhelm had returned from his sailing holiday in Norway after learning of the Austrian suspension of diplomatic relations with Serbia on 25 July. He arrived at Potsdam on the 27th. Early the following morning he read the Serbian answer

417

Geiss

THE FIRST
WORLD WAR
AND GERMAN
WAR AIMS

to Austria's ultimatum. Like nearly everybody else in Europe outside Germany and Austria, the Kaiser was impressed by Serbia's answer, which had conceded practically everything except one point, and made only a few reservations. Suddenly all his warlike sentiments vanished and he minuted:

> a brilliant achievement in a time-limit of only 48 hours! It is more than one could have expected! A great moral success for Vienna; but with it all reason for war is gone and Giesl ought to have quietly stayed on in Belgrade! After that I should never have ordered mobilization.

He immediately ordered the Auswärtiges Amt to draft a note for Vienna, telling the Austrians that they should accept the Serbian answer. To satisfy the army, and at the same time as a guarantee for what the Serbians had conceded, the Kaiser suggested that Austria should content herself with occupying Belgrade only and negotiate with the Serbians about the remaining reservations.

Apparently the Auswärtiges Amt took fright at their sovereign's weakness. The moment that had come during both Moroccan crises threatened to come again: that the Kaiser would lose his nerve and beat the retreat. This time, however, Bethmann Hollweg and the Auswärtiges Amt did not listen to their sovereign as they had done on 5 July. The Chancellor despatched the instructions to Tschirschky on the evening of 28 July, i.e., after he had learned that Austria had declared war on Serbia. Furthermore, he distorted the Kaiser's argument by omitting the crucial sentence that war was now no longer necessary. The occupation of Belgrade was not meant to be, in Bethmann's words, a safeguard for the implementation of Serbian concessions, but a means to enforce Serbia's total acceptance of the Austrian ultimatum. Finally, the Chancellor added a comment which was sure to defeat any conciliatory effect of his démarche, if any chance of this had remained.

In these circumstances, the démarche, when executed by Tschirschky, had no effect whatsoever, nor did a later British proposal along similar lines.

When developments had gone so far, Bethmann Hollweg undertook his most important move, the bid for British neutrality. On 29 July he had despatched the ultimatum to Belgium to the German minister in Brussels. The violation of Belgian neutrality made it vital for Germany that at least British acquiescence be secured. During the evening of 29 July, Bethmann, returning from talks with the Kaiser and his military advisers at Potsdam, summoned the British ambassador. The Chancellor asked for England's neutrality in return for the promise that Germany would not annex French or Belgian territory. The reaction of the Foreign Office was scathing, as is borne out by Crowe's comment.

A British answer to the German demand was no longer needed, for, just after Goschen left the Chancellor, a telegram from London arrived: Lichnowsky reported Grey's warning that Britain would not remain neutral if France were involved in a continental war. Now Grey—at last —had spoken in such a way that even the German Chancellor had to abandon his cherished hope of British neutrality, which would have meant certain victory for Germany in the imminent continental war. Bethmann Hollweg was dumbfounded, for he saw clearly the consequences of Grey's warning—a world war which Germany could hardly win. In his panic, he tried to salvage what seemed possible. He now pressed the Austrians in all sincerity to modify their stand, but did not go so far as to advise the Austrians to drop the whole idea of war against Serbia. He only pleaded with them to accept the British version of the 'halt-in-Belgrade' proposal and to open conversations with the Russians. In such conversations the Austrians were to repeat their promise not to annex Serbian territory, a pledge which, as the Chancellor knew quite well, was regarded by Russia as insufficient. Bethmann made his proposals in the vague hope that by shifting the blame to Russia the British might stay out after all. At the same time he wanted to persuade the German public, especially the social-democrats, to follow his policy by demonstrating his peaceful intentions. The Chancellor did not want to put an end to the local war, which had just seen its second day; what he wanted was to improve Germany's position in a major conflict.

Bethmann Hollweg failed in his first objective; he succeeded in his second only too well. The social-democrats supported the German war effort, and the Russians are still blamed in Germany today for having started the war. For this same reason—to shift the blame to Russia—Bethmann also resisted the pressure of the General Staff who pleaded for immediate German mobilization. The Chancellor urged that Russia be allowed to mobilize first against Germany, since, as he put it, he could not pursue military and political actions at the same time. In other words, he could not simultaneously put the blame on Russia and order German mobilization before Russian general mobilization.

On 29 July, the German generals still appreciated Bethmann Hollweg's policy. But during the 30th they became impatient. In the evening, about two hours after Russian general mobilization had been definitely ordered, they told the Chancellor that he had to make up his mind about German mobilization immediately. The Chancellor won a delay until noon next day, but there was little doubt which way the decision was meant to go. Bethmann Hollweg agreed, in the hope that the Russians might order general mobilization beforehand. During the morning of 31 July the Germans waited for the news of Russian general mobilization as their cue to rush into military action themselves. Luckily enough for Bethmann Hollweg and generations of German historians, Sazonov lost his nerve and had, in fact, already ordered Russian general mobilization.

At 11 a.m. Bethmann, Moltke, and Falkenhayn met again, anxiously waiting for news from Russia with only one hour left before the deadline they had set themselves. At five minutes to twelve a telegram from Pourtalès, the German ambassador to St Petersburg, was handed to them. It

419

Geiss

THE FIRST
WORLD WAR
AND GERMAN
WAR AIMS

confirmed the rumours that Russian general mobilization had been ordered. Now they could order German mobilization with what they thought a clear conscience. Immediately after the receipt of the telegram the state of threatening war, the phase of military operations which immediately preceded general mobilization, was declared in Germany. The same afternoon, two ultimata went off—one to Russia demanding that she stop all military preparations not only against Germany but also against Austria, the other to France, asking about the stand France would take in a war between Germany and Russia. At the same time the Auswärtiges Amt prepared the declarations of war on both countries. Thus war had become inevitable, even more so since German general mobilization, according to the famous Schlieffen plan, meant opening hostilities against neutral Belgium a few days after mobilization had actually started.

After noon on 31 July, therefore, the catastrophe could no longer be averted. On 1 August, Germany ordered general mobilization, at the same hour as France. In the evening of that day, Germany declared war on Russia. An hour before, a curious and revealing incident had occurred. A telegram from Lichnowsky arrived suggesting that Britain might remain neutral if Germany were not to attack France. The Kaiser and his military, naval, and political advisers were happy, since their tough line during the July crisis seemed to be paying off after all. Only Moltke demurred. He was shocked by the idea of having to change his plan, and even feared that Russia might drop out as well. Late in the evening another telegram from London arrived, making the true position clear.

The French answer was evasive in form but firm in content: France would not forsake her ally. At the same time, France tried desperately to secure British support. The Russians, the French, and Crowe in the Foreign Office, urged Grey to make Britain's stand quite clear, that she would not remain neutral in a continental war. Grey had warned Germay before, but his language had not been straightforward enough to destroy German illusions. When Grey made the British policy unmistakably clear, even to the German Chancellor, it was too late.

How much Germany up to the last hour still hoped for British neutrality can be seen by the invention of a whole series of alleged border incidents, some of which were so crudely presented that outside Germany nobody believed them. They were part of the German manoeuvre to put the blame this time on France and to impress Britain. The German invasion of Belgium, however, removed the last hesitations: Britain sent an ultimatum to Germany demanding the immediate withdrawal of German troops from Belgium. When Germany refused, Britain entered the war automatically after the time-limit of the ultimatum had expired, i.e., at 11 p.m. Greenwich time on 4 August.

In trying to assess the shares of responsibility for the war two basic distinctions have to be made: on the one hand between the three stages of war connected with its outbreak: local war (Austria v. Serbia), continental war (Austria and Germany v. Russia and France), and world war

(Britain joining the continental war). On the other hand, one has to distinguish between the will to start any of those three stages of war and the fact of merely causing them.

Since the world war developed out of a local war, then a continental war, the major share for causing it lies with that power which willed the local and/or continental war. That power was clearly Germany. She did not will the world war, as is borne out by her hopes of keeping out Britain, but she did urge Austria to make war on Serbia. Even if Austria had started the local war completely on her own—which, of course, she had not—Germany's share would still be bigger than Austria's, since a German veto could have effectively prevented it. Germany, furthermore, was the only power which had no objection to the continental war. So long as Britain kept out, she was confident of winning a war against Russia and France. Germany did nothing to prevent continental war, even at the risk of a world war, a risk which her government had seen from the beginning.

Austria, of course, wanted the local war, after—with German prodding—she had made up her mind, but feared a continental war. In fact, she hoped that Germany, by supporting her diplomatically, might frighten Russia into inaction.

Russia, France, and Britain tried to avert continental war. Their main argument for mediation between Serbia and Austria was precisely that to prevent the local war would be the best means of averting continental war. On the other hand, they contributed to the outbreak, each in her own way: Russia by committing the technical blunder of providing the cue for German mobilization, instead of waiting until Germany had mobilized. The French attitude was almost entirely correct; her only fault was that she could not hold back her Russian ally from precipitate general mobilization. Britain might have made her stand clear beyond any doubt much earlier, since this might have been a way of restraining Germany, although it is doubtful whether this would have altered the course of events to any appreciable degree. The share of the Entente powers is much smaller than Germany's, for it consisted mainly in reacting—not always in the best manner—to German action.

Looking back on the events from the mid-sixties, the outbreak of the first world war looks like the original example of faulty brinkmanship, of rapid escalation in a period of history when the mechanisms of alliances and mobilization schedules could still work unchecked by fear of the absolute weapon and the absolute destruction its use would bring in what would now be the third world war.

421

Geiss

THE FIRST
WORLD WAR
AND GERMAN
WAR AIMS

GEORGE F. KENNAN

Fifty years ago there occurred, in the Bosnian capital of Sarajevo, the assassination of the Austrian heir apparent, the Archduke Ferdinand, the event that touched off World War I. It was far from being the war's actual cause. The real causes were of great complexity. They reached back into the past, as the historical roots of great events always do. They have been the subject of exhaustive study and of long controversy among the historians.

If the question were to be posed, What were the broad historical circumstances out of which the war arose? one would probably be safe in naming two: first, the failure to find an acceptable place in the European order for the united Germany which had come into existence in 1870; and, second, the rivalry between Russia and Austria-Hungary over the succession to the disintegrating Turkish empire in the Balkans. The European order emerging from the Napoleonic Wars proved insufficiently flexible, in other words, to stand the subtraction of one great power in the southeast of the continent and the addition of a new one in the northwest.

History, it has often been observed, tends to be written by the victors. Certainly this was to some extent true in the English-speaking countries in the case of World War I. Many of us were brought up on a view of the war that depicted the Germans as those most responsible for its outbreak. The confession of Germany's primary guilt in this respect was embedded in the Versailles Treaty, over the violent protest of an entire generation of Germans.

There can be no question that the statesmanship of the imperial German government of the post-Bismarckian period was guilty of grievous mistakes which entered importantly into the origins of the world war. Outstanding among these were the insistence on challenging British naval power by the attempt to build a fleet of comparable strength; the uncritical support given at crucial moments to an aggressive Austrian policy in the Balkans; and the fatal decision to inaugurate hostilities against France in 1914 by moving through Belgium, thus assuring Britain's entry into the war.

But it would be an oversimplification to accept these mistakes as proof of Germany's primary guilt. The tragedy of Germany's situation lay in the fact that the establishment of the German Reich was practically coincidental with the conduct of the Franco-Prussian War of 1870–1871, and that this war ended with the incorporation into the new, united Germany

Source: George F. Kennan, "The Price We Paid for War," *Atlantic,* CCXIV, No. 4 (October 1964), pp. 50–54. Copyright © 1964 by The Atlantic Monthly Company, Boston, Mass. Reprinted with permission.

of two provinces, Alsace and Lorraine, which had previously been part of France. This territorial change was never really accepted by the French. And this meant, in effect, that the French never really reconciled themselves to the presence of a united Germany in the family of the European powers. In the decades just prior to World War I, France was actually more hostile to the existing status quo in Europe than was Germany. Germany was a satiated power in Europe; France was not. Germany had no territorial aspirations anywhere on the continent; France did.

These two situations—the Franco-German tension and the rivalry in the Balkans—were brought together for the first time in the Franco-Russian Alliance, concluded in 1894. This flowed directly from the French unwillingness to accept the loss of Alsace and Lorraine. Had France been willing to accept this loss, no alliance with Russia would have been required for France's protection. Germany, after all, had no further territorial designs on France.

Ostensibly, the Franco-Russian Alliance was a defensive one. Almost every alliance is defensive—on paper. Actually, this one was conceived by the French as a framework within which, eventually, when the time was ripe, they could move toward the recovery of the lost provinces.

In several respects, the Franco-Russian Alliance had unfortunate consequences. It constituted the first link in that encirclement of which the Germans so bitterly complained. It was the first great step toward Germany's isolation. But this isolation increased Germany's dependence on its one faithful ally, Austria-Hungary, and caused Germany to feel that there was no choice but to support that ally faithfully, even when the latter's policies were reckless and aggressive.

For the Russians, on the other hand, the alliance with France was an unnatural commitment. It reflected no real Russian interest. Russia's acceptance of the alliance initially, and adherence to it down through the years, were simply consequences of financial weakness. It represented a political price Russia was obliged to pay for France's financial support in a period of rapid economic development in Russia, a period in which the need of the Russian economy for investment capital was great and indigenous sources of capital were inadequate. And it had the dual effect of causing the Russians to lose much of the independence of their policy vis-à-vis Germany, where an independence of policy might have been helpful in preventing a world war, and yet to gain too much independence of policy in the Balkans, where an active Russian policy could only increase the danger of war.

Originally, the Franco-Russian Alliance was not supposed to be applicable to the contingency of a war between Russia and Austria. But it led to such extreme political tensions that any Balkan war in which Russia should be involved could no longer be isolated. It was, after all, over just such a Russian-Austrian conflict, not over any German attack on either Russia or France, that the alliance was finally invoked in 1914. There can be no question that Russian policy in the Balkans in the years from 1906 to 1914 was strengthened and made sharper by the knowledge on the part of Russian statesmen that Germany could not come to the aid of Austria in a Balkan conflict without inviting the intervention of France on its western frontier.

As for the conflict between Russian and Austro-Hungarian interests in the Balkans, here again it is not a simple matter to assess the rights and wrongs from a distance of fifty years. It must be recognized that Austrian interests were more vitally affected than were those of Russia by the disintegration of Turkish power and the emergence of the South Slav peoples to independent political activity. This development constituted no threat to Russia, which was itself a Slavic state. To Austria, on the other hand, which already had great Slavic minorities within its borders, the establishment of new, independent Slavic states on the immediate southern periphery of the empire could have dangerous consequences.

The Russian interest in the Balkans was occasioned at that time not by any real defensive interests, but by two sentimental enthusiasms of the Russian educated class: a romantic sympathy for fellow Slavs, and the long-standing desire to control the straits at the entrance to the Black Sea. Neither of these aspirations looks very impressive from a distance of fifty years. Membership in the Slavic branch of the human family is not really, as history has shown, a very important bond. Cultural and religious traditions, varying widely among the Slavic peoples, are more important as determinants of national policy, over the long run. And as for the Russian yearning to control the straits, it is hard to view this as anything more than a matter of prestige. The regime of the straits that existed in the period prior to the war occasioned no difficulties for Russian commerce. And if one looks at the matter from the military standpoint, one can only say that this regime, barring as it did the passage of foreign warships through the straits, was a positive advantage to a country which had lost most of its naval strength at Tsushima.

All these considerations lead to the conclusion that it was indeed the Austrians, not the Russians, whose interests were most vitally concerned in the development of events in the Balkans in the first years of the century. And one cannot blame the Austrians for wishing to assure that the liberation of the Balkan Slavs from the Turkish hegemony should not occur in a manner likely to endanger the integrity of the Austro-Hungarian empire. But one can and must blame them for the reckless and aggressive measures by which they attempted to assure this: measures which offended the South Slavs themselves, relied on naked force far more than on persuasion, alarmed the international community, and made it much more difficult than it need otherwise have been for Russia to remain aloof without suffering real damage to its prestige. If it be true, as I believe it to be, that in the relations between governments the "how" is, generally at least, as important as the "what," then one must indeed charge the Austro-Hungarian statesmen of that day with a responsibility second to none for the outbreak of the world war in 1914.

Such, in the main, were the political origins of the war. They point, as one can readily see, to the conclusion that none of the four greatest continental powers involved was without blame in the complicated process of its origins. But behind these specific political circumstances, there was a deeper deficiency which lay in the spirit and the outlooks of the time and pervaded the diplomacy of all four of these powers. This was the disparity between the real implications and possibilities of major warfare as an instrument of policy in the modern age, and what people supposed these implications and possibilities to be.

The international society of that day was still dominated by romantic concepts of warfare, and these concepts embraced two great errors. First, they exaggerated the role of personal bravery and determination in a war fought with modern weapons. Under the influence of this misimpression, they pictured warfare too much as a test of the personal qualities and spirit of a nation and too little as a test of its manpower and resources and its capacity for social discipline. It was thought that if a nation's people were brave enough, spirited enough, determined enough, a nation won. People failed to realize that in a war where military realities would be governed so extensively by the machine gun and barbed wire, excessive personal valor would be only a wasteful form of foolhardiness; victory or defeat would depend primarily on the grisly mathematics of mutual destruction and, above all, on who was prepared to expend and to sacrifice the greatest quantity of men and matériel. In many of the offensives undertaken in that war, it could be, and was, calculated in advance that so and so many tens of thousands of men, one's own men as well as those of the enemy, would inevitably perish in the course of the offensive. They would perish from shells and bullets fired by men whom they could not even see. It would make no difference, or very little difference, whether they were brave as lions; they would perish anyway. War was no longer a matter just of valor and enthusiasm.

This lesson could have been learned, one would think, from the Russo-Japanese War. It does not seem to have been. As a result, governments moved lightheartedly into the horror of war in 1914, and millions of young men went singing to their death, encouraged to believe that they were embarking on a great martial adventure, as in the days of chivalry.

Second, the statesmen of the period preceding World War I had no idea of the destructiveness of modern war. They had no idea how long it would last or how many lives and resources it would consume. They deceived themselves in believing that the fruits of victory would easily overweigh the attendant sacrifices. But they grievously misestimated both elements. It did not occur to them that the losses of life—the losses, above all, of young life, of the flower of the male youth—would be so great that no conceivable fruits of victory could possibly justify them. No defeat could have carried with it disasters worse than the sacrifice of young manhood actually incurred in pursuit of victory. And no victory could have been so glorious as to justify this sacrifice. History reveals that every one of the warring powers would have been better off to have concluded peace in the early stages of the war *on the adversary's terms* rather than to accept the loss of life attendant on continuation of the war to 1918. This loss inflicted on each of the belligerents a subjective damage from which it could not recover, even superficially, for at least a generation. In a deeper sense, some may be said to have not fully recovered to the present day.

Any loss of young manhood on the scale that was incurred by the major belligerents in World War I inflicts both genetic and spiritual damage on the nation that incurs it. The age structure of the population is disbalanced. The spirit of the older people is terribly affected. They cannot stand this slaughter of their sons. A portion of themselves—of their taste for life, their capacity for hope—dies with those in whom so much of themselves was invested. Great damage is done to the youth, who are forced to grow up in an unsettled world without the steadying hand of the fathers. On the political scene, the continuity of the tradition is destroyed. The field is left to be contended for by the very old and the very young, among whom there is no intimacy. We shall never know how many of the troubles and failures of European civilization in the 1920s and 1930s, including the drift into a new world war, were attributable to these conditions.

All these are subjective damages which no victory could have made good, even if it had been as glorious as the statesmen of 1914 pictured it to themselves, and even if it had accorded fully with the objectives they had in mind when they entered the war. But actually, the war ended with results which nobody could have predicted, and which did not correspond at all with the aims for which the victor powers entered the war.

The war, as it turned out, produced the destruction of all three of the great empires so prominently involved in its outbreak: the Austro-Hungarian, the Russian, and the German. This was something which no one —not even the French and British, but least of all the statesmen of those three empires themselves—wished or expected to achieve when they went to war in 1914, and from which no one really profited.

The destruction of the Austro-Hungarian empire led merely to the establishment in Central and Eastern Europe of a new status quo even less stable than the one that had existed prior to the war. It involved the establishment of an entire tier of independent states in Central and Eastern Europe, lying between Germany and Austria, on the one hand, and Russia, on the other. The idea was that these states, in alliance with France, would keep Germany helpless and would serve as a barrier to the spread of Russian Communism into Europe. This was, therefore, a status quo predicated on the weakness of both Germany and Russia. It was bound to break down as soon as that weakness was overcome. And break down it did, in a manner that contributed greatly to the outbreak of World War II. In addition to that political defect, the new status quo represented a deterioration from the standpoint of the integration of the economies of that area. No new form of international unity could be found to replace the unity which the Austro-Hungarian empire had once given to the economic life of the peoples of the Danubian Basin. None has been found to this day.

If we turn to the collapse of the Russian empire, we have to note that the Russian Revolution of 1917 was the direct result of the war. The Revolution would probably never have occurred at all at that juncture had the Czar's government not involved itself in the war. It would certainly not have ended in a seizure of power by the Communists if the Allies had not insisted that the Provisional Government continue the war effort. The Russian Revolution: the estrangement of Russia, the conversion of Russia, with its great resources, from the status of a friend to that of an opponent of the Western nations for a period of at least half a century—all this must be regarded as part of the price paid by the victors of 1918 for the privilege of smashing Germany. A higher price, surely, it would be difficult to imagine.

And the significance of the Russian Revolution was of course not restricted to Russia's relations with the West. This Revolution represented only the first phase of that great revolt, moral and political, of "non-Europe" against Europe which has been a dominating development of this century and has included other Communist revolutions, notably the Chinese, as well as the worldwide anticolonial movement. All these processes were greatly hastened, if not caused, by the Russian Revolution.

Finally, there was the destruction of the German empire itself. Who gained from this? True, the Germans were thoroughly defeated. For a number of years they could no longer threaten Britain on the seas. They were obliged to return Alsace and Lorraine to France. But these were perhaps the only Allied gains of any importance from the four long years of war. It proved impossible to collect from the Germans anything more than a fraction of the reparations the Allies once thought to collect. Even when the reparations could be collected, the transfer of them turned out to present serious financial difficulties. The restrictions placed on German rearmament were only temporarily effective. So long as they were observed, their principal result was to free the Germans from the financial strain of maintaining armed forces, thus giving them a competitive advantage over the Western Allies in economic recovery. The moral and political effect of the effort to impose a punitive peace on Germany in the 1920s was just enough, together with the economic crisis, to overstrain the resources of moderate, democratic government in Germany, and to render the political life of that country vulnerable to capture by extremist forces.

We all know the result. Within less than two decades after the world war came to an end, the Allies were faced with a revived and rearmed Germany, but this time under a leadership—that of Adolf Hitler— far more hostile and dangerous to the remainder of the West than the Kaiser's Germany they had been so concerned to defeat in the period from 1914 to 1918.

In the damage it did to the structure of international life, and in the even deeper damage it inflicted on the biological and spiritual condition of the European peoples, World War I still looms on the historical horizon as *the* great determining tragedy of our century. There are many lessons to be gained from it for our own generation. But one stands out in importance. It is the lesson of the unsuitability of major war as an instrument of policy in the modern age. In that period of 1914 to 1918, thirty years before the development of the nuclear weapon, it was demonstrated that war, conducted in the grand manner and as a means of achieving major political objectives, was no longer a rational means of procedure. Defensive war might still have a rational purpose, as long as it remained exclusively and truly defensive and as long as one hoped for nothing from it but sheer survival. Limited war—war for limited objectives—might still have a rational purpose, provided the actual military effort could be held to modest dimensions and provided one could be sure of stopping in time. But all-out war, involving the total commitment of a nation's manpower and resources and aimed at the total destruction of an enemy's will to resist and the complete power to order his life and to shape his behavior, had already, in 1914, lost its rationale.

It had lost its rationale because of the terrible destructiveness of modern weapons, because of the enormous cost of cultivating and employing such weapons, because of the great complexity of modern society, because of the impossibility, the sheer technical impossibility, of one great country holding another great country in subjection for any long period of time and shaping its life in ways contrary to the will of the people.

In the 1930s, this lesson was widely forgotten or ignored. The result was tragedy and great suffering. Today, when the destructiveness of weaponry is many times greater than it was in 1914, one can no longer afford to ignore it. If people today will ponder the meaning of the great conflagration that occurred a half century ago, and will learn to take it into account in the conduct of statesmanship, then, perhaps, the eight and a half million young men who laid down their lives at that time will not have died entirely in vain.

27. The Well-Spring of Our Discontents

WILLIAM L. LANGER

28. Containment and Counterrevolution at Versailles, 1918-1919

ARNO J. MAYER

World War I knocked the European Humpty-Dumpty off the wall and in the Paris Peace Conference at war's end all the king's horses and all the king's men could not put Humpty-Dumpty together again. Nor could the world's statesmen and diplomatists. Perhaps no major peace conference has had such a dismal record. Instead of healing the disruption and dislocation brought by the war, the peace settlement perpetuated or reinforced them. In twenty-five years world war came again. That war followed so soon almost makes it appear that any other settlement—the harsh crushing of German might that Clemenceau wanted or an appeasement of Germany with a Wilsonian "peace without victory"—would have stood a better chance of keeping the peace. Instead, the peacemakers seemed to have taken the worst features of each alternative to arrive at a settlement which antagonized Germany enough to demand revision of it without weakening Germany enough to prevent revision from happening. At the same time the settlement created a power vacuum of weak states in eastern Europe with great powers—Germany and the Soviet Union—on either side and no real means to deter them from filling that vacuum whenever they desired. The sorry record of the Paris Peace Conference of 1919 continues to raise two questions: What was so bad about the settlement, and why did not the peacemakers do better?

Source: William L. Langer, "The Well-Spring of Our Discontents," *Journal of Contemporary History*, III, No. 4 (October 1968), 3–17. Reprinted by permission of George Weidenfeld and Nicolson.

The first of the following two selections on the peace settlement deals with half of that double question. In it Professor William L. Langer, who wrote the selection on the 1848 revolutions, reviews the principal terms of the settlement and evaluates them from the vantage point of fifty years distance. For him, as for George F. Kennan in the preceding selection, the effects of the war and peace settlement were so disastrous that they form "the well-spring of our discontents." According to Langer, why were the provisions of the settlement, especially regarding reparations, war guilt, and self-determination, so bad for subsequent history? What attitudes and aims did such leaders as Clemenceau, Lloyd George, and Wilson take into the conference which caused them to make such provisions? In what ways did the peace settlement's attempt "to break the power of Germany" work to the opposite effect? To what extent did the "specter of Bolshevism and social revolution" haunt the peacemakers and shape the settlement? From the article as a whole, how would you sum up the negative efforts of the war and peace settlement on western civilization? Were there any positive effects?

The second selection is a new attempt to describe the atmosphere in which the peacemakers worked. It is the prologue to one of several books by Arno J. Mayer of Princeton University which promise to reinterpret twentieth-century diplomatic history. He holds that this century witnessed a "new diplomacy." Peacemaking and warmaking were no longer mere technical efforts to adjust the balance of power among rival national states as they had been for Metternich, Talleyrand, or Castlereagh. Diplomatists were now politicians of the people who found their options for solving international problems inexorably tied to domestic politics. By 1919 domestic politics in the victor nations had brought about right-wing majorities determined to halt the prewar tide of socialism and moderate reform. At the other end of the political spectrum loomed the Bolshevik menace, frightening not only because of what it was doing in Russia, but because of what it might do in the political vacuum of central Europe and even in the stable politics of the victor powers. In the interplay of domestic and international politics which resulted from these complex developments moderates like Wilson increasingly found themselves in a world polarized between Left and Right with little choice but to join with one or the other in a kind of "cold war" mentality at home and abroad. What does Mayer's account add to Langer's to explain the decision-making process of the world leaders in 1919? How had both problems and problem-solving changed since the Congress of Vienna in 1815? How did "the start of the Bolshevik Revolution in Russia, the collapse of political authority in Central Europe, the threat of revolution throughout defeated Europe, and the right-wing upsurge inside the victor nations" affect the decisions of the peacemakers? Taking Langer and Mayer together, why could the peacemakers not make a settlement according to the principles Henry Kissinger set forth in his account of the Congress of Vienna?

WILLIAM L. LANGER

The problem of perspective is one of the historian's chronic concerns. He knows that events look different when viewed in a millennial setting from what they seem at close hand. Take the French Revolution as a striking and instructive example. Contemporaries had strong opinions as well as violent feelings about it. But no one would contend that these contemporaries could have seen the larger import of that great cataclysm. If it were so, historians would be wasting their time and effort. In actual fact they are still groping, after the lapse of almost two centuries, for a fuller and deeper understanding of this truly drastic turn in human affairs. Indeed, the wealth of data and the refinement of argument deriving from their efforts make one wonder at times whether perhaps greater emphasis should not be given to earlier and simpler interpretations.

Half a century has now elapsed since the conclusion of the First World War and the ensuing peace settlements. This is perhaps an ideal time for reviewing this great conflict, for fifty years gives us enough perspective to see things in the light of later developments, and yet we are not so far removed that we cannot recapture the hopes, the disillusions, and the enmities of that time. There are still many men alive, including the present writer, who fought in the First World War and have, over the years, observed its effects. Assuming, then, that the time is ripe for review and revaluation, let us attempt to determine what the impact of those years has been on European and world history.

431

Langer

THE
WELL-SPRING
OF OUR
DISCONTENTS

Some historians see the First World War as a watershed and consider the period 1914–19 as marking a halt in the headlong advances, political and social, of the nineteenth century. They stress the destruction of material and spiritual values, the release of forces of evil, and the revamping of Europe in such a way as to court future trials and disasters.

There is certainly much to be said in support of this interpretation. On the other hand it must be said that, viewed in perspective, the major tribulations of the world today do not by any means all flow from the First World War. The march of modern science, on which so much of our civilization depends, has continued at the accelerating tempo set long before 1914, only to culminate in the nuclear threat to society and all mankind. Similarly, the phenomenal and frightening growth of the world population, one of the most ominous features of our times, had its origins in the eighteenth century and has proceeded quite independently of the World War tragedy and the very considerable human losses which that conflict entailed. Again, the urbanization of western society and the mounting racial tensions throughout the world were affected in only a minor way, if at all, by the events of 1914–19. And finally, the nationalistic fervour rampant in the world today drew its inspiration from developments long anteceding the great war. No doubt that conflagration stimulated national feeling and provoked national antagonisms, but the examples of India and Egypt, to mention only two cases, will suffice to demonstrate the rapid spread of nationalist principles well before the outbreak of hostilities in Europe.

It is clear, then, that some of the major concerns of modern society have deep roots in the historical evolution of recent centuries. To a large extent they are the inescapable concomitants of that fundamental transformation familiarly known as the Industrial Revolution which, while it brought humanity an untold enrichment in goods and an unprecedented rise in the standard of living, entailed dislocations and tensions of such magnitude as almost to defy non-violent solutions.

Leaving these larger considerations aside, we must apply ourselves to the analysis of the impact of the war and the repercussions of the peace settlements. In so doing, we are struck at once by the stimulus provided by the war to various forces already operative. Looking back, we can distinguish the rising tide of totalitarianism, that is, the ominous antecedents of both Fascism and Bolshevism, as well as the recrudescence of revolutionary socialism which eventuated in Bolshevism. We can recognize the impact of Nietzschean teaching and the influence of Sorel, and we can see also the significance of such movements as the Action Française and Futurism. On the other side we can note in the labour movements the revulsion against the revisionism of Bernstein, the persuasive argumentation of Luxemburg and Hilferding, and the emergence of Lenin as a dominant leader.

Taken all in all, though, it is most unlikely that any of these extremist movements would have scored an early success had there been no major upheaval. The proto-fascist movements were spectacular, but not very influential. They were certainly far from shaking the general confidence of people in democracy and the forms of constitutional government. By many they were regarded as the demonstrations of cranks. On the other side, socialism and the labour movements were becoming steadily more domesticated. Despite all the party programmes and congresses, despite all the revolutionary oratory, the labouring classes were more and more taking on the trade union mentality so hateful to Marx and Lenin, and were taking advantage of universal suffrage and parliamentary institutions to move from one success to another. By 1914 socialism had lost much of its bite and was rapidly becoming a liberal progressive movement directed by sober, intelligent leaders. At the same time the middle classes were becoming converted to the principles of the welfare state, to social security, and to the sharing of the product of labour. The extremists and their programme were voted down in the party congresses and when, in 1914, the internationalism of the socialist parties was put to the test, the representatives of those parties voted almost to a man exactly like their bourgeois associates. It is surely no exaggeration to say that without the shattering impact of the great war the revolutionary elements would not for a long time, if ever, have been able to subvert any major government, not even the Russian.

The liquidation of the war and the forging of the peace settlements, too, must be viewed in the light of the animosities, the rancour, and the vindictiveness engendered by four years of desperate fighting. All wars tend to arouse the worst of human passions, and it was inevitable that so prolonged a holocaust as the First World War should inflame hatreds of all kinds. Modern war, it has often been pointed out, involves the mobilization of all the varied forces of a nation and requires the utmost exertion of the entire people. In order to bring this about governments feel impelled to stimulate effort by fostering antipathies and revengefulness. They did this in the First World War not only by perfecting the techniques of traditional psychological warfare, but also by the falsification of documents and by atrocity propaganda cut from whole cloth.

The French, who suffered particularly high losses in men and goods and who had behind them a long history of Franco-German hostility, were most uncompromising in the hour of victory. Clemenceau, who did not spare his own countrymen in the drive to win the war, was most obdurate in his insistence on revenge. A politician who even in 1870 was one of the mayors of Paris, who saw his country prostrate while the enemy marched victoriously down the Champs Elysées, and who witnessed the horrors of the Paris Commune, Clemenceau had ever since dreamed of the day of retribution. For him nothing should be allowed to stand in the way of a drastic reduction in German power for as long a period as possible, and of guarantees of French security. He and Foch could not hope to satisfy all their desires, but they did attain many of their ends and persisted in their demand that Germany pay the costs of the war. The continuance of the 'hunger blockade' of Germany, in violation of the armistice, was regarded by Clemenceau as a convenient weapon to enforce acceptance of harsh peace terms. Similarly the creation of new states in eastern Europe was thought of as providing a system of French satellites to replace Tsarist Russia as a bulwark against German expansion. The logic of the French position is not hard to grasp, but it does not alter the fact that Clemenceau obstructed all efforts to transcend the wartime mentality so as to shape the settlements with an eye to the future rather than to the satisfaction of time-worn enmities.

433

Langer

THE
WELL-SPRING
OF OUR
DISCONTENTS

Lloyd George and Orlando were cooler and less emotional in their approach to the problems of peace, though they were more exposed to political pressure at home than was Clemenceau. The British prime minister is often given credit for having realized, at least towards the end, that the reconstruction of Europe was going awry and that French aims and claims threatened to provoke further tensions and crises. But Lloyd George was the man of the 'knock-out' blow, the man who had skilfully avoided all efforts at mediation, the man who even in December 1916, when he replaced Asquith, had called for a peace on the basis of 'complete restitution, full reparation and effectual guarantees.' He did nothing to disabuse his countrymen of the idea that the Germans could and would pay for everything, and in the sequel of the all-too-successful elections of December 1918, he never showed any willingness to defy the forces demanding a draconian peace. Furthermore, if the prime minister belatedly softened in his attitude towards the German treaty, it was only after the decision had been reached by the conference to destroy German naval power, and to cripple German economic life by the surrender of the merchant fleet, of railroad rolling stock, and of valuable natural resources. In addition, the liquidation of the German colonial empire and the division of the spoils (greatly in Britain's favour) under the guise of the mandate system had already been decreed. In short, Lloyd George's conversion came only after essential British interests had been secured, when the threat of French domination of the Continent became truly ominous. Even then he was hardly ever willing to go to bat for the policy of moderation which he now advocated.

As for Woodrow Wilson, his figure still remains enigmatic, despite much excellent work that has been done of late in the study of his career and policy. In retrospect one cannot help being impressed with the depth of his understanding. Though he had a low opinion of European alliances and balance of power and secret diplomacy, though he thought as late as 1918 that the Europeans should be left to settle their specific territorial and other problems by themselves, he had a keen perception of the larger problems of peace-making. Before the intervention of the United States in the conflict, he had exposed himself to obloquy by calling for peace without victory, by which he meant a compromise peace negotiated between equals. In his address to the senate on 22 January 1917 he argued that 'the right state of mind, the right feeling between nations, is as necessary for a lasting peace as is the just settlement of vexed questions of territory or of racial and national allegiance. . . . Victory would mean peace forced upon the loser, a victor's terms imposed upon the vanquished. It would be accepted in humiliation, under duress, at an intolerable sacrifice, and would have a sting, a resentment, a bitter memory upon which terms of peace would rest, not permanently, but only as upon quicksand.' And later, in a speech of 27 September 1918, he called for impartial justice which 'must involve no discrimination between those to whom we wish to be just and those to whom we do not wish to be just.' Finally, on the very eve of the armistice, Sir William Wiseman reported the president as saying in conversation (16 October 1918): 'If we humiliate the German people and drive them too far, we shall destroy all form of government, and Bolshevism will take its place. We ought not to grind them to powder or there will be nothing to build up from.' He disliked, he said, the idea of settling peace terms without the enemies being present to state their case, and thought that Germany should be a member of the League of Nations, which 'should be the very centre of the Peace Settlement, the pillar upon which the house will stand.'

Wilson, then, saw all the dangers of a complete victory, and of a draconian peace dictated to the defeated. For that very reason he felt that an international organization to revise and rectify provisions of the treaties, as well as to forestall future conflict, was of transcendent importance. One can hardly question the sincerity of his purpose or the nobility of his vision. The question is rather whether at Paris he made full use of his great power and immense prestige to implement his programme. Why, after being hailed in December 1918 by the peoples of Europe as the harbinger of a new order, did he yield step by step to the pressures of his fellow-statesmen? In the matter of the League Covenant he did persist. While Lloyd George and Clemenceau argued that the settlement of concrete issues was the necessary foundation for international organization, Wilson insisted that it be taken up first and that the covenant of the League be made an integral part of the peace treaty. It is more than likely that if he had yielded on this crucial issue the sceptics and opponents of the League idea would eventually, after securing what they wanted, have scuttled the entire project. But preoccupation with the League covenant of necessity distracted the attention of the president from other more mundane matters and made it difficult for him not to reciprocate in making concessions.

If, with respect to concrete issues, Wilson lent himself to mistaken decisions, it must be remembered that until a late date he thought of leaving these matters to the Europeans and still reckoned on the Germans being brought into the discussions when a draft of the treaty was completed. It is worth noting, too, that he was by upbringing decidedly Anglophil, that he shared the common American devotion to France, and that, without looking much into the matter, he accepted the prevalent conviction that the German government, if not the German people, was responsible for the catastrophe. He himself had a very limited acquaintance with continental countries and but little knowledge of their problems. An American committee of experts (the Inquiry) had been studying important issues for some time, and in the course of the peace conference American commissioners were sent to many central European countries to report on conditions as they developed. But the president was not the man to turn readily to others for an opinion, and when he did so it might often be when the fat was already in the fire. Besides, it must be confessed that the American experts and commissioners were not all immune to the wartime fever. Some of their opinions and recommendations would not in retrospect meet with much approval.

More important, however, than these considerations was the political pressure under which Wilson worked at Paris. The national elections of November 1918 had returned Republican majorities in both houses of the legislature, and Republican leaders, rightly or wrongly, interpreted this result as popular endorsement of a harsh peace. Former president Theodore Roosevelt and Senator Henry Cabot Lodge called for unconditional surrender and the stiffest possible terms. 'No peace that satisfies Germany in any degree can ever satisfy us,' declared Lodge in August 1918; 'it cannot be a negotiated peace. It must be a dictated peace.' This was only the opening shot in a steadily spreading campaign. It may well be that Wilson underestimated the strength of the opposition, but he must have noticed that his fellow-statesmen in Paris questioned whether in fact he could speak for his country. We may assume that this made it seem to

435
Langer
THE
WELL-SPRING
OF OUR
DISCONTENTS

him all the more imperative to clinch the League issue, for which there was far more support in the United States than for a moderate negotiated peace. Actually the very fact that the president had insisted on the inclusion of the covenant in the Treaty of Versailles gave his opponents a welcome opening for attack. The battle of the amendments began. Some of them made good sense from the standpoint of American interests, and others, while not of crucial import, were at least reasonable and would indubitably have been accepted by the European governments in order to secure the adherence of the United States to the new organization. The dispute, it might be said, hinged less on the animosity of men such as Lodge to the president or to the League project, than on Wilson's obduracy. Before as well as after his collapse the president refused to yield even a tittle of his sacred text, probably as a matter of prestige, but also because of his unshakable belief that the sentiment of the country would support him. Having retreated from the pinnacle of his idealism, Wilson was determined to stand his ground, come what come may, and so the treaty, with the League covenant, was lost in the Senate. The tragedy of this outcome it would be hard to overstate, for the United States, after overcoming its isolationism in 1917 in order to rescue western Europe, now rejected its newly acquired leadership, eschewed all participation in world organization, and declined all responsibility for collective action on behalf of peace. Who would now deny that the United States, by the Senate's final rejection of the Versailles Treaty and its desertion of the League, underlined all the shortcomings of the peace settlements, and assumed a heavy responsibility for the weakness and ineffectuality of the world organization, that is for the return of international anarchy in more aggravated form than ever.

The Treaty of Versailles violated the spirit and in some respects the letter of Wilson's Fourteen Points, on which the surrender of Germany and the armistice were based. This was presumably of little concern to Clemenceau and Lloyd George, who had never endorsed the Wilsonian programme and who resented the president's high-handed assumption of the role of sole negotiator for the Allied powers. This violation of solemn agreements, however, undermined Wilson's position and cost him the support of many who had looked upon him as the harbinger of a new age and a more just order. Increasingly, as the weeks went by, the president was impelled to yield on vital items of the settlement, until in the end the sum total of the treaty was a punitive document indeed, and one which was imposed on the Germans on a take-it-or-leave-it basis.

This is hardly the place to attempt a summary of the hundreds of articles by which the defeated enemy, charged with sole responsibility for the outbreak of the war (article 231), was shorn of substantial territories, obliged to assume heavy servitudes, disarmed except for a paltry 100,000 man army for domestic security, and burdened with a preposterous but purposely undefined bill for reparations, the effect of which was intended to be the long-term debility of the country. It will long remain a mystery how, in the circumstances, the new German republic was able to survive and successfully repel the rising forces of desperation and revolt. Looking back, one can hardly escape the conclusion that the entire reparations programme was an international calamity of the first order. Not only Keynes but also other experts foresaw the disastrous consequences for the victors as well as the vanquished. Despite successive adjustments, such as the Dawes and Young Plans, the issue had not been fully disposed of when the great depression broke over the western world. No doubt the economic tribulations and financial confusion engendered by the reparations problem played a significant role in undermining the post-war order.

To the material items of the settlement must be added the moral obloquy and shock to German self-respect involved in the so-called war-guilt clause, and the sense of betrayal and outrage provoked by the violations of the Fourteen Points and the prolongation of the hunger blockade. Psychologically the scene was set for the stab-in-the-back agitation, the great war-guilt debate, and the emergence of Nazism. In addition the excesses of the peace treaty contributed mightily to the growing tensions of the ensuing twenty years. They help to explain the rising uncertainty as to the justice of the treatment meted out to the defeated in 1919 and the steadily mounting feeling that concessions should be made to rectify acknowledged injustices. This sense of guilt on the part of the erstwhile victors was of course an integral part of the policy of appeasement, and this policy in its turn served only to strengthen Hitler's hand and encourage him to press further and further along the road that led to the Second World War.

The peace settlements (the secondary treaties as well as the Versailles Treaty) were designed, in the constructive sense, to ensure the triumph of nationalism and democracy. All peoples were to be accorded the right of self-determination and were to be supported in establishing popular, representative government. The defeated Germans, to be sure, especially those of the former Habsburg Monarchy, were considered an exception. Clemenceau was adamant in his refusal to see Germany enlarged by the addition of the German provinces of Austria. Elsewhere, however, the principle of nationalism was given full expression and high hopes were placed on a world made safe for democracy. In retrospect it is plain that much of this programme and policy was pursued uncritically. Experience has taught how far most of the Continent was from being prepared for democratic government. Furthermore, it might be argued that the new nations, although they have proved durable, by disrupting the eastern empires sapped the stability of the entire area and destroyed a well-established balance of power. None of the succession states, not even Poland, was strong enough politically or economically or militarily to withstand the pressures of Nazi Germany or Soviet Russia. No doubt many people in these states have asked themselves the question whether the game was worth the candle—whether a factitious independence ending in foreign domination and reduction to satellite status was preferable to the pre-1914 regime.

437

Langer

THE
WELL-SPRING
OF OUR
DISCONTENTS

In this context it must be remembered that this disruption of central and eastern Europe was not foreordained. Nationalism had been a potent and effective instrument for unifying the numerous small states of the area in the nineteenth century, and there had been a recrudescence of nationalist ardour in the immediate pre-war period, due in part to conflicting imperialist claims but even more to the opposition of conservative forces to the growing internationalism of both capital and labour. The effect of the war was to arrest the trend towards international cooperation and European unity and at the same time to raise the issue of weakening the enemy by fostering centrifugal forces within its boundaries. Both sides resorted to these tactics, but the Allied powers had by far the most to offer, and it was their policy that eventually produced the break-up of the Habsburg Monarchy and the emergence of the new states. It is often said that they had relatively little to do with this business; that the new states had already proclaimed their independence and set up their governments before the Paris peace conference even met. But this is surely only a half-truth. The national movements in central and eastern Europe had before the war been modest and limited in their aspirations. Their aim was to secure greater autonomy and increased cultural freedom. Only a few extremists talked of independence, which most of the leaders recognized as impracticable, if only for economic reasons. And so the situation remained during most of the war, the French government in particular favouring the preservation of the Habsburg Monarchy as an important factor in the balance of power. Only after efforts to secure the defection of the Vienna government had failed and after Wilson had proclaimed the Fourteen Points did the Allied governments abandon the policy of sustaining the Austrian Empire in favour of the various national committees, which were then encouraged to set their sights on full independence.

The defection of Russia and France's need for new friends and supporters in the east may well have influenced Clemenceau to change his mind in favour of Poland, Czechoslovakia, and the other succession states, but Wilson's policy was probably the decisive force. The president was positively obsessed with the principle of self-determination, without having much notion of the difficulties in the way of its realization. It was in this respect that his ignorance of European conditions bore its bitterest fruit. Had he learned sooner that there were three million Germans in Bohemia, he might have been less hasty in accepting and backing the new Czechoslovak state. By 1919 it was too late. When he finally stood out against the Italian claims in the Adriatic, he cut a sorry figure. In any event, as we look back from the vantagepoint of fifty years and review the countless trials and tribulations which these new states have had to endure, to say nothing of the international tensions occasioned by their very existence, we are certainly justified in asking whether the peace conference's role in the fragmentation of much of Europe was a blessing or a misfortune.

Many issues raised by the war and the peace must be passed over in a summary essay of this kind, but the Russian problem was of such overriding importance as to deserve special consideration and emphasis. The charge often levelled against the peace-makers, that they failed to understand the Russian problem and to come to grips with it, is hardly tenable. Numerous recent studies, based on the official records, have highlighted the fact that, on the contrary, the statesmen at Paris were all too conscious of the problem and wrestled with it as best they could. It is hardly an exaggeration to say that the spectre of Bolshevism and social revolution hovered in the background of the peace conference from beginning to end and that, furthermore, many different moves were made in the effort to exorcize it.

It stands to reason that the Bolshevik seizure of power in November 1917 came as a surprise, for, despite the chaotic situation in Russia in the summer of 1917, it seemed unlikely that a small minority group should be able to outmanoeuvre much stronger parties such as the Social Revolutionaries, should establish control of a major European state, proclaim a communist regime which theretofore had been of only theoretical interest, and presently desert Russia's western allies in the hour of their greatest need. Naturally the Bolshevik Revolution profoundly changed the complexion of the war and at the same time loosed forces which had hitherto been dormant. Labour everywhere could hardly avoid the fascination of an experiment which promised so much of what the working classes had been striving for. During the year 1918 the lower classes in all countries were becoming war-weary and restless. It was a question how long they could be counted on to support the struggle. At the same time the propertied classes were profoundly disturbed and soon apprehensive of possible social upheaval. In the larger sense the Bolshevik victory, while it tended to divide and so to weaken the forces of labour, provoked a recrudescence of conservative forces. While on the left the Bolshevik programme of no annexations and no indemnities made a genuine appeal and strengthened the demand for a new order along Wilsonian lines, on the right there was an ever more insistent demand for drastic action and harsh terms, to say nothing of military intervention to crush Bolshevism in its infancy.

As for the statesmen, it would appear that initially they believed that so extreme and radical a movement as Bolshevism could not long maintain itself; that in fact a strict quarantine would suffice to strangle it. But when, in the winter of 1918–19, the whole of central and eastern Europe sank into chaos, and the Bolsheviks, though hard pressed at home, launched an aggressive propaganda appeal to all peoples to rise against the upper classes, the threat of subversion became formidable and immediate. It is well known that Lenin's great hope and expectation was that defeated and hungry Germany would revolt and carry much of the Continent with it. The German provisional government itself raised the spectre of a German-Russian alliance in the hope of securing more favourable treatment, but in reality proved itself uncompromisingly hostile to Spartacism and other radical movements. The Germans could certainly have done their former enemies no greater favour than to stamp out the forces of social subversion and stand guard against the Bolshevik advance in the Baltic area. Nonetheless, the situation in the spring of 1919 was touch

439

Langer

THE
WELL-SPRING
OF OUR
DISCONTENTS

and go, as demonstrated by the establishment of communist regimes in Bavaria and Hungary.

Conservatives, such as Winston Churchill, persistently urged the destruction of the Bolshevik regime by military force as the only safeguard against the triumph of communism in much of Europe. But none of the leading statesmen, least of all Wilson, would countenance such drastic action, chiefly from fear lest the working classes rise in revolt against their governments, but also because of the impossibility of finding enough troops for so formidable an operation. A limited intervention, chiefly of a defensive nature, had already taken place in 1918. But even this met with vigorous opposition from the war-weary peoples, who made it clear that they would not allow a new war, for whatever purposes, to be foisted upon them. Mutinous outbreaks among the British and French troops in Russia made it equally clear that large-scale military action was entirely out of the question.

Efforts were made by the peace conference to find a solution in conjunction with exiled Russian statesmen such as Sazonov, but these proved fruitless. Like most emigré groups, the Russian was rent by dissension and none of its leaders was willing or able to commit himself to such a democratic programme as the Allies required. Similarly, moves made to deal directly with the Bolsheviks ran into countless difficulties, and the Allies saw no alternative to the programme of financial and military support of the various counter-revolutionary generals. Of these, it is clear, none had much popular support or much chance of success. The Paris peace-makers desired nothing more ardently than the destruction of the Bolshevik regime. Their action against the communist rule of Bela Kun in Hungary shows that they would shrink from no course that was feasible and promising. However, in the case of Russia there was no such possibility. Nothing they could do was really effective. In the end all they achieved was the distrust and enmity of the Bolsheviks, which was to colour all international relations for decades to come and which, more than anything else, provided the foundation for the division of Europe and later the world into opposing ideological camps.

Many of the peace terms so passionately formulated at Paris were soon obliterated and others were presently serving purposes diametrically opposed to those intended by the framers. The reparations programme proved a dismal failure, the Rhineland occupation was abandoned before its term, the disarmament of Germany, which was to be the prelude to general disarmament, was never susceptible of enforcement and soon lost its *raison d'être*. Furthermore, Germany, deprived of so many capital goods, was able to start afresh and, with the support of former enemies, to build an ultra-modern industrial plant. Shorn of its colonies, Germany was spared the agony and expense attending the gradual liquidation of European imperialism. The triumph of nationalism in the Danube Basin served among other things to facilitate the resumption of the traditional *Drang nach Osten*. The German professional army provided the officer corps for the vast expansion and high standards of the great military machine that was to stage the Blitzkriegs of 1939–41. All told, it would seem in retrospect that much of the effort of 1919 to break the power of Germany for at least a generation actually accrued to the benefit of that country in an even shorter time. Apparently a Carthaginian peace, if it falls short of the actual destruction of the enemy, is about the least profit-able settlement imaginable.

Over the long term the greatest contribution of the war and the peace seems to have been the launching of the League of Nations. This can be said even with full realization of the weaknesses of that institution, for we can easily see that the League marked an important departure in the conduct of international relations. Had the three great powers—isolationist United States, defeated Germany, and outlawed Russia—been present at its councils from the very beginning, it might well have progressed instead of gradually failing and ultimately disintegrating. It is one more irony of history that, in the 1930s, when the decay of the international order was already well advanced, Russia was admitted and the United States, though still only an 'observer,' began to show a greater readiness to cooperate—too late, too late. However, the eclipse of the League was to be shortlived, for the second great world conflict underlined even more heavily the overriding need for international organization and action. This is the most eloquent testimony to the achievement, however partial, of the original effort. The United Nations, too, has its weaknesses and its frustrations, yet it marks a further advance towards effective international authority, without which modern society cannot hope long to survive.

Beyond these particulars there are still imponderable and immeasurable effects of the war and the peace which cannot be left out of account. Even the appalling human losses and the vast destruction of hard-won goods were probably of less account than the impact of fratricidal war on the European community and the ensuing division of western society by ideological antagonisms as well as by the distrust and animosity that flourish in times of conflict. How shall we evaluate the revival of ruthlessness and violence, the disillusionment about progress, the profound spiritual deflation which were the legacy of the war and the peace? Nor were these effects confined to Europe itself. They reached out to all corners of the earth, destroyed the image of Europe as the vanguard of modern civilization, and prepared the backlash against imperialism with which we are all familiar. The massacres on the battlefields of Europe were witnessed by hundreds of thousands of non-European troops and labourers, who no doubt contributed to the loss of respect for the white peoples which soon seized on the peoples of Asia and Africa. From the extreme nationalism fostered by the warring powers, non-Europeans were to draw the inspiration for their new, often immature and sometimes preposterous nationalisms. To be sure, the time had not yet come to challenge European rule with any real chance of success, but the seed had been planted and by 1939 had already germinated. It took only another severe shock to the European order to destroy the primacy of that continent and encompass the

441

Langer

THE
WELL-SPRING
OF OUR
DISCONTENTS

liquidation of imperialism, the hallmark of European ascendancy. Whatever the reservations one might wish to make, the conclusion is incontestable that the First World War, and more particularly the crucial years 1917–19 marked a major turning point in European and world affairs and, furthermore, that they helped substantially to undermine the foundations on which our civilization now so precariously stands.

ARNO J. MAYER

For quite some time reasoning by historical analogy has been the stock in trade of modern statesmen and their advisers, particularly when confronted with big questions. In 1918–19 the history of the Congress of Vienna was considered to be the most pertinent guide to the making of peace; and the history of the French Revolution, including Europe's reaction to it, the most pertinent guide to dealing with the Russian Revolution. Of course, each statesman's interpretation of these paradigms was marked by his own ideological preferences, national interest calculations, political exigencies, and personal tastes. But all alike searched the history of the Vienna Congress and the French Revolution for policies to be emulated, shunned, or applied in modified form. All participants both used and abused historical analogies precisely because then as now such analogies were vital aids in the analysis and discussion of the quagmire of contemporary history.

The peacemakers of 1814–15 and 1918–19 convened to settle the accounts of a multilateral, unlimited, and ideological conflict; to legalize a new territorial status quo; to agree on safeguards and sanctions against future transgressions by the major defeated enemy; and to explore ways of putting the peace and concert of Europe on more enduring foundations. In both Vienna and Paris each statesman pursued these overarching objectives while simultaneously striving to maximize the national interest of his own country.

These two sets of constantly jarring objectives were pursued within a framework of power politics. Conflicting national interests were accommodated through mutual compensations and concessions. In 1814–15 as in 1918–19 the major powers assumed responsibility for bringing and maintaining in balance the international system of sovereign states. They arrogated to themselves the right to settle all basic territorial, military, economic, and political issues before securing approval for their decisions from the plenary congress or conference. The secondary and minor powers were cast in the role of suitors, suppliants, or satellites. They promoted

Source: Arno J. Mayer, *Politics and Diplomacy of Peace-Making: Containment and Counterrevolution at Versailles, 1918–1919* (New York: Alfred A. Knopf, 1967), pp. 3–30. Copyright © 1967 by Arno J. Mayer. Reprinted by permission of Alfred A. Knopf, Inc. [Footnotes omitted.]

their interests primarily by deftly capitalizing on the jockeyings, rivalries, and needs of the big powers.

Not surprisingly, on the eve of the Paris Peace Conference Charles K. Webster urged the British Foreign Office to look for precedents to the negotiations that had concluded the Napoleonic Wars. At Vienna the assembled statesmen had upheld the cardinal distinction between major and minor powers; had adjusted borders according to the dictates of the balance of power; and had agreed on diplomatic procedures to be followed in the future. Shortly after the Conference Webster also claimed that "however puny" the problems of 1814–15 appeared next to those of 1918–19, the Vienna settlement was the only one which in "scope and importance" could be compared to the Versailles settlement: "the boundaries of almost every state in Europe were remodelled; a barrier was erected against and reparations were inflicted upon the dominant military power; colonial territories were redistributed; new international organizations were erected; and even schemes for the perpetuation of world peace were considered."

As a conventional diplomatic historian with a passion for the functional, procedural, and technical aspects of peacemaking, Webster tendered advice to a foreign office dominated by practitioners of the Old Diplomacy, most of whom were of gentlemanly background. These and other factors predisposed him to stress the important but in the last analysis surface similarities between Vienna and Paris.

At the turn of the century Woodrow Wilson had joined the New Historians in their rebellion against this one-dimensional political and legal history. He was interested "not so much in what happened as in what underlay the happening; not so much in the tides as in the silent forces that lifted them." For him law and government were "regulative rather than generative," and he refused to be satisfied with legal and political history that got at "the surface only, not at the heart of affairs."

In any case, given his progressive *Weltanschauung,* which was solidly rooted in this New History, Wilson was bound to probe into the direction in which a re-enactment of history was likely to take the world. Early in the deliberations he explicitly rejected the Congress of Vienna as a valid precedent. His reasons were that this Congress had presided over a vast restoration, both national and international, and had charted the Holy Alliance which sought to "extend the system of monarchical and arbitrary government in the world." Wilson impassionately begged that "such would not be the purpose of the present conference."

Ideologically and temperamentally the President would readily have reconciled himself to an enlightened restoration calculated to head off a White reaction. But a restoration had been difficult to launch and sustain after 1814–15, at the end of a revolutionary cycle. How much more difficult to launch and sustain one in 1918–19, at the beginning of such a cycle! In 1814–15 the peacemakers were secure in having the support of powerful and influential political, social, economic, and administrative strata which craved domestic order and international stability; they could build on governmental organisms which had survived almost intact; and they needed concern themselves almost exclusively with territorial divisions.

The peacemakers at Paris were not nearly so well served. To begin with, in 1918–19 the leaders and forces favoring moderate reconstruction at home and abroad were fatally buffeted by *enragés* of the Left as well as of the Right. This erosion of conservative liberalism had been well advanced by 1914; the war and revolution merely exacerbated it. Moreover, in Germany, throughout the Danubian basin, in the Balkans, and in Turkey governmental structures were shaky, in ruins, or embryonic. Also, though by no means least important, in both defeated and victor Europe questions of economic and social reconstruction and reform were generating intense political heat. Needless to say, these divisive and explosive domestic conditions were bound to affect the work of the Peace Conference, thereby complicating the assignment of the assembled statesmen far beyond what had faced their predecessors after Napoleon's fall.

According to Ferrero, the Big Four were confronted with a Himalayan task.

Everything was destroyed, commercial treaties and treaties of alliance, conventions between State and State relating to the most jealously guarded interests, the public and private law of every single State. The elite of the greater European nations, and more especially its youth who would have been called to govern in ten or fifteen years' time, were mown down. The Prussian, no less than the English and French, aristocracy were decimated. The same was true of the middle classes both in France and Germany. The better part of the Russian nation was dispersed or dead. Everywhere the balance of wealth was upset; vast fortunes were made without labour by ignorant, incapable, or cowardly persons, while the flower of the population was ruined or perished in the trenches. The national fortune even of the richest peoples, was heavily mortgaged in order to meet gigantic war obligations. It is by no means rash to estimate these burdens as amounting to more than half their total possessions. Finally, during the war there was revealed to all eyes the double soul—which wishes for power and at the same time for justice—of the State created by the French Revolution and by the nineteenth century. In this war all the most generous sentiments which make life dear to men were exalted; but at the same time the most terrible offensive weapons which the world has ever seen were brought into action. The States of Western Civilization finally dared to do what to previous ages would have seemed madness if not a crime, and that was, to arm the masses.

Ferrero went on to warn that the apprenticeship of the successor states, which would be arduous and tedious even under the most favorable of circumstances, would be doubtly difficult in the "midst of a Europe devastated, bled white, convulsed, and impoverished by the war." *The New Eu-*

rope refused to share this pessimism, even though it conceded that Central Europe was "as nearly a *tabula rasa* as a civilized continent could be."

This awareness of the unparalleled scope and complexity of peacemaking in the wake of the world war and the world revolution was widespread. According to Villard of *The Nation,* the statesmen were charged not with simply closing a war but with fully recasting the inherited world order. Notwithstanding Wilson's ecumenical promise, at this juncture the world was "less safe for democracy than at any previous period in modern times . . . and the whole modern order of society was on trial for its life." For the Paris correspondent of the *Philadelphia Ledger* the Conference had to balance and square "the accounts of a whole epoch, the deeds and misdeeds of an exhausted civilization."

As early as May 1918 H. G. Wells, who in September 1914 had held out the promise of *The War That Will End War,* could "conceive no such Peace Congress as those that had settled up after other wars settling up after this War." There were no precedents to go by because this war had been "enormously bigger than any other war . . . and had struck deeper at the foundations of social and economic life." With commendable candor Wells confessed that he doubted that the Western intelligentsia and political class even began "to realize how much of the old system was dead today, how much had to be remade." This doubt was confirmed once the Paris Conference began to flounder. Wells promptly joined thirty prominent Western intellectuals who compared themselves to those "gloomy prophets and the first apostles" who in experiencing the "agony of Babylonia and Imperial Rome" had cried out that the decomposition of these great powers "was due less to the [shock] of [external] invasion than to the weight of their own [internal] crimes." These modern brainworkers saw themselves as more "despairing and paralyzed" than the witnesses of past political cataclysms because the decadence confronting them was "more universal, more profound, and more incurable" than that of ancient Greece and Rome.

These and similar expressions of the post-Armistice *Weltschmerz, crise de conscience,* or failure of nerve serve to call attention to the deep and multivarious crisis that, starting in 1917, the Great War precipitated throughout the world: the Bolshevik Revolution in Russia, the nationalist rebellions throughout the Dual Monarchy, the November Revolution in Germany, the post-Armistice neurasthenia in the Allied nations, the Kemalist revolution in Turkey, the rice riots in Japan, the May Fourth Movement in China, and Gandhi's first Swaraj campaign in India. In each of these countries an old order was being jostled by a new one; in some, revolution and counterrevolution were squaring off. It was with this crisis-torn world, particularly with a crisis-torn Europe, swirling about them, that the Big Four were expected to negotiate a lasting diplomatic settlement.

As of the mid-nineteenth century the inseparability of strain or defeat in war and reform or revolution became increasingly apparent. Russia's defeat in the Crimean War was followed by the reforms of the sixties; Austria's defeat at Sadowa led to the compromise of 1867; France's defeat in 1870–1 brought first the fall of the Second Empire, then the Commune, and eventually the birth of the fragile Third Republic; China's defeat in the Sino-Japanese War stimulated an outburst of anti-imperialist nationalism and prepared the ground for the "Hundred Days" of 1898; Russia's defeat in the war with Japan contributed to the revolution of 1905, followed by the Octobrist reforms; and, finally, Russia's exhaustion in the Great War precipitated first the March uprising and then the November Revolution of 1917.

The Russian Revolution came as a timely reminder of the costs of military exhaustion and defeat under conditions of mounting political tensions. Otherwise both the Allies and the Central Powers might well have held out for unconditional surrender. Had it not been for the demonstration effect of the Bolshevik Revolution neither side would have considered the Wilsonian points as an acceptable basis for armistice negotiations. In the event the Armistice was concluded just in time to limit the political consequences of military defeat in Central and East Central Europe to less than revolutionary proportions. But even with this eleventh-hour finish the legacy of disruption and convulsion was far from negligible.

Granted, neither Germany nor Austria went Spartacist; and Hungary remained Bolshevik for only 133 days. Even so, particularly since Allied policies contributed to this outcome, it would be wrong to dismiss the danger of revolution as having been at best a sham or at worst a conspiracy. Admittedly, the social and political carriers as well as the precipitants of unrest varied in composition and intensity from country to country, and from month to month. But, the fact remains that there were grave disorders, rebellions, and strikes throughout defeated Europe, notably because politicians and labor leaders had ready-made organizational weapons with which to capitalize on political instability, unemployment, food shortages, and runaway prices.

In her diary Beatrice Webb raised a question that haunted Europe's political class, including the chief statesmen, throughout the Peace Conference: "Are we confronted with another Russia in Austria, possibly even in Germany—a Continent in rampant revolution . . . ?" For General Smuts Europe was reduced to her "original atoms," with no hint of the "new political forms" within which these might be joined. Curiously, it was the conservative liberal and legalistic David Hunter Miller who stressed, quite properly, that whereas the peacemakers of 1814–15 only had to reconcile disputes "between well-known and established powers," those of 1918–19 had to bring about "order out of chaos in practically all of Europe east of the Rhine, and north of the Danube, as well as restoration and a new life in various other parts of Europe and Asia." Likewise, Walter Lippmann noted the absence of "stable government anywhere east of the Rhine," warning that no one knew "what Germany would be, nor Russia, nor the twenty odd nationalities of Eastern Europe and New Asia." With good reason Woodrow Wilson acknowledged the wisdom and necessity of postponing the Conference "until there were governments in Germany and Austria-Hungary which could enter into binding agreements." While Smuts exuberantly proposed that the League be made the trustee of the politically untrained peoples "left behind by the decomposition of Russia, Austria, and Turkey," Wilson and his advisers did their best to press the Allies into helping the "receiver" and successor governments of the defeated empires to consolidate themselves.

Of course, even without the force of the Soviet Russian example and the activities of local Bolshevik parties this chaos would have developed and caused concern. But as it was, the Bolshevik regime, by its mere survival as well as through its flaming manifestoes, provided encouragement to all far-Left radicals and stirred especially Independent Socialists into greater militancy. In addition, Lenin offered food to the Ebert-Scheidemann government, sent the Radek mission to Berlin, charted the Third International in early March 1919, and built up the Red Army. Counterrevolutionaries in particular vastly exaggerated the scope and aggressive nature of these steps, thereby making the specter which was haunting Europe doubly terrifying.

Naturally not only the Big Four or Five but also the experts within each delegation differed among themselves in their estimates of the nature and seriousness of the revolutionary threat, and hence in their prescriptions for containing it. Moreover, as in 1792–4, the coherence and unity of the counterrevolutionary crusade were undermined by rival national interests, uneven material capabilities, and shifting domestic pressures. Even so, in spite of these grave dissonances, the Paris Peace Conference made a host of decisions, all of which, in varying degrees, were designed to check Bolshevism: the victors made territorial concessions to Poland, Rumania, and Czechoslovakia for helping to stem the revolutionary tide beyond their own borders; they gave military assistance and economic aid to these and other border lands as well as to the Whites for their armed assault on Soviet Russia and Hungary; they stepped up their direct military intervention in Russia; they rigorously enforced the blockade against Bolshevik Russia and Hungary; they rushed economic assistance to Austria and the successor states to help stabilize their governments; and they drafted the charters of the International Labor Organization (I.L.O.) and the League of Nations with a view to immunizing the non-Bolshevik Left against the ideological bacillus of the Bolshevik Revolution.

Some of these measures constituted a defensive containment policy, a *cordon sanitaire* calculated to prevent the Revolution from spreading beyond Bolshevik-controlled areas; other measures were aimed at the outright overthrow of Lenin and Béla Kun. But all alike were decided, orchestrated, sanctioned, or condoned by the peacemakers in Paris. Furthermore, all alike—intentionally or unintentionally—contributed to sparing defeated Europe further revolutionary infections. During the pivotal year of 1918–19, when defeated Europe was most vulnerable, the armed intervention, reinforced by the blockade, forced Lenin to exhaust his scarce military and economic resources in defensive operations. Outside Russia he was reduced to countering the massive material intervention by the Allies with ideological appeals.

At the time, the outcome of this first round in the international civil war of the twentieth century seemed to be very much in the balance. According to Ray Stannard Baker, "at all times, at every turn in the negotiations, there rose the specter of chaos, like a black cloud out of the east, threatening to overwhelm and swallow up the world. There was no Russia knocking at the gates of Vienna! At Vienna, apparently, the revolution was securely behind them; at Paris it was always with them." At one time or another every delegation played on this fear of the Bolshevik specter for its own purposes, thereby making the threat even more pervasive than it needed have been.

The uses and abuses of this spuriously inflated bogy of Bolshevism were as numerous then as they are today. With intermittent support from Lloyd George, President Wilson sought to convince Georges Clemenceau that Germany would succumb to Spartacism unless the Allies promptly lifted the blockade and proffered moderate peace terms. Back home, when Congress threatened to refuse his first major foreign aid bill, Wilson reluctantly but successfully frightened Capitol Hill with tales of the horrors of Bolshevism sweeping over the entire European continent.

Naturally, the vulnerable "receiver" governments of Germany, Austria, and Hungary were the most boisterous advocates of this Wilson line, insisting that should their countries be swallowed up by Bolshevism the advancing flood would not stop at the borders of the victor nations. Ironically, the German government itself diminished the blackmail value of Spartacism by repressing it sternly at home and by fighting Bolshevism eagerly in the *Baltikum*. On the other hand, Count Michael Károlyi invited the Bolsheviks into the Hungarian government in order to make his threats more credible. As for the Poles and the Rumanians, they received vast amounts of financial, economic, and military aid from the Allies for their assault on Soviet Russia and Soviet Hungary. Roman Dmowski and John Brătianu, supported by Ferdinand Foch and Winston Churchill, styled themselves as selfless champions of anti-Bolshevism, all the time extorting exorbitant territorial annexations for their counterrevolutionary services. Even Eleutherios Venizelos, whom Harold Nicolson mysteriously paired with Lenin as "the only two great men in Europe," was not above trading on the Bolshevik scare; neither were Thomas Masaryk and Eduard Beneš.

In brief, at one time or another most delegations at the Paris Peace Conference wielded the specter of Bolshevism as a weapon and a threat. In each instance the assault on or containment of Bolshevism was calculated to advance a government's foreign policy goals while at the same time fortifying its political position at home. *Contra communismo saepe; pro patria et politica semper.*

This twin assignment of stabilizing governments throughout defeated

Europe and of containing if not destroying the Russian Revolution called for day-to-day consultations, decisions, and directives. Here, then, was one of the chief sources of that "vast quantity of executive work which was thrust upon the Conference of Paris and which found no parallel at Vienna." Once the Paris Conference is placed in its historical context this executive work can no longer be deplored as a festering diversion from the real stuff of diplomacy, from negotiations of frontier adjustments, colonial redistributions, and reparations. In fact, this diversion, which vastly complicates diplomacy, may yet turn out to be the essence of peacemaking in an era of international civil war. It certainly deserves more than passing mention that the peacemakers of 1918–19 manipulated blockades, wielded military and economic aid, and ordered counterrevolutionary military interventions. Properly to carry out this assignment of preventing Europe "from going to smash under [their] feet," they established the Supreme Economic Council, the Directory for Relief, the Blockade Committee, and the Supreme Council.

The tight interlocking of international and domestic policies in both defeated and victor nations complicated the diplomacy of peacemaking still further.

Since in the defeated nations governments had to be formed before plenipotentiaries could be sent to the Paris Peace Conference, foreign policy platforms became decisive weapons in the struggle for political control. In November 1917 the Bolsheviks had seized power in Russia primarily though not exclusively on a promise of immediate peace; and they were determined to maintain themselves in power without external aid until fellow revolutionary regimes could come to their rescue.

After the Armistice, in Germany, Austria, Hungary, and the successor states, rival political parties, notably those which eventually formed or controlled the governments, claimed that they were best qualified to secure favorable terms from the Big Four. The essential corollary of this pledge was the insistence that successful performance in the peace negotiations was the passkey to domestic rehabilitation, reconstruction, and reform.

But whereas in Russia the Bolsheviks had seized power from below, in Germany, Austria, and Hungary inveterate power elites invited the leaders of the nonrevolutionary forces of movement to act as receivers for bankrupt regimes. They pressed Friedrich Ebert, Friedrich Adler, and Károlyi into accepting these receiverships, not only because at home each was an ideal foil against revolutionary and anarchist excesses, but above all also because each was alone likely to inspire confidence in the Allies, notably in Wilson.

The promise and, in the case of Austria, the fulfillment of Allied goodwill and aid played a crucial role once these provisional governments tried to transform their receiverships from above into popular mandates from below. The Social Democrats and their collaborators forewarned the electorates—and the Allies punctuated these warnings—that in case of chaos or revolution their countries could expect neither food, nor

449
Mayer
CONTAINMENT
AND COUNTER-
REVOLUTION AT
VERSAILLES

credits, nor favorable peace terms, with the result that there would be massive starvation, especially in the large cities. On the other hand, they promised that provided order was maintained and reformist republican regimes established the victors, under pressure from Wilson and the Allied Left, would provide economic aid and grant moderate peace terms. By mid-January the triumph of the parties of the July Coalition in the campaign for the German Constituent Assembly best attested to the nature and successful application of this political formula. Within two months Károlyi's withdrawal in favor of Béla Kun, which was precipitated by the peremptory Vix Note, demonstrated the failure of the same formula in Hungary.

Just as the peacemakers could ill afford to ignore this interplay of national and international politics in the defeated countries, they could not ignore it in their own. In 1814–15 the peace was negotiated "in elegant and ceremonious privacy . . . [by] a group of Aristocrats, life-trained as statesmen or diplomats," who considered themselves responsible to crowned sovereigns and barely worried about partisan pressures. The situation was not so serene a century later, when seasoned party politicians of *petit-bourgeois* background—two professors, a journalist, a solicitor—gathered around the conference table. The Big Four were responsible to parliaments, and they never seriously considered insulating themselves from the political parties, pressure groups, mass media, and mass electorates, which were highly agitated over the peace question. To be sure, compared to Metternich, Castlereagh, and Talleyrand, the Big Four were "amateur" diplomats. It does not follow, however, that because they aligned the methods and procedures of diplomacy with the prevailing requirements of party and mass politics they understood less about international affairs than their illustrious predecessors.

Churchill rightly emphasized that the peacemakers of 1918–19 were orators, mass leaders, and men of action, "each of whom had to produce a triumph for himself and his Party and give satisfaction to national fears and passions well founded or not." But why go on and call them "embarrassed demagogues," as Churchill did? Probably nostalgia for both cabinet diplomacy and status politics accounts for the still widely espoused defamation that these "plenipotentiaries were essentially politicians, old parliamentary hands, and therefore expedient-mongers whose highest qualifications for their own profession were drawbacks which unfitted them for their self-assumed [diplomatic] mission."

Even during the prewar decades the growth of party, mass, and crisis politics had substantially eroded cabinet diplomacy, with politically based foreign policy actors superseding professional diplomats. By 1918–19 this erosion of the methods, procedures, style, and personnel of the Old Diplomacy was completed. There was no going back, least of all at the opening of a revolutionary era with soaring class and party strife at home and abroad. And yet, the very day the Conference was formally inaugurated the *Temps* called on the Central Powers not to allow party conflicts to disturb international relations; not to use foreign intervention "to upset the internal equilibrium of nations"; and not to bring into play polemics in the peace deliberations. At the same time it inveighed against making partisan use of half-accurate information about these negotiations. *Mirabile dictu.*

With the Armistice the political truce burst wide open in the victor nations, the forces of order and reaction seizing the offensive. In the United States the congressional elections of November 1918 returned a Republican Senate, thereby undermining domestic support for Woodrow Wilson's moderate peace project; in England the coupon election of mid-December 1918 returned a grim House of Commons, resolved to hold Lloyd George to a Carthaginian course; in Italy, in late December, Leonida Bissolati, Italy's foremost Wilsonian, resigned from Orlando's cabinet. Heartened by these developments, on December 29 Clemenceau defiantly proclaimed his skepticism of the Wilsonian program, certain that the war-hardened Chamber of 1914 was determined to have a punitive settlement.

According to Nicolson this upsurge of vindictiveness was a spontaneous prolongation of wartime passions into the post-Armistice period. Irrational hatreds swelled up and consumed "alert but ignorant electorates," which thereafter made it "impossible even for supermen to devise a peace of moderation and righteousness." But was this outburst of revengeful jingoism all that spontaneous? And, if it was, did the governments and their supporters, which had known how to mobilize these hatreds, do anything to revaluate these mass sentiments?

There are numerous indications that the clamor for a punitive peace was stirred up as part of a vast political design. Except for the protofascist new Right the leaders, parties, pressure groups, patriotic leagues, and newspapers that sparked this agitation also favored rigorously conservative or outright reactionary social and economic policies. In fact, the forces of order appear to have taken advantage of the intoxication of victory either to preserve or advance their class interests and status positions under an ideological cover which was a syncretism of jingoist nationalism, baleful anti-Wilsonianism, and rabid anti-Bolshevism. Whoever was not a super-patriot was denounced as a fellow traveler of the Bolsheviks and stood accused not only of disloyalty but also of advocating a sellout peace.

The revolutionary segments of the Socialist and labor movements were not the primary target of the jingoist *cum* anti-Bolshevik campaign. Its aim was to rout and disconcert the very core of the forces of change, to do so now, pre-emptively, before the fast-growing Left had a chance to rally around Wilson and to make political gains from the high cost of living, rising taxes, and the strains of reconversion. In addition to championing a Wilsonian peace, this Left—this non-Communist Left—was battling for the forty-eight-hour week, collective bargaining, graduated income taxes, and social welfare measures.

Already in the prewar decade the Left and the Right in Britain, France, and Italy had faced each other with mounting bitterness over these same issues. Compared to then, of course, in 1918–19 the eco-

451

Mayer

CONTAINMENT
AND COUNTER-
REVOLUTION AT
VERSAILLES

nomic and fiscal crisis was infinitely more acute; the membership and following of the labor movement was vastly greater; the Russian Revolution stood forth both as an invigorating and a frightening example; and the Right was able to claim credit for timely preparedness as well as victory. But notwithstanding these important permutations and mutations the continuities with the prewar situation were all too apparent. Specifically, in the struggle over labor, tax, and welfare issues, the extremists of the Right frightened Conservatives into inflexibility by deliberately exaggerating the revolutionary posture and the foreign policy pacifism of the Left. In turn, this creeping inflexibility played into the hands of the radical Left, which charged the Right with domestic reaction and warmongering. By mid-1914 the moderate leaders of both camps were rapidly becoming hostages to their respective extremists, with the result that the politics of compromise and accommodation became increasingly deadlocked. Witness the threatened strike by the Triple Industrial Alliance and the Ulster crisis in Britain, the impasse over the three-year law in France, and Red Week in Italy.

The war merely sharpened this polarization of politics and labor-management relations, at the expense of the conservative-reformist center. Victory strengthened, hardened, and emboldened the refractory Right; the Russian Revolution had a similar impact on the militant Left. Both extremes left indelible marks on the politics and diplomacy of the victor powers in 1918–19. Because the jingoist Right had champions or sympathizers in the legislatures, foreign offices, interior ministries, armed services, conservative parties, and editorial offices, its preemptive thrust was felt in a vast range of developments: in America, in the November elections, in congressional obstruction of a Wilsonian peace, in the Red Scare, and in the drive for "normalcy"; in England, in the coupon election, in Parliamentary opposition to the appeasement of Germany and Soviet Russia, and in the government's sham reconstruction program; in France, in the gestation of the *chambre bleu horizon,* in Clemenceau's intransigence toward Germany and Soviet Russia, in the resolute repression of strikes, and in Parliament's obstinate refusal to approve nonregressive taxes; and in Italy, in Sidney Sonnino's domination of the peace delegation, in Gabriele d'Annunzio's expedition to Fiume, in the growth of the *Fasci de combattimento,* and in Orlando's failure to check inflation.

Except for frightening established governments and societies and serving as a pretext for the excesses of the avant-garde of anti-Bolshevism, the extreme Left had no leverage outside the labor movement. Its leaders, most of them nationally unknown, concentrated their organizational, propagandist, and conspiratorial activities on the rapidly expanding Socialist parties and trade unions, making special efforts to enlist the new recruits. They fed on each and every grievance, sparked local strikes, participated prominently in mass demonstrations, and worked their propaganda presses overtime. In 1918–19 these zealots helped generate a mood of impatience among the rank and file, thereby goading their Majoritarian and Independent rivals into a greater sense of urgency about the labor cause. These political and syndicalist militants should not be denied their share of the credit for the enactment of the forty-eight-hour week by the Allied parliaments and for the labor movement's concerted and partially successful opposition to direct military intervention in Russia.

Without this impatience and activism on the Left Woodrow Wilson's moderating influence would have been completely nullified. As it was, precisely because the moderate forces of movement were so decisively checked even before the start of the Conference, Wilson had only limited leverage. Moreover, he was hesitant to appeal to the Left for help for fear that the militants would seize the initiative for themselves. Wilson was condemned to labor in a political field, both national and international, in which measured reformism, so essential to the achievement of his diplomatic aims, was fatally emasculated.

Wilson's principles and aims, like all such pronunciamentos, were destined to be honored in the breach. The conditions that had prompted their formulation and acceptance in early 1918 had passed into history: there was no longer any need to restrain the Soviet government from signing a separate peace with the Central Powers; with the success of the revolution from above in Berlin the rebellion against the Kaiser and Erich Ludendorff no longer required encouragement; and after the Armistice the Allied Governments could dispense with the support of their own forces of movement. Above all, the Allied cabinets were much less prone to bend to the ideological and diplomatic wishes of the Wilson Administration once victory had drastically reduced their dependence on American military and economic power. Besides, no programmatic guidelines had complicated the labors of the peacemakers of 1814–15.

Even so, the President's Fourteen Points and subsequent pronouncements were not simply shunted aside. By making their two reservations with regard to the freedom of the seas and reparations the Allies conceded that Wilson's prescriptions had crystallized into a public touchstone for the coming peace negotiations; and the pre-Armistice exchanges with Germany even endowed them with a measure of contractual force.

But quite apart from any moral or legal obligation to Germany, until May 1919 the Allied Governments could not afford to disavow Woodrow Wilson publicly. The President's ideology and America's economic bounty were expected to exercise a moderating influence on revolutionary conditions in defeated Europe and on the post-Armistice neurasthenia in the victor nations. Without the still potent spell of Wilsonianism the swing toward Leninism within the Left might well have assumed considerable proportions. Especially the Independents, but also the Majoritarians, trusted in the President to block a punitive peace, thereby thwarting the offensive of the Allied Right, consolidating the reformist regimes in the defeated nations, and giving the lie to Lenin's charge that Wilsonianism was but an insidious bourgeois-capitalist smoke screen.

The frenzied enthusiasm that greeted the President upon his arrival in Europe was not without political and class overtones. While Socialist, labor, and radical-bourgeois leaders and their followers wildly cheered

453
Mayer
CONTAINMENT
AND COUNTER-
REVOLUTION AT
VERSAILLES

him, their opponents berated them for apotheosizing Wilson for selfish, partisan purposes. On the eve of the Conference the Allied Governments were sufficiently apprehensive about this united front of Wilson and the Left that they purposely obstructed contacts between them. On the other hand, the governments of the defeated nations continued to profess their faith in Wilson until well after they knew that his cause was lost. As for the governments of the successor states, they courted Wilson's favor in their bid for favorable frontiers and economic aid. In sum, throughout most of the Conference the President and his arsenal of spiritual and material resources were considered indispensable by each delegation as well as by the Berne International. Significantly, even Clemenceau was careful not to risk a break with Wilson; and notwithstanding his anti-Wilsonian tirades, Lenin was eager for the President to blunt the military edge of the counterrevolutionary intervention.

At the time of the Congress of Vienna Tsar Alexander I certainly did not play such a pivotal role as did Wilson. Quite apart from the fact that the League of Nations was to serve as an instrument for peaceful change in the international arena while the Holy Alliance was designed to freeze the new status quo at home and abroad, the Tsar had considerably less leverage than Wilson. Whereas Alexander was confined to cooperation with fellow sovereigns and to military means of intervention, Wilson could marshal popular support for the League and dispose of substantial economic and financial resources which were of critical importance to the exhausted nations of Europe.

R. S. Baker quite rightly stressed that the use of the "economic weapon" to achieve diplomatic and political ends "was only in its crude beginnings at Paris," and that the world would get "a fuller taste of it in the future." During the Conference all nations—large and small, old and new—brought their economic resources into play; and the Conference as a whole, supported by the neutrals, enforced a strict blockade against Bolshevik Russia and Hungary.

But America's use of the economic weapon was particularly noteworthy. She had a vast reservoir of instantly available capital, food, and manufactures, and her delegation had a precocious understanding of economic power as an instrument of control in the international politics of this dawning era of civil war.

The Armistice was not signed as yet when U.S. officials in Europe advised Washington that since America's "economic and financial support would be essential to the Allies in the post-war period" material pressures might be used to force an acceptable interpretation of "our own principles and policies." Wilson himself chose Armistice Day solemnly to declare that it would be America's "fortunate duty to assist by example, by sober, friendly counsel and by *material aid* in the establishment of a just democracy throughout the world"; and he may well have had the economic weapon in mind when he told his advisers, during the crossing to Europe, that the U.S. would fight for a new order "agreeably if we can, disagreeably if necessary."

Colonel House shared the view of many U.S. officials and business leaders that the Allies were "vitally interested in what manner we propose to use our great strength" in finance, commerce, shipping, raw materials, and food. As for D. H. Miller, he confidently predicted that Wilson's covenant would be accepted without any American concessions because "Europe was bankrupt financially and her Governments were bankrupt morally . . . [and] the mere hint of the withdrawal of America . . . would see the fall of every government in Europe without exception, and a revolution in every country of Europe with one possible exception."

Members of the British Delegation confirmed this diagnosis. According to Keynes, in early 1919 "Europe was in complete dependence on the food supplies of the United States; and financially she was even more absolutely at their mercy." In Nicolson's judgment this economic dependence made the Allies "entirely subservient to the dictates of Washington" and gave Wilson an "overwhelming force of compulsion." In retrospect, both Keynes and Nicolson recall that it never occurred to them that, "if need arose, Wilson would hesitate to use" America's economic and financial power, and both attribute this hesitancy to his having been a prophet instead of a man of power.

In actual fact, the American Delegation played a leading role in the formulation and implementation of diplomatically and politically intended economic policies toward Soviet Russia, Bolshevik Hungary, the successor states, and the new regimes in Germany and Austria. But whereas Wilson readily used the economic weapon to strangle Bolshevism, to support fledgling nations, and to stabilize the governments of the defeated nations, he hesitated to exert pressure on the Allies. This hesitation, however, was due to political considerations, both domestic and foreign, rather than to his prophetic disposition.

At home influential senators, the patriotic leagues, the jingoist press, and select interest groups mounted a campaign against the use of the economic weapon for a Wilsonian peace of the sort advocated by the European Left. To make matters worse, the three Allied premiers were well informed about this opposition and proposed to foster and harness it for their own purposes. By early December 1918 the London *Spectator* assured its readers that Wilson did not have the "least chance of getting any treaty ratified which was repugnant to the sentiments of the Republican party"; and that since the opinions of that party were "framed in unreserved support of Great Britain and France" the Allies could approach the Conference "with all confidence." Within a month the Boston *Transcript* (independent Republican) hinted that since the Allied statesmen were familiar with the American opposition as well as with the American Constitution they might be "inclined to heed rather the view of the American majority than that of a President whose general policies had been discredited by the popular vote." Meanwhile Senator Henry Cabot Lodge set out to encourage the Allied Carthaginians to join him in standing up to Wilson.

As the *Springfield Republican* suggested, in order to "neutralize the in-

455

Mayer

CONTAINMENT
AND COUNTER-
REVOLUTION AT
VERSAILLES

fluences working against him in his own country" the President would have "to rally sympathetic elements in Great Britain, France and Italy." In fact, the Right on both sides of the Atlantic was apprehensive about the progressive *domestic* implications of a peace of reconciliation, just as the Left was nervous about the conservative domestic consequences of a vindictive settlement.

Radical publicists called attention to this political struggle "not between nations but between parties whose constituency transcended all national boundaries." For the purposes of peacemaking "the progressive wings of the American parties, British labor and liberals, French and Italian and Belgian liberals and socialists were one party; the Lodges and Milners and Carsons and Clemenceaus and their following of imperialists and protectionists constituted the opposing party." To be sure, Radicals were blind to the broad popular support of the Right and crudely divided the political spectrum into two monolithic blocs. But except for these blind spots this characterization of the transnational political confrontation had considerable merit, not least because it acknowledged the inevitability of the politics of intervention. Frederick Jackson Turner quite rightly anticipated that the conservative forces of different nations were on the verge of cooperating internationally, in imitation of their Socialist rivals.

Theoretically the Right indignantly and violently objected to external intervention in the internal affairs of nations. In practice, however, it championed counterrevolutionary intervention in Bolshevik countries and relied on informal transnational contacts elsewhere. Naturally Lenin and Karl Radek disdainfully rejected this principle of the nonintervention in the internal affairs of other nations and proceeded to devise organizational mechanisms with which to maximize the effectiveness of their predesigned interference abroad. Meanwhile, Wilson searched for political support for the material and ideological intervention for which he was so much better equipped than Lloyd George, Clemenceau, Orlando, and even Lenin.

As noted before, his supporters were in retreat in the United States as well as in Europe. In America *The New Republic, The Nation,* the League of Free Nations Society, the Committee of 48, segments of organized labor, and internationally minded businessmen and financiers were fighting a rear-guard battle against onrushing conservatives, superpatriots, and anti-Communists. Simultaneously in the Allied nations the non-Communist Left and the radical bourgeoisie were in disarray. Perhaps this narrow political base at home and in the Allied countries accounts for Wilson's hesitancy to go over the heads of the Big Three. The hardening of opinion in his own country sensitized him to the hardening of opinion in London, Paris, and Rome. Moreover, quite apart from being careful not to encourage the revolutionary Left, Wilson was worried about weakening governments, including the Polish and Rumanian governments, that carried the brunt of the containment of and the intervention in Russia.

In sum, a frontal attack on the victory-hardened Allies, which Socialists and Radicals on both sides of the Atlantic urged upon the President, was not to be undertaken lightly. The task and responsibility would have been staggering, the risk immense—the more so for a statesman and politician sworn to reason rather than passion, to agreement by consent rather than coercion, to reform rather than revolution. The issue is hardly whether or not Wilson was sincere about his principles and aims; nor is the issue one of the quality of his strategic and tactical skills as diplomatist and politician. Even assuming Wilson scored exceptionally high on all these counts, a prior question must be considered: how pertinent and consequential was Wilson's reformist project in the crisis setting of 1918–19?

Unlike Clemenceau, the President strained to understand this crisis in its world historical context. Both he and Lloyd George consistently rejected the conspiratorial view of the Russian Revolution, which they saw as a variant of the French Revolution in scale, ecumenical appeal, and duration.

Wilson's concern was less with the importance of the Revolution for Russia than for Europe and the world. He saw the example of the Revolution, embellished by stirring manifestoes, acting upon crisis-torn societies which in the prewar years had been rife with discontent and agitated by revolutionary parties and ideologies. According to Isaiah Bowman, the President told his advisers on the S.S. *George Washington* that the poison of Bolshevism was spreading because it was "a protest against the way in which the world had worked." William Bullitt, who was present on this same occasion, recorded Wilson as saying that the only way he could "explain the susceptibility of the people of Europe to the poison of Bolshevism, was that their Governments had been run for wrong purposes." Wilson then added his prediction that unless the peace were made "on the highest principles of justice it would be swept away by the peoples of the world in less than a generation." In that event he intended "to run away and hide on the Island of Guam or somewhere else remote, for there would follow not mere conflict but cataclysm." A bit later, when pleading with the Big Three for an accommodation with Lenin, he warned that "there was certainly a latent force behind Bolshevism which attracted as much sympathy as its more brutal aspects caused general disgust." Wilson attributed this sympathy to "a feeling of revolt throughout the world against large vested interests which influence the world both in the economic and in the political sphere."

It was precisely because the Russian Revolution was "a menace to others" that Wilson was so reluctant to leave Russia to "settle her own affairs in her own way." With the help and encouragement of his key advisers, notably of Herbert Hoover, Wilson spearheaded various Allied efforts to tame the Russian Revolution. In fact, these efforts came to be central to Wilson's overall peacemaking strategy.

Whereas the Entente Governments tended to advocate either direct or indirect military intervention—with America providing most of the funds, the material, and the food supplies—the American Delegation gave first priority to diplomatic, economic, and ideological intervention.

Not that the Wilson Administration backed out of or cut back the armed intervention started in mid-1918. Still, by comparison it was particularly intent on exploring those avenues that might obviate military measures partially or altogether. Of course this nonmartial approach suited Wilson's view of the dynamics of the Russian Revolution, his diplomatic style, and America's foreign policy capabilities.

Rather than denounce the Bolshevik Revolution as either a sinister conspiracy or a vile crime, Wilson saw it as the natural and fitting culmination of lingering popular dissatisfactions with the tsarist regime, catalyzed by the strains of war and enthusiasm for the seductive promises of the Bolshevik ideology. Such dissatisfaction and ardor could not be conquered by force of arms, not least because a military onslaught threatened to restore the *ancien régime*. Clemenceau and, to a lesser extent, Lloyd George were not particularly bothered by the prospect of the Whites replacing Lenin, so that the irresolution of their intervention in the Russian Civil War was not a function of political scruples but of overstrained resources and anti-interventionist pressures. Wilson, however, refused to close his eyes to the ideological and political aftergrowth of the destruction of the Soviet regime. The qualified recognition of Alexander Kolchak, which was delayed until late May 1919, mirrored his desperate but unrealistic and self-deceiving attempt to transform the unmistakably counterrevolutionary intervention into a crusade for the democratization of Russia. That even his worst fears were justified was amply demonstrated once the Allied-sponsored overthrow of Béla Kun was followed by a White terror and by anti-Semitic pogroms.

On the intellectual plane the President understood that revolution and counterrevolution inevitably incited and needed each other. In terms of policy, however, he simply could not admit the impossibility of a moderate middle course. Like it or not, America was one of the senior partners in a coalition resolved to contain or destroy the Bolshevik Revolution. To achieve this objective the Allies needed the military services of Finland, Poland, Rumania, and Germany, even at the price of allowing conservative and reactionary forces in these countries to benefit from this anti-Bolshevik campaign.

It was to avoid paying this distasteful political price that the American delegates wanted to explore the use of nonmilitary methods of intervention. Their aim was to moderate and domesticate rather than destroy the revolutionary regime in Russia. In their judgment the ideological canons of Bolshevism and the lust for power of the Bolshevik leaders were not the primary moving force of the Soviet dictatorship. According to some American officials Lenin's iron rule at home and revolutionary agitation abroad were part of a *levée en masse* by a revolutionary government fighting for its life against internal insurgents and foreign invasion in a country bled white by war. Provided these mainsprings of revolutionary dictatorship were removed or reduced, the Soviet leaders could afford to relax their iron grip and agree to a united front of the Left for the reconstruction, modernization, and reform of Russia. The Allies could contribute to this relaxation of revolutionary discipline and terror not only by stopping their intervention and lifting the blockade but also by providing economic and technical assistance.

The Buckler-Litvinov conversations, the Prinkipo proposal, and the Bullitt Mission were so many efforts in this direction. All alike were opposed and sabotaged by the entire French Delegation, by key members of the American and British delegations, by antiappeasement forces in the Allied parliaments, by all but one of the Russian *émigré* groups in Paris, by the Whites in Russia, and by the governments of most of the new states along Russia's western borders. Some were motivated by power-political considerations and others by age-old national hatreds, but all alike called forth and embodied counterrevolutionary economic, social, and political forces. There was no corresponding reservoir of support for moderation. Wilson knew this; and so did Lenin.

Chances for a negotiated accommodation were never very good. The Big Four, including Wilson, insisted on military conditions that were designed to favor the Whites and their borderland allies and sought to extract debilitating political concessions in exchange for lifting the blockade and providing food. In turn, Lenin was careful not to play any of his spare trumps, notably critical and advanced military positions and control of the railways. Whereas strictly territorial issues might have been compromised, mutual distrust stemming from irreconcilable political, economic, and social persuasions stood in the way of an overall settlement —at a time that both sides still hoped for total victory. Lenin was not about to trust Wilson, whom he rightly suspected of being a prisoner— even if a reluctant prisoner—of the counterrevolution.

With the March-April crisis the Russian question once again became acute. The stand of the Right toward Bolshevism both inside and outside Russia stiffened still further in the face of rising labor unrest in the Allied countries, renewed Spartacist outbreaks in Germany, the establishment of a Soviet outpost in Bavaria, the triumph of Béla Kun in Hungary, and the explosive instability in Vienna. This rigidification was well under way when rumors of the Bullitt Mission incited the die-hards to protest furiously against any dealings with Lenin and to urge stepped-up military measures.

Once again caught between the appeasers and the irreconcilables, Wilson abandoned a direct diplomatic approach in favor of an untried economic formula. The Nansen Plan for a commission of neutrals to feed Russia originated in the American Delegation. At first, in order to broaden its ideological appeal, the letter drafted by Hoover for Fridtjot Nansen's signature was supposed to be countersigned by Karl Hjalmar Branting. But the leader of the Second International preferred to stay in the background. Under the Nansen scheme the Russian Bolsheviks were asked to halt military operations "against our allies" on all fronts and to waive "political recognition or negotiation" in exchange for food and other essential supplies to be provided by a neutral relief agency. Obviously, the arrangements for the distribution in Russia of this "wholly

459

Mayer

CONTAINMENT
AND COUNTER-
REVOLUTION AT
VERSAILLES

non-political" relief would be decisive, primarily because their political implications were the crux of this proposal.

In fact, political rather than humanitarian purposes were at the heart of the Nansen Plan. This political design was forcefully sketched out by Hoover in a remarkable letter to President Wilson, dated March 28, 1919.

As the result of Bolshevik economic conceptions, the people of Russia are dying of hunger and disease at the rate of some hundreds of thousands monthly in a country that formerly supplied food to a large part of the world.

I feel it is my duty to lay before you in just as few words as possible my views as to the American relation to Bolshevism and its manifestations. These views at least have the merit of being an analysis of information and thought gleaned from my own experience and the independent sources which I now have over the whole of Europe, through our widespread relief organization.

It simply cannot be denied that this swinging of the social pendulum from the tyranny of the extreme right to the tyranny of the extreme left is based on a foundation of real social grievance. The tyranny of the reactionaries in Eastern and Central Europe for generations before the war, and the suffering of their common people is but a commonplace to every social student. This situation was thrown into bold relief by the war and the breakdown of those reactionary tyrannies. After fighting actually stopped on the various fronts the famine which followed has further emphasized the gulf between the lower and upper classes. The poor were starved and driven mad in the presence of extravagance and waste.

It is to be noticed that the Bolshevik ascendancy or even their strong attempts so far are confined to areas of former reactionary tyranny. Their courses represent the not unnatural violence of a mass of ignorant humanity, who themselves have learned in grief of tyranny and violence over generations. Our people, who enjoy so great liberty and general comfort, cannot fail to symphathize to some degree with these blind gropings for better social condition. If former revolutions in ignorant masses are any guide, the pendulum will yet swing back to some moderate position when bitter experience has taught the economic and social follies of present obsessions. No greater fortune can come to the world than that these foolish ideas should have an opportunity somewhere of bankrupting themselves.

It is not necessary for any American to debate the utter foolishness of these economic tenets. We must all agree that our processes of production and distribution, the outgrowth of a hundred generations, in the stimulation to individual initiative, the large equality of opportunity and infinite development of mind and body, while not perfect, come about as near perfection as is possible from the mixture of avarice, ambition, altruism, intelligence, ignorance and education, of which the human animal is today composed. The Bolshevik's land of illusion is that he can perfect these human qualities by destroying the basic processes of production and distribution instead of devoting himself to securing a better application of the collective surplus.

Politically, the Bolsheviki most certainly represent a minority in every country where they are in control, and as such they constitute a tyranny that is the negation of democracy, for democracy as I see it must rest on the execution of the will of the majority expressed by free and unterrified suffrage. As a tyranny, the Bolshevik has resorted to terror, bloodshed and murder to a degree long since abandoned even amongst reactionary tyrannies. He has even to a greater degree relied upon criminal instinct to support his doctrines than even autocracy did. By enveloping into his doctrines the cry of the helpless and the downtrodden, he has embraced a large degree of emotionalism and has thereby given an impulse to his propaganda comparable only to the impulse of large spiritual movements. This propaganda, however, in my view will stir other populations only in ratio to their proportions of the suffering and ignorant and criminal. I feel myself, therefore, that the political danger of spread of Bolshevism by propaganda is a direct factor of the social and political development of the population which they attempt to impregnate. Where the gulf between the middle classes and the lower classes is large, and where the lower classes have been kept in ignorance and distress, this propaganda will be fatal and do violence to normal democratic development. For these reasons, I have no fear of it in the United States, and my fears as to other countries would be gauged by the above criterion. It is possible that the Soviet type of government might take hold in some other countries as a primitive form of democracy, but its virulence will be tempered by their previous degree of political subversion.

There remains in my mind one more point to be examined, that is as to whether the Bolshevik centers now stirred by great emotional hopes will not undertake large military crusades in an attempt to impose their doctrines on other defenseless people. This is a point on which my mind is divided with the evidence at hand, and it seems to me that the whole treatment of the problem must revolve on the determination of this one question. If this spirit is inherent in their doctrine, it appears to me that we must disregard all other questions and be prepared to fight, for exactly the same reasons that we entered the European War against Germany. If this is not the case, then it appears to me that from an American point of view we should not involve ourselves in what may be a ten year military entanglement in Europe. The American people cannot say that we are going to insist that any given population must work out its internal social problems according to our particular conception of democracy. In any event, I have the most serious doubt that

461

Mayer

CONTAINMENT
AND COUNTER-
REVOLUTION AT
VERSAILLES

outside forces entering upon such an enterprise can do other than infinite harm, for any great wave of emotion must ferment and spread under repression. In the swing of the social pendulum from the extreme left back toward the right, it will find the point of stabilization based on racial instincts that could never be established by outside intervention.

I think we have also to contemplate what would actually happen if we undertook military intervention in, say, a case like Hungary. We should probably be involved in years of police duty, and our first act would probably in the nature of things make us a party to reestablishing the reactionary classes in their economic domination over the lower classes. This is against our fundamental national spirit, and I doubt whether our soldiers under these circumstances could resist infection with Bolshevik ideas. It also requires consideration as to whether or not our people at home, on gradual enlightenment as to the social wrongs of the lower classes in these countries, would stand for our providing power by which such reactionaries held their position, and we would perchance be thrown in to an attempt as governors to work out some social reorganization of these countries. We thus become a mandatory with a vengeance. We become, in fact, one of four mandatories, each with a different political and social outlook, for it would necessarily be a joint Allied undertaking. Furthermore, in our present engagements with France, England and Italy, we become a junior in this partnership of four. It is therefore inevitable that in these matters where our views and principles are at variance with the European Allies we would find ourselves subordinated and even committed to policies against our convictions.

In all these lights, I have the following three suggestions:

First: We cannot even remotely recognize this murderous tyranny without stimulating actionist radicalism in every country in Europe and without transgressing on every National ideal of our own.

Second: That some Neutral of international reputation for probity and ability should be allowed to create a second Belgian Relief Commission for Russia. He should ask the Northern Neutrals who are especially interested both politically and financially in the restoration of better conditions in Russia, to give to him diplomatic, financial and transportation support; that he should open negotiations with the Allied governments on the ground of desire to enter upon the humane work of saving life, and ask the conditions upon which ships carrying food and other necessaries will be allowed to pass. He should be told that we will raise no obstructions and would even help in his humanitarian task if he gets assurances that the Bolsheviki will cease all militant action across certain defined boundaries and cease their subsidizing of disturbances abroad; under these conditions that he could raise money, ships and food, either from inside or outside Russia; that he must secure an agreement covering equitable distribution, and he might even demand that Germany help pay for this. This plan does not involve any recognition or relationship by the Allies of the Bolshevik murderers now in control any more than England recognized Germany in its deals with the Belgian Relief. It would appear to me that such a proposal would at least test out whether this is a militant force engrossed upon world domination. If such an arrangement could be accomplished it might at least give a period of rest along the frontiers of Europe and would give some hope of stabilization. Time can thus be taken to determine whether or not this whole system is a world danger, and whether the Russian people will not themselves swing back to moderation and themselves bankrupt these ideas. This plan, if successful, would save an immensity of helpless human life and would save our country from further entanglements which today threaten to pull us from our National ideals.

Third: I feel strongly the time has arrived for you again to reassert your spiritual leadership of democracy in the world as opposed to tyrannies of all kinds. Could you not take an early opportunity to analyze, as only you can, Bolshevism from its political, economic, humane and its criminal points of view, and, while yielding its aspirations, sympathetically to show its utter foolishness as a basis of economic development; show its true social ends; rap our own reactionaries for their destruction of social betterment and thereby their stimulation of Bolshevism; point, however, to the steady progress of real democracy in these roads of social betterment. I believe you would again align the hearts of the suffering for orderly progress against anarchy, not alone in Russia but in every Allied country.

If the militant features of Bolshevism were drawn in colors with their true parallel with Prussianism as an attempt at world domination that we do not stand for, it would check the fears that today haunt all men's minds.

463

Mayer

CONTAINMENT
AND COUNTER-
REVOLUTION AT
VERSAILLES

In this letter Hoover brilliantly summarized the key tenets of the Wilsonian view of the Bolshevik problem: Russian Bolshevism was a condition to be cured rather than a conspiracy to be destroyed; there were considerable sources of Bolshevik contagion outside Russia; the spiritual appeals of the Bolshevik ideology were far from negligible; the reactionary consequences of a military crusade against Bolshevism could not be ignored; and a military truce combined with economic aid was most likely to redirect the revolutionary currents into reformist channels in Russia.

But the letter also struck some novel chords. Above all, Hoover made an insidious comparison of the "foolishness" of Bolshevik economic doctrines with the unequaled excellence of the American economic system. Moreover, he envisaged the possibility that doctrinally the Bolsheviks were sworn to export their economic and political system, if need be even by force of arms. Without abandoning the view that the Bolshevik system was primarily a product of historical conditions Hoover now stressed the doctrinal sources of Soviet conduct.

As a result, while Hoover's policy recommendations dovetailed with Wilson's drive to give priority to nonmilitary intervention, they also embodied a new departure. Accordingly, Wilson was urged to couple his economic intervention with an ideological counteroffensive. Hoover wanted the President to issue a manifesto criticizing the doctrine, promise, and practice of Bolshevism and setting forth the aims and methods of reformist and democratic capitalism. In other words, just as the recently completed crusade against the Central Powers had required and profited from the Fourteen Points, so this incipient crusade against the rival social-political system required an anti-Bolshevik manifesto.

Even though Wilson successfully insisted on certain political assurances as a precondition for recognizing Kolchak, he never went on to issue a full-blown manifesto proclaiming the objectives of the Big Powers' participation in armed containment and intervention. Perhaps he never did so because he could at best be halfhearted about an operation whose carriers and objectives were too counterrevolutionary for his own liking. The words and principles of a Wilsonian pronouncement would have been blatantly incompatible with the whole thrust of the enterprise, thus making it that much easier for Lenin and his champions to expose the hypocrisy of the democratic-reformist ideology. A declaration like that issued at Pillnitz against the French Revolution would have been more appropriate, but Foch or Churchill, rather than Wilson, would have had to formulate it.

It may well be that the democratization and moderation of the counterrevolutionary side in a civil war is a historical impossibility. In any case, Wilson lacked the courage, the political support, and the diplomatic leverage to force a credible effort for accommodation with Lenin; or, failing this, to make the operation essentially *defensive*. The intervention continued, with each participant's contribution determined by a variety of factors—among them power capabilities, domestic political pressures, national rivalries, and changing estimates of chances for the overthrow of the Bolshevik regime.

The military operations of this intervention impinged only occasionally on the politics and diplomacy of peacemaking. On the other hand, precisely because peacemaking and the containment of Bolshevism were so tightly interlocked the one could never be separated from the other. Once again it was Baker, the participant-historian of liberal persuasion, who faced up to this dilemma.

The effect of the Russian problem on the Paris Conference . . . was profound: Paris cannot be understood without Moscow. Without ever being represented at Paris at all, the Bolsheviki and Bolshevism were powerful elements at every turn. Russia played a more vital part at Paris than Prussia. For the Prussian idea had been utterly defeated, while the Russian idea was still rising in power.

The Revolution in Russia and the specter of revolution over liberated and defeated Europe left its mark on the entire settlement. Still according to Baker, the President could not risk breaking up the Conference because of "the need to hold the world steady, keep order and fight both extremes —militarism on the one hand and Bolshevism on the other." This policy of caution benefited the counterrevolution more than it benefited the Revolution. Wilson wound up giving his consent to a diplomatic course that was decidedly right of center and not halfway between Foch and Lenin, as Baker implied.

Thorstein Veblen was the first to note that the compact to reduce Soviet Russia and contain Bolshevism "was not written into the text of the Treaty [but] may rather be said to have been the parchment upon which that text was written." In his view this was the only objective that the Big Four held in common. Veblen suggested, furthermore, that Wilson's "apparent defeat . . . was not so much a defeat, but rather a strategic alignment designed to compass what was indispensable, even at some cost to his own prestige—the main consideration being the defeat of Bolshevism at any cost—so that a well-considered view of the President's share in the deliberations of the Conclave would credit him with insight, courage, facility, and tenacity of purpose. . . ."

In order to appreciate the world historical importance of the Paris Peace Conference, it is necessary to view it against the background of the extreme complexity of the international and domestic politics of 1918–19. This complexity was due to the convergence of the end of the Great War with the start of the Bolshevik Revolution in Russia, the collapse of political authority in Eastern and Central Europe, the threat of revolution throughout defeated Europe, and the right-wing upsurge inside the victor nations. These unanticipated and unintended consequences of the war produced conditions of national and international disequilibrium that rendered this peacemaking task more extensive and more intricate than any previously on record. Moreover, the interplay of national and international politics reached unequaled intensity. As a result, more than ever before, peacemakers had to be politicians in addition to being diplomatists. Also, the opportunities, purposes, and instruments for intervention in the internal affairs of other states assumed unparalleled proportions.

The debates and decisions of the Conference cannot be studied, therefore, as if these new conditions had not existed. The analytic framework of conventional diplomatic history simply must be enlarged to accommodate the complexities of international relations in an age of mass and crisis politics, in an age of international civil war. Furthermore, its scope must be broadened in order to show the impact of the dialectic between revolution and counterrevolution on the national and international

465

Mayer

CONTAINMENT
AND COUNTER-
REVOLUTION AT
VERSAILLES

level upon the processes of diplomacy. Thirdly, diplomatic history must abandon its national or bilateral perspective in favor of a multilateral, comparative, and transnational approach.

In any event, only a comprehensive diplomatic history can explicate the politics and diplomacy of peacemaking after the Great War. Without slighting the customary personal jealousies, national rivalries, and security dilemmas at the Paris conference table, it will then have in its purview the domestic politics in the participant nations, the specter of Bolshevism, and the intervention in Russia. Moreover, this updated diplomatic history will note that while the Peace Conference was in session in Paris, the charter meeting of the Third International was held in Moscow, the precursors of German Nazism fought Bolshevism through the Free Corps, Benito Mussolini scored his first fascist triumphs in Italy, and an awakening India provoked the British into the Amritsar massacre.

29. Westernization, Revolution and the Search for a Basis of Authority — Russia in 1917

THEODORE H. VON LAUE

30. A Historical Turning Point: Marx, Lenin, Stalin

EDWARD HALLETT CARR

As the selections on World War I and the Paris Peace Conference have pointed out, twentieth-century total war created a revolutionary situation throughout Europe. In Russia it was massive enough for revolution to triumph. Elsewhere revolution failed, but the war's destruction of the old order and the threat of revolutionary communism inspired counterrevolutionary movements. These took power in Italy and Germany as fascism and Nazism and, like communism, threatened the forces of liberal democracy elsewhere. In the period between the world wars, then, Europe was beset by new varieties of revolution and counterrevolution.

In 1967 the Soviet Union celebrated the fiftieth anniversary of the Russian Revolution. Western scholars commemorated it by analyzing its impact from the viewpoint of fifty years later. By 1967 both fascism and the Cold War

Source: Theodore H. Von Laue, "Westernization, Revolution and the Search for a Basis of Authority—Russia in 1917," *Soviet Studies*, XIX (October 1967), 155–80. Reprinted by permission of the author and Basil Blackwell, Publisher. [Footnotes omitted.]

were over. Although the threat of Soviet power remained, communism as
an ideology had neither won western Europe nor was it any longer a menace.
As a result, the impact of the Russian Revolution seemed different than it had
in the 1917–1945 period. Its greatest influence had not been on the developed
nations of western Europe, but on the undeveloped or developing nations of
Asia and Africa. These selections are two of the most distinguished examples
of the many articles and papers written on its fiftieth anniversary. In the first
selection and in his other work on modern Russian history Theodore H. Von
Laue of Clark University views the events of 1917 as Russia's revolutionary
response to the problem of westernization. The second selection is by British
historian Edward Hallett Carr, whose masterly multi-volume standard history
of the Soviet Union has now been completed through 1928. He suggests that by
making a revolution of westernization and modernization Lenin and Stalin
changed the direction of Marxism.

Von Laue's article limits itself to the events of 1917 and how Lenin's Bol-
sheviks were able to seize control of the revolution made in February of that
year. For him the February revolution was "a product of westernization." What
does he mean by that? At the same time, he continues, that revolution thrust
up enormous mass revolutionary energies which, as they are wont to do, created
chaos. The problem that dominated Russia in 1917 between the February and
October revolutions was to find "a fresh source of authority" upon the collapse
of tsardom which could preserve both order and the revolution. How and in
what ways did it happen that "the February revolution, instead of introducing
a superior efficiency, created disruption and chaos in every aspect of the econ-
omy"? In the "search for a basis of authority" in those months why did each of
the major non-Bolshevik parties and leaders—Milyukov's Kadets, Kerensky,
Soviet and Menshevik leaders like Tsereteli—fail to convince Russia of its
authority? In contrast, what was Lenin's view of the basis of authority and how
was he able to impose his view on Russia? According to Von Laue, why did
not the Russian Revolution adopt a western solution to the problems of freedom
and authority?

Carr's selection casts a similar problem in a much broader framework of
Marxism, Leninism, and Stalinism. He argues that the Russian Revolution was
not only "the first great revolution to be deliberately planned and made" and
"a political revolution in an economically unripe country," but that the "most
significant of all the achievements" of this political revolution was industrializa-
tion through economic planning. His thesis raises at least two important ques-
tions. First of all, how and why did Marx, Lenin, and Stalin differ from each
other on how the revolution would take place and on the relationship between
party and class? Secondly, how did the Russian Revolution and Soviet develop-
ment differ so much from previous revolutions in goals, methods, and accom-
plishments that, according to Carr, it ended the era of the French Revolution?
One might also consider Carr's suggestion that the Chinese Communist revolu-
tion of 1949, in turn, ended the era of the Russian Revolution.

THEODORE H. VON LAUE

I. Westernization and the Problem of Freedom

In the half-century that has elapsed since the Russian revolutions of 1917, the world has learned much not only about the portents of these events in Russia but also about the continued viability in the world at large of the so-called 'capitalist system'. Certain ingredients of that 'system' seem to be basic to a successful urban industrial society anywhere, even under 'socialism'. The Leninist dialectics have been refuted by the course of events. Around much of the globe the contrasts are now no longer between a young Russia and an old West, an ascending socialist system and a moribund capitalism, but between the 'developing' and the 'advanced' countries. The new terminology has reversed the order of promise implicit in the prophecies of Marx or Lenin. The prestige has shifted back to the 'capitalist' pace-setters.

The new framework suggests a new approach. The Soviet experiment should be examined also in the perspective of the 'developing' countries, which—whatever the marvels of their native heritage—find themselves grievously inept at mastering the secrets that have given Western civilization its ascendancy. In this new perspective the tables are turned for once, and Westerners are congenitally handicapped. They cannot easily put themselves into the position of large-scale borrowers of culture. Yet this approach, difficult though it is, would seem to offer the best insight into the problems and tragedies of the gifted and long-suffering peoples that inhabit northern Eurasia.

Whatever the traditional theories about Russia's relations to the West, Russia belongs among the developing countries in one crucial respect: the Western pattern of development which now for better or worse has become the global prototype and which continues to shame the various efforts of native, non-Western modernization, does not organically mesh with indigenous traditions. Like all developing countries, Russia, even Soviet Russia, suffers from a deep cleavage between the turbulent spontaneity of the native temperament and the Western-imposed and Western-oriented necessities, between heart and head, instinct and reason, between the native value structure and imported ideals and goals. One can trace such a fault-line in every continental country of Europe, but in the case of Russia it has long assumed classic proportions. It shows up at every turning-point in modern Russian history; it is writ large over the year 1917.

For a specific illustration of that forever unhealing fracture we may take a statement made by A. F. Kerensky at a conference of provincial commissars and other public officials shortly before the Moscow State Conference early in August 1917. By that time the February revolution lay behind by roughly five months; the Provisional Government had accomplished as much legislation as it ever would, and the unsettling effects of a regime dedicated to freedom and democracy in the Western sense were daily becoming more patent in a Russia still at war. As Kerensky told his audience: the country was in danger and worse calamities lay ahead. Then he poured forth his lament:

> I cannot say that there turned out to be not enough of reason and conscience, but I can say one thing with absolute certainty that *in questions of State administration there turned out to be too much ignorance and too little experience among the free people, or among those free people who are now called upon to forge their destiny under the blows of the formidable and irreconcilable external foe.*

Yet in his next sentence he reversed himself:

> *There is no greater, no more vital task for the Russian State, for the future of the Russian people and the peoples of Russia, as well as for the future of the Revolution than the creation, at all costs, of a stable, resolute, and single revolutionary authority.*

This contradictory sequence reveals more than the routine antagonism between freedom and authority so common in Western political experience. It lays bare a clash of two different worlds. On the one hand we see—if we scan the entire horizon—the emergency of the First World War and the need for total mobilization under a strong government employing the most advanced techniques of production and organization; on the other, the ignorance and lack of experience of the Russian people, their penchant for anarchy. Kerensky, to be sure, would have denied the existence of any contradiction. He would not be pushed to the seemingly obvious conclusion that, if the Russian people were too ignorant and inexperienced, a truly democratic and progressive government authority of the Western type was impossible in Russia, and particularly a Russia at war; even now he clings to his idea. Yet by August 1917 the mounting evidence of disorganization (*razrukha*) had made him hesitate: the realization of his goals was a more difficult task than he had expected. The Russian people did not respond to the supreme crisis of their country with a united and knowledgeable upsurge.

We shall return to Kerensky later. At the moment the point was merely to demonstrate the existence of a painful cultural gap at the most important—and final—level of human interaction, in the political relations between individuals and groups of individuals and in the forging of a new state. The concept of good government held by Kerensky (and essentially by all public figures who backed the Provisional Government) did not meet with sufficient support from the population at large for whose benefit it was intended. But more was challenged: Kerensky's faith in the automatic combination of freedom with effective public authority.

Was such a combination, derived from Western practice, to be taken for granted anywhere outside its original setting?

At this point let us define our terms. 'The West' is used here hypothetically, denoting the formula that gave global predominance to Western civilization. We may think of it as a vastly complex compound like one of the vast molecules of organic chemistry in which all components are mutually attuned to each other. Separated from each other they waste or turn sour. To be sure, certain achievements of the West, its technology, its institutions or ideas—the hard, visible surfaces in short—have long been lifted from their contexts; but their fate outside the original matrix is uncertain; they cannot find the deeper affinities that have sustained them before.

'Westernization' then stands for the massive transfer of these hard visible aspects of Western civilization from England (and the United States), France, Germany, etc., into unprepared societies where the molecule of indigenous society is composed differently and where the impact is bound to fester. The history of Westernization, I think, makes clear that such a transfer has always stemmed from an unwelcome necessity rather than from preference. It is forced on the recipient for the sake of survival (although it is doubtful in the end what native tradition will survive). Everywhere Westernization has come as a subversive force undermining native authority; for native authority obviously did not endow the country with the political or cultural ascendancy which enabled it to export rather than import basic guidelines of human development. In modern Russian history we can see that Western subversion clearly at work, never more powerfully than in the half-century before 1914. It spread its nets in terms of government, society, economic wellbeing, expectations of the good life, in terms of literary taste or fashion. Against this current the tsarist regime had no recourse, try as it might. Indeed, there were powerful forces within the government pressing for more drastic modernization; Russia, they said, was rapidly falling behind in the competition with the industrialized Great Powers. If proof was needed for these alarms, the world war amply supplied it. Of all the prompters of Westernization, military defeat by a more Westernized power is the most persuasive. It compels the sacrifice of any tradition that obstructs the adoption of the Western techniques of powers. But what are the Western techniques of power?

The question is not easily answered, because the Western model is by no means clear-cut or precise. To start with, the Western model offers a bewildering choice, English, American, French, German, to mention but the chief sub-models at the time of the first world war, and within each of these a whole keyboard of attitudes and convictions. Yet there is worse confusion. On the one hand Westernization encourages imitation of its instruments of power, its institutions and other visible and transferable details. On the other hand it teaches that the greatest strength of a people lies within itself, in its sovereignty: the English (or the Americans) do not imitate; they are wholly themselves, both culturally and politically.

This form of imitation, the deliberate assertion of native ways, sometimes encourages the most deep-seated nativism and a return to backwardness which in the end defeats itself. The same paradox occurs as the result of yet another Western import: democracy. Democracy encourages self-expression, self-determination, freedom and spontaneity. These temptations inevitably stir up the depths of tradition, sometimes to the fullness of anti-Westernism. They also affirm and harden every shade of native variety, imperilling whatever precarious unity a country had evolved in the past. Westernization thus always implies a mixture at best, an uneasy merger of native and Western elements as the imports infiltrate into the non-Western environment, and at worst a mortal conflict between incompatible sources of basic inspiration (or authority). What we find then in any society under Western influence is a wide spectrum of inchoate combinations, ambiguity, contradiction, indecision, and a wrangle of many souls in one breast. Thus Westernization enters as a divisive force into a society already burdened with discord.

And finally, Westernization cannot but draw state and society into closer ties with the advanced Western model. This implies more strenuous interaction in terms of economic relations and power politics in peace and war. Whatever form such interaction takes—and it is most arduous in times of war—it will put the country under a tighter necessity of efficiency. It will impose a higher degree of specialization, extort a harder and seemingly more self-denying work discipline, compel a more subtle rationality among individuals and institutions and demand more cohesion and common purpose in society at large just when they are more than ever lacking as a result of Westernization. Such are the unsettling effects of Westernization, and Russia in the throes of revolution showed all of them (though only a few can be pointed out here).

The February revolution itself might be interpreted as the product of Westernization. It embodied the political ideals of constitutional government and democracy as practised in the West and the heightened expectations derived from the prewar contacts with Western Europe; it was fed from the tensions built up by a rapid Westernization and industrialization since the 1890s. It also reflected the wartime pressure for still more rapid modernization, particularly of the army and the economy. The tsarist regime had patently failed to protect the country. It was the task of its successor to introduce a superior efficiency, first in the political framework of the country, and then in everything else that mattered for the national welfare in war and peace.

Let the term revolution be applied, however, more specifically to the eight months between the collapse of the tsarist regime and the Bolshevik coup, when even Lenin would boast that Russia was the freest country in the world. Let it also stand for the lengthy revolutionary chain reaction set off by the February revolution. Since March the people of Russia possessed the freedom to agitate and organize, to express at last their deepest thoughts and feelings, without fear of consequences. In both its dual centres the new government left no doubt that it welcomed such self-expression. As the Provisional Government announced on 7 March, while defending the country 'the Government will at the same time deem it to be its primary duty to open a way to the expression of the popular will with regard to the form of government . . . and . . . to provide the country with laws safeguarding civil liberty and equality in order to enable all citizens to apply freely their spiritual forces to creative work for the benefit of the country'. The Petrograd Soviet trumpeted a more drastic version of the same message to its following: 'We must take the fullest advantage of the present state of affairs. Everyone must form associations, a free press must be created, and meetings must be called where the freedom of speech must be exercised in a tireless struggle against the old order. . . . Form associations, call meetings—agitate! Remember that every minute is valuable during a revolution. . . . The chief strength of the democracy lies in its organization!' The order of the day was: agitate, activate, organize, and agitate again with redoubled strength and make your influence felt to the limits of your organization. And the inhabitants of the empire did organize after March as they had never before.

Propertied and educated Russia was well organized already. Its agencies were ready, the Fourth Duma supplemented by members of its predecessors, the State Council still hovering in the background, the many organizations of trade and industry, and, of course, the party organization of the Kadets now enlarged and strengthened. Among those who had hitherto been deprived of the opportunity, new organizations sprang up like mushrooms; the soviets were only the chief among innumerable lesser groups. It was inevitable that this process of articulating public opinion under the Western slogan of democratic freedom should stir up layers of the population that had traditionally stood entirely outside politics. This process, called 'the deepening of the revolution', must be judged the single most crucial corollary of the revolution of freedom. It was bound to mobilize the furthest recesses of Russian tradition and throw all varieties of outlook and interest and levels of civilization within the empire into stark surface relief.

Let it be pointed out next that in this frenzy of agitation and organization all competitors started with equal opportunities. The race was wide open to what was called 'all the live creative forces of the country'. Only time would reveal where the handicaps lay. At the outset at least the 'censitary' elements patently possessed the strongest assets in their social position and their widely acknowledged experience of public affairs. Yet once under way the process was entirely a matter of trial and error, an exploration of the hidden opportunities of mass politics in the Russian setting. No one could foresee at the time whither it would lead.

Thus the peoples of Russia, with unprecedented suddenness, were propelled into the age of mass politics and thrust up, unprepared, against the problem of reconstituting their government by voluntary agreement. It was a staggering challenge: how in all the seething agitation through the length and breadth of the country could there emerge a central authority sufficient for preserving law and order, preventing the collapse of the economy, and carrying the war to a solution reasonably in line with national interest? The progress of the revolution between February and October added up to an elemental search for a basis of 'a stable, resolute and single revolutionary authority' as an alternative to chaos and the annihilation of Russia's sovereignty. It is important to note, however, that all spokesmen, from the Kadet right to the Bolshevik left, accepted the basic premise that such authority was to express the will of the people, or at least their majority. Yet how this could be done or whether it was possible at all, remained to be seen. Here lay the crux of the political experiment set off by the February revolution.

Pointing to the repeated and mounting demands for a firm and stable authority is not to deny the existence of a strong counter-strain of anarchy. The sudden grant of full freedom encouraged among all layers of the population a penchant for unilateral and precipitious action not cleared with the Provisional Government. The months between February and October abounded with such licence; the unresolved dualism at the centre set a bad example. The same political leaders who called for a firm authority, furthermore, often took the lead in provoking disorders. Wherever one looks in Russia in these months, authority and anarchy were closely intertwined, and any effort to create or assert authority often aggravated the anarchy. The anarchy in turn intensified the search for authority and forced authority to become more authoritarian.

The search for a convincing authority pervaded all aspects of Russian life and government in the months after the February revolution. For a brief illustration of the consequences of that revolution this essay now turns to two vital tasks of the government: providing food and stabilizing the economy.

II. Freedom and the Economy

The supply of food to the army and to the population in the food-importing parts of Russia had posed a grave problem already before the revolution; it had led, in 1915, to the creation of a special Council on Food Supply attached to the Ministry of Agriculture. After the revolution this body was reorganized as the State Committee on Food Supplies; in early April, under strong pressure from the Soviet, it was finally transformed into a fully-fledged state grain monopoly, advised by a central State Food Committee, on which sat—under the new principle of parity representation—the spokesmen of the major forces in public opinion. As a further step towards effective administration, on 19 May a special Ministry of Food Supplies was created. In order to facilitate the work of these agencies the Provisional Government encouraged the establishment of a network of local groups, called the food committees, in the provinces, districts and towns. Eventually much of the work of the grain monopoly devolved upon these bodies: taking charge of local reserves, conducting a census of the crop lands in cultivation and supervising distribution and transportation of the grain under prices fixed by the central government. As it emerged after March, the basic pattern seemed rational enough—on paper.

In reality there was growing chaos. In the first place, one has to remember that the food monopoly was foisted on the Provisional Government by the Soviet. The business community, particularly that group which in the past had conducted the grain trade, was strongly opposed. It wanted more, not less, freedom from the revolution. Barely rid of tsarist meddling, it took the grain monopoly as an entering wedge of an ever more constringent socialism. Its opposition soon came to a head in the State Food Committee, which thus turned into a political forum. Considering the variety of groups represented on it and the widening divergence of their views, it was not surprising that this body, which was to rally public opinion to the support of the grain monopoly, became instead a mere debating society.

The local food committees were even less effective. They were created in only half the provinces (mostly the food-consuming ones), where they rarely acted according to official instructions. The food-producing provinces, on the other hand, proved for the most part extremely uncooperative, even to the point of sabotaging the government's efforts. Where local food committees were established, they became involved in all the tensions of their community and changed their political complexion as opinions became more inflamed. By the autumn they were often taking the law into their own hands, after breaking all ties with the capital. It was no wonder then that as early as May the Provisional Government tried to shift their function to the zemstvos, hoping thereby to introduce greater orderliness. But the zemstvos, too, were caught in the turmoil and incapable of shouldering additional burdens. And as if it had no confidence in its local organs, already in April the government had begun to dispatch special emissaries into the countryside. As S. N. Prokopovich admitted in May: 'We have to extract the grain from the people with the assistance of special expeditions.'

In Western Europe—to put the matter into perspective—the problem of gathering and distributing food for the purposes of war was comparatively easy. The state made use of existing commercial channels for the grain trade, endowing them with the necessary additional controls. In Russia, however, it quickly became apparent that the services of private business were not wanted. The local food committees and other public elements associated with them, like the soviets, were particularly hostile to any participation by commercial agents; the grain merchants were among the most hated of all 'capitalists'. Here and there, to be sure, their cooperation was solicited; but most committees would have nothing to do with them, even to the detriment of their duties. There were cases where local committees were dissolved under local pressure, just because they had relied on 'capitalists'. A. V. Peshekhonov, the Minister of Food, conceded in June that sometimes these merchants had earned this hostility by speculation and dishonesty so that even the tsarist government had begun to bypass them.

Needless to say, the deep-seated hostility between large elements of the population and the grain traders undermined the grain monopoly. By October it was about to collapse. Its abolition was openly discussed in the Ministry of Trade and Industry, which wanted to substitute a bureaucratic apparatus working through commercial channels. This new approach (never carried out) was a part of the hardening of the liberal attitude in the last months before the Bolshevik seizure of power. Another indication of the failure of the grain monopoly was a doubling of the fixed prices of food in September, which could only benefit the producers, particularly the large ones, at the expense of the small consumers. In the absence of a more effective authority, the step may have been necessary in order to bring the hidden reserves to market, but it undermined the public confidence in the grain monopoly. The peasants, too, hastened its débâcle by evading the crop census ordered by the government, by forcibly preventing the transport of grain, or by illegally distilling it and thereby contributing to the drunken orgies that sometimes accompanied rural disorders. The grain monopoly thus ran up against the innate localism, the anticapitalism and the plain anarchy of peasant life.

It was not, however, all stubbornness and ignorance that made the peasant and other producers so anarchic. As long as they received ever less in return for their labours they could not be expected to part with their stores. This realization had prompted the Minister of Agriculture at the very start of the grain monopoly to set up a section in his ministry aiming to provide the peasants with cheap consumer goods, as well as with machinery and fertilizers. This task was taken over in May by the new Ministry of Food Supplies; it became in effect the Ministry of Supplies and Consumer Goods in general (not without competition from the Ministry of Trade and Industry, a far more 'capitalist' ministry, which soon created its own supply committee). The ambition to supply Russia with all necessities, however, had vast implications; it called for no less than state control of the entire enconomy, of production, distribution, consumption and transportation.

It should be remembered in this context that the chief problem facing the Provisional Government in the administration of the grain monopoly was not an overall shortage of grain. Sufficient reserves were left over from the 1916 harvest; and the next harvest was by no means as disastrous as one might deduce from the drift of politics in the summer and autumn of 1917. The problem was primarily one of organizing the collection and distribution of existing stores. That, however, called for a firm and stable authority capable not only of overcoming the conflicting social and political pressures at work among the local and central agencies of the grain monopoly, but also of finding a speedy solution to the land problem, as well as of salvaging Russia's collapsing economy.

Turning now to the economy as a whole, one might well argue that, given the weakness of the transportation systems and the strains of the war, nothing could have stopped the galloping breakdown. The more the railways were worn out by the over-use of equipment, the more trade and industry were bound to suffer; the more their activities were curtailed, the less fuel and metal would reach the railways—in an ever narrowing spiral leading to a dead end. This, however, was not the prognosis of the leading public figures in any camp; they were full of hope. Unfortunately they could not agree over the proper remedies; and their wrangle over economic policy revealed yet another facet of the search for a strong authority.

For the guidance of the economy the Provisional Government had inherited the machinery of economic mobilization devised in 1915 by the Progressive Bloc and its allies among the public and the bureaucracy. Essentially it consisted of the four Special Councils (for defence, fuel, transport and food—the latter already mentioned), and in addition the Central War Industries Committee, altogether a rather uncoordinated and somewhat ineffectual set of agencies. The reason for the confusion and overlapping of competence lay in the fact that the Progressive Bloc had thought the tsarist bureaucracy incapable of achieving the fullest mobilization of Russian industry. The question after March 1917 was whether the new government could impose more effective and better coordinated controls.

The Provisional Government started on its difficult task with the basic assumption that more public participation in the controlling agencies, both central and local, would liberate the creative energies of the Russian people. Thus the bureaucrats on the afore-mentioned councils were largely replaced by delegates from public bodies, from the soviets, the various organizations of trade, industry and finance, the cooperatives (whose role was rapidly increasing), the trade unions, the peasant soviets and similar organizations. At the same time the Provisional Government tried to liberate private initiative through the enactment, immediately after the revolution, of a new corporation law, which gave rise to a minor speculative boom. From March to the summer an unusually large number of new enterprises were incorporated—in the eyes of Russian businessmen the long-awaited opportunity had at last come. Now they hoped to acquire the prosperity and social prestige appropriate to their position in the capitalist era. There was nothing reactionary in their outlook. Following the Western model, they were for the most part ready to support a progressive labour policy, provided, of course, that the rights of management went unchallenged.

Whether this programme could have reversed the drift towards collapse depended on the loyal compliance of the working class. Yet the Russian workers were hardly in the mood to accept the authority of the capitalists, for they too expected to make the most of their new freedom. The February revolution introduced democracy into the very heart of private enterprise. In one of its first measures the Provisional Government, under the pressure of the Soviet, had legalized the factory committees, elected bodies of workers all too ready to encroach on the rights of management. These factory committees sprang up with great speed, more rapidly than the more elaborate trade unions, and were patently more expressive of the mentality of the workers. They instinctively tended to tighten the cohesion of the work force, sometimes by throwing out men of non-working class (or non-peasant) background. They were also likely to view the factory as the peasants viewed the land, as a source of livelihood that rightly belonged to them. When the management threatened to shut down production, for lack of fuel, raw materials, operating funds, or of plain entrepreneurial energy in exceedingly difficult times, the factory committees often attempted to run the factories themselves. Under these conditions the relations between the *fabkomy* and the management were strained at best, and production inevitably suffered. This was obviously no time to impose tight labour discipline. The incessant political activities of hitherto passive workers, the uncertainties of the time, the falling purchasing power of their wages, the material difficulties of life in general, which always hit the workers hardest—all contributed to the growing anarchy in the factories, mills and mines. Was it a wonder that in their new freedom the workers were speaking their own minds, untutored though they were in the rationalities of industry and commerce or in the complexities of modern society, and if they spoke with a vengeance?

In May the crisis in industrial relations exploded into the government through the resignation of the Minister of Trade and Industry, A. I. Konovalov, one of the most enlightened spokesmen of the Russian business community. In a speech shortly before his resignation he issued a sharp warning: 'The slogans which are being thrust into the midst of the workers, exciting the dark instincts of the mob, are followed by destruction, anarchy, and the annihilation of public and national life.' In other words, democracy as the workers saw it was incompatible with industrial production sufficient to carry on the war and to supply the population with the necessities of life.

Yet there was another threat that drove Konovalov to despair: undue pressure on the Provisional Government from the Soviet and from its representative in the cabinet, the new Minister of Labour, M. I. Skobelev. For under Menshevik inspiration the Soviet, too, had analysed the economic crisis and drawn up its own recommendations (formulated by V. G. Groman).

The Soviet leadership viewed the economic goals of the revolution very differently from the business community. It felt no scruples over the extension of government control. Groman admired the British and still more the German system of wartime industrial mobilization; as a Marxist he rejoiced in phrases like 'the planned regulation of economic life'. In May the Soviet stepped forward with plans for 1) the compulsory cartellization of the industries concerned with coal, oil, metals, sugar, paper; 2) governmental control of all banks and credit institutions; and 3) universal labour conscription after the German model 'in order to combat idleness'. Finally, it demanded greatly stepped-up taxation of income and profits. Even Lenin found these plans somewhat extreme; they were unacceptable, of course, to the Provisional Government. Prokopovich, eventually Konovalov's successor, argued that, while such things were possible in England or Germany, Russia was not ready for them.

Under Soviet pressure, however, the Provisional Government ordered the four ministries most directly concerned (Trade and Industry, Finance, Labour and Food Supply) to draft a proposal for an effective economic policy. One of the results was a memorandum written by V. A. Stepanov, the acting minister of trade and industry. It was a curious document containing two contradictory recommendations. On the one hand, it said that the Provisional Government must make it clear once and for all that Russia was heading for a 'capitalist order'. On the other hand he admitted that 'the government cannot recommend to the country a return to a free economy. . . . The economic disorder does not allow a predominance of private interests.' He went so far as to advocate the imitation of the German model for compulsory cartellization for whole branches of industry, and Government regulation of labour relations as well.

This memorandum revealed the confusion created by dual power in the field of economic policy. Neither a clear-cut principle of action nor a forthright authority arose to guide the economic development in times of disintegration. Was it surprising then that the government favoured a debilitating compromise? In June it created an Economic Council charged with drafting 'a general plan for the organization of the national economy and of labour' and a subsidiary Central Economic Committee charged with carrying out its recommendations. At the same time it packed these bodies with a majority of 'capitalists' under the leadership of leading industrialists.

The Economic Council was a large body containing, besides the representatives of the ministries concerned, the delegates of the Soviet, the Congresses of Trade and Industry, of the banks, cooperatives, the grain traders, trade unions, zemstvos and professional economists. With such diversity of outlook the Economic Council shared the fate of the State Food Committee and quickly degenerated into a debating society. In September it was dissolved, under the pressure of the business community, having accomplished nothing. Its functions were absorbed by the Central Economic Committee, which had less ambitious tasks and did not raise ideological questions. The suppression of the Economic Council, incidentally, was yet another step in the efforts of the propertied elements to consolidate their position in the interval between the failure of Kornilov and the Bolshevik coup.

The currency and the budget, too, faced chaos in those months. It came as a shock when N. V. Nekrasov, the Minister of Finance, announced at the Moscow State Conference that the revolution had been far more extravagant financially than the autocracy. This was not entirely surprising, considering that the revolt against the tsarist regime had been, in some respects, also a revolt against poverty. Now that the former penny-pinching authority had been overthrown, the many new public authorities that succeeded it spent more freely and irresponsibly. But something more ominous was involved. A zemstvo official reported on the same occasion that he had found a strange attitude in the countryside: money was a bourgeois institution and therefore could be spent to one's heart's content. 'Never', so he reported, 'had there been such reckless spending.' Thus state expenditures skyrocketed while tax receipts fell off sharply, compelling the government to resort ever more freely to the printing press for its supply of money.

Taxation was another political issue undermining the authority of the Provisional Government. The tsarist government had introduced the income tax in 1916; in May and June of 1917, under pressure from the Soviet, its successor sharply increased the income tax as well as the tax on war profits, though not as radically as the Soviet had desired. Before the Bolshevik coup the high rates, however, were reduced again in view of the financial distress of the propertied classes (this again was part of the hardening of the liberal attitude). The Liberty Loan, proclaimed soon after the February revolution, was a further effort on the part of the new government to tap the financial reserves of the country and to limit the rampant inflation. Yet it did not catch hold. The working classes could not and would not save, and the 'capitalists' in their apprehension held back. By autumn the loan was considered a relative failure. The slow returns on the loan prompted plans for a more drastic capital levy, which, however, were not carried out either. The 'egotism' of the propertied classes did not go unobserved and uncriticized, even among moderates. Yet in the absence of a firm and stable authority one can hardly blame the 'capitalists' for taking what private precautions they could: their worst traits were reinforced by the general insecurity. This meant widespread speculation, black-market operations and sometimes irresponsibly high living.

The economic decline accentuated the traditional sharp inequalities in Russian society. The government and every important political leader, including Lenin, constantly urged the utmost sacrifices for the cause of the country. But it remained an open question who was making such sacrifices and who was to judge how real and extensive they were. From May onwards, each group was accusing the others of 'narrow class feeling', but in the end the opinion of the largest number, i.e. of the workers, soldiers and peasants, carried the day. The deep-seated egalitarianism of the peasant *soslovie* was running stronger than ever, now that it could be openly expressed. Anybody living in a better style, so peasant opinion argued, should be making a proportionately greater sacrifice until he had reached the common level; and who could deny that from the material point of view the toilers were still worse off than the *burzhui?* In these months of rapidly deteriorating conditions hunger and cold thus divided the Russian polity ever more deeply and broke down whatever authority and prestige had accrued to the privileged classes during the good years before the war. Hunger and cold also aggravated the divisions over basic economic policy.

One may describe the opposing positions in the economic struggle roughly as follows. On the one hand we find the supporters of a system of free enterprise modified, as in England, by progressive labour legislation and by the necessities of the war cautiously interpreted. They wanted to leave the right of management untouched; workers' control was anathema to them, as was central control by a state planning agency. They knew from experience that the workers were not qualified to run the factories according to the demands of modern competitive efficiency (within the country as well as in the international market); and they agreed with Prokopovich that under Russian conditions effective planning, even of the kind at work in wartime Germany, was hopelessly utopian. Finally, they argued that after the war Russia would need large foreign loans; these could be obtained only from Western capitalists for capitalist purposes.

Their opponents, on the other hand, marshalled an equally strong rebuttal. Given the conditions of Russia, it was obvious that all aspects of the economy were interdependent. If there was to be enough food, manufactured goods had to reach the village; they had to be produced in sufficient quantities, under priorities determined by the needs of state and society. Given the scarcities, furthermore, consumption too would have to be regulated. Under the hard necessities of the moment, therefore, the socialist economists might seem to have had the best of the argument. Only a central and all-encompassing authority could undertake the rational revival of the economy. The socialist view, however, was deficient in regard to the details of planning: how were the central plans to be carried out at the grass-roots? Thus again the question of authority was raised. The Menshevik planners assumed, of course, that with the widest possible democratic participation the problem could be solved. But that assumption the 'capitalists', with a more realistic experience of the working class, knew to be false.

The conflict of rival interests and panaceas dissolved whatever central authority over the Russian economy the Provisional Government had inherited. Eventually production and distribution became a matter of catch-as-catch-can. Even before the Bolshevik coup Petrograd was informed that in certain areas of the country the economy was lapsing into a state of barter. Manufactured goods of local production were being exchanged against local foodstuffs. Only a strong central authority with strong local agents and an effective administrative apparatus could restore an effective national economy.

III. Mass Politics and the Problem of Leadership

The foregoing has given a few examples showing how the February revolution, instead of introducing a superior efficiency, created disruption and chaos in every aspect of the economy (not to mention here state administration, the war effort or foreign policy). At the same time the growing disorganization intensified the search, in each separate branch of public service as well as in state and society in general, for an authority capable of restoring order and strengthening the country. The question now arises: what were the positions taken in regard to this search by a few of

the leading public figures of the day? The traditional authority of the tsarist regime was ended forever, and all the lesser authorities like landlord,
employer and even priest, who at critical moments had derived a considerable part of their power from the police or the army, were discredited
too. The new men had to find a fresh source of authority and tap new
well-springs of cohesion amidst the deepening revolution for an ever
more exacting government if Russia was to survive as a Great Power.
How did they propose, in the competition for leadership, to solve this
problem?

Beginning with P. N. Milyukov's party, the 'Party of Popular Freedom', as it also called itself, we find that its official programme, adopted
in late March, went over unreservedly to the premises of democratic politics. It proclaimed as its guiding objectives 'the inviolability of civil liberty and equality, . . . the guarantee of the complete rule of the popular
will', and finally and more vaguely, the achievement of 'social justice'. Yet
Milyukov, the party's leader, revealed a strange misjudgement of the implications of this programme when, early in May, he insisted that his
party stood to the left of centre in the political spectrum of the day. So
strong was the pull of the old order and so little known the essence of the
new! At the same time, however, Milyukov made a shrewder observation,
saying, with his eyes on people like Chernov and Lenin: 'It should be recognized that the old conspirators, who have applied their experience
under the new conditions which are extremely favourable to them, are
more experienced in the matter of organizing the masses.'

If the secret of success lay in mass organization, the Kadets were
strongly handicapped. Although the party had officially declared itself in
favour of a republic, Milyukov, a monarchist at heart, did not trust the
masses. Nor did his party accept the consequences of its professions. Its
spokesmen began to play down the boons of freedom and urged more discipline, restraint, sacrifice and patriotism. By May many Kadets had become disillusioned with freedom. What then was left for Milyukov and
his party to do?

Their answer was apparent in their subsequent words and deeds. In
the first place they tried to broaden their popular support from among all
propertied and educated elements, to become, in other words, the conservative party *par excellence*. They also strove, by admonition and action, to
bolster the authority of the Provisional Government and of the state as
the historic body of Russia. Increasingly they cast themselves in the role
of 'the party of the principle of statesmanship', presuming to stand above
party and self-interest, without, however, losing faith that the masses were
with them. 'In the end', V. A. Maklakov predicted in August, 'the masses,
whose voice . . . is the voice of God . . . , will instinctively understand
who is destroying them and who is leading them to salvation.' Without
this self-deception the Kadets, one suspects, would have been unable to
face the prospect of a Constituent Assembly based on universal suffrage.
Yet at the time of the Moscow State Conference some more realistic Kadets were turning to the authority of the machine gun.

By temperament and conviction, as well as by his work, Kerensky stood closer to the masses, 'the hostage of democracy' in the Provisional Government, as he was called in the weeks after February, always 'heeding the voice of [his] socialist and revolutionary conscience'.

His authority derived from the February revolution. Secure in the support of the Temporary Committee of the Duma he had brought to its support the active revolutionary thrust of the Soviet of workers and soldiers. He had succeeded in doing so largely by his sheer inexhaustible energy, by his reputation as the defender of freedom and justice under the tsarist regime and by the reach of his magnificent voice. He alone had seemed to be in control of the rapidly unfolding events. In that grand moment, when the hatred of the old regime united the most diverse social and political outlooks, he had received his baptism of mass politics; the exultation of that historic hour cemented his conviction that on this basis a new and better Russia could be built.

As time went by, and the revolutionary democracy shifted to the left, he moved to the right, relatively speaking. But he always tried to bridge the widening gap between 'capitalists' and 'socialists'. As he has recently written: 'From the moment of the collapse of the monarchy . . . until the downfall in October, I found myself in the center of events. I was in fact the focal point, the center of the vortex of human passions and conflictive ambitions which raged around me in the titanic struggle to erect a new state. . . .' In an earlier volume he referred to himself at the time of the Moscow State Conference as 'the mathematical point of unity'.

Though pinpointing himself at the hub, it was his ambition to wheel far and wide both right and left. Like the Kadets he felt above party, aiming to represent the whole of Russia, yet with a keener eye on the revolutionary masses and the soviets. At the Moscow State Conference he hopefully spoke of 'those obscure levels of socio-political life, for which the time has not yet come perhaps to express themselves aloud'. Like the Kadets he hoped that eventually, at the time of the Constituent Assembly, they would rally around him. His faith in the masses, acquired in the glorious days of February, never entirely forsook him, even though in early August he had passed through a mood of disillusionment. He remained wedded to the democratic premise that the only true source of political authority lay in public opinion, and to the delusion that public opinion would back him up at the decisive moment.

What enabled him to rise above the bitter conflicts that surrounded him and to overlook the ambiguities and contradictions in his own programme was, one might surmise, his confidence in the sway of his oratory. He was the first great spellbinder of modern mass politics. By working himself into an emotional frenzy and pouring out his innermost self he tried to reach into the same depths among his listeners, hoping to find there at last the common ground on which to establish his ascendancy and to create unity. Maurice Paléologue has left us a description of Kerensky's effectiveness as an orator:

The fierce intensity of his features, the flow of words alternately halting and torrential, the sudden vagaries of his train of thought, the somnambulistic deliberation of his gesture, the fixity of his gaze and his twitching lips and bristling hair made him look like a monomaniac or one possessed. At such time his audience shudders visibly. All interruptions cease, all opposition is brushed aside, individual wills melt into nothingness and the whole assembly communes together in a sort of trance.

The effects of such success were soon showing in Kerensky's behaviour. As early as March Sukhanov and others on the left had suspected him of Bonapartist designs. By August, after he had established himself in the Winter Palace, everyone began to notice how he struck several of Napoleon's favourite poses. He had come upon a tempting model—a historic figure creating, by the power of his own personality, the authority necessary for summing up a great revolution. Years later a chastened Kerensky likened himself to more modest contemporaries who symbolized in their persons the resilience of their countries at war: Lloyd George and Clemenceau. But there was really no parallel.

The fact was that in trying to cast his spell over all 'the live creative forces of Russia' his voice did not carry far or deep enough. Despite his frantic appeals to patriotism he did not strike any common ground at all. His frenzy did not lay bare, as did Hitler's, the hidden layers of a common instinct; he did not speak to the condition of the Russian masses.

One reason for this failure, no doubt, was that his speech lacked clarity. He was caught in all the compromises and contradictions of the coalition government, and he suffered from a lack of reality. When, for instance, he said at the Moscow State Conference that 'Russian democracy is imbued with the spirit of love for the State, with the idea of freedom', he voiced a patent contradiction: popular freedom and a strong government did not go together, as he himself had pointed out to the commissars a few days before. The phrase was pure verbiage, typical of Kerensky's Western-oriented idealism. What fantastic idealism! As he told the Ukrainian nationalist, Professor Hrushevsky: 'With good will one can get anywhere; a socialist can persuade his people to do anything.' And what illusion! To this day Kerensky denies the existence of dual power, calling it 'a legend' put forth by the enemies of the Provisional Government. After the Kornilov plot he was clearly out of touch with the drift of events.

One can hardly argue that the Soviet leaders like Tsereteli and other prominent Mensheviks possessed more realism, although they enjoyed one advantage. Their following, at least at the start, was more clearly defined than Kerensky's. It consisted almost exclusively of members of the peasant *soslovie* in the cities and towns, mills and factories, and in the armies of Russia, with the soldier-peasants heavily over-represented, as even Lenin complained. From the start this category of citizens arrogated to itself the term 'democracy', and the presumption spoke volumes about the soviet state of mind. The term claimed that the masses were overwhelmingly behind the Petrograd Soviet, and that it represented the voice of the people down to 'those obscure levels of socio-political life' to which Kerensky had alluded. The claim unwittingly undercut—or at least challenged —the monopoly of the Constituent Assembly. It established a rival authority, presumably with an absolute majority of the popular vote, and, what was even more important, with a modicum of social cohesion. That cohesion was born of centuries of oppression and legal segregation from the rest of the population, a very real force in 1917, yet—we must add —a negative one, unfortunately, strongest in opposition to innovation and modern statehood in general.

The soviets also stood out, at least intermittently, as an overwhelming political force at the seat of government, in Petrograd, and to a lesser extent in other industrial and military centres. Their constituents had made the revolution, whatever the subsequent explanations of the Kadets, and they showed their might again in April and May. Thereafter their influence declined, because they lost some of their original unity when parts of the garrison and of the working class turned towards the Bolsheviks, and their leaders ceased to trust them. These leaders, it should be added, had never fully recognized the soviets as a suitable basis for state authority because, like the liberals, they judged their following incapable of sustaining the responsibilities of government. They praised the soviets as a truly Russian and revolutionary institution, but would not explore their potentials; they adhered to the view that the government must represent *all* groups of society, not only those gathered in the soviets. Whether this conviction could be squared with the majority principle of democracy was an issue which they never raised. Like Milyukov, they never seemed to have analysed rationally the quantitative distribution of votes once 'the obscure levels of socio-political life' had been activated. And deep in their hearts they feared the implications for the democratic Russia which was their ideal. Thus they would not let go of their alliance with 'censitary' Russia, which in their eyes possessed the qualities that the masses lacked.

Neither would they let go of their source of power. They did, however, shift their ground, as their soviet constituency became more radical. From August onwards they searched for a wider representation of 'the democracy', even occasionally dropping the customary adjective 'revolutionary'. Now they appealed to *all* 'democratic' groups, such as the cooperatives, trade unions, peasant organizations, zemstvo workers, land committees and the like, none as revolutionary as the soviets. Yet could the All-Russian Central Executive Committee of the All-Russian Congress of Soviets reconstruct on this new basis the cohesion and authority that had so readily emerged from the Petrograd Soviet when it first gathered?

The test for this experiment came after the failure of the Kornilov putsch, when the Second Coalition collapsed and the political initiative for a spell fell to Tsereteli and the Menshevik leaders (at a time when they were fatally losing ground in local elections). At that moment Tsereteli urged 'all the real, vital forces of the country' to 'unite around a single revolutionary power' emerging from a body representing all democratic organization. This new attitude prompted the calling of the Democratic Conference. Yet as it convened, the boldness of the Mensheviks, caused by the Kornilov crisis and the mobilization of resistance from below, had already melted away. The Democratic Conference was left without firm leadership. And after much confused balloting on the issue of a renewal of the coalition, 'There turned out to be no agreement, no unity of will that could be translated into reality by the force of the whole democracy or by its greater majority'. In these words Tsereteli himself expressed the results of the experiment in a devastating indictment of its futility. Soon after Kerensky again seized the initiative and called the Council of the Republic (or preparliament) which absorbed most of the democratic organizations and fell back into the familiar rut of compromise.

The episode proved not only that there existed no effective organization of 'the democracy' outside the soviets, but also that the Menshevik leaders could not bring themselves to entrust the future of the country to the masses. Their failure showed that—whatever the adumbrations of the ideologists—the crucial dividing line between the opposing forces in Russia at the time did not lie between 'capitalists' and 'socialists', or even between moderates and maximalists. It lay rather between those who knew that the masses were incapable of coping, by their own initiative and wisdom, with the monumental tasks of statehood and modernization that confronted Russia, and those who, however foolishly, thought that the masses could cope or—more likely in this age of mass politics and total mobilization—that the masses *must be made* to cope with these tasks. It was over this issue that men decided whether Russia was to stay capitalist or go socialist. Only Lenin took the latter view.

From the start of the revolution Lenin had been more clearly aware than his rivals that politics in the age of imperialism was mass politics. His whole thought and action were geared to the twin propositions that the war had stirred up the masses of all belligerent countries to their depths and that this had created a potent and still unexploited source of political power which he could use for his own ends.

Even before his return to Russia he ordered his followers in Petrograd to 'counter the magnificent organisation of the Russian bourgeoisie and the entire bourgeois intelligentsia with an equally magnificent organisation of the proletariat, which must lead the entire vast mass of urban and rural poor, the semi-proletariat and small proprietors'. The task of the moment, so he told them, was to draw the 'unprecedentedly broad masses of the oppressed classes into an organisation that would take over the military, political and economic functions of the state'. After his arrival in April he became the most astute practitioner of mass politics in the country, rivalling and eclipsing Kerensky.

In these months of agitation it was he rather than Kerensky who probed into 'the obscure levels of socio-political life' in order to win over the 'unprecedentedly large masses of proletarians who have just awakened to political life', as the April Theses put it. The slogans which he set for the party that month spelled out the charge in further detail: 'To carry on propaganda and agitation from group to group in every regiment, in every factory and, particularly, among the most backward masses. . . . To organise, organise, and once more organise the proletariat in every factory, in every district, in every city quarter.' This became Bolshevik routine, to be stepped up to the utmost after Trotsky became president of the Petrograd Soviet. In Lenin and particularly in Trotsky the Bolsheviks possessed rhetorical talent almost as brilliant as Kerensky's. But they preferred the persistent and more direct pressure of the ubiquitous small agitators—there was no loudspeaker as yet to carry the leaders' voice into the masses everywhere.

It was not clear, however, from Lenin's analyses who exactly belonged to the masses. He always included the proletariat (whatever that signified in the Russian setting), but also added the semi-proletarian elements, the poorest peasantry, and the petty bourgeoisie that might be won over to the proletariat. His terminology remained highly ambiguous from a strict Marxist point of view; it became even vaguer as time went by, although perhaps more realistic in view of Russian conditions. The aptest term in his political vocabulary was perhaps 'the toiling masses'—obviously of *narodnik* inspiration—which in essence meant the members of the peasant *soslovie,* particularly those in cities, towns, mills and factories, and in the army.

It cannot be said, however, that Lenin viewed these masses with unqualified admiration. While still in Switzerland, he raised the crucial question: 'Do the masses of the Russian workers possess sufficient class consciousness, fortitude and heroism to perform' the miracles of organization necessary for the future? He answered frankly: 'We don't know.' But he leapt boldly and willingly forward into the unknown: experience alone could tell, he wrote, and also what he called 'the locomotive of history', the progress of the war, starvation and incalculable hardship. 'Let the masses be tormented hard enough, and they will play at last their predestined role as a constructive social force.' Thus, roughly, one may rephrase his revolutionary faith. Yet he too had his doubts. In April he despaired of Russia as the most petty bourgeois country in Europe, and he did so again in September. In those moments Tsereteli and other Mensheviks always flinched and fell back on the 'capitalists' for their superior knowledge. Lenin, with the courage of his conviction, took a different turn. He put his confidence in the organization of the proletarian vanguard, the Bolshevik party, to guide the erring masses. 'The less the organizational experience of the Russian people', he wrote in April, 'the more resolutely must we proceed to organizational development by the people themselves.'

Yet, if we look closely at Lenin's writings in this period, we perceive an unconscious duplicity in his thought. On the one hand he dwelt with pride on the creative power of the Russian masses; on the other he retained his misgivings about their petty-bourgeois or plain anarchist character and fell back on the power of organization concentrated in the vanguard. The first was the dominant theme in 1917. Over and over again he expressed his trust in the creative energies of the proletarian masses. But one could also hear a persistent note of desperation in the praise of revolutionary enthusiasm.

It was desperation which strengthened the authoritarian element opposed to the untrammelled creativity of the masses in Lenin's thought. Even when calling for revolutionary enthusiasm he stressed the need for strict organization and comradely discipline. He used the word discipline almost as often as Kerensky. The qualifying adjectives were different, but the meaning essentially the same. How far he might go in this direction was revealed in his speech to the All-Russian peasant congress in May when he stressed that the transition to a better way of life 'requires the greatest labour effort, . . . concentration, determination and energy on the part of each peasant and worker at his own place, at his own particular job, which he knows and has been working at for years'. This would indicate an endorsement of specialization and contradict his views as subsequently expressed in *State and Revolution*.

The fact was that both strands of thought were present side by side. It was Lenin's predicament that he tried to square the circle. He wanted democratic centralism, to combine control with spontaneity, trust the masses and not trust them, use their experience and ability and yet call for the services of bourgeois experts at above-scale wages and for the brotherly assistance of the more highly-developed Western proletariat. And more, like his rivals Lenin was never free of the fear of chaos that might overtake Russia. In October one of his arguments in favour of a speedy Bolshevik seizure of power was just that: 'a wave of real anarchy may become stronger than we are'.

Thus even in Lenin we find no unqualified acceptance of the soviets or of the masses as a firm and reliable basis for authority. What he stood for was the recognition 1) that the crisis of Russia—as well as of civilization in the era of imperialism—required a political solution that worked with and through the masses, not against them, and 2) that the only effective basis of authority in Russia lay in the institution which the revolutions of 1905 and 1917 had thrust up from amidst the urbanized and industrialized segments of the peasant *soslovie*. He alone of all competing public figures was willing to make use of what measure of social cohesion he could find in the soviet clientele. He tried to strengthen it further by a strong infusion of nationalism, first cultivated by the Socialist Revolutionaries and soon adopted by the Bolsheviks for their own ends, and by constantly stoking the fire under the old fears and hatreds. Yet he was fully aware of the weakness of that base. It needed constant rallying through the élan of leadership, through decision, control, prodding and education coming from a disciplined body that stood outside and ahead of it. At best the contradictory elements of Lenin's appraisal of the soviets as a source of authority were held in an uneasy balance. The slightest crisis would upset it, always in favour of more organization and sterner discipline.

Let us now return to our beginnings, to Kerensky's lament about the free people of Russia who were too ignorant and inexperienced for the tasks of government confronting them, and to our reflections on freedom and authority which were much further apart in Russia than in the Western model. If we bring Lenin into that context, we find, I think, that he was hardly less utopian than Kerensky in trying to harness freedom and authority. Though Lenin proved more in command of the conditions under which they worked and more successful in imposing a harness, the congenital flaw in the mixture of the Western model with Russian realities was (and still is) imprinted in all his achievements.

After half a century's experience with global Westernization we should say, however, that the fault was not really his. The flaw is inherent in any effort to fuse the two incompatible cultural molecules of Western order and native tradition. Good government based on consensus—to take but the political facet of the Western model—does not fit the home-grown moulds of mind and institutions, particularly not when native traditions in state and society are under great strain to defend their sovereignty. In the alien setting freedom—and even reason and conscience (to hark back once more to Kerensky's words quoted at the outset)—degenerate into anarchy, for the invisible restraints that make freedom into a constructive force by limiting its application to certain well-circumscribed channels are not exported along with the temptations of liberation.

The tasks confronting the leaders in non-Western societies, we might conclude, are thus radically different from those of Western statesmanship. Kerensky and Lenin were trying to hitch together two disparate universes of value rather than reform or adjust existing traditions. But in mixing the Western and the native worlds they could not escape the basic paradox of Westernization: because they were willing to undertake the mastery of mass politics in the Russian setting, they liberated the largest volume of native sentiment ever released into the Russian polity in modern history. Westernization in politics inevitably led to political 'nativization' as well—which meant that the job of modernization in the larger sense had barely started. The process of Westernization had to begin from scratch. If it was to succeed, it had to be carried through on a mass basis and through a native authority, by a revolution from above that pretended to be guided from below in the name of an un-Western or anti-Western people.

With the Bolshevik coup the pressure of modernization had barely been met. The revolutionary chain-reaction set off in February had been brought under control, at least in principle, and revolutionary spontaneity had been tamed by a strong authority capable of safeguarding Russian interests in the global competition. Yet only the political takeoff point had been secured. The job of bringing Russia up to the most advanced contemporary standards of state, society and the economy lay still ahead. The efficiency and power of the model had—and has—yet to be matched.

EDWARD HALLETT CARR

The idea of progress and belief in history as a meaningful process, issuing from the Enlightenment and consecrated by the French Revolution, were a dominant creed of the nineteenth century. Marx fortified the belief in progress and the belief in history with the belief in revolution as "the locomotive of history" and, in so doing, created the first theory of revolution. It was appropriate that his name and doctrine should serve as the beacon for the next great revolution. In the interval between the final elaboration of Marx's system and the next revolution of 1917 much had changed, but much also had survived, so that, when we consider the historical significance of the Russian Revolution, we see the interaction of a Marxist or pre-Marxist revolutionary tradition and a neo-Marxist or post-Marxist revolutionary environment. One thing that had not changed— or, rather, that had been greatly intensified—was the emphasis on productivity. Marx stood on the shoulders of the Enlightenment thinkers and of the classical economists in treating production as the essential economic activity, to which all other categories were subsidiary: and he was in essence right when he saw the key to the future in the hands of the industrial worker and treated the individual peasant cultivator of the soil as an obsolescent unit of production. The Russian Revolution for the first time explicitly proclaimed the goal of increased production and identified it with socialism: Lenin's remark that socialism meant electrification plus the Soviets was the first primitive formulation of this idea. It was repeated over and over again by Lenin and other Bolsheviks that the test of socialism was that it could organize production more efficiently than capitalism. One of the few glimpses afforded by Marx of the Communist utopia was that there the springs of wealth would flow more abundantly. The success of the Soviet campaign for industrialization, which in 30 years, starting from a semi-literate population of primitive peasants, raised the USSR to the position of the second industrial country in the world and the leader in some of the most advanced technological developments, is perhaps the most significant of all the achievements of the Russian Revolution. Nor can the achievement be measured purely in material terms. In the time span of half a century, a population almost 60 percent urban has replaced a population more than 80 percent peasant; a high standard of general education has replaced near illiteracy; social services have been built up; even in agriculture, which remains the stepchild— or problem child—of the economy, the tractor has replaced the

Source: Edward Hallett Carr, "A Historical Turning Point: Marx, Lenin, Stalin," in Richard Pipes, ed., *Revolutionary Russia* (Cambridge: Harvard University Press, 1968), pp. 282–94. Copyright © 1968 by Richard Pipes. Reprinted by permission of the publishers.

wooden plough as the characteristic instrument of cultivation. It would be wrong to minimize or condone the sufferings and the horrors inflicted on large sections of the Russian people in the process of transformation. This was a historical tragedy, which has not yet been outlived, or lived down. But, however the reckoning is made, it would be idle to deny that the sum of human well-being and human opportunity is immeasurably greater in Russia today than it was fifty years ago. It is this achievement that has most impressed the rest of the world and has inspired in industrially undeveloped countries the ambition to imitate it.

The world in which the USSR embarked on industrialization was, however, a very different world from that of Marx. It was not only technology that had advanced. Man's attitude to nature and his conception of his place in the economic process had also radically changed. The neo-Marxist world was a world of self-consciousness. The Russian Revolution was the first great revolution in history to be deliberately planned and made. The English revolution received its name *ex post facto* not from the politicians who made it, but from the intellectuals who theorized about it. The men who brought about the French Revolution did not want to make a revolution; the Enlightenment was not in intention or in essence a revolutionary movement. The self-declared revolutionaries appeared only after the revolution had begun. The revolution of 1848 was a conscious imitation of the French Revolution: this is presumably why Namier called it a "revolution of the intellectuals." Its one positive achievement was to extend to some parts of Central Europe some of the results of the French Revolution. The Russian Revolution was also a revolution of intellectuals, but of intellectuals who not only sought to make a revolution, but to analyze and prepare the conditions in which it could be made. It is this element of self-consciousness that gives the Russian Revolution its unique place in modern history.

The nature of the change can be analyzed in terms of the differences between Marx and Lenin, of the transition from Marxism to Leninism. Although nearly everything that Lenin wrote can be supported by quotations from Marx, the differences between them were profound and significant. The differences are sometimes explained as being due to the transplantation of Marxism to Russian soil: Leninism is Marxism adapted to Russian needs and conditions. There is much truth in this view. But it is more fruitful to think of the differences as the product of a difference in time: Leninism is Marxism of the epoch no longer of objective and inexorable economic laws, but of the conscious ordering of economic and social processes for desired ends.

The growth of consciousness begins in the economic sphere. So long as the individual producer and the small entrepreneur predominated, nobody seemed to control the economy as a whole, and the illusion of impersonal laws and processes was preserved. Marx's world picture was firmly grounded in the past. He learned from Adam Smith that individual entrepreneurs and owners of capital were the essential agents of production in bourgeois society; and he followed Adam Smith and Hegel in believing that the activity of individuals, acting in their own interests, led in virtue of objective laws—the counterpart of the "hidden hand" or the "cunning of reason"—to results independent of their own will and purpose.

Although Marx rejected the providential harmony of interests, he did believe that ultimate harmony would result from the economically motivated action of individuals: this absolved him from any deliberate planning for the future. All economic thinkers from Adam Smith to Karl Marx believed in objective economic laws and in the validity of predictions derived from them. This was the essence of "classical economics." The change came when technological advance gave birth to large-scale capitalism. With the arrival of the mammoth manufacturing corporation and trading cartel, the economic scene was dominated by what, in a masterly understatement, was described as "imperfect competition." Economics had become instrumental—a matter not so much of scientific prediction as of conscious manipulation. Spontaneous price adjustment through the law of supply and demand was replaced by price regulation for specific economic ends. It was no longer possible to believe in a world governed by objective economic laws. The hidden hand that pulled the strings was barely concealed by the velvet glove of the great corporations.

These developments made quite unrealistic the old conception of the "night-watchman" state, mounting guard to ensure fair play between a host of small independent competitive producers. The socialists, though they appear to have invented the term "planning," were far behind German industrialists, bankers, and academic economists in their recognition of the direction and the inevitability of the processes at work. The first more or less fully planned national economy in modern times was the German economy at the height of World War I, with the British and French economies lagging not far behind. When the revolution proved victorious in Russia, the case for planning rested both on socialist precept and on the example of the German war economy. The first long-term plan to be formally adopted in Soviet Russia was the plan of electrification in 1920. The first "five-year plan of the national economy" was adopted for the period 1928–29 to 1932–33. Since then the USSR, except in the war period, has never been without its five-year plan; and five-year plans (or sometimes six- or seven-year plans) have proliferated around the world. If one wishes to assess the historical significance of the Russian Revolution in terms of the influence exercised by it, productivity, industrialization, and planning are key words.

The transition from economic *laissez faire* to economic management (whether management by corporations or management by the state), from spontaneity to planning, from the unconscious to the conscious, had corresponding repercussions on social policy. The *Communist Manifesto* had accused the bourgeoisie of "naked, shameless, direct, brutal exploitation" of the worker. Yet, so long as poverty or bad housing or unemployment could be attributed to the operation of objective economic laws, consciences were appeased by the argument that anything done to remedy these misfortunes would be done in defiance of economic laws and would therefore in the long run only make things worse. Once, however, everything that happened in the economy was seen as the result of a deliberate human decision, and therefore avoidable, the argument for positive action became irrefutable. Compassion for unavoidable suffering was replaced by indignation at unnecessary suffering. The concept of exploitation acquired a new dimension. For Marx exploitation was not an incidental abuse of which individuals were guilty, but an essential characteristic of the capitalist system, ineradicable so long as that system lasted. Exploitation now became a misdemeanor that could be prevented or mitigated by remedial action. A perceptive English conservative writer in the last volume of the Cambridge Modern History, published in 1910, diagnosed the change of climate and defined by implication the character of the next revolution:

> The belief in the possibility of social reform by conscious effort is the dominant current of the European mind; it has superseded the belief in liberty as the one panacea. . . . Its currency in the present is as significant and as pregnant as the belief in the rights of man about the time of the French revolution.

The Russian Revolution of 1917 was the first revolution in history committed to establish social justice through economic controls organized by political action.

The reassertion, due to the advance of technology and economic organization, of the need for political action to direct and control the economy, was reflected in a change of emphasis in Marxist doctrine. Marx's nineteenth-century belief in the primacy of economics over politics had been cautiously qualified, after his death, by Engels' famous remarks about the mutual interaction of base and superstructure. The change fitted readily into Russian conditions. At the turn of the century, the controversy between the orthodox Russian Social Democrats and the Economists, who wanted to give priority to the economic demands of the workers, helped shape and influence early Bolshevik thinking and encouraged Lenin, in *What Is to Be Done?* and elsewhere, to stress the primary need for political action. The Russian trade unions were too feeble to play any role in Bolshevik schemes of revolution. The Russian Revolution was a political revolution in an economically unripe country. Lenin, in a remarkable *obiter dictum* of May 1918, observed that one half of socialism—the political half—had been realized in Russia, the other half—a planned economy—in Germany. Political action, the dictatorship of the proletariat, was needed to promote an economic result, the building of a socialist economy. The assumption that, once the political revolution had triumphed, the economic consequences would look after themselves was, however, falsified. After the political episode of war communism, the introduction of NEP in 1921 meant a partial reinstatement of economic forces; and throughout the 1920's the battle went on between the market principle as the guiding force of the economy and the principle of planning. In theory everyone accepted the assumption that it was preferable to achieve the socialist goal through economic rather than through adminis-

493

Carr

A HISTORICAL
TURNING POINT:
MARX, LENIN,
STALIN

trative action. In practice market forces proved unable to carry the strain of intensive industrialization, and by 1929 had completely broken down. The use of direct and conscious political means to bring about economic ends has been since 1929 a persistent leitmotif of Soviet history, scarcely modified by the play-acting of so-called "market socialism."

The dichotomy between economics and politics characteristic of Western nineteenth-century thought was reflected in the familiar issue of society versus the state. When the Physiocrats in France sought to free trade from the frustrating restrictions of state power, when Adam Smith had his vision of a vast economic process working independently of the state for the greatest benefit of all, when Hegel set "bourgeois society" over against the state and made this dichotomy the foundation of his political theory, the distinction between economics, which meant bourgeois society, and politics, which meant the state, was clearly established. Bourgeois society was the realm of economic man. Throughout the nineteenth century the argument proceeded about the desirable and practicable relation between society and the state, but not about the reality of the distinction. In the English-speaking world, in particular, the opposition between society and the state, and the natural priority of society, became a fundamental category of political thinking. But Marx fully shared the same view: "Only political superstition [he wrote in *The Holy Family*] today supposes that social life must be held together by the state, whereas in reality the state is held together by social life."

In nineteenth-century Russia an embryonic bourgeois society was too weak to withstand the hypertrophy of state power; and after the revolution of 1917 a paradoxical situation developed. In Western countries the persistence of the nineteenth-century liberal democratic tradition continued to encourage a negative attitude toward the state and an eagerness to denounce "bureaucratic" abuses of its power, even while the constant encroachments of that power were recognized and accepted. In the USSR the Marxist tradition also embodied a deep-seated hostility to the state, enshrined in Lenin's *State and Revolution* and in widespread denunciations of "bureaucratism." But here the worldwide strengthening of the role of the state and its officials was reinforced by the Russian tradition of an absolute power, and, in a period where the state was everywhere extending its function and its authority, the critics of bureaucracy fought a losing battle. What is happening everywhere today is not so much the assertion of the primacy of the state, by way of reaction against the nineteenth-century assertion of the primacy of society, as a gradual obliteration of the distinction between them. The state becomes predominantly social and economic in character. Society identifies itself with the power of the state. The dividing line between economics and politics that was the essential feature of bourgeois society ceases to exist. These changes are strikingly illustrated by the way in which Soviet thought and practice has turned away from the Marxist attitude to the state.

Here we come to Lenin's most distinctive innovation in revolutionary theory and practice—the substitution of party for class as the motive force of revolution. Lenin once again found himself in verbal agreement, at any rate with the earlier Marx. The *Communist Manifesto* foresaw "the organization of the proletarians into a class, and consequently into a political party"; and Lenin, of course, constantly spoke of the class of which the party was the spearhead or vanguard. But the change of emphasis was marked and corresponded to the shift from the world of objective economic laws to the world of political action designed to mold and modify the economy. A class was a loose economic group without clear definition or organization or program. A party was a closely knit political organization defined by a common conscious purpose.

Both for Marx and for modern sociologists, class remains an elusive concept. A class, for Marx, was an economic and social group bound together by a common relation to the means of production. It had no legal existence and no institutions. Its common action was the unconscious product of innumerable spontaneous actions of individuals pursuing their particular interests. It was these unplanned and unconscious common actions that determined the policies of bourgeois governments and constituted "the dictatorship of the bourgeoisie." This view of class fitted into the *laissez-faire* conceptions of economic action and thought, and of the sharp dichotomy between society and state, that were dominant in the advanced countries throughout the nineteenth century and was scarcely comprehensible in any other context. The embarrassments of attempting to apply the concept of class to earlier historical periods or to other continents are notorious. The only class that really comes to life in Marx's writings is the bourgeoisie; nearly everything written by him about class in general relates, consciously or unconsciously, to the bourgeoisie in particular. The proletariat as a class was envisaged by Marx on the same model. Increasingly intolerable economic conditions would drive the workers to take action in defense of their interests. The workers of the world would spontaneously unite; and this common action would bring about the overthrow of the bourgeoisie and the dictatorship of the proletariat. Marx made it clear that this did not imply consciously planned action: "The question is not what this or that proletarian, or even the whole proletariat at the moment, *considers* as its aim. The question is, *what the proletariat is,* and what, consequent on that *being,* it will be compelled to do."

Marx knew well that only a small proportion of the proletariat was as yet class-conscious (though, living in England, he may have tended to exaggerate this proportion); and he recognized the existence of a *Lumpenproletariat,* an unorganized and unreliable mass of low-grade workers. At the other end of the scale, Engels noted the birth in England of what he called "a bourgeois working class," of a stratum of workers who showed signs of making common cause with the capitalists. But Marxists as a whole were not troubled by these threats to the international solidarity of the proletariat. It was assumed that time would correct these anomalies, and that at the right moment the workers would play their historical role, like the bourgeoisie before them, as a unified class. The contradictions of

495
Carr

A HISTORICAL
TURNING POINT:
MARX, LENIN,
STALIN

the capitalist system and the pressures engendered by it would sap its progressive and expansive capacities and provoke a revolt by an increasingly numerous and increasingly impoverished proletariat. This would be the last revolution, which would overthrow the last ruling class, the bourgeoisie, and usher in the classless society.

When Lenin surveyed the scene—and the Russian scene in particular—at the turn of the century, the prospect was obscure. In the countries of the Second International, although few signs had appeared of an imminent proletarian revolution, the organization of the workers had made giant strides; and everyone appeared to agree that this was an encouraging token of their growing solidarity and revolutionary potential. In Russia, workers' organization was primitive, and revolutionary hopes seemed infinitely remote. Logically, Lenin set to work to create a party to galvanize the Russian workers into action; and in Russian conditions the work of a party on Russian soil was necessarily secret and conspiratorial. These preparations seemed in no sense a departure from the Marxist tradition or from the models created by the great Social Democratic parties of the West; they were merely another desperate Russian attempt to "catch up" with the West. What was bewildering and decisive was what happened in 1914 and 1917—the negative and positive sides of the same medal. The outbreak of war in 1914 struck a crucial and long-awaited blow at the nineteenth-century capitalist system and found the workers of the advanced countries rallying to its defense in their respective national uniforms; the traumatic effect on Lenin of this incredible experience is well known. The Revolution of 1917 put in power the first government professing allegiance to Marxism and dedicated to the overthrow of capitalism; and this occurred in an economically backward country with a small, undeveloped, and relatively unorganized proletariat. This reversal of the expected order of events confronted the Bolsheviks with the task of maintaining and defending the victorious Russian Revolution in a hostile environment with woefully inadequate resources, human and material, at their disposal.

This crisis evoked a response already familiar in Russian revolutionary history. For the best part of a century, the Russian intelligentsia—a group without precise counterpart elsewhere—had provided the leadership and the inspiration for a series of revolutionary movements. Lenin's *What Is to Be Done?*, published in 1902, was a plea for a party of professional revolutionaries under intellectual leadership to spearhead the proletarian revolution; and Trotsky, in a famous polemic two years later, accused the Bolshevik party of attempting "to *substitute* itself for the working class." When therefore the survival of the revolutionary regime was placed in jeopardy by the inadequacy, quantitative and qualitative, of the proletariat, the party, led and organized mainly by intellectuals, stepped into the gap. The Russian Revolution was made and saved not by a class, but by a party proclaiming itself to be the representative and vanguard of a class. It was a solution consonant with the Russian revolutionary tradition. But, more important, it was a solution that marked the distance traveled since the days of Marx. It belonged to an age in which effective force was thought of as the product, no longer of the spontaneous action of mass of individuals, but of conscious political planning.

The *Communist Manifesto* recognized the role of leadership exercised by Communists as the only fully class-conscious members of the proletariat and of proletarian parties. But it was a condition of the proletarian revolution that Communist consciousness should spread to a majority of the workers. Marx attributed to Blanqui, and rejected as heretical, a belief in the revolutionary seizure of power by a disciplined minority. Lenin's conception of the party as the vanguard of the class contained *elitist* elements absent from Marx's writings and was the product of a period when political writers were turning their attention more and more to the problem of *elites*. The party was to lead and inspire the mass of workers; its own membership was to remain small and select. It would, however, be an error to suppose that Lenin regarded the revolution as the work of a minority. The task of leading the masses was not, properly understood, a task of indoctrination, of creating a consciousness that was not there, but of evoking a latent consciousness; and this latent consciousness of the masses was an essential condition of revolution. Lenin emphatically did not believe in revolution from above. His fullest account of what created a revolutionary situation was given in the pamphlet *The Infantile Disease of "Leftism,"* which he prepared for the Second Congress of Comintern in 1920.

> Only when the "lower layers" (*nizy*) *are not willing* to put up with the old, and the "top layers" (*verkhi*) *are not able to go on in the old way,* only then can the revolution triumph. In other words this truth can be expressed as follows: revolution is impossible without a general national crisis affecting both exploited and exploiters.

Some critics have found an element of political casuistry in this attempt to combine an elite leadership with mass consciousness. The embarrassed and sometimes contradictory utterances of the Bolshevik leaders about class contrast with their precise and rigid conceptions of party. After Lenin's death, Lenin's successors lacked the capacity or the patience to evoke that measure of mass consciousness and mass support that Lenin had had behind him in the period of the revolution and the Civil War and took the short cut—always the temptation that lies in wait for an elite—of imposing their will, by measures of increasingly naked force, on the mass of the population and on the mass of the party. Stalin's once famous short history of the Communist party called the collectivization of agriculture "a revolution from above, on the initiative of state power, with direct support from below"; and, although the phrase "revolution from above" has since been condemned as heretical, it was symptomatic of the Stalinist epoch.

These developments were due in part to the peculiarly exacting nature of the problems that the revolutionary regime in Russia had to face and

497
Carr

A HISTORICAL
TURNING POINT:
MARX, LENIN,
STALIN

in part to the peculiar conditions of a country were primitive peasants formed more than 80 percent of the population, and the number of trained and politically conscious workers, comparable to the organized workers of the West, was infinitesimally small. But they were also, and more significantly, a product of the period. The French revolutionary slogan of equality was a necessary and effective protest against privilege in a highly stratified society. For Marx this problem, like every social problem, was a problem of the relations of production. Capitalist society was based on the exploitation of man by man; the principle of inequality was built into the capitalist division of labor. The Marxist utopia contemplated the breaking down of the differentiation between different forms of labor—notably between manual and intellectual work. Lenin's *State and Revolution*, with its vision of the work of administration performed by ordinary workers in rotation and the initial experiments of the Bolshevik revolution in workers' control in the factories were the last and most famous tributes to this conception. Their failure heralded the advent of a new epoch. In the mass industrial society of today, the old stratified society against which nineteenth-century radicals of every complexion protested may have disappeared or be obsolescent. But a new kind of stratification has entered into every branch of administration and production. The need for technological and administrative elites declares itself at every level—in government, in industrial organization, on the factory floor, and on the farm—and is likely to increase with the increasing complexity of administrative and productive processes. When Stalin shocked the world in June 1931 by denouncing egalitarianism or "levelling" (*uravnilovka*) and remarked that "every industry, every enterprise, every workshop" had its "leading groups," and later accused supporters of egalitarianism of "petty bourgeois views," he struck a shrewder blow than was realized by his critics at the time. But this does not dispose of the difficulty of reconciling the need for administrative and technological elites with the egalitarian aspirations that mass democracy inherited from the French Revolution. The fact that many of these elites would call themselves nonpolitical does not mean that they do not wield decisive political power. "Bureaucracy" and "technocracy" are not empty words. The autocrats of the past have been replaced by anonymous Kafka-like figures, whom we cannot control and often cannot identify. The need, with which Lenin wrestled and which Stalin contemptuously dismissed, of reconciling elite leadership with mass democracy has emerged as a key problem in the Soviet Union today. Nor is the problem, though spotlighted by the sequel of the Bolshevik revolution, of exclusive significance to a single country. It would be rash to dismiss the Russian experience as irrelevant to our own or to be unduly complacent about our own solutions.

The educational function of the elite was strongly emphasized by Lenin in *What Is to Be Done?* Marx, like Adam Smith and Hegel, believed that individuals conformed to, and were the agents or victims of, objective social and economic laws of which they were, nevertheless, unconscious. "The conceptions formed about the laws of production in the hands of the agents of production and circulation will differ widely from these real laws"; and, *a fortiori,* "The workers are enslaved to a power which is unknown to them." These conceptions, which did not correspond with reality, were what Marx called "ideology." Ideology for Marx was necessarily false consciousness—the false idea of their motives formed by men who were unconscious of the real laws governing their actions. Marx did not consider it his function to issue positive injunctions—much less to propound a new ideology. His aim was to unmask error and illusion. Marx, following Hegel, identified the historical process with the growth of consciousness, and the growth of consciousness with the growth of freedom. Thus the final revolution leading to the Marxist utopia of the class-less society would also mean the ending of the rift between reality and ideology and the realization of true freedom and true consciousness.

Lenin remained in one respect rooted in the nineteenth century. While Lenin proclaimed the need to instruct and influence the masses, he continued to believe in instruction by rational persuasion or by force of experience. By the middle of the twentieth century this belief had lost much of its validity both in the Soviet Union and elsewhere. This was perhaps the fundamental difference that marked the transition from Lenin to Stalin. Lenin regarded persuasion or indoctrination as a rational process in the sense that it sought to implant a rational conviction in the minds of those to whom it was directed. Stalin regarded it as a rational process only in the sense that it was planned and conducted by a rational elite. Its aim was to induce large numbers of people to behave in a desired way. How to achieve this aim was a technical problem, which was the object of rational study. But the most effective means to employ in achieving this aim did not always, or not often, appeal to the reason. It would be erroneous to suppose that this transition from rational persuasion to technical indoctrination was peculiar to the USSR, or to any particular form of government. A similar development in Western democratic countries has often been attributed to the influence of commercial advertising, the practices of which, and sometimes the practitioners who apply them, are transferred from the commercial world to that of politics. The candidate is sold to the voter by the same means used to sell patent medicines or refrigerators. The enormous expansion of media of mass communication has clearly fostered this process. But deeper underlying causes have been at work. The professional, politically neutral, public relations consultant, setting out to create a favorable image for his clients and to mold opinion, by every known technical and psychological device, in the sense desired by them is a now familiar phenomenon, difficult to reconcile with the principles of Lincoln or Gladstone, but apparently inseparable from contemporary mass democracy. The future of democracy, in any part of the world, is today a disturbing problem. Here, as in other respects, the transition from liberal democracy to mass democracy in the Western world has reflected the experience of the Russian Revolution.

The problem has been further complicated by the course of revolution since 1917. Had the Russian Revolution been quickly followed—as the

499

Carr

A HISTORICAL
TURNING POINT:
MARX, LENIN,
STALIN

Bolsheviks at first expected—by revolutions in Western Europe, its priority would have been no more than a chronological anomaly in the total scheme. But when the cause of revolution, having proved barren in the West, flourished in the fertile soil of Asia, the shape of things to come changed radically. Much more was involved in the change than a mere geographical transposition. The Marxist revolution reached the peoples of Asia and Africa in its Leninist incarnation. Industrialization had to be pursued in these countries in conditions far closer to those experiences in the Soviet Union than to those envisaged by Marx. More significant still was the weakness, or sometimes total absence, of a bourgeoisie or of any of the concepts of a bourgeois society. In these countries, the bourgeois revolution, still unfinished in the Russia of 1917, had not even begun. Here the Russian problem was reproduced in an extreme form, and could be met only by the Leninist solution of a small intellectual elite to assume the leadership of the revolution. Many of these new leaders had received their education and made their first acquaintance with Marxism in Western countries or under Western auspices. But, in practice, local conditions made Marxism applicable only in its Leninist transformation. The absence of a bourgeoisie and of an established bourgeois tradition meant rejection, in practice if not in theory, of bourgeois liberal democracy and a return to Rousseauistic or Jacobin conceptions of democracy.

It is perhaps too early to attempt to place these ambiguous events in historical perspective. What is clear is that the Russian Revolution has triggered off a revolutionary movement of revolt against the nineteenth century capitalist order, in which the challenge is directed not against its exploitation of the industrial workers of the advanced countries, but against its exploitation of backward colonial peoples. It never occurred to Lenin, and was never admitted later, that a revolution under these auspices, although it might be directed against capitalism and have aims that could be described as socialist, had moved far away from the Marxist premises. The post-Leninist reorientation of the socialist revolution on neo-Marxist or non-Marxist lines implied that the final overthrow of capitalism would be the work not of its proletarian victims in the advanced countries (who had somehow become its allies), but of its colonial victims in the undeveloped countries, and that it would be the work not of an economic class, but of a political movement. The era of the French Revolution ended in 1917, and a new revolutionary epoch opened. Historians of the future may debate whether that epoch ended in 1949, when the Asian and African revolutions effectively began, or whether these events can be interpreted as a slightly unorthodox prolongation of the Russian Revolution. Such debates are not very fruitful, and it is unnecessary to anticipate them. But so long as man is interested to explore his past, nobody will doubt the credentials of the Russian Revolution as one of the great turning points in his history.

31. The Genesis of Fascism

GEORGE L. MOSSE

32. National Socialism: Totalitarianism or Fascism?

WOLFGANG SAUER

The extremely diverse use of the word fascist *as a political epithet in recent years has produced a great deal of confusion. Whatever can fascism mean when groups as varied as student rebels, "Weathermen," and "Yippies" have been called fascist by their enemies while some of them, in turn, have used the term to describe their enemies, such as J. Edgar Hoover and the police. It can only mean that the word is being used so indiscriminately that it can describe anything or anybody that someone does not like.*

Although historians disagree about its nature—a session on fascism at the American Historical Association's 1970 convention found all four partici-pants basically disagreeing—great strides in understanding fascism began in the 1960s when historians started taking a comparative rather than a national approach to the subject. Particularly helpful were Ernst Nolte's Three Faces of Fascism *(a 1966 translation of a German work published in 1963),* Eugen Weber's *Varieties of Fascism (1964),* Weber's *and* Hans Rogger's *The Euro-pean Right: A Historical Profile *(1964),* John Weiss's *The Fascist Tradition (1967),* and the first issue of the *Journal of Contemporary History *(1966), which was entirely devoted to the subject. This approach recognized the serious differences between the various national movements but saw fascism as a worldwide reaction to liberal democracy in developed and developing*

Source: George L. Mosse, "The Genesis of Fascism," *Journal of Contemporary History*, I, No. 1 (1966), 14–26. Reprinted by permission of George Weidenfeld and Nicolson. [Footnotes omitted.]

nations. Fascism likewise rejected the other opponents of liberal democracy such as communism, socialism, and reaction. Sometimes, but not everywhere, it was racist. Generally fascist movements appealed mainly to the lower middle class and were antirational in outlook.

Indeed, the most fruitful approach to understanding fascism appears to lie in examining its intellectual and socioeconomic composition, and the next two selections do just that. The first is by George L. Mosse, who teaches intellectual history at the University of Wisconsin and who wrote a major work on Nazism, The Crisis of German Ideology: Intellectual Origins of the Third Reich *(1964). For him, "the key to fascism is not only the revolt but also its taming." Against what features of industrial society did fascism revolt? What were the ingredients of fascism's response to that society? What kind of people became fascists and what did they have in common? How did the fascist response to industrial society differ from reaction? How could fascism reconcile revolt and taming, movement and tradition? To what extent were racism, mass terror, and war ingredients of the fascist response?*

The selection by University of California (Berkeley) professor Wolfgang Sauer reviews the literature of fascism and Nazism and focuses on the socio-economic composition of fascism. He sees Nazism as the German variant of a more universal fascism. In doing so he raises certain fundamental questions regarding the nature of the movement. What evidence does he use to show that socially "fascism can be defined as a revolt of those who lost—directly or indirectly, temporarily or permanently—by industrialization"? Whom does that include and exclude? Why did fascism attract lower middle class "losers," but not upper class ones? How was it that fascist regimes both "fostered industrialization and yet insisted, ultimately, on setting the clock back"? How do they differ from communist regimes? Why did the German variety of fascism become more radical and "neobarbaric" than varieties elsewhere? At the same time, why did fascism not become strong in France and Britain? Why does Sauer believe World War I so important to understanding both the birth of fascism and the kind of people attracted to it? Considering Mosse's discussion of fascist "taming" of its revolt against industrial society and Sauer's view of fascism's appeal to some but not all "losers" in the industrialization of society, should fascism be considered revolutionary or counterrevolutionary? Does your perception of the world indicate that fascism is dead as Sauer claims, or if not, who can be called fascist today?

GEORGE L. MOSSE

In our century two revolutionary movements have made their mark upon Europe: that originally springing from Marxism, and fascist revolution. The various Marxisms have occupied historians and political scientists for many decades, but fascism has been a neglected movement. The reason for this seems plain: the war and the pre-eminent position of Germany within this revolution have obscured its European-wide importance. That is why, in this special number on fascism, we have not concentrated on Germany but have, for once, given space to the rest of the story. For by the 1930s there was no nation without a native fascist party, and by 1936 a fascist Europe seemed within the realms of possibility—this even before Germany came to exercise its dominance over the movement. To be sure, Italy provided an important model and even tried (if unsuccessfully) to form a fascist international, but the national fascist parties had their own élan and their own problems to deal with. Yet if we want to get closer to the essence of the fascist revolution we must analyse it on a European-wide scale, taking into account important variations, but first trying to establish what these movements had in common. Fascism lacked a common founder, but all over Europe it sprang out of a common set of problems and proposed a common solution to them.

Fascism (although of course the word was not used at the time) originated in the attack on positivism and liberalism at the end of the nineteenth century. This was a general European phenomenon and examples readily spring to mind. In Italy, for example D'Annunzio praised man's instincts: 'Never had the world been so ferocious'.

The writings of these men reflect the same basic paradox of industrial society: man seems on the one hand robbed of his individuality but on the other it is precisely this individuality which he wants to assert once more. The phenomena of mass man were accompanied by a feeling that the bourgeois age had culminated in conformity while those personal relationships upon which bourgeois morality and security were built had dissolved into nothingness. The tone among many intellectuals and among the young was one of revolt, of a desire to break out of the fetters of a system which had led to such an impasse. Much has been written about the aspect of this revolt which found its clearest reflection in expressionism; it is not often realized that fascism had its origins in the same spirit of rebellion.

Indeed, the idea of both fascism and expressionism share the urge to recapture the 'whole man' who seemed atomized and alienated by society, and both attempt to reassert individuality by looking inwards, towards instinct or the soul, rather than outwards to a solution in those positivist, pragmatic terms which bourgeois society prized. There is nothing surprising in the fact that fascism felt an affinity with expressionist art and literature, and that even a not wholly unimportant segment of national-socialism tried to embrace them.

The key to fascism is not only the revolt but also its taming. For the problem before the fascist leaders was how to make this attitude towards society effective, and to counter the chaos which it might produce. How could the 'constant feeding of one's own exaltation' which D'Annunzio advocated, or the instinctualism of Nietzsche be captured and redirected into politically effective channels? That fascism could find an answer to this dilemma, play the cowboy to this widespread *fin de siècle* mood, explains much of its later success.

Both Georges Sorel and Gustave Le Bon had suggested answers, for they had shown concern for precisely this problem in the 1890s. A political movement must be based upon the instincts of men and these instincts harnessed to a dedicated leadership. Sorel's myth was the overt rationalization of the deepest feeling of the group. For Le Bon politics had to be based upon the fact of mass man and his irrationality. These two Frenchmen accepted as 'given' the view of human nature which the revolt of the *fin de siècle* had posited and proceeded from there. Fascism shared the ground Sorel and Le Bon had prepared not only by accepting their view of human nature, but also by following out the content they gave to it and the prescription they made for it. Gustave Le Bon believed in the conservatism of crowds clinging tenaciously to traditional ideas. The appeal must be made to this irrational conservatism and it must be combined with the 'magic' influence of mass suggestion through a leader. In this way mass man can be harnessed to a political mass movement, his tendency towards chaos can be curbed, and he can be redirected into positive action.

Le Bon describes admirably how to tame the revolt. The conservatism of crowds was reborn in fascism itself as the instinct for national traditions and for the restoration of personal bonds, like the family, which seemed fragmented in modern society. This conservatism was closely connected with the longing for an end to alienation, for belonging to a definite group. But the group had to be a traditional one, and it had to represent the restoration of the traditional morality. Hitler, for example, believed mass movements necessary because they enabled man to step out of his workshop, where he feels small, and to be surrounded by 'thousands and thousands of people with like convictions'. Alienation was to be exorcized, but on the basis of accepting a view of man as both irrational and conservative. Similarly in Italy an historically centred nationalism was to provide the 'national consensus'.

But the taming was always combined with activism, and this kind of conservatism inevitably went hand in hand with revolution. Both Hitler and Mussolini disliked drawing up party programmes, for this smacked of 'dogmatism'. Fascism stressed 'movement'—Hitler called his party a 'Bewegung', and Mussolini for a time favoured Marinetti's futurism as an artistic and literary form which stressed both movement and struggle. All European fascisms gave the impression that the movement was open-ended, continuous Nietzschean ecstasy. But in reality definite limits were provided to this activism by the emphasis upon nationalism, racism, and the longing for a restoration of traditional morality. The only variety of fascism of which this is not wholly true we find in France. There a man like Drieu La Rochelle exalted the 'provisional', the idea that all existing reality can be destroyed in one moment. But elsewhere that reality was 'eternal', and the activism was directed into destroying the existing order so that the eternal verity of *Volk* or nation could triumph, and with it the restoration of traditional morality.

The impact of the first world war shows this rhythm of fascism, just as it gave the movement a mass base. The *élan* of the battlefield was transformed into activism at home. The *fasci,* the German storm troopers, and the Iron Guard in Rumania all regarded their post-war world as an enemy which as shock troops they must destroy. Indeed, the leaders of these formations were in large part former front-line officers: Roehm, the head of the SA; Codreanu, founder of the Iron Guard; De Bono in Italy and Szalasi in Hungary—to give only a few examples. But this activism was tamed by the 'magic' of the leadership of which Le Bon had written so much earlier. Among the returned veterans it was tamed all the more easily, for they sought comradeship and leadership with some desperation. Not only because of the war experience, but also because of their sense of isolation within a nation which had not lived up to their expectations.

The 'cult element' was central to the taming process; it focused attention upon the eternal verities which must never be forgotten. The setting was a vital part: the balcony of the Palazzo Venezia, the Casa Rossa, the window of Hitler's new Chancellery. Activism there must be, enthusiasm is essential, but it must focus upon the leader who will direct it into the proper 'eternal' channels.

The liturgical element must be mentioned here, for the 'eternal verities' were purveyed and reinforced through the endless repetition of slogans, choruses, and symbols. These are the techniques which went into the taming of the revolution and which made fascism, even that which leaned on a Christian tradition, a new religion with rites long familiar in traditional religious observance. Fascist mass meetings seemed something new, but in reality contained predominantly traditional elements in technique as well as in the ideology.

To be sure, this taming did not always work. The youthful enthusiasm which presided at the beginning of the movement was apt to be disappointed with its course. Italy, where fascism lasted longest, provides the best example, for the danger point came with the second fascist generation. There the young men of the 'class of 35' wanted to return to the beginnings of the movement, to its activism and its war on alienation—in short, to construct the fascist utopia. By 1936 such youths had formed a resistance movement within Italian fascism which stressed that 'open-endedness' the revolution had seemed to promise: to go to 'the limits of fascism where all possibilities are open'. They would have felt at home in the French fascism of Drieu La Rochelle and Robert Brasillach, but they were not pleased with the fascism in power. We can discern similar signs as Nazism developed, but here the SS managed to capture the activist spirit. Had it not been for the war, Hitler might well have had difficulty with the SS, which prized ideology less than power of the will as expressed in naked and brutal action. But then fascism never had a chance to grow old, except in Italy; given the ingredients which went into the revolution, old age might have presented the movement with a severe crisis.

Fascism was a movement of youth, not only in the sense that it covered a short span of time, but also in its membership. The revolt of the *fin de siècle* had been a revolt of the young against society, but also against parents and school. They longed for a new sense of community, not for a 'chaos of the soul'. They were of bourgeois background, and their dominant concern for several generations had been with national unity and not with social and economic change—something for which they felt little need. Thus they were quite prepared to have their urge to revolt directed into national channels, on behalf of a community which seemed to them one of the 'soul' and not an artificial creation. Such were the young who streamed not only into the German youth movement, but also into the *fasci* and the SA, and made up the cadres of the Iron Guard as well as the Belgian Rexists. Returned from the war, they wanted to prolong the camaraderie they had experienced in the trenches. Fascism offered it to them. It is well to note in this connection that fascists were a new grouping, not yet bureaucratized, and the supposed open-endedness made them more dynamic than the other and rival political parties. The fascist leaders too were young: Mussolini was 39 when he became Prime Minister, Hitler 44 on attaining the Chancellorship, Léon Degrelle was in his early thirties, and Primo de Rivera as well as Codreanu were in their late twenties.

Youth symbolized vigour and action: ideology was joined to fact. Fascist heroes and martyrs died at an early age in order to enter the pantheon, and symbolic representations of youth expressed the ideal type in artistic form. Hitler liked speed and was a motorcar and airplane enthusiast; Mussolini loved his motor bicycle, but when it came to directing their movements, both stressed the rootedness of the true community. Indeed, when they inveighed against the bourgeoisie they meant merely the older generation which could never understand a movement of youth.

The traditionalism of the fascist movement coincided with the most basic of bourgeois prejudices. When Hans Naumann spoke at the Nazi book-burning in 1933 he praised action; the more books burned the better. But he ended his speech by exalting the traditional bonds of family and *Volk*. Such a traditionalism was in the mind of Giuseppe Bottai when he called for a 'spiritual renewal', or when the leading Rexist, Jean Denis, held that without a moral revolution there can be no revolution at all. Some fascisms defined the moral revolution within the context of a traditional Christianity: this is true of the Belgian Rexist movement, for example, as well as of the Rumanian Iron Guard. The Nazis substituted racism for religion, but, once more, the morality was that shared with the rest of the bourgeoisie.

The revolution of youth, of a virile activism, ends up as a revolution of the 'spirit', asserting the primacy of ideology. It is the shared world-view which binds the Nation together and it is this which must be realized. The world-view restores the dignity of the individual because it unites him with those of his fellow men whose souls function in a similar manner, and they do so because all are part of the *Volk,* the race, or the nation.

This is an organic view of the world. It is supposed to take in the whole man and thus end his alienation. A fundamental redefinition of politics is involved in such a view of man and his place in the world.

'Politics', the Italian fascist Bottai wrote, 'is an attitude towards life itself', and this phrase can be repeated word for word from national-socialist literature. The leader of the Iron Guard, Horia Sima, summed it up: 'We must cease to separate the spiritual man from the political man. All history is a commentary upon the life of the spirit.' Such an emphasis meant that cultural expressions of the true community moved to the forefront as symbols of the new society. The national-socialist emphasis upon art and literature did not stand alone; for the leader of Flemish fascism, Joris van Severen, culture was the principle of unity and coordination. He added, typically enough, that culture presupposes a tradition.

The emphasis upon the organic, the creative national community, was supposed to overcome not only political but also class divisions. Georges Valois, the founder of French fascism, made the point when, before the first world war, he described the differences between his beliefs and Marxism. Marxism stressed one class, but he wanted to harness the energy even of the bourgeoisie to the new society. Valois' statement was prophetic, for fascism not only harnessed the energy of the bourgeois class but indeed became a movement whose spiritual revolution, the quest for organic, rooted man, coincided with bourgeois longings, at least in most of the West. It is significant that the classless society was always supposed to be a hierarchial one as well.

Fascism believed in hierarchy, not in terms of class but in terms of service to the *Volk* or nation as exemplified by the leader. In Western, but not German, fascism, the ideal of a corporate state was adopted; a state operating not through parliamentary representation (with its divisive political parties) but through workers and managers sitting together. However they did not sit together as equals; the manager was the 'leader'. Though there exists a considerable fascist literature about such a shaping of the state, in the last resort it was secondary. For if all members of *Volk* and nation shared a common myth, a common soul, then their participation in government need only be symbolized by the leader who has activated their shared human natures through his own activism, his 'heroic will'.

Fascism did stress the aim of social justice, but it would bring this about through the nation, the *Volk,* and not through the imposition of equality. The political and social hierarchies were to be open to all who served. This meant opposition to the old ruling circles whether bourgeois or noble, and the substitution of new men for the old. Economic hierarchy was also preserved but within this framework a note of social justice was struck: Mussolini had his Charter of Labour and other fascisms drew up similar documents. Once again, fascism offered the best of all possible worlds: order and hierarchy would be maintained, private property would not be expropriated, but social justice would be done nevertheless. Once more this meant the primacy of ideology, ending spiritual alienation as a prerequisite for improving economic conditions.

Lest we brush this aside as inconsequential and lacking in appeal for the workers, it should be remembered that some fascisms did attempt, and successfully, to base themselves on the workers and peasants rather than the bourgeoisie. This was true in those countries where the working classes or the peasants had not been preempted by Marxist movements. Spain and Argentina provide examples in the West, and it is true of the Iron Guard as well as of the Hungarian fascist movement. To be sure, in those countries the bourgeoisie was not as strong as elsewhere, but another factor is of greater importance in explaining the fascist appeal to the labouring classes. Here, for the first time, was a movement which tried to bring these segments of society into political participation. In underdeveloped countries, the stress upon the end to alienation, the belief in the organic community, brought dividends—for the exclusion of workers and peasants from society had been so total that purely economic considerations could take second place.

Economics was indeed one of the least important fascist considerations. Jose Primo di Rivera, the founder of the Spanish Falange (which attracted much lower-class support), believed that 'people have never been moved by anyone save the poets', while the Belgian fascist Léon Degrelle called Hitler, Mussolini, and Codreanu 'poets of revolution'. The mystical side of the ideology dominated, the 'magic'; a fascist revolution must recognize the 'primacy of the spiritual'. Not control over the means of production was important, but the 'new man' about whom all fascists talked. He was man made whole once more, aware of his archetype and of those with whom he shared it, an activist in that he was not afraid to join in a revolution which would make society correspond to the longings of his soul. These longings were for unity with the group, for the recapturing of those virtues which were being submerged in the modern world. As Hitler stated clearly throughout his career: a man rooted in the world-view to which he belonged was not afraid to make it come true. Once he had joined he released his creative instincts, his power of will, in the common cause. Triumph meant that the whole nation would now share this creativity and renew itself. Economic well-being was subordinate to the stress upon art, literature, indeed the total cultural endeavour. Fascism was a revolution, but one which thought of itself in cultural, not economic terms.

In spite of the working-class support which it attracted in the more backward countries, in the West this was primarily a bourgeois revolution. The bourgeoisie could have a revolution as an outlet for their frustrations, and at the same time rest assured that order and property would be preserved. But for all that we must sharply distinguish fascism from the reactionary regimes in Europe. To be sure, the Rexists supported the Belgian monarchy and the Flemish fascists did likewise, but the differences are nevertheless far-reaching. Reaction rejected all revolution, opted for the *status quo,* and looked back to the *ancien régime* for its models. It stressed hierarchy, but this was the traditional hierarchy of entrenched privilege. It needs no demonstration that such regimes discouraged activism and mass movements. Moreover, they thought in strictly territorial terms and the 'shared soul' of all nationals or of the *Volk* would have had little meaning for them. For such regimes were not interested in bringing the disfranchised into politics or in ending man's alienation from his society. Their efforts were directed towards keeping men away from politics in order to maintain the monopoly of the traditional ruling class. Culture was not important here, and reactionary regimes gave wide latitude to all sorts of artistic expression so long as it did not encroach upon the monopoly of political power. The description of the Horthy regime by a modern historian is significant in this regard: Horthy did not intend to allow opposition to challenge his own will, but he did not think it any part of the duty of government to pry into and regiment each detail of his subjects' conduct, much less their thoughts.

Just so the French fascists split from the Action Française because it was not revolutionary enough, as shown by its inaction in February 1934. Francisco Franco destroyed his fascist movement, the Falange, in favour of a Horthy-like dictatorship. Fascism and reaction had different visions, and the two must not be confused.

But what of the differences between the diverse fascisms from nation to nation? These are best exemplified in the problem of racism and anti-semitism. Neither of these was a necessary component of fascism, and certainly not of those sections of the movement which looked to Italy for a model. There, until 1936, racism did not exist. In Belgium and the Netherlands the fascist situation was, in this respect, similar to that of Italy. Léon Degrelle explicitly repudiated racism—hardly surprising in a multi-national nation. What, he asked, is the 'true race'—the Belgian, the Flamand, or the Walloon? From the Flemish side, the newspaper *De Daad* inveighed against race hatred and called on 'upright Jews' to repudiate the Marxists in their midst.

Even Dutch national-socialism under Anton Adrian Mussert at first did not write racism on its banner, and kept silent about the Jews, a silence that the German Nazis were later to find incomprehensible. The French fascist group around the newspaper *Je Suis Partout* did go in for anti-semitism, but even here the Germans were accused of exaggerating the racial issue, for one could have good relations with a foreign people like the Jews. It is not astonishing that the early Falange was free from such ideas, for there were hardly any Jews in Spain. Yet the actual existence of Jewish groups cannot be linked too closely to fascist anti-semitism—for example both Belgium and the Netherlands had a relatively sizeable Jewish population. To be sure, in those countries a single-minded concentration on Marxism as the enemy tended to exclude all other considerations. But even this does not provide a satisfactory explanation, for the Marxist-Jewish equation could easily have been drawn there as it was in Germany.

This state of affairs did not last. By 1936 Mussolini had turned racist, and not merely because of German influence. Through racism he tried to reinvigorate his ageing fascism, to give a new cause to a youth becoming disillusioned with his revolution. The Italian reversal of attitude on this question seems to have affected the Falange as well, in spite of the absence of a native Jewish population. But here also a need coincided with this change of attitude—namely to make a more powerful appeal to the lower classes. As in Italy, so in Spain, anti-semitism helped to give the movement a greater and renewed dynamic. However, the Falange always rejected secular racism and based itself on the militant Catholic faith of Spain's crusading tradition. Similarly Oswald Mosley's fascists adopted anti-semitism when they found that this could give them a greater dynamic, a true feeling of struggle (and much free publicity) as they paraded through London's predominantly Jewish East End.

It was only in central and eastern Europe that racism was from the beginning an integral part of fascist ideology. Here were to be found the masses of Jewry, and still under quasi-ghetto conditions. They were a wholly distinct part of the population and vulnerable to attack. Moreover, in countries like Rumania or Hungary, the Jews had become *the* middle class, forming a distinct entity within the nation as that class which seemed to exploit the rest of the population through its commercial activites. No wonder the Iron Guard, in appealing to the nationalism of the peasants, became violently anti-semitic and even racist despite their Christian orientation—for they had begun as the legion of the 'Archangel Michael'.

After the First World War, the masses of east European Jewry began to emigrate into the neighbouring countries, predominantly Germany and Austria. The account in *Mein Kampf* of how Hitler reacted to the sight of such strangers in Vienna, may well have been typical. However that may be, the facts of the situation in that part of Europe gave fascism an enemy who could be singled out as symbolizing the forces which must be overcome. Moreover, in eastern Europe the struggle for national liberation had become associated with romanticism and racism long before fascism made its appearance on the scene. Hitler captured this tradition, and built upon the 'Jewish question'. This led to a further differentiation of national-socialism from Western fascism. For Hitler the enemy was not a vague Marxism; it was physically embodied by the Jews. Building on the Central-European tradition of a racist-orientated nationalism, he could give to the enemy of his world-view a concrete and human shape. Thus mass terror, and eventually mass extermination, could be built into German fascism as it was not built into other western fascisms. Both in Germany, and during the short-lived dominance of the Iron Guard, mass terror and pogroms became the manifestation of an activism which identified a distinct human group as the enemy.

Mass terror cannot, therefore, be a part of the definition of fascism as a European-wide movement. Hannah Arendt's *Origins of Totalitarianism* is wrong in this regard, and forced to concentrate solely on the German example. There is a difference between fascist violence and street fighting on the one hand, and mass terror on the other, which is explained partly by the predominance of the racial and anti-Jewish direction of the movement in central and eastern Europe.

Mass terror and violence were restrained by another factor within several of the fascist movements. A certain moderation was forced upon the fascisms which identified the nation with the existing state as over against those which sought to liquidate all existing political institutions for the sake of the *Volk*. Thus in Italy Mussolini never attempted to depose the monarchy, and in England, Belgium, and Holland fascism proclaimed its loyalty to the symbol of the state. This was not the case in central and eastern Europe, and as a consequence the activism there could have greater play and a more consistent goal, since *all* existing political institutions were to be abolished and founded anew.

The fascist revolution cannot be understood if we see it merely in negative terms or judge it entirely by the dominance which national-socialism achieved over it by the late 1930s. For millions it did satisfy a deeply-felt need for activism combined with identification, it seemed to embody their vision of a classless society. The acceptance of the irrational seemed to give man roots within his inner self, while at the same time making him a member of a spontaneous not artificial community. Bourgeois youth streamed into its ranks because to them it seemed to offer a positive solution to the problems of industrial and urban society.

The negative side of fascism triumphed in the end. How can the activist dynamic be tamed once the 'eternal verities' have triumphed? Can the emphasis on liturgy overcome the emptiness of a programme fulfilled? The answer was war upon the internal enemy, the adoption of racism; but another general solution lay in the realm of foreign policy. The activism must now be tamed by being directed towards the outside world. Hitler dreamed of his new Europe, Mussolini of the *Mare Nostrum*, Perón of an Argentine-dominated South America, and in Eastern Europe there were enough irridentas to fulfil this function.

The 'new man' of whom fascism had dreamed went down to defeat, the victim of a dynamic which had, after all, not been satisfactorily curbed. The dream turned out to be a nightmare.

511

Sauer

NATIONAL
SOCIALISM:
TOTALITARIANISM
OR FASCISM?

WOLFGANG SAUER

It is only two decades since National Socialism has left the scene, and yet the literature dealing with it is already immense. The fifty-year rule, never much respected by historians, has been quickly ignored in the face of so provoking a subject. This was all the more easy since, in this case, no Cerberus guarded the gates of the archives. Never before in the history of historiography did the documentary record of events become accessible to historians so quickly and comprehensively. One of the thought-provoking

Source: Wolfgang Sauer, "National Socialism: Totalitarianism or Fascism?" *American Historical Review*, LXXIII (1967), 404–24. Reprinted by permission of the author. [Most footnotes omitted.]

effects of this state of affairs is that historians suddenly have begun to wonder whether this surfeit of documents may not be, as one of them put in a recent review, "a source of confusion rather than clarification."

One way to avoid confusion is to define clearly the concepts and theories used in interpreting Nazism and to evaluate them in terms of the available evidence. Such an enterprise may seem all the more urgent since well-established concepts have become questionable in recent years. The following discussion attempts to clarify the problem. It first surveys past efforts of interpretation, then reviews present studies in this field, and, finally, develops some suggestions for further interpretive analyses.

The study of Nazism has so far traversed three periods with the two turning points being the outbreak of the Second World War and the start of the cold war. In the first period, prior to 1939, scholars tended to explain National Socialism in terms of fascism. Adolf Hitler seemed merely a German variant of Benito Mussolini, and both appeared, during the Great Depression and the popular front, to be but varieties of the agony of capitalism. Many writers were strongly influenced by socialist thought and, what is more, by socialist hopes. They sensed a profound revolutionary change in their time and interpreted it in terms of Marx's prophecies of the coming of the classless society. From this point of view, the rise of fascism in many parts of Europe appeared as a desperate last effort of monopoly capitalists to reassert their control over the masses against the tide of socialism, using the stick of terror and the carrot of pseudo socialism.

Fascism, in this view, was understood as a mere manipulation by big business. The outstanding example of this approach was Franz L. Neumann's *Behemoth* with its emphasis on social and economic analysis.

Historiography proper started with the Second World War. Under the impact of the war situation and in view of a growing awareness among social scientists of the differences between Nazism and other forms of fascism, authors tended to interpret the former as a Germanism, that is, some particularly German form of social disease. Studies focused, consequently, on the historical roots of Nazism and analyzed them especially in terms of intellectual history. The tendency of scholars in this field to stress logical sequences in historical developments may have contributed to the well-known deterministic interpretation of German history. A. J. P. Taylor's *Course of German History* is characteristic of this determinism, though Taylor did not emphasize intellectual history. German responses after 1945 varied from the apologetic tone of Gerhard Ritter to the searching analysis of Friedrich Meinecke and the universal view of Ludwig Dehio.

In the third period, starting with the cold war, the prevalent interpretation was that of totalitarianism. Nazism now appeared as but one form of a more general disease of modern society similar to Communism. Socialist hopes had yielded to deep pessimism in light of such staggering and embarrassing experiences as World War II, the rule of Stalinism in Russia and in Eastern Europe, and the rise of mass society, automation, and managerial bureaucracy in the West. Instead of the end of capitalism, the end of civilization seemed to loom ahead. Characteristic is the change in the attitude of Neumann who referred, in the early 1950's, to Sigmund Freud's idea that "conflicts deepen with the process of civilization, for . . . the increasing technical progress which in itself ought to make possible a greater measure of instinct gratification, fails to do so." What was true of former Marxists was no less true of conservatives. To writers such as Hannah Arendt, Carl Joachim Friedrich, and Jacob L. Talmon, totalitarianism appeared more or less a kind of suicide of civilization, a dialectical reversal by which progress turned against itself. Their studies stressed the omnipotence and the monolithic structure of totalitarian regimes and analyzed them in terms of the relationships between ideology and terror and between elites and masses.

It should be noted, however, that this survey deals with shifts in emphasis among interpretations and not with the replacement of one interpretation by another. Actually, the theories of fascism, Germanism, and totalitarianism coexisted to a degree from the outset. In addition, a fourth interpretation that has emerged since the war defines Nazism as but a modern variant of classical tyranny. Held mainly by British historians, this view rejects the thesis advanced by Friedrich and others that totalitarian dictatorship is an entirely new phenomenon, unprecedented in history; the British school stresses, instead, historical continuity. In this regard it approaches the thesis of Dehio who interpreted Nazism as the last link in a long chain of European struggles for hegemony. The case of tyranny has been most powerfully argued by Alan Bullock in his biography of Hitler, but similar views have been held both by Hugh Trevor-Roper, who compared what he called Hitler's court to the late Roman monarchy, and by Taylor, who recently argued that Hitler was but a traditional statesman. The discontinuity thesis has been rejected, interestingly enough, also for Communism. Karl Wittfogel, for example, has maintained that a continuity runs from Oriental despotism to modern Communist totalitarianism in Russia and China.

These historicist interpretations in terms of classical tyranny or Oriental despotism have so far been what might be called a minority opinion. Yet they should be noted the more carefully since the totalitarianism approach has generally begun to lose ground since the end of the 1950's. Khrushchev's anti-Stalinist and coexistence policies, the conflict between Russian and Chinese Communism, and a growing awareness in the West that industrial society might eventually produce mass prosperity rather than deadly conflict—all these developments militated against the apocalyptic visions of the totalitarianism theory. In addition, scholars had meanwhile begun to penetrate the mountains of documentary material and had gained a closer view of the historical realities of the Third *Reich*. These realities proved to be quite different from the monolithic image of totalitarianism. If we compare, for example, the view of Nazi rule as it emerges from Friedrich's studies to that which appears in Robert Koehl's article on "Feudal Aspects of National Socialism," we might wonder whether the two authors are talking about the same subject.

An unfortunate effect of using the totalitarianism approach is the

513

Sauer

NATIONAL
SOCIALISM:
TOTALITARIANISM
OR FASCISM?

emergence of a striking imbalance in covering the field of Nazi history. While we have an abundance of studies on the Nazi terror system, on military and war history, and on the history of the resistance, we know little or nothing about the problems of Nazi domestic politics and social history after 1934. The feuds within and between the bureaucracy and the party, the organization and social composition of the party and most of its affiliated organizations, the Nazi economic policy, particularly the Four-Year Plan, the effects of this policy and of the war on German society, and the attitude of various social groups, particularly of the workers, toward the Nazi government are subjects of major importance that are neglected to a surprising degree by studies of Nazism.[1] Even in the case of Nazi ideology, we know more about its roots and about its propaganda system than about its structure and its functional role in the social system.

Such evidence seems clearly to suggest that a revision of the existing conceptual framework is needed. To be sure, the totalitarianism theory cannot be dismissed entirely. Modern dictatorships have undoubtedly developed new characteristics, and totalitarianism is certainly one of them. It is, however, hardly as important as the totalitarianism theory has maintained. The theory of Germanism has been abandoned already as a possible alternative; William Shirer's attempt to revive it was a popular rather than a scholarly success. The question as to why Nazism rose just in Germany certainly remains, but scholars seem generally to agree that the understanding of the problem needs a wider horizon than a mere national perspective can provide.

Recent writings even show a tendency to conceive the responsibility for the Nazi atrocities in a broader way than before. This problem has caused three of the most passionate debates in recent years: the controversies over Arendt's comment on Adolph Eichmann, over Rolf Hochhuth's criticism of Pope Pius XII, and over Taylor's new *coup de main* on the established thesis regarding the origins of the Second World War. Historiography has gained from these debates mainly by the stimulation they provided. Books like Raul Hilberg's *The Destruction of the European Jews* and Ernst-Wolfgang Böckenförde's critical article on German Catholicism in 1933 had dealt even earlier with similar problems. Taylor's book, however, raises a major historiographical problem that deserves brief discussion here.

Taylor's thesis is professedly an attempt to anticipate a revision of historical opinion, which he believes will eventually occur as it did after World War I. But the idea of revision arose after 1918 from original research rather than from a consideration of what future historians might say. Taylor's results are not, however, too convincing in terms of research. His thesis seems to be, therefore, but an attempt to escape a condition

[1] For some recent studies indicating a change, see note 2, below. One of the neglected topics is the story of rescuers of Jews. Research in this field has recently been organized by Rabbi Harold M. Schulweis in the Institute for the Righteous Acts, Oakland, California. For an earlier attempt, see Kurt R. Grossmann, *Die unbesungenen Helden: Menschen in Deutschlands dunkelsten Tagen* (Berlin, 1957).

that is at least uncommon, if not unprecedented, in historiography. In Nazism, the historian faces a phenomenon that leaves him no way but rejection, whatever his individual position. There is literally no voice worth considering that disagrees on this matter, and it is probably not accidental that Taylor felt the stress of the situation most strongly. Does not such fundamental rejection imply a fundamental lack of understanding? And if we do not understand, how can we write history? The term "understanding" has, certainly, an ambivalent meaning; we can reject and still "understand." And yet, our intellectual, and psychological, capacities reach, in the case of Nazism, a border undreamed of by Wilhelm Dilthey. We can work out explanatory theories, but, if we face the facts directly, all explanations appear weak.

Thus, the attempt to write the history of Nazism confronts the historian with an apparently unsolvable dilemma and raises the question of what historical understanding and historical objectivity may mean in the face of Nazism. One of the merits of the totalitarianism theory was that it took care of this condition; from this point of view, one might be tempted to define it as a scholarly formulation of our lack of understanding.

Is there a better way to conceal our weakness? Among the established concepts one remains: fascism. To be sure, the theory of fascism has also suffered severely from both the politics of and the historical studies on Nazism. This concerned, however, the Marxist-Leninist interpretation of fascism, and it may be worthwhile to ask if this interpretation is the only possible one. Attempts have indeed been made recently to repair the damaged tool for use. Some outstanding examples are Seymour Lipset's *Political Man,* which contains a comprehensive study of fascism on the basis of election analyses; Irving Fetscher's article on *Faschismus und Nationalsozialismus,* in which the author explicitly aims at a refutation of the Marxist concept of fascism; Eugen Weber's works on the *Action Française* and the European Right; and Ernst Nolte's volume *Der Faschismus in seiner Epoche* of which an English translation has meanwhile appeared. Mention must also be made in this context of Arthur Schweitzer's *Big Business in the Third Reich* in which the author attempts, unsuccessfully, I believe, to fuse elements of Max Weber's and Marxist theories. These works constitute, as a whole and despite differences in approach and position, the first serious attempt to develop a workable, non-Marxist concept of fascism. Their results are less conclusive regarding the relationship between fascism and totalitarianism; this issue needs further clarification. A shift in emphasis toward an interpretation in terms of fascism is, nevertheless, unmistakable. In this context it is notable that works like William S. Allen's study of Nazi rule in a northern German town, Schweitzer's study, and Alan S. Milward's brilliant book on *The German Economy at War* [2] show a disposition of historians to turn to the neglected topics of Nazi history.

515
Sauer

NATIONAL
SOCIALISM:
TOTALITARIANISM
OR FASCISM?

[2] William S. Allen, *The Nazi Seizure of Power: The Experience of a Single German Town 1930–1935* (Chicago, 1965); Alan S. Milward, *The German Economy at War* (London, 1965). Since the completion of this article in May 1966, further studies have been published confirming this trend and covering many of the hitherto neglected subjects.

In the case of Schweitzer the turn is obviously related to the fascism approach; his book continues the earlier analysis of Neumann. Allen and Milward, by contrast, seem to have chosen their subjects without major theoretical considerations. But whatever the reasons for this turn, the tendency expressed in all of these works seems to be the most characteristic development in recent studies of Nazism.

Leaving aside the mainly empirical studies of Allen and Milward, we may ask what image of fascism emerges from these works. A summary is naturally difficult in view of the differences in individual positions, and yet there are two closely related points of agreement. First, the authors agree that fascism is not, as the Marxist interpretation holds, merely a manipulation of monopoly capitalists: it is a mass movement with a character and aim of its own, indicating a major crisis in liberal democracy and capitalism. Whether or not this crisis is temporary remains controversial. Second, it is now established beyond doubt that the lower middle classes, both rural and urban, were at least one of the major social components of fascist movements.

There are also many divergences and discrepancies, however. Some confusion exists regarding the distinction between fascist movements and fascist regimes. Fetscher's analysis shows that fascist movements can ally, in view of their basic opportunism, with a wide variety of other groups; Schweitzer has exemplified this in the case of Nazism. Consequently, there may be a marked difference between the original, relatively homogeneous fascist movements prior to the seizure of power and what emerges as fascist regimes after that event. This leads to the equally important problem of the relationships between fascist movements and their allies. For example, Lipset's interesting definition of fascism as the extremism of the liberal Center, in contrast to Right-wing extremism and Left-wing extremism (Communism), does not sufficiently explain why fascist regimes were frequently built on alliances with conservatives while alliances with Communists never materialized. Which social groups, then, were likely to become allies of fascist movements, and what functional role did these alliances play in the structure of the individual fascist regimes?

Other questions concern the social composition and the revolutionary aims of the movements. On the first question, most authors limit their analysis to the lower middle class and the problems of its definition. This is, indeed, an important issue since the concept of the lower middle class still needs clarification, both in itself and in relation to the varieties of fascist supporters. Historical evidence shows that support of fascism may not be confined to the classical elements of the lower middle class (*Mittelstand* —peasants, artisans, small businessmen, and so forth), but may extend to a wide variety of groups in the large field between the workers on the one hand and big business, the aristocracy, and the top levels of bureaucracy on the other. This evidence agrees, interestingly enough, with Leo Baeck's statement that it was among the workers, the aristocracy, and the upper strata of the civil servants that the Jews found strongest support against persecution in Germany.

Important as such an analysis is, however, it is still incomplete; it neglects the military element as a major social component of fascist movements. The military is apparently still not a category for social analysts. Among the authors quoted, only Fetscher recognizes its importance to fascism. It may even be said that a distinct interest group was formed within the fascist mixture by what might be called the military desperadoes, veterans of the First World War and the postwar struggles, who had not been reintegrated into either the civilian society or the armed forces. In an age of mass armies they were a sizable minority. Having become primitive warriors in four years and more of struggles, they sought to return into the arms of the mother army and to reform it according to their own model. Their conflict with society was, hence, not mainly economic, though this factor certainly was not absent. The main conflict was that between militarism and pacifism. In a time when the League of Nations appealed to the widespread war-weariness and the rising pacifism of the masses, the military desperadoes fought, not only for their own survival, but for the survival of soldiery in general.

The desperadoes were, thus, natural participants in the fascist revolution, but they did not merge entirely in the movement. Both in Italy and Germany the social differentiation was reflected in varying degrees in organizational differentiations between the party and the militia or the *Sturmabteilung* (SA), respectively. This indicates that the conflict over militarism re-emerged in varied form within the fascist movements. What was a conflict of principles in the relationship between the military desperadoes and society was a conflict of preferences in the fascist movements. The lower-middle-class groups and the military desperadoes considered each other as tools. The lower-middle-class members regarded the military desperadoes as a weapon to force their way into government; the military desperadoes hoped that the lower-middle-class members would provide the mass basis without which they could not expect to rule.

After the seizure of power the smoldering conflict within the fascist movements had to be resolved if the fascist regimes were to last. In Germany the conflict was terminated by Hitler when, in June 1934, he crushed the Röhm "revolt" which was, as I should like to maintain against Hermann Mau and others, predominantly a movement of the military desperadoes. To be sure, the SA contained in its rank and file large parts of the lower-middle-class Nazi supporters, but Ernst Röhm had ousted their representative in the leadership of the SA, Chief of Staff Otto Wagener, immediately after he assumed office in 1931. Röhm was, and always remained, the leader of the military desperadoes, and he defended their interests in 1934. He may have received some lower-middle-class support, so that his opposition might appear, consequently, as an embryonic revolt of the movement against Hitler's alliance with big business and the *Reichswehr*. Yet Röhm's opposition was aimed as much against the Nazi party as against Hitler, and his victory would invariably have led to a conflict with, and possibly a defeat of, the lower-middle-class forces. They were not better off with Hitler, however; the party won against

517
Sauer

NATIONAL
SOCIALISM:
TOTALITARIANISM
OR FASCISM?

Röhm, but lost against Hitler (and, *nota bene,* Heinrich Himmler and Hjalmar Schacht). Hitler's victory prevented the pending conflict within the movement from breaking through the façade of the *Volksgemeinschaft,* and rearmament "resolved" the conflict by securing occupations both for all types of business and for the desperadoes. It may be added that basically the same situation existed in Italy, though things were somewhat different, and, above all, less radical, there. One wonders whether Mussolini's imperialist adventure in Abyssinia did not play a role equivalent to Hitler's crushing of the Röhm revolt.

The control fascist regimes achieved over the dynamism of their movements creates doubts concerning the revolutionary character of fascist movements. There is virtual agreement among scholars that fascist movements contained, contrary to the Marxist thesis, a true revolutionary potential. This seems to conflict, however, with the noted opportunism of these movements. Rudolph Heberle's well-known study of the Schleswig-Holstein peasants, recently republished in its unabridged German form, first revealed this point, and Lipset has now been able to generalize Heberle's results. A look at the fascist regimes in operation, moreover, would show that, whatever the revolutionary potential of the movements, the revolutionary results were meager.

How can this problem be resolved? May an answer be found by setting fascism in a wider historical framework? This is the way Nolte approaches his subject, but his answer is suggestive rather than conclusive. He advances the thesis that fascism was a revolt against the universal process of secularization, democratization, and international integration in the modern era. When this process reached its critical stage in the period of the two world wars, those elements in the culture that were doomed to perish revolted, according to Nolte, with increasing radicalism and decreasing rationality, or, in national terms, from the French *Action Française* through Italian Fascism to German National Socialism. On the last, most radical stage, fascism turned, Nolte argues, into a resistance against what he calls the "transcendence." He does not succeed, however, in clarifying this point sufficiently.

Nolte's thesis is not new in terms of facts. Its originality lies in assigning a metaphysical dimension to the fascist revolt and definitely attaching this revolt to a historical period. Fascism, Nolte suggests, is dead. This is, on the one hand, a more optimistic variation of the totalitarianism analysis; on the other hand, he tries to ascribe a historical meaning to fascism, which would provide a starting point for historical understanding. Much of this remains abstract and vague, however—mere *Ideengeschichte.* If the modernization process was universal, was fascist revolt also universal? If so, why does Nolte deal only with France, Italy, and Germany? If not, why did the fascist revolt occur only in these (and some other) countries? And what was the cause for differentiation? Why was this revolt most radical in Germany? Or, to put the question in a sociological rather than a national form, which social groups provided the mass basis for fascism, and why were just these groups antimodernist in this ori-

entation? Why did the antimodernist fascist revolt frequently foster industrialization? And, finally, what exactly does "transcendence" mean, and
by which concrete means did the fascist resistance against it manifest itself?

Nolte's neglect of these questions can be attributed primarily to his
method, which he calls "phenomenological" and which he conceives as an
attempt to return to G. W. F. Hegel's integration of philosophy and history. This attempt is, however, problematical. Hegel's striking success in
synthesizing philosophy and history depended on his dialectical "logic";
Nolte's method is not dialectical. Nor does Nolte develop an alternative.
He has not succeeded, therefore, in invalidating Leopold von Ranke's argument against Hegel that philosophy in itself does not produce a method
for the analysis and organization of empirical facts. Philosophy alone was,
indeed, not sufficient for Nolte; his phenomenological method turns out,
under scrutiny, to be essentially Dilthey's good, old method of empathy,
supplemented by some fragmentary social-scientific concepts formed *ad
hoc* to satisfy immediate needs.

To be sure, Nolte makes this method operative by confining his study
mainly to an interpretation of the ideas of the fascist leaders—Charles
Maurras, Mussolini, Hitler—and he achieves much in this way, especially with regard to psychological and ideological analysis. Such a biographical approach is too narrow, however, to support Nolte's generalizations. What is true of the fascist leaders is not necessarily true of the
masses of their followers. Their attitudes and motivation can be recognized only by a social analysis that includes economic factors. Nolte would
perhaps respond to such a suggestion with as much contempt as he
shows for the use of the concept of industrialization. What does his
concept of "practical transcendence" mean, however, if not that economic
factors have adopted in modern societies a significance that transcends
their "materialistic" meaning? And if this is true, how can we expect to gain
meaningful results about modern societies without taking these factors
into account? Nolte's method, in fact, seems to conflict heavily with
his concept of "practical transcendence."

This must raise some doubts about the origin of Nolte's thesis of fascism as an antimodernist revolt. Indeed, he seems to have obtained his
thesis, not through his biographical analyses, but rather through an analysis of Maurras's ideas. Nolte's decision, not too plausible at first glance,
to raise the *Action Française* to a prominent position in the history of the
origins of fascism, has, actually, methodological rather than historical reasons. The *Action Française* is important to Nolte because Maurras succeeded in building an intellectual bridge between the counterrevolutionary tradition and fascism, thereby establishing a unified concept of
antimodernism that Nolte found apparently suggestive as an analytical
concept for his own study. His chapter on the *Action Française* is, thus,
actually a part of his methodological introduction.

The conclusion that Nolte arrived at his thesis in a methodologically
irregular way does not necessarily imply that the thesis is wrong. It does
imply, however, that he has not proven his case. Fascism and counterrevo-

519

Sauer

NATIONAL
SOCIALISM:
TOTALITARIANISM
OR FASCISM?

lution are actually different social phenomena, the latter being the earlier position of a part of what has been defined here as the allies of fascism. Fascism had its own independent antecedents: pseudo revolutionaries like Father Jahn and the anti-Semites of the 1880's and 1890's (as examples in Germany). To be sure, counterrevolution showed a combination of revolutionary and reactionary elements similar to fascism, but it was a revolution from above while fascism is a revolution from below. The discussion of Maurras by Nolte explains, therefore, the possibility of the fascist-conservative alliance, but it does not explain fascism. Nor does Nolte provide a satisfying answer to the question of the origins of fascism, especially in the German case. Nolte's chapters on pre-1914 Germany and Austria are in fact among the weakest in his book, though this is owing partly to Nolte's general weakness in historical knowledge.

These criticisms do not, however, detract from the value of the book, which is a major step forward in the study of fascism. If verified, Nolte's hypothesis can offer, for example, an explanation for the fascist tendencies in the military; its metaphysical implications might, in addition, open a way to understand certain aspects in the relationship between the churches and fascism. Nolte might indeed have achieved his aim of developing a comprehensive theory of fascism had it not been for his mistaken conception of the relationship of philosophy and history and his refusal to consider the socioeconomic aspects of the problem.

The task is, then, to provide the non-Marxist theory of fascism with a socioeconomic dimension; more precisely, the task is to bring the earlier attempts of this kind up to date. Some contributors to the discussion in the 1930's have already laid important foundations for a socioeconomic theory of fascism. We have only to adjust these foundations to today's advanced stage of practical experience, historical research, and theoretical thought. With regard to theory the most important recent contribution probably comes from economic historians who have worked out, on the basis of the experiences of both the Great Depression and the underdeveloped countries, a non-Marxist concept of economic development that is highly suggestive to the analysis of fascism.

The attempt to use this concept for the interpretation of fascism poses, of course, certain problems. The Marxist trap of economic determinism is but a minor difficulty. Apart from the fact that the difference between causes and conditions in social developments has meanwhile become sufficiently familiar to social scientists, it must also be stressed that the main purpose in using, here, an economic theory for a historical analysis is merely a heuristic one. In addition, the "theory of economic growth" is, in the last analysis, not strictly an economic theory. It is rather a historical synthesis of the process of industrialization on the basis of a socioeconomic analysis. Consequently, it already implies that the relationship between social and economic factors is a reversible one. In applying this theory to the interpretation of fascism, we merely shift the perspective without abandoning reversibility.

A more important problem arises because we have to face, as usual, several conflicting formulations of that theory. Only those formulations that focus on continental European conditions, however, are useful to the analysis of fascism. This reduces the number of alternatives to two: the models of Alexander Gerschenkron and W. W. Rostow. If we analyze the results of these two theories with regard to the social context of industrialization, we find that they are complementary. Gerschenkron's theory of "relative backwardness" provides a model of historical differentiation missing in Rostow's "stage" theory, and the latter offers a model for periodization not developed by Gerschenkron.

The critical problem is the development of a model for the advanced period of the industrialization process. Gerschenkron's model of relative backwardness cannot be directly extended to it since it deals with the starting conditions, while Rostow's definition as a stage of "high mass consumption" is still unsatisfactory. Rostow hits, certainly, the essential point: that industry, if it exceeds a certain limit of growth, must turn to mass production. He is also aware that private mass consumption is not the only possible response. Rostow's idea, however, that societies on the stage of mass production have a choice between high mass consumption and national political expansion (or, between private mass consumption and mass consumption by the state), does not entirely agree with the historical evidence. There is certainly an element of choice in the situation; yet it may well be that there are also constraints working against a choice. They may be owing to the consequences of relative backwardness, or to differential national developments and resulting international tensions and crises such as war. Rostow neglects the impact of national economic growth on international relations and vice versa; this seems to be, in fact, the major weakness of his theory. If we analyze twentieth-century history from this point of view, we do indeed find a period of world crises (World War I, the Great Depression, World War II) spreading between Rostow's stages of industrial maturity and high mass consumption.

In terms of a theory of economic growth revised in this way, fascism can be defined as a revolt of those who lost—directly or indirectly, temporarily or permanently—by industrialization. Fascism is a revolt of the *déclassés*. The workers and industrialists do not fall under this definition; it applies mainly to most of the lower middle class as defined above. They indeed suffered, or feared they would suffer, from industrialization —peasants who opposed the urbanizing aspects of industrialism; small businessmen and those engaged in the traditional crafts and trades that opposed mechanization or concentration; white-collar workers (at least as long as they felt the loss of economic independence); lower levels of the professions, especially the teaching profession, which opposed changing social values; and so forth. Also the military joins here, with opposition against the industrialization of war, which tended to destroy traditional modes of warfare and which by its increasing destructiveness intensified pacifism and antimilitarism. On the other hand, groups like the aristocracy, the large landlords, the higher bureaucrats, and so on,

521

Sauer

NATIONAL
SOCIALISM:
TOTALITARIANISM
OR FASCISM?

who lost also by industrialization, generally did not turn to fascism. In continuing the counterrevolutionary position, they defended hierarchical society and abhorred, therefore, the egalitarian elements in fascism. In exact distinction, then, fascist movements represented the reaction of the lower-class losers, while the upper-class losers tended to react in a nonfascist way, but were potential allies of fascist regimes.

Such an analysis seems to be a way of explaining the intriguing paradox of a revolutionary mass movement whose goals were antirevolutionary in the classical sense. As a movement of losers, it turned against technological progress and economic growth; it tried to stop or even to reverse the trend toward industrialization and to return to the earlier, "natural" ways of life. In this respect the movement was reactionary, but, as a movement of the lower classes, its means were necessarily revolutionary. In defining fascism as a revolt of losers, we can also understand better both fascist atavism and fascist opportunism. Since the process of industrialization as a whole is irresistible, the existence of civilization is inextricably bound to it. Fascist revolt against industrialization must, therefore, eventually turn against civilization too. This was most evident in Germany, where Nazism developed into full-fledged neobarbarism, but it is also true of the other fascist movements, though for various reasons neobarbarism remained, there, more or less underdeveloped. Such a definition of fascism as a neobarbaric revolt against civilization seems to describe in more concrete terms what Nolte calls the resistance against the "transcendence."

The same condition led to fascist opportunism. Since fascists acted, as losers, essentially from a position of weakness, they were compelled, in spite of their tendency toward violence, to compromise with their environment, even with their industrial enemy. This accounts for the contradiction that fascist regimes often fostered industrialization and yet insisted, ultimately, upon setting the clock back. The dialectic that resulted from this condition led eventually to a point at which the movement assumed suicidal proportions. Industrialization was sought in order to destroy industrial society, but since there was no alternative to industrial society, the fascist regime must eventually destroy itself. This was the situation of Nazism. The Nazis built an industrial machinery to murder the Jews, but once in operation the machine would have had to continue and would have ruined, indirectly at least, first the remnants of civilized society and then the fascist regime. Industrialization of mass murder was, thus, the only logical answer Nazism had to the problems of industrial society.

The analysis of fascism in terms of economic growth also offers a way to define more precisely the fallacy in the Marxist-Leninist concept of fascism. The fallacy lies in that Marxism blurs the distinction between early commercial and late industrial capitalism. Fascism indicated a conflict within capitalism, between traditional forms of commercialism and the modern form of industrialism. The fact that the former had survived in the twentieth century only on the lower levels of the middle classes accounted for the social locus of fascism. It is true, therefore, that fascism was capitalistic by nature; it is not true that it was industrial. It is also true that fascist regimes often were manipulated in varying ways and degrees, but the share of industrialists in manipulation was rather small. Fetscher shows convincingly that the share was indeed larger in industrially underdeveloped Italy than it was in industrially advanced Germany.

On the other hand, the difference between fascism and Bolshevism appears, in light of this analysis, more fundamental than the totalitarianism analysis would admit. Neither V. I. Lenin nor Joseph Stalin wished to turn the clock back; they not merely wished to move ahead, but they wished to jump ahead. The Bolshevik revolution had many elements of a developmental revolution not unlike those now under way in the underdeveloped countries. One of the striking differences between the two systems appears in the role of the leaders. The social and political order of Bolshevism is relatively independent from the leadership; it is, so to speak, more objective. Fascist regimes, by contrast, are almost identical with their leaders; no fascist regime has so far survived its leader. This is why Bullock's interpretation of Hitler in terms of traditional tyranny has some bearing. The limits of this approach would become evident, I believe, if scholars could be persuaded to balance their interest in Hitler's secret utterances and political and military scheming by also stressing his role as a public speaker. The Nazi mass rallies with their immediate, ecstatic communication between leader and followers were, indeed, what might be called a momentary materialization of the Nazi utopia, at least so far as the "Nordic race" was concerned.

Finally, it is plain from an analysis in terms of economic growth that the degree of radicalization must somehow be related to the degree of industrialization. The more highly industrialized a society, the more violent the reaction of the losers. Thus Germany stood at the top, Italy lagged behind, and Spain and others were at the bottom. In Germany, fascism gained sufficient momentum to oust its allies. By the dismissal of Schacht, Werner von Blomberg, Werner von Fritsch, and Konstantin von Neurath in 1937–1938, the Nazis assumed control over the economy, the army, and the diplomacy, those exact three positions that their conservative allies of January 30, 1933, had deemed it most important to maintain. In Italy a fairly stable balance was sustained between the movement and its various allies until the latter, relying on the monarchy and assisted by Fascism's defeat in war, finally ousted the Fascists. In Spain, a borderline case, the allies assumed control from the outset and never abandoned it. Similar observations can be made with the many cases of pre-, proto-, and pseudofascist regimes in Central, Eastern, and Southeastern Europe.

The thesis of the parallel growth of industrialization and fascist radicalization seems to conflict, however, with the evidence of some highly industrialized societies such as France and England where fascist opposition never gained much momentum. The problem can be solved only by adding a broader historical analysis involving the specific national, social, and cultural traditions that industrialization encountered in individual socie-

523

Sauer

NATIONAL
SOCIALISM:
TOTALITARIANISM
OR FASCISM?

ties. It is perhaps not accidental that the industrialization process ran relatively smoothly in West European nations whose political rise concurred with the rise of modern civilization since the late Middle Ages. Fascist opposition, by contrast, was strongest in the Mediterranean and Central European regions where the premodern traditions of the ancient Roman and the medieval German and Turkish Empires persisted. The religious division between Protestantism and Catholicism may also have some relevance: one remembers both Max Weber's thesis on the correlation of Protestantism and capitalism and the recent controversy on the attitude of Pope Pius XII toward Fascism and Nazism. In other words, fascism emerged where preindustrial traditions were both strongest and most alien to industrialism and, hence, where the rise of the latter caused a major break with the past and substantial losses to the nonindustrial classes.

This definition is still incomplete, however, since it does not tell why fascism emerged rather simultaneously throughout Europe though the countries affected were on different levels of economic growth. We face here the question of the "epoch" of fascism, raised but not answered by Nolte. The general conditions of fascism as defined above existed, after all, earlier. In Germany, for example, lower-middle-class opposition against industrialization had already emerged in the mid-nineteenth century and accompanied economic growth in varying degrees through all its stages. Why did it not turn into fascism prior to 1914, though it did so on parallel stages of growth in Italy and Spain after the First World War? At this point the importance of the military element for the analysis of fascism becomes apparent again: Only after total war had militarized European societies and had created large military interests were the conditions required for fascism complete. The First World War had tremendously strengthened industrialization in technical terms, but it had diverted it from production to destruction. After the war the victorious nations of the West managed, on the whole, to stabilize industrial society and to return to production, but the defeated nations and those industrially underdeveloped found it extremely difficult to follow the same course. When they met with economic crises, many of them abandoned whatever advance they had made toward democracy and turned to fascism.

This breakdown occurred roughly along the social and cultural lines defined above. If we examine the geographical distribution of fascist regimes in Europe between the two world wars, we find that they emerged mainly in three areas: the Mediterranean coast; the regions of Central, Eastern, and Southeastern Europe; and Germany. In the first area, the original and highly developed Mediterranean urban and commercial civilization that reached back to antiquity faced destruction by the invasion of industrialism as released or accelerated by World War I. Defeat, either imagined as in the case of Italy or real as in the case of Spain at the hands of Abd-el-Krim at Anual in 1921, played an additional role. In the second area, an old feudal civilization struggled with the problems arising out of sudden liberation from Habsburg or tsarist dominations as well as from competition with both Western industrialism and Eastern Bolshevism. Both regions were predominantly Catholic. In the third area, a technologically fully developed industrial society clashed violently with the stubborn resistance of surviving remnants of preindustrial forms of society over who was to pay for defeat and economic crises. Catholicism played, here, a dual and partly contradictory role. On the one hand, it seems to have influenced indirectly Nazism as such top Nazi leaders as Hitler, Himmler, and Goebbels were Catholic by origin, and the Vatican was quick to compromise with the Hitler regime. On the other hand, the vast majority of the Catholic population was relatively immune to Nazi temptations. Significantly enough, Protestantism also split, though along somewhat different lines.

These differentiations suggest a division into three subtypes of fascism: the Mediterranean as the "original" one; the various and not too long-lived regimes in Central, Eastern, and Southeastern Europe as a mixed, or not full-fledged, variation; and German Nazism as a special form.

The "epoch" of fascism starts, thus, with the aftermath of the First World War, but when does it end? Eugen Weber and Lipset agree with many scholars who believe that there is no epoch of fascism, that fascism is a general condition of modern society contingent upon crises in liberal democracy. This is certainly indisputable as far as fascist attitudes and movements are concerned; it is quite another problem, however, whether fascist regimes will emerge again. This emergence seems unlikely for two reasons. First, the socioeconomic development in the highly industrialized societies of the West generally rules out the re-emergence of the historical condition of fascism—a disarrangement of society in which the rise of large masses of *déclassés* coincides with the rise of a sizable group of military desperadoes. There are no longer economic losers of industrialization, at least not on a mass scale, and Charles de Gaulle's victory over the rebellious French military shows that military desperadoes alone will not get very far.[3] In addition, the horrible experience of neobarbarism puts a heavy burden on all attempts at imitation. If the success of fascism under modern, Western conditions is unlikely, there remain, theoretically, the underdeveloped countries as possible breeding grounds of fascism. Yet it is doubtful whether opposition against industrialization will assume there the form of fascism since these countries lack the specific traditions of the ancient and medieval civilizations that conditioned the antimodernist revolt in Europe. The second reason working against fascist regimes is, thus, that fascism is inseparable from its Central and South European conditions; it is, in fact, one of the products of the dialectical movement of European civilization.

Some remarks on specific characteristics of Nazism and its German origins may be added as a conclusion to this discussion of fascism. The

525

Sauer

NATIONAL
SOCIALISM:
TOTALITARIANISM
OR FASCISM?

[3] It would be different in case of large-scale war which might, of course, drastically change present social conditions.

specialty of the German case may be seen, in light of this analysis, in that Germany was the only highly industrialized society in which a fascist regime emerged. Some authors have tried to explain this by pointing to the dominant role the state played in German industrialization. Yet Gerschenkron has convincingly shown that a relatively strong role of the state is a general characteristic of industrialization under conditions of "relative backwardness." We must look, therefore, for other causes, and it seems that they can be found in social rather than in political conditions of industrialization. A comparison with developments in France and Russia shows that the state in these countries changed its social basis by revolutionary means either prior to or during the process of industrialization; in Germany, however, preindustrial social traditions proved so strong and so flexible that they maintained influence on, if not control over, the state up to and beyond the stage of what Rostow calls industrial maturity. The ambivalent social structure that resulted from this twisted process was so fragile that it broke apart under the impact of the series of severe crises from World War I to the Great Depression. One of the conditions that complicated German industrialization may be seen in the fact that Wilhelm von Humboldt's reform of the German educational system favored, at the very moment when Germany began to industrialize, an aesthetic-aristocratic idea of culture over an idea of civilization compatible with industrialism. The tensions resulting from this divergence are reflected in German nineteenth-century intellectual history and its complex relationship to the intellectual roots of Nazism. Fritz Stern and George L. Mosse, among others, have recently made important contributions to this subject. Mosse has taken up the issue of the *Völkisch* ideology and has convincingly shown how deeply it had penetrated into German society already prior to 1914. In focusing on the *Völkisch* ideology alone, Mosse has, however, by-passed what appears to be the real problem. Parallel to the rise of the *Völkisch* ideology, Germany experienced one of the greatest intellectual flowerings in its history during the first three decades of this century. In many cases it reached the level of the classical period around 1800, and it certainly surpassed it in breadth. The real question is, then, why this parallelism occurred and why the *Völkisch* ideology eventually triumphed. As far as intellectual history is concerned, there was, in fact, no gradual decline toward Nazism; there was a clear rupture in 1933.

Stern's study is less ambitious and more penetrating. Its results might lend some support to Nolte's thesis of metaphysical despair, but they are valuable especially because they draw attention to the crisis of self-confidence in the academic establishment. This seems to correspond to Allen's findings that indicate a deep and violent resentment on the "grass root" level of the Nazi party against the "educated" classes, and both studies together may hint at some reasons for the triumph of the *Völkisch* ideology analyzed by Mosse. Synthesized in this way, the results of the three authors may draw attention to one of the unduly neglected class divisions in Germany: between the educated and the uneducated. In the classical country of *Bildung* where the professor held and still holds one of the top positions in public prestige, such a division was highly important in itself. It became still more important, even in a political sense, when the aristocracy partially adopted during the nineteenth century the bourgeois idea of *Bildung*. Most telling in this respect is the rise of the idea of the army as a "school of the nation," indicating that even the Prussian army felt advised after 1848 to engage in a competition for education with the bourgeoisie. The civil bureaucracy had already adopted the educational ideal earlier; now, the military and part of the aristocracy followed in an attempt to maintain their position and to provide for the cooptation of "suitable" bourgeois elements.

In view of these facts, the hypothesis seems to arise that the division between the educated and uneducated may have developed in the nineteenth century into the true dividing line between the ruling oligarchy and its subjects. If this is true, subjects seeking emancipation had two ways to respond: either forming a subculture or resorting to barbarism. The first was the solution of the socialist labor movement; the second was the way of the Nazis, and it was the true revolutionary way. Evidence suggests that Hitler's prestige with the masses did not rest exclusively on economic and foreign policy successes; it also appears to have been supported by the fact that Hitler succeeded again and again in defeating and humiliating the members of the old oligarchy. Hitler's frequent invectives against this class in his speeches are usually explained as motivated merely by his own personal resentments. The motive may well have been more sophisticated, however. Such considerations must lead to the perplexing question of whether the Nazi movement did involve some elements of the completion, terribly distorted indeed, of Germany's age-old-unfinished revolution. This would open some new perspectives on the resistance movement, and it would perhaps explain the intriguing fact that the Nazi regime, in contrast to the Hohenzollern monarchy in 1918 and the Fascist regime in Italy in 1943–1944, was not overthrown by a mass upheaval from within. The question cannot be answered here, but it is crucial. The answer will determine not only our understanding of the nature of Nazism in terms of the problem of fascism, but also our interpretation of Nazism as an element in German history.

527

Sauer

NATIONAL
SOCIALISM:
TOTALITARIANISM
OR FASCISM?

33. Hitler and the Origins of the Second World War

ALAN BULLOCK

Within ten years after the end of World War I a whole body of revisionist history began to be written which objected to exclusively German "war guilt." Although that revisionist view has come under considerable attack, as we have seen in earlier selections, no one at the end of World War II would have predicted a similar revisionism regarding Hitler's war. His responsibility seemed too clear-cut. The unconditional surrender of Germany in 1945 had placed in the hands of historians and war crimes tribunals almost complete documentation of Hitler's and Germany's foreign policy and war plans. No similar evidence existed for World War I's origins until just recently. The unique full documentation of Nazi Germany's actions and the enormity of the crimes of Hitler and his lieutenants seemed to preclude any revisionism regarding the origins of the Second World War.

Yet, in the early 1960s revisionism came anyway. Usually revisionism follows the revelation of new documents, as was the case with the publication in the 1920s of the pre-World War I diplomatic documents of all the great powers. But the World War II revisionism came without new documentation; the German material was already complete and that of the victorious powers only began to dribble out in the 1960s. It came instead by a reworking of what was already known. The most highly publicized revisionist work was British historian A. J. P. Taylor's Origins of the Second World War *(1961).*

Source: Alan Bullock, "Hitler and the Origins of the Second World War," *Proceedings of the British Academy,* LIII (1967), 259–87. Reprinted by permission.

*Although it was almost universally condemned in its reviews, the most
memorable one being that by Professor Hugh Trevor-Roper in* Encounter
*(July, 1961), it continues to prosper. If we are to believe D. C. Watt's article
in* Political Quarterly *in 1965 (pp. 191—213), it has become part of an entire
revisionist school.*

*At the risk of oversimplifying Taylor's argument, we may summarize it
thus: he insists that Hitler was a "traditional" German statesman, albeit a
more "wicked" one than his predecessors. As such, his ambition was German
expansion in eastern Europe, first to recover the territory lost at the Treaty
of Versailles, and then to recover what Germany won at the Treaty of Brest-
Litovsk, victorious Germany's peace settlement with Russia in 1918 which
turned Poland, the Baltic, and the Ukraine into German spheres of influence.
From the time he published* Mein Kampf *Hitler's enemies were Poland and
the Soviet Union, not Britain and France. He had no "blueprint" for defeating even those powers, let alone a master plan for world conquest. Rather,
he made up policy as he went along, capitalizing on the weakness and mis-
judgments of his opponents. The Munich pact, for example, rather than being
his aggression was the "triumph" of a British policy determined to pin down
Hitler to specific aims. His seizure of the rest of Czechoslovakia six months
later merely resulted from Munich's ungluing of the Czech state. In Taylor's
view World War II was only a "war for Danzig," brought about because
Hitler miscalculated the depth of British and French commitment to Poland.
Even then, as his lack of war preparedness illustrates, he embarked on what
he mistakenly assumed would be a short and limited war. In short, World
War II was a result of blunder, accident, and miscalculation on all sides
rather than a planned Hitlerian drive for world domination. What made
Taylor's book such a sensation was both his interpretation of the documents
and his previous anti-German record in two earlier books,* The Course of
German History *(1946) and* Struggle for Mastery in Europe, 1848—1918
(1954).

*A revisionist work like Taylor's is valuable because it extends historical
knowledge whether or not its interpretation finds wide acceptance. Either by
finding new evidence or by reinterpreting old, it forces everyone to look at
a historical event afresh. In that important way historical knowledge advances.
The example of British historian Alan Bullock is a case in point. His biography
of Hitler, the most distinguished one in English, had argued that World War II
was Hitler's war. The publication of the books by Taylor and others caused
him to reexamine his position. You will discover that he still comes down
against Hitler, but with more depth and nuance than he had before. Why does
Bullock believe that the "two contrasted views of Hitler's foreign policy,"
the "fanatic" and the "opportunist," need to be combined into one? How does
he then combine them in dealing with such historical evidence and events as
the Hossbach conference, the level of German rearmament, and the* Anschluss?
*How do both the Czech crisis of 1938 and the Polish one of 1939 illustrate
Hitler's mixture of aims and opportunism? What light do Hitler's actions
after the outbreak of the war in 1939 shed on his responsibility before the war
began?*

529
Bullock
**HITLER AND
THE ORIGINS OF
THE SECOND
WORLD WAR**

In the twenty years since the end of the war and the Nuremberg Trials, historical controversy has been largely concerned with the share of the other Powers in the responsibility for allowing war to break out in 1939. Thus, the British and French Governments of the 1930s have been blamed for their policy of appeasement and for failing to secure an agreement with Russia; Mussolini for his alliance with Hitler; Stalin for the Nazi-Soviet Pact; the Poles for the illusions which encouraged them to believe that they could hold Russia as well as Germany at arm's length. Taking a wider sweep, historians have turned for an explanation of the origins of the Second World War to the mistakes made in the peace settlement that followed the First; to the inadequacies of British and French policy between the wars; the retreat of the United States into isolation; the exclusion of the Soviet Union; the social effects of the Great Depression, and so on.

All this is necessary work, in order to establish the historical situation in which the war began, but as the catalogue grows, I find myself asking what is left of the belief universally held outside Germany twenty years ago that the primary responsibility for the war rested on Hitler and the Nazis?

No one suggests that theirs was the sole responsibility. Hitler would never have got as near to success as he did if it had not been for the weakness, the divisions, the opportunism of the other governments, which allowed him to build up such power that he could not be prevented from conquering Europe without a major war. Still, there is a lot of difference between failing to stop aggression, even hoping to derive side profits from it—and aggression itself. Indeed, much of the criticism directed at the other Powers for their failure to stop Hitler in time would fall to the ground if there proved to have been nothing to stop.

Is the effect of filling in the historical picture to reduce this difference to the point where it no longer appears so important, where the responsibility for the war becomes dispersed, or is shifted on to the shortcomings of an anarchical system of international relations, or of militarism or of capitalism, as happened after the First World War? Is Mr. A. J. P. Taylor [1] the harbinger of a new generation of revisionist historians who will find it as anachronistic to hold Hitler—or anyone else—responsible for the outbreak of the Second World War as to hold the Kaiser responsible for the outbreak of the First?

The question is an important one, for to an extent which we only begin to realize when it is questioned, the accepted version of European

---

[1] In *The Origins of the Second World War* (rev. ed. 1963). See also the article by T. W. Mason, 'Some Origins of the Second World War', in *Past and Present,* no. 29, Dec. 1964, and Mr. Taylor's reply in the same journal, no. 30, Apr. 1965. For a German view of Mr. Taylor's book, see the review article by Gottard Jasper in *Vierteljahrshefte für Zeitgeschichte,* July 1962, pp. 311–40.

history in the years between 1933 and 1945 has been built round a particular view of Hitler and of the character of German foreign policy, and if the centrepiece were removed, far more than our view of Hitler and German foreign policy would have to be revised—our view of the foreign policies of all the Powers and of the substantiality of the dangers which the other governments, and their critics, believed they confronted.

It occurred to me, therefore, when I was invited to deliver this lecture, that it would be interesting to take a fresh look at Hitler's foreign policy in the light of the new evidence that has become available in the twenty years since the Nuremberg Trials (and, no less important, of new ways of looking at familiar evidence) and then to go on and ask, in what sense, if at all, it is still possible to speak of Hitler's and the Nazis' responsibility for what became a Second World War.

II

There are two contrasted versions of Hitler's foreign policy which for convenience's sake I will call the fanatic and the opportunist.

The first [2] fastens upon Hitler's racist views and his insistence that the future of the German people could be secured, neither by economic development nor by overseas colonization, not even by the restoration of Germany's 1914 frontiers, but only by the conquest of living space (*Lebensraum*) in Eastern Europe. Here the scattered populations of Germans living outside the Reich could be concentrated, together with the surplus population of the homeland, and a Germanic empire established, racially homogeneous, economically self-sufficient, and militarily impregnable. Such *Lebensraum* could only be obtained at the expense of Russia and the states bordering on her and could only be won and cleared of its existing population by force, a view which coincided with Hitler's belief in struggle as the law of life, and war as the test of a people's racial superiority.

Hitler first set these views down in *Mein Kampf*, elaborated them in his so-called *Zweites Buch*,[3] and repeated them on almost every occasion when we have a record of him talking privately and not in public, down to the Table Talk of the 1940s [4] and his final conversations with Bormann in the early months of 1945 [5] when his defeat could no longer be disguised. Not only did he consistently hold and express these views over twenty years, but in 1941 he set to work to put them into practice in the most literal way, by attacking Russia and by giving full rein to his plans,

531
Bullock
HITLER AND
THE ORIGINS OF
THE SECOND
WORLD WAR

[2] This view is well stated by Professor H. R. Trevor-Roper in an article 'Hitlers Kriegsziele', ibid., Apr. 1960.

[3] Written in 1928 but not published until 1961. An English translation has been published by Grove Press Inc., N.Y., *Hitler's Secret Book*. This book is almost entirely concerned with foreign policy.

[4] An English version, *Hitler's Table Talk 1941–44*, was published in 1953, with an introduction by H. R. Trevor-Roper.

[5] *The Testament of Adolf Hitler. The Hitler–Bormann Documents* (London, 1961).

which the S.S. had already begun to carry out in Poland, for the resettlement of huge areas of Eastern Europe.

The alternative version[6] treats Hitler's talk of *Lebensraum* and racist
empire in the East as an expression of the fantasy side of his personality
and fastens on the opportunism of Hitler's actual conduct of foreign policy. In practice—so this version runs—Hitler was an astute and cynical politician who took advantage of the mistakes and illusions of others
to extend German power along lines entirely familiar from the previous
century of German history. So little did he take his own professions seriously that he actually concluded a pact with the Bolsheviks whom he had
denounced, and when Hitler belatedly began to put his so-called programme into practice, it marked the point at which he lost the capacity to
distinguish between fantasy and reality and, with it, the opportunist's
touch which had been responsible for his long run of successes. Thereafter
he suffered nothing but one disaster after another.

These two versions of Hitler's foreign policy correspond to alternative
versions of his personality. The first stresses his insistence on a fanatical
will, force, and brutality of purpose, his conviction that he was a man of
destiny, his reliance on intuition, his scorn for compromise, his declaration after the occupation of the Rhineland: 'I go the way that Providence
dictates with the assurance of a sleepwalker.'[7]

The second takes this no more seriously than the rest of Nazi and Fascist rhetoric and insists that in practice Hitler relied for his success upon
calculation, total lack of scruple, and remarkable gifts as an actor. The

suggestion that his opponents had to deal with a man who was fanatical
in his purposes and would stop at nothing to accomplish them was part of
the act, and a very successful part. His threats were carefully timed as part
of a war of nerves, his ungovernable rages turned on or off as the occasion
demanded, his hypnotic stare and loss of control part of a public *persona*
skilfully and cynically manipulated. And when Hitler, carried away by his
triumphs, himself began to believe in his own myth, and no longer to manipulate it, success deserted him.

It is a mistake, however, I believe, to treat these two contrasting views
as alternatives, for if that is done, then, whichever alternative is adopted,
a great deal of evidence has to be ignored. The truth is, I submit, that
they have to be combined and that Hitler can only be understood if it is
realized that he was at once both fanatical *and* cynical; unyielding in his
assertion of will-power *and* cunning in calculation; convinced of his role
as a man of destiny *and* prepared to use all the actor's arts in playing it.
To leave out either side, the irrational or the calculating, is to fail to grasp
the combination which marks Hitler out from all his imitators.

The same argument, I believe, applies to Hitler's foreign policy which
combined consistency of aim with complete opportunism in method and

[6] For this view, see A. J. P. Taylor, *The Origins of the Second World War*.
[7] 14 Mar. 1936, in a speech at Munich. For the context, cf. Max Domarus, *Hitler, Reden und Proklamationen*, vol. 1 (Würzburg, 1962), p. 606.

tactics. This is, after all, a classical receipt for success in foreign affairs. It was precisely because he knew where he wanted to go that Hitler could afford to be opportunistic and saw how to take advantage of the mistakes and fears of others. Consistency of aim on Hitler's part has been confused with a time-table, blueprint, or plan of action fixed in advance, as if it were pinned up on the wall of the General Staff offices and ticked off as one item succeeded another. Nothing of the sort. Hitler frequently improvised, kept his options open to the last possible moment, and was never sure until he got there which of several courses of action he would choose. But this does not alter the fact that his moves followed a logical (though not a predetermined) course—in contrast to Mussolini, an opportunist who snatched eagerly at any chance that was going but never succeeded in combining even his successes into a coherent policy.

III

Hitler had established his power inside Germany by the late summer of 1934. By securing the succession to President Hindenburg, he became Head of State and Commander-in-Chief of the Armed Forces as well as leader of the only party in the country and head of a government in which no one dared to oppose him. From now on, apart from the one thing which he put before everything else, his own supremacy, Hitler took no great interest in internal affairs or administration. He turned his attention almost wholly to foreign policy and rearmament.

Shortly after he became Chancellor, on 3 February 1933, Hitler had met the leaders of the armed forces privately and told them that, once his political power was secure, his most important task would be to rearm Germany and then move from the revision of the Versailles Treaty to the conquest of *Lebensraum* in the East.[8]

Just over a year later, on 28 February 1934, Hitler repeated this at a conference of Army and S.A. leaders, declaring that here was a decisive reason for rejecting Roehm's plan for a national militia and for rebuilding the German Army. The Western Powers would never allow Germany to conquer *Lebensraum* in the East. 'Therefore, short decisive blows to the West and then to the East could be necessary', tasks which could only be carried out by an army rigorously trained and equipped with the most modern weapons.[9]

None the less, in the first two years, 1933 and 1934, Hitler's foreign policy was cautious. Politically, he had still to establish his own supremacy

533

Bullock

HITLER AND
THE ORIGINS OF
THE SECOND
WORLD WAR

[8] General Liebmann's note of Hitler's speech on this occasion is reprinted in *Vierteljahrshefte für Zeitgeschichte*, Oct. 1954, pp. 434–5. Cf. K. D. Bracher, W. Sauer, and G. Schulz, *Die Nationalsozialistische Machtergreifung* (Köln, 1962), p. 748, and Robert J. O'Neill, *The German Army and the Nazi Party, 1933–1939* (London, 1966), pp. 125–6.

[9] A report of Hitler's speech on this occasion, made by Field Marshal von Weichs, is printed by O'Neill, ibid., pp. 39–42. For further discussion of the reliability of this report see Bracher, Sauer, and Schulz, op. cit., p. 749, n. 14.

at home. Diplomatically, Germany was isolated and watched with suspicion by all her neighbours. Militarily, she was weak and unable to offer much resistance if the French or the Poles should take preventive action against the new régime.

These were all excellent reasons for Hitler to protest his love of peace and innocence of aggressive intentions. As he told Rauschning, now that Germany had left Geneva, he would more than ever speak 'the language of the League'.[10] There is, in fact, a striking parallel between his conduct of foreign policy in this early period and the tactics of 'legality' which he had pursued in his struggle for power inside Germany. By observing the forms of legality, staying within the framework of the constitution, and refusing to make a *Putsch*—which would have brought the Nazis into open conflict with the Army—Hitler was able to turn the weapons of democracy against democracy itself. His appeal to Wilsonian principles of national self-determination and equality of rights had precisely the same effect—and those who believed him were to be as sharply disillusioned as those who supposed Hitler would continue to observe the limits of legality in Germany once he had acquired the power to ignore them.

Although Nazi propaganda made the most of them, none of Hitler's foreign policy moves in his first two years did much to improve Germany's position. Leaving the Disarmament Conference and the League was a gesture; the Pact with Poland clever but unconvincing, and more than counter-balanced by Russia's agreement to join the League and start negotiations for an alliance with France. The hurried repudiation of the Austrian Nazis in 1934 was humiliating, and the Saar plebiscite in January 1935 was largely a foregone conclusion. When Hitler announced the reintroduction of conscription in March 1935, Germany's action was condemned by the British, French, and Italian governments meeting at Stresa, as well as by the League Council, and was answered by the conclusion of pacts between Russia and France, and Russia and France's most reliable ally Czechoslovakia.[11]

Between 1935 and 1937, however, the situation changed to Hitler's advantage, and he was able not only to remove the limitations of the Versailles Treaty on Germany's freedom of action but to break out of Germany's diplomatic isolation.

It is true that the opportunities for this were provided by the other Powers: for example, by Mussolini's Abyssinian adventure and the quarrel to which this led between Italy and the Western Powers. But Hitler showed skill in using the opportunities which others provided, for example, in Spain where he reduced the policy of non-intervention to a farce and exploited the civil war for his own purposes with only a minimum commitment to Franco. He also provided his own opportunities: for ex-

[10] Hermann Rauschning, *Hitler Speaks* (London, 1939), p. 116.
[11] A critical review of Hitler's foreign policy in these years is made by K. D. Bracher in *Vierteljahrshefte für Zeitgeschichte*, Jan. 1957: 'Das Anfangsstadium der Hitlerschen Außenpolitik' (pp. 63–76).

ample, the offer of a naval treaty to Britain in 1935 and the military reoccupation of the Rhineland in 1936. This was a bold and risky stroke of bluff, taken against the advice of his generals, without anything like sufficient forces to resist the French if they had marched, and accompanied by a brilliantly contrived diversion in the form of the new peace pacts which he offered simultaneously to the other Locarno Powers.

Of course, there were failures—above all, Ribbentrop's failure to get an alliance with Britain. But between April 1935, when the Powers, meeting at Stresa, had unanimously condemned German rearmament, and Mussolini's state visit to Germany as a prospective ally in September 1937, Hitler could claim with some justification to have transformed Germany's diplomatic position and ended her isolation.

IV

The German Foreign Ministry and diplomatic service were well suited to the international equivalent of the policy of 'legality', but Hitler soon began to develop instruments of his own for a new style of foreign policy.[12] One was the Nazi groups among the Volksdeutsche living abroad. The two most obvious examples are the Nazi Party in Austria and Henlein's *Sudetendeutsche Partei* in Czechoslovakia. The former had to be hastily disavowed in the summer of 1934, when the *Putsch* against Dolfuss failed, but the subsidies to the Austrian Nazis continued and so did the many links across the frontier from Munich and Berlin. Henlein's Sudeten Party was also secretly in receipt of subsidies from Germany from early 1935,[13] and was to play a key role in the campaign against Czechoslovakia. These links were maintained outside the regular Foreign Ministry system and there were a number of Nazi agencies—Bohle's *Auslandsorganisation,* Rosenberg's *Außenpolitisches Amt,* VOMI (*Volksdeutsche Mittelstelle*) competing with each other, and with the Foreign Ministry, to organize the German-speaking groups living abroad.

At the same time Hitler began to make use of envoys from outside the foreign service for the most important diplomatic negotiations: Goering, for instance, who frequently undertook special missions to Italy, Poland, and the Balkans, and Ribbentrop whose Büro, originally set up to deal with disarmament questions in 1933, soon moved into direct competition with the *Auswärtiges Amt.* It was Ribbentrop who negotiated the naval treaty with London; Ribbentrop who was given the key post of ambassador in London in order to secure a British alliance; Ribbentrop who represented Germany on the Non-Intervention Committee, who negotiated and signed the Anti-Comintern Pact with Japan in 1936 and a year later brought in Italy as well.

[12] I am indebted in this section to Dr. H. A. Jacobsen who allowed me to see a forthcoming article: 'Programm und Struktur der nationalsozialistischen Außenpolitik 1919–1939.'

[13] *Documents on German Foreign Policy,* Series C, vol. 3, no. 509.

It was not until the beginning of 1938 that Hitler appointed Ribbentrop as Foreign Minister: until then he left the German Foreign Ministry and diplomatic service as a respectable façade but increasingly took the discussion of policy and the decisions out of their hands and used other agents to carry them out. In Hitler's eyes the diplomats—like the generals, as he came to feel during the war—were too conservative, too preoccupied with the conventional rules of the game to see the advantages of scrapping rules altogether and taking opponents by surprise. Hitler's radicalism required a new style in the conduct of foreign affairs as different from old style diplomacy as the Nazi Party was from the old style political parties of the Weimar Republic.

This new style did not emerge clearly until 1938–9, but there were unmistakable signs of it before then in the changed tone in which Hitler and German propaganda were speaking by 1937. Hitler receiving Mussolini and showing off the strength of the new Germany,[14] Hitler beginning to talk of Germany's 'demands', was speaking a very different language from that of the man who only three or four years before had used all his gifts as an orator to convince the world of Germany's will to peace. German national pride and self-confidence had been restored, and, instead of trying to conceal, Nazi propaganda now boasted of her growing military strength.

V

The Nazis' claims about German rearmament were widely believed. Phrases like 'Guns before butter'—'total war'—'a war economy in peacetime' made a deep impression. When Goering was appointed Plenipotentiary for the Four Year Plan in October 1936, this was taken to mean the speeding up of rearmament, and Hitler's secret memorandum to Goering found among Speer's papers after the war confirms this view.[15] Irritated by Schacht's opposition to his demands, he declared that the shortage of raw-materials was 'not an economic problem, but solely a question of will'. A clash with Bolshevik Russia was unavoidable: 'No State will be able to withdraw or even remain at a distance from this historical conflict. . . . We cannot escape this destiny.'

Hitler concluded his memorandum to Goering with the words:

I thus set the following task:
1. The German Army must be operational (*einsatzfähig*) within 4 years.

[14] Mussolini's visit to Germany took place in the last ten days of Sept. 1937 and left an indelible impression on the Italian dictator. A few weeks later, in Nov. 1937, Mussolini agreed to sign the Anti-Comintern Pact, a further step in committing himself to an alliance with Hitler.

[15] It is printed in *Documents on German Foreign Policy*, Series C, vol. 5, no. 490. Cf. Gerhard Meinck, *Hitler und die deutsche Aufrüstung* (Wiesbaden, 1959), p. 164. Meinck's book is a valuable guide to the problems connected with German rearmament. Reference should also be made to Georg Tessin, *Formationsgeschichte der Wehrmacht 1933–39*, Schriften des Bundesarchivs, Bd. 7 (Boppard/Rhein, 1959). A convenient summary is provided by O'Neill, op. cit., ch. 6.

2. The German economy must be fit for war (*kriegsfähig*) within 4 years.

Yet the evidence now available does not bear out the widespread belief in Germany's all-out rearmament before 1939.[16] The figures show that the rearmament programme took a long time to get under way and did not really begin to produce the results Hitler wanted until 1939. Even then Germany's military superiority was not as great as both public opinion and the Allies' intelligence services assumed.

The really surprising fact, however, is the scale of German rearmament in relation to Germany's economic resources. At no time before September 1939 was anything like the full capacity of the German economy devoted to war production. The figures are well below what German industry could have achieved if fully mobilized, below what German industry had achieved in 1914–18, and below what was achieved by the British when they set about rearmament in earnest.

The immediate conclusion which one might well draw from these facts is that they provide powerful support for the argument that Hitler was not deliberately preparing for war but was thinking in terms of an armed diplomacy in which he relied on bluff and the *threat* of war to blackmail or frighten the other Powers into giving way to his demands.

Before we accept this conclusion, however, it is worth while to carry the examination of the rearmament figures beyond the date of 1 September 1939. The attack on Poland may or may not have been due to mistaken calculation on Hitler's part (I shall come back to this later), but no one can doubt that the German attack on France and the Low Countries on 10 May 1940 was deliberate, not hastily improvised but prepared for over a six months' period. And this time it was an attack not on a second-class power like Poland but on two major Powers, France and Britain. Yet the interesting fact is that the proportion of Germany's economic resources devoted to the war hardly went up at all. Even more striking, the same is true of the attack on Russia in 1941. In preparation for Operation Barbarossa, the Army was built up to 180 divisions, but this was not accompanied by an all-out armaments drive and on the very eve of the invasion of Russia (20 June 1941) Hitler actually ordered a reduction in the level of arms production. This was put into effect and by December 1941, when the German Army was halted before Moscow, the over-all level of weapons production had fallen by 29 per cent. from its peak in July of that year.[17]

In fact, it was not until 1942, the year in which Hitler lost the initiative and Germany was pushed on to the defensive, that Hitler was persuaded to commit the full resources of the German economy to an all-out effort.

537
Bullock

HITLER AND
THE ORIGINS OF
THE SECOND
WORLD WAR

[16] The evidence has been admirably summarized and reviewed by Alan S. Milward in *The German Economy at War* (London, 1965). Further details are to be found in Burton H. Klein, *Germany's Economic Preparations for War* (Cambridge, Mass., 1959).

[17] Klein, op. cit., pp. 191–5; Milward, op. cit., pp. 43–5.

This puts the facts I have mentioned in a different light. For, if Hitler believed that he could defeat the Western Powers, subdue the Balkans, and conquer Russia without demanding more than a partial mobilization from the German people, then the fact that German rearmament before the war had limited rather than total objectives is no proof that his plans at that time did not include war.

The truth is that, both before and after September 1939, Hitler was thinking in terms of a very different sort of war from that which Germany had lost in 1914–18 or was to lose again between 1942 and 1945. With a shrewder judgement than many of his military critics, Hitler realized that Germany, with limited resources of her own and subject to a blockade, was always going to be at a disadvantage in a long-drawn-out general war. The sort of war she could win was a series of short campaigns in which surprise and the overwhelming force of the initial blow would settle the issue before the victim had time to mobilize his full resources or the other Powers to intervene. This was the sort of war the German Army was trained as well as equipped to fight, and all the German campaigns between 1939 and 1941 conformed to this pattern— Poland, four weeks; Norway, two months; Holland, five days, Belgium, seventeen; France, six weeks; Yugoslavia, eleven days; Greece, three weeks. The most interesting case of all is that of Russia. The explanation of why the German Army was allowed to invade Russia without winter clothing or equipment is Hitler's belief that even Russia could be knocked out by a blitzkreig in four to five months, before the winter set in. And so convinced was Hitler that he had actually achieved this that in his directive of 14 July 1941 [18] he spoke confidently of reducing the size of the Army, the Navy, and the armaments programme in the near future.

This pattern of warfare, very well adapted both to Germany's economic position and the advantages of secrecy and surprise enjoyed by a dictatorship, fits perfectly the pattern of German rearmament. What was required was not armament in depth, the long-term conversion of the whole economy to a war footing which (as in Britain) would only begin to produce results in two to three years, but a war economy of a different sort geared (like German strategy) to the concept of the blitzkrieg. It was an economy which concentrated on a short-term superiority and the weapons which could give a quick victory, even when this meant neglecting the proper balance of a long-term armament programme. What mattered, as Hitler said in his 1936 memorandum, was not stocks of raw materials or building up productive capacity, but armaments ready for use, plus the will to use them. How near the gamble came to success is shown by the history of the years 1939–41 when Hitler's limited rearmament programme produced an army capable of overrunning the greater part of Europe, and very nearly defeating the Russians as well as the French.

[18] Reprinted in the English translation of Walter Hubatsch's *Hitlers Weisungen, Hitler's War Directives, 1939–45,* edited by H. R. Trevor-Roper (London, 1964), pp. 82–51.

VI

But we must not run ahead of the argument. The fact that Germany was better prepared for war, and when it began proceeded to win a remarkable series of victories, does not prove that Hitler intended to start the war which actually broke out in September 1939. We have still to relate Hitler's long-term plans for expansion in the East and his rearmament programme to the actual course of events in 1938 and 1939.

A starting-point is Colonel Hossbach's record of Hitler's conference with his three Commanders-in-Chief, War Minister, and Foreign Minister on 5 November 1937.[19] It was an unusual occasion, since Hitler rarely talked to more than one Commander-in-Chief or minister at a time, and he came nearer to laying down a programme than he ever had before. Once again he named *Lebensraum* in the East and the need to provide for Germany's future by continental expansion as the objective, but instead of leaving it at that, he went on to discuss how this was to be achieved.

The obstacles in the way were Britain and France, Germany's two 'hate-inspired antagonists'. Neither was as strong as she seemed: still, 'Germany's problems could only be solved by force and this was never without attendant risk.'

The peak of German power would be reached in 1943–5: after that, their lead in armaments would be reduced. 'It was while the rest of the world was preparing its defences that we were obliged to take the offensive.' Whatever happened, he was resolved to solve Germany's problem of space by 1943–5 at the latest. Hitler then discussed two possible cases in which action might be taken earlier—one was civil strife in France, disabling the French Army: the other, war in the Mediterranean which might allow Germany to act as early as 1938. The first objective in either case 'must be to overthrow Czechoslovakia and Austria simultaneously in order to remove the threat to our flank in any possible operation against the West'. Hitler added the comment that almost certainly Britain and probably France as well had already tacitly written off the Czechs.

To speak of this November meeting as a turning-point in Hitler's foreign policy at which Hitler made an irreversible decision in favour of war seems to me as wide of the target as talking about time-tables and blueprints of aggression. Hitler was far too skilful a politician to make irreversible decisions in advance of events: no decisions were taken or called for.

But to brush the Hossbach meeting aside and say that this was just Hitler talking for effect and not to be taken seriously seems to me equally wide of the mark. The hypotheses Hitler outlined—civil strife in France, a Mediterranean war—did not materialize, but when Hitler spoke of his determination to overthrow Czechoslovakia and Austria, as

539
Bullock
**HITLER AND
THE ORIGINS OF
THE SECOND
WORLD WAR**

---

[19] Text in *Documents on German Foreign Policy,* Series D, vol. 1, no. 19. Cf. also Friedrich Hossbach, *Zwischen Wehrmacht und Hitler* (Hanover, 1949), pp. 207–20.

early as 1938 if an opportunity offered, and when both countries *were* overthrown within less than eighteen months, it is stretching incredulity rather far to ignore the fact that he had stated this as his immediate programme in November 1937.

The next stage was left open, but Hitler foresaw quite correctly that everything would depend upon the extent to which Britain and France were prepared to intervene by force to prevent Germany's continental expansion and he clearly contemplated war if they did. Only when the obstacle which they represented had been removed would it be possible for Germany to carry out her eastward expansion.

This was a better forecast of the direction of events in 1938–41 than any other European leader including Stalin made at the end of 1937— for the very good reason that Hitler, however opportunist in his tactics, knew where he wanted to go, was almost alone among European leaders in knowing this, and so kept the initiative in his hands.

The importance of the Hossbach conference, I repeat, is not in recording a decision, but in reflecting the change in Hitler's attitude. If the interpretation offered of his policy in 1933–7 is correct, it was not a sudden but a gradual change, and a change not in the objectives of foreign policy but in Hitler's estimate of the risks he could afford to take in moving more rapidly and openly towards them. As he told the Nazi Old Guard at Augsburg a fortnight later: 'I am convinced that the most difficult part of the preparatory work has already been achieved. . . . To-day we are faced with new tasks, for the *Lebensraum* of our people is too narrow.'[20]

There is another point to be made about the Hossbach conference. Of the five men present besides Hitler and his adjutant Hossbach, Goering was certainly not surprised by what he heard and Raeder said nothing. But the other three, the two generals and Neurath, the Foreign Minister, showed some alarm and expressed doubts. It is surely another remarkable coincidence if this had nothing to do with the fact that within three months all three men had been turned out of office—the two generals, Blomberg and Fritsch, on bare-faced pretexts. There is no need to suppose that Hitler himself took the initiative in framing Blomberg or Fritsch. The initiative seems more likely to have come from Goering and Himmler, but it was Hitler who turned both Blomberg's *mésalliance* and the allegations against Fritsch to his own political advantage. Blomberg, the Minister of War, was replaced by Hitler himself who suppressed the office altogether, took over the OKW, the High Command of the armed forces, as his own staff and very soon made clear that neither the OKW nor the OKH, the High Command of the Army, would be allowed the independent position of the old General Staff. Fritsch, long regarded by Hitler as too stiff, conservative, and out of sympathy with Nazi ideas, was replaced by the much more pliable Brauchitsch as Commander-in-Chief of the Army, and Neurath, a survivor from the original coalition, by Ribbentrop

[20] Speech at Augsburg, 21 Nov. 1937. Domarus, op. cit., pp. 759–60.

who made it as clear to the staff of the Foreign Ministry as Hitler did to the generals that they were there to carry out orders, not to discuss, still less question the Fuehrer's policy.

VII

I find nothing at all inconsistent with what I have just said in the fact that the timing for the first of Hitler's moves, the annexation of Austria, should have been fortuitous and the preparations for it improvised on the spur of the moment in a matter of days, almost of hours. On the contrary, the *Anschluß* seems to me to provide, almost in caricature, a striking example of that extraordinary combination of consistency in aim, calculation, and patience in preparation with opportunism, impulse, and improvisation in execution which I regard as characteristic of Hitler's policy.

The aim in this case was never in doubt: the demand for the incorporation of Austria in the Reich appears on the first page of *Mein Kampf*. After the Austrian Nazis' unsuccessful *Putsch* of 1934, Hitler showed both patience and skill in his relations with Austria: he gradually disengaged Mussolini from his commitment to maintain Austrian independence and at the same time steadily undermined that independence from within. By the beginning of 1938 he was ready to put on the pressure, but the invitation to Schuschnigg to come to Berchtesgaden was made on the spur of the moment as the result of a suggestion by an anxious Papen trying hard to find some pretext to defer his own recall from Vienna. When Schuschnigg appeared on 12 February, Hitler put on an elaborate act to frighten him into maximum concessions with the threat of invasion, but there is no reason to believe that either Hitler or the generals he summoned to act as 'stage extras' regarded these threats as anything other than bluff. Hitler was confident that he would secure Austria, without moving a man, simply by the appointment of his nominee Seyss-Inquart as Minister of the Interior and the legalization of the Austrian Nazis—to both of which Schuschnigg agreed.

When the Austrian Chancellor, in desperation, announced a plebiscite on 9 March, Hitler was taken completely by surprise. Furious at being crossed, he decided at once to intervene before the plebiscite could be held. But no plans for action had been prepared: they had to be improvised in the course of a single day, and everything done in such a hurry and confusion that 70 per cent of the tanks and lorries, according to General Jodl, broke down on the road to Vienna. The confusion was even greater in the Reich Chancellery: when Schuschnigg called off the plebiscite, Hitler hesitated, then was persuaded by Goering to let the march in continue, but without any clear idea of what was to follow. Only when he reached Linz, did Hitler, by then in a state of self-intoxication, suddenly decide to annex Austria instead of making it a satellite state, and his effusive messages of relief to Mussolini show how unsure he was of the consequences of his action.

No doubt the *Anschluß* is an exceptional case. On later occasions the plans were ready: dates by which both the Czech and the Polish crises must be brought to a solution were fixed well in advance, and nothing like the same degree of improvisation was necessary. But in all the major crises of Hitler's career there is the same strong impression of confusion at the top, springing directly (as his generals and aides complained) from his own hesitations and indecision. It is to be found in his handling of domestic as well as foreign crises—as witness his long hesitation before the Roehm purge of 1934—and in war as well as peacetime.

The paradox is that out of all this confusion and hesitation there should emerge a series of remarkably bold decisions, just as, out of Hitler's opportunism in action, there emerges a pattern which conforms to objectives stated years before.

VIII

The next crisis, directed against Czechoslovakia, was more deliberately staged. This time Hitler gave preliminary instructions to his staff on 21 April 1938 [21] and issued a revised directive on 30 May.[22] Its first sentence read: 'It is my unalterable decision to smash Czechoslovakia by military action in the near future.' It was essential, Hitler declared, to create a situation within the first two or three days which would make intervention by other Powers hopeless: the Army and the Air Force were to concentrate all their strength for a knock-out blow and leave only minimum forces to hold Germany's other frontiers.

It is perfectly true that for a long time in the summer Hitler kept out of the way and left the other Powers to make the running, but this was only part of the game. Through Henlein and the Sudeten Party, who played the same role of fifth column as the Austrian Nazis, Hitler was able to manipulate the dispute between the Sudeten Germans and the Czech Government, which was the ostensible cause of the crisis, from within. At a secret meeting with Hitler on 28 March, Henlein summarized his policy in the words: 'We must always demand so much that we can never be satisfied.' The Fuehrer, says the official minute, approved this view.[23]

At the same time through a variety of devices—full-scale press and radio campaigns, the manufacture of incidents, troop movements, carefully circulated rumours, and diplomatic leaks, a steadily mounting pressure was built up, timed to culminate in Hitler's long-awaited speech at the Nuremberg Party Congress. Those who study only the diplomatic documents get a very meagre impression of the war of nerves which was maintained throughout the summer and which was skilfully directed to play on the fear of war in Britain and France and to heighten the Czechs' sense of isolation. It was under the pressure of this political warfare,

[21] *Documents on German Foreign Policy,* Series D, vol. 2, no. 133. Cf. also Series D, vol. 7, pp. 635–7.

[22] Ibid., vol. 2, no. 221.   [23] Ibid., vol. 2, no. 107.

something very different from diplomacy as it had been traditionally practised, that the British and French governments felt themselves impelled to act.

What was Hitler's objective? The answer has been much confused by the ambiguous use of the word 'war'.

Western opinion made a clear-cut distinction between peace and war: Hitler did not, he blurred the distinction. Reversing Clausewitz, he treated politics as a continuation of war by other means, at one stage of which (formally still called peace) he employed methods of political warfare—subversion, propaganda, diplomatic and economic pressure, the war of nerves—at the next, the threat of war, and so on to localized war and up the scale to general war—a continuum of force in which the different stages ran into each other. Familiar enough now since the time of the Cold War, this strategy (which was all of a piece with Hitler's radical new style in foreign policy) was as confusing in its novelty as the tactics of the Trojan horse, the fifth column, and the 'volunteers' to those who still thought in terms of a traditionally decisive break between a state of peace and a state of war.

So far as the events of 1938 go, there seem to be two possible answers to the question, What was in Hitler's mind?

The first is that his object was to destroy the Czech State by the sort of blitzkrieg for which he had rearmed Germany and which he was to carry out a year later against Poland. This was to come at the end of a six months' political, diplomatic, and propaganda campaign designed to isolate and undermine the Czechs, and to manœuvre the Western Powers into abandoning them to their fate rather than risk a European war. The evidence for this view consists in the series of secret directives and the military preparations to which they led, plus Hitler's declaration on several occasions to the generals and his other collaborators that he meant to settle the matter by force, with 1 October as D-day. On this view, he was only prevented from carrying out his attack by the intervention of Chamberlain which, however great the cost to the Czechs, prevented war or at least postponed it for a year.

The other view is that Hitler never intended to go to war, that his objective was from the beginning a political settlement such as was offered to him at Munich, that his military preparations were not intended seriously but were designed as threats to increase the pressure.

The choice between these two alternatives, however—*either* the one *or* the other—seems to me unreal. The obvious course for Hitler to pursue was to keep both possibilities open to the very last possible moment, the more so since they did not conflict. The more seriously the military preparations were carried out, the more effective was the pressure in favour of a political settlement if at the last moment he decided not to take the risks involved in a military operation. If we adopt this view, then we remove all the difficulties in interpreting the evidence which are created either by attempting to pin Hitler down on any particular declaration and say *now,* at this point, he had decided on war—or by the dog-

543

Bullock

HITLER AND
THE ORIGINS OF
THE SECOND
WORLD WAR

matic assumption that Hitler *never* seriously contemplated the use of force, with the consequent need to dismiss his military directives as bluff.

Neither in 1938 nor in 1939 did Hitler deliberately plan to start a general European war. But this was a risk which could not be ignored, and in 1938 it was decisive. The generals were unanimous that Germany's rearmament had not yet reached the point where she could face a war with France and Britain. The Czech frontier defences were formidable. Their army on mobilization was hardly inferior at all, either in numbers or training, to the thirty-seven divisions which the Germans could deploy and it was backed by a first-class armaments industry.[24] To overcome these would require a concentration of force which left the German commander in the West with totally inadequate strength to hold back the French Army.

While the generals, however, added up divisions and struck an unfavourable balance in terms of material forces, Hitler was convinced that the decisive question was a matter of will, the balance between his determination to take the *risk* of a general war and the determination of the Western Powers, if pushed far enough, to take the *actual decision* of starting one. For, however much the responsibility for such a war might be Hitler's, by isolating the issue and limiting his demands to the Sudetenland, he placed the onus of actually starting a general war on the British and the French. How far was Hitler prepared to drive such an argument? The answer is, I believe, that while he had set a date by which he knew he must decide, until the very last moment he had not made up his mind and that it is this alternation between screwing up his demands, as he did at his second meeting with Chamberlain in Godesberg, and still evading an irrevocable decision, which accounts both for the zigzag course of German diplomacy and for the strain on Hitler.

In the end he decided, or was persuaded, to stop short of military operations against Czechoslovakia and 'cash' his military preparations for the maximum of political concessions.

No sooner had he agreed to this, however, than Hitler started to regret that he had not held on, marched his army in, then and there, and broken up the Czechoslovak State, not just annexed the Sudetenland. His regret sprang from the belief, confirmed by his meeting with the Western leaders at Munich, that he could have got away with a localized war carried out in a matter of days, and then confronted the British and French with a *fait accompli* while they were still hesitating whether to attack in the West—exactly as happened a year later over Poland.

Almost immediately after Munich, therefore, Hitler began to think about ways in which he could complete his original purpose. Every sort of excuse, however transparent, was found for delaying the international guarantee which had been an essential part of the Munich agreement. At

[24] For the strength of the Czech forces, see David Vital, 'Czechoslovakia and the Powers', *Journal of Contemporary History,* vol. 1, no. 4, Oct. 1966.

the same time, the ground was carefully prepared with the Hungarians, who were eager to recover Ruthenia and at least part of Slovakia, and with the Slovaks themselves who were cast for the same role the Sudeten Germans had played the year before. The actual moment at which the crisis broke was not determined by Hitler and took him by surprise, but that was all. The Slovaks were at once prodded into declaring their independence and putting themselves in Hitler's hands. The Czech Government, after Hitler had threatened President Hacha in Berlin, did the same. The 'legality' of German intervention was unimpeachable: Hitler had been invited to intervene by both the rebels and the government. War had been avoided, no shots exchanged, peace preserved—yet the independent state of Czechoslovakia had been wiped off the map.

IX

Within less than eighteen months, then, Hitler had successfully achieved both the immediate objectives, Austria and Czechoslovakia, which he had laid down in the Hossbach meeting. He had not foreseen the way in which this would happen, in fact he had been wrong about it, but this had not stopped him from getting both.

This had been true at every stage of Hitler's career. He had no fixed idea in 1930, even in 1932, about how he would become Chancellor, only that he would; no fixed idea in 1934–5 how he would break out of Germany's diplomatic isolation, again only that he would. So the same now. Fixity of aim by itself, or opportunism by itself, would have produced nothing like the same results.

It is entirely in keeping with this view of Hitler that, after Czechoslovakia, he should not have made up his mind what to do next. Various possibilities were in the air. Another move was likely in 1939, if only because the rearmament programme was now beginning to reach the period when it would give Germany a maximum advantage and Hitler had never believed that time was on his side. This advantage, he said in November 1937, would only last, at the most until 1943–5; then the other Powers with greater resources would begin to catch up. He had therefore to act quickly if he wanted to achieve his objectives.

Objectives, yes; a sense of urgency in carrying them out, and growing means to do so in German rearmament, but no timetable or precise plan of action for the next stage.

Ribbentrop had already raised with the Poles, immediately after Munich, the question of Danzig and the Corridor. But there is no evidence that Hitler had committed himself to war to obtain these, or to the dismemberment of Poland. If the Poles had been willing to give him what he wanted, Hitler might well have treated them, for a time at any rate, as a satellite—in much the same way as he treated Hungary—and there were strong hints from Ribbentrop that the Germans and the Poles could find a common objective in action against Russia. Another possibility, if

545
Bullock
HITLER AND
THE ORIGINS OF
THE SECOND
WORLD WAR

Danzig and the Corridor could be settled by agreement, was to turn west and remove the principal obstacle to German expansion, the British and French claim to intervene in Eastern Europe.

After Prague, the German-Polish exchanges became a good deal sharper and, given the Poles' determination not to be put in the same position as the Czechs, but to say 'No' and refuse to compromise, it is likely that a breach between Warsaw and Berlin would have come soon in any case. But what precipitated it was the British offer, and Polish acceptance, of a guarantee of Poland's independence. In this sense the British offer is a turning-point in the history of 1939. But here comes the crux of the matter. If Mr. Taylor is right in believing that Hitler was simply an opportunist who reacted to the initiative of others, then he is justified in calling the British offer to Poland a revolutionary event.[25] But if the view I have suggested is right, namely, that Hitler, although an opportunist in his tactics, was an opportunist who had from the beginning a clear objective in view, then it is very much less than that: an event which certainly helped—if you like, forced—Hitler to make up his mind between the various possibilities he had been revolving, but which certainly did not provoke him into an expansionist programme he would not otherwise have entertained, or generate the force behind it which the Nazis had been building up ever since they came to power. On this view it was Hitler who still held the initiative, as he had since the *Anschluß,* and the British who were reacting to it, not the other way round: the most the British guarantee did was to give Hitler the answer to the question he had been asking since Munich, Where next?

The answer, then, was Poland, the most probable in any event in view of the demands the Nazis had already tabled, and now a certainty. But this did not necessarily mean war—yet.

Hitler expressed his anger by denouncing Germany's Non-Aggression Pact with Poland and the Anglo-German Naval Treaty, and went on to sign a secret directive ordering the Army to be ready to attack Poland by 1 September.[26] The military preparations were not bluff: they were designed to give Hitler the option of a military solution if he finally decided this way, or to strengthen the pressures for a political solution—either direct with Warsaw, or by the intervention of the other powers in a Polish Munich. Just as in 1938 so in 1939, Hitler kept the options open literally to the last, and until the troops actually crossed the Polish frontier on 1 September none of his generals was certain that the orders might not be changed. Both options, however: there is no more reason to say dogmatically that Hitler was aiming all the time at a political solution than there is to say that he ruled it out and had made up his mind in favour of war.

Hitler's inclination, I believe, was always towards a solution by force,

[25] Taylor, op. cit., ch. 10.
[26] International Military Tribunal Document C-120. Cf. also Walter Warlimont, *Inside Hitler's Headquarters* (London, 1964), p. 20.

the sort of localized blitzkrieg with which in the end he did destroy Poland. What he had to weigh was the risk of a war which could not be localized. There were several reasons why he was more ready to take this risk than the year before.

The first was the progress of German rearmament—which was coming to a peak in the autumn of 1939. By then it represented an eighteen-fold expansion of the German armed forces since 1933.[27] In economists' terms this was not the maximum of which Germany was capable, at least in the long run, but in military terms it was more than adequate, as 1940 showed, not just to defeat the Poles but to deal with the Western Powers as well. The new German Army had been designed to achieve the maximum effect at the outset of a campaign and Hitler calculated—quite rightly—that, even if the British formally maintained their guarantee to Poland, the war would be over and Poland crushed before they could do anything about it.[28]

A second reason was Hitler's increased confidence, his conviction that his opponents were simply not his equal either in daring or in skill. The very fact that he had drawn back at Munich and then regretted it made it all the more likely that a man with his gambler's temperament would be powerfully drawn to stake all next time.

Finally, Hitler believed that he could remove the danger of Western intervention, or at least render the British guarantee meaningless, by outbidding the Western Powers in Moscow.

In moments of exaltation, e.g. in his talks to his generals after the signature of the Pact with Italy (23 May) and at the conference of 22 August which followed the news that Stalin would sign, Hitler spoke as if the matter were settled, war with Poland inevitable, and all possibility of a political settlement—on his terms—excluded. I believe that this was, as I have said, his real inclination, but I do not believe that he finally made up his mind until the last minute. Why should he? Just as in 1938, Hitler refused to make in advance the choice to which historians have tried to pin him down, the either/or of war or a settlement dictated under the threat of war. He fixed the date by which the choice would have to be made but pursued a course which would leave him with the maximum of manœuvre to the last possible moment. And again one may well ask, Why not—since the preparations to be made for either eventuality—war or a political settlement under the threat of war—were the same?

Much has been made of the fact that for the greater part of the summer Hitler retired to Berchtesgaden and made no public pronouncement. But this is misleading. The initiative remained in Hitler's hands. The pro-

547
Bullock

HITLER AND
THE ORIGINS OF
THE SECOND
WORLD WAR

[27] O'Neill, op. cit., ch. 6.

[28] It is noticeable that there were far fewer doubts in the Army in 1939 than in 1938—and the major reason for this (apart from the fact that a war with Poland fitted in far better with the generals' traditionalist ideas than one with Czechoslovakia) was their belief that a war in 1939 involved fewer risks than in 1938.

paganda campaign went ahead exactly as planned, building up to a crisis by late August and hammering on the question, Is Danzig worth a war? So did the military preparations which were complete by the date fixed, 26 August. German diplomacy was mobilized to isolate Poland and, if the pact with Italy proved to be of very little value in the event, and the Japanese failed to come up to scratch, the pact with Stalin was a major coup. For a summer of 'inactivity' it was not a bad result.

Hitler's reaction when the Nazi-Soviet Pact was signed shows clearly enough where his first choice lay. Convinced that the Western Powers would now give up any idea of intervention in defence of Poland, he ordered the German Army to attack at dawn on 26 August: i.e. a solution by force, but localized and without risk of a general European war, the sort of operation for which German rearmament had been designed from the beginning.

The unexpected British reaction, the confirmation instead of the abandonment of the guarantee to Poland—this, plus Mussolini's defection (and Mussolini at any rate had no doubt that Hitler was bent on a solution by force) upset Hitler's plans and forced him to think again. What was he to do? Keep up the pressure and hope that the Poles would crack and accept his terms? Keep up the pressure and hope that, if not the Poles, then the British would crack and either press the Poles to come to terms (another Munich) or abandon them? Or go ahead and take the risk of a general war, calculating that Western intervention, if it ever took place, would come too late to affect the outcome.

It is conceivable that if Hitler had been offered a Polish Munich, on terms that would by now have amounted to capitulation, he would still have accepted it. But I find it hard to believe that any of the moves he made, or sanctioned, between 25 August and 1 September were seriously directed to starting negotiations. A far more obvious and simple explanation is to say that, having failed to remove the threat of British intervention by the Nazi-Soviet Pact, as he had expected, Hitler postponed the order to march and allowed a few extra days to see, not if war could be avoided, but whether under the strain a split might not develop between the Western Powers and Poland and so leave the Poles isolated after all.

Now the crisis had come, Hitler himself did little to resolve or control it. Characteristically, he left it to others to make proposals, seeing the situation, not in terms of diplomacy and negotiation, but as a contest of wills. If his opponents' will cracked first, then the way was open for him to do what he wanted and march into Poland without fear that the Western Powers would intervene. To achieve this he was prepared to hold on and bluff up to the very last minute, but if the bluff did not come off within the time he had set, then this time he steeled his will to go through with the attack on Poland even if it meant running the risk of war with Britain and France as well. All the accounts agree on the strain which Hitler showed and which found expression in his haggard appearance and temperamental outbursts. But his will held. This was no stumbling into war. It was neither misunderstanding nor miscalculation which sent the German Army over the frontier into Poland, but a calculated risk, the gambler's bid—the only bid, Hitler once told Goering, he ever made, *va banque,* the bid he made when he reoccupied the Rhineland in 1936 and when he marched into Austria, the bid he had failed to make when he agreed to the Munich conference, only to regret it immediately afterwards.

X

Most accounts of the origins of the war stop in September 1939. Formally, this is correct: from 3 September 1939 Germany was in a state of war with Britain and France as well as Poland, and the Second World War had begun. But this formal statement is misleading. In fact, Hitler's gamble came off. The campaign in which the German Army defeated the Poles remained a localized war and no hostilities worth speaking of had taken place between Germany and the Western Powers by the time the Poles had been defeated and the state whose independence they had guaranteed had ceased to exist.

If Hitler had miscalculated at the beginning of September or stumbled into war without meaning to, here was the opportunity to avoid the worst consequences of what had happened. It is an interesting speculation what the Western Powers would have done, if he had really made an effort to secure peace once the Poles were defeated. But it is a pointless speculation. For Hitler did nothing of the sort. The so-called peace offer in his speech of 6 October was hardly meant to be taken seriously. Instead of limiting his demands, Hitler proceeded to destroy the Polish State and to set in train (in 1939, not in 1941) the ruthless resettlement programme which he had always declared he would carry out in Eastern Europe.

Even more to the point, it was Hitler who took the initiative in turning the formal state of war between Germany and the Western Powers into a real war. On 9 October he produced a memorandum in which he argued that, instead of waiting to see whether the Western Powers would back their formal declaration of war with effective force, Germany should seize the initiative and make an all-out attack on the French and the British, thereby removing once and for all the limitations on Germany's freedom of action.

The German generals saw clearly what this meant: far from being content with, and trying to exploit the good luck which had enabled him to avoid a clash with the Western Powers so far, Hitler was deliberately setting out to turn the localized campaign he had won in Poland into a general war. Their doubts did not deter him for a moment and, although they managed on one pretext or another to delay operations, in May 1940 it was the German Army, without waiting for the French or the British, which launched the attack in the West and turned the *drôle de guerre* into a major war.

Even this is not the end of the story. Once again, Hitler proved to be a better judge than the experts. In the middle of events, his nerve faltered, he became hysterical, blamed everyone, behaved in short in exactly the

549
Bullock
HITLER AND
THE ORIGINS OF
THE SECOND
WORLD WAR

opposite way to the copybook picture of the man of destiny: but when the battle was over he had inflicted a greater and swifter defeat upon France than any in history. And it is no good saying that it was 'the machine' that did this, not Hitler. Hitler was never the prisoner of 'the machine'. If 'the machine' had been left to decide things, it would never have taken the risk of attacking in the West, and, if it had, would never have adopted the Ardennes plan which was the key to victory. Pushing the argument further back, one can add that, if it had been left to 'the machine', German rearmament would never have been carried out at the pace on which Hitler insisted, or on the blitzkrieg pattern which proved to be as applicable to war with the Western Powers as to the limited Polish campaign.

Once again, the obvious question presents itself: what would have happened if Hitler, now as much master of continental Europe as Napoleon had been, had halted at this point, turned to organizing a continental New Order in Europe, and left to the British the decision whether to accept the situation—if not in 1940, then perhaps in 1941—or to continue a war in which they had as yet neither American nor Russian allies, were highly vulnerable to attack, and could never hope by themselves to overcome the disparity between their own and Hitler's continental resources. Once again—this is my point—it was thanks to Hitler, and no one else that this question was never posed. It was Hitler who decided that enough was not enough, that the war must go on—Hitler, not the German military leaders or the German people, many of whom would have been content to stop at this point, enjoy the fruits of victory, and risk nothing more.

If the war had to continue, then the obvious course was to concentrate all Germany's—and Europe's—resources on the one opponent left, Britain. If invasion was too difficult and dangerous an operation, there were other means—a Mediterranean campaign with something more than the limited forces reluctantly made available to Rommel, or intensification of the air and submarine war, as Raeder urged. The one thing no one thought of except Hitler was to attack Russia, a country whose government had shown itself painfully anxious to avoid conflict and give every economic assistance to Germany. There was nothing improvised about Hitler's attack on Russia. Of all his decisions it was the one taken furthest in advance and most carefully prepared for, the one over which he hesitated least and which he approached with so much confidence that he even risked a five-week delay in starting in order to punish the Yugoslavs and settle the Balkans.[29]

Nor was it conceived of solely as a military operation. The plans were ready to extend to the newly captured territory the monstrous programme of uprooting whole populations which the S.S.—including Eichmann—had already put into effect in Poland.[30] Finally, of all Hitler's deci-

[29] See G. L. Weinberg, *Germany and the Soviet Union 1939–41* (The Hague, 1954).

[30] See Robert L. Koehl, *RKFDV, German Resettlement and Population Policy*

sions it is the one which most clearly bears his own personal stamp, the culmination (as he saw it) of his whole career.

It will now be evident why I have carried my account beyond the conventional date of September 1939. Between that date and June 1941, the scope of the war was steadily enlarged from the original limited Polish campaign to a conflict which, with the attack on Russia, was now on as great a scale as the war of 1914–18. The initiative at each stage— except in the Balkans where he was reluctant to become involved— had been Hitler's. Of course he could not have done this without the military machine and skill in using it which the German armed forces put at his disposal, but the evidence leaves no doubt that the decision where and when to use that machine was in every case Hitler's, not his staff's, still less that all Hitler was doing was to react to the initiative of his opponents.

Now, it may be that the Hitler who took these increasingly bold decisions after September 1939 was a different person from the Hitler who conducted German foreign policy before that date, but this is surely implausible. It seems to me far more likely that the pattern which is unmistakable after September 1939, using each victory as the basis for raising the stakes in a still bolder gamble next time, is the correct interpretation of his conduct of foreign policy before that date. And this interpretation is reinforced by the fact that at the same time Hitler was carrying out the rearmament and expansion of the German armed forces on a pattern which exactly corresponds to the kind of war which he proceeded to wage after September 1939.

Let me repeat and underline what I said earlier in this lecture: this has nothing to do with time-tables and blueprints of aggression. Throughout his career Hitler was an opportunist, prepared to seize on and exploit any opportunity that was offered to him. There was nothing inevitable about the way or the order in which events developed, either before or after September 1939. The annexation of Austria and the attempt to eliminate Czechoslovakia, by one means or another, were predictable, but after the occupation of Prague, there were other possibilities which might have produced a quite different sequence of events—as there were after the fall of France. Of what wars or other major events in history is this not true?

But Hitler's opportunism was doubly effective because it was allied with unusual consistency of purpose. This found expression in three things:

First, in his aims—to restore German military power, expand her frontiers, gather together the scattered populations of Volks-

551
Bullock

**HITLER AND
THE ORIGINS OF
THE SECOND
WORLD WAR**

1939–45 (Cambridge, Mass., 1957), and Alexander Dallin, *German Rule in Russia, 1941–45* (London, 1957).

deutsche, and found a new German empire in Eastern Europe, the inhabitants of which would either be driven out, exterminated, or retained as slave-labour.

Second, in the firmness with which he grasped from the beginning what such aims entailed—the conquest of power in Germany on terms that would leave him with a free hand, the risk of pre-emptive intervention by other Powers, the need to shape German rearmament in such a way as to enable him to win a quick advantage within a limited time by surprise and concentration of force, the certainty that to carry out his programme would mean war.

Third, in the strength of will which underlay all his hesitations, opportunism, and temperamental outbursts, and in his readiness to take risks and constantly to increase these by raising the stakes—from the reoccupation of the Rhineland to the invasion of Russia (with Britain still undefeated in his rear) within the space of no more than five years.

Given such an attitude on the part of a man who controlled one of the most powerful nations in the world, the majority of whose people were prepared to believe what he told them about their racial superiority and to greet his satisfaction of their nationalist ambitions with enthusiasm—given this, I cannot see how a clash between Germany and the other Powers could have been avoided. Except on the assumption that Britain and France were prepared to disinterest themselves in what happened east of the Rhine and accept the risk of seeing him create a German hegemony over the rest of Europe. There was nothing inevitable about either the date or the issue on which the clash actually came. It half came over Czechoslovakia in 1938; it might have come over another issue than Poland. But I cannot see how it could have been avoided some time, somewhere, unless the other Powers were prepared to stand by and watch Hitler pursue his tactics of one-at-a-time to the point where they would no longer have the power to stop him.

If the Western Powers had recognized the threat earlier and shown greater resolution in resisting Hitler's (and Mussolini's) demands, it is possible that the clash might not have led to war, or at any rate not to a war on the scale on which it had finally to be fought. The longer they hesitated, the higher the price of resistance. This is their share of the responsibility for the war: that they were reluctant to recognize what was happening, reluctant to give a lead in opposing it, reluctant to act in time. Hitler understood their state of mind perfectly and played on it with skill. None of the Great Powers comes well out of the history of the 1930s, but this sort of responsibility even when it runs to appeasement, as in the case of Britain and France, or complicity as in the case of Russia, is still recognizably different from that of a government which deliberately creates the threat of war and sets out to exploit it.

In the Europe of the 1930s there were several leaders—Mussolini, for instance—who would have liked to follow such a policy, but lacked the toughness of will and the means to carry it through. Hitler alone possessed the will and had provided himself with the means. Not only did he create the threat of war and exploit it, but when it came to the point he was prepared to take the risk and go to war and, then when he had won the Polish campaign, to redouble the stakes and attack again, first in the West, then in the East. For this reason, despite all that we have learned since of the irresolution, shabbiness, and chicanery of other governments' policies, Hitler and the nation which followed him still bear, not the sole, but the primary responsibility for the war which began in 1939 and which, before Hitler was prepared to admit defeat, cost the lives of more than 25 million human beings in Europe alone.

Bullock

HITLER AND THE ORIGINS OF THE SECOND WORLD WAR

34. The Impact of Total War

GORDON WRIGHT

*"Every modern war, someone has said, is also a revolution." Thus begins
Stanford University Professor Gordon Wright on the impact of World
War II. Because modern war is total war it cannot help but cause
revolutionary changes on the societies of both the victorious and defeated
powers. Victory comes to the powers that can mobilize the most human
and material resources for the longest possible time. Such total mobilization
and the enormous human and material costs of modern war destroy or alter
the old order quite as much as victory or defeat. This was certainly true of
World War I. Defeat so weakened the authority of the old order in Russia
and the Hapsburg empire that social revolution triumphed and the dynasties
disintegrated. The first planned economies were introduced in Germany and
Britain. Everywhere economies, governmental finances, and international
stability were disrupted. Repression or concessions were used to contain the
rising expectations of those classes left out of the prewar ruling establishment.*

*Events since 1945 have shown that World War II also worked a revolution.
The most obvious alterations have been the end of European hegemony, as
a result of successful African and Asian anticolonialism and that bipolar struggle between the United States and the Soviet Union called the Cold War, and
the replacement of a fascist Europe by one divided between liberal-democratic*

Source: Gordon Wright, *The Ordeal of Total War 1939–1945* (New York:
Harper & Row, 1968), "The Impact of Total War," pp. 234–67. Copyright © 1968
by Gordon Wright. Reprinted by permission of Harper & Row, Publishers, Inc.

*western Europe and communist eastern Europe, each engaging in some sort
of permanent planned economy and welfare state for the first time. The triumph
of economic planning and welfare-statism indicate that the old order would
have been destroyed by the war whether or not there had been a Cold War.*

*The impact of total war between 1939 and 1945 in creating these and other
changes is the subject of Professor Wright's selection. It is a chapter from his*
Ordeal of Total War, *one of the finest books written on World War II or any
other war. No understanding of the Cold War or contemporary western civilization is possible without seeing the impact of the Second World War, an impact Wright analyzes here in an excellent fashion. What does he see as the political impact of the war on the various participating powers? What was the
social impact in the way of fostering the "garrison state," a mood for reform,
increased social mobility, and the rise of new leaders against the old order?
To what extent did the war make a lasting psychological impact? How did
the war affect such thinkers as Mounier, Bonhoeffer, Sartre, and Camus? What
was the cost of the war for Europe in terms of people, property, and prestige?*

I. The War as Revolution

Every modern war, someone has said, is also a revolution. It could hardly
be otherwise; the stress and strain of total and protracted conflict unavoid-
ably works profound changes in men and institutions. Some might argue
that for the most part, these changes represent no drastic shift in direction, but only a speeding up of trends already under way in the prewar
years. Yet even when existing processes are merely hastened, the unsettling impact may produce results equal to those of major revolutions. Neither the boatman nor the historian can afford to ignore "the difference in
character and consequence between a gentle current and a cataract." [1]

At the outset, no European could possibly foresee the depth and
breadth of the war's impact on his life and on the lives of his successors.
True, there were a few hopeful doctrinaires like the Russian refugee Victor Serge who rejoiced at this "war of social transformation" which would
introduce an era of controlled and planned economies. There were the
Axis leaders, too, for whom the war would be a constructive cataclysm
bulldozing away the debris of "decadent" Europe and opening the way for
a totally new age. And in the West, there were those who spoke in panicky or apocalyptic fashion about the imminent end of civilization.

But it was the fall of France that shocked many western Europeans into
the first dim realization that the Europe they had known had little chance
of surviving Hitler's war. Some of them—notably the collaborationists
in the defeated countries—saw a German victory as inevitable now,
and concluded that they must adapt to whatever revolutionary changes
Hitler might dictate. But even those Westerners who refused to capitulate
were shaken into a new awareness. Charles de Gaulle in 1940 described
the war as "the greatest revolution the world has ever known." The Brit-

[1] Hancock and Gowing, *British War Economy*, p. 555.

ish too, jolted out of their lethargy, began to express not only a new resoluteness but also a clearer realization that the basic values of Western culture were at stake. Churchill, who now became their official spokesman, had insisted from the outset on this broader and deeper nature of the struggle. "This is not a question of fighting for Danzig or for Poland," he had told the House of Commons in September 1939. "We are fighting to save the whole world from the pestilence of Nazi tyranny and in defense of all that is most sacred to man. . . . It is a war, viewed in its inherent quality, to establish, on impregnable rocks, the rights of the individual, and it is a war to establish and revive the stature of man." [2] But along with this British determination to defend traditional values, there emerged in 1940 a new consciousness that traditional ways and structures could never be restored *in toto*. The venerable and conservative *Times* of London, in a lead article just after Dunkirk, issued a call for a redefinition of values to fit the twentieth century. The day of narrow, clashing nationalisms was over, said the *Times;* and so was the day of "rugged individualism which excludes social organization and economic planning. . . . The new order cannot be based on the preservation of privilege, whether the privilege be that of a country, of a class, or of an individual." [3]

This urge for renovation, for building a new and better Europe on the ruins of the old, grew over the years into a persistent theme not only in Britain but also in the German-occupied countries. Resistance movements, governments-in-exile, and individual citizens sought sustenance and comfort by lifting their eyes to the future, and drafting plans for new institutions and refurbished ideals. Indeed, one hardheaded British official complained in 1944 that "the time and energy and thought which we are all giving to the Brave New World is wildly disproportionate to what is being given to the Cruel Real World." [4] But while cynics might scoff at this kind of wartime theorizing, the genuineness of the wartime urge for change can scarcely be doubted. And the expectations built up by this mood of revolutionary reform could not fail to operate as a powerful force in postwar Europe.

Yet the changes for which men consciously thirst and work and die are not the only ones produced by a great war. More profound and more sweeping, perhaps, are those that are unintended and even unforeseen. Mass warfare in the industrial age possesses its own powerful impetus, twisting and distorting the political and social institutions of the peoples caught up in the whirlwind. Peacetime limits on the powers of government give way to an increased centralization of authority, which narrows the individual's role and rights. Furthermore, deep beneath the surface of men's consciousness lie attitudes and impulses that may be altered, often in incalculable ways, by the strain of protracted war. Thus the Second World War seems to have initiated or reinforced trends toward a mood of

[2] Great Britain, *Parliamentary Debates: Commons,* CCCLI (Sept. 3, 1939), 297.
[3] *Times* (London), July 1, 1940.
[4] Hancock and Gowing, *British War Economy*, p. 542.

lawlessness, toward a confusion and corruption of values, toward a decline in man's belief in a rational universe. The mechanization of warfare brought a concurrent deterioration in the methods of waging war: the old restraints (feeble enough at best) began to lose their force in an era of long-range weapons and air bombardment. The battlefield, no longer limited and defined, was everywhere; it was occupied by civilians and soldiers alike. Chance alone seemed to determine not only who gained and lost status and security, but even who died and who survived. Old beliefs in causality tended to dissolve before these evidences of chaos; there was a growing sense that irrational forces rule man's fate. No scientist, no historian has yet discovered a technique for measuring the enduring after effects of war; but no thoughtful man can doubt their severity or their persistence.

II. The Impact on Political Structures

"No protracted war," Tocqueville once wrote, "can fail to endanger the freedom of a democratic country. . . . War does not always give over democratic communities to military government, but it must invariably and immeasurably increase the powers of civil government; it must almost compulsorily concentrate the direction of all men and the management of all things in the hands of the administration. If it does not lead to despotism by sudden violence, it prepares men for it more gently by their habits. All those who seek to destroy the liberties of a democratic nation ought to know that war is the surest and the shortest means to accomplish it." [5]

Tocqueville's dictum, appropriate enough in his own day, is even more applicable in the twentieth century. When nations must mobilize their total resources for a long struggle, the normal tensions between authority and liberty are intensified, and the trend toward dictatorship affects even the most democratic of nations. Where parliaments survive, their usual functions are sharply restricted; decision-making becomes increasingly concentrated in the hands of a small executive group, or even in those of one man.

Such had been the experience of the European nations during the First World War; such was even more clearly the case during the Second. In the totalitarian states, of course, this process had already taken place before 1939, the German, Italian, and Soviet political systems were, in a sense, on a war footing even in peacetime, and needed little adaptation when war came. The democratic states, on the other hand, had to grope their way toward some kind of workable compromise. Thanks to the experience of the 1914 war, they were able to convert more rapidly and more efficiently this time. Both the British and the French parliaments had anticipated such an emergency, and had laid plans before 1939 for vesting their governments with emergency powers. These special arrange-

[5] Alexis de Tocqueville, *Democracy in America* (New York, 1945), II, 284.

ments were promptly voted into effect in September 1939: Neville Chamberlain was authorized to set up a small War Cabinet, while Premier Daladier was partially freed from parliamentary control by an extensive grant of wartime decree powers.

The period of the twilight war demonstrated, however, that even more centralization of control was needed—not merely to match that of the totalitarian enemy, but simply to ensure the most effective use of national power. The problem was particularly grave in France, where political divisions and personal rivalries in the cabinet hamstrung the government's activity. When Paul Reynaud replaced Daladier as premier in March 1940, his efforts to act with more vigor and dispatch were frustrated by internal dissension that threatened to wreck the cabinet if he moved too brusquely. Reynaud dared not even replace his army commander, General Maurice Gamelin, in whom the new premier lacked confidence. The failings of the French political system in the crisis weeks of 1940 appalled even many sound republicans, and paved the way for Marshal Pétain and Pierre Laval to substitute a frankly authoritarian system after France's defeat. It also enabled Charles de Gaulle to establish his Free French movement on essentially autocratic lines. Although de Gaulle eventually made some grudging concessions to the idea of democratic controls, these limitations remained more theoretical than real during the war years. Only a strong regime, de Gaulle argued, could speak out effectively for France's right to great-power status in the postwar world. Thus both Pétainist and Gaullist Frenchmen were given a taste of authoritarian rule for the first time in several generations. Some of them were to find that taste attractive; others grew increasingly restive, and looked forward to the restoration of a more responsive peacetime democracy.

In Great Britain, the tank-trap called the English Channel provided enough respite to allow a strengthening of political authority after France fell. The change was partly one of personal style: Winston Churchill was a far more forceful and assertive leader than Chamberlain. It was partly a natural reaction to the intensification of the war; any British prime minister after May 1940 would have had to take a bolder lead. But the Churchill era brought some important structural changes as well. Churchill combined with the prime ministership the newly created post of minister of defense, thus absorbing direct control of all three branches of the armed services, and becoming in effect both supreme commander and head of government. The War Cabinet was reduced in size from nine to five members (though it later expanded again). An Emergency Powers Act, adopted by Parliament after a single day's debate, gave the government "practically unlimited authority over all British citizens and their property." [6]

The sweeping character of Churchill's personal authority was almost unprecedented in a modern democracy. He was confronted by no powerful rival: neither a civilian minister of defense, nor a single "economic

[6] A. J. P. Taylor, *English History 1914–1945* (London, 1965), p. 479.

czar," nor a military chief of staff speaking for the armed forces as a whole. He operated through his small War Cabinet (which rarely if ever challenged him) and through a four-member Chiefs of Staff Committee (C.O.S.) representing the three branches of the armed services. As the war went on, the War Cabinet was gradually stripped of any role in the formulation of strategy, and found itself confined to matters of foreign and economic policy. An extensive network of some sixty War Cabinet committees handled much of the routine work of wartime government. Meanwhile the authority of the C.O.S. rapidly expanded, until it shared with Churchill the real direction of the war. The unprecedented concentration of power in the hands of Churchill and the C.O.S. led to sporadic protest in press and Parliament, especially at times when the fortunes of war were low. The goal of most of the critics was to strip Churchill of strategic direction of the war by substituting a supreme military commander for the C.O.S. Such a change would have reduced Churchill's role to that of official rhetorician and morale-builder, leaving the supreme commander to run the war. But these pressures were resisted to the end; and the Churchill-C.O.S. combination (despite sporadic tensions and even sharp clashes) developed an effectiveness that won the admiration of the Germans as well as of Britain's allies. Its achievements reconciled Parliament to a sharply reduced though not insignificant wartime role as occasional critic and outlet for popular irritations.

Britain's wartime system of government meshed smoothly with that of the United States when the latter became an ally in 1941. The Americans promptly set up a new committee called the Joint Chiefs of Staff (J.C.S.) on the model of the British C.O.S., and Anglo-American coordination was provided through a Combined Chiefs of Staff Committee composed of the J.C.S. and the C.O.S. From 1942 onward, this body became the vital center of Anglo-American military planning and operations. Many of the usual problems of coalition warfare were thus avoided from the outset. But it was not the machinery alone that made the system work smoothly. The personal relationship between Churchill and Roosevelt was of crucial importance, along with the fact that the coalition operated as a real partnership of equals throughout most of the war. Britain's two-year advantage over the United States in military buildup and experience counterbalanced the enormous American preponderance in manpower and resources. Toward the end, however, that preponderance was seriously undermining the equality of the partnership, and was forcing the British into reluctant acceptance of joint responsibility for certain decisions that ran against their better judgment. Perhaps another year or two of war might have threatened the harmony of the coalition. Victory in 1945 averted that danger, and gave both the British and the Americans the right to boast that few coalitions in history had worked so well.

In the Axis states and the Soviet Union, the war brought fewer problems of political adaptation, since authority there was already highly concentrated. Yet there remained one vital area of uncertainty: the wartime relationship between the political leaders and the professional soldiers.

The tradition of military predominance in time of war was especially strong in Germany, where during the First World War there had emerged a kind of dictatorship of the high command. No such tradition existed in Italy or Russia; yet there, too, it seemed that the conditions of war might offer the soldiers a chance to demand a major share in shaping policy.

Such an increase in army influence did occur in the Soviet Union—though certainly not by Stalin's choice. At the outset, Stalin lost no time in formalizing the absolute power which he already possessed *de facto*. The direction of the war was vested in a new five-man State Defense Committee under Stalin's chairmanship; and a few weeks later Stalin named himself both commissar for defense and commander-in-chief of the armed forces. He was also a member (along with Molotov) of the new supreme military headquarters called the Stavka—the nearest Soviet equivalent to the British C.O.S. To ensure party control over the armed forces, a decree in July re-established the authority of the party's watchdogs, the political commissars, who would henceforth share command of each military unit. The Kremlin clearly remained suspicious of the loyalty of its military cadres, even after the drastic purge of 1937–1938.

But the demands of war were to force a gradual softening of Stalin's grip. The initial defeats suffered in 1941 seem to have had a chastening effect, for they revealed the disastrous consequences of the purge. The incapacity of Stalin's political generals—many of them old comrades of civil war days—threatened the survival of the Soviet regime. Beginning in the autumn of 1941, a quiet "purge by battle" was carried out; new commanders were chosen not for their political reliability but by the sole criterion of ability demonstrated in the field. Meanwhile the authority of the Stavka slowly but steadily expanded. Its representatives functioned as a kind of mobile C.O.S. as they were dispatched to key battle areas (e.g., Stalingrad) to supervise operations. True, Stalin at no time relinquished his right to the final word in strategic matters. He showed an obsessive concern for minutiae, and at times he interfered with, harassed, and browbeat his generals in rather startling fashion.[7] Yet by the time of Stalingrad, the relationship between Stalin and his high command seems to have evolved into something not vastly different from that between Churchill and the C.O.S. Despite occasional friction, the strategic and operational direction of the war in the Soviet Union had become a cooperative enterprise, in which the soldiers had an effective voice. As a symbol of this new relationship, Stalin in October 1942 freed his commanders from the galling control of the political commissars. "Out of its subordination, the army marched into equality with the Party." [8]

This growth of reasonably confident collaboration within the USSR was never extended to cover general inter-Allied direction of the war.

---

[7] E.g., see Marshal Georgi Zhukov in *Voenno-Istoricheskii Zhurnal, No. 10* (1966), pp. 75–76.

[8] J. Erickson, *The Soviet High Command* (London, 1962), p. 667.

Neither the Western powers nor the USSR was interested in broadening the Anglo-American Combined Chiefs of Staff Committee to include Soviet representatives. Late in 1943, the Americans did suggest the creation of a four-power United Chiefs of Staff Committee to exist alongside the Combined Chiefs of Staff and to function "when necessity arose." The proposal was dropped when the British pointed out that the new body might try to claim superiority over the C.C.S. Some months later, in July 1944, the Soviet authorities suggested the creation of a tripartite military committee in Moscow to coordinate matters of military importance. The Western powers, after some discussion, agreed on condition that the tripartite committee be merely advisory to the C.C.S. and the Soviet general staff. No Soviet response came; and the war ended without any formal coordinating machinery. Stalin preferred, on the whole, to fight his own "parallel war." Perhaps it was just as well. A broadening of the Anglo-American command machinery might have seriously hampered or destroyed its effectiveness; probably the C.C.S. functioned well because it included only two well-suited partners. For somewhat similar reasons, it was probably fortunate that the great powers excluded the smaller associated powers from the direction of the war. Coalition wars are undoubtedly the most difficult kind to fight. If a broadly inclusive supreme allied council had been organized to discuss and shape the strategic conduct of the war, the enterprise might have degenerated into constant bickering and fatal delays. Happily, most representatives of the smaller allies accepted their uncomfortable role in good spirit, and rested their confidence in the good faith of the Anglo-Americans.

It was Adolf Hitler who faced the greatest test of the totalitarian leader's ability to dominate his army in wartime. There, the army's sense of pride and independence was deeply rooted, and the public was conditioned to expect military control once the guns began to speak. In the circumstances, Hitler's total triumph over the soldiers was impressive, but also costly. His monopoly of power equaled that of Stalin, and increased as the war moved on. Hitler developed no equivalent of the British War Cabinet or the Soviet State Defense Committee. A Ministerial Council for National Defense, set up at the outbreak of the conflict, withered away after December 1939; as for the Reich cabinet, it never met during the war.

Nor did the Germans develop any equivalent of the British C.O.S. In February 1938, Hitler had dismissed the minister of defense without appointing a successor, and had personally assumed command over the armed forces as a whole. He had simultaneously created a new High Command of the Armed Forces (*Oberkommando der Wehrmacht*, or OKW) which appeared to be the nucleus of a unified command system destined to coordinate the army, navy, and air force. But the demarcation of roles was not clear-cut, and it became increasingly confused during the course of the war. The OKW, which might have developed into an agency even more powerful and effective than the British C.O.S., shriveled into little more than Hitler's military working staff, destined not to help plan overall strategy but to translate the Fuehrer's inspirations into the form of operational orders and to transmit them to the three service commands (or even over the heads of those commands to an individual commander at the front). The OKW chiefs, Field Marshal Wilhelm Keitel and General Alfred Jodl, preened themselves on their absolute loyalty to Hitler and slavishly followed his orders. The army's high command (OKH), though restive and bitter at this high-handed and capricious treatment, had no effective spokesman in Hitler's immediate entourage, and found no other way to bring its potential influence to bear. Meanwhile, much to the army's irritation, the commanders-in-chief of the *Luftwaffe* (Goering) and of the navy (Raeder and Doenitz) enjoyed direct personal access to the Fuehrer. From December 1941 Hitler made things still worse by naming himself commander-in-chief of the army as well as supreme commander of the armed forces; he thus took over complete charge of army operations, issuing detailed as well as general instructions. In 1942 he even assumed active command of an army group in the Caucasus while remaining in his headquarters more than a thousand miles away. Compounding the confusion was the fact that OKH was given operational control of the war in Russia, while OKW was in charge on all the other fronts. Since Hitler laid down the law to both agencies, there could be no ultimate rivalry; but the arrangement was awkward and inefficient. No wonder some high-ranking soldiers in Germany envied the smooth-working and simple command organization developed by their enemies in the west.

Hitler's solution for the problems of conducting a coalition war was no more effective. The German and Italian high commands were not linked by any equivalent of the Anglo-American Combined Chiefs of Staff; military consultations occurred sporadically, at the irregular summit conferences between the two dictators. Mussolini's desire to fight his own "parallel war" was matched by Hitler's determination to give the Italians no voice in his strategical planning. Mussolini, whose direct personal control of Italian strategy and operations was as complete as Hitler's in Germany, found himself increasingly dependent on his German ally for war matériel and military support. The Italian fiasco in Greece, and the dispatch of General Rommel to Libya, reduced the idea of a "parallel war" to a mere facade for German domination of the Mediterranean theater. The effect was increasing ill-will between the Axis partners. Hitler's relations with the Japanese were even more tenuous; machinery for military coordination was totally lacking.

In the management and the strategic direction of the war, the Atlantic democracies and the Soviet Union clearly outdid the Axis powers in effectively adapting their systems to the demands of the epoch. The presumed superiority of dictatorship in time of crisis was belied by the course of events; constitutional systems proved flexible enough to borrow such authoritarian techniques as were necessary for survival and victory. One result of that success was to bolster the confidence of many Europeans in free government—a confidence that had been widely shaken during the interwar years. But it also inspired a disturbing fear that in an age of chronic crisis, the distinction between wartime and peacetime conditions might become increasingly blurred, and that the traditional balance between authority and liberty, sharply shifted by the demands of the Second World War, might suffer a permanent change.

III. The Social Impact

Wars leave their mark not only on political structures, but on every aspect of human organization. Indeed, their effects on social structures may be even deeper and more durable. On the other hand, measuring those effects is clearly more difficult; for societies are complex things, and the changes that occur may reveal themselves only gradually, well after the last shot is fired.

One obvious effect of total mobilization is a certain militarizing of society, at least for the duration of the war. The long strain calls for intensified social discipline: a greater regimentation of the citizen's life, a more hierarchical set of relationships, a partial replacement of civilian by military values. The altered demands of war also bring sharp changes in mores and in social values, new kinds of achievement are highly honored and yield fame and status, while others are pushed into the background. The normal channels of social mobility are twisted or blocked as by an earthquake, and new channels are suddenly wrenched open for heretofore obscure citizens. A reordering of social relationships inevitably follows —sometimes in the direction of greater leveling, sometimes in the direction of increased inequalities. As a rule, the chief social benefits of modern war have gone to the professional soldier at the expense of those who practice the peacetime arts. Midway through the First World War, the German officer Wilhelm Groener rather smugly remarked: "The uniform counts more among us now than the black coat of the civilian, and the cry for dictatorship by the military is raised on every side." [9] Early in the Second World War, an American social scientist somberly predicted that the conflict would produce a world of "garrison states" in which the "specialists in violence" would fix a durable grip on societies everywhere.[10]

Some of the foregoing changes did occur in Europe during the Second World War—though with particular nuances from one society to another, and with some rather surprising aberrations. One notable fact was that while the usual militarizing of society did occur in the broad sense of that term, it failed to put the military into the saddle anywhere, and in one case even reduced the political and social authority enjoyed by the armed forces. That case was Germany. During the war of 1914–1918, the German military had fixed its grip on almost every aspect of domestic

[9] Quoted in G. A. Craig, "The Impact of the German Military on the Political and Social Life of Germany during World War II," *Rapports du XIIe Congrès International des Sciences Historiques* (Vienna, 1965), IV, 297.

[10] H. J. Lasswell, "The Garrison State," *American Journal of Sociology,* XLVI (1941), 455–68.

life, from political decision-making to industrial production, food ration-ing, labor policy, the control of public information, and censorship. After 1939, the armed forces found themselves excluded from all such functions, and even from such responsibilities as the raising and training of reserves. Just as Hitler himself increasingly monopolized the strategic and even the operational conduct of the war, so the various agencies of the Nazi party absorbed all domestic administrative tasks—police and security, man-power allocation, psychological mobilization and indoctrination. "The Fuehrer," wrote Goebbels in 1943, "is totally opposed to the Wehrmacht engaging in tasks that are not germane to it. . . . The Wehrmacht is to limit itself to conducting the war in a military sense and to leave every-thing else to civilians." [11] If the conflict further increased Germany's "gar-rison state" qualities, it did so at the expense and not to the advantage of the professional soldier. The traditional prestige of the German officer corps, and its assumption of a dominant role in past wars, worked against the army at a time when the nation's new political elite jealously refused to share authority with any potential rival.

In the Soviet Union, on the other hand, the war did bring a carefully controlled shift in status and authority to the advantage of the military. The vast influx of Soviet citizens into the armed forces after 1941, and the Kremlin's increased dependence on the generals' courage and loyalty, as-sured the soldiers of greater deference and higher status. But although honors and praise were dealt out generously, the officer corps was given no expanded role outside the sphere of military operations; the tasks of social control and of adapting Soviet society to wartime needs were exclu-sively reserved to the political elite. Even though the bloodiest fighting and the greatest destruction of the war occurred on the Russian front, the war's effects on the Soviet political system and social structure were prob-ably slighter than in any other participating country. For unlike the West-ern democracies, the Soviet Union had already become a garrison state be-fore the war; and unlike Germany, the Soviet Union did not have to face the postwar social upheaval caused by defeat.

One would expect the war to have had a far greater impact on the liberal societies of the West, where the transition from peace to war was bound to be more unsettling. Such was indeed the case; yet the changes were not always the ones that might have been predicted. The apparent shift toward a garrison state in Great Britain (the only western European nation to endure the long strain of protracted war as an independent bel-ligerent) brought increased status and authority to the military, but not at the expense of civilian officialdom or of the civilian population as a whole. Survival and victory depended on the united effort of the British people, whether in or out of uniform; total mobilization put everyone onto the front lines. Episodes like the Battle of Britain were peculiarly im-portant in eroding the differences between civilians and soldiers. And when the war effort depended as much on the production and delivery of

[11] Lochner, *The Goebbels Diaries*, pp. 540–41.

goods as on battlefield heroics, special privileges for men in uniform would have been difficult to justify.

The war brought, too, a drastic process of leveling, a kind of flattening of the social pyramid. British leadership had no choice but to practice what someone has called "demostrategy"; it implied an intensified state concern for the health and morale of the whole population. From the early months of the war, the government ordered a marked broadening of social services provided to all citizens, regardless of class or military status. The emergency evacuation of millions of women and children from Greater London suddenly brought to light a number of social deficiencies of which few Britons had been consciously aware. It was clear that the nation's hospital facilities were desperately inadequate, and that hundreds of thousands of urban refugee children had in the past been inadequately fed, clothed, and cared for. The government introduced a whole series of emergency welfare measures; but more important still, the conditions of war stimulated a nationwide mood of reform. From this mood emerged the welfare-state concept in its modern form. So great was its appeal that when Sir William Beveridge issued his famous report in 1943, outlining a postwar plan for universal social security, the bulky and austere document became an overnight best seller; queues of citizens stood before bookstores to get their copies.

Wartime government controls contributed, too, to the leveling process. Critical shortages of consumer goods after 1940 forced an austerity standard for all; and changing mores reinforced government regulation to impose a growing uniformity in standards of living, of dress, and of public conduct generally. Long years of war required rigorous social discipline, and such discipline was made more bearable when it was shared by everyone. Yet along with the flattening of the social pyramid, there occurred a marked increase in social mobility. New opportunities were opened to many men and women whose roles had been humble or obscure in peacetime. The rise of the scientists was perhaps the most striking example. Only a few years before the war, a British cabinet minister had remarked condescendingly, "What I like about scientists is that they are a team, so that one need not know their names." [12] Suddenly, in the war years, the names of certain scientists came to be almost as well known among the cognoscenti as those of generals and ministers. On a broader scale, the rise of women in social status was equally notable. The increase in the number of British women employed in industry, government, and the armed forces exceeded that of any other warring country; it profoundly altered the role and the self-image of British women. The new technological aspect of the war also had its effect (in Britain as elsewhere) in pushing forward men of technical and managerial talent, both in the government and in the armed services. Sir John Anderson, a highly skilled career civil servant without experience as a politician, held important cabinet posts

[12] Earl of Birkenhead, *The Professor and the Prime Minister* (Boston, 1962), p. 198.

throughout the war, and in 1945 was even nominated by Churchill to succeed to the prime ministership in case Churchill and Eden were killed en route to Yalta. Likewise, the new-style armed forces enabled the military managers to assert a right to equality with charismatic battlefield leaders.

Perhaps the most drastic immediate impact of the war on social structures occurred in the German-occupied countries of the Continent. Defeat and occupation radically transformed the dominant value systems and the relationships among social groups. Some previously favored elements suddenly found themselves transformed into outsiders, threatened by physical destruction as well as social ruin. Others found the channels of upward mobility suddenly opened wide to those who were opportunistically inclined. In areas like Poland and occupied Russia, the conquerors consciously endeavored to liquidate the whole intellectual and professional elite, and to substitute an imported German ruling class. In western Europe, favors often went to men who had been disgruntled misfits or frustrated failures in their prewar societies. But the deeper social effects in the occupied countries were aftereffects, to be felt during the postwar years. For the nucleus of a new elite gradually emerged from the various resistance movements; its members were catapulted after 1944 into positions of political, economic, and social prominence to which only a few of them could have aspired without the upheaval of the war. Nowhere were they to attain a monopoly of postwar power or status; many would be shunted back into obscurity after a few months or years of fleeting notoriety. But the long-range effect was to produce a kind of circulation of the elites, out of which would come an amalgam of old-established and newly-arrived elements in roles of authority and status.

In the defeated Axis nations, too, the social effects of the war were mainly aftereffects; but the impact was no less profound for being delayed. Germany and Italy had already undergone a partial social revolution during the prewar years—a revolution that had brought the new Fascist or Nazi party elite into uneasy partnership with those elements of the older elites that chose to collaborate. In Germany, a radical wing of the Nazi movement had favored a much more sweeping social revolution that would liquidate most of the older elite and would culminate in a thoroughly totalitarian system. This impulse was strongest within the SS, some of whose leaders talked of creating an "SS-state" in which all the key positions would be monopolized by members of that elite formation. The war did bring an impressive growth in the size and influence of the SS, but at the same time forced postponement of its leaders' ambitions. So long as the fighting lasted, they concentrated their energies on the task of creating and consolidating a German empire in the east, while deferring their domestic goals for implementation after victory was won.

But the social revolution that eventually followed Germany's defeat was to be of a quite different sort. The destruction of much of the Nazi elite, the temporary disgrace of those powerful elements that had collaborated with Hitler, and the massive influx of a huge uprooted refugee population from the east were to produce a kind of social disintegration out of which a largely new social order would eventually emerge. The refugees (mostly from Protestant regions) were scattered in camps throughout the western zones of occupied Germany, and many eventually settled in what had been solidly Catholic areas. The effect was a somewhat greater religious and social "homogenization" of the western zones. On the other hand, the permanent division of Germany that split off the heavily Protestant eastern part led to a sharp increase of Catholic influence in the segment that eventually came to be governed from Bonn.

Still more profound were the social changes that emerged from the massive physical destruction of the country, and from the disastrous blows suffered by the old ruling elites. The rebuilding of the German economy opened the way to the creation, for the first time in German history, of a thoroughly capitalist system in place of the old uneasy mixture of industrial capitalism and quasi-feudal traditionalism. The industrial-managerial group rapidly emerged as the unchallenged upper stratum of society, able to assert its individualistic, competitive values as those of the new Germany. Greater social mobility, a personal success ideology, and a somewhat exaggerated materialism seemed on the way to replacing the more rigid and status-ridden order of the past. What kind of amalgam would eventually emerge remained somewhat uncertain, but it was clear enough that the war had opened the way to a quite unintended kind of social revolution in Germany.

IV. The Psychological Impact

That modern war strains and disrupts the political, social, and economic fabric of a highly organized continent is too obvious to be doubted. Its effects on the psychological fabric are much more controversial. Common sense and experience testify that an individual may be traumatized by a shattering personal experience; and certainly millions of individual Europeans suffered some kind of traumatic experience during the Second World War. But whether whole societies may be traumatized by a collectively experienced catastrophe is more open to debate. Those who believe that communities of men possess a kind of collective mind or psychological fabric will be more likely to seek out and to accept evidence of the generalized impact of disaster. Yet even those who are skeptical of the idea of "socially-shared psychopathology" will recognize that the long strain and the terrifying climaxes of modern war must leave their mark on tens of thousands of survivors.

Such evidence as emerged from the Second World War relates not to entire populations but to special groups: members of the armed forces, children separated from their families, prisoners of war, civilians subjected to heavy bombing raids, and concentration camp inmates. The data, though extensive, is spotty, and rarely permits confident generalization. Only the Americans and the British compiled information and made studies of psychological responses during the war itself; as for the data from Germany, most of it was gathered immediately after the war by American teams, or was contributed by survivors of the concentration camps. Probably the surest conclusions are those that concern the short- and long-range effects of mass bombing.

The approach of war had inspired panicky fears in Britain and France about the anticipated consequences of air attacks. The British Air Ministry estimated that air-raid casualties during the early weeks of war would run into the millions, and would produce widespread neurosis and panic. Indeed, a committee of psychiatrists had predicted in 1938 that psychological casualties might exceed physical injuries by a ratio of three to one, so that the former might approach three or four million cases during the first six months. When war was declared, therefore, more than three million women and children were hastily evacuated from Greater London to the country districts or to smaller towns. When the expected air raids failed to materialize, the majority of the refugees found their own way back to London. By the time the German blitz of 1940–1941 began, the initial panic had passed. This time there was no organized evacuation; many Londoners preferred the risks of bombing to the dislocation and tensions of life as unwelcome guests in a crowded rural or small-town home. In fact, there is fairly persuasive evidence that children suffered more severely from the psychological effects of separation from their families than from the rigors of the air raids.

The impact of the bombing, when it came at last, seemed to belie the fears and predictions of the experts. There was no mass hysteria, no social disruption inspired by panic or shock. The nearest approach to spontaneous mass action or "civil disobedience" was the occupation of London subway stations by thousands of citizens who lacked airraid shelters. Civil defense officials worked tirelessly and efficiently to care for the injured, to clear street obstructions, and to restore disrupted public utilities. There was no increase in the number of mental disorders reported; the number of suicides and of arrests for drunkenness or disorderly conduct actually decreased during the war years. On the other hand, cases diagnosed as "temporary traumatic neurosis" were frequent in heavily-bombed areas, and increased absenteeism from work on grounds of illness often followed an air attack. There was also a rise in the incidence of such psychosomatic disorders as peptic ulcers in bombed areas.

Fortunately for the British, the air blitz tapered off after about ten months, and there was a long respite before the period of V–1 and V–2 attacks in 1944. No doubt this interlude reduced the nervous strain in British cities, and helped to keep the number of psychological casualties low. Meanwhile, the Germans were beginning to confront a steadily intensifying barrage of air raids both more severe and more protracted than anything the British—or any other people heretofore—had known. Here, too, the experience seemed to prove the remarkable capacity of human beings to bear up under unprecedented strain and terror. As in England, there was neither mass panic nor social disruption (save in a few instances when the municipal authorities failed to respond effectively to emergency conditions following an air raid). Even in the massive Hamburg raids, which laid waste half the city and left 48 percent of the population homeless, the effect was widespread shock rather than mass hysteria or economic breakdown. Berlin, which underwent the longest period of almost uninterrupted raids (eighteen months) and which by 1945 was reduced largely to rubble, continued to function as an organized community until the very end. In Germany as in England there seems to have been no increase in the number of mental disorders. But here, too, the number of ulcer cases rose in bombed areas, and work absenteeism was more common after raids. Signs of tension and strain were general; the German authorities finally had to abandon the use of air-raid sirens to warn against isolated attacks, in an effort to reduce fatigue caused by unnecessary alarm.

The remarkable resilience of both the English and the Germans when subjected to intense air warfare blasted the prewar myth about the devastating effects of terror bombing; but perhaps it tended to create a new myth in place of the old. It was easy to conclude, during and after the war, that mass bombing had been a relatively ineffective weapon, and that its psychological effect had actually been to improve the morale of an attacked population, to intensify its will to resist. Such a conclusion can be neither affirmed nor denied on the basis of the evidence from the Second World War. Even though mass hysteria did not occur, there was widespread shock that amounted to temporary traumatic neurosis, and that produced a kind of numb indifference rather than a heightened determination to fight and win. As for the long-range consequences of these temporary psychological disorders, the evidence is scanty. One British study of mental cases carried out in 1948 showed only 3 percent of this sample to be clearly connected with air-raid experience during the war. It is quite possible, however, that hidden damage of a deeper sort went undetected.

The psychological impact of the war on members of the armed forces is difficult to assess, since only the British and the Americans kept detailed statistics. British psychiatric casualties seem to have averaged about 10 percent of total battle casualties; but this average concealed a wide variation, ranging from 2 to 30 percent, depending on the particular conditions and the duration of a given battle. Long periods of severe strain produced serious effects. For example, in the garrison at Malta, under intense air bombardment in 1942–1943, more than one man in four eventually showed some kind of pathological response. In 1940, a ship loaded with exhausted and demoralized British troops who had fought in the French campaign was sunk near Bordeaux, and the soldiers dumped into a sea coated with flaming oil; every man who was rescued suffered severe psychological aftereffects. Many of the Dunkirk survivors reached home in a state of total neurotic collapse, "suffering from acute hysteria, reactive depression, functional loss of memory or of the use of their limbs, and a variety of other psychiatric symptoms. . . ." [13]

[13] William Sargant, "Psychiatry and War," *Atlantic Monthly,* CCXIX (1967), p. 102.

During the First World War, all such disorders had been lumped under the misleading label "shell shock," and it was assumed that such men were either weaklings or cowards. At best, they had been given a spell of rest and then sent back to the front lines, where they often broke down completely, and became incurable casualties. This mistake was corrected in the Second World War by improved understanding and better methods of treatment. Both the British and the Americans soon learned that it was essential to treat acute hysteria cases as quickly as possible, before the abnormal behavior patterns had time to become stabilized in the nervous system. They learned, too, that to send "cured" neurotics back into action was almost always futile, and that a transfer or a discharge was the only alternative to permanent damage. They learned, finally, that not only weaklings were susceptible to psychological battle disorders; that "practically everyone has his neurotic breaking point if the stresses are severe enough." [14] The advance of psychiatric knowledge had at least one clearly favorable result: it sharply reduced the number of permanent psychological casualties in the British and American armed forces, as compared to the record of 1914–1918.[15]

No experience of strain and terror during the Second World War exceeded that of the men and women confined in German concentration camps. Inadequate food, brutal treatment, harsh labor assignments, constant uncertainty about the future seem to have produced radical personality changes in many inmates. The program of calculated terror used by the SS guards was evidently designed to strip the prisoner of all human traits, to destroy his self-respect, to "depersonalize" him. The effect of the treatment varied widely: regression toward infantile traits was perhaps the commonest result, while others managed some sort of adaptation in order to survive. In most cases, the central concern after the first few weeks came to be self-preservation; all other values faded before this urge to live, no matter what the cost. Some long-time prisoners even came to model themselves after the SS guards, and to ape their conduct and values. Only a few managed to cling, despite the inhuman conditions in the camp, to those altruistic traits that mark normal human conduct. The en-

[14] Sargant, "Psychiatry and War," p. 106; *cf.* R. H. Ahrenfeldt, *Psychiatry in the British Army during the Second World War* (New York, 1958), p. 256.

[15] Churchill, however, viewed the work of psychiatrists with a jaundiced eye. "I am sure it would be sensible [he wrote in 1942] to restrict as much as possible the work of these gentlemen, who are capable of doing an immense amount of harm with what may very easily degenerate into charlatanry. . . . There are no doubt easily recognizable cases which may benefit from treatment of this kind, but it is very wrong to disturb large numbers of healthy, normal men and women by asking the kind of odd questions in which the psychiatrists specialise. There are quite enough hangers-on and camp-followers already" (Churchill, *Second World War,* IV, 918).

German and Soviet leaders shared Churchill's prejudices in even greater measure. The German armed forces used psychologists to administer tests to officer candidates, but abandoned even this practice in 1942. No information is available on the incidence of war-induced neuroses or psychoses in Germany or the USSR.

during effects of the concentration camp experience were to be demonstrated after the war by the frequency of psychological disorders among former inmates. Chronic anxiety and panic were frequent, while certain mental and physical diseases that occurred ten or twenty years later have been diagnosed as the result of brain injury caused by malnutrition and prolonged, intense fear experienced during the concentration camp years.

The full breadth and depth of the war's psychological impact on the peoples of Europe will, of course, never be measured. At least one psychiatrist, on returning to the Continent in 1945, contended that almost every inhabitant of occupied Europe showed some traits that might be described as neurotic or even psychotic. Others spoke of a new set of impenetrable "psychological boundaries" that would henceforth separate those with sharply differing sets of wartime experiences. Still others spoke with a touch of awe of the unexpected power of adaptation shown by ordinary human beings in time of crisis. On the surface, Europe after the end of the war seemed to return quite rapidly to a kind of normalcy, and its citizens a decade later no longer appeared to be haunted by the terrible memory of their wartime experiences. Yet who is to say whether deeper lesions may not have persisted, marring and distorting the psyche of the "normal" European who survived the conflict? "Perhaps," suggests Richard M. Titmuss, "more lasting harm was wrought to the minds and to the hearts of men, women and children than to their bodies. The disturbances to family life, the separation of mothers and fathers from their children, of husbands from their wives, of pupils from their schools, of people from their recreation, of society from the pursuits of peace—perhaps all of these indignities of war have left wounds which will take time to heal and infinite patience to understand." [16] Thucydides remarked long ago that ". . . war, which takes away the comfortable provision of daily life, is a hard master and tends to assimilate men's characters to their conditions." It may be that characters warped by the experience of protracted total war will never quite return to their former shape, and that from these warped qualities may emerge the neuroses of the next generation.

V. The Impact on Intellectual and Cultural Life

Epochs of war are rarely times of creativity in the realm of the spirit. Men's thoughts and energies tend to be swallowed up by the harsh demands of the struggle; it absorbs or annihilates most intellectual activities. Yet even in such times, the life of the mind goes on, though at reduced intensity; some individuals find occasion to reflect and to create, if only as a way to retain their sanity. And in a more practical sphere, governments often find advantage in encouraging the arts in wartime, although this encouragement is likely to be inspired by such instrumental motives as to maintain morale or to convey a desired message to the masses.

Almost every government that was caught up in the war gave some at-

[16] R. M. Titmuss, *Problems of Social Policy* (London, 1950), p. 538.

tention to stimulating the arts. In Germany and the Soviet Union, which already enjoyed managed cultures, the enterprise was particularly orthodox and utilitarian. Joseph Goebbels, whose authority as minister of people's enlightenment encompassed cultural life, insisted that the outbreak of war should alter nothing—that because of Germany's cultural preeminence through the ages, "the muses should not be silenced as elsewhere by the clash of arms." Besides, for Goebbels the arts were no mere pastime for peace, but "a sharp spiritual weapon for war." [17] Theaters remained open in surprising number until the very last phase of the war; glossy art magazines continued to appear, despite restrictions on paper and manpower. National Socialist art, literature, and drama continued to be custom built to reinforce party doctrine; its purpose was to inculcate a sense of massiveness and power, of group unity and passionate self-righteousness. Spontaneity and originality were the most obvious casualties, but they had already succumbed in 1933.

One of Germany's few wartime innovations in culture was the establishment in 1941 of a staff of uniformed war artists destined to immortalize on canvas the nation's victorious campaigns. Eventually this staff grew to include eighty painters, who spend three-month tours of duty at the front and produced an enormous mass of "combat art." Hitler hailed their work as proof that direct personal experience far outweighed the results of cloistered study under the uninspired "daubers" of the art academies. "This war," he declared with more enthusiasm than accuracy, "is stimulating the artistic sense much more than the last war." [18] Hitler was less concerned with uncovering new talent, however, than with planning the Supermuseum of German Art which he intended to build in Linz after the victory. His brief last will, found in the ruins of Berlin in 1945, contained a plaintive appeal that this project be carried to completion by his successors. Instead, only the Volkswagen factory lived on as a monument to the Fuehrer's creative genius.

Of all the arts, it was the cinema that lent itself most effectively to the cultural policy of the Nazi state at war. Goebbels' interest in the film as a propaganda device led him to sponsor not only a remarkable series of war documentaries recording each successive campaign, but also a number of enormously costly pseudohistorical pageants designed to justify the German war effort and, toward the end, to bolster the nation's flagging morale. The first and probably the most successful of these was Veit Harlan's *Der Jud Süss,* a virulently anti-Semitic epic. *Ohm Krüger,* a tale of the Boer War, was designed to stir up hatred of the devious and oppressive English, inventors of the concentration camp. Biographical films of Frederick the Great and Bismarck, inflated to superhuman stature, provided examples of German leadership and military success. Toward the end of the war, Goebbels pinned his fading hopes of victory on the film entitled *Kolberg:* an account of a small East Prussian city under French siege in

[17] H. Heiber, *Joseph Goebbels* (Berlin, 1952), p. 299.
[18] *Hitler's Secret Conversations,* p. 507.

1807, stubbornly holding out against overwhelming odds until the last-minute arrival of a relieving army. *Kolberg* was given a gala double premiere on January 30, 1945: one showing in half-ruined Berlin, the other in the French town of La Rochelle, where a small German force had been cut off by the Allied advance.

In the Soviet Union, literature and the arts were likewise expected to play major roles as auxiliary weapons in the war. "What is of paramount importance today," asserted the official organ of Soviet writers and artists, ". . . is the *activizing* function of art which possesses the invaluable faculty of inspiring men to fight." [19] The goal, it added, was not military literature but militant literature. Soviet writers responded with an enormous outpouring of novels, plays, poetry, and journalistic pieces that only occasionally rose above aesthetic mediocrity but that struck a responsive chord in a nation fighting for survival. With few exceptions, writers found their subject matter in episodes of the current war—especially variations on the theme of the common man caught up in the conflict and transfigured, somewhat to his own surprise, into a hero. Historical studies glorifying Russia's past also began to appear; in Leningrad under siege, a new 500,000-copy edition of *War and Peace* was published in an effort to bolster morale. Most of the literature of the time strongly reflected the powerful wave of national consciousness, of love for the Russian motherland, that was inspired by the war. Konstantin Simonov's semi-journalistic novels and plays and simple, highly emotional poetry made him the most widely read author of the war years, though Alexey Surkov rivaled his popularity as a poet, and Vassily Grossman, Alexander Korneichuk, and Leonid Leonov were equally successful playwrights. Ilya Ehrenburg, best known of the literary journalists, devoted his facile talents to essays filled with the most virulent hatred of the Germans. "Two eyes for an eye," "a pool of blood for a drop of blood," were typical of Ehrenburg's passionate cries for vengeance upon those "gray-green slugs," the invaders of Russia. The cinema, a field in which the USSR had already pioneered before the war, was also mobilized in the service of morale. The most notable masterpieces of the war years were undoubtedly Sergei Eisenstein's last films, *Alexander Nevsky* (completed just before the invasion) and *Ivan the Terrible,* a monumental pageant glorifying that controversial tsar from Russia's dark past. Even the composers were swept along by the flood tide of wartime emotion. Dimitri Shostakovich's enormously popular Seventh ("Leningrad") Symphony, composed during the siege of the city in 1941, echoed the mood and even the events of the time.

In German-occupied Europe and in Fascist Italy, the arts profited little from government sponsorship—with the possible exception of the cinema, which experienced a kind of renaissance almost everywhere. Opportunities for diversion were rare in wartime Europe; the cinema provided almost the only easy escape from the reality and drudgery of daily exis-

[19] Quoted in G. Struve, *Soviet Russian Literature 1917–1950* (Norman, Okla., 1951), p. 300.

tence. Everywhere, theaters were crowded and attendance steadily rose. Since the Continent was cut off from American and British films, new fields were opened to European producers. Mussolini moved at once to take advantage of the opportunity; in 1941 and 1942, Italy produced more films than any other European country. Their quality was generally mediocre; but the rapid expansion of the industry eventually opened the way to a new younger generation of directors—notably Roberto Rossellini and Vittorio de Sica—who took the first steps toward the neo-realistic style that was to put its mark on postwar Italian films.

In France, an even more remarkable wave of new talent appeared, and was matched by successful experimentation by some of the established directors. Goebbels, who was determined to assert Germany's dominance in the entire European film industry, was sufficiently concerned at this burst of French creativity to take countermeasures. He set up a German-owned film company in Paris, and planned gradually to tempt the most talented French actors to work for the new firm or for Berlin producers. One of the most brilliantly executed wartime films, H. G. Clouzot's *Le Corbeau* (a characterological study of a small French town), was produced by the German-owned company. Most of the outstanding French films, however, were made by independent French directors and firms who owed nothing to either German or Vichy sponsorship; and almost none were devoted to wartime themes. Notable among them were Jean Delannoy's *L'Eternel Retour,* Jacques Becker's *Goupi-Mains-Rouges,* and Marcel Carné's *Les Visiteurs du Soir* and *Les Enfants du Paradis.*

Of all governmental efforts to stimulate the wartime arts, those in Great Britain may have produced the most remarkable and lasting changes. The outbreak of war temporarily disrupted British cultural life; most places of entertainment were closed by the blackout, and a great many professional musicians and actors found themselves out of work. The Board of Education and a small private foundation stepped in with funds to tide them over the emergency, and to keep alive some amateur musical groups as well. Out of this accidental beginning was to grow the state-supported Council for the Encouragement of Music and the Arts, chaired after 1942 by no less a figure than John Maynard Keynes, and endowed with a government subsidy that grew larger in each wartime year. Instead of expiring in 1945, the CEMA was to live on into peacetime under a new name—the first long-term experiment (except in totalitarian states) in subsidizing the arts.

During the war years, the CEMA sponsored a broad and varied program of dramatic, musical, and artistic entertainment. Concerts and plays were staged by both professional and amateur groups in dozens of British cities, as well as in armaments factories and in bombed-out areas (where, for morale purposes, an orchestra was often dispatched immediately after the all-clear signal). The National Gallery, left vacant when its collections were stored for safekeeping, was taken over for daily concerts at noon, under the guidance of the gallery director Sir Kenneth Clark and the noted pianist Dame Myra Hess. The CEMA also subsidized a group of "war artists"—among them men of the caliber of Henry Moore, who spent a year or more sketching scenes in bomb shelters and munitions plants. The theater continued to function in lively fashion, and the British cinema, like that of the Continent, underwent a kind of rejuvenation. Indeed, some British historians have argued that the war actually increased the tempo of intellectual and cultural activity in Britain. This may have been true in a quantitative sense, as well as in the sense that there was a certain democratizing of culture as good music, art, and theater were made easily available to all. It would be more difficult to contend that the war brought an outburst of creativity. Neither public sponsorship nor private inspiration managed to produce any outstanding works of literature, of music, or of art in wartime Britain. Wartime novels and poetry lacked the sentimental and heroic rhetoric of the literature of 1914–1918; their dominant note, rather, was low-keyed restraint. The most representative novels were those of J. B. Priestley—though Evelyn Waugh's sardonic trilogy written just after the war probably came closer to catching the mood of wartime Britain. Perhaps A. J. P. Taylor is right in suggesting that to the British the Second World War was not a profound spiritual experience, and that a prosaic war, accepted by all and fought in businesslike fashion as a job that must be done, is not likely to produce general intellectual ferment. At most, the war stimulated British artists, writers, and composers to reflect the new mood of national pride and unity, and to seek inspiration in the native British tradition rather than in Continental models.

But the real impact of any war on intellectual and cultural life is not revealed in the somewhat artificial and manipulative efforts of governments to stimulate artistic expression. It must be sought elsewhere, in the moods and attitudes of thoughtful and creative men whose view of themselves and of the world is altered by the experience. Such effects are not easy to detect while the war continues; they are more likely to reveal themselves in the postwar years, when a chastened older generation and a restless, questioning new generation are suddenly freed from the stresses of the conflict, yet find that its burdens still weigh upon their spirits. Only the tentative beginnings of such postwar manifestations belong in a book whose chronological limits are the war years.

The war struck Europe at a time of low resistance to infection by intellectual doubt and despair. For two generations, the dominant values and beliefs of the post-Enlightenment era had been under attack; old certainties had been dissolving without being replaced by positive new values and convictions. The interwar years had been most strongly marked by this mood of cultural despair—a mood from which fascist movements (especially in Germany) had profited greatly. True, the decade of the 1930's had brought some signs of a resurgent humanism, an attempt to reassert Enlightenment values against the anti-rationalists and the cultural pessimists. Many European intellectuals, writers, and artists turned back toward social and political commitment in these years of economic breakdown and rising barbarism. And the outbreak of war seemed for a moment to strengthen this resurgence, for a war against Hitler could be seen as a crusade for humane values against the new savagery.

Hitler's triumphant course from 1939 to 1941 came as a profound shock to many thoughtful Europeans, for it seemed to suggest that the enemies of the Enlightenment tradition, the spokesmen for the mood of cultural despair, had been right all along. The deepest impact was felt in the countries overrun by the Nazis; in Britain and the Soviet Union, on the other hand, the fight for survival left little time for the luxury of introspection. On the occupied Continent, however, men were forced to re-examine all that they had believed, and to seek new explanations. A few took the easy way out: they accepted the Nazi *Weltanschauung* as the spirit of the new age, and rivaled Hitler in proclaiming its merits. The largest group of intellectual converts (some of whom had already become fascist sympathizers before the war) was to be found in France: writers like Robert Brasillach, Pierre Drieu la Rochelle, Abel Bonnard, Alphonse de Chateaubriant, and (in more ambiguous fashion) Louis-Ferdinand Céline. Others, like the German essayist Ernst Jünger and the French satirist Marcel Aymé, sought refuge in ironic detachment or sheer escapism. But there were still others who continued to grope in the gloom for another exit. It was here, in the conquered countries (and to a lesser degree in Germany as well, when the early victories gave way to exhausting deadlock), that the war really did become a profound spiritual experience; and it was here that some faint signs of intellectual renewal made their appearance.

For some of these lonely spirits, reflecting in solitude or communing in small groups, the crisis of Europe and of the West seemed to derive from the abandonment of what was true and good in the Enlightenment tradition. Decades of derogatory or fearful talk about the rise of the mass-man, they believed, had devalued the worth of the individual and the concept of basic human rights. The rising tide of anti-rationalism had submerged the less dramatic fact that even the mass-man retains a spark of rationality. Because the world sometimes seems to lack system and sense, too many Europeans had concluded that it could not be subjected to man's purposes through the use of science and reason. The goal, then, must be to reassert a kind of traditional humanism with a strongly socialist cast, concerned less for the techniques of social change than for its human goals. In both western and eastern Europe, flickering signs of this new mood could be seen emerging, principally among heirs of the positivist tradition and among younger Marxians. Its most widely read literary expression was Vercors's *Silence de la mer,* published underground in France in 1942.

A second current of renewal was rooted in Christian belief. For several decades the various Churches had seemed to be losing their effectiveness in grappling with modern problems, and their influence had been in serious decline. When neither Protestants nor Catholics offered strong resistance to Hitler's new paganism, and when part of the hierarchy readily collaborated with the Nazi conqueror, it began to seem that the Churches must have reached an advanced state of moral decay. Yet the challenge was now severe enough to produce a healthy reaction. In France, Italy, and the Low Countries, small groups of Catholic laymen, supported by a considerable number of parish priests and regular clergy as well as a few members of the hierarchy, embarked not only on active resistance but also on an attempt to re-examine the Christian's role in the modern world. In France Emmanuel Mounier, a young lay Catholic who in the prewar decade had developed the doctrine he called personalism, began to emerge as *spiritus rector* of the young Christian democrats. Mounier challenged both the "established disorder" of bourgeois democracy and the introspective advocates of cultural despair; he talked of "rediscovering man-as-a-social-being," of the need for "community" and *engagement,* or commitment to a cause. In Germany, a few hardy Protestant pastors (of whom Dietrich Bonhoeffer was to become best known) struck out on the even more dangerous and difficult path of moral resistance to their own government at war. Bonhoeffer's *Letters from Prison,* written prior to his execution by the Nazis early in 1945, argued that even though men must learn to live as though God were dead, they must not lose their determination to bear witness to the values of Christian humanism. In his cell, he remarked, he had discovered "religion-less Christianity"—a faith that could survive without the apparatus of the Church. Only the familiar Christian virtues could gird men to confront the darkness of the secular world that men had made.

Still a third current of resurgent humanism may have been even more representative of the mood induced by the war. Loosely and popularly labeled existentialism, it grew directly out of the prewar *Kulturpessimismus* that had driven some intellectuals to fascism and others to nihilism. The existentialists, for whom neither Marxian nor Christian doctrine offered a comforting set of certainties, found themselves adrift in what they saw as an absurd world, a world without meaning, beyond man's comprehension or control. Jean-Paul Sartre, their most talented and influential spokesman, had provided literary expression to their somber outlook in his prewar novel *La nausée* (1938), which offered only the meager consolations of artistic creativity as a palliative for total despair. Albert Camus reflected this same grim mood in his prewar writings, including his first novel *L'étranger,* completed just before the fall of France (though not published until 1942).

The irrational horror of total war could not fail to enrich the soil for the existentialists' seed. It assured them of a vastly broadened postwar audience, conditioned to accept the idea of an absurd and incomprehensible world. Yet that same experience of war somehow affected the leading spokesmen of existentialism, and pulled them back into at least the edges of the older humanistic current. Sartre during the war years moved toward Mounier's concept of *engagement,* seen as the obligation of the thoughtful man to assert his own freedom, to give his life meaning by dedicating himself to action for the cause of humanity. His play *Les Mouches,* staged in German-occupied Paris in 1943, hinted at the direction of his thought, though its full development was to come only after the war. As for Camus, who always rejected the existentialist label, his wartime transition was still more rapid and profound. A moralist in the old European tradition, an old-fashioned liberal humanist born after his time, Camus found himself reverting to a belief in certain fundamental values even in a world of absurdity. As early as 1941, his private notebooks show him seeking a way to rally "the community of men" against absurdity, against despair; "a pessimist with respect to the human condition," he mused, "I am an optimist with respect to man." Already he had completed his essay *Le mythe de Sisyphe,* an assertion of man's invincible courage and self-reliance; he was about to become an active participant in the anti-German underground; and he was reflecting on the ideas that would shape his postwar novel *La Peste,* whose powerful evocation of men's varying responses to evil was to stir the sensibilities of a whole new generation whose formative years had been those of the war.

Whether these three currents of resurgent humanism could merge successfully into one, and whether their combined force would be great enough to carry postwar Europe toward recovery and renewal, was beyond any European's powers of divination in 1945. For the hope they offered was clouded by the signs of political and ideological conflict among the victors, and by the awareness of many European intellectuals that war—particularly a war like that of 1939–1945—is not likely to condition men's minds and spirits for the practice of the humane values. Perhaps that awareness underlay the musings of the still obscure French Jesuit Pierre Teilhard de Chardin, as he viewed the scene from his enforced exile in distant China:

> At the root of the greatest disturbance on which the nations have embarked today, I distinguish the signs of a change in the human age. Like it or not, the age of the "lukewarm pluralisms" finally has passed. Either, then, a single people will succeed in destroying or absorbing the others or else the peoples will join in a common soul in order to become more human. Unless I deceive myself, that is the dilemma set by the present crisis. In the collision of events, may the passion to unite be lighted in us and become more ardent each day as it faces the passion to destroy. . . .[20]

VI. The End of the European Age?

On May 8, 1945, the fragmentary remnant of Hitler's Germany surrendered. Many years earlier, in anticipation of war, Hitler had remarked privately: "We may be destroyed, but if we are, we shall drag a world with us—a world in flames."[21] Joseph Goebbels had also warned grimly that in case of defeat, the Nazis would know how to slam the door behind

---

[20] M. Picón-Salas, *The Ignoble Savages* (New York, 1965), pp. 166–67.
[21] H. Rauschning, *The Voice of Destruction* (New York, 1940), p. 5.

them and not be forgotten for centuries.[22] Some Europeans like Léon Blum sensed uneasily that Goebbels might be right, and that the Nazis' downfall might even conceal a deeper victory. "I tremble [wrote Blum] at the thought that you are already conquerors in this sense: you have breathed such terror all about that to master you, to prevent the return of your fury, we shall see no other way of fashioning the world save in your image, your laws, the law of Force." [23]

Hitler had embarked on the war with the aim of remaking Europe according to some new design—a design to be fashioned by the Germans alone, and to endure for a thousand years. He is said to have prophesied, however, that "if Germany does not win this war, it will not be won by Britain or France but by the non-European powers." Perhaps, behind his self-confidence and bluster, there lurked a dim realization of the truth: that his attempt to consolidate Europe under German control might not be countenanced by the non-European peoples. Perhaps he sensed that the men and the resources of overseas continents might come pouring into the European theater of war, and that the outcome then might be to end the brief epoch of European dominance of the world—a dominance already threatened by the rise of newer nations overseas.

Six years of war more destructive than any in human history could scarcely fail to speed the downward spiral of European power and influence. The human and material losses alone seemed almost irreplaceable. The dead in Europe approximated 30 million—a toll half again as great as that of the First World War.[24] The Soviet Union alone probably lost some 16 million citizens; central and western Europe, over 15 million. Poland's casualty rate—15 percent of the total population—exceeded that of any other nation. The Polish dead (in majority Jews) totalled 5.8 million; Germany lost 4.5 million, Yugoslavia 1.5 million, France 600,000, Rumania 460,000, Hungary 430,000, Czechoslovakia 415,000, Italy 410,000, the United Kingdom almost 400,000, the Netherlands 210,000. Never before had civilians so widely shared with soldiers the bloody risks of war: almost half of Europe's dead were civilians, as compared to one-twentieth in the First World War. Europe's prewar Jewish population had been reduced from 9.2 million to 3.8 million; and only about 1 million of these survivors lived west of the Russian frontier. Accompanying the carnage was an uprooting of populations of unprecedented scope in Europe's history. Between 1939 and 1947, sixteen million Europeans were permanently transplanted from their homelands to other parts of the continent. Eleven million of these were Germans who fled or were driven out of eastern Europe in 1945–1946. This massive German retreat from the east seemed to mean the end of an epoch, of a sporadic *Drang nach Osten* that had begun in the Middle Ages. It transformed the ethnographic map of eastern Europe.

[22] H. Arendt, *The Origins of Totalitarianism* (New York, 1958), p. 332.

[23] L. Blum, *L'Oeuvre de Léon Blum* (Paris, 1955), V, 514.

[24] There are no generally accepted casualty figures, official or unofficial, for either of the world wars. Civilian casualties are particularly controversial.

The destruction of physical property was also unprecedented in scope. In the Soviet Union, seventeen hundred cities and towns and seventy thousand villages had been devastated; so were 70 percent of the industrial installations and 60 percent of the transportation facilities in the invaded areas. In Berlin, 75 percent of the houses were destroyed or severely damaged; someone estimated that to clear the city's rubble would require the use of ten fifty-car freight trains per day for sixteen years. In some cities (e.g., Düsseldorf), 95 percent of the homes were uninhabitable. In France and the Low Countries as well as in Germany, most waterways and harbors were blocked, most bridges destroyed, much of the railway system temporarily unusable. In England, whole sections of central London and of other industrial cities had been laid waste by incendiary bombs. Almost everywhere on the Continent, industrial and agricultural production was down by more than half; food, clothing, and consumer necessities were in desperately short supply; circuits of trade had been almost totally disrupted. Except for a few cases like Sweden and Switzerland, Europe seemed destined to be, at least for some years, a vast dilapidated slum and poorhouse.

Europe's financial plight was equally dismaying. Although the British had managed to finance almost half of their war effort on a pay-as-you-fight basis, Britain in 1945 had the dubious distinction of being the world's largest debtor nation. The European allies were technically liable to pay for American Lend-Lease supplies worth $30 billion, of which $13.5 billion had gone to the British and $9 billion to the USSR. Britain was also heavily in debt to the dominions and other members of the sterling bloc. France, whose currency had been virtually ruined by German occupation exactions, owed less under Lend-Lease, but desperately needed continued outside help to avert financial disaster; the same was true of the Netherlands and Italy. The Germans, who had maintained a fictitious financial stability during the war and had counted on victory to bail them out, lay prostrate with a public debt that had increased almost tenfold since 1939, and with a currency inflated sevenfold.

Europe's dismal state seemed even more grave when contrasted with the unprecedented wealth and power of the triumphant United States. American battlefield casualties (300,000 dead) had been relatively small in absolute figures, and seemed even slighter when calculated on a per capita basis. American industry, far from being ravaged by the war, had grown in hothouse fashion; the index of industrial production rose from 100 to 196 during the war years, while the gross national product increased from $91 billion to $166 billion. The American share of the world's merchant marine, which in 1939 had stood at 17 percent compared to Europe's 63 percent, now exceeded that of all the European nations combined.

This shattered Europe was confronted not only by a transatlantic rival of overwhelming power, but also by a restless and newly assertive Africa and Asia, no longer willing to accept a role of colonial subjection. The war had undermined the moral influence as well as the economic and military power of the European states. Japan's early victories had shattered the old image of Western invincibility, and had encouraged other Asiatic peoples to agitate for change. The Americans, preaching the gospel of anti-colonialism, had contributed to this new mood. Some of the colonial peoples—the Indians, the Congolese, the inhabitants of French Africa —had made important contributions in manpower or resources to the Allied victory, and felt justified in presenting their bill for payment. For the exhausted Europeans, colonial empires might still appear to be a base upon which to rebuild their status as world powers; but this appearance was shadowed by the threat that the cost of holding empires might soon outweigh the benefits.

Thus the end of the conflict in Europe, viewed through the wild and sometimes hysterical jubilation of V-E day, could not fail to leave most Europeans sobered and gloomy. If the war had been fought to preserve a workable balance of power in Europe, there was some reason to doubt that the goal had been achieved; for the advance of Soviet control almost to the heart of the Continent might eventually prove as disruptive as Germany's conquest of eastern Europe. If, on the other hand, the war had been fought to preserve the values of Western culture against destruction by a brutal tyranny, there was some reason to wonder whether those values could survive so harrowing an experience, and could harness the passions aroused by the struggle.

For some Europeans, escape seemed the only way out; they looked to the chance of emigrating to some relatively unscathed part of the overseas world, where they might make a new start. For others, the consolations of faith offered a stronger appeal; there was a significant reawakening of interest in religion. A far more striking phenomenon, however, was the temporary decline of nationalist sentiment in favor of some kind of supranational ideal. The intense nationalistic fervor normally stimulated by any war was in this case partially counterbalanced by the sense that in Europe the sovereign nation-state had seen its day, and could survive only if merged into a larger entity, massive enough to exert some influence in an altered world. During the latter months of the war, some tentative explorations into the federal idea were inaugurated, mainly by private citizens, but also by governments. In London, the Belgian, Dutch, and Luxembourg governments-in-exile even managed to work out plans for a postwar economic union, which emerged after 1945 as Benelux. But the future of these hopes on the morrow of victory remained opaque, for alongside them could be seen signs of a vigorously assertive nationalism, embodied for example in de Gaulle's followers in France and in the victorious British who had stood fast for so long against the tempest.

Europeans in May 1945 could not anticipate what the postwar years would bring. There was no precedent for the state to which they had been reduced by the most savage and destructive war in Europe's history. They could hope that Soviet power in eastern Europe would be exercised with restraint, and would gradually be relaxed in order to restore a reasonably stable European balance. They could hope that the United States, made wise by the record of error after another great war, would this time show a generous and sympathetic understanding of Europe's needs, and would use its power and wealth to constructive ends. They could hope that the vanquished Germans, beaten to their knees and temporarily outlawed from European society, would eventually emerge chastened and "Europeanized" in outlook, rather than humiliated and filled with a paranoid urge for revenge. Of these hopes, some were to be fulfilled in large measure; others would long remain clouded by uncertainty. But even the most optimistic Europeans in 1945 could not foresee the speed and vigor of economic recovery and expansion that would quickly heal the physical scars of war, that would convert most of the continent from potential slum and poorhouse into a society of unprecedented affluence and renewed self-confidence. Perhaps men are always inclined to underestimate the resilience of the human race, its stubborn capacity to scramble back from the pit into which it has been cast by its own follies. Perhaps those observers who in 1945 had talked gloomily of "the end of Europe" had overlooked the possibility of a new beginning.

35. Origins of the Cold War

ARTHUR M. SCHLESINGER, JR.

36. The Cold War, Revisited and Re-visioned

CHRISTOPHER LASCH

From the vantage point of the 1970s the Cold War looks more and more like a thing of the past. Most of the containers which held its definitions, be they communism v. "free world" or US–USSR bipolar power struggle, have become sieves. Bipolarity increasingly gives way to a multipower world which includes China, Japan, and a western Europe changing from a super-market to a super-power. The Sino-Soviet quarrel, revolts within the Soviet bloc in Europe, rifts within NATO, and the lack of significant great power backing for American involvement in southeast Asia all show that neither the "communist world" nor the "free world" has much solidarity any more. If the Cold War is still on, it is difficult to tell one side from the other without a program. In the 1971 Indo-Pakistan war, for example, "free world" United States lined up with Communist China to support "free world" Pakistan against a "free world" India backed by communist Soviet Union. If the Cold War was primarily a struggle between the United States and the Soviet Union over Europe, it more and more appears that the last confrontations in that struggle were over the Berlin wall in 1961 and the Cuban missile crisis of 1962.

During the Cold War there was but one widely held interpretation of it, an

Source: Arthur M. Schlesinger, Jr., "Origins of the Cold War," *Foreign Affairs*, XLVI, No. 1 (October 1967), 22–52. Reprinted by permission from *Foreign Affairs*, October 1967. Copyright © 1967 by the Council on Foreign Relations, Inc., New York.

*interpretation that the following two selections term "orthodox." That view
holds that the Cold War resulted from the response of an innocent United
States to an aggressive Soviet Union whose motives stemmed from great
power ambitions or communist ideology. A modified statement of that position is set forth in the selection by Arthur M. Schlesinger, Jr., the distinguished City University of New York historian of the Franklin D. Roosevelt
and John F. Kennedy administrations and a former adviser to President
Kennedy. It is the version probably held by most historians, political liberals
for the most part, and certainly that held by both the liberal and conservative
political establishments.*

*T*he orthodox position is the only one. The ebbing of
US–USSR confrontations has sped the advancement of a revisionist interpretation of the Cold War. It holds that American policy was just as aggressive
and responsible for the Cold War as was Russian policy. The Cold War began
in 1945 with a series of mutually hostile American and Russian actions and
was in full operation by the 1947 dropping of communists from the coalition
governments of Italy and France and the communist seizure of power in
Hungary in 1947 and in Czechoslovakia in 1948. The rise of a revisionist
interpretation is traced in the second selection by Christopher Lasch, a University of Rochester historian of American radicalism. It was written in part
to refute Schlesinger's article and his earlier letter to the New York Review of
Books. While revisionism generally has been the work of the so-called New
Left historians, it has been as critical of the liberal mainstream as have the
conservatives. For example, William Appleman Williams, the grandfather if
not the father of the revisionists and presently professor at Oregon State
University, has found more to admire in the foreign policy of conservative
presidents like Hoover and Eisenhower than in that of liberal presidents like
Truman and Kennedy. A similar view of Hoover was expressed in Arno
Mayer's selection on the Treaty of Versailles.*

*I*n evaluating the orthodox and revisionist positions one should keep in
mind that between 1945 and 1947 communism fared differently in different
areas. In those areas occupied by the Red Army in 1945, the Soviet Union
permanently allowed "friendly" democratically elected governments in Finland and Austria, temporarily allowed them in Czechoslovakia and
Hungary, and imposed communist regimes on Rumania, Bulgaria, and Poland,
while Yugoslavian and Albanian communists both liberated their nations
from German occupation and established communist regimes without significant help from the Soviet Union. Interestingly enough, Austria, like Germany,
had been divided into four occupation zones, with Vienna, like Berlin, being a
four-power "island" in the middle of the Soviet zone.*

*T*aking Schlesinger and Lasch together, the reader might consider these
questions: What evidence points to the Cold War's having originated from a
breakdown of communications between the United States and the Soviet
Union? What evidence points to just the opposite, that each side knew exactly
the other side's intentions? Does the evidence indicate that American policy
can best be characterized by "universalism" or by "open door"? According
to the evidence available to us, were Russian aims and intentions marked*

by a sphere-of-influence policy or one characterized by a "universalism" of its own? In its relations with the West, where did the Soviet Union show flexibility, where firmness?

ARTHUR M. SCHLESINGER, JR.

The Cold War in its original form was a presumably mortal antagonism, arising in the wake of the Second World War, between two rigidly hostile blocs, one led by the Soviet Union, the other by the United States. For nearly two somber and dangerous decades this antagonism dominated the fears of mankind; it may even, on occasion, have come close to blowing up the planet. In recent years, however, the once implacable struggle has lost its familiar clarity of outline. With the passing of old issues and the emergence of new conflicts and contestants, there is a natural tendency, especially on the part of the generation which grew up during the Cold War, to take a fresh look at the causes of the great contention between Russia and America.

Some exercises in reappraisal have merely elaborated the orthodoxies promulgated in Washington or Moscow during the boom years of the Cold War. But others, especially in the United States (there are no signs, alas, of this in the Soviet Union), represent what American historians call "revisionism"—that is, a readiness to challenge official explanations. No one should be surprised by this phenomenon. Every war in American history has been followed in due course by skeptical reassessments of supposedly sacred assumptions. So the War of 1812, fought at the time for the freedom of the seas, was in later years ascribed to the expansionist ambitions of Congressional war hawks; so the Mexican War became a slaveholders' conspiracy. So the Civil War has been pronounced a "needless war," and Lincoln has even been accused of manoeuvring the rebel attack on Fort Sumter. So too the Spanish-American War and the First and Second World Wars have, each in its turn, undergone revisionist critiques. It is not to be supposed that the Cold War would remain exempt.

In the case of the Cold War, special factors reinforce the predictable historiographical rhythm. The outburst of polycentrism in the communist empire has made people wonder whether communism was ever so monolithic as official theories of the Cold War supposed. A generation with no vivid memories of Stalinism may see the Russia of the forties in the image of the relatively mild, seedy and irresolute Russia of the sixties. And for this same generation the American course of widening the war in Viet Nam—which even non-revisionists can easily regard as folly—has unquestionably stirred doubts about the wisdom of American foreign policy in the sixties which younger historians may have begun to read back into the forties.

It is useful to remember that, on the whole, past exercises in revisionism have failed to stick. Few historians today believe that the war hawks caused the War of 1812 or the slaveholders the Mexican War, or that the Civil War was needless, or that the House of Morgan brought America into the First World War or that Franklin Roosevelt schemed to produce the attack on Pearl Harbor. But this does not mean that one should deplore the rise of Cold War revisionism.[1] For revisionism is an essential part of the process by which history, through the posing of new problems and the investigation of new possibilities, enlarges its perspectives and enriches its insights.

More than this, in the present context, revisionism expresses a deep, legitimate and tragic apprehension. As the Cold War has begun to lose its purity of definition, as the moral absolutes of the fifties become the moralistic clichés of the sixties, some have begun to ask whether the appalling risks which humanity ran during the Cold War were, after all, necessary and inevitable; whether more restrained and rational policies might not have guided the energies of man from the perils of conflict into the potentialities of collaboration. The fact that such questions are in their nature unanswerable does not mean that it is not right and useful to raise them. Nor does it mean that our sons and daughters are not entitled to an accounting from the generation of Russians and Americans who produced the Cold War.

II

The orthodox American view, as originally set forth by the American government and as reaffirmed until recently by most American scholars, has been that the Cold War was the brave and essential response of free men to communist aggression. Some have gone back well before the Second World War to lay open the sources of Russian expansionism. Geopoliticians traced the Cold War to imperial Russian strategic ambitions which in the nineteenth century led to the Crimean War, to Russian penetration of the Balkans and the Middle East and to Russian pressure on Britain's "lifeline" to India. Ideologists traced it to the Communist Manifesto of 1848 ("the violent overthrow of the bourgeoisie lays the foundation for the sway of the proletariat"). Thoughtful observers (a phrase meant to exclude those who speak in Dullese about the unlimited evil of godless, atheistic, militant communism) concluded that classical Russian imperialism and Pan-Slavism, compounded after 1917 by Leninist messianism, confronted the West at the end of the Second World War with an inexorable drive for domination.[2]

[1] As this writer somewhat intemperately did in a letter to *The New York Review of Books,* October 20, 1966.

[2] Every student of the Cold War must acknowledge his debt to W. H. McNeill's remarkable account, "America, Britain and Russia: Their Cooperation and Conflict, 1941–1946" (New York, 1953) and to the brilliant and indispensable series by Herbert Feis: "Churchill, Roosevelt, Stalin: The War They Waged

The revisionist thesis is very different.[3] In its extreme form, it is that, after the death of Franklin Roosevelt and the end of the Second World War, the United States deliberately abandoned the wartime policy of collaboration and, exhilarated by the possession of the atomic bomb, undertook a course of aggression of its own designed to expel all Russian influence from Eastern Europe and to establish democratic-capitalist states on the very border of the Soviet Union. As the revisionists see it, this radically new American policy—or rather this resumption by Truman of the pre-Roosevelt policy of insensate anti-communism—left Moscow no

and the Peace They Sought" (Princeton, 1957); "Between War and Peace: The Potsdam Conference" (Princeton, 1960); and "The Atomic Bomb and the End of World War II" (Princeton, 1966). Useful recent analyses include André Fontaine, "Histoire de la Guerre Froide" (2 v., Paris, 1965, 1967); N. A. Graebner, "Cold War Diplomacy, 1945–1960" (Princeton, 1962); L. J. Halle, "The Cold War as History" (London, 1967); M. F. Herz, "Beginnings of the Cold War" (Bloomington, 1966) and W. L. Neumann, "After Victory: Churchill, Roosevelt, Stalin and the Making of the Peace" (New York, 1967).

[3] The fullest statement of this case is to be found in D. F. Fleming's voluminous "The Cold War and Its Origins" (New York, 1961). For a shorter version of this argument, see David Horowitz, "The Free World Colossus" (New York, 1965); the most subtle and ingenious statements come in W. A. Williams' "The Tragedy of American Diplomacy" (rev. ed., New York, 1962) and in Gar Alperovitz's "Atomic Diplomacy: Hiroshima and Potsdam" (New York, 1965) and in subsequent articles and reviews by Mr. Alperovitz in *The New York Review of Books*. The fact that in some aspects the revisionist thesis parallels the official Soviet argument must not, of course, prevent consideration of the case on its merits, nor raise questions about the motives of the writers, all of whom, so far as I know, are independent-minded scholars.

I might further add that all these books, in spite of their ostentatious display of scholarly apparatus, must be used with caution. Professor Fleming, for example, relies heavily on newspaper articles and even columnists. While Mr. Alperovitz bases his case on official documents or authoritative reminiscences, he sometimes twists his material in a most unscholarly way. For example, in describing Ambassador Harriman's talk with President Truman on April 20, 1945, Mr. Alperovitz writes, "He argued that a reconsideration of Roosevelt's policy was necessary" (p. 22, repeated on p. 24). The citation is to pp. 70–72 in President Truman's "Years of Decision." What President Truman reported Harriman as saying was the exact opposite: "Before leaving, Harriman took me aside and said, 'Frankly, one of the reasons that made me rush back to Washington was the fear that you did not understand, as I had seen Roosevelt understand, that Stalin is breaking his agreements.' " Similarly, in an appendix (p. 271) Mr. Alperovitz writes that the Hopkins and Davies missions of May 1945 "were opposed by the 'firm' advisers." Actually the Hopkins mission was proposed by Harriman and Charles E. Bohlen, who Mr. Alperovitz elsewhere suggests were the firmest of the firm—and was proposed by them precisely to impress on Stalin the continuity of American policy from Roosevelt to Truman. While the idea that Truman reversed Roosevelt's policy is tempting dramatically, it is a myth. See, for example, the testimony of Anna Rosenberg Hoffman, who lunched with Roosevelt on March 24, 1945, the last day he spent in Washington. After luncheon, Roosevelt was handed a cable. "He read it and became quite angry. He banged his fists on the arms of his wheelchair and said, 'Averell is right; we can't do business with Stalin. He has broken every one of the promises he made at Yalta.' He was very upset and continued in the same vein on the subject."

alternative but to take measures in defense of its own borders. The result was the Cold War.

These two views, of course, could not be more starkly contrasting. It is therefore not unreasonable to look again at the half-dozen critical years between June 22, 1941, when Hitler attacked Russia, and July 2, 1947, when the Russians walked out of the Marshall Plan meeting in Paris. Several things should be borne in mind as this reëxamination is made. For one thing, we have thought a great deal more in recent years, in part because of writers like Roberta Wohlstetter and T. C. Schelling, about the problems of communication in diplomacy—the signals which one nation, by word or by deed, gives, inadvertently or intentionally, to another. Any honest reappraisal of the origins of the Cold War requires the imaginative leap—which should in any case be as instinctive for the historian as it is prudent for the statesman—into the adversary's viewpoint. We must strive to see how, given Soviet perspectives, the Russians might conceivably have misread our signals, as we must reconsider how intelligently we read theirs.

For another, the historian must not overindulge the man of power in the illusion cherished by those in office that high position carries with it the easy ability to shape history. Violating the statesman's creed, Lincoln once blurted out the truth in his letter of 1864 to A. G. Hodges: "I claim not to have controlled events, but confess plainly that events have controlled me." He was not asserting Tolstoyan fatalism but rather suggesting how greatly events limit the capacity of the statesman to bend history to his will. The physical course of the Second World War—the military operations undertaken, the position of the respective armies at the war's end, the momentum generated by victory and the vacuums created by defeat—all these determined the future as much as the character of individual leaders and the substance of national ideology and purpose.

Nor can the historian forget the conditions under which decisions are made, especially in a time like the Second World War. These were tired, overworked, aging men: in 1945, Churchill was 71 years old, Stalin had governed his country for 17 exacting years, Roosevelt his for 12 years nearly as exacting. During the war, moreover, the importunities of military operations had shoved postwar questions to the margins of their minds. All—even Stalin, behind his screen of ideology—had became addicts of improvisation, relying on authority and virtuosity to conceal the fact that they were constantly surprised by developments. Like Eliza, they leaped from one cake of ice to the next in the effort to reach the other side of the river. None showed great tactical consistency, or cared much about it; all employed a certain ambiguity to preserve their power to decide big issues; and it is hard to know how to interpret anything any one of them said on any specific occasion. This was partly because, like all princes, they designed their expressions to have particular effects on particular audiences; partly because the entirely genuine intellectual difficulty of the questions they faced made a degree of vacillation and mind-changing eminently reasonable. If historians cannot solve their problems in retrospect, who are they to blame Roosevelt, Stalin and Churchill for not having solved them at the time?

III

Peacemaking after the Second World War was not so much a tapestry as it was a hopelessly raveled and knotted mess of yarn. Yet, for purposes of clarity, it is essential to follow certain threads. One theme indispensable to an understanding of the Cold War is the contrast between two clashing views of world order: the "universalist" view, by which all nations shared a common interest in all the affairs of the world, and the "sphere-of-influence" view, by which each great power would be assured by the other great powers of an acknowledged predominance in its own area of special interest. The universalist view assumed that national security would be guaranteed by an international organization. The sphere-of-interest view assumed that national security would be guaranteed by the balance of power. While in practice these views have by no means been incompatible (indeed, our shaky peace has been based on a combination of the two), in the abstract they involved sharp contradictions.

The tradition of American thought in these matters was universalist —*i.e.* Wilsonian. Roosevelt had been a member of Wilson's subcabinet; in 1920, as candidate for Vice President, he had campaigned for the League of Nations. It is true that, within Roosevelt's infinitely complex mind, Wilsonianism warred with the perception of vital strategic interests he had imbibed from Mahan. Morever, his temperamental inclination to settle things with fellow princes around the conference table led him to regard the Big Three—or Four—as trustees for the rest of the world. On occasion, as this narrative will show, he was beguiled into flirtation with the sphere-of-influence heresy. But in principle he believed in joint action and remained a Wilsonian. His hope for Yalta, as he told the Congress on his return, was that it would "spell the end of the system of unilateral action, the exclusive alliances, the spheres of influence, the balances of power, and all the other expedients that have been tried for centuries —and have always failed."

Whenever Roosevelt backslid, he had at his side that Wilsonian fundamentalist, Secretary of State Cordell Hull, to recall him to the pure faith. After his visit to Moscow in 1943, Hull characteristically said that, with the Declaration of Four Nations on General Security (in which America, Russia, Britain and China pledged "united action . . . for the organization and maintenance of peace and security"), "there will no longer be need for spheres of influence, for alliances, for balance of power, or any other of the special arrangements through which, in the unhappy past, the nations strove to safeguard their security or to promote their interests."

Remembering the corruption of the Wilsonian vision by the secret treaties of the First World War, Hull was determined to prevent any sphere-of-influence nonsense after the Second World War. He therefore fought all proposals to settle border questions while the war was still on and, excluded as he largely was from wartime diplomacy, poured his not inconsiderable moral energy and frustration into the promulgation of virtuous and spacious general principles.

In adopting the universalist view, Roosevelt and Hull were not indulging personal hobbies. Sumner Welles, Adolf Berle, Averell Harriman, Charles Bohlen—all, if with a variety of nuances, opposed the sphere-of-influence approach. And here the State Department was expressing what seems clearly to have been the predominant mood of the American people, so long mistrustful of European power politics. The Republicans shared the true faith. John Foster Dulles argued that the great threat to peace after the war would lie in the revival of sphere-of-influence thinking. The United States, he said, must not permit Britain and Russia to revert to these bad old ways; it must therefore insist on American participation in all policy decisions for all territories in the world. Dulles wrote pessimistically in January 1945, "The three great powers which at Moscow agreed upon the 'closest coöperation' about European questions have shifted to a practice of separate, regional responsibility."

It is true that critics, and even friends, of the United States sometimes noted a discrepancy between the American passion for universalism when it applied to territory far from American shores and the preëminence the United States accorded its own interests nearer home. Churchill, seeking Washington's blessing for a sphere-of-influence initiative in Eastern Europe, could not forbear reminding the Americans, "We follow the lead of the United States in South America"; nor did any universalist of record propose the abolition of the Monroe Doctrine. But a convenient myopia prevented such inconsistencies from qualifying the ardency of the universalist faith.

There seem only to have been three officials in the United States Government who dissented. One was the Secretary of War, Henry L. Stimson, a classical balance-of-power man, who in 1944 opposed the creation of a vacuum in Central Europe by the pastoralization of Germany and in 1945 urged "the settlement of all territorial acquisitions in the shape of defense posts which each of these four powers may deem to be necessary for their own safety" in advance of any effort to establish a peacetime United Nations. Stimson considered the claim of Russia to a preferred position in Eastern Europe as not unreasonable: as he told President Truman, "he thought the Russians perhaps were being more realistic than we were in regard to their own security." Such a position for Russia seemed to him comparable to the preferred American position in Latin America; he even spoke of "our respective orbits." Stimson was therefore skeptical of what he regarded as the prevailing tendency "to hang on to exaggerated views of the Monroe Doctrine and at the same time butt into every question that comes up in Central Europe." Acceptance of spheres of influence seemed to him the way to avoid "a head-on collision."

A second official opponent of universalism was George Kennan, an eloquent advocate from the American Embassy in Moscow of "a prompt and clear recognition of the division of Europe into spheres of influence and of a policy based on the fact of such division." Kennan argued that nothing we could do would possibly alter the course of events in Eastern Europe; that we were deceiving ourselves by supposing that these countries had any future but Russian domination; that we should therefore relinquish Eastern Europe to the Soviet Union and avoid anything which would make things easier for the Russians by giving them economic assistance or by sharing moral responsibility for their actions.

A third voice within the government against universalism was (at least after the war) Henry A. Wallace. As Secretary of Commerce, he stated the sphere-of-influence case with trenchancy in the famous Madison Square Garden speech of September 1946 which led to his dismissal by President Truman:

> On our part, we should recognize that we have no more business in the *political* affairs of Eastern Europe than Russia has in the *political* affairs of Latin America, Western Europe, and the United States. . . . Whether we like it or not, the Russians will try to socialize their sphere of influence just as we try to democratize our sphere of influence. . . . The Russians have no more business stirring up native Communists to political activity in Western Europe, Latin America, and the United States than we have in interfering with the politics of Eastern Europe and Russia.

Stimson, Kennan and Wallace seem to have been alone in the government, however, in taking these views. They were very much minority voices. Meanwhile universalism, rooted in the American legal and moral tradition, overwhelmingly backed by contemporary opinion, received successive enshrinements in the Atlantic Charter of 1941, in the Declaration of the United Nations in 1942 and in the Moscow Declaration of 1943.

IV

The Kremlin, on the other hand, thought *only* of spheres of interest; above all, the Russians were determined to protect their frontiers, and especially their border to the west, crossed so often and so bloodily in the dark course of their history. These western frontiers lacked natural means of defense—no great oceans, rugged mountains, steaming swamps or impenetrable jungles. The history of Russia had been the history of invasion, the last of which was by now horribly killing up to twenty million of its people. The protocol of Russia therefore meant the enlargement of the area of Russian influence. Kennan himself wrote (in May 1944), "Behind Russia's stubborn expansion lies only the age-old sense of insecurity of a sedentary people reared on an exposed plain in the neighborhood of fierce nomadic peoples," and he called this "urge" a "permanent feature of Russian psychology."

In earlier times the "urge" had produced the tsarist search for buffer states and maritime outlets. In 1939 the Soviet-Nazi pact and its secret protocol had enabled Russia to begin to satisfy in the Baltic states, Karelian Finland and Poland, part of what it conceived as its security requirements in Eastern Europe. But the "urge" persisted, causing the friction between Russia and Germany in 1940 as each jostled for position in the area which separated them. Later it led to Molotov's new demands on Hitler in November 1940—a free hand in Finland, Soviet predominance in Rumania and Bulgaria, bases in the Dardanelles—the demands which convinced Hitler that he had no choice but to attack Russia. Now Stalin hoped to gain from the West what Hitler, a closer neighbor, had not dared yield him.

It is true that, so long as Russian survival appeared to require a second front to relieve the Nazi pressure, Moscow's demand for Eastern Europe was a little muffled. Thus the Soviet government adhered to the Atlantic Charter (though with a significant if obscure reservation about adapting its principles to "the circumstances, needs, and historic peculiarities of particular countries"). Thus it also adhered to the Moscow Declaration of 1943, and Molotov then, with his easy mendacity, even denied that Russia had any desire to divide Europe into spheres of influence. But this was guff, which the Russians were perfectly willing to ladle out if it would keep the Americans, and especially Secretary Hull (who made a strong personal impression at the Moscow conference), happy. "A declaration," as Stalin once observed to Eden, "I regard as algebra, but an agreement as practical arithmetic. I do not wish to decry algebra, but I prefer practical arithmetic."

The more consistent Russian purpose was revealed when Stalin offered the British a straight sphere-of-influence deal at the end of 1941. Britain, he suggested, should recognize the Russian absorption of the Baltic states, part of Finland, eastern Poland and Bessarabia; in return, Russia would support any special British need for bases or security arrangements in Western Europe. There was nothing specifically communist about these ambitions. If Stalin achieved them, he would be fulfilling an age-old dream of the tsars. The British reaction was mixed. "Soviet policy is amoral," as Anthony Eden noted at the time; "United States policy is exaggeratedly moral, at least where non-American interests are concerned." If Roosevelt was a universalist with occasional leanings toward spheres of influence and Stalin was a sphere-of-influence man with occasional gestures toward universalism, Churchill seemed evenly poised between the familiar realism of the balance of power, which he had so long recorded as an historian and manipulated as a statesman, and the hope that there must be some better way of doing things. His 1943 proposal of a world organization divided into regional councils represented an effort to blend universalist and sphere-of-interest conceptions. His initial rejection of Stalin's proposal in December 1941 as "directly contrary to the first, second and third articles of the Atlantic Charter" thus did not spring entirely from a desire to propitiate the United States. On the other hand, he had himself already reinterpreted the Atlantic Charter as applying only to Europe (and thus not to the British Empire), and he was, above all, an empiricist who never believed in sacrificing reality on the altar of doctrine.

So in April 1942 he wrote Roosevelt that "the increasing gravity of the war" had led him to feel that the Charter "ought not to be construed so as to deny Russia the frontiers she occupied when Germany attacked her." Hull, however, remained fiercely hostile to the inclusion of territorial provisions in the Anglo-Russian treaty; the American position, Eden noted, "chilled me with Wilsonian memories." Though Stalin complained that it looked "as if the Atlantic Charter was directed against the U.S.S.R.," it was the Russian season of military adversity in the spring of 1942, and he dropped his demands.

He did not, however, change his intentions. A year later Ambassador Standley could cable Washington from Moscow: "In 1918 Western Europe attempted to set up a *cordon sanitaire* to protect it from the influence of bolshevism. Might not now the Kremlin envisage the formation of a belt of pro-Soviet states to protect it from the influences of the West?" It well might; and that purpose became increasingly clear as the war approached its end. Indeed, it derived sustenance from Western policy in the first area of liberation.

The unconditional surrender of Italy in July 1943 created the first major test of the Western devotion to universalism. America and Britain, having won the Italian war, handled the capitulation, keeping Moscow informed at a distance. Stalin complained:

> The United States and Great Britain made agreements but the Soviet Union received information about the results . . . just as a passive third observer. I have to tell you that it is impossible to tolerate the situation any longer. I propose that the [tripartite military-political commission] be established and that Sicily be assigned . . . as its place of residence.

Roosevelt, who had no intention of sharing the control of Italy with the Russians, suavely replied with the suggestion that Stalin send an officer "to General Eisenhower's headquarters in connection with the commission." Unimpressed, Stalin continued to press for a tripartite body; but his Western allies were adamant in keeping the Soviet Union off the Control Commission for Italy, and the Russians in the end had to be satisfied with a seat, along with minor Allied states, on a meaningless Inter-Allied Advisory Council. Their acquiescence in this was doubtless not unconnected with a desire to establish precedents for Eastern Europe.

Teheran in December 1943 marked the high point of three-power collaboration. Still, when Churchill asked about Russian territorial interests, Stalin replied a little ominously, "There is no need to speak at the present time about any Soviet desires, but when the time comes we will speak." In the next weeks, there were increasing indications of a Soviet determination to deal unilaterally with Eastern Europe—so much so that in early February 1944 Hull cabled Harriman in Moscow:

> Matters are rapidly approaching the point where the Soviet Government will have to choose between the development and exten-

sion of the foundation of international cooperation as the guiding principle of the postwar world as against the continuance of a unilateral and arbitrary method of dealing with its special problems even though these problems are admittedly of more direct interest to the Soviet Union than to other great powers.

As against this approach, however, Churchill, more tolerant of sphere-of-influence deviations, soon proposed that, with the impending liberation of the Balkans, Russia should run things in Rumania and Britain in Greece. Hull strongly opposed this suggestion but made the mistake of leaving Washington for a few days; and Roosevelt, momentarily free from his Wilsonian conscience, yielded to Churchill's plea for a three-months' trial. Hull resumed the fight on his return, and Churchill postponed the matter.

The Red Army continued its advance into Eastern Europe. In August the Polish Home Army, urged on by Polish-language broadcasts from Moscow, rose up against the Nazis in Warsaw. For 63 terrible days, the Poles fought valiantly on, while the Red Army halted on the banks of the Vistula a few miles away, and in Moscow Stalin for more than half this time declined to coöperate with the Western effort to drop supplies to the Warsaw Resistance. It appeared a calculated Soviet decision to let the Nazis slaughter the anti-Soviet Polish underground; and, indeed, the result was to destroy any substantial alternative to a Soviet solution in Poland. The agony of Warsaw caused the most deep and genuine moral shock in Britain and America and provoked dark forebodings about Soviet postwar purposes.

Again history enjoins the imaginative leap in order to see things for a moment from Moscow's viewpoint. The Polish question, Churchill would say at Yalta, was for Britain a question of honor. "It is not only a question of honor for Russia," Stalin replied, "but one of life and death. . . . Throughout history Poland had been the corridor for attack on Russia." A top postwar priority for any Russian régime must be to close that corridor. The Home Army was led by anti-communists. It clearly hoped by its action to forestall the Soviet occupation of Warsaw and, in Russian eyes, to prepare the way for an anti-Russian Poland. In addition, the uprising from a strictly operational viewpoint was premature. The Russians, it is evident in retrospect, had real military problems at the Vistula. The Soviet attempt in September to send Polish units from the Red Army across the river to join forces with the Home Army was a disaster. Heavy German shelling thereafter prevented the ferrying of tanks necessary for an assault on the German position. The Red Army itself did not take Warsaw for another three months. None the less, Stalin's indifference to the human tragedy, his effort to blackmail the London Poles during the ordeal, his sanctimonious opposition during five precious weeks to aerial resupply, the invariable coldness of his explanations ("the Soviet command has come to the conclusion that it must dissociate itself from the Warsaw adventure") and the obvious political benefit to the Soviet Union from the destruction of the Home Army—all these had the effect of suddenly dropping the mask of wartime comradeship and displaying to the West the hard face of Soviet policy. In now pursuing what he grimly regarded as the minimal requirements for the postwar security of his country, Stalin was inadvertently showing the irreconcilability of both his means and his ends with the Anglo-American conception of the peace.

Meanwhile Eastern Europe presented the Alliance with still another crisis that same September. Bulgaria, which was not at war with Russia, decided to surrender to the Western Allies while it still could; and the English and Americans at Cairo began to discuss armistice terms with Bulgarian envoys. Moscow, challenged by what it plainly saw as a Western intrusion into its own zone of vital interest, promptly declared war on Bulgaria, took over the surrender negotiations and, invoking the Italian precedent, denied its Western Allies any role in the Bulgarian Control Commission. In a long and thoughtful cable, Ambassador Harriman meditated on the problems of communication with the Soviet Union. "Words," he reflected, "have a different connotation to the Soviets than they have to us. When they speak of insisting on 'friendly governments' in their neighboring countries, they have in mind something quite different from what we would mean." The Russians, he surmised, really believed that Washington accepted "their position that although they would keep us informed they had the right to settle their problems with their western neighbors unilaterally." But the Soviet position was still in flux: "the Soviet Government is not one mind." The problem, as Harriman had earlier told Harry Hopkins, was "to strengthen the hands of those around Stalin who want to play the game along our lines." The way to do this, he now told Hull, was to

be understanding of their sensitivity, meet them much more than half way, encourage them and support them wherever we can, and yet oppose them promptly with the greatest of firmness where we see them going wrong. . . . The only way we can eventually come to an understanding with the Soviet Union on the question of non-interference in the internal affairs of other countries is for us to take a definite interest in the solution of the problems of each individual country as they arise.

As against Harriman's sophisticated universalist strategy, however, Churchill, increasingly fearful of the consequences of unrestrained competition in Eastern Europe, decided in early October to carry his sphere-of-influence proposal directly to Moscow. Roosevelt was at first content to have Churchill speak for him too and even prepared a cable to that effect. But Hopkins, a more rigorous universalist, took it upon himself to stop the cable and warn Roosevelt of its possible implications. Eventually Roosevelt sent a message to Harriman in Moscow emphasizing that he expected to "retain complete freedom of action after this conference is over." It was now that Churchill quickly proposed—and Stalin as quickly accepted—the celebrated division of southeastern Europe: ending (after further haggling between Eden and Molotov) with 90 percent

Soviet predominance in Rumania, 80 percent in Bulgaria and Hungary, fifty-fifty in Jugoslavia, 90 percent British predominance in Greece.

Churchill in discussing this with Harriman used the phrase "spheres of influence." But he insisted that these were only "immediate wartime arrangements" and received a highly general blessing from Roosevelt. Yet, whatever Churchill intended, there is reason to believe that Stalin construed the percentages as an agreement, not a declaration; as practical arithmetic, not algebra. For Stalin, it should be understood, the sphere-of-influence idea did not mean that he would abandon all efforts to spread communism in some other nation's sphere; it did mean that, if he tried this and the other side cracked down, he could not feel he had serious cause for complaint. As Kennan wrote to Harriman at the end of 1944:

> As far as border states are concerned the Soviet government has never ceased to think in terms of spheres of interest. They expect us to support them in whatever action they wish to take in those regions, regardless of whether that action seems to us or to the rest of the world to be right or wrong. . . . I have no doubt that this position is honestly maintained on their part, and that they would be equally prepared to reserve moral judgment on any actions which we might wish to carry out, i.e., in the Caribbean area.

In any case, the matter was already under test a good deal closer to Moscow than the Caribbean. The communist-dominated resistance movement in Greece was in open revolt against the effort of the Papandreou government to disarm and disband the guerrillas (the same Papandreou whom the Greek colonels have recently arrested on the claim that he is a tool of the communists). Churchill now called in British Army units to crush the insurrection. This action produced a storm of criticism in his own country and in the United States; the American Government even publicly dissociated itself from the intervention, thereby emphasizing its detachment from the sphere-of-influence deal. But Stalin, Churchill later claimed, "adhered strictly and faithfully to our agreement of October, and during all the long weeks of fighting the Communists in the streets of Athens not one word of reproach came from *Pravda* or *Izvestia*," though there is no evidence that he tried to call off the Greek communists. Still, when the communist rebellion later broke out again in Greece, Stalin told Kardelj and Djilas of Jugoslavia in 1948, "The uprising in Greece must be stopped, and as quickly as possible."

No one, of course, can know what really was in the minds of the Russian leaders. The Kremlin archives are locked; of the primary actors, only Molotov survives, and he has not yet indicated any desire to collaborate with the Columbia Oral History Project. We do know that Stalin did not wholly surrender to sentimental illusion about his new friends. In June 1944, on the night before the landings in Normandy, he told Djilas that the English "find nothing sweeter than to trick their allies. . . . And Churchill? Churchill is the kind who, if you don't watch him, will slip a kopeck out of your pocket. Yes, a kopeck out of your pocket! . . . Roosevelt is not like that. He dips in his hand only for bigger coins." But whatever his views of his colleagues it is not unreasonable to suppose that Stalin would have been satisfied at the end of the war to secure what Kennan has called "a protective glacis along Russia's western border," and that, in exchange for a free hand in Eastern Europe, he was prepared to give the British and Americans equally free hands in their zones of vital interest, including in nations as close to Russia as Greece (for the British) and, very probably—or at least so the Jugoslavs believe—China (for the United States). In other words, his initial objectives were very probably not world conquest but Russian security.

V

It is now pertinent to inquire why the United States rejected the idea of stabilizing the world by division into spheres of influence and insisted on an East European strategy. One should warn against rushing to the conclusion that it was all a row between hard-nosed, balance-of-power realists and starry-eyed Wilsonians. Roosevelt, Hopkins, Welles, Harriman, Bohlen, Berle, Dulles and other universalists were tough and serious men. Why then did they rebuff the sphere-of-influence solution?

The first reason is that they regarded this solution as containing within itself the seeds of a third world war. The balance-of-power idea seemed inherently unstable. It had always broken down in the past. It held out to each power the permanent temptation to try to alter the balance in its own favor, and it built this temptation into the international order. It would turn the great powers of 1945 away from the objective of concerting common policies toward competition for postwar advantage. As Hopkins told Molotov at Teheran, "The President feels it essential to world peace that Russia, Great Britain and the United States work out this control question in a manner which will not start each of the three powers arming against the others." "The greatest likelihood of eventual conflict," said the Joint Chiefs of Staff in 1944 (the only conflict which the J.C.S., in its wisdom, could then glimpse "in the foreseeable future" was between Britain and Russia), ". . . would seem to grow out of either nation initiating attempts to build up its strength, by seeking to attach to herself parts of Europe to the disadvantage and possible danger of her potential adversary." The Americans were perfectly ready to acknowledge that Russia was entitled to convincing assurance of her national security—but not this way. "I could sympathize fully with Stalin's desire to protect his western borders from future attack," as Hull put it. "But I felt that this security could best be obtained through a strong postwar peace organization."

Hull's remark suggests the second objection: that the sphere-of-influence approach would, in the words of the State Department in 1945, "militate against the establishment and effective functioning of a broader system of general security in which all countries will have their part." The United Nations, in short, was seen as the alternative to the balance of power. Nor did the universalists see any necessary incompatibility between the Russian desire for "friendly governments" on its frontier and the American desire for self-determination in Eastern Europe. Before Yalta the State Department judged the general mood of Europe as "to the left and strongly in favor of far-reaching economic and social reforms, but not, however, in favor of a left-wing totalitarian regime to achieve these reforms." Governments in Eastern Europe could be sufficiently to the left "to allay Soviet suspicions" but sufficiently representative "of the center and *petit bourgeois* elements" not to seem a prelude to communist dictatorship. The American criteria were therefore that the government "should be dedicated to the preservation of civil liberties" and "should favor social and economic reforms." A string of New Deal states—of Finlands and Czechoslovakias—seemed a reasonable compromise solution.

Third, the universalists feared that the sphere-of-interest approach would be what Hull termed "a haven for the isolationists," who would advocate America's participation in Western Hemisphere affairs on condition that it did not participate in European or Asian affairs. Hull also feared that spheres of interest would lead to "closed trade areas or discriminatory systems" and thus defeat his cherished dream of a low-tariff, freely trading world.

Fourth, the sphere-of-interest solution meant the betrayal of the principles for which the Second World War was being fought—the Atlantic Charter, the Four Freedoms, the Declaration of the United Nations. Poland summed up the problem. Britain, having gone to war to defend the independence of Poland from the Germans, could not easily conclude the war by surrendering the independence of Poland to the Russians. Thus, as Hopkins told Stalin after Roosevelt's death in 1945, Poland had "become the symbol of our ability to work out problems with the Soviet Union." Nor could American liberals in general watch with equanimity while the police state spread into countries which, if they had mostly not been real democracies, had mostly not been tyrannies either. The execution in 1943 of Ehrlich and Alter, the Polish socialist trade union leaders, excited deep concern. "I have particularly in mind," Harriman cabled in 1944, "objection to the institution of secret police who may become involved in the persecution of persons of truly democratic convictions who may not be willing to conform to Soviet methods."

Fifth, the sphere-of-influence solution would create difficult domestic problems in American politics. Roosevelt was aware of the six million or more Polish votes in the 1944 election; even more acutely, he was aware of the broader and deeper attack which would follow if, after going to war to stop the Nazi conquest of Europe, he permitted the war to end with the communist conquest of Eastern Europe. As Archibald MacLeish, then Assistant Secretary of State for Public Affairs, warned in January 1945, "The wave of disillusionment which has distressed us in the last several weeks will be increased if the impression is permitted to get abroad that potentially totalitarian provisional governments are to be set up without adequate safeguards as to the holding of free elections and the realization of the principles of the Atlantic Charter." Roosevelt believed that no administration could survive which did not try everything short of war to save Eastern Europe, and he was the supreme American politician of the century.

Sixth, if the Russians were allowed to overrun Eastern Europe without argument, would that satisfy them? Even Kennan, in a dispatch of May 1944, admitted that the "urge" had dreadful potentialities: "If initially successful, will it know where to stop? Will it not be inexorably carried forward, by its very nature, in a struggle to reach the whole—to attain complete mastery of the shores of the Atlantic and the Pacific?" His own answer was that there were inherent limits to the Russian capacity to expand—"that Russia will not have an easy time in maintaining the power which it has seized over other people in Eastern and Central Europe unless it receives both moral and material assistance from the West." Subsequent developments have vindicated Kennan's argument. By the late forties, Jugoslavia and Albania, the two East European states farthest from the Soviet Union and the two in which communism was imposed from within rather than from without, had declared their independence of Moscow. But, given Russia's success in maintaining centralized control over the international communist movement for a quarter of a century, who in 1944 could have had much confidence in the idea of communist revolts against Moscow?

Most of those involved therefore rejected Kennan's answer and stayed with his question. If the West turned its back on Eastern Europe, the higher probability, in their view, was that the Russians would use their security zone, not just for defensive purposes, but as a springboard from which to mount an attack on Western Europe, now shattered by war, a vacuum of power awaiting its master. "If the policy is accepted that the Soviet Union has a right to penetrate her immediate neighbors for security," Harriman said in 1944, "penetration of the next immediate neighbors becomes at a certain time equally logical." If a row with Russia were inevitable, every consideration of prudence dictated that it should take place in Eastern rather than Western Europe.

Thus idealism and realism joined in opposition to the sphere-of-influence solution. The consequence was a determination to assert an American interest in the postwar destiny of all nations, including those of Eastern Europe. In the message which Roosevelt and Hopkins drafted after Hopkins had stopped Roosevelt's initial cable authorizing Churchill to speak for the United States at the Moscow meeting of October 1944, Roosevelt now said, "There is in this global war literally no question, either military or political, in which the United States is not interested." After Roosevelt's death Hopkins repeated the point to Stalin: "The cardinal basis of President Roosevelt's policy which the American people had fully supported had been the concept that the interests of the U.S. were worldwide and not confined to North and South America and the Pacific Ocean."

VI

For better or worse, this was the American position. It is now necessary to attempt the imaginative leap and consider the impact of this position on the leaders of the Soviet Union who, also for better or for worse, had reached the bitter conclusion that the survival of their country depended on their unchallenged control of the corridors through which enemies had so often invaded their homeland. They could claim to have been keeping their own side of the sphere-of-influence bargain. Of course, they were working to capture the resistance movements of Western Europe; indeed, with the appointment of Oumansky as Ambassador to Mexico they were even beginning to enlarge underground operations in the Western Hemisphere. But, from their viewpoint, if the West permitted this, the more fools they; and, if the West stopped it, it was within their right to do so. In overt political matters the Russians were scrupulously playing the game. They had watched in silence while the British shot down communists in Greece. In Jugoslavia Stalin was urging Tito (as Djilas later revealed) to keep King Peter. They had not only acknowledged Western preëminence in Italy but had recognized the Badoglio régime; the Italian Communists had even voted (against the Socialists and the Liberals) for the renewal of the Lateran Pacts.

They would not regard anti-communist action in a Western zone as a *casus belli;* and they expected reciprocal license to assert their own authority in the East. But the principle of self-determination was carrying the United States into a deeper entanglement in Eastern Europe than the Soviet Union claimed as a right (whatever it was doing underground) in the affairs of Italy, Greece or China. When the Russians now exercised in Eastern Europe the same brutal control they were prepared to have Washington exercise in the American sphere of influence, the American protests, given the paranoia produced alike by Russian history and Leninist ideology, no doubt seemed not only an act of hypocrisy but a threat to security. To the Russians, a stroll into the neighborhood easily became a plot to burn down the house: when, for example, damaged American planes made emergency landings in Poland and Hungary, Moscow took this as attempts to organize the local resistance. It is not unusual to suspect one's adversary of doing what one is already doing oneself. At the same time, the cruelty with which the Russians executed their idea of spheres of influence—in a sense, perhaps, an unwitting cruelty, since Stalin treated the East Europeans no worse than he had treated the Russians in the thirties—discouraged the West from accepting the equation (for example, Italy = Rumania) which seemed so self-evident to the Kremlin.

So Moscow very probably, and not unnaturally, perceived the emphasis on self-determination as a systematic and deliberate pressure on Russia's western frontiers. Moreover, the restoration of capitalism to countries freed at frightful cost by the Red Army no doubt struck the Russians as the betrayal of the principles for which *they* were fighting. "That they, the victors," Isaac Deutscher has suggested, "should now preserve an order from which they had experienced nothing but hostility, and could expect nothing but hostility . . . would have been the most miserable anti-climax to their great 'war of liberation.'" By 1944 Poland was the critical issue; Harriman later said that "under instructions from President Roosevelt, I talked about Poland with Stalin more frequently than any other subject." While the West saw the point of Stalin's demand for a "friendly government" in Warsaw, the American insistence on the sovereign virtues of free elections (ironically in the spirit of the 1917 Bolshevik decree of peace, which affirmed "the right" of a nation "to decide the forms of its state existence by a free vote, taken after the complete evacuation of the incorporating or, generally, of the stronger nation") created an insoluble problem in those countries, like Poland (and Rumania), where free elections would almost certainly produce anti-Soviet governments.

The Russians thus may well have estimated the Western pressures as calculated to encourage their enemies in Eastern Europe and to defeat their own minimum objective of a protective glacis. Everything still hung, however, on the course of military operations. The wartime collaboration had been created by one thing, and one thing alone: the threat of Nazi victory. So long as this threat was real, so was the collaboration. In late December 1944, von Rundstedt launched his counter-offensive in the Ardennes. A few weeks later, when Roosevelt, Churchill and Stalin gathered in the Crimea, it was in the shadow of this last considerable explosion of German power. The meeting at Yalta was still dominated by the mood of war.

Yalta remains something of an historical perplexity—less, from the perspective of 1967, because of a mythical American deference to the sphere-of-influence thesis than because of the documentable Russian deference to the universalist thesis. Why should Stalin in 1945 have accepted the Declaration on Liberated Europe and an agreement on Poland pledging that "the three governments will jointly" act to assure "free elections of governments responsive to the will of the people"? There are several probable answers: that the war was not over and the Russians still wanted the Americans to intensify their military effort in the West; that one clause in the Declaration premised action on "the opinion of the three governments" and thus implied a Soviet veto, though the Polish agreement was more definite; most of all that the universalist algebra of the Declaration was plainly in Stalin's mind to be construed in terms of the practical arithmetic of his sphere-of-influence agreement with Churchill the previous October. Stalin's assurance to Churchill at Yalta that a proposed Russian amendment to the Declaration would not apply to Greece makes it clear that Roosevelt's pieties did not, in Stalin's mind, nullify Churchill's percentages. He could well have been strengthened in this supposition by the fact that *after* Yalta, Churchill himself repeatedly reasserted the terms of the October agreement as if he regarded it, despite Yalta, as controlling.

Harriman still had the feeling before Yalta that the Kremlin had "two approaches to their postwar policies" and that Stalin himself was "of two minds." One approach emphasized the internal reconstruction and development of Russia; the other its external expansion. But in the meantime the fact which dominated all political decisions—that is, the war against Germany—was moving into its final phase. In the weeks after Yalta, the military situation changed with great rapidity. As the Nazi threat declined, so too did the need for coöperation. The Soviet Union, feeling itself menaced by the American idea of self-determination and the borderlands diplomacy to which it was leading, skeptical whether the United Nations would protect its frontiers as reliably as its own domination in Eastern Europe, began to fulfill its security requirements unilaterally.

In March Stalin expressed his evaluation of the United Nations by rejecting Roosevelt's plea that Molotov come to the San Francisco conference, if only for the opening sessions. In the next weeks the Russians emphatically and crudely worked their will in Eastern Europe, above all in the test country of Poland. They were ignoring the Declaration on Liberated Europe, ignoring the Atlantic Charter, self-determination, human freedom and everything else the Americans considered essential for a stable peace. "We must clearly recognize," Harriman wired Washington a few days before Roosevelt's death, "that the Soviet program is the establishment of totalitarianism, ending personal liberty and democracy as we know and respect it."

At the same time, the Russians also began to mobilize communist resources in the United States itself to block American universalism. In April 1945 Jacques Duclos, who had been the Comintern official responsible for the Western communist parties, launched in *Cahiers du Communisme* an uncompromising attack on the policy of the American Communist Party. Duclos sharply condemned the revisionism of Earl Browder, the American Communist leader, as "expressed in the concept of a long-term class peace in the United States, of the possibility of the suppression of the class struggle in the postwar period and of establishment of harmony between labor and capital." Browder was specifically rebuked for favoring the "self-determination" of Europe "west of the Soviet Union" on a bourgeois-democratic basis. The excommunication of Browderism was plainly the Politburo's considered reaction to the impending defeat of Germany; it was a signal to the communist parties of the West that they should recover their identity; it was Moscow's alert to communists everywhere that they should prepare for new policies in the postwar world.

The Duclos piece obviously could not have been planned and written much later than the Yalta conference—that is, well before a number of events which revisionists now cite in order to demonstrate American responsibility for the Cold War: before Allen Dulles, for example, began to negotiate the surrender of the German armies in Italy (the episode which provoked Stalin to charge Roosevelt with seeking a separate peace and provoked Roosevelt to denounce the "vile misrepresentations" of Stalin's informants); well before Roosevelt died; many months before the testing of the atomic bomb; even more months before Truman ordered that the bomb be dropped on Japan. William Z. Foster, who soon replaced Browder as the leader of the American Communist Party and embodied the new Moscow line, later boasted of having said in January 1944, "A postwar Roosevelt administration would continue to be, as it is now, an imperialist government." With ancient suspicions revived by the American insistence on universalism, this was no doubt the conclusion which the Russians were reaching at the same time. The Soviet canonization of Roosevelt (like their present-day canonization of Kennedy) took place after the American President's death.

The atmosphere of mutual suspicion was beginning to rise. In January 1945 Molotov formally proposed that the United States grant Russia a $6 billion credit for postwar reconstruction. With characteristic tact he explained that he was doing this as a favor to save America from a postwar depression. The proposal seems to have been diffidently made and diffidently received. Roosevelt requested that the matter "not be pressed further" on the American side until he had a chance to talk with Stalin; but the Russians did not follow it up either at Yalta in February (save for a single glancing reference) or during the Stalin-Hopkins talks in May or at Potsdam. Finally the proposal was renewed in the very different political atmosphere of August. This time Washington inexplicably mislaid the request during the transfer of the records of the Foreign Economic Administration to the State Department. It did not turn up again until March 1946. Of course this was impossible for the Russians to believe; it is hard enough even for those acquainted with the capacity of the American government for incompetence to believe; and it only strengthened Soviet suspicions of American purposes.

The American credit was one conceivable form of Western contribution to Russian reconstruction. Another was lend-lease, and the possibility of reconstruction aid under the lend-lease protocol had already been discussed in 1944. But in May 1945 Russia, like Britain, suffered from Truman's abrupt termination of lend-lease shipments—"unfortunate and even brutal," Stalin told Hopkins, adding that, if it was "designed as pressure on the Russians in order to soften them up, then it was a fundamental mistake." A third form was German reparations. Here Stalin in demanding $10 billion in reparations for the Soviet Union made his strongest fight at Yalta. Roosevelt, while agreeing essentially with Churchill's opposition, tried to postpone the matter by accepting the Soviet figure as a "basis for discussion"—a formula which led to future misunderstanding. In short, the Russian hope for major Western assistance in postwar reconstruction foundered on three events which the Kremlin could well have interpreted respectively as deliberate sabotage (the loan request), blackmail (lend-lease cancellation) and pro-Germanism (reparations).

Actually the American attempt to settle the fourth lend-lease protocol was generous and the Russians for their own reasons declined to come to an agreement. It is not clear, though, that satisfying Moscow on any of these financial scores would have made much essential difference. It might have persuaded some doves in the Kremlin that the U.S. government was genuinely friendly; it might have persuaded some hawks that the American anxiety for Soviet friendship was such that Moscow could do as it wished without inviting challenge from the United States. It would, in short, merely have reinforced both sides of the Kremlin debate; it would hardly have reversed deeper tendencies toward the deterioration of political relationships. Economic deals were surely subordinate to the quality of mutual political confidence; and here, in the months after Yalta, the decay was steady.

The Cold War had now begun. It was the product not of a decision but of a dilemma. Each side felt compelled to adopt policies which the other could not but regard as a threat to the principles of the peace. Each then felt compelled to undertake defensive measures. Thus the Russians saw no choice but to consolidate their security in Eastern Europe. The Americans, regarding Eastern Europe as the first step toward Western Europe, responded by asserting their interest in the zone the Russians deemed vital to their security. The Russians concluded that the West was resuming its old course of capitalist encirclement; that it was purposefully laying the foundation for anti-Soviet régimes in the area defined by the blood of centuries as crucial to Russian survival. Each side believed with passion that future international stability depended on the success of its own conception of world order. Each side, in pursuing its own clearly indicated and deeply cherished principles, was only confirming the fear of the other that it was bent on aggression.

Very soon the process began to acquire a cumulative momentum. The impending collapse of Germany thus provoked new troubles: the Russians, for example, sincerely feared that the West was planning a separate surrender of the German armies in Italy in a way which would release troops for Hitler's eastern front, as they subsequently feared that the Nazis might succeed in surrendering Berlin to the West. This was the context in which the atomic bomb now appeared. Though the revisionist argument that Truman dropped the bomb less to defeat Japan than to intimidate Russia is not convincing, this thought unquestionably appealed to some in Washington as at least an advantageous side-effect of Hiroshima.

So the machinery of suspicion and counter-suspicion, action and counter-action, was set in motion. But, given relations among traditional national states, there was still no reason, even with all the postwar jostling, why this should not have remained a manageable situation. What made it unmanageable, what caused the rapid escalation of the Cold War and in another two years completed the division of Europe, was a set of considerations which this account has thus far excluded.

VII

Up to this point, the discussion has considered the schism within the wartime coalition as if it were entirely the result of disagreements among national states. Assuming this framework, there was unquestionably a failure of communication between America and Russia, a misperception of signals and, as time went on, a mounting tendency to ascribe ominous motives to the other side. It seems hard, for example, to deny that American postwar policy created genuine difficulties for the Russians and even assumed a threatening aspect for them. All this the revisionists have rightly and usefully emphasized.

But the great omission of the revisionists—and also the fundamental explanation of the speed with which the Cold War escalated—lies precisely in the fact that the Soviet Union was *not* a traditional national state.[4] This is where the "mirror image," invoked by some psychologists, falls down. For the Soviet Union was a phenomenon very different from America or Britain: it was a totalitarian state, endowed with an all-explanatory, all-consuming ideology, committed to the infallibility of government and party, still in a somewhat messianic mood, equating dissent with treason, and ruled by a dictator who, for all his quite extraordinary abilities, had his paranoid moments.

Marxism-Leninism gave the Russian leaders a view of the world according to which all societies were inexorably destined to proceed along appointed roads by appointed stages until they achieved the classless nirvana. Moreover, given the resistance of the capitalists to this development, the existence of any noncommunist state was *by definition* a threat to the Soviet Union. "As long as capitalism and socialism exist," Lenin wrote, "we cannot live in peace: in the end, one or the other will triumph—a funeral dirge will be sung either over the Soviet Republic or over world capitalism."

Stalin and his associates, whatever Roosevelt or Truman did or failed to do, were bound to regard the United States as the enemy, not because of this deed or that, but because of the primordial fact that America was the leading capitalist power and thus, by Leninist syllogism, unappeasably hostile, driven by the logic of its system to oppose, encircle and destroy Soviet Russia. Nothing the United States could have done in 1944–45 would have abolished this mistrust, required and sanctified as it was by Marxist gospel—nothing short of the conversion of the United States into a Stalinist despotism; and even this would not have sufficed, as the experience of Jugoslavia and China soon showed, unless it were accompanied by total subservience to Moscow. So long as the United States remained a capitalist democracy, no American policy, given Moscow's theology, could hope to win basic Soviet confidence, and every American action was poisoned from the source. So long as the Soviet Union re-

---

[4] This is the classical revisionist fallacy—the assumption of the rationality, or at least of the traditionalism, of states where ideology and social organization have created a different range of motives. So the Second World War revisionists omit the totalitarian dynamism of Nazism and the fanaticism of Hitler, as the Civil War revisionists omit the fact that the slavery system was producing a doctrinaire closed society in the American South. For a consideration of some of these issues, see "The Causes of the Civil War: A Note on Historical Sentimentalism" in my "The Politics of Hope" (Boston, 1963).

mained a messianic state, ideology compelled a steady expansion of communist power.

It is easy, of course, to exaggerate the capacity of ideology to control events. The tension of acting according to revolutionary abstractions is too much for most nations to sustain over a long period: that is why Mao Tse-tung has launched his Cultural Revolution, hoping thereby to create a permanent revolutionary mood and save Chinese communism from the degeneration which, in his view, has overtaken Russian communism. Still, as any revolution grows older, normal human and social motives will increasingly reassert themselves. In due course, we can be sure, Leninism will be about as effective in governing the daily lives of Russians as Christianity is in governing the daily lives of Americans. Like the Ten Commandments and the Sermon on the Mount, the Leninist verities will increasingly become platitudes for ritual observance, not guides to secular decision. There can be no worse fallacy (even if respectable people practiced it diligently for a season in the United States) than that of drawing from a nation's ideology permanent conclusions about its behavior.

A temporary recession of ideology was already taking place during the Second World War when Stalin, to rally his people against the invader, had to replace the appeal of Marxism by that of nationalism. ("We are under no illusions that they are fighting for us," Stalin once said to Harriman. "They are fighting for Mother Russia.") But this was still taking place within the strictest limitations. The Soviet Union remained as much a police state as ever; the régime was as infallible as ever; foreigners and their ideas were as suspect as ever. "Never, except possibly during my later experience as ambassador in Moscow," Kennan has written, "did the insistence of the Soviet authorities on isolation of the diplomatic corps weigh more heavily on me . . . than in these first weeks following my return to Russia in the final months of the war. . . . [We were] treated as though we were the bearers of some species of the plague"—which, of course, from the Soviet viewpoint, they were: the plague of skepticism.

Paradoxically, of the forces capable of bringing about a modification of ideology, the most practical and effective was the Soviet dictatorship itself. If Stalin was an ideologist, he was also a pragmatist. If he saw everything through the lenses of Marxism-Leninism, he also, as the infallible expositor of the faith, could reinterpret Marxism-Leninism to justify anything he wanted to do at any given moment. No doubt Roosevelt's ignorance of Marxism-Leninism was inexcusable and led to grievous miscalculations. But Roosevelt's efforts to work on and through Stalin were not so hopelessly naïve as it used to be fashionable to think. With the extraordinary instinct of a great political leader, Roosevelt intuitively understood that Stalin was the *only* lever available to the West against the Leninist ideology and the Soviet system. If Stalin could be reached, then alone was there a chance of getting the Russians to act contrary to the prescriptions of their faith. The best evidence is that Roosevelt retained a certain capacity to influence Stalin to the end; the nominal Soviet acquiescence in American universalism as late as Yalta was perhaps an indi-

cation of that. It is in this way that the death of Roosevelt was crucial
—not in the vulgar sense that his policy was then reversed by his successor, which did not happen, but in the sense that no other American could
hope to have the restraining impact on Stalin which Roosevelt might for
a while have had.

Stalin alone could have made any difference. Yet Stalin, in spite of the
impression of sobriety and realism he made on Westerners who saw him
during the Second World War, was plainly a man of deep and morbid
obsessions and compulsions. When he was still a young man, Lenin had
criticized his rude and arbitrary ways. A reasonably authoritative observer
(N. S. Khrushchev) later commented, "These negative characteristics of
his developed steadily and during the last years acquired an absolutely in-
sufferable character." His paranoia, probably set off by the suicide of his
wife in 1932, led to the terrible purges of the mid-thirties and the wanton
murder of thousands of his Bolshevik comrades. "Everywhere and in
everything," Khrushchev says of this period, "he saw 'enemies,' 'double-
dealers' and 'spies.' " The crisis of war evidently steadied him in some
way, though Khrushchev speaks of his "nervousness and hysteria . . .
even after the war began." The madness, so rigidly controlled for a time,
burst out with new and shocking intensity in the postwar years. "After
the war," Khrushchev testifies,

> the situation became even more complicated. Stalin became even
> more capricious, irritable and brutal; in particular, his suspicion
> grew. His persecution mania reached unbelievable dimensions. . . .
> He decided everything, without any consideration for anyone or
> anything.
>
> Stalin's wilfulness showed itself . . . also in the international
> relations of the Soviet Union. . . . He had completely lost a sense of
> reality; he demonstrated his suspicion and haughtiness not only in
> relation to individuals in the USSR, but in relation to whole parties
> and nations.

A revisionist fallacy has been to treat Stalin as just another Realpolitik
statesman, as Second World War revisionists see Hitler as just another
Stresemann or Bismarck. But the record makes it clear that in the end
nothing could satisfy Stalin's paranoia. His own associates failed. Why
does anyone suppose that any conceivable American policy would have
succeeded?

An analysis of the origins of the Cold War which leaves out these
factors—the intransigence of Leninist ideology, the sinister dynamics of
a totalitarian society and the madness of Stalin—is obviously incomplete. It was these factors which made it hard for the West to accept the
thesis that Russia was moved only by a desire to protect its security and
would be satisfied by the control of Eastern Europe; it was these factors
which charged the debate between universalism and spheres of influence
with apocalyptic potentiality.

Leninism and totalitarianism created a structure of thought and behavior which made postwar collaboration between Russia and America—in any normal sense of civilized intercourse between national states— inherently impossible. The Soviet dictatorship of 1945 simply could not have survived such a collaboration. Indeed, nearly a quarter-century later, the Soviet régime, though it has meanwhile moved a good distance, could still hardly survive it without risking the release inside Russia of energies profoundly opposed to communist despotism. As for Stalin, he may have represented the only force in 1945 capable of overcoming Stalinism, but the very traits which enabled him to win absolute power expressed terrifying instabilities of mind and temperament and hardly offered a solid foundation for a peaceful world.

VIII

The difference between America and Russia in 1945 was that some Americans fundamentally believed that, over a long run, a modus vivendi with Russia was possible; while the Russians, so far as one can tell, believed in no more than a short-run modus vivendi with the United States.

Harriman and Kennan, this narrative has made clear, took the lead in warning Washington about the difficulties of short-run dealings with the Soviet Union. But both argued that, if the United States developed a rational policy and stuck to it, there would be, after long and rough passages, the prospect of eventual clearing. "I am, as you know," Harriman cabled Washington in early April, "a most earnest advocate of the closest possible understanding with the Soviet Union so that what I am saying relates only to how best to attain such understanding." Kennan has similarly made it clear that the function of his containment policy was "to tide us over a difficult time and bring us to the point where we could discuss effectively with the Russians the dangers and drawbacks this status quo involved, and to arrange with them for its peaceful replacement by a better and sounder one." The subsequent careers of both men attest to the honesty of these statements.

There is no corresponding evidence on the Russian side that anyone seriously sought a modus vivendi in these terms. Stalin's choice was whether his long-term ideological and national interests would be better served by a short-run truce with the West or by an immediate resumption of pressure. In October 1945 Stalin indicated to Harriman at Sochi that he planned to adopt the second course—that the Soviet Union was going isolationist. No doubt the succession of problems with the United States contributed to this decision, but the basic causes most probably lay elsewhere: in the developing situations in Eastern Europe, in Western Europe and in the United States.

In Eastern Europe, Stalin was still for a moment experimenting with techniques of control. But he must by now have begun to conclude that he had underestimated the hostility of the people to Russian dominion. The Hungarian elections in November would finally convince him that the Yalta formula was a road to anti-Soviet governments. At the same time, he was feeling more strongly than ever a sense of his opportunities in Western Europe. The other half of the Continent lay unexpectedly before him, politically demoralized, economically prostrate, militarily defenseless. The hunting would be better and safer than he had anticipated. As for the United States, the alacrity of postwar demobilization must have recalled Roosevelt's offhand remark at Yalta that "two years would be the limit" for keeping American troops in Europe. And, despite Dr. Eugene Varga's doubts about the imminence of American economic breakdown, Marxist theology assured Stalin that the United States was heading into a bitter postwar depression and would be consumed with its own problems. If the condition of Eastern Europe made unilateral action seem essential in the interests of Russian security, the condition of Western Europe and the United States offered new temptations for communist expansion. The Cold War was now in full swing.

It still had its year of modulations and accommodations. Secretary Byrnes conducted his long and fruitless campaign to persuade the Russians that America only sought governments in Eastern Europe "both friendly to the Soviet Union and representative of all the democratic elements of the country." Crises were surmounted in Trieste and Iran. Secretary Marshall evidently did not give up hope of a modus vivendi until the Moscow conference of foreign secretaries of March 1947. Even then, the Soviet Union was invited to participate in the Marshall Plan.

The point of no return came on July 2, 1947, when Molotov, after bringing 89 technical specialists with him to Paris and evincing initial interest in the project for European reconstruction, received the hot flash from the Kremlin, denounced the whole idea and walked out of the conference. For the next fifteen years the Cold War raged unabated, passing out of historical ambiguity into the realm of good versus evil and breeding on both sides simplifications, stereotypes and self-serving absolutes, often couched in interchangeable phrases. Under the pressure even America, for a deplorable decade, forsook its pragmatic and pluralist traditions, posed as God's appointed messenger to ignorant and sinful man and followed the Soviet example in looking to a world remade in its own image.

In retrospect, if it is impossible to see the Cold War as a case of American aggression and Russian response, it is also hard to see it as a pure case of Russian aggression and American response. "In what is truly tragic," wrote Hegel, "there must be valid moral powers on both the sides which come into collision. . . . Both suffer loss and yet both are mutually justified." In this sense, the Cold War had its tragic elements. The question remains whether it was an instance of Greek tragedy—as Auden has called it, "the tragedy of necessity," where the feeling aroused in the spectator is "What a pity it had to be this way"—or of Christian tragedy, "the tragedy of possibility," where the feeling aroused is "What a pity it was this way when it might have been otherwise."

Once something has happened, the historian is tempted to assume that it had to happen; but this may often be a highly unphilosophical assumption. The Cold War could have been avoided only if the Soviet Union had not been possessed by convictions both of the infallibility of the communist word and of the inevitability of a communist world. These convictions transformed an impasse between national states into a religious war, a tragedy of possibility into one of necessity. One might wish that America had preserved the poise and proportion of the first years of the Cold War and had not in time succumbed to its own forms of self-righteousness. But the most rational of American policies could hardly have averted the Cold War. Only today, as Russia begins to recede from its messianic mission and to accept, in practice if not yet in principle, the permanence of the world of diversity, only now can the hope flicker that this long, dreary, costly contest may at last be taking on forms less dramatic, less obsessive and less dangerous to the future of mankind.

CHRISTOPHER LASCH

More than a year has passed since Arthur Schlesinger Jr. announced that the time had come "to blow the whistle before the current outburst of revisionism regarding the origins of the cold war goes much further." Yet the outburst of revisionism shows no signs of subsiding. On the contrary, a growing number of historians and political critics, judging from such recent books as Ronald Steel's *Pax Americana* and Carl Oglesby's and Richard Shaull's *Containment and Change,* are challenging the view, once so widely accepted, that the cold war was an American response to Soviet expansionism, a distasteful burden reluctantly shouldered in the face of a ruthless enemy bent on our destruction, and that Russia, not the United States, must therefore bear the blame for shattering the world's hope that two world wars in the twentieth century would finally give way to an era of peace.

"Revisionist" historians are arguing instead that the United States did as much as the Soviet Union to bring about the collapse of the wartime coalition. Without attempting to shift the blame exclusively to the United States, they are trying to show, as Gar Alperovitz puts it, that "the cold war cannot be understood simply as an American response to a Soviet challenge, but rather as the insidious interaction of mutual suspicions, blame for which must be shared by all."

Not only have historians continued to re-examine the immediate origins of the cold war—in spite of attempts to "blow the whistle" on their efforts—but the scope of revisionism has been steadily widening. Some scholars are beginning to argue that the whole course of American diplomacy since 1898 shows that the United States has become a counter-revolutionary power committed to the defense of a global status quo.

Source: Christopher Lasch, "The Cold War, Revisited and Re-visioned," *New York Times Magazine* (January 14, 1968), pp. 26–27, 44–47, 54, 59. Copyright © 1968 by The New York Times Company. Reprinted by permission.

Arno Mayer's monumental study of the Conference of Versailles, *Politics and Diplomacy of Peacemaking,* which has recently been published by Knopf and which promises to become the definitive work on the subject, announces in its subtitle what a growing number of historians have come to see as the main theme of American diplomacy: *Containment and Counterrevolution.*

Even Schlesinger has now admitted, in a recent article in *Foreign Affairs,* that he was "somewhat intemperate," a year ago, in deploring the rise of cold-war revisionism. Even though revisionist interpretations of earlier wars "have failed to stick," he says, "revisionism is an essential part of the process by which history . . . enlarges its perspectives and enriches its insights." Since he goes on to argue that "postwar collaboration between Russia and America [was] . . . inherently impossible," and that "the most rational of American policies could hardly have averted the cold war," it is not clear what Schlesinger thinks revisionism has done to enlarge our perspective and enrich our insights; but it is good to know, nevertheless, that revisionists may now presumably continue their work (inconsequential as it may eventually prove to be) without fear of being whistled to a stop by the referee.

The orthodox interpretation of the cold war, as it has come to be regarded, grew up in the late forties and early fifties—years of acute international tension, during which the rivalry between the United States and the Soviet Union repeatedly threatened to erupt in a renewal of global war. Soviet-American relations had deteriorated with alarming speed following the defeat of Hitler. At Yalta, in February, 1945, Winston Churchill had expressed the hope that world peace was nearer the grasp of the assembled statesmen of the great powers "than at any time in history." It would be "a great tragedy," he said, "if they, through inertia or carelessness, let it slip from their grasp. History would never forgive them if they did."

Yet the Yalta agreements themselves, which seemed at the time to lay the basis of postwar cooperation, shortly provided the focus of bitter dissension, in which each side accused the other of having broken its solemn promises. In Western eyes, Yalta meant free elections and parliamentary democracies in Eastern Europe, while the Russians construed the agreements as recognition of their demand for governments friendly to the Soviet Union.

The resulting dispute led to mutual mistrust and to a hardening of positions on both sides. By the spring of 1946 Churchill himself, declaring that "an iron curtain has descended" across Europe, admitted, in effect, that the "tragedy" he had feared had come to pass. Europe split into hostile fragments, the eastern half dominated by the Soviet Union, the western part sheltering nervously under the protection of American arms. NATO, founded in 1949 and countered by the Russian-sponsored Warsaw Pact, merely ratified the existing division of Europe.

From 1946 on, every threat to the stability of this uneasy balance produced an immediate political crisis—Greece in 1947, Czechoslovakia and the Berlin blockade in 1948—each of which, added to existing tensions, deepened hostility on both sides and increased the chance of war. When Bernard Baruch announced in April, 1947, that "we are in the midst of a cold war," no one felt inclined to contradict him. The phrase stuck, as an accurate description of postwar political realities.

Many Americans concluded, moreover, that the United States was losing the cold war. Two events in particular contributed to this sense of alarm—the collapse of Nationalist China in 1949, followed by Chiang Kai-shek's flight to Taiwan, and the explosion of an atomic bomb by the Russians in the same year. These events led to the charge that American leaders had deliberately or unwittingly betrayed the country's interests. The Alger Hiss case was taken by some people as proof that the Roosevelt Administration had been riddled by subversion.

Looking back to the wartime alliance with the Soviet Union, the American Right began to argue that Roosevelt, by trusting the Russians, had sold out the cause of freedom. Thus Nixon and McCarthy, aided by historians like Stefan J. Possony, C. C. Tansill and others, accused Roosevelt of handing Eastern Europe to the Russians and of giving them a preponderant interest in China which later enabled the Communists to absorb the entire country.

The liberal interpretation of the cold war—what I have called the orthodox interpretation—developed partly as a response to these charges. In liberal eyes, the right-wingers made the crucial mistake of assuming that American actions had been decisive in shaping the postwar world. Attempting to rebut this devil theory of postwar politics, liberals relied heavily on the argument that the shape of postwar politics had already been dictated by the war itself, in which the Western democracies had been obliged to call on Soviet help in defeating Hitler. These events, they maintained, had left the Soviet Union militarily dominant in Eastern Europe and generally occupying a position of much greater power, relative to the West, than the position she had enjoyed before the war.

In the face of these facts, the United States had very little leeway to influence events in what were destined to become Soviet spheres of influence, particularly since Stalin was apparently determined to expand even if it meant ruthlessly breaking his agreements—and after all it was Stalin, the liberals emphasized, and not Roosevelt or Truman, who broke the Yalta agreement on Poland, thereby precipitating the cold war.

These were the arguments presented with enormous charm, wit, logic and power in George F. Kennan's *American Diplomacy* (1951), which more than any other book set the tone of cold-war historiography. For innumerable historians, but especially for those who were beginning their studies in the fifties, Kennan served as the model of what a scholar should be—committed yet detached—and it was through the perspective of his works that a whole generation of scholars came to see not only the origins of the cold war, but the entire history of twentieth century diplomacy.

It is important to recognize that Kennan's was by no means an uncritical perspective—indeed, for those unacquainted with Marxism, it seemed the only critical perspective that was available in the fifties. While Kennan insisted that the Russians were primarily to blame for the cold war, he seldom missed an opportunity to criticize the excessive moralism, the messianic vision of a world made safe for democracy, which he argued ran "like a red skein" through American diplomacy.

As late as 1960, a radical like Staughton Lynd could still accept the general framework of Kennan's critique of American idealism while noting merely that Kennan had failed to apply it to the specific events of the cold war and to the policy of containment which he had helped to articulate. "Whereas in general he counseled America to 'admit the validity and legitimacy of power realities and aspirations . . . and to seek their point of maximum equilibrium rather than their reform or their repression'—'reform or repression' of the Soviet system were the very goals which Kennan's influential writings of those years urged."

Even in 1960, however, a few writers had begun to attack not the specific applications of the principles of *Realpolitik* but the principles themselves, on the grounds that on many occasions they served simply as rationalizations for American (not Soviet) expansionism. And whereas Lynd in 1960 could still write that the American demand for freedom in Eastern Europe, however misguided, "expressed a sincere and idealistic concern," some historians had already begun to take a decidedly more sinister view of the matter—asking, for instance, whether a country which demanded concessions in Eastern Europe that it was not prepared to grant to the Russians in Western Europe could really be accused, as the "realist" writers had maintained, of an excess of good-natured but occasionally incompetent altruism.

Meanwhile the "realist" interpretation of the cold war inspired a whole series of books—most notably, Herbert Feis's series (*Churchill-Roosevelt-Stalin; Between War and Peace; The Atomic Bomb and the End of World War II*); William McNeill's *America, Britain and Russia: Their Cooperation and Conflict;* Norman Graebner's *Cold War Diplomacy;* Louis J. Halle's *Dream and Reality* and *The Cold War as History;* and M. F. Herz's *Beginnings of the Cold War.*

Like Kennan, all of these writers saw containment as a necessary response to Soviet expansionism and to the deterioration of Western power in Eastern Europe. At the same time, they were critical, in varying degrees, of the legalistic-moralistic tradition which kept American statesmen from looking at foreign relations in the light of balance-of-power considerations.

Some of them tended to play off Churchillian realism against the idealism of Roosevelt and Cordell Hull, arguing, for instance, that the Americans should have accepted the bargain made between Churchill and Stalin in 1944, whereby Greece was assigned to the Western sphere of influence and Rumania, Bulgaria and Hungary to the Soviet sphere, with both liberal and Communist parties sharing in the control of Yugoslavia.

These criticisms of American policy, however, did not challenge the basic premise of American policy, that the Soviet Union was a ruthlessly aggressive power bent on world domination. They assumed, moreover, that the Russians were in a position to realize large parts of this program, and that only counterpressure exerted by the West, in the form of containment and the Marshall Plan, prevented the Communists from absorbing all of Europe and much of the rest of the world as well.

It is their criticism of these assumptions that defines the revisionist historians and distinguishes them from the "realists." What impresses revisionists is not Russia's strength but her military weakness following the devastating war with Hitler, in which the Russians suffered much heavier losses than any other member of the alliance.

Beginning with Carl Marzani's *We Can Be Friends: Origins of the Cold War* (1952), revisionists have argued that Russia's weakness dictated, for the moment at least, a policy of postwar cooperation with the West. Western leaders' implacable hostility to Communism, they contend, prevented them from seeing this fact, a proper understanding of which might have prevented the cold war.

This argument is spelled out in D. F. Fleming's two-volume study *The Cold War and Its Origins* (1961); in David Horowitz's *The Free World Colossus* (1965), which summarizes and synthesizes a great deal of revisionist writing; in Gar Alperovitz's *Atomic Diplomacy: Hiroshima and Potsdam* (1965); and in the previously mentioned *Containment and Change.*

But the historian who has done most to promote a revisionist interpretation of the cold war, and of American diplomacy in general, is William Appleman Williams of the University of Wisconsin, to whom most of the writers just mentioned owe a considerable debt. Williams's works, particularly *The Tragedy of American Diplomacy* (1959), not only challenge the orthodox interpretation of the cold war, they set against it an elaborate counterinterpretation which, if valid, forces one to see American policy in the early years of the cold war as part of a larger pattern of American globalism reaching as far back as 1898.

According to Williams, American diplomacy has consistently adhered to the policy of the "open door"—that is, to a policy of commercial, political and cultural expansion which seeks to extend American influence into every corner of the earth. This policy was consciously and deliberately embarked upon, Williams argues, because American statesmen believed that American capitalism needed ever-expanding foreign markets in order to survive, the closing of the frontier having put an end to its expansion on the continent of North America. Throughout the twentieth century, the makers of American foreign policy, he says, have interpreted the national interest in this light.

The cold war, in Williams's view, therefore has to be seen as the latest phase of a continuing effort to make the world safe for democracy— read liberal capitalism, American-style—in which the United States finds itself increasingly cast as the leader of a world-wide counterrevolution.

After World War II, Williams maintains, the United States had "a vast proportion of actual as well as potential power vis-à-vis the Soviet Union." The United States "cannot with any real warrant or meaning claim that it has been forced to follow a certain approach or policy." (Compare this with a statement by Arthur Schlesinger: "The cold war could have been avoided only if the Soviet Union had not been possessed by convictions both of the infallibility of the Communist word and of the inevitability of a Communist world.")

The Russians, by contrast, Williams writes, "viewed their position in the nineteen-forties as one of weakness, not offensive strength." One measure of Stalin's sense of weakness, as he faced the enormous task of rebuilding the shattered Soviet economy was his eagerness to get a large loan from the United States. Failing to get such a loan—instead, the United States drastically cut back lend-lease payments to Russia in May, 1945—Stalin was faced with three choices, according to Williams:

He could give way to accept the American peace program at every point—which meant, among other things, accepting governments in Eastern Europe hostile to the Soviet Union.

He could follow the advice of the doctrinaire revolutionaries in his own country who argued that Russia's best hope lay in fomenting world-wide revolution.

Or he could exact large-scale economic reparations from Germany while attempting to reach an understanding with Churchill and Roosevelt on the need for governments in Eastern Europe not necessarily Communist but friendly to the Soviet Union.

His negotiations with Churchill in 1944, according to Williams, showed that Stalin had already committed himself, by the end of the war, to the third of these policies—a policy, incidentally, which required him to withdraw support from Communist revolutions in Greece and in other countries which under the terms of the Churchill-Stalin agreement had been conceded to the Western sphere of influence.

But American statesmen, the argument continues, unlike the British, were in no mood to compromise. They were confident of America's strength and Russia's weakness (although later they and their apologists found it convenient to argue that the contrary had been the case). Furthermore, they believed that "we cannot have full employment and prosperity in the United States without the foreign markets," as Dean Acheson told a special Congressional committee on postwar economic policy and planning in November, 1944. These considerations led to the conclusion, as President Truman put it in April, 1945, that the United States should "take the lead in running the world in the way that the world ought to be run"; or more specifically, in the words of Foreign Economic Administrator Leo Crowley, that "if you create good governments in foreign countries, automatically you will have better markets for ourselves." Accordingly, the United States pressed for the "open door" in Eastern Europe and elsewhere.

In addition to these considerations, there was the further matter of the atomic bomb, which first became a calculation in American diplomacy in July, 1945. The successful explosion of an atomic bomb in the New Mexican desert, Williams argued, added to the American sense of omnipotence and led the United States "to overplay its hand"—for in spite of American efforts to keep the Russians out of Eastern Europe, the Russians refused to back down.

Nor did American pressure have the effect, as George Kennan hoped, of promoting tendencies in the Soviet Union "which must eventually find their outlet in either the break-up or the gradual mellowing of Soviet power." Far from causing Soviet policy to mellow, American actions, according to Williams, stiffened the Russians in their resistance to Western pressure and strengthened the hand of those groups in the Soviet Union which had been arguing all along that capitalist powers could not be trusted.

Not only did the Russians successfully resist American demands in Eastern Europe, they launched a vigorous counterattack in the form of the Czechoslovakian coup of 1948 and the Berlin blockade. Both East and West thus found themselves committed to the policy of cold war, and for the next 15 years, until the Cuban missile crisis led to a partial detente, Soviet-American hostility was the determining fact of international politics.

Quite apart from his obvious influence on other revisionist historians of the cold war and on his own students in other areas of diplomatic history, Williams has had a measurable influence on the political radicals of the sixties, most of whom now consider it axiomatic that American diplomacy has been counterrevolutionary and that this fact reflects, not a series of blunders and mistakes as some critics have argued, but the basically reactionary character of American capitalism.

Some radicals now construe these facts to mean that American foreign policy therefore cannot be changed unless American society itself undergoes a revolutionary change. Carl Oglesby, for instance, argues along these lines in *Containment and Change*. From Oglesby's point of view, appeals to conscience or even to enlightened self-interest are useless; the cold war cannot end until the "system" is destroyed.

Williams thought otherwise. At the end of the 1962 edition of *The Tragedy of American Diplomacy,* he noted that "there is at the present time no radicalism in the United States strong enough to win power, or even a very significant influence, through the processes of representative government"—and he took it for granted that genuinely democratic change could come about only through representative processes. This meant, he thought, that "the well-being of the United States depends— *in the short-run but only in the short-run*—upon the extent to which calm and confident and enlightened conservatives can see and bring themselves to act upon the validity of a radical analysis."

In an essay in *Ramparts* last March, he makes substantially the same point in commenting on the new radicals' impatience with conservative critics of American diplomacy like Senator Fulbright. Fulbright, Williams says, attracted more support for the position of more radical critics than these critics had attracted through their own efforts. "He hangs tough over the long haul, and that is precisely what American radicalism has never done in the twentieth century."

As the New Left becomes more and more beguiled by the illusion of its own revolutionary potential, and more and more intolerant of radicals who refuse to postulate a revolution as the only feasible means of social change, men like Williams will probably become increasingly uncomfortable in the presence of a movement they helped to create. At the same time, Williams's radicalism, articulated in the fifties before radicalism came back into fashion, has alienated the academic establishment and prevented his works from winning the widespread recognition and respect they deserve. In scholarly journals, many reviews of Williams's work—notably a review by Oscar Handlin of *The Contours of American History* in the *Mississippi Valley Historical Review* a few years ago—have been contemptuous and abusive in the extreme. The result is that Williams's books on diplomatic history are only beginning to pass into the mainstream of scholarly discourse, years after their initial publication.

Next to Williams's *Tragedy of American Diplomacy,* the most important attack on the orthodox interpretation of the cold war is Alperovitz's *Atomic Diplomacy.* A young historian trained at Wisconsin, Berkeley and King's College, Cambridge, and currently a research fellow at Harvard, Alperovitz adds very little to the interpretation formulated by Williams, but he provides Williams's insights with a mass of additional documentation. By doing so, he has made it difficult for conscientious scholars any longer to avoid the challenge of revisionist interpretations. Unconventional in its conclusions, *Atomic Diplomacy* is thoroughly conventional in its methods. That adds to the book's persuasiveness. Using the traditional sources of diplomatic history—official records, memoirs of participants, and all the unpublished material to which scholars have access—Alperovitz painstakingly reconstructs the evolution of American policy during the six-month period March to August, 1945. He proceeds with a thoroughness and caution which, in the case of a less controversial work, would command the unanimous respect of the scholarly profession. His book is no polemic. It is a work in the best—and most conservative —traditions of historical scholarship. Yet the evidence which Alperovitz has gathered together challenges the official explanation of the beginnings of the cold war at every point.

What the evidence seems to show is that as early as April, 1945, American officials from President Truman on down had decided to force a "symbolic showdown" with the Soviet Union over the future of Eastern Europe. Truman believed that a unified Europe was the key to European recovery and economic stability, since the agricultural southeast and the industrial northwest depended on each other. Soviet designs on Eastern Europe, Truman reasoned, threatened to disrupt the economic unity of Europe and therefore had to be resisted. The only question was whether the showdown should take place immediately or whether it should be delayed until the bargaining position of the United States had improved.

At first it appeared to practically everybody that delay would only weaken the position of the United States. Both of its major bargaining counters, its armies in Europe and its lend-lease credits to Russia, could be more effectively employed at once, it seemed, than at any future time. Accordingly, Truman tried to "lay it on the line" with the Russians. He demanded that they "carry out their [Yalta] agreements" by giving the pro-Western elements in Poland an equal voice in the Polish Government (although Roosevelt, who made the Yalta agreements, believed that "we placed, as clearly shown in the agreement, somewhat more emphasis" on the Warsaw [pro-Communist] Government than on the pro-Western leaders). When Stalin objected that Poland was "a country in which the U.S.S.R. is interested first of all and most of all," the United States tried to force him to give in by cutting back lend-lease payments to Russia.

At this point, however—in April, 1945—Secretary of War Henry L. Stimson convinced Truman that "we shall probably hold more cards in our hands later than now." He referred to the atomic bomb, and if Truman decided to postpone the showdown with Russia, it was because Stimson and other advisers persuaded him that the new weapon would "put us in a position," as Secretary of State James F. Byrnes argued, "to dictate our own terms at the end of the war."

To the amazement of those not privy to the secret, Truman proceeded to take a more conciliatory attitude toward Russia, an attitude symbolized by Harry Hopkins's mission to Moscow in June, 1945. Meanwhile, Truman twice postponed the meeting with Churchill and Stalin at Potsdam. Churchill complained, "Anyone can see that in a very short space of time our armed power on the Continent will have vanished."

But when Truman told Churchill that an atomic bomb had been successfully exploded at Alamogordo, exceeding all expectations, Churchill immediately understood and endorsed the strategy of delay. "We were in the presence of a new factor in human affairs," he said, "and possessed of powers which were irresistible." Not only Germany but even the Balkans, which Churchill and Roosevelt had formerly conceded to the Russian sphere, now seemed amenable to Western influence. That assumption, of course, had guided American policy (though not British policy) since April, but it could not be acted upon until the bombing of Japan provided the world with an unmistakable demonstration of American military supremacy.

Early in September, the foreign ministers of the Big Three met in London. Byrnes—armed, as Stimson noted, with "the presence of the bomb in his pocket, so to speak, as a great weapon to get through" the conference—tried to press the American advantage. He demanded that the Governments of Bulgaria and Rumania reorganize themselves along lines favorable to the West. In Bulgaria, firmness won a few concessions; in Rumania, the Russians stood firm. The American strategy had achieved no noteworthy success. Instead—as Stimson, one of the architects of that strategy, rather belatedly observed—it has "irretrievably embittered" Soviet-American relations.

The revisionist view of the origins of the cold war, as it emerges from the works of Williams, Alperovitz, Marzani, Fleming, Horowitz, and others, can be summarized as follows. The object of American policy at the end of World War II was not to defend Western or even Central Europe but to force the Soviet Union out of Eastern Europe. The Soviet menace to the "free world," so often cited as the justification of the containment policy, simply did not exist in the minds of American planners. They believed themselves to be negotiating not from weakness but from almost unassailable superiority.

Nor can it be said that the cold war began because the Russians "broke their agreements." The general sense of the Yalta agreements—which were in any case very vague—was to assign to the Soviet Union a controlling influence in Eastern Europe. Armed with the atomic bomb, American diplomats tried to take back what they had implicitly conceded at Yalta.

The assumption of American moral superiority, in short, does not stand up under analysis.

The opponents of this view have yet to make a very convincing reply. Schlesinger's recent article in *Foreign Affairs,* referred to at the outset of this article, can serve as an example of the kind of arguments which historians are likely to develop in opposition to the revisionist interpretation. Schlesinger argues that the cold war came about through a combination of Soviet intransigence and misunderstanding. There were certain "problems of communication" with the Soviet Union, as a result of which "the Russians might conceivably have misread our signals." Thus the American demand for self-determination in Poland and other East European countries "very probably" appeared to the Russians "as a systematic and deliberate pressure on Russia's western frontiers.

Similarly, the Russians "could well have interpreted" the American refusal of a loan to the Soviet Union, combined with cancellation of lend-lease, "as deliberate sabotage" of Russia's postwar reconstruction or as "blackmail." In both cases, of course, there would have been no basis for these suspicions; but "we have thought a great deal more in recent years," Schlesinger says, ". . . about the problems of communication in diplomacy," and we know how easy it is for one side to misinterpret what the other is saying.

This argument about difficulties of "communications" at no point engages the evidence uncovered by Alperovitz and others—evidence which seems to show that Soviet officials had good reason to interpret American actions exactly as they did: as attempts to dictate American terms.

In reply to the assertion that the refusal of a reconstruction loan was part of such an attempt, Schlesinger can only argue weakly that the Soviet request for a loan was "inexplicably mislaid" by Washington during the transfer of records from the Foreign Economic Administration to the State Department! "Of course," he adds, "this was impossible for the Russians to believe." It is impossible for some Americans to believe. As William Appleman Williams notes, Schlesinger's explanation of the "inexplicable" loss of the Soviet request "does not speak to the point of how the leaders could forget the request even if they lost the document."

When pressed on the matter of "communications," Schlesinger retreats to a second line of argument, namely that none of these misunderstandings "made much essential difference," because Stalin suffered from "paranoia" and was "possessed by convictions both of the infallibility of the Communist word and of the inevitability of a Communist world."

The trouble is that there is very little evidence which connects either Stalin's paranoia or Marxist-Leninist ideology or what Schlesinger calls "the sinister dynamics of a totalitarian society" with the actual course of Soviet diplomacy during the formative months of the cold war. The only piece of evidence that Schlesinger has been able to find is an article by the Communist theoretician Jacques Duclos in the April, 1945, issue of *Cahiers du communisme,* the journal of the French Communist party, which proves, he argues, that Stalin had already abandoned the wartime policy of collaboration with the West and had returned to the traditional Communist policy of world revolution.

Even this evidence, however, can be turned to the advantage of the revisionists. Alperovitz points out that Duclos did not attack electoral politics or even collaboration with bourgeois governments. What he denounced was precisely the American Communists' decision, in 1944, to withdraw from electoral politics. Thus the article, far from being a call to world revolution, "was one of many confirmations that European Communists had decided to abandon violent revolutionary struggle in favor of the more modest aim of electoral success." And while this decision did not guarantee world peace, neither did it guarantee 20 years of cold war.

Schlesinger first used the Duclos article as a trump card in a letter to the *New York Review of Books,* Oct. 20, 1966, which called forth Alperovitz's rejoinder. It is symptomatic of the general failure of orthodox historiography to engage the revisionist argument that Duclos's article crops up again in Schlesinger's more recent essay in *Foreign Affairs,* where it is once again cited as evidence of a "new Moscow line," without any reference to the intervening objections raised by Alperovitz.

Sooner or later, however, historians will have to come to grips with the revisionist interpretation of the cold war. They cannot ignore it indefinitely. When serious debate begins, many historians, hitherto disposed to accept without much question the conventional account of the cold war, will find themselves compelled to admit its many inadequacies. On the other hand, some of the ambiguities of the revisionist view, presently submerged in the revisionists' common quarrel with official explanations, will begin to force themselves to the surface. Is the revisionist history of the cold war essentially an attack on "the doctrine of historical inevitability," as Alperovitz contends? Or does it contain an implicit determinism of its own?

Two quite different conclusions can be drawn from the body of revisionist scholarship. One is that American policy-makers had it in their power to choose different policies from the ones they chose. That is, they could have adopted a more conciliatory attitude toward the Soviet Union, just as they now have the choice of adopting a more conciliatory attitude toward Communist China and toward nationalist revolutions elsewhere in the Third World.

The other is that they have no such choice, because the inner requirements of American capitalism *force* them to pursue a consistent policy of economic and political expansion. "For matters to stand otherwise," writes Carl Oglesby, "the Yankee free-enterpriser would . . . have to . . . take sides against himself. . . . He would have to change entirely his style of thought and action. In a word, he would have to become a revolutionary Socialist whose aim was the destruction of the present American hegemony."

Pushed to what some writers clearly regard as its logical conclusion, the revisionist critique of American foreign policy thus becomes the obverse of the cold-war liberals' defense of that policy, which assumes that nothing could have modified the character of Soviet policy short of the transformation of the Soviet Union into a liberal democracy—which is exactly the goal the containment policy sought to promote. According to a certain type of revisionism, American policy has all the rigidity the orthodox historians attribute to the USSR, and this inflexibility made the cold war inevitable.

Moreover, Communism really did threaten American interests, in this view. Oglesby argues that, in spite of its obvious excesses, the "theory of the International Communist Conspiracy is not the hysterical old maid that many leftists seem to think it is." If there is no conspiracy, there is a world revolution and it *"does* aim itself at America"—the America of expansive corporate capitalism.

Revisionism, carried to these conclusions, curiously restores cold-war anti-Communism to a kind of intellectual respectability, even while insisting on its immorality. After all, it concludes, the cold warriors were following the American national interest. The national interest may have been itself corrupt, but the policy-makers were more rational than their critics may have supposed.

In my view, this concedes far too much good sense to Truman, Dulles and the rest. Even Oglesby concedes that the war in Vietnam has now become irrational in its own terms. I submit that much of the cold war has been irrational in its own terms—as witness the failure, the enormously costly failure, of American efforts to dominate Eastern Europe at the end of World War II. This is not to deny the fact of American imperialism, only to suggest that imperialism itself, as J. A. Hobson and Joseph Schumpeter argued in another context long ago, is irrational—that even in its liberal form it may represent an archaic social phenomenon having little relation to the realities of the modern world.

At the present stage of historical scholarship, it is of course impossible to speak with certainty about such matters. That very lack of certainty serves to indicate the direction which future study of American foreign policy might profitably take.

The question to which historians must now address themselves is whether American capitalism really depends for its continuing growth and survival on the foreign policy its leaders have been following throughout most of the twentieth century. To what extent are its interests really threatened by Communist revolutions in the Third World? To what extent can it accommodate itself to those revolutions, reconciling itself to a greatly diminished role in the rest of the world, without undergoing a fundamental reformation—that is, without giving way (after a tremendous upheaval) to some form of Socialism?

Needless to say, these are not questions for scholars alone. The political positions one takes depend on the way one answers them. It is terribly important, therefore, that we begin to answer them with greater care and precision than we can answer them today.

Correlation of *Western Civilization: Recent Interpretations,* Volume II, with Western Civilization Texts

	Langer et al., WESTERN CIVILIZATION, Vol. II	Clough et al., A HISTORY OF THE WESTERN WORLD, 2nd ed., Vol. II	Brinton, Christopher, and Wolff, A HISTORY OF CIVILIZATION, 4th ed., Vol. II	Palmer and Colton, HISTORY OF THE WEST WORLD, 4th ed
Text Chapters	Related selections in *Western Civilization: Recent Interpretations,* Volume II			
1				
2				
3				
4				
5				1
6				1
7	2, 3			
8	1			2–3
9	1			4–6
10	4–6			7–8
11	7	1–3, 9		9–10, 12
12	8	4–7		11, 13, 17, 2
13	9, 10	8, 10–12, 14, 17–18, 22		18–19
14	12	15–16, 19–21, 23–26, 13		14–16, 20–
15	11, 17–19	27–34		24
16	14	35–36	1	25–28
17			2–3	29–30
18	22–23		4–7	
19	13, 22–23		8, 11	31–32
20	20–21		9–10, 12–13, 22–23	33–34
21	24		17–18, 21	35–36
22	25–26		19–20	
23	29–30		14–16	
24	15–16		24	
25			25–28	
26	27–28		29–30	
27	31–32		31–32	
28				
29	33–34		33–34	
30	35–36		35–36	
31				
32			15–16	

Text Chapters	Wallbank and Taylor, CIVILIZATION PAST AND PRESENT, 5th ed., Vol. II	Ferguson and Bruun, A SURVEY OF EUROPEAN CIVILIZATION, 4th ed., Vol. II	Text Chapters	Ferguson and Bruun (con't)
	Related selections in *Western Civilization: Recent Interpretations*, Volume II			
1				
2	1			
3	2–3			
4	4–8		63–64	25–26
5	12		65	27–28
6	9–10, 13		66	
7	11, 22		67	29–30
8	17–18		68	
9	24		69	31–32
10	24		70	
11	14–16		71	33
12	19–21		72	34
13	22–23, 25–26		73–74	35–36
14	25–26, 27–28		78	15–16
15	29–30, 31–32			
16				
17	31–32, 33–34			
18	35–36			
41–44		1		
45		2–3		
46–48		4–6		
49–50		7		
51		8		
52		12		
53		9–10		
54		11, 17		
55		18		
56				
57		19		
58				
59		13–14		
60		20–23		
61		24		
62				